Fast Guide to

CUBASE 5

Simon Millward

PC Publishing

PC Publishing
Keeper's House
Merton
Thetford
Norfolk IP25 6QH
UK

Tel +44 1953 889900
email info@pc-publishing.com
web site http://www.pc-publishing.com

First published 2010

© Simon Millward

ISBN 13: 978-1-906005-146

British Library Cataloguing in Publication Data
A catalogue record for this book is available from the British Library

Printed and bound in Great Britain by The Cromwell Press Group, Trowbridge, Wilts

Introduction

Welcome to the *Fast Guide to Cubase 5*.

Cubase is the ultimate professional music production system for music creation and sound recording. It is renowned for its user-friendliness, flexibility and innovative design. This book aims to help you get the most from the software.

The *Fast Guide to Cubase 5* is not a retread of the manual. It supplies the essential information to get you up and running in the shortest possible time but, more importantly, explores advanced techniques and a wide range of theoretical knowledge which help you get better results. Topics covered include: recording, editing and arranging in the Project window; slicing and looping in the Sample editor; MIDI editing in the MIDI editors; and mixing and mastering in the Mixer. Other subjects include: recording techniques, EQ, compression, gating, limiting, plug-in effects, automation, surround sound, pattern-based arranging, quantizing, beat design, audio warping, pitch correction, tempo manipulation, synchronisation, media management and VST instruments. The book is packed full of hints, tips and tutorials and includes a comprehensive website list and glossary. 100 speed tips and a powerful macro library take your music production and programming skills to the next level.

Combining extensive Cubase know-how and theoretical knowledge from the worlds of sound recording and music technology, this book helps take your projects from conception and multi-track recording right through to mixing and mastering.

The *Fast Guide to Cubase 5* is the ideal companion for all users of the software, including musicians, producers, sound recordists and audio professionals.

Contents

Description and overview

This chapter provides an overall description of Cubase and gives a brief preview of the Project window, Transport panel and Mixer. This helps you become familiar with the main points of contact before moving on to a more detailed exploration of the program.

What is Cubase?

Cubase is a music creation and production system for the recording, editing and processing of MIDI data and digital audio. It belongs to a type of software sometimes referred to as a MIDI+audio sequencer and, when installed on your computer, is also known as a 'digital audio workstation' (DAW). In its simplest form, a sequencer is a device which allows you to chain together sequences of musical notes or events. However, Cubase is infinitely more capable than this. It allows you to perform a multitude of music production tasks within a single, streamlined software environment. Cubase is at once a MIDI sequencer, a powerful multitrack digital audio recorder, a fully featured mixing console, a music for video production workstation, a post production workstation, an audio analysis tool, an audio loop creation tool and a multimedia tool.

Cubase can be interfaced with the usual range of MIDI devices, such as synthesizers, samplers and drum machines, and is also a digital audio recorder for recording vocals, acoustic musical instruments, line level signals from electronic musical instruments, electric guitar and bass, and anything else you can imagine. In addition, it allows the mixing of both audio and MIDI recordings in a virtual mixing console offering effects, EQ and automation. The program features the use of native audio processing which means that most of the audio processing is performed by the CPU (central processing unit) of the computer. Audio recording and processing can therefore be performed with less hardware. The program runs on PC and Macintosh computers.

Cubase provides simultaneous playback of hundreds of audio and MIDI tracks (depending on the overall speed and efficiency of the host computer). It features a central Project window which allows the management of most routine recording, editing and processing within a single-page environment. A virtual mixing console provides adaptable screen views within which all audio or MIDI based tracks can be viewed and mixed in the same order as they appear in the Project window. Each audio track features 4-band parametric EQ, eight send effect slots and eight real-time insert effect slots. MIDI tracks feature four send and four insert effect slots. Plug-in architecture is provided for VST instruments, audio effects, and MIDI processors. A wide range of audio effects plug-ins (with side chain capability), MIDI processors and VST instruments are supplied with the program. There is sample accurate automation for all mixer, VST instrument and effects parameters and an audio mixdown facility. Offline audio processes include time-stretch, pitch shift, envelope, fade, noise gate, normalise, reverse and other processes. Special audio manipulation tools include pitch correction, audio looping, audio warping, audio quantize and groove extraction. For MIDI, there are Key, In-place, Drum, List, Logical, Score and Sysex editors, along with quantize and groove manipulation functions. Unlimited undo/redo, off-line process history, user-configurable key commands, workspaces, universal presets and advanced media management help complete the picture.

Cubase supports all standard digital audio recording resolutions up to 32-bit float/96kHz. Support for ASIO allows the use of low-latency audio cards and hardware.

When was Cubase developed?

The Cubase family of sequencers already has a long history. Steinberg developed their first sequencer, the Pro 16, in 1984 on the Commodore 64 computer. This was followed by the Pro 24 for the Atari computer in 1986. The very first version of Cubase began life in 1989 as a radical new update to the Pro 24. It featured the revolutionary Arrange window which allowed musicians to visualise and arrange their musical compositions in a dynamic graphical display of time on the horizontal axis against tracks on the vertical axis. All these early applications were concerned with the recording of MIDI data only. However, as the processing power of computers increased during the 1990s Steinberg was able to add audio recording capability to the program. During the same period, the code was ported to PC and Apple Macintosh computers.

In 1996, Steinberg introduced the concept of VST (Virtual Studio Technology) and Cubase became known as Cubase VST. VST aims to bring all those elements normally found within a real-world recording studio into a single virtual environment inside your computer. This design principle remains one of the cornerstones of the Cubase range of sequencers. With Cubase SX (introduced in 2002), Steinberg further refined and streamlined the Cubase concept into a package which is more powerful, more flexible and more logical than its predecessors. In 2006, the 'SX' was dropped from the name and the program became known simply as 'Cubase', followed by a version number. This marked the arrival of a more mature and complete Cubase, including VST3 technology, improved audio routing, side chaining, advanced media management and a new collection of plug-ins.

Who can use Cubase?

Newcomers to the software and also experienced sequencer users may have to learn new skills in order to have meaningful contact with the many aspects of Cubase. The MIDI sequencer element of the package requires knowledge

Info

Steinberg, the company behind Cubase, was formed in 1984 by Karl Steinberg and Manfred Rurup. Cubase, therefore, benefits from a background of over 20 years of music software research and development.

of the normal techniques associated with MIDI recording but the audio aspects require knowledge from a wider range of music technology disciplines. Of course, anyone can use Cubase but, since the package involves the concept of a self-contained virtual recording studio, it follows that having knowledge of the skills required to operate a real-world recording studio is useful. This encompasses such things as sound engineering and music production. However, even users with limited sound recording skills are able to quickly benefit from the advantages of Cubase.

Why use Cubase?

There are many reasons why Cubase is an excellent music software choice. The seamless integration of MIDI and audio recording and real-time processing together with the possibility of recording large numbers of tracks, the inclusion of 4-band parametric EQ on every audio channel and the supply of a wide range of effects and processors are just some of the advantages encompassed by the program. The package is also very cost-effective since most of the audio processing takes place in the computer's main processor, which reduces the need for additional hardware. Cubase can produce excellent results using a fast PC or Mac computer and an ASIO low-latency audio card. The convenience of this compact arrangement is an obvious advantage.

How do I use Cubase?

This is the key question! Before you can use Cubase you must have some idea of how to record and manipulate MIDI data, how to record and manipulate audio signals, how you are going to get an audio signal into the computer and how you are going to feed it back out into the real world. These matters, and many other details related to Cubase, form the subject matter of this book.

The big picture

Primary functions

A simple graphical representation of Cubase helps us understand its essential elements. Figure 1.1 shows the two primary functions of the program: MIDI recording and audio recording.

MIDI (Musical Instrument Digital Interface) is a note-based interface, originally developed so that electronic keyboards and synthesizers could talk to each other. MIDI contains no audio. MIDI is a sequence of digital instructions related

Figure 1.1
Simple visualisation of Cubase

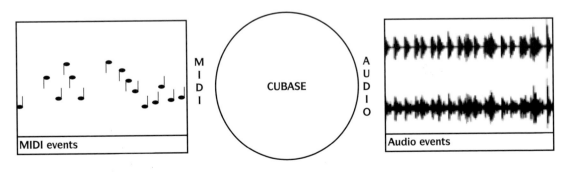

MIDI events   CUBASE   Audio events

to a musical performance. The data contains information such as the pitch and velocity of the notes being played and travels through a cable from one keyboard to another or from a keyboard into a computer-based sequencer like Cubase. Music recorded in this way is represented primarily as individual note events. In Cubase these events are displayed as notes on a score or as symbols in a piano-roll style editor, and are grouped together within graphical containers known as MIDI parts. The primary uses for MIDI data in Cubase are for triggering internal VST instruments or external MIDI devices.

Audio recording involves the recording of the actual audio signal itself. In Cubase, the audio data is shown as waveforms representing the recorded signal. These waveforms are displayed within graphical containers known as audio events. The audio aspects of the program also include the virtual studio features of mixing, routing, processing and adding effects to the material.

Overview

The MIDI and audio functions of Cubase are seamlessly integrated. The recording of both kinds of data can take place in the Project window, the main window of Cubase, and both kinds of data can be mixed in the same virtual mixing console, known as the Mixer. The Project window and Mixer form the central hub of activity for most Cubase projects. You can fulfil most routine recording, editing, mixing and processing tasks within the Project window and Mixer, but for editing in fine detail the system contains a wide range of specialist editors and functions (see Figure 1.2 for a basic overview).

In the MIDI domain, Figure 1.2 shows the main MIDI-based editors; the Key, Score, List and Drum editors. These are used to edit note and controller data in fine detail and the Score editor can also produce high quality printed scores. There is also a comprehensive range of other features for the editing and processing of MIDI data including the SysEx editor, MIDI plug-in effects and advanced quantize functions (not shown in the diagram).

In the audio domain, the Sample editor forms the main editing environment for audio material. There are also many audio processing features such as EQ, plug-in effects and off-line audio processing. The management of audio files takes place in the Pool and the Media Bay.

Somewhere in between the MIDI and audio sides of Cubase we find VST Instruments (Virtual Studio Instruments) which are played using conventional MIDI data but produce their sounds using the system's audio engine. Some plug-in effects also respond to MIDI data but process audio. You can use the Mixer to mix audio, MIDI, VST Instrument, Group and other tracks. For the overall management of audio files and presets there is the Media Bay.

Brief preview

Figure 1.2 provides a graphical overview of the main parts of Cubase which is useful for an appreciation of what the system includes. But what does Cubase actually look like on screen, where are the main areas of activity and how do you interact with the program?

You can change the appearance of Cubase to suit your own requirements but when you first launch a project you might see the Project window displayed in a

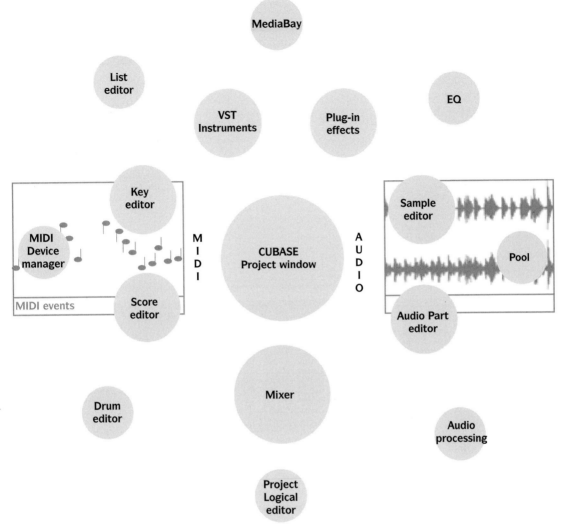

Figure 1.2
Cubase: graphical overview

similar manner to Figure 1.3. The Project window is the uppermost window. By default, computer keys F2 and F3 open the Transport panel and Mixer. These are shown above and below the Project window in Figure 1.3.

The Project window is where you see a graphical representation of your audio and MIDI material in the form of rectangular blocks known as parts or events. These are containers which hold either audio or MIDI data. Parts and events are found on tracks. There are a number of different track types including audio, MIDI, instrument, group, FX, automation, video and others. Tracks are displayed vertically in the track list and time is represented horizontally on a ruler which displays bars and beats, seconds, timecode or samples. There is a toolbar at the top of the display and an optional control area to the left of the track list, known as the Inspector. The Inspector shows additional details for the currently selected track. The Project window is the centre of activity for most Cubase operations.

Figure 1.3

Cubase Project window, Mixer and
Transport panel

The Mixer displays the tracks in the same order as they appear in the
Project window but laid out as channels with volume faders, pan controls, EQ
controls, effects sends and so on, similar to a conventional mixing console.
Both audio and MIDI tracks are mixed in the Mixer and the mixing environment can be configured and scaled to suit your requirements and the available screen space.

The Transport panel features the normal rewind, fast-forward, stop, play,
cycle and record controls and manages most playback and recording functions. The current song position is shown by a vertical line which moves
across the Project window. This is known as the Project cursor.

The Cubase user interface is intuitive and direct. It features a comprehensive set of menus and icon buttons, and a large number of mouse functions,
user-configurable keyboard shortcuts, and drag-and-drop editing techniques
with which to control operations in the Project and other windows. These
functions and a whole lot more are described in detail throughout the course
of this book.

Patience, practice and understanding

This chapter gives you a foretaste of the power and elegance of Cubase. Its streamlined and easy-to-use design is the result of many years of research and development and the program represents the leading edge in native audio music software. It provides a logical and adaptable framework within which you can operate intuitively and creatively. However, despite being one of the more user-friendly music software applications, there is still a learning curve and there are still techniques with which to become familiar and concepts to understand. This requires some initial effort from the user. Achieving the best results requires patience, practice and understanding.

Setting up the system

This chapter describes the hardware you need to run Cubase, how to install the software and what kinds of overall system setups are suitable for the program.

General computer requirements

Cubase runs on PC or Apple Macintosh computers. In order to use the program comfortably you are advised to choose a computer with a very fast processor, a particularly large and fast hard drive and a large amount of RAM. The more audio tracks, effects and VST Instruments you wish to use, the more powerful your computer must be. The system should also include suitable audio hardware, preferably featuring its own dedicated ASIO driver, and a suitable MIDI interface if you intend to record MIDI data. Your computer should also feature a USB port since Cubase is protected by a special key which plugs into a USB socket.

The program has been optimised for the latest operating systems on both platforms. Windows XP is required for the PC and OSX is required for the Mac. The recording of multi-track digital audio makes special demands of a computer system so it is worth considering the details (see Appendix 1). PC users are advised to obtain a PC which has been built specifically for audio purposes. The final choice of platform (PC or Mac) is purely a matter of personal preference.

Info

For those who need more details about computer requirements please consult your user manuals and the latest computer and music technology magazines. See also Appendix 1 at the back of this book.

Installation

Before proceeding

Before proceeding with the installation of any audio hardware and software, verify that you already have one of the recommended operating systems running on the computer and that it is functioning correctly. Before installing Cubase itself, the intended audio hardware and associated driver should have already been installed on the computer.

Audio hardware and drivers

There are various ways in which Cubase can communicate with your audio hardware. This depends as much on the hardwares drivers as on the design of the hardware itself. A driver is a short software program which provides the communication link between the hardware device and the operating sys-

tem (or a specific application like Cubase). The hardware is set up and initialised via the driver software. In the case of Cubase, the program commu-
nicates with the audio hardware according to what kind of driver has been
installed. The main options include:

1 A dedicated ASIO (Audio Stream Input Output) driver supplied with the
   audio hardware. This provides direct communication between Cubase
   and the hardware. This is the preferred choice since it reduces the delay
   between user input and the computer's response. This delay is commonly
   known as latency. Lower latency means smoother and more accurate
   real-time operation of Cubase. A well-written dedicated ASIO driver
   should provide a latency of less than 10ms.
2 A Direct X driver supplied with the audio hardware allowing communication
   with Microsoft Windows Direct X. Direct X handles multimedia operations
   under Windows. When Cubase is installed on a PC computer system, its own
   ASIO Direct X driver is automatically installed. There are, therefore, two
   drivers involved with this option, one for the audio hardware and one for
   Cubase. To communicate with the audio hardware via Direct X you must
   choose the ASIO Direct X Full Duplex driver option for your audio device
   within Cubase. This option provides adequate performance but with inferior
   latency figures to dedicated ASIO drivers.
3 A standard Windows multimedia driver allowing communication between
   Windows compatible audio cards and the Windows multimedia system. This
   is supplied with the audio card. When Cubase is installed on a PC computer,
   its own ASIO Multimedia driver is automatically installed. There are,
   therefore, two drivers involved with this option, one for the audio hardware
   and one for Cubase. To communicate with the Windows multimedia
   compatible hardware you must choose the ASIO Multimedia driver option for
   your audio device within Cubase. This option provides inferior latency
   performance and is not recommended for professional applications.

Option 1 is strongly recommended for all Cubase systems. The best audio cards
and professional audio hardware are supplied with dedicated ASIO drivers.

MIDI interface and drivers
If MIDI functionality is not included in your audio hardware, you will need to install
a separate MIDI interface to record MIDI-based music. Installation of MIDI
devices is usually a simple procedure involving the connection of the hardware
interface to the computer, switching it on and installing the driver (usually supplied on a CD-ROM). All standard MIDI interfaces function with Cubase. See the
documentation supplied with the MIDI interface for full details.

Before installing Cubase
Before installing Cubase you should:

• Preferably defragment the hard disk.
• If you have not already done so, install your audio hardware and driver(s)

according to the supplied documentation (see Audio hardware and drivers, above).

- Test the functionality of the audio hardware outside of Cubase if you have other suitable software already installed (as part of the operating system, for example). This assumes that you already have your hardware's audio outputs connected to an amplifier and loudspeakers (or headphones).
- If needed, install your MIDI interface and driver according to the supplied documentation (see MIDI interface and drivers, above).

Installing Cubase

Cubase is supplied on a DVD-ROM and is easily installed onto a suitably prepared computer. The following steps outline what you need to do:

- Insert the Cubase DVD-ROM and open the Cubase start centre.
- Click on the Cubase Install icon and follow the instructions in the Cubase setup dialogue. Typically, all elements required for Cubase are automatically installed, including an application called the Syncrosoft Licence Control Centre (LCC) which is used to manage your Steinberg software licences.
- Activate your Cubase licence according to the supplied instructions. Your licence is stored on the supplied Steinberg USB protection key.
- Launch Cubase by double-clicking on the Cubase logo on the desktop.

System verification

Upon first launching Cubase you may immediately ask one important question. Where, within Cubase, do I find references to my audio hardware and MIDI interface? The answer lies in firstly knowing the type of ASIO driver supplied with the hardware and the number of audio and MIDI inputs and outputs. You can then set about finding the locations within the software where the ASIO driver and the various inputs and outputs are activated.

Verifying the ASIO driver

Cubase chooses its ASIO driver according to what hardware and driver(s) are already installed in the computer. To inspect the ASIO driver configuration select Device Setup / VST Audio System from the Devices menu. Verify which ASIO driver has been installed in the ASIO driver field (Figure 2.1). If supplied with your audio hardware, make sure that its dedicated ASIO driver is selected here. A special ASIO driver written exclusively for the hardware gives better latency performance than the other options.

Figure 2.1
Finding the ASIO driver in the Device setup window

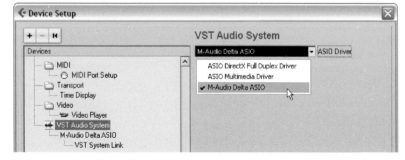

Finding the audio inputs and outputs

When using a typical ASIO driver, the inputs and outputs of your audio hardware are shown within the software at two locations:

1 All available input/output ports are shown in Device setup / << Name of your chosen ASIO driver >> (Devices menu). By default, all ports are made visible within the system (marked by a cross in the 'Visible' column). Input/output ports that you do not need may be de-selected here by clicking in the corresponding box to de-activate the cross. The number of input/output ports depends upon the number of physical inputs and outputs on your audio hardware (Figure 2.2).

Figure 2.2
All the available inputs and outputs of your audio hardware are shown in the Device Setup window.

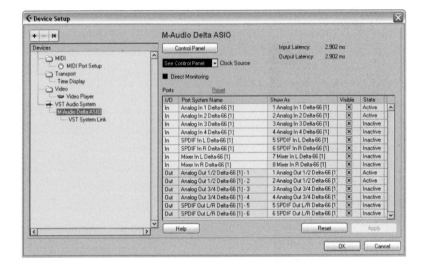

Info

In Cubase, audio input and output routing is based upon buses. Input signals must enter the program via an input bus and output signals must exit via an output bus.

2 The input/output ports are connected in the input and output sections of the VST Connections window (Devices menu). This is where you assign the input and output ports to input and output buses (Figure 2.3). Buses are added using the 'Add bus' button. A bus added in the VST Connections window appears in the Mixer as a channel strip to the left and right of the other channel strips. Only those input/output ports which are actually connected become active within the system and these are marked as such in the 'State' column of the input/output port list in Device Setup.

Figure 2.3
Input and output ports are connected in the inputs and outputs sections of the VST Connections window

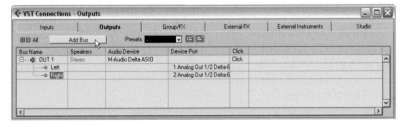

Finding the MIDI inputs and outputs

The available MIDI input and output ports are found in Device Setup / MIDI Port Setup (Devices menu). Here you can show/hide the available ports by clicking in the 'Visible' column (Figure 2.4). Verify that the required MIDI ports are visible. A port becomes active in the 'State' column when the corresponding port is activated on any MIDI track.

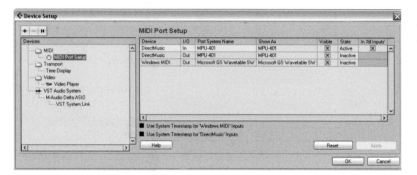

Figure 2.4
The MIDI Port Setup window showing the available MIDI ports

The MIDI ports are available in the pop-up input and output menus found in the Inspector for each MIDI track. Selecting 'All MIDI inputs' allows you to assign multiple MIDI inputs to the same track. The MIDI inputs included when you use 'All MIDI inputs' are specified in the "In 'All Inputs'" column in the MIDI Port Setup window.

Overall system setup

The overall system used for Cubase may vary enormously and depends on the precise requirements of each user. By overall system we mean Cubase and all the peripheral MIDI and audio equipment which surround it (apart from the audio card/hardware already installed).

Basic system elements

The minimum overall setup needed to record and play back both MIDI and audio material involves the following elements (see Figure 2.5):

• For MIDI-based recording, you need some kind of MIDI input device such as a MIDI keyboard/synthesizer or a MIDI guitar.
• For audio recording, the bare minimum is a single microphone connected to a microphone input of the audio card/hardware, or a line-level signal connected to a line input of the audio card/hardware.
• For monitoring purposes, you normally need some kind of amplifier and speaker system (or headphones) to hear the sounds you create within Cubase. In the simplest of cases, the main stereo outputs from your audio card/hardware pass directly to the amplifier / speaker system for monitoring purposes.

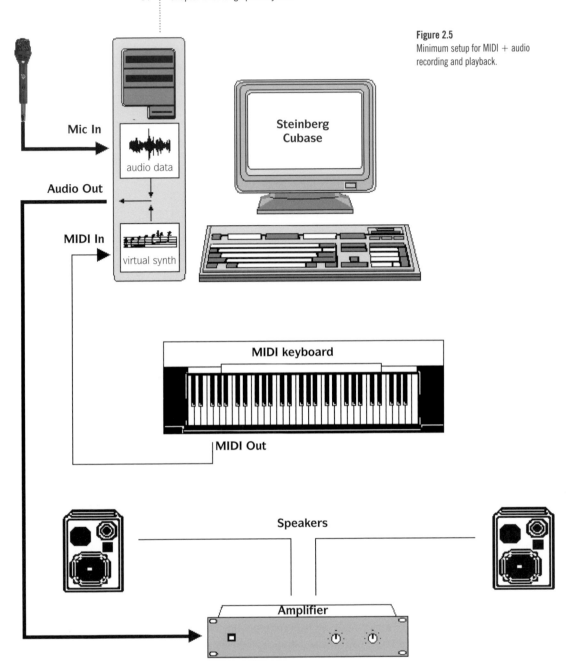

Figure 2.5
Minimum setup for MIDI + audio
recording and playback.

Mic In

audio data

Audio Out

MIDI In

virtual synth

Steinberg
Cubase

MIDI keyboard

MIDI Out

Speakers

Amplifier

MIDI keyboard choice

To make real-time MIDI recordings you need some kind of MIDI triggering
device like a MIDI keyboard, a MIDI guitar, MIDI drum pads or a MIDI wind-
blown instrument. The device should preferably be velocity sensitive and, in
the case of a keyboard, have at least a five octave key span, although two
octave mini-keyboards are excellent for small desktop systems where space
is limited. Those keyboards which have their own sound-making circuitry
should be equipped with MIDI in, out and thru sockets (now standard on reg-

ular MIDI keyboards). Some budget keyboards with no sound-making circuitry may only feature a single MIDI output, which may be all you need to trigger the other MIDI devices and VST instruments within a simple system. Other things to look out for in MIDI keyboards are high quality on-board sounds and effects, ease of programmability and keys which are comfortable to play.

Microphone matters

The microphone is the very first stage in the recording path when you are recording live vocals, musical instruments and other real-world sources so, if you are serious about your recording, it is worth investing in a well-specified model. A bad quality input signal cannot be corrected in Cubase and cannot be improved later, no matter how good the quality of your plug-ins and audio hardware.

For good all-round performance and for the recording of vocals, large diaphragm capacitor microphones usually produce the best results. These invariably require phantom power to drive the microphone. However, microphone choice depends very much on the source which is being recorded and only knowledge and experience can help make the appropriate decision.

The basic techniques for connecting a microphone to a Cubase system include the following:

1 Connection of the microphone directly to the microphone input of the audio hardware device or audio card. Many high-end audio devices feature mic inputs (or mixed mic/line inputs) with phantom power which are suitable for the direct connection of professional microphones.
2 Connection of the microphone to the audio hardware device via a separate mic pre-amp. A mic pre-amp is a unit specialised in optimising the signal from a microphone. The inputs of a mic pre-amp are suitable for the connection of most types of microphone, and line level or digital outputs provide the connection to the audio hardware device.
3 Connection of the microphone to an external mixing console. Most mixing consoles provide microphone and line inputs for the connection of a variety of sources. A line level output signal from the console (e.g. a group out) is then routed to the line inputs of the audio hardware device.

For small-scale systems which do not feature a mixing console, option 2 is the preferred choice. A mic pre-amp can significantly improve the quality of the source signal and some units include built-in compression, EQ, gating or valve simulation effects. However, for non-mixing console systems, option 1 also provides good results but with less flexibility. The quality of the results of option 3 depend very much upon the quality of the mixing console. There is an additional practical problem when using a microphone connected to a small-scale computer recording system: fan noise. Most computers make enough noise to interfere with a microphone recording taking place in the same room. The immediate solution is to place the microphone as great a distance away from the computer as is practical and acoustically desirable, or to use screening between the computer and the microphone. Never attempt to dampen the noise of the fan by blocking the ventilation of the computer case as this could cause your computer to overheat. Of course, the ideal solution is to make all the recordings in a separate (preferably acoustically treated) room, as takes place in a professional recording studio. See Chapter 7 for more details about recording with microphones.

Recording non-microphone sources

If you are recording an electric guitarist or bassist, it is possible to route the signal directly into the line inputs of your audio card / hardware via a guitar or bass pre-amp. Many of the mic pre-amps from the manufacturers mentioned above are dual mic/line devices which can be used for both kinds of sources. This is particularly useful for the small home recording setup and for guitarists who wish to take advantage of computer based recording technology, which tends to be MIDI and keyboard centred. External electronic keyboards, synthesizers and sound modules can normally be linked to the audio card / hardware directly via line level cables or via a mixing console or pre-amplifier. See Chapter 7 for more details about recording non-microphone sources.

Monitoring

The use of high-quality audio monitoring equipment is essential for the best results and is a pre-requisite for all professional Cubase installations. This normally includes either active monitors or a power amplifier with passive monitors placed in an acoustically balanced room. A studio monitoring system is designed to give a clear, neutral sound so that you can make truly accurate judgements during each stage of the recording process.

Large, highly accurate monitors with a wide, flat frequency response which does not significantly colour the sound are normally chosen for professional recording studios. A pair of small near field monitors are often sufficient for home studio setups. These also serve as a second reference in larger setups where the monitoring can be switched between the main speakers and the near field speakers. The final choice of monitor is based upon its technical specifications and your own judgements about its fidelity.

The positioning of the monitors is extremely important. A good starting point is that of an equilateral triangle formed by the listening position and the two speakers. Normally, the monitors are angled slightly towards the listening position. Ideally, the distance between the two monitors should not exceed the distance from the monitors to the listener as this can affect the perception of the stereo image. It is also desirable to have the monitors placed on a non-resonant, rigid surface which does not produce any direct physical vibrations in the actual structure of the room. Also of primary importance is the use of a high quality amplifier which comfortably produces a clear, undistorted signal. The amplifier should not have to be driven to its maximum volume in order to achieve the desired listening level, so a model with sufficient headroom above the average listening level should be chosen.

Info

High-quality monitoring is essential for making accurate judgements about the sound. You are likely to find what you need among the monitors supplied by Adam, Audix, Dynaudio, FAR, Fostex, Genelec, JBL, Klein and Hummel, KRK, M Audio, Mackie, Miller and Kreisel, PMC, Quested, Samson, Tannoy and Yamaha.

Info

Traditional home hi-fi speakers usually produce significant colouration in the sound resulting in confusion when attempting to make accurate judgements about recordings and the mix. A mix sounding excellent on these speakers in your own studio may well sound terrible when you play it on any other system. They are, therefore, best avoided.

Tip

Place your monitors away from walls and reflective surfaces, and, above all, do not place them directly in the corners of your control room.

Complex system considerations

Larger-scale overall setups for Cubase involve a wider range of variables. A large-scale setup is likely to include a mixing console and / or external control hardware, external sound processing equipment and effects, one or more mic pre-amps, high-quality studio monitors and a network of MIDI devices. These items significantly improve the functionality of Cubase. An example setup is shown in Figure 2.6.

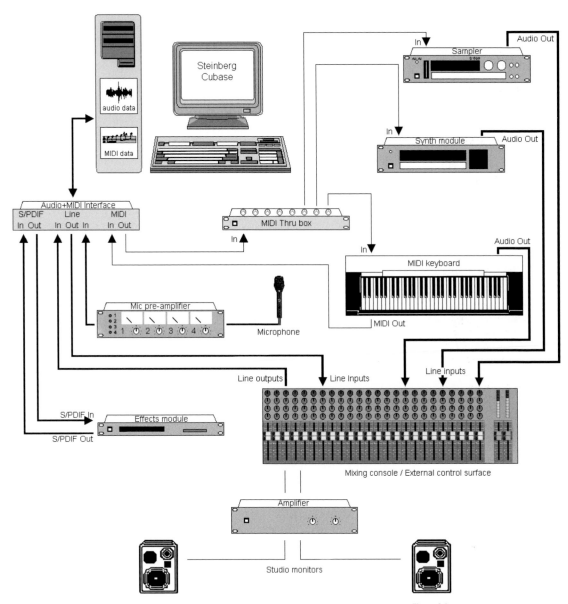

Figure 2.6
A complex Cubase system

Do I need a mixer?

One of the first questions which might be asked when setting up a larger overall system is why do I need an external mixer when there is a virtual mixer in Cubase? The answer is that it depends upon how you want to link Cubase to the external world. Cubase's interconnectivity with the external world is limited by the installed audio hardware and the equipment in the overall system. Simple systems featuring a microphone and mic pre-amp, for example, do not really need an external mixer. In this case, Cubase's mixer might be viewed as being primarily concerned with playback and mixing.

However, an external mixing console is often more flexible for all kinds of recording, playback and routing tasks. For example, the majority of users need a way of interfacing and routing the wide range of equipment which is commonly used in the recording process. This might include one or more microphones, a lead or bass guitar, an electronic keyboard, a multi-track recorder, a CD player or any number of other musical instruments or sound sources. Any combination of these sources might be routed into Cubase via the line-outs of the external mixer. The use of an external mixer also provides direct, hands-on control of multiple faders and control knobs, which is especially convenient for recording multiple sources.

A project studio may require only a small mixer, providing enough inputs for several microphone and line signals (such as those from MIDI keyboards and modules) and enough I/O sockets to be able to interface external units and Cubase (as shown in Figure 2.6, above). For Cubase, a small, high quality external mixer with flexible routing functions is often preferable to a large console with many channels. A small mixer is fine for most recording purposes although it may not be able to handle a large-scale automated mix. In this context, the mixing facilities of Cubase become extremely useful since its virtually unlimited number of mixer channels and advanced automation facilities mean that the mix can be performed entirely within Cubase ('mixing in the box'). The use of Cubase with a small mixer therefore cuts down on the cost and space requirements of a large console.

External control surfaces

One of the limitations of computer-based multi-track audio systems is that manipulation of the controls is achieved mainly via the mouse and keyboard. This is not practical or convenient for the manipulation of some of the common audio control parameters. This is immediately apparent if you try to simultaneously move two faders in Cubase's Mixer. A mouse only allows you to move one fader at a time and a conventional computer keyboard does not feature hardware sliders. The installation of an additional hardware control surface can overcome these problems.

Hardware control surfaces include a number of hardware buttons, faders and control knobs designed for various levels of functional integration with the software. For example, the more sophisticated dedicated control surfaces include transport controls, faders, pan pots and control knobs which can be assigned to the majority of Cubases functions. They may also provide microphone and line inputs, MIDI I/O and routing capability and may therefore replace the necessity for more traditional external mixing console solutions.

Alternatively, some regular mixing consoles can double as control surfaces for Cubase (e.g. Yamaha's 01v, 02r96 and DM series consoles).

Cubase includes support for CM Motormix, Euphonix MC Mix and MC Control, JL Cooper MCS-3000 series, Mackie Control, Radikal SAC 2.x series, Roland MCR8, Steinberg Houston, Tascam US-428, Yamaha 01x, 01v, 02r96, DM1000 and DM2000, many of which feature a high level of functional integration with the program including motorised faders and other controls which reflect the current settings within Cubase. A generic remote setup option allows communication with a wide range of other control surfaces. Open the Device Setup window (Devices menu) and click on the Add device button to see the available options.

MIDI networks
Many Cubase systems include some kind of MIDI network. This is simply a collection of MIDI devices connected together using MIDI cables, usually in a 'star' network similar to that shown in Figure 2.6. Larger star networks feature a MIDI thru box (also called a MIDI splitter box) or some other central MIDI hub which enables the channelling of MIDI data to specific devices within the system. For example, the MIDI network in Figure 2.6 features a master keyboard from which the MIDI Out is sent to the MIDI In of the computer. The MIDI input data passes through Cubase and is passed back out of the computer, along with any other data which has already been recorded, to the MIDI input of the MIDI thru box. The data is then distributed to the respective outputs of the thru box and thus passed 'through' to the MIDI inputs of the master keyboard and to the other modules in the system.

Since the introduction of software-based MIDI instruments, large scale physical MIDI networks are becoming less common. Software-based instruments are commonly referred to as VST Instruments (Virtual Studio Instruments) and a number of examples are included with Cubase. VST Instruments are virtual equivalents of real-world MIDI samplers, synthesizers and drum machines. They reside in the memory of your computer and are triggered via MIDI in much the same way as their external counterparts. They do not suffer from the usual wear and tear of the physical world and they do not need any physical cabling. A vast range of VSTi products are available from Steinberg and other developers and these considerably expand the available sound palette.

CD and DVD recording
Of all the peripheral equipment surrounding Cubase, DVD and CD recorders are among the most useful. These are most often installed as DVD/CD drives within the computer itself rather than as stand-alone separate units. Using a DVD/CD recorder you can create your own Red Book audio CDs for demo or mastering purposes. DVD and CD are also invaluable for routine data back-up where the audio is stored as computer data files. DVDs are particularly appropriate for backup and archiving due to their large storage capacity.

For the creation of audio CDs, audio material may be mixed down directly as audio files onto hard disk using Cubase's Export / Audio mixdown function (this technique is often referred to as 'mixing in the box'). The audio files are

Red Book refers to the technical specifications which govern the correct creation and manufacture of an audio CD, as defined by Sony and Philips. An actual copy of the Red Book is usually only available to CD manufacturing plants. Other CD types have similar colour coded books which govern their creation, such as Yellow Book for CD-ROM, Green Book for CD-i, Orange Book for write-once CD-R, White Book for video CD and Blue Book for CD-Extra.

later burnt onto CD using a separate mastering / burning application, such as Steinberg Wavelab or Bias Peak. For mastering purposes the chosen application must be capable of burning Red Book audio CDs. For reliable results a good quality CD burner is required.

Summary

This chapter has explained some of the variables involved in setting up the software and overall system for Cubase. Any combination of hardware might be included, depending upon the application. Inevitably, setting up uncovers a wide range of issues from the worlds of music production, sound recording and studio design. Knowledge of these subjects not only helps you get the most out of your Cubase system, it also helps you make the right choices of audio hardware. Those readers who wish to enrich their knowledge further are advised to consult the latest music technology magazines and the recommended reading list at the back of this book.

First steps

This chapter shows you how to set up a new project, how to record MIDI and audio tracks, and explores some of the general features of the system. Most users are keen to make their first recording as soon as possible and many attempt to do this without ever having read the manual. This is certainly possible since Cubase has been designed to make the recording process as trouble-free as possible. However, it is not always certain that things will go according to plan since recording is controlled by many parameters. The following step-by-step guides help avoid some of the common problems which may arise during your first attempts at recording.

Recording in Cubase

Creating a new project

The Cubase environment is based upon the idea of organising all your recording, editing and processing endeavours into a project. All the data for a project is normally stored in a single directory on your hard disk, the location of which is chosen before you start recording. The directory for the project contains the project file itself (recognised by its .cpr file extension) and all the associated audio, edit, fade and image files. To ensure a trouble-free journey through the recording processes outlined below it is best to set up a new empty project using the Project Assistant. Proceed as follows:

Figure 3.1
Open the Project Assistant and select Empty

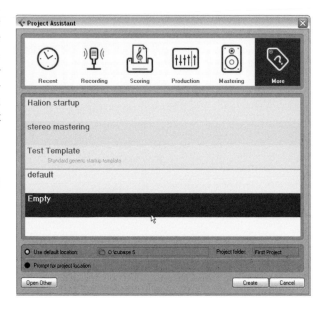

1 Select New Project from the File menu to open the Project Assistant. Select the 'More' icon and choose Empty from the list (Figure 3.1).
2 In the lower section of the Project Assistant, select Use Default Location and click in the folder field (centre) to choose your audio drive or directory

where you intend to store all your projects. Enter a suitable name for the new project folder in the Project Folder field (Figure 3.2).

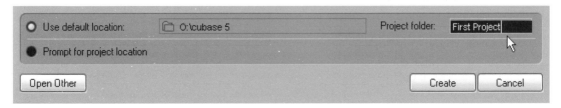

Figure 3.2
Enter the new project folder name in the Project Folder field

3   Click on Create to create the new empty project. An empty Cubase project with various default settings is opened on the screen (Figure 3.3). Immediately save the new project under a new name using File / Save As. The Cubase project file is saved in the project folder you just created. You are now ready to start work.

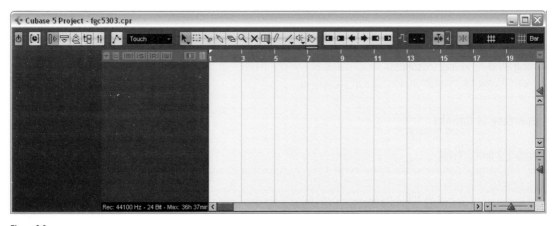

Figure 3.3
The resulting empty project

Project setup

When you create a new project, Cubase gives you a working environment with various default settings. Many of these are found in the Project setup window (Figure 3.4), opened by selecting Project setup from the Project menu. The Project setup determines the settings for a number of fundamental global parameters. Whenever you start a serious project it is best to verify that the values are suitable. Most of the settings could be changed half-way through a project but the sample rate should be set once only before commencing. For the purposes of making your first recordings, as outlined below, configure your Project setup window to match the values shown in Figure 3.4.

The values in the Project setup window are saved as part of each Cubase project file. The parameters include the following:

- Start – determines the start time of the project (hours : minutes : seconds : frames). This allows you to set the start time to values other than zero and to regulate the start time when Cubase is synchronised to an external device.

- Length – determines the overall length of the project (hours : minutes : seconds : frames). Ten minutes is a good default length but this depends entirely upon the kind of project you are creating.
- Frame rate – sets the frame rate for Cubase when it is slaved to external time code.
- Display format – sets the global time line format for all ruler and position displays in Cubase.
- Display offset – allows you to set an offset for the ruler display when working with Cubase slaved to external time code (hours : minutes : seconds : frames).
- Bar offset – allows you to set a bar offset value relative to the start time chosen above. Only relevant when bars and beats are displayed in the ruler.
- Sample rate – determines the sample rate for the project. All audio playback and recording occurs at this sample rate. Here you would normally use 44.1kHz for audio-only projects and 48kHz for sound-to-picture projects. 88.2 and 96kHz help optimise audio quality and suit projects destined for high-end mastering and high-resolution formats such as DVD-Audio and SACD (see 'What bit resolution and sample rate should I use?' in Chapter 7 for more details).
- Record format – determines the bit depth for the project. Although 16-bit provides good quality, 24-bit and 32-bit float are recommended for serious projects.
- Record file type – sets the file format for all audio files recorded within the project.
- Stereo pan law – determines how the level is attenuated when audio signals are panned centre. The default setting is -3dB.

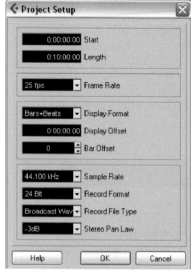

Figure 3.4
Project setup window

Info

It is not necessary to understand all the details of the parameters in the Project setup window before proceeding with your first recordings. The details are explained in other chapters. For the purposes of this chapter, configure your Project window to match the values shown in Figure 3.4. See the glossary in the back pages for an explanation of some of the jargon and terminology used here.

Your first MIDI recording

Connect the MIDI Out of your MIDI keyboard (or other MIDI device) to the MIDI In of your MIDI interface. Verify the connection by checking the MIDI activity indicator on the Transport panel while playing the MIDI keyboard (right-click on the Transport panel and select 'MIDI Activity' if no MIDI Activity indicator is visible). Connect the MIDI Out of your MIDI interface to the MIDI In of the keyboard. Activate the global MIDI Thru function in File / Preferences / MIDI.

1 Add a MIDI track and activate the record enable button

Add a new MIDI track by selecting Add track / MIDI in the Project menu. Select a track count of one and click OK. A new MIDI track is added to the track list. If preferred, you may add an Instrument track instead. An Instrument track gives you a quick connection to one of the VST Instruments

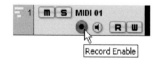

available in your system (see Chapter 4 for more details). Activate the record enable button on the new MIDI track (illuminated in red = active). The record enable button is automatically activated when each track is selected, if 'Enable record on selected track' in File / Preferences / Editing / Project & Mixer is ticked (the default setting). When a track is record enabled MIDI data passes through the track, from the MIDI input to the MIDI output, allowing you to trigger the target MIDI device. Recording takes place on all record enabled tracks when you press the record button on the Transport panel.

2 Set MIDI input/output ports and MIDI channel

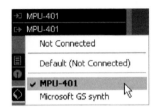

If it is not already visible, open the Inspector for the selected MIDI track by clicking on the Show Inspector button in the top left corner of the Project window. Set the MIDI input port to your chosen MIDI input device in the pop-up MIDI input routing menu. Set the MIDI output port to the desired MIDI output device in the pop-up MIDI output routing menu. The target device could be an external MIDI instrument such as a synthesizer, or it could be an internal VST instrument. There could be several input and output ports available, depending on the hardware and software you have installed or activated in your computer. If applicable, select a MIDI channel in the channel field of the Inspector (normally the same channel as set on the target device).

3 Set metronome

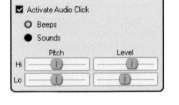

Set up an appropriate precount and guide click by activating Precount and adjusting the settings of the Metronome setup dialogue (Transport menu / Metronome setup). Try ticking 'Precount' in the Transport menu and 'Activate Audio click' in the Metronome setup dialogue. Select 'Beeps' for a standard audio beep. Alternatively, you could use a MIDI device for the click sound by ticking 'Activate MIDI click' and setting the MIDI click channel and output port to an appropriate MIDI device. Set the MIDI notes as required (C#1/37 and F#1/42 are the usual positions for a rimshot and a closed hi-hat respectively). Set a precount of 2 bars.

4 Adjust the tempo and activate click

In the Transport panel, set the tempo to Fixed mode and enter the desired value in the tempo field. Also, activate the click button and de-activate the punch in and punch out buttons (Locators section). Leave all other Transport panel settings in their default positions.

5 Start recording

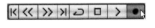

To record, select the record button on the Transport panel. Cubase outputs a two bar count, (as set in the metronome), and then recording commences from bar 1. The selected track turns red to indicate that recording has been implemented. Anything played on your MIDI keyboard is recorded.

6 Stop recording

Stop recording by selecting the stop button on the Transport panel. A graphical strip known as a part remains on the track and this contains the MIDI events you have just recorded (Figure 3.13).

7 Rewind

Rewind the song position in the conventional manner using the Transport panel rewind button or, alternatively, select '.' on the computer's numeric keypad which takes you back to the beginning of the project.

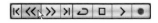

8 Now play it back

To replay the performance select the Transport panel play button.

Save your work by selecting save from the file menu or use Ctrl + S (PC) / Command + S (Mac) on the computer keyboard. The above steps should get you into MIDI recording with the minimum of fuss. Cubase has been supplied with most of the parameters already sensibly set so, in most cases, only the last few steps are necessary to actually make the recording. However, the details outlined here help you become aware of some of the other parameters involved.

Figure 3.13
Resulting MIDI part in the Project window

If you experience problems with this process verify that:

- the MIDI cables are not faulty and have been connected correctly
- the MIDI interface has been correctly installed and is active in Device Setup / MIDI Port Setup
- the relevant ports are selected in the input and output routing menus of the selected MIDI track
- the MIDI channel is appropriate in the channel field of the selected MIDI track
- any external equipment connected to the system is switched on and configured to receive MIDI information on the appropriate channel(s)

Your first audio recording

Make sure that your audio hardware is installed correctly. Open the control panel for the audio hardware and verify the settings. Make sure the first pair of audio outputs are connected to your amplifier and speaker system so that you can hear any audio output. Connect the source signal cable to the first pair of line inputs of your audio hardware. For this exercise, try recording a stereo line level source such as the stereo audio output from an electronic keyboard instrument or a CD player. Select VST Connections from the Devices menu and, in the input and output sections, verify that there is at least one input bus and one output bus assigned to the appropriate ports of your audio hardware.

1 Add an Audio track and activate the record and monitor enable buttons

Add a new Audio track by selecting Add track / Audio in the Project menu. Select stereo in the configuration menu of the pop-up Add dialogue. A new

Record Enable

stereo Audio track is added to the track list. Select Tape Machine Style in File / Preferences / VST / Auto Monitoring. Activate the record enable button on the new Audio track (illuminated in red = active). The record enable button is automatically activated when each track is selected, if Enable record on selected track in File / Preferences / Editing / Project & Mixer is ticked (the default setting). This makes the channel record ready. In Tape Machine Style mode, activating the record enable button also automatically activates the monitor button when you are in stop or record modes. This allows you to hear the input signal and visually monitor the level on the channel level meters. Recording takes place on all record enabled tracks when you press the record button on the Transport panel.

2 Open the Mixer and select Meter input in Global meter settings

Open the Mixer from the Devices menu or select F3 on the computer keyboard. Here you find the input bus which is connected to your audio hardware inputs (on the left) and the channel strip for the Audio track you created in step 1 (to the right). Right-click (PC) / Control + click (Mac) in blank space in the Mixer and select 'Meter input' in the Global meter settings section of the pop-up menu. In the input bus you now see the level of the incoming signal at the input of your audio hardware (before any level changes or other processing takes place within Cubase).

3 Adjust the input level while monitoring the signal in the input bus

The signal level at the input of your audio hardware is visually monitored in the meters of the input bus when the Global meter settings have been set to Meter input. At this stage, the level is adjusted using the output fader of your external mixer or directly on the output faders of the device or instrument you are recording. Some audio hardware allows adjustment of the input signal via its own control panel. The source level at the input is NOT adjusted using the input bus fader or input gain control.

Carefully adjust the source level so that no clipping occurs on the level meter of the input bus channel strip. The peak level value of the incoming signal is shown just below the channel meters. Clipping has occurred if the clip indicator under the fader is illuminated in red. The peak level should not exceed 0dBFS. Signals which exceed this level produce an unpleasant audible distortion. If you are recording at 24-bit resolution it is normal to leave a healthy amount of headroom by aiming for peaks between -10 and -6dBFS and an average signal level of around -18dBFS.

To aurally monitor the signal make sure that the monitor enabled audio channel you created in step 1 is set to receive the signal from the appropriate input bus in the input routing menu above the channel strip (see step 5 below for details). There may be a delay between the moment the signal enters the audio hardware and the moment you hear it via Cubase. This delay is known as latency and varies according to the audio hardware and driver which is installed in your system. Audio hardware devices with special dedicated ASIO drivers give the best performance and are the preferred option.

Overall, this step ensures that the incoming signal is not producing distortion at the input of your audio hardware and is being recorded at the optimum level. This is often a once-only calibration.

Info

Some ASIO drivers allow the use of the Direct Monitoring option in the VST Audio System section of the Device Setup dialogue. This virtually cuts out latency altogether but does not allow the monitoring of the whole signal path which passes through Cubase.

4 Switch to Meter post-fader setting

Now that you know that there is no distortion at the input of your audio hardware, it is appropriate to switch the meter setting back to the default Meter post-fader position. You are now monitoring the signal after it has passed through the input gain, fader and any other processing on the input bus and it is this signal which is recorded to hard disk. If you have not changed any of the controls on the input bus then the post-fader output signal is identical to the input signal. If you are suffering from a particularly weak source signal, you may at this stage wish to adjust the input gain on the input bus. Hold Shift or Alt and adjust the input gain control as required. You may also apply insert effects or EQ on the input bus. This allows you to print effects and processing to hard disk (such as a signal with compression and EQ). Adding effects may result in an increase in signal level which is too hot to be recorded on hard disk. If this is the case reduce the level slightly using the input bus fader.

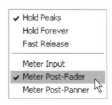

5 Select an input on the record channel

Verify that the record enabled audio channel you created in step 1 is set to receive the signal from the appropriate input bus (i.e. that to which you have connected your stereo audio source). The input bus for audio channels is chosen by clicking in the input routing menu above the channel strip (found in the Mixer or in the Inspector). You may need to extend the view of the Mixer if the input/output routing menus are not visible. The default names for the first pair of inputs for your audio hardware usually read 'S In 1'. By default, a stereo audio channel is routed to the first stereo output bus found in your system which, in turn, is connected to the first pair of outputs on the audio hardware. Note that the fader and other controls of the target record channel come *after* the signal is recorded to hard disk and are therefore used purely for monitoring and mixing purposes. The record level and record quality of the incoming audio signal is not affected by any settings you make here.

6 Adjust the metronome and tempo

Adjust the Metronome to give the desired pre-count before recording commences. It is possible to record audio with no concern for the current tempo but here it is assumed you are using the tempo of the click to keep in time. In the Transport panel, activate the click button and de-activate the punch in and punch out buttons (Locators section). Set the tempo to Fixed mode and enter the desired value in the tempo field. Leave all other Transport panel settings in their default positions.

7 Start recording

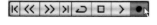

To record, select the record button on the Transport panel. After the pre-count, commence the musical performance (or send the audio signal). In this exercise, recording commences at bar 1. The selected record-enabled track turns red when recording commences.

8 Stop and play back the recording

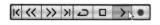

Stop recording by selecting the stop button on the Transport panel. A graphical strip remains on the track containing a waveform which represents the audio you have just recorded. This is known as an audio event. To play back the audio, rewind and press the play button (note that in Tapemachine Style mode, as chosen in step 1 above, playback automatically deactivates the monitor button so that you can hear the recorded audio).

Figure 3.22
Resulting audio event in the Project window

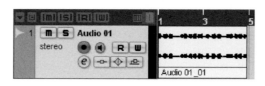

The resulting audio event appears in a similar manner to that shown in Figure 3.22. Save your work by selecting save from the file menu or use Ctrl + S (PC) / Command + S (Mac) on the computer keyboard.

First impressions

Creating a new project and recording with Cubase reveals some of the primary features of the program. The MIDI and audio recording processes operate in a similar fashion and, once you become familiar with the parameters, recording can be accomplished with fewer steps than those outlined above. You may have also noticed that you can achieve a great deal without ever leaving the Project window. The Project window is at once a powerful multi-track recorder and a sophisticated multi-track editor in a single ergonomic environment. Its streamlined approach speeds up your production time and enhances your creativity. However, before exploring the Project window in more detail, lets look at the system in a more generalised way.

Testing the controls

Some users miss many of the peripheral features of Cubase by using only the mouse in a misguided quest for quick results. Relying on the mouse alone is not the best way of using the program. There are also a wide range of key commands which make editing and navigating around the system faster and easier. Many of these are already assigned by default and some of the most useful are shown in Table 3.1.

Tip

In many cases, using key commands is faster and easier than using the mouse. You can at any time change the default settings or assign new key commands in the Key Commands dialogue (File / Key commands).

Table 3.1 Default key commands

QWERTY keyboard		Function
PC	**Mac**	
F2	F2	open/close Transport panel
F3	F3	open/close Mixer
F4	F4	open/close VST Connections
F8	F8	open/close video
F9	F9	select previous tool
F10	F10	select next tool
F11	F11	open/close VST instruments rack
F12	F12	open/close VST performance meter
ctrl + O	command + O	open project
ctrl + S	command + S	save project
ctrl + W	command + W	close current window
ctrl + Q	command + Q	quit program
ctrl + E	command + E	open default editor associated with the event type
ctrl + R	command + R	Score edit
ctrl + X	command + X	cut
ctrl + C	command + C	copy
ctrl + V	command + V	paste
ctrl + Z	command + Z	undo
ctrl + P	command + P	open Pool
ctrl + T	command + T	open Tempo track
alt + I	option + I	show/hide Inspector
backspace	backspace	delete selected track, part or event
return	return	open/close editor
C	C	metronome click on/off
F	F	autoscroll on/off
G	G	zoom out
H	H	zoom in
J	J	snap on/off
M	M	mute on/off
P	P	move locators to selection
R	R	record enable track
S	S	solo on/off

Learning to use Cubase is rather like learning to drive a car. In the same way as it's a good idea to become familiar with the controls of a car before taking it out on the road, it's a good idea to become familiar with the controls of Cubase before you start using it for serious projects. For example, try the following steps to get used to manipulating some of the key areas of the Project window and Mixer:

- Start a new empty project as outlined in the recording exercises above.
- Select Project / Add Track / Audio. In the dialogue which appears, enter a count of four and press OK. Four audio tracks appear in the track list.
- Press the up or down arrows on the computer keyboard to select different tracks. The selected track is highlighted.
- Press F9 / F10 to select the previous / next tool in the toolbar.
- Press F11 to open / close the VST instruments rack. This is where you load VST instruments.
- Press F12 to show / hide the VST performance meter. This is where you keep an eye on the CPU load and disk performance in projects which make heavy use of your computer's resources.
- Press F2 to open / close the Transport panel. Try leaving the Transport panel open and drag it to a convenient location on screen.
- Press Alt+I to open / close the Inspector for a track (the Inspector opens to the left of the track list).
- Now press F3 to open the Mixer. The Mixer displays all tracks as channel strips in the same order in which they appear in the Project window.
- With the Mixer still open on screen, press the left / right arrows on the computer keyboard to select different channel strips.
- Press the up / down arrows on the computer keyboard to change the level of the fader of the currently selected channel strip.
- Press the M key to mute / unmute the channel.
- Press the S key to solo / unsolo the channel.
- Press the R key to record enable / record disable the channel.
- Press F3 a second time to close the Mixer.

Note that many of the key commands are on / off or open / close toggle switches for their respective functions. You can therefore handle Cubase in a very quick and logical fashion. Other immediately useful key commands include the C key for turning the guide click on and off, and the G and H keys for horizontal zoom out and zoom in.

The numeric keypad

The numeric keypad may be used as a remote control for the transport functions. This provides a quick and handy alternative to the Transport panel which is particularly helpful when the latter is hidden from view (see Table 3.2).

Table 3.2 Numeric keypad shortcuts

Numeric keypad		Function
PC	Mac	
*	*	record
Enter	Enter	play
0	0	stop
–	–	rewind
+	+	fast forward
1	1	go to left locator
2	2	go to right locator
•	•	go to bar 1.1.1.0
/	/	cycle on/off

Mouse and computer keyboard ergonomics

The mouse is, above all, useful for drag-and-drop functions, changing values, using tools, selecting objects, opening menus and fine editing in the editors. It is also convenient for setting the project cursor position by clicking once in the ruler above the track display. In addition, double-clicking in the ruler starts playback from the point at which you clicked, and double-clicking a second time in the ruler stops playback. However, for the quickest and most efficient use of the program it is best not to rely exclusively on the mouse.

The best overall approach for the manipulation of the controls, tools and functions of Cubase is an intelligent combination of mouse moves and key commands. This requires a practical and ergonomic approach to the physical workspace. Arrange your equipment on your work surface so that you use your left hand for key commands on your typewriter keyboard and your right hand for mouse manipulations (or vice versa for left-handed users). This two-handed approach dramatically speeds up editing and other processes.

The menus

The menus are found under various headings at the top of the computer screen and it is well worth browsing through the menu contents to find out what is available. It is apparent from the range of menu items that Cubase is extremely versatile. Some of the most important elements include the file save and open functions; the import options; the undo and select options; project setup and media options; audio menu and audio processing options; the MIDI editors; the quantize functions; and the score, transport and VST functions. Most of the important menu items are explored throughout the course of this book.

Cubase startup options

You can set Cubase to behave in various different ways when the program is launched by changing the selection in the 'On Startup' option in File / Preferences / General (Figure 3.23).

Figure 3.23
Changing the startup options in the general preferences dialogue.

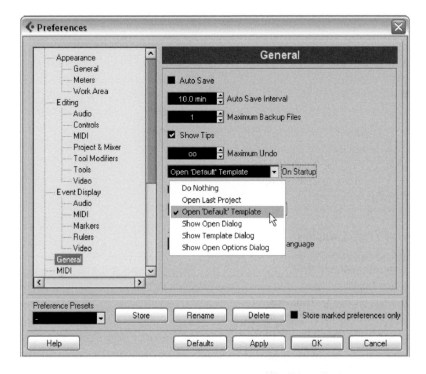

The available options are as follows:

- Do nothing – Cubase is launched as an empty environment with no open Project window.
- Open last project – opens the last project which was worked upon in Cubase.
- Open default project – opens the Cubase default project file (named as default.cpr).
- Show open dialogue – automatically opens a Project file selection dialogue when Cubase is launched.
- Show template dialogue – opens a project template dialogue.
- Show open options dialogue – opens an options dialogue, allowing you to choose from a list of your most recent projects.

These options help manage how you start your Cubase sessions. If you are working on a single long-term project then 'Open last project' is the best option. If you are using Cubase as a musical notepad then you may prefer to start with the same default project at the beginning of each session, in which case you should select 'Open default project'. If you continually change between a number of simultaneous projects on the same system then try using 'Show open options dialogue'.

The Project window

This chapter provides information about the Project window, the Project window tools, track types, the Transport panel, the Inspector, event and part editing, and file handling. The Project window is the central hub of activity within Cubase and, as such, this chapter is essential reading for those not yet familiar.

The Project window

Project window basics

The Project window (Figure 4.1) features time on the horizontal axis and tracks on the vertical axis. Tracks are added to the project using the Add command in the Project menu. A number of different track types are available including audio, instrument, MIDI, arranger, FX, folder, group, marker,

Figure 4.1
The Project window

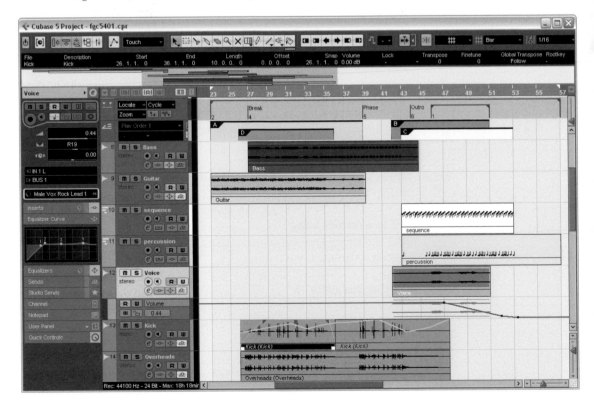

ruler, signature, tempo, transpose, automation and video types. A track can be re-named by double-clicking on its name field. Various buttons surround the track name including (for audio and MIDI tracks) the mute and solo buttons (M and S), the record and monitor buttons (circular record and speaker icons), and the read and write buttons for track automation (R and W). Tracks contain events in the form of graphical blocks, lines, waveforms and symbols arranged along the time line in the central area of the Project window. This central area is known as the event display.

The current time position is shown by a vertical line known as the project cursor. When in play mode, the project cursor moves along the time line which is marked by a ruler located just above the event display. By default, the ruler displays time in bars and beats but by clicking on the arrow to the right of the ruler you can also find options for displaying time in seconds, time code or samples. There can be only one active Project window at any one time. An active Project window is designated by an illuminated blue indicator in the top left corner of the toolbar. A new project may be created at any time by selecting New Project in the File menu or by pressing Ctrl (PC) / Command (Mac) + N on the computer keyboard.

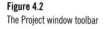

Info

Several projects could be opened within Cubase at the same time. However, only one can be active at any given moment (designated by an illuminated blue indicator in the top left corner of the toolbar).

The toolbar

The Project window features a toolbar above the event display which contains a number of function buttons and tools (Figure 4.2). These provide easy access to the display and editing properties of the Project window.

Figure 4.2
The Project window toolbar

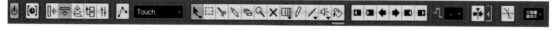

Let's take a look at the most commonly used buttons and the editing tools, as found in the default setup of the toolbar. From left to right the first five buttons include:

The show Inspector button

This shows/hides the information and editing area to the left of the event display known as the Inspector (see The Inspector (below) for more details).

The show Infoline button

This shows/hides an information line above the display which shows the details of the currently selected event.

The show Overview button

This shows/hides an overview strip above the display used for sizing and navigating within the event display.

The Open Pool button

This opens the Pool, a file display and organisation window which shows all the audio and video clips used in the active Project (see Chapter 10 for more details).

The Open Mixer button

This opens the Mixer, a virtual mixing console for the mixing of all audio, MIDI, Instrument and Group tracks and the setting up of EQ, effects and automation (see Chapter 11 for more details).

The Infoline

The Infoline (shown by clicking on the Infoline button in the toolbar) displays information about the currently selected event or part. The contents vary according to what kind of event or part is chosen. For a MIDI part the Infoline includes (from left to right) the name, start time, end time, length, offset, mute status, lock status, transpose and velocity values. Most of these are self explanatory. Offset is an amount by which the contents can be moved back and forth in time relative to the start and end of the part. Lock allows various attributes of the part, such as position and size, to be locked to avoid accidental changes to important material.

Figure 4.3
Infoline for a MIDI part

Name	Start	End	Length	Offset	Mute	Lock	Transpose	Global Transpose	Velocity	Rootkey
MIDI part	43. 1. 1. 0	55. 1. 1. 0	12. 0. 0. 0	0. 0. 0. 0 -		-	-	0	Follow	0	-

The infoline is particularly useful for detailed editing since all fields can be directly edited using the mouse and computer keyboard. When more than one event is selected the infoline text is shown in yellow and contains the information relevant to the first of the selected events. Editing any of the yellow values applies the changes relatively to all selected events (i.e. changing the start position from, for example, bar 17 to bar 18 moves all selected events one bar later than their current position). To apply the edits in an absolute sense hold down Ctrl while making the changes (this time, changing the start position from bar 17 to bar 18 moves all selected events to the same absolute position at bar 18).

The Infoline for an audio event is very similar but contains a greater number of data fields including the file name which is referenced by the audio event; a description field; the start, end and length; offset, snap and volume fields; fade, mute and lock fields; and transpose and fine tune. See Chapter 8 for more information about the audio event Infoline.

The Overview strip

The Overview strip (shown by clicking on the show overview button in the toolbar) shows a thumbnail view of the event display. The blue selection box outlines the horizontal bar range shown in the event display and by grabbing either end of the selection box (a double arrow appears) you can change the range. You can also grab the whole box (a hand symbol appears) and drag it to a new position within your arrangement.

Figure 4.4
Overview

Other toolbar functions

The buttons and functions visible on the toolbar may be shown/hidden using the options shown in the pop-up menu which appears when you right click (PC) / Ctrl + click (Mac) anywhere on the toolbar. Other functions include

Constrain delay compensation, Performance meter, Locators, Time display, Markers, Nudge palette and the Colour menu. Constrain delay compensation helps minimise additional latency which may be caused by the automatic delay compensation of the program while monitoring live audio or a VSTi on channels with insert effects. The Performance meter allows you to see the current load on the CPU and hard drive. The Locators option shows the left and right locator positions. The Markers option provides a numerical display of the first ten markers. The Nudge palette allows you to trim the start and end points of the current event selection or move the event back and forth in time. The colour menu provides a colour palette for changing the colour of the currently selected track or event. The order in which the buttons and functions appear on the toolbar is edited in the Setup dialogue.

The Project window tools

To choose a tool in the Project window make a selection from the tool buttons in the toolbar or click with the right mouse button (PC) / Ctrl + click (Mac) in the event display to open a pop-up tool selection menu known as the Quick menu. The tools are for the manipulation and editing of events and parts and they include the following:

Object selection tool (pointer tool)

The object selection tool (or pointer tool) is the default, general purpose tool for the selection, moving and copying of events and parts, and for the manipulation of data anywhere in the Project window. Its button has a small downward pointing arrow in the lower right corner. This indicates a multi-function tool. Click on the tool button a second time to reveal the other functions. There are two additional options: sizing moves contents and sizing applies time stretch. Sizing moves contents moves the contents of an event or part forward or backward in time according to whether you size the object by sliding the start or end handles, (this effectively locks the start or end of the contents to the start or end of the object). Sizing applies time stretch stretches (or compresses) the contents of an object when you re-size it. For MIDI parts the notes are re-positioned accordingly and for audio events the audio is time-stretched (or compressed).

Range selection tool

The range selection tool is for making event-independent selections of any material in the Project window. Once selected, the material can be cut, copied and pasted as required (moving range selected data automatically splits events where applicable). This is in contrast to the object selection tool which always selects whole events and parts.

Split tool

The split tool is for splicing events/parts into smaller portions. Events/parts are split at the mouse position and according to the current snap settings. Holding Alt while clicking with the split tool automatically divides the event/part into a number of smaller events at the resolution of the snap settings.

Glue tool

The glue tool is used to join together two or more events/parts. In the case of MIDI material, parts are joined to make one longer MIDI part. In the case of audio material, events/parts are grouped into one longer audio part. Holding Alt while clicking on an event glues all the following events on that track into one long event.

Erase tool

The erase tool is for deleting events by clicking on any single object or selected group of objects in the event display. Holding Alt while clicking on an event (or while clicking in blank space) deletes all the following events on that track.

Zoom tool

The zoom tool is for zooming in and out of the event display. To zoom in, select the zoom tool and click once in the event display. This zooms in to the display horizontally around the position at which you clicked. To zoom out, click with the zoom tool while holding Alt. By clicking and dragging a selection box with the zoom tool you can zoom in to specific areas of the event display. Holding Ctrl (PC) / Command (Mac) while clicking with the zoom tool steps back through the previous zoom views you have used. Holding Shift while clicking in the event display with the zoom tool gives you a view of all events in the project. By default, the zoom tool acts upon the display horizontally. For simultaneous horizontal and vertical zooming deactivate zoom tool standard mode in File / Preferences / Editing / Tools.

Mute tool

The mute tool is for muting events and parts. Click on objects individually or drag a selection box over several to implement muting. When an object is muted it is displayed in grey. Muting actions are not stored in the undo list and so cannot be undone using Ctrl / Command + Z. To undo a mute, click on the muted object a second time.

Time warp tool

The time warp tool is for dragging a bar position to a time position. This might be used to line up the start or end of a musical passage to a visual cue in a video or it might equally be used to make a musical sequence fit a specific time duration. The time warp tool operates between the left and right locators in two modes; default mode and musical events follow mode. In the default mode, all tracks are automatically switched to linear time base and do not move when you drag the warp tool in the display. In musical events follow mode, the events on all tracks which are set to musical time base mode are moved as you drag the warp tool in the display. The time warp tool is used most effectively when you set the snap mode to Events, at which time it becomes easier, for example, to drag a bar position to the start or end of an event. Inserting markers in the Marker track also helps navigate the Warp tool to the desired time position. Holding Shift while clicking in the Project window display with the Time warp tool inserts a tempo event. Holding Shift with the time warp tool in the ruler allows the deleting of tempo events. To use the time warp tool, tempo track mode must be selected in the Transport bar (time warp does not function in fixed tempo mode). For more details on the use of the time warp tool see Chapter 18.

Draw tool

The draw tool is used for drawing new empty parts by dragging the tool in the event display, adding markers in the Marker track (see below for details) and freely drawing such things as volume and pan curves on automation tracks.

Line tool

The line tool features straight line, parabola, sine, triangle and square forms which may be used to draw their respective shapes on automation tracks according to the current snap resolution.

Play/scrub tool

The play/scrub tool is a dual function tool. In its default play mode, clicking on an audio or MIDI event plays back the material from the position at which you click and continues for as long as you hold the mouse button. In scrub mode clicking and dragging over an audio or MIDI event plays back the material at the speed with which you drag, much like rocking the tape back and forth over the playback heads of a tape machine. You can change the characteristics of the scrub behaviour in File / Preferences / VST / Scrub.

Colour tool

The colour tool allows you to apply different colours to events in the display. The colour is chosen from a pop-up colour palette which appears when you click on the colour strip just below the tool button. Double-clicking on the colour strip opens the event colour dialogue where you can create your own custom colours. To change an event back to the default colour chosen for the track, click on the event with the colour tool with 'default colour' chosen from the colour palette.

Autoscroll and snap functions

Autoscroll and Suspend Autoscroll button

The Autoscroll button status is managed using the mouse or by pressing 'F' on the computer keyboard. When activated, the event display follows the project cursor. When de-activated, the event display remains static regardless of the project cursor position. An activated Suspend Autoscroll button automatically suspends autoscroll behaviour when you proceed with any kind of editing operation. The suspend status is cancelled by re-starting the transport or by clicking on the suspended autoscroll button.

The snap button

The snap button is found to the right of the autoscroll button and is activated/de-activated using the mouse or by pressing J on the computer keyboard. When activated, all tool manipulations and editing moves are sensitive to the snap settings. Snap describes the manner in which event manipulations and editing with the tools is pulled onto the nearest bar or beat (or other subdivision) of the grid. This occurs according to a chosen snap resolution.

The snap to zero crossing button

When activated, the global Snap to zero crossing button forces all editing of audio events onto the zero crossing points of the waveform. Zero crossing points are where there are the least amounts of energy in the audio signal. Editing here reduces the occurrence of audible clicks and makes for a good join when one section of audio is joined to another. This effects the re-sizing and splitting of audio events. However, when both the Snap button and the Snap to zero crossing button are activated, re-sizing or splitting audio events occurs at the nearest zero crossing point to the Snap point and not directly on the beat specified by the snap resolution, as usually happens. This may cause unforeseen side-effects when working with audio events which you expect to start or end on precise bar or beat divisions. As a general rule, the global Snap to zero crossing button is best left in its default disabled state, unless you have a specific reason for activating it.

The snap, grid and quantize menus

There are a number of menus and parameters which govern snap behaviour. Most of these are found to the right of the snap button in three menus known as the Snap type menu, the Grid type menu and the Quantize type menu (Figure 4.5).

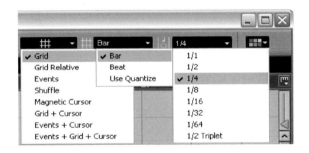

Figure 4.5
The Snap type, Grid type and Quantize type menus

Snap type menu

The Snap type menu contains the following options:

- Grid – the snap resolution is governed by the setting of the Grid type menu to the right.
- Grid relative – the snap resolution is governed by the setting of the Grid type menu but dragged objects maintain their relative position to the nearest snap point. For example, dragging an event whose initial position is bar 1 beat 2, with Grid relative enabled and Bar selected in the Grid type menu, snaps the event to bar 2 beat 2, bar 3 beat 2, bar 4 beat 2 and so on, as you drag the event across the display. This mode is excellent for moving and copying events whose positions do not begin on precise divisions of the bar.
- Events – the start and end positions of objects become magnetic. Any events dragged near to these points are snapped onto the start or end of the nearest object.
- Shuffle – objects moved on a track are snapped tightly one against the

> **Tip**
>
> Snap might be viewed as a magnetic grid which you impose upon the event display. With the snap button activated, objects moved or edited in the display are attracted to the nearest magnetic grid line.

other with no space in between. This mode may be used for changing the order of consecutive events by inserting an object in between two others. Objects to the right of the insert point are automatically moved forward to make room for the newly inserted event.

- Magnetic cursor – the project cursor becomes magnetic and any objects dragged nearby are snapped to its position.
- Grid + cursor – grid and magnetic cursor modes combined.
- Events + cursor – event and magnetic cursor modes combined.
- Events + grid + cursor – event, grid and magnetic cursor modes combined.

Grid type menu

The Grid type menu changes according to which time line format has been chosen in the ruler. Click on the downward pointing arrow to the right of the ruler to change the time format. This is most commonly set to bars and beats, in which case the menu contains the following:

- Bar – tool editing and event placement snaps to the nearest 1 bar division on the ruler.
- Beat – tool editing and event placement snaps to the nearest 1 beat division on the ruler.
- Use quantize – tool editing and event placement snaps to the nearest division as chosen in the Quantize type menu (see below).

Quantize type menu

The Quantize type menu contains a list of note values which may be used to define the snap resolution. However, the quantize value is only relevant to snap behaviour when all three of the following selections are made:

- grid is selected in the Snap mode type menu (see above)
- use quantize is selected in the Grid type menu (see above)
- bars and beats is chosen as the time format on the ruler.

If any of these is not the case then the Quantize type becomes irrelevant to the snap behaviour.

Managing snap behaviour is an alternative function of the Quantize type menu, which is normally used for the main Quantize function in the MIDI menu. When used to govern the snap resolution in the Project window, quantize allows the editing and moving of events to be locked to musically meaningful positions along the time scale. This helps you complete your musical arrangement with maximum speed and accuracy. The main quantize functions (MIDI menu) automatically move recorded musical events onto the divisions of the bar chosen in the Quantize type menu. Quantize was first devised as a purely corrective function for MIDI recordings but, in Cubase, it is also used to affect the timing of audio material and govern the snap resolution for editing in general. Cubase provides two main quantize functions known as Over quantize and Iterative quantize (see the MIDI menu). Over quantize moves recorded events onto the exact divisions of the bar as chosen in the Quantize type menu, whereas Iterative quantize moves recorded events towards the chosen value according to a strength percentage (see Chapters 5 and 6 for more details about quantizing).

The ruler and the left and right locators

The Project window features a ruler above the event display to help you navigate within your project and to specify the timing divisions which Cubase takes into account for transport and editing operations. Click on the downward pointing arrow to the right of the ruler to change the time format (Figure 4.6). This is most commonly set to bars and beats but the time line may also be displayed in seconds, timecode and samples.

The ruler also displays the left and right locators. These are shown as pointers at each end of a shaded area in the ruler and event display. The locators are used for defining the positions you want to start and stop recording and for setting up cycle playback and cycle recording operations (Figure 4.7). The positions of the left and right locators are set in the

Figure 4.6
Choosing the time format in the Project window ruler.

Figure 4.7
The left and right locators in the ruler.

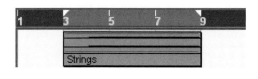

Transport panel or by clicking and dragging in the upper half of the ruler (a pencil tool appears). Moving the right locator to a position before the left locator implements skip mode where playback jumps between the start and end points of the shaded area. This is good for quickly testing alternative musical arrangements.

Split, divide, size and track colour functions

Vertical split point
The Project window features a vertical split point at the left edge of the event display. Pulling the split point to the left maximises the size of the event display, giving you more space to work. Pulling the split point to the right reveals more of the buttons and functions associated with the tracks.

Divide track list
Clicking on the Divide track list button divides the track list into two separate displays. This is useful when working with video tracks where the video track can be placed in the upper display while all the audio and MIDI tracks are placed in the lower display. This allows you to freely scroll within the musical arrangement while always keeping the video track visible in the upper part of the display. Similarly, the Marker track might be better placed in the upper display so that it is always visible. The divided track list is also good for using Ruler tracks set to different time displays (e.g. one set to SMPTE time in the upper display and another set to bars and beats in the lower display).

Track size
The vertical size of the tracks is scaleable. Clicking and dragging on the lower edge of a track allows you to change its vertical size. Holding Ctrl (PC) /

Command (Mac) while dragging on the lower edge sets all tracks to the same row size. Greater track size reveals more of the tracks buttons and expands the waveform or MIDI events view in the event display. By default, Cubase sizes the tracks in terms of rows but if you need to resize freely, de-activate 'Snap Track Heights' in the Track scale pop-up menu (found just above the vertical zoom control).

Track colours

Clicking on the small colour palette above the track list toggles between standard and colour-coded track displays. When colour is activated, the tracks show their default colours in the Project window, Mixer and Inspector. This helps clarify the screen display and allows you to change the default track colour from the pop-up colour palette which appears when you click in each track's colour box in the track list. Colour may be applied to all tracks.

Zoom and sizing functions in the Project window

There are a wide range of functions available for zooming in and out of the event display. This section outlines a number of techniques designed to help you manage the zoom status and general look of the display more easily.

Using the zoom tool

> **Info**
>
> If you prefer the traditional, no nonsense way of zooming in and out, use the horizontal and vertical zoom sliders found in the lower right corner of the Project window.

Among the simplest ways to zoom in is to select the zoom tool and click in the event display. This zooms in to the display around the position at which you clicked. Holding Alt while clicking with the zoom tool zooms back out again. Standard horizontal or combined vertical/horizontal zooming takes place according to the zoom tool mode chosen in File / Preferences / Editing. Clicking and dragging a selection box with the zoom tool allows you to zoom in to specific areas of the event display. To zoom back out again hold Ctrl (PC) / Command (Mac) while clicking in the event display with the zoom tool. This steps you back to the previous zoom view you have used.

Zoom in the ruler

> **Tip**
>
> To achieve a full horizontal and vertical view of all events in the project, select the Zoom tool, hold Shift and click once in the event display.

Clicking in the ruler and moving the mouse position up or down while keeping the mouse button pressed allows you to zoom in and out horizontally in the event display. Drag down to zoom in and drag up to zoom out. Note that the project cursor is automatically moved to the position of the mouse, and for the function to work correctly, Zoom while locating in time scale must be activated File / Preferences / Transport.

Zoom default key commands

There are a number of default key commands which provide quick and convenient zoom control. Press H to zoom in horizontally and G to zoom out horizontally. Press Alt + H to zoom in vertically and Alt + G to zoom out vertically. Shift + F gives you a full horizontal zoom up to the end of the events currently present in the display.

Zoom with the overview strip

The overview strip provides a graphical way of zooming and navigating within your project. The strip is shown by clicking on the Show overview button in the toolbar. The overview features a blue selection box which can be dragged to new positions and re-sized. The selection box outlines the horizontal bar range shown in the event display and by grabbing either end of the selection box (a double arrow appears) you can change the horizontal zoom. (See also The Overview Strip, above).

Zoom presets menu

The Zoom presets menu (Figure 4.8) is revealed when you click on the small downward pointing arrow to the right of the horizontal scroll bar. The menu features a number of presets for full horizontal zoom, zooming to the section inside the left and right locators and, if they are present, you can zoom in to cycle marker positions (see The Marker track below for more details about cycle markers). You can also store your own horizontal zoom presets. To achieve this, set up your desired horizontal zoom, open the Zoom presets menu, select Add and type in a suitable name in the dialogue which appears. Try setting up presets in terms of time. Horizontal zoom factors of 1sec, 10secs and 1min can prove quite useful. To help still further key commands may be assigned to the first five presets in File / Key Commands (try Alt + 1-5).

Track scale menu

The Track scale menu (Figure 4.9) is revealed when you click on the small downward pointing arrow below the vertical scroll bar. The menu features a number of presets for scaling the vertical zoom in terms of rows. Various preset row values are available and you can also use 'Zoom tracks N rows' and 'Zoom N tracks' to achieve the vertical scale of your choice.

The Quick menu

The Quick menu is a context sensitive pop-up menu opened by clicking with the right mouse button on the area of interest. The contents of the menu vary according to where you click and include only options which are relevant to the chosen area. For example, clicking in the event display opens a menu containing the Project window tools and a wide range of general editing options (Figure 4.10). This menu also varies according to whether there is an event selected and what kind of event this is. When a MIDI part is selected the Quick menu includes more MIDI related items such as the MIDI functions and advanced quantize. When an audio event is selected it contains more audio related items such as the audio processing and audio plug-in options.

Clicking with the right mouse button in the Track list opens a Quick menu with functions relevant to tracks such as the Add functions and Show/Hide automation options (Figure 4.11). Additional functions are added to the menu if you right click directly on a track.

Figure 4.8
The Zoom presets menu.

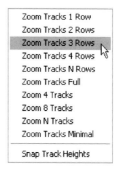

Figure 4.9
The Track scale menu.

Figure 4.10
The Quick menu in the event display.

Figure 4.11
The Quick menu in the track list

The Transport panel

The Transport panel is a user-configurable strip for the control of standard transport operations such as record, play, stop, rewind, and various record, playback and cycle modes. It is opened by selecting Transport panel in the Transport menu or by pressing F2 on the computer keyboard (Figure 4.12). It can be dragged to any screen position and each section of the panel can be shown/hidden by right clicking anywhere on the panel and making the desired selection from the pop-up menu. All of its parameters may be updated or manipulated in some way using either the mouse or computer keyboard commands.

Figure 4.12
The Transport panel

Apart from the obvious tape recorder style controls the Transport panel also features the following:

Virtual keyboard

This is a virtual MIDI keyboard played by clicking the on-screen keys or by pressing the appropriate keys on your computer keyboard. Output is directed to any monitor-enabled MIDI or instrument track. When Virtual Keyboard is active, normal computer keyboard function is suspended since key strokes

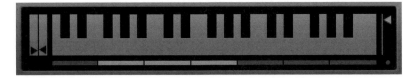

now trigger MIDI output. Virtual Keyboard is particularly useful for musicians who compose on the move and for those who need a quick and convenient method of triggering and auditioning sounds on-screen, without additional hardware. To get to know Virtual Keyboard try the following key commands:

- Press Alt + K to toggle Virtual Keyboard on or off.
- Press the Tab key to toggle the virtual keyboard display between computer key and musical key views.
- Press the left / right arrow keys to change the octave.
- Press the up / down arrow keys to change the note output velocity.
- Play and hold a note with the mouse and move the cross hair symbol up / down for modulation and left / right for pitch bend.

Linear record mode selector

This determines how Cubase behaves when recording audio or MIDI events which overlap existing events in the project. There are three modes as follows:

- Normal – any audio or MIDI recording which takes place over a passage where there is existing material does NOT overwrite the previously recorded events. It produces a new event which overlaps the existing material. In the case of MIDI events, both the new and previously recorded material is heard simultaneously. In the case of audio events, only the audio event which takes playback priority is heard (normally the event which is on top in the event display).
- Merge – for audio recording, merge produces identical behaviour to normal mode (as described above). For recording MIDI over an existing MIDI part, any new events are merged with the existing events in the part and no new MIDI part is created.
- Replace – any audio or MIDI recording which overlaps a passage where there is existing material replaces the previously recorded events in the overlapped section.

Cycle record mode selector

The cycle record mode selector determines the manner in which recordings are made when in Cycle mode. Mix and Overwrite modes are relevant mainly to MIDI recording. Keep Last and Stacked modes are relevant to both audio and MIDI recording. The modes function as follows:

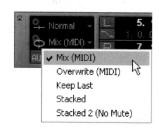

- Mix (MIDI) – the current MIDI input is added to any existing recording in the same part. This is the default mode for quickly building up a rhythm part, for example, when different elements of a drum kit can be added on each lap of the cycle.
- Overwrite (MIDI) – any MIDI input replaces any existing recordings in the same part and deletes any data which occurs after the drop-in point for the current lap of the cycle.
- Keep Last (audio and MIDI) – for MIDI recordings, each completed lap of the cycle in which there is MIDI input replaces the previously recorded lap. If you do not play anything, the existing events recorded on a previous lap are kept. For audio recordings, the last lap in the cycle which is recorded up to the end of the cycle range is kept as an audio event. All previously recorded laps are kept within the audio file and may be accessed via the regions settings or other manipulations of the audio event (see Chapter 8 for more details).

• Stacked (audio and MIDI) – for MIDI recordings, a MIDI part for each lap of the cycle appears on its own lane within the vertical space of the MIDI track. The stacked MIDI parts can be directly spliced, muted or otherwise edited in the Project window, or edited in the Key editor. Edited parts may be later merged into a single composite part using Merge MIDI in Loop (MIDI menu). For audio recordings, an audio event for each lap of the cycle appears on its own lane within the vertical space of the audio track. The stacked events can be edited directly in the event display, making it easy to quickly build up a composite take while remaining in the Project window.

• Stacked 2 (no mute) – similar to the regular stacked mode outlined above except that previous takes are not automatically muted on each lap of the cycle. This is relevant mainly to MIDI recording and means that all recorded events are heard simultaneously (similar to overwrite mode except that the recordings are stored in separate events).

The left and right locator positions

These show the current positions of the left and right locators. Clicking on either of the L and R boxes moves the project cursor to the respective positions in the event display. Clicking and on any part of the locator position number or double-clicking the whole number allows you to enter a numerical value from the computer keyboard. The left and right locators can also be set by dragging the locator pointers in the ruler.

The automatic quantize button (AQ)

Used to automatically quantize a performance as it is recorded according to the quantize value set in the Quantize type menu.

The punch in and out buttons

For automatically dropping in and out of record mode at the left and right locator positions. If 'Start record at left locator' is activated in the Transport menu, Cubase always starts recording from the left locator position and when record mode is implemented the punch in button is automatically selected. However, if Cubase is rewound to a point some bars before the left locator and put into play with the punch in button manually selected, Cubase drops in to record when it reaches the left locator position. If the punch out button has also been selected, Cubase drops out of record at the right locator position. Otherwise it remains in record mode until you stop the sequencer.

Pre and post-roll parameters

The pre-roll field determines the number of bars of pre-roll which occurs when you implement playback or record. The post-roll field determines the number of bars of post-roll which occurs after dropping out of record. The latter is only relevant when you use the punch out button. To enable pre and post roll, activate 'pre/post roll' in the Transport menu or click on the pre/post roll buttons on the Transport panel.

Shuttle speed and jog wheels

The Transport panel features a useful dual dial control which helps you find specific audio material and locations within your project. This is useful for lining up

the project cursor to audio cues prior to using split at cursor (Edit menu) or dropping a marker, for example. The outer dial is the shuttle speed dial which allows
you to monitor the audio as you move the project cursor forwards or backwards
within the material. This is a bit like standard fast forward and rewind except you
can still hear the audio. The further round you drag the dial from its centre position the faster the playback speed (normal or reverse playback depending on
which side of the centre position you drag the dial). The inner dial is the jog
wheel. This also allows you to move the project cursor while still hearing the audio
but, this time, is designed for jogging back and forth over a smaller section of
material, much like a traditional jog wheel designed for lining up the playback
heads of a tape machine to a specific location on tape. The jog wheel is an infinite wheel with no minimum or maximum positions so you can continuously
rotate it in either direction to find the desired audio point. The centre of the dial
features + and – nudge buttons. These allow you to nudge the project cursor
position backwards or forwards one frame at a time (according to the current
time code frame rate). These buttons are useful for fine tuning the position of the
project cursor to very precise locations.

The position display and position slider

The position display shows the current project cursor position in two displays;
the primary and secondary time displays. The primary time display is selected for the project in Project setup (Project menu) or by making a selection
from the pop-up menu to the right of the primary time display or to the right
of the ruler. The secondary time format is selected from the pop-up menu to
the right of the secondary time display. Clicking on any part of the position
display or double-clicking on it allows you to enter a numerical value from the
computer keyboard. The + and – buttons allow you to move the cursor position forwards or backwards one bar, one frame, one second or one sample at
a time depending on which time format has been chosen. The position slider
is found just below the position display and can be used to quickly slide back
and forth within the project.

The click on/off and pre-count buttons

The click button enables / disables the guide click and the pre-count button
enables / disables a pre-count click for recording purposes. The number of
bars for the pre-count is defined in the Metronome setup dialogue. When
pre-count is activated, pre-roll is de-activated, and vice versa.

The tempo track mode and tempo/time signature displays

The tempo track mode allows the changing of the tempo behaviour between
fixed and track modes. In fixed mode, the tempo follows the single tempo
and time signature settings as shown in the Transport panel. In tempo track
mode, the tempo follows any tempo and time signature changes as found in
the Tempo track. The tempo is shown in beats per minute (BPM).

The sync button

For activating or de-activating synchronisation to an external time code generating device. When de-activated (set to INT), Cubase uses the internal tim-

ing clock of the computer for all tempo and time-based functions. When activated, Cubase may be slaved to an external clock for synchronisation with other sequencers, tape machines and drum machines.

Track types

Cubase features a number of different track types, each specialised in the handling of its own kind of data, and each displayed with a unique graphical symbol in the track list of the Project window (Figure 4.13). The main track types are described in the following sections.

Audio tracks

To create an Audio track select Add track/Audio in the Project menu. In the dialogue which appears you can choose the track count and the mono, stereo or multi-channel attributes of the track. You can also make a choice from the Track presets list by activating Browse presets. Audio tracks are for the recording and playback of audio signals. Recorded audio data is stored on hard disk and represented in the Project window within graphical blocks known as audio events. The audio data within each event is shown as a waveform. Audio events may also be grouped within other graphical blocks known as Audio parts. These are useful for grouping events together for editing purposes and the simplification of the display. Audio events and parts may be selected, moved, split and edited in a multitude of different ways using the editing tools and other functions. Audio tracks and audio recording are explained in more detail in Chapters 3, 7 and 8.

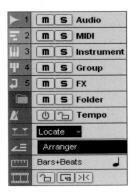

Figure 4.13
The different track types in the track list

Figure 4.14
Acoustic piano and voice recorded on stereo and mono audio tracks

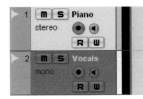
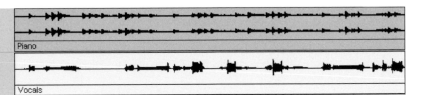

MIDI tracks

To create a MIDI track select Add track/MIDI in the Project menu. In the dialogue which appears you can choose the track count and, if desired, make a choice from the Track presets list by activating Browse presets.

MIDI tracks are for the recording and playback of MIDI data. MIDI data is a sequence of digital instructions representing a musical performance, such as the sequence of keys pressed on your MIDI keyboard. MIDI data is represented in the Project window within graphical blocks known as MIDI parts. The MIDI data within each part is shown as notes, lines or

Figure 4.15
MIDI tracks in the Project window

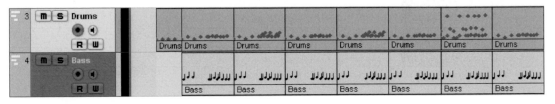

drum symbols. MIDI parts may be selected, moved, split and edited in a multitude of different ways using the editing tools and other functions. MIDI tracks and MIDI recording are explained in more detail in Chapters 3, 5 and 6.

Instrument tracks

Instrument tracks are a hybrid track type for the recording and playback of MIDI data which exclusively triggers a single VST Instrument.

To create an Instrument track select Add track/Instrument in the Project menu. In the dialogue which appears you can choose the track count and VST Instrument and, if desired, make a choice from the presets list by activating Browse presets. If you also activate the MIDI Input button in the Viewer section of the Browser, you can preview the presets by playing your MIDI keyboard before you actually create the Instrument track.

An Instrument track provides one MIDI input and one stereo audio output, linking a MIDI-based track in the Project window to a VST instrument-based channel in the Mixer.

Tip

Similar VST Instrument tracks are created when you load a VST instrument in the VST Instrument panel (F11). These are displayed with the same colour and symbol as normal Instrument tracks but they are automatically grouped within the VST Instruments folder. These do not feature MIDI functionality and exist to provide audio output and mixing controls for the VST instrument. VST instruments activated in this way must be separately triggered via conventional MIDI tracks.

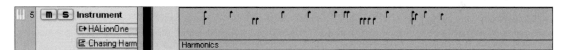

Figure 4.16
An Instrument track set up to trigger the supplied HalionOne sampler

Arranger track

Description and user guide

The Arranger track is a special non-linear playback track which allows you to play different sections of your musical arrangements in any order and with any number of repeats. This could be likened to a pattern-based sequencer where various preset patterns can be chained together to form a musical composition.

There can be only one Arranger track in each Cubase project. It is managed in the Project window, the Inspector or the Arranger editor. To start using the Arranger track proceed as follows:

- Add the Arranger track to an existing project by selecting Add Track / Arranger track in the Project menu. The Arranger track appears in the Project window.

Figure 4.17
Arranger parts in the event display

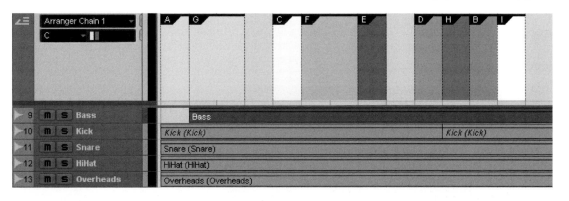

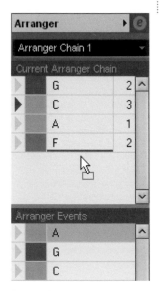

Figure 4.18
Drag and drop Arranger events into the current Arranger chain in the Inspector

- Create some events in the new Arranger track which correspond musically with the existing arrangement by dragging across the Arranger track display with the draw tool (Figure 4.17). By default, new Arranger events are named with the letters of the alphabet but the name may be changed on the infoline.
- Select the Arranger track and open the Inspector by clicking on the Show Inspector button on the toolbar. Alternatively, open the Arranger editor by clicking on the edit button in the Arranger track header.
- Drag and drop Arranger events from the Arranger events section of the Inspector (or Arranger editor) into the current Arranger chain (Figure 4.18). You can arrange the parts in any order you wish and adjust the number of repeats for each event in the right-hand column.
- Activate Arranger mode by clicking on the Arranger mode button in the track header of the Arranger track or in the Arranger section of the Transport panel. Playback is now governed by the order of events in the Arranger chain.

Arranger track creative techniques

The Arranger track is a great tool for remixing and loop-based dance styles. It would normally be used to re-order the sequence of events in an existing musical arrangement. For example, rather than start at the beginning of the song, you could start on the ad-lib chorus section at the end, and if the second and third bar of the solo section contains a great hook line, you could loop it twice before the start of the first verse. When working with repetitive loops, it is easy to chain your patterns together with the desired number of repeats in the Arranger chain. There are a wide range of possibilities for creatively re-arranging any existing musical structure.

The Arranger track may also be used in a more experimental way to generate new ideas. For example, try setting up an Arranger sequence within a drum loop using relatively short Arranger events of one, two and four beats in length. This is a good loop mangling technique and can help create new drum rhythms (Figure 4.19). The same technique can be used for the creative manipulation of abstract and time-stretched sound effects. Remember that Arranger events can be nested inside each other allowing you to use events of varying lengths repeatedly over the same passage (see parts E and F in Figure 4.19).

Several Arranger chains may be held in memory at the same time allowing you to develop a number of different musical arrangements within the same project. When you are happy with a new Arranger chain of events you may wish to convert it into a conventional linear arrangement. This is achieved by selecting Flatten Chain in the pop-up Arranger menu in the Inspector, or by clicking on the

Figure 4.19
Experimenting with Arranger events on a drum loop to create a new rhythm

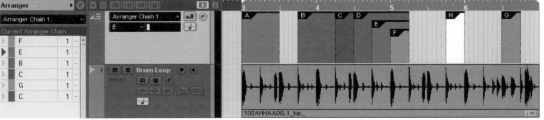

Flatten button in the Arranger editor. Upon selection, all relevant events are re-arranged, split and repeated as necessary across the event display in a linear manner corresponding to the order of events in the current Arranger chain, and the Arranger track itself is closed. All material which is not used in the Arranger chain is deleted from the event display. Use the standard undo command if you wish to go back to the original linear version of the project.

Folder tracks

Folder tracks are much like the folders you use to store files within Windows Explorer or OSX Finder. A folder track is thus a container for storing any number of other tracks. In the same way that creating a filing system on your hard disk helps organise your data, adding folder tracks helps organise complex musical arrangements and keeps the event display uncluttered.

To create a folder track, use Add track in the Project menu and select Folder. A new folder track appears in the event display. Once the folder track is available you can drag and drop other tracks into the folder track. A green arrow appears each time you drag a track over the folder track.$ All track types may be dragged into a folder track, including other folder tracks. A closed folder track looks similar to that shown in Figure 4.20. The folder track can be sized and named like any other track and most basic tool editing tech-

Figure 4.20
A closed folder track

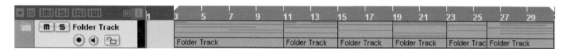

niques are still valid, such as splitting, erasing, muting and so on. You can open or close a folder track by clicking on the folder icon. Figure 4.21 shows the event display when the folder track in Figure 4.20 is opened. Folder tracks are generally used for keeping different instrument categories in the same location to help clarify the display and the musical structure. Common Folder track categories include drums, percussion, strings, brass and vocals for popular music or, for an orchestra, you might choose double bass, cellos, violas, violins, woodwinds, brass and percussion. Folder tracks can free up

Figure 4.21
The same folder track opened in the event display

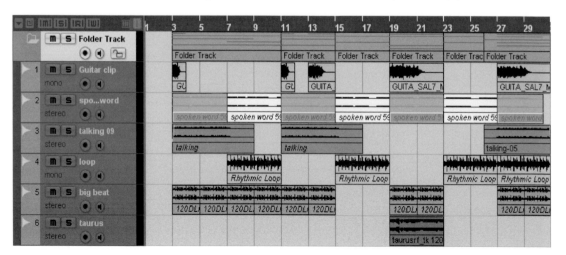

lots of space in the event display and are therefore indispensable for projects with large track counts. They are also good for soloing and muting purposes where you might like to solo or mute whole sections of the arrangement rather than individual tracks. Or if you are working on a lead vocal part, you might like to put all the instrumental tracks into a separate folder so that you can focus on the vocal track alone.

Info

Cubase also supports input / output bus and video tracks. The input / output bus tracks are for the management of any mix automation data from the input / output buses. Video tracks are for the display of video files when you are working on sound to picture projects. These elements are covered in other chapters.

Group tracks

Info

Group tracks should not be confused with Folder tracks. Folder tracks are concerned with visual presentation and editing in the event display, whereas Group tracks are concerned with audio signal routing. For more information on Group tracks, see Chapter 11.

To create a Group track select Add track / Group in the Project menu. In the dialogue which appears you can choose the track count and the mono, stereo or multi-channel attributes of the track. Group tracks are analogous to the Group channels found on traditional mixing consoles. Group tracks provide a logical routing bus when you wish to group a number of audio signals onto a single fader in the Mixer. For example, it is common practice to group all the audio tracks of a drum kit onto a single stereo Group track, allowing level, EQ and effects changes for the whole drum kit to be achieved more easily. Since Group tracks are primarily concerned with how you route your signals they are more relevant in the Mixer, where they appear as channel strips. In the Project window, a Group track appears in a similar fashion to other track types except that it can never contain audio events. However, its presence there allows you to automate its level and other parameters using the automation curves.

Figure 4.22
Group tracks do not contain audio events but their presence in the event display allows you to create and edit Group track automation

The Marker track and Marker window

The Marker track and Marker window are for managing guide markers inserted along the time line of your project. Markers allow you to quickly move to any position within your project and to set up cycle loops (for recording and playback purposes). To open the Marker track select Add track/Marker in the Project menu (Figure 4.23). The Marker track differs from the other track types in the sense that only one Marker track can be present for each project. Deleting the track merely removes it from view, it does not delete the data and all marker data is still present when you re-open the track. The Marker window provides a list-based overview of all markers and allows you to edit and name them as desired. There are three different types of markers: the left and right locators, cycle markers and standard markers. The

Figure 4.23
The Marker track in the event display

Marker track and Marker window essentially deal with the same data but the Marker track allows a graphical approach whereas the Marker window provides a text-based list.

Adding markers

There are a number of ways to add markers as follows:

1 To add standard markers, click on the add marker button found in the track list section of the Marker track, press the insert key on the computer keyboard or click in the Marker track with the draw tool. You can also add standard markers by clicking with the object selection tool while holding Alt. Standard markers are placed at the current location of the project cursor and are automatically numbered in ascending order as they are added. Standard markers appear as vertical blue lines. They can be added on the fly (while in playback mode) or while Cubase is static. Standard markers are named in the Infoline.

2 To add cycle markers, click on the add cycle marker button found in the track list section of the Marker track. You can also assign a key command to this function in File / Key Commands. The latter functions insert the cycle markers between the left and right locators and they are automatically numbered in ascending order as they are added. Alternatively, cycle markers may be added by dragging in the Marker track with the draw tool. They appear as downward facing brackets between the left and right locator positions and may be colour coded. Cycle markers are named in the Infoline.

Editing markers

Markers are edited in a similar manner to other events in the event display. Marker events are selected by clicking on them with the object selection tool, they are deleted using the erase tool, and cycle marker events are split into two by clicking with the split tool on the horizontal line between the two cycle points. Markers may also be viewed and edited in the Inspector and the Project Browser.

The Marker window

The Marker window displays the Marker track data in list format. Any changes made in either the Marker window or the Marker track are reflected in both. Select Markers from the Project menu or Ctrl + M (PC) / Command + M (Mac) to open the Marker window (Figure 4.24).

Tip

You can drag the Marker track to any position in the track list. If you use the divide track list button, the Marker track automatically appears in the upper pane.

Tip

When the snap button is active, all marker input and editing is magnetic to the current snap resolution.

Info

Removing the Marker track from the track list does not remove the marker data. All data remains intact and available in other parts of the program.

Figure 4.24
The Marker window

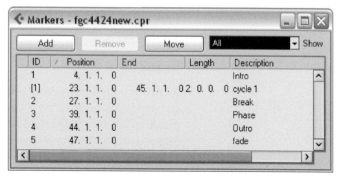

The Marker window features a number of columns for the display of marker information. These include the following:

- ID – shows the ID number for the marker.
- Position – shows the ruler position for the marker (or the start position in the case of cycle markers).
- End – shows the end position of cycle markers.
- Length – shows the length of cycle markers.
- Description – allows you to enter a description or name for the marker or cycle marker. The left and right marker names cannot be changed.

The Marker window provides a useful overview of all the markers in the project and allows you to filter the different marker types in the show menu.

Using the markers

There are a wide range of uses for markers including marking points of interest within your music, labelling sections of your arrangement so that you can see its structure more clearly and setting up cycle loops for playback and recording purposes. For example, one classic use of markers is to mark the intro, verse, chorus, bridge, break (and so on) of a song structure. In addition, there are a number of techniques associated with markers which make navigating within your project a whole lot easier. Try the following:

- Double click between any two markers with the pointer tool to select all events in the bars between them.
- Double click between any two markers with the range selection tool to select the precise range in the bars between them.
- Double click on any standard marker to move the project cursor to the markers location.
- Double click inside any cycle marker to move the left and right locators to the start and end of the cycle range.
- Select numeric keypad numbers 3 to 9 to move the project cursor to marker numbers 3 to 9.
- In the Marker track header in the track list, open the locate pop-up menu to navigate to any one of the available markers. Open the cycle marker pop-up menu to move the left and right locators to the start and end of a chosen cycle marker range. Open the zoom pop-up menu to zoom in to a chosen cycle marker range.

Track presets

Introduction

As well as including a wide range of presets for the on-board VST instruments and audio effects, Cubase also includes a special category of preset known as a Track preset. Presets in general are handled via the VST Sound universal media management features which aim to centralise the handling of all audio files, MIDI files, Track presets, VST plug-in presets, video files and Cubase project files found on the hard disk(s) of the host computer. Track presets are relevant to audio, instrument and MIDI tracks (or multiple numbers of these track types) and are accessible from various locations within the Project window. They are also handled in the MediaBay, Loop browser or Sound browser (Media menu). Track presets allow you to store or recall all the important channel settings for a track, including combinations of the insert effects, EQ, volume, gain, phase, VST instrument setup, MIDI Modifiers, MIDI Input Transformer, and MIDI output routing parameters, depending upon the track type.

The advantages of Track presets

The advantages of Track presets include:

- convenient addition of tracks which are already set up for specific sounds or instruments
- rapid modification of multiple settings for comparative or experimental purposes
- easy exchange of track settings between projects
- direct drag and drop from the Sound browser onto the track list.

Adding a track using a Track preset

To create an Audio, MIDI or Instrument track from a Track preset, select Add track followed by the chosen track type in the Project menu. In the dialogue which appears, open the browser by clicking on the Browse presets button. The browser window includes the filter section (left) where you can filter the display according to name and category, and the viewer (right) where you can select from a list of presets (Figure 4.25). For MIDI and Instrument tracks, activating the MIDI Input button allows you to preview the presets by playing your MIDI keyboard before you actually create the track. When you are happy with your choice click on OK to add the track and close the window.

Figure 4.25
The Track preset browser for an Instrument track filtered to show only those presets in the Bass category

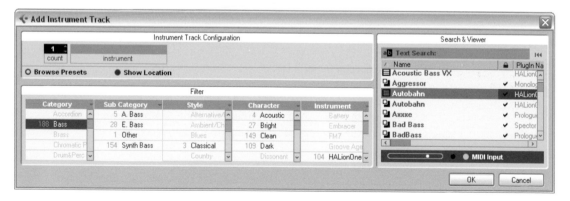

Applying a track preset to an existing track

Track presets may be applied to existing tracks using the Apply Track preset field in the Inspector or by right-clicking on the track to open the Quick menu and selecting Apply Track preset. This opens the Apply Track preset window which operates in the same manner as the Track preset browser shown in Figure 4.25, above. Great care must be taken when applying Track presets to existing tracks since confirming your preset choice by clicking on the OK button sets the track permanently to the new settings. The rule here is to 'try before you apply'. In other words, always audition the presets while still remaining in the Apply presets dialogue. If you are not happy with the new settings click on the Cancel button to close the dialogue. This reverts to the original track settings as set before you opened the dialogue.

Creating your own track presets

To create your own Track preset, set up the track with the desired effects, EQ, and so on and right-click on the track in the track list to open the Quick menu. Select Create Track preset to open the Create Track preset dialogue (Figure 4.26). Click on the Tag button to open the Tag editor. The Tag editor allows you to define the Category, Character, Style and Sub Category for the preset (if required). This helps you recall presets from the Track presets browser more easily by filtering the data (as shown in Figure 4.25, above).

Figure 4.26
The Create Track preset dialogue for a MIDI track

The Inspector

The Inspector is found in the Project window to the left of the track list. It is opened and closed by clicking on the Show Inspector button in the toolbar. The Inspector contains a number of parameters and sub-sections associated with the currently selected track. It varies according to what type of track is selected. Among the two most important Inspector configurations are those for MIDI and audio tracks and these are outlined below.

The Inspector for MIDI tracks

For MIDI tracks, the Inspector features a basic settings section and seven optional sections. The tabs for the optional sections are made visible from a pop-up menu which appears when you right-click anywhere on the Inspector. Each section is opened by clicking on the corresponding tab.

Basic track settings

The basic track settings section features the MIDI track name, the mute and solo buttons, the read and write buttons for track automation, the Input Transformer button for real-time MIDI data transformation, the record and monitor buttons for record-enabling and monitor enabling, the linear/musical timebase button for switching between time (non-tempo dependent) or beat based (tempo dependent) positioning of events, the lock button for locking the attributes of events on the selected track and the lane display type but-

ton for managing lanes within the vertical space of the track. The edit channel settings button next to the name opens the channel settings window
where you see a combined overview of the channel fader, insert effects, send
effects and other elements within a separate window. Below the buttons there
are mini-faders for controlling the MIDI volume, pan and delay time (in milliseconds). Below this there are fields for input and output routing, MIDI
channel and edit instrument functions (if a VST instrument is triggered from
the channel), program name (or number), MIDI drum map setup and Track
preset fields.

Volume and pan are useful for quickly setting up the basic level and pan
position without opening the Mixer. Delay is good for shifting the track backwards or forwards relative to the others, thus changing the feel of the music.
This might include adjusting a snare or hi-hat track to be late or early, or
shifting a slow strings sound earlier to anticipate the beat. The program field
changes the program number / patch in the target MIDI unit / VST instrument. This is good for quickly searching for the desired patch on a synth while
still remaining within the convenient environment of the Project window.

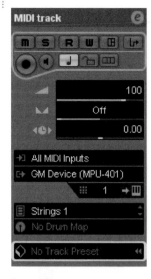

Figure 4.27
Basic track settings (Inspector for MIDI
tracks)

MIDI modifiers

The MIDI modifiers section features controls for the real-time manipulation of
MIDI data. These include the following:

- Transpose – for transposing MIDI notes up or down (range: -127 to +127)
- Velocity shift – for adding / subtracting an amount to the velocity of MIDI
  notes (range: -127 to +127)
- Velocity compression – for compressing / expanding the velocity of MIDI
  notes according to a ratio.
- Length compression – for compressing / expanding the length of MIDI
  notes according to a ratio.
- Random – for adding / subtracting random numbers between a chosen
  minimum and maximum value. Random acts upon position, pitch,
  velocity or length and features two independent random fields.
- Range – for limiting / filtering MIDI notes (or notes of a chosen velocity)
  between a chosen minimum and maximum value. Range features a
  choice of velocity limit, velocity filter, note limit or note filter with two
  independent range fields.

Transpose can be used for trying out simple harmonies or shifting the octave for
any given sound, as well as corrective transposing. Velocity shift affects the overall velocity of the MIDI data and is useful for increasing / decreasing the global
intensity of a performance. Velocity shift and velocity compression might be used
together to flatten out the dynamics of an over-excited track (try settings of +60
for velocity shift with 2/3 for velocity compression). Length can emphasise the
staccato feel of a track by using a setting of 1/3 or 1/4. To increase a tracks legato try a value of 3/1 or more. The random section is good for humanising a MIDI
performance. Try setting the first random field to position with minimum at 0 and
maximum at 6, and the second random field to velocity with minimum at -20 and
maximum at +20. This avoids robotic MIDI parts.

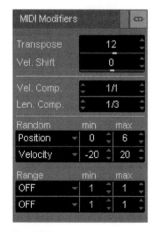

Figure 4.28
MIDI modifiers (Inspector for MIDI
tracks)

Figure 4.29
MIDI Inserts (Inspector for MIDI tracks)

MIDI Inserts

The Inserts section features four slots for inserting MIDI effects plug-ins into the MIDI data path. This is a duplicate of the MIDI inserts section as found in the extended part of the Mixer. To load a MIDI effect, click on an empty Insert slot to open the effects menu. When an effect is chosen from the menu it is immediately activated and its GUI is automatically opened. Adjust the parameters as required or choose an existing preset from the presets menu of the chosen effect. Activate playback to hear the results. MIDI insert effects transform the data in real-time. The original MIDI data remains intact unless you use Merge MIDI in loop in the MIDI menu to make the effects permanent. With Insert effects the MIDI data is routed through each activated effect in turn. MIDI Insert effect combinations may be stored as presets or recalled from Track presets using the pop-up preset management menu.

MIDI Sends

The Sends section features four slots for assigning MIDI send effects (Figure 4.30). This is a duplicate of the MIDI sends section as found in the extended part of the Mixer. Each MIDI track can have its own unique set of send effects and settings. The MIDI Send effects menu is the same as that for MIDI Insert effects and choosing and setting up sends is the same as for MIDI Insert effects. Similarly, the original MIDI data remains intact unless you use Merge MIDI in loop in the MIDI menu. Each send effect takes its input from the original MIDI data and both the original data and the effect data appear at the output.

MIDI Fader

The MIDI fader section (Figure 4.31) features a fader which is a duplicate of the track's fader as found in the Mixer, with an overview strip alongside. This is convenient for changing the level and pan position of the track and for applying mute, solo, read, write, bypass inserts, disable sends, record and monitoring functions, all without needing to open the Mixer.

Figure 4.30 (right)
MIDI Sends (Inspector for MIDI tracks)

Figure 4.31 (far right)
MIDI fader section (Inspector for MIDI tracks)

The Inspector for audio tracks

For audio tracks, the Inspector features a basic settings section and eight optional sections. The tabs for the optional sections are made visible from a pop-up menu which appears when you right-click anywhere in the Inspector. Each section is opened by clicking on the corresponding tab.

Basic track settings

The basic track settings section for Audio tracks features a similar group of buttons and functions as the basic track settings section for MIDI tracks (see MIDI basic track settings above). The audio basic track settings also include: an Open Device panels button for setting up graphical interfaces for audio effects and track parameters. These may be activated in the User panels sections of the Inspector or Mixer; an Auto Fades settings button for setting up a short automatic cross-fade between adjacent audio events on the track; and a Freeze Audio Channel button for freezing the pre-fader insert effects on the

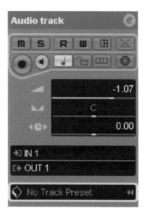

Figure 4.32
Basic track settings (Inspector for audio tracks)

channel when you need to reduce the load on the CPU. There are also in and out fields for selecting the input and output ports for the track.

Info

Auto fade produces glitch-free transitions between adjacent audio events by applying a short automatic crossfade. This is set globally for the project in Auto fades settings in the Project menu or it can be adjusted individually for the track in the Inspector by clicking on the auto fades settings button.

Inserts

The Inserts section features eight slots for inserting audio effects plug-ins into the audio signal path. The inserts section is a duplicate of that which is found in the extended part of the Mixer. To find out more, choose an audio track and experiment with one or more audio effects in the Inserts section. To load an audio effect, click on an empty effects slot to open the effects menu. The menu features a wide range of audio effects organised into various categories including delay, distortion, dynamics, EQ, filter, modulation and others. When an effect is chosen from the menu it is immediately activated and its GUI is automatically opened.

Figure 4.33
Inserts section (Inspector for audio tracks)

Tip

To move the contents of any insert slot to another, drag from the source insert slot number and release over the target slot. This gives total freedom to change the order of effects. Hold Alt to copy rather than move the contents.

Adjust the parameters as required or choose an existing preset from the presets browser. Activate playback to hear the results. The effects processing takes place in real-time. With Insert effects the audio signal is routed through each effect in turn. (See Chapter 12 for more details about audio effects).

Equalizers

The Equalizers section features a four band EQ which is a duplicate of that which is found in the extended part of the Mixer. The EQ section includes four numbered modules intended for low, lower-mid, high-mid and high frequency bands with Q, frequency and gain controls. Adjustments are made by dragging the mini-faders horizontally or by editing the parameter values. There is also an Equalizer curve section where you can adjust the equaliser settings graphically by dragging handles in the display. Click on the VST Sound symbol to open the EQ presets menu. ().

Sends

The Sends section (Figure 4.35) features eight slots for audio send effects each with a mini-fader for regulating the audio track signal level which is sent to the effect. The choice of send effects is determined by the number of FX channel tracks which have already been created for the project. Edit buttons for each effect allow you to open its GUI directly from the Inspector. The sends section is a duplicate of that which is found in the extended part of the Mixer. The supplied effects are the same as those for the audio Insert effects (see above). To find out more, choose an audio track and experiment with one or more audio send effects. Audio send effects transform the signal in real-time. With send effects the original audio signal (dry signal) is mixed with the FX channel signal (wet signal) at the master output faders.

Studio Sends

Cubase features a special monitoring and signal distribution mixer known as the Control Room Mixer. This allows you to manage monitoring levels, multiple mix configurations, talk-back and listen functions separately from the main mixer. The setup for the Control Room Mixer takes place in the VST Connections window in the Studio section. This is where you activate the Studio sends (Figure 4.36). Once activated, a Studio Send module becomes visible in the Control Room Mixer, and the corre-

> **Info**
>
> For more information about EQ see Chapter 12.

> **Info**
>
> Sends may also be used to send the channel signal to effect side chains, to groups or to output buses. When these are active within Cubase they become available in the pop-up menu of the send slot.

> **Info**
>
> See Chapter 12 for more details about audio effects).

Figure 4.34
Equalizers and Equalizer curve sections (Inspector for audio tracks)

Figure 4.35
Sends section (Inspector for audio tracks)

sponding Studio Send is available in the Studio
Sends section of all audio-based channels. You
can have up to four Studio Sends, each of which
may be sent to a different destination (for example, to headphone mixes, to performance area
monitoring speakers or any other suitable destination). What we see in the Inspector is a duplicate of the Studio Sends section as found in the
extended part of the Mixer. Each Studio Send
slot features a mini-fader for level control and a
pan parameter. These are all you need to set up
separate mixes for each Studio Send. See
Chapter 11 for more details about the Control
Room Mixer and Studio Sends.

Figure 4.36
Studio Sends section (Inspector for
audio tracks)

Channel

The Channel section (Figure 4.37) features a fader
which is a duplicate of the channel fader as found
in the Mixer, with an overview strip alongside. This
is convenient for changing the level and pan position of the track and for activating
mute, solo, listen, read, write, edit, bypass inserts, bypass EQ, disable sends, record
and monitoring functions, all without needing to open the Mixer.

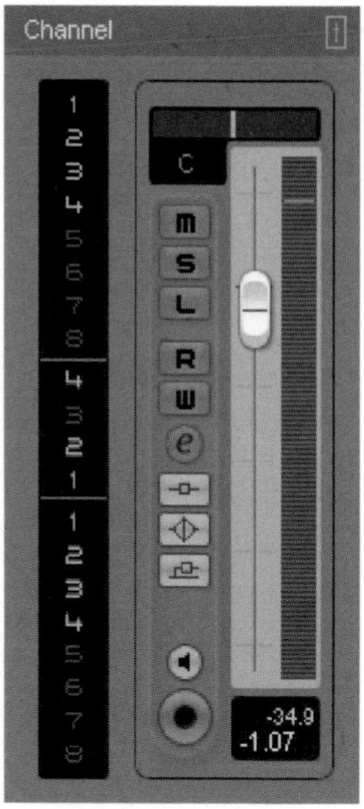

Figure 4.37
Channel section (Inspector for audio
tracks)

The Inspector Quick controls

The Inspector for MIDI, Audio and Instrument tracks includes a Quick controls section (Figure 4.37b). This features eight mini sliders which can be
controlled via an external control surface using MIDI messages and assigned
to the available parameters for the track type. External device control is set
up in Devices / Device setup / Remote devices / Quick controls. For example,
for an audio track you could assign the parameters for one or two modules
of the on-board paramteric EQ, or for an instrument track you could assign
the parameters for the filter section of a VST instrument.

The key advantage is that you can use the same physical faders and dials
on the external control surface to modify the parameters of both these channels, and you can set up any number of additional channels to respond to the
same physical controls. Editing is directed to the channel which is currently
in focus. The Quick controls are thus convenient for editing sounds and
recording automation.

Figure 4.37b
The Inspector Quick controls of an
Instrument track assigned to the filter
section of the supplied Prologue
synthesizer

Tip

o open a menu for selecting the parameters of tracks other than the currently selected one, hold any
modifier key while clicking in a Quick control field.

Info

o set up your own presets for what sections are available in the Inspector, right click / Ctrl click
anywhere in the Inspector panel and select Setup in the pop-up menu. This opens a dialogue where you
can manage what tabs are visible or hidden. Each combination may be saved as a preset.

Using the tools

Arranging and editing the events in the event display is among the principal functions of the Project window and once you have recorded a number of audio events or MIDI parts you will almost certainly wish to edit them in some way. This requires a good knowledge of how to use the tools in the toolbar. Using the tools is among the most important skills in the confident handling of Cubase. See Table 4.1 for a summary of the main tool functions.

Table 4.1 Tool function table

Tool	Keys held PC	Mac	Mouse action	Result
object selection	-	-	double-click between locators	creates a new empty part
	-	-	click on event	selects event
	-	-	click in empty space and drag	opens rectangular selection box
	-	-	click on event(s) and drag	moves event(s)
	alt	alt	click on event(s) and drag	copies event(s)
	alt	alt	drag lower right corner of event	repeats event
	alt + shift	alt + shift	click on event and drag	copies event as a shared copy
range selection	-	-	click and drag	selects event-independent range
split	-	-	click on event	splits event at mouse position
	alt	alt	click on event	splits event into several events
glue	-	-	click on event	joins event to the next event
	alt	alt	click on event	joins event to all those following
erase	-	-	click on event(s)	erases event(s)
	alt	alt	click on event	erases all following events
zoom	-	-	click in display	zooms in
	alt	alt	click in display	zooms out
mute	-	-	click on event	mutes the event
draw	-	-	click in empty space and drag	creates a new empty part
	-	-	drag within audio event	creates volume curve
play	-	-	click on event	plays event data at normal speed
scrub	-	-	drag over event	plays event data at drag speed

Common event editing operations include selecting, moving, duplicating, splitting, joining, resizing, fading, muting and erasing. Try the following techniques with events in the Project window using a test project.

Selecting

Selecting is often necessary before other editing operations take place. For selecting, Cubase provides the object selection and range selection tools. Any object in the event display may be selected by clicking on it with the object selection tool. Dragging a selection box around a number of events allows you to select a number of objects in one move. Holding the Shift key on the computer keyboard allows you to add to (or subtract from) an existing selection by clicking on single objects one at a time. All selections made with the object selection tool involve whole events. Conversely, the range selection tool allows event-independent selections. To use the range selection tool, drag the capture zone across the required bar and track range in the event display.

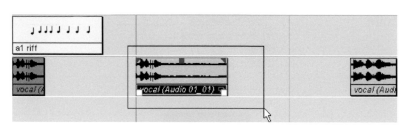

Figure 4.38
Selecting an event in the event display

Info

The range sub-menu of the Edit menu becomes active when you make a selection using the Range tool. This is useful for cut, copy and paste operations and also features special delete time, cut time and paste time options. Delete time deletes the range selection and moves all following events on the track leftwards to close the gap. Cut time is similar but also copies the deleted range to the clipboard. Paste time copies the clipboard onto a track at the start point of the range selection and moves all following events rightwards to make room for the pasted data.

Tip

Right-click in empty space in the event display to open the Quick menu. This contains the tools and a wide range of editing functions.

Moving

To move an event to a new position in the display, select the object selection tool, click on the event and drag it to a new position. More than one event can be moved simultaneously by clicking in empty space and dragging a selection box around several events. Clicking and dragging on any one of the selected events allows you to move all the events to a new location. Alternatively, try using the range selection tool to select an event-independent range within the display. The selection can then be moved to a new position in the same way, (events are automatically split at the appropriate positions). If the snap button is active, dragged events are magnetic to the snap resolution.

Tip

To move an event one tick at a time, select the event, place the pointer over the start tick value on the info line, and turn the mouse wheel. Alternatively, create a preset in the Project Logical editor as outlined in Chapter 21.

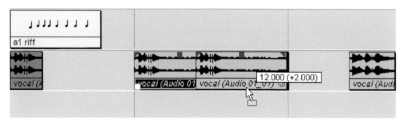

Figure 4.39
Moving an event

Duplicating

To duplicate an event, select the object selection tool, click on the event and drag while holding Alt on the computer keyboard. A duplicate event is created which can be placed at a new location in the event display. Holding Shift + Alt while dragging the event creates a shared copy. Any subsequent audio or MIDI processing which takes place on one of the shared copies affects all the others simultaneously. Duplicating audio events always results in shared copies since the events are always referenced to the same audio clip. Shared copies can be converted to independent events by selecting convert to real copy in the edit menu.

Figure 4.40
Duplicating an event

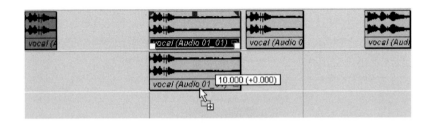

Info

To duplicate a number of consecutive events (i.e. to repeat the events) select Repeat in the Edit menu (Ctrl / Command + K) and enter the number of repeats required in the pop-up dialogue. Alternatively, select Duplicate in the Edit menu (Ctrl / Command + D).

Splitting

To split an event, select the split tool (scissors) and click on the event at the point you wish to implement the split. If the snap button is active, the split point is magnetic to the snap resolution. The event is divided into two separate events. Holding Alt while clicking on an event, splits the event into a number of smaller parts at the resolution of the snap setting.

Figure 4.41
Splitting an event

Joining

To join one event to a following event, select the glue tool and click on the first of the events. In the case of MIDI material, the first part is joined to the second to make one longer MIDI part. In the case of audio material, the audio events are grouped together within a single audio part. Holding Alt while clicking on an event, joins all following contiguous events into one long event.

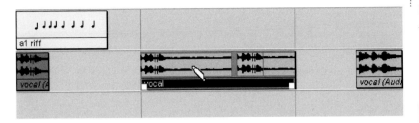

Figure 4.42
Joining events

Resizing

To resize events drag one of the small square handles which appear in the lower corners of the start and end points of the event when it is selected. A double arrow appears when you have placed the mouse in the correct position to begin resizing. For this purpose, the object selection tool is available in three modes; normal sizing, sizing moves contents and sizing applies time stretch. 'Normal sizing' resizes the object without making any changes to the data; it simply hides existing data when you reduce the size and adds blank space when you increase it. 'Sizing moves contents' moves the contents of an event forward or backward in time by locking the start or end of the contents to the start or end of the object. 'Sizing applies time stretch' stretches (or compresses) the contents of an object when you re-size it.

Normal resizing is helpful when you need to quickly top and tail an event to hear only the desired part of the audio. This applies to audio recordings where unwanted noise may have been recorded before or after the musical performance. 'Sizing moves contents' is useful when you do not want the contents at the start or end of the event to change when you drag the start and end handles. 'Sizing applies time stretch' is sometimes convenient for changing the length and tempo of drum loops to fit the current tempo of Cubase. Extreme time stretching manipulations are good for experimentation and producing sound effects.

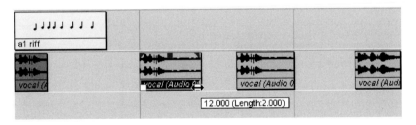

Figure 4.43
Resizing an event

Fading and volume control

To fade an audio event in or out, select the event with the object selection tool and drag the blue handle in the upper left corner to create a fade in, or drag the blue handle in the upper right corner to create a fade out. The fade curve can be modified by double clicking above the curve in the display and changing the settings in the fade dialogue which appears. The middle blue handle is for modifying the volume of the event. The fade and volume handles are available for audio events only.

> **Tip**
>
> Most of the tools are endowed with alternative behaviour when used in combination with the modifier keys (Shift, Ctrl, Alt, Apple command). Check out Table 4.1 for some the commonly used combinations.

Figure 4.44
Creating a fade in for an event

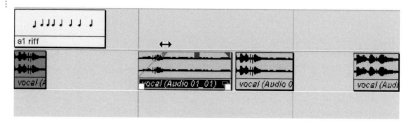

If you need to create elaborate volume curves for audio events, Cubase features volume events. These provide a basic alternative to regular automation and have the advantage of being attached permanently to the event. To create a volume curve for an audio event proceed as follows: select the draw tool and place it within the event (a small volume curve symbol appears beside the tool). Select the event and click with the tool to insert volume handles. Drag the handles within the event to form the desired curve (see Figure 4.45). Volume events are deleted by holding the Shift key while clicking upon a volume handle.

Figure 4.45
Creating volume events within an audio event

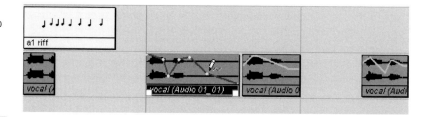

Figure 4.46
Muting an event

Muting

To mute an event, select the mute tool and click on the event. You can also drag a selection box over several events to mute a number of objects simultaneously. A muted event is displayed in grey.

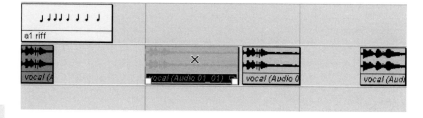

Erasing

To erase an event, select the erase tool and click once on the event. Multiple events can be deleted by selecting a group of objects and clicking once on any one of them. Holding Alt while clicking on an event deletes the event and all those which follow it on the same track.

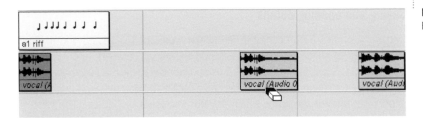

Figure 4.47
Erasing an event

Visual clarification

The above outlines some of the tool-based event editing techniques in the Project window. More elaborate techniques in the various editors are explored in chapters 6 and 8. Figure 4.36 provides visual clarification of the basics.

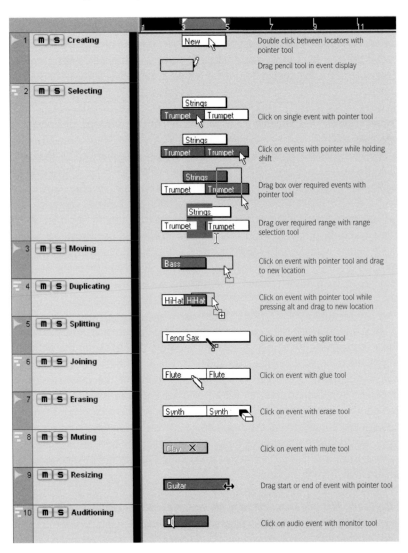

Figure 4.48
Basic event editing

Saving and opening details

Cubase supports a number of different file types for the saving and loading of data. These should be fully understood before you embark upon any serious projects. Most files are handled using the options in the File menu which include regular open and save options for native Cubase files and import and export options for file types which are not exclusive to Cubase. The type of file to be opened or saved is often recognised by its file extension and the following are the main possibilities:

Cubase project files (file extension: cpr)

Cubase project files are used to save and load all the relevant data of a Cubase project, except for the audio files themselves and various Cubase global preference settings. Cubase project files are also used to create templates. Templates are preset environments which you can prepare in advance for specific types of projects (such as 24 track audio recording, 16 track surround mixing or stereo mastering). To save a template select Save as Template in the File menu. To open a template select New project in the File menu.

Import audio files (file extensions: wav, aif, aifc, aiff, rex, rx2, sd2, mp3, mp2, mpeg, ogg, wma, w64)

Cubase can import a wide range of audio file formats including wav, aif and mp3. Wav is the standard audio file format used in PC Windows, aif is the standard audio file format used in Mac OSX, and mp3 (mpeg layer 3) is a compressed audio file format suitable for websites and recreational playback. Audio files may be imported directly into the event display by selecting Import Audio file in the File menu or by dragging and dropping an audio file from the Media Bay. When using Import Audio File, the audio material is inserted at the current position of the project cursor in the event display. When dragging and dropping files, the audio is dropped at the position where the mouse is released taking the current snap setting into consideration. Mp3 files are first converted into wav files before they can be used within Cubase.

Rex and rx2 are the file extensions for files created in Propellerheads Recycle program. Recycle is a separate program specialised in the processing of audio loops. A rex file is an audio file which has been sliced up into its constituent parts according to the rhythmic pulse of the material. When imported into Cubase, the rex file automatically adjusts itself to the project tempo without affecting the pitch of the sound, so the tempo can be freely changed without worrying too much about the consequences. You can make your own rex files if you have Recycle or alternatively they are supplied on sample CDs. Rex files cannot be created within Cubase and it is therefore an import-only format.

Export audio files (file extensions: wav, aif, mp3, wma, wav [broadcast wave])

File / Export / Audio Mixdown allows the exporting of audio between the left and right locators in the Project window in most of the standard audio file formats. The Export Audio Mixdown dialogue includes options for mono, split channel, stereo interleaved, and multi-channel exports. Bit depths between 8-bit and 32-bit float with sample rates between 8 and 96kHz ensure compatibility with just about any possible digital audio standard. A channel batch export function allows exporting of multiple channels to separate files which is useful for transferring projects to a different DAW.

Import and export of standard MIDI files (file extension: mid)

A MIDI file is a special file format designed to allow the transfer of music between different makes of MIDI sequencer and between different platforms.

MIDI files come in two formats: type 0 and type 1. Type 0 files always contain only one track which plays back on many MIDI channels. Type 1 files contain the original track structure of the material and include two or more tracks on separate MIDI channels.

To export a MIDI file, select File / Export / MIDI file. After choosing a name for the file, an Export options dialogue appears. To save as a type 0 file select the type 0 box. De-select the type 0 box to save as type 1. Select the other options in the dialogue as appropriate. All settings in the Tempo track are saved in the MIDI file and all un-muted parts are included.   To import a MIDI file, select File / Import / MIDI file. Cubase recognises both MIDI file formats when importing and files may be imported into the current project at the left locator position or into a new Project.

Drum map setup files (file extension: drm)

Drum map setup files are used to load and save drum maps. A drum map defines which MIDI notes correspond with which drum sounds in the target device. Drum maps are designed and managed within the Drum Map setup window (MIDI menu / Drum Map Setup). Open the Functions menu above the map list to load or save a drum map.

Progress report

This chapter has helped you become familiar with the primary functions of the Project window. This is essential for the successful handling of the program. The Project window provides a comfortable, streamlined software environment where you can execute a wide range of tasks within a small amount of screen space. You can configure the controls to suit your own particular way of working and you can run most routine recording, playback and editing tasks without ever leaving the window. Many of the techniques and tools used here are transferable to other parts of the program. We have only just scratched the surface of the available possibilities, but we are now armed with some of the essential skills with which to go on to more musically meaningful pursuits and serious recording tasks.

MIDI recording

This chapter outlines basic MIDI theory, explains how to set up a MIDI network and features some practical MIDI recording techniques for Cubase. Understanding the theory behind MIDI and setting up a logical MIDI network help when you record MIDI or Instrument tracks.

MIDI basics

What is MIDI?

MIDI (Musical Instrument Digital Interface) is a data communication standard, first established in 1983, for the exchange of musical information between electronic musical instruments and, subsequently, computers. It involves the serial transfer of digital information via cables terminated with 5 pin DIN connectors.

MIDI messages

MIDI is governed by a pre-defined set of rules known as the MIDI Specification. Just as the grammatical rules found in a regular language tell us how to form a sentence, the MIDI specification tells us how MIDI data should be sent and received in packets known as 'MIDI messages'. The first MIDI message to understand is that which describes the action of pressing a key on a musical keyboard. In MIDI 'talk', this is known as a 'Note on' message. A similar message needs to be sent to describe the action of releasing the key, and this is known as a 'Note off' message. Note on and note off messages contain information about the pitch of the key being pressed and the force with which it was pressed (known as the velocity). The duration of each note is governed by the length of time between the note on and note off messages. If a note off message is not sent at some stage after the note on message then the note continues to play indefinitely.

MIDI, therefore, is like a language. MIDI devices, such as synthesizers, samplers and drum machines can 'talk' to each other using MIDI messages. The sending of these messages involves two or more MIDI devices, one which is transmitting the data and the other(s) receiving it. It is important to grasp that the transmitted data consists of a series of instructions only, there is NO audio signal within the data. Note on and off messages instruct the receiving unit(s) about which note should be played, its velocity and duration. The actual sound is chosen on the receiving unit.

MIDI connections

MIDI devices normally include In, Out and Thru ports. To transmit messages from one device to another, a MIDI Out is connected to a MIDI In of a second device (using a correctly wired MIDI cable). The MIDI Thru port passes on a copy of the messages received at the MIDI In port. This is often used to daisy-chain several units together in a simple MIDI network. So, in its simplest form, hooking up a MIDI cable from the MIDI Out of your keyboard to the MIDI In of a synth module allows you to play the two devices simultaneously. The MIDI keyboard is being triggered in the normal way from its own keyboard and the synth module is being triggered by the MIDI messages it receives via the MIDI cable.

Great! But how does this help us use the MIDI side of Cubase? Well, instead of hooking up the MIDI cable from your MIDI keyboard to a synth module, plug it into the MIDI interface of your computer setup. You can now send MIDI messages into Cubase and thereby record a musical performance.

MIDI data in Cubase

MIDI-based music recorded in Cubase is displayed as individual events. These events are grouped together in the event display inside graphical blocks known as MIDI parts. They may also be viewed in more detail in the MIDI editors, as notes on a score or graphical events on a piano-roll style grid.

Changing the sound

Once the MIDI data has been recorded, it can be transmitted to any of the MIDI devices present in your system. The actual sound you hear is chosen in the receiving device where it is usually stored as a preset. Presets are also known as programs or patches and are recalled by manual selection on the unit or by sending a Program Change message via MIDI. Separating performance data and preset selection means you can change the sound long after the original recording has been made.

MIDI message types

What happens to the outgoing MIDI data if you turn the pitch wheel of your keyboard while playing a note? It is tempting to think that the MIDI note data itself is modified in some way. In fact, the note data remains the same and the pitch data is sent separately as another type of MIDI message known, not surprisingly, as a Pitch bend message. Pitch bend messages instruct the receiving unit how to bend the note(s) in question. A similar thing happens if you turn the modulation wheel. This sends out another type of message known as a Control change message (Continuous Controller). Other types of messages include Aftertouch (Channel Key pressure) and Program Change.

MIDI message types fall into two main categories: Channel and System messages. Channel messages have two sub categories known as Channel Voice messages and Channel Mode messages.

Channel Messages

Channel Voice messages

All the message types described so far come under the same category within the MIDI specification and are known as Channel Voice messages. Channel Voice messages are characterised by the fact that MIDI channel information (see below) is embedded within the message. 'Voice' means that this type of message is directed to and controls the receiving instrument's voices (or sounds). Channel Voice messages are likely to be the message types with which you most often come into contact in the routine use of Cubase. To summarise, Channel Voice messages include the following message types:

- Note off – the releasing of a key to terminate the playing of a note.
- Note on – the pressing of a key to begin the playing of a note.
- Polyphonic Key pressure (Aftertouch) – key pressure taking into consideration the pressure applied to each individual key.
- Control Change (Continuous Controller) – for the control of various non-note parameters like modulation (vibrato), breath control, volume and pan.
- Program Change – changes the sound preset in the receiving unit.
- Channel key pressure (Aftertouch) – key pressure taken as an overall pressure reading for the MIDI channel.
- Pitch Bend – instructs the receiving unit to change (bend) the pitch of any currently sounding notes (normally sent using the pitch bend wheel of the master keyboard).

Channel Mode messages

Channel mode messages are a group of reserved control change messages (between controllers 120 and 127). These reset and change the mode of operation of the receiving device. They include the following:

- Controller 120 (All sound off) – switches off sounds on all channels.
- Controller 121 (Reset all controllers) – resets all controllers to their default parameters.
- Controller 122 (Local on/off) – Local off disconnects the keyboard from the sound-making circuitry in the receiving device. Local on re-connects the keyboard to the sound-making circuitry
- Controller 123 (All notes off) – switches off all currently sounding notes. This is MIDI's panic button and is used to switch off hanging notes.
- Controller 124 (Omni mode off, all notes off) – the receiving device responds to messages on a single MIDI channel. This message also switches off all currently sounding notes. (Normally corresponds with a MIDI mode 3 status in the receiver, see below).
- Controller 125 (Omni mode on, all notes off) – the receiving device responds to messages on all MIDI channels. This message also switches off all currently sounding notes. (Normally corresponds with a MIDI mode 1 status in the receiver, see below).
- Controller 126 (Mono mode on/poly mode off, all notes off) – the receiving device responds to messages monophonically. This message also determines the number of monophonic MIDI channels used to process incoming MIDI notes. It switches off all currently sounding notes. (Normally corresponds with a MIDI mode 4 status in the receiver, see below).
- Controller 127 (Poly mode on/mono mode off, all notes off) – the

receiving device responds to messages polyphonically. This message also switches off all currently sounding notes. (Normally corresponds with a MIDI mode 3 status in the receiver, see below).

MIDI Modes

Controller messages 124 to 127 can be combined to produce four modes known as MIDI modes. These are operational modes governing how a MIDI device manages data on different channels and whether it responds polyphonically or monophonically. The MIDI modes are as follows:

- Mode 1 (Omni On/Poly) – the receiver responds to messages on all MIDI channels polyphonically. Commonly known as Omni mode.
- Mode 2 (Omni On/Mono) – the receiver responds to messages on all MIDI channels monophonically. Rarely used mode.
- Mode 3 (Omni Off/Poly) – the receiver responds to messages on the chosen MIDI channel polyphonically. Commonly known as Poly mode.
- Mode 4 (Omni Off/Mono) – the receiver responds to messages on the chosen MIDI channel(s) monophonically. In this mode, response to incoming MIDI notes is shared between a number of monophonic channels. Commonly known as Mono mode.

The MIDI modes are slightly outdated but are still implemented in some form on most devices. Mode 1 might be used for troubleshooting and testing. Mode 2 is rarely used. Mode 4 is useful for guitar synthesizers (and similar instruments) since it allows you to assign each string to a different monophonic MIDI channel, thereby more closely approximating the performance behaviour of the real-world instrument. Most MIDI devices power up in MIDI Mode 3. Multi-timbral functionality (now common in many devices) is not covered by the standard MIDI modes. Multi-timbral mode is therefore assigned on the instrument itself and is normally known as 'Multi Mode'. Multi Mode operation might be viewed as a number of separate polyphonic instruments within a single device (each set to MIDI Mode 3).

System messages

System messages form the other main type of message in the MIDI specification. These include System Common, System Real Time and System Exclusive messages. System Common messages include such things as MIDI Time Code, song position pointer, song select and tune request messages. System Real Time includes timing clock (24 ppqn) and start, stop and continue messages for sequencer synchronisation purposes. System Exclusive involves manufacturer-specific messages and Universal System Exclusive messages like MIDI file dump, sample dump, GM system on/off, MIDI Show Control and MIDI Machine Code. System Common and System Real Time messages are transmitted globally to all units in the MIDI network and do not use a MIDI channel for transmission or reception purposes. System Exclusive is used for transferring manufacturer and model-specific data to/from individual units and is generally only recognised by a single targeted device. This is typically used for dumping sounds and setup configurations from the MIDI device into a sequencer (like Cubase).

MIDI channels

In order to transmit MIDI messages to different targets within the same network, MIDI adopts a system of sixteen different channels. Channel Voice messages can be transmitted on any one of these channels. MIDI devices are usually set to receive polyphonically on one channel (Mode 3) or polyphonically on several channels simultaneously (multi-timbral). Messages on all sixteen MIDI channels can be transmitted simultaneously via a single MIDI cable.

To understand MIDI channels, it is helpful to think of your network of MIDI devices as a number of televisions. The signals from the TV broadcasting stations are being transmitted on a continuous basis, but you decide which one you are going to watch on screen by changing the channel on your TV. If you have several televisions you can set each one to a different channel. You can do exactly the same with your network of MIDI devices. Each unit is like a television which can be tuned to the appropriate channel. In such a system, Cubase is like a group of TV broadcasting stations. It transmits multiple channel MIDI data to the whole network. However, only those units which are tuned to the appropriate channels produce the appropriate sound. Certain MIDI devices can be set to receive on several channels simultaneously. This is known as multi-timbral or multi mode (as mentioned above) and allows a single unit to perform polyphonically on several channels at once. This means that you can trigger a number of different sounds simultaneously to hear a whole musical arrangement from a single unit (such as drums, bass, piano, strings and brass).

What MIDI is not

MIDI is NOT audio. MIDI data is a sequence of digital instructions related to a musical performance whereas audio data is a recording of the actual sound itself.

MIDI network details

For recording MIDI events, Cubase is normally connected to a MIDI keyboard and a number of other external MIDI devices and / or internal software-based VST instruments, such as synth modules, samplers and drum machines. Typically, the main keyboard is used to trigger the other devices and is usually referred to as the master keyboard. The master triggering device may also be a MIDI guitar or MIDI drum pads. The overall MIDI system and how all the devices are connected together is known as the MIDI network.

A simple MIDI network

Figure 5.1 shows a very simple MIDI network. The MIDI output from the master keyboard is routed directly into the MIDI input of the computer's MIDI interface. The diagram assumes that a MIDI interface is installed inside the computer (e.g. a PCI card featuring MIDI input and output ports). The MIDI input data passes through Cubase (via the activated global MIDI Thru in the program, see below) and is routed back out, along with any other data which has already been recorded, to the MIDI input of the master keyboard. A copy of the data arriving at the MIDI In is sent out from the MIDI Thru port of the master keyboard and routed to a synth module. The data arriving at the MIDI

Info

Cubase is supplied with a number of VST (Virtual Studio) Instruments and others can be installed from the vast range of VSTi products available from Steinberg and other developers. These are triggered via MIDI in much the same way as their real-world counterparts and they form a valuable extension to your MIDI network (see Chapter 18 for more details).

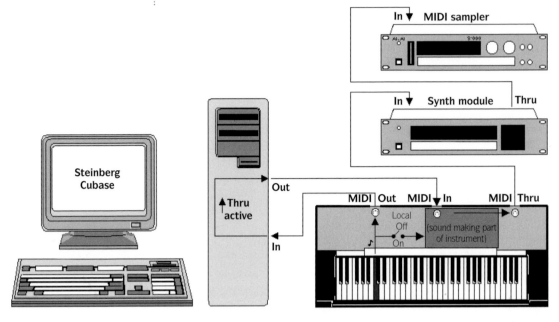

Figure 5.1
A simple MIDI 'daisy chain' network

In of the synth module is passed on to a MIDI sampler in the same manner (via the MIDI Thru of the synth module). This type of configuration is known as a 'daisy-chain' network.

A daisy-chain network is easy to set up but suffers from two disadvantages:

1 Inflexibility – although it may suit very simple setups, more complex MIDI routing tasks may require awkward re-plugging of the MIDI cables.
2 Data corruption risk – if the data passes through several units in the daisy-chain there is more risk of MIDI delays and data corruption.

A complex MIDI network

More complex MIDI networks typically feature a MIDI thru box (also called a MIDI splitter box) which enables the channelling of MIDI data to specific locations in the system. The MIDI network in Figure 5.2 shows a master keyboard whose MIDI Out is connected to the MIDI In of a computer via a MIDI thru box. The diagram assumes that a MIDI interface is installed inside the computer (e.g. a PCI sound card featuring MIDI input and output ports). The MIDI input data passes through Cubase via the activated global MIDI Thru in the program and is passed back out, along with any other data which has already been recorded, to the MIDI input of the MIDI thru box. The data is split among the outputs of the MIDI thru box and routed to the various devices in the system (including back to the master keyboard itself). This type of configuration is known as a MIDI 'star' network. In such a system, the MIDI thru box allows the connection of any input to any number of outputs and often includes MIDI data merge functionality. This allows the merging of two or more MIDI inputs into one MIDI data stream. In Figure 5.2, the master instrument's keyboard has been disconnected from its sound making circuitry (commonly known as Local off mode). In this mode, the sound making cir-

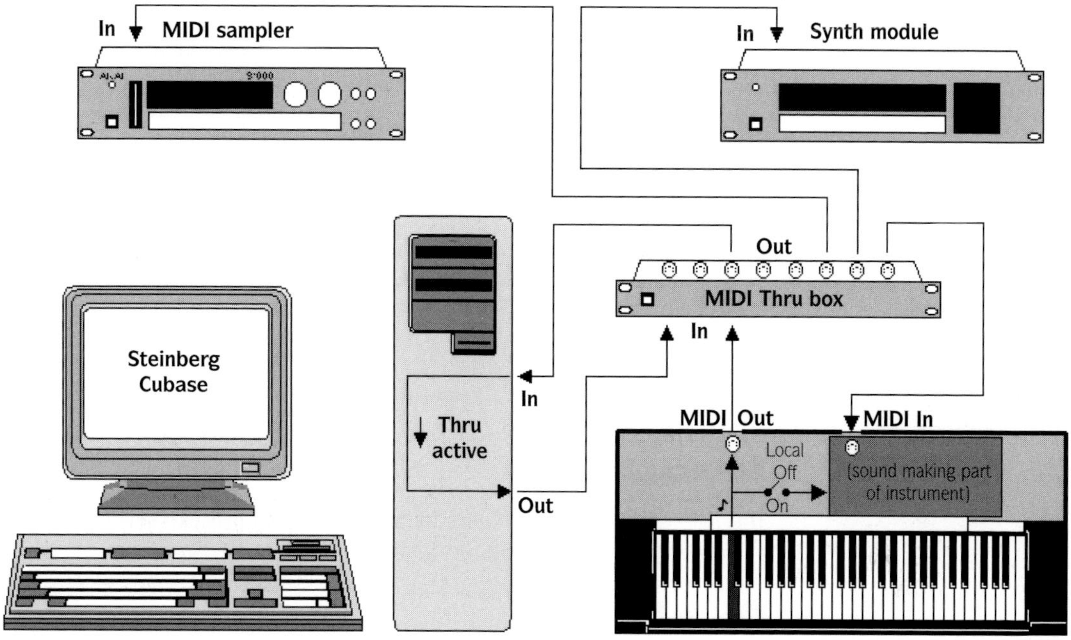

Figure 5.2
A complex MIDI 'star' network

cuitry is triggered by incoming MIDI messages only. The master keyboard, therefore, triggers its sound making circuitry via Cubase. Note also that MIDI outputs are always connected to MIDI inputs and involve single cables between each output / input pair of sockets.

A MIDI star network is recommended for ensuring better MIDI timing, particularly for systems featuring more than two modules in addition to the master keyboard. It is also more flexible since, with a sufficiently well-specified MIDI thru box, any MIDI output can be routed to any MIDI input. This allows two-way handshaking operations when dumping MIDI data from an external unit into the computer and vice versa.

If you have not already done so, try making a clear, logical diagram of your own MIDI network with all the MIDI inputs and outputs clearly labelled. This helps clarify your own setup and is invaluable for troubleshooting if you run into problems. It is also helpful to include all the peripheral audio equipment and audio connections, once again clearly labelling all the inputs and outputs. (See Figure 2.6 for an example). If you have the opportunity use colour in your diagram to colour code the MIDI and audio connections.

Info

Making a clear, logical diagram of your own Cubase MIDI and audio connections and peripheral equipment helps clarify the structure of your system and is valuable for troubleshooting. In such a diagram, be sure to label all inputs and outputs clearly and, if possible, use colour-coding to differentiate between the MIDI and audio connection cables.

Record modes for MIDI recording

The precise manner in which MIDI recording takes place is governed by the record mode section of the Transport panel. You are advised to become familiar with the record modes before commencing any serious recording projects. These affect both the linear and cycle recording behaviour of the program. The linear record modes determine what happens when a new MIDI recording overlaps an existing part on the same track. The cycle record modes determine what happens when you record multiple takes over the same range in a continuous cycle (when the Transport panel cycle button is activated). The function of each record mode is outlined in the following table:

Record modes for MIDI recording			
Linear record modes		**Cycle record modes**	
Mode	*Overlap behaviour*	*Mode*	*Cycle behaviour*
Normal	pastes new part on top	Mix	mixes with previous lap data
Merge	merges data into existing part	Overwrite	overwrites to end of lap
Replace	replaces data in existing part	Keep Last	keeps last lap only
		Stacked	records laps in lanes

MIDI recording in detail

The following steps help clarify the MIDI recording process beyond the level achieved in earlier chapters. Proceed as follows:

Preparing the system

Create a new project

To create a new project, select 'New Project' from the File menu and choose 'Empty' from the dialogue which appears. In the Select directory dialogue, choose your audio drive or an appropriate existing directory and click on the Create button to create a new directory for this particular project. Choose an appropriate name. The directory is created on the hard disk. Click on OK to leave the Select directory dialogue. An empty Cubase project is opened.

Verify MIDI Thru and set MIDI filter

It is standard practice to pass MIDI data through Cubase. To achieve this, tick the MIDI Thru Active box in File / Preferences / MIDI. This ensures that all data received at the MIDI In port(s) is echoed to the MIDI Out port(s). Also make sure that SysEx is filtered in the record and thru sections of the MIDI filter in File / Preferences / MIDI / Filter. This avoids recording any unnecessary data in the recording exercises outlined below.

Set Local Off

Set your master keyboard to Local Off. Most MIDI keyboards include a parameter for Local on/off control. Local Off means that the musical keyboard is disconnected from the sound making part of the instrument. All sound is now triggered via incoming MIDI only. This avoids double notes and stops the master keyboard being triggered inappropriately when other instruments in the network are being played live via MIDI.

Add a MIDI track and set the input and output

Select Project / Add Track / MIDI to add a new MIDI track. Once created, choose an appropriate MIDI input and output port in the input and output fields of the Inspector for the track (Figure 5.3). These would normally correspond to the MIDI input and output ports of the MIDI interface you have installed in your computer. You can now play any of the external devices in the MIDI network by changing the MIDI channel in the channel field.

It is also possible to play any available VST instruments (Virtual Studio instruments) by selecting the instrument in the output menu. For a VST instrument to be available it must have already been activated in the VST instruments panel (opened from the Devices menu). Alternatively, if you intend to use a single track which triggers a VST instrument you may prefer to add an Instrument track instead of a MIDI track. An Instrument track is already set up to trigger the chosen instrument and depending on your needs may be a better option than a standard MIDI track.

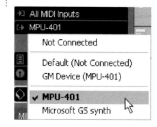

Figure 5.3
Set the MIDI input, output and channel in the Inspector

Troubleshooting

If you experience difficulties with triggering your real-world or virtual instruments verify that:

- the target devices are switched on and are functioning correctly.
- the MIDI cables are of the approved type, are correctly connected between Cubase and the devices in the network, and are not faulty.
- the record enable or monitor enable button for the chosen MIDI track is active. This allows MIDI data to pass from the MIDI input to the MIDI output.
- the MIDI activity indicator in the Transport panel registers MIDI input and output activity when you play your keyboard.
- the correct output device and channel is selected in the output menu.
- the target devices are set to the correct MIDI channels.

Set the metronome, click and tempo

In Transport / Metronome Setup activate the audio click and select beeps. Activate Metronome in record and Metronome in play, and set a precount of two bars. To ensure predictable results, activate 'Precount on' and 'Start Record at Left Locator' in the Transport menu. Activate the click button on the Transport panel by pressing the 'C' key on the computer keyboard or by clicking on the button with the mouse. Start playback to test the click and verify the tempo of Cubase. In Fixed tempo mode you can adjust the tempo on the fly by double-clicking on the Transport panel tempo field and pressing the up/down arrows on the computer keyboard to increase/decrease the tempo. When you are satisfied with the tempo, press enter on the computer keyboard.

Name the track and choose a sound

Double-click on the name of the MIDI track (or Instrument track) you created above and enter an appropriate name. Select an appropriate sound for your MIDI device on the unit itself or remotely using the patch selector field in the Inspector. The patch selector sends out MIDI program change messages when you change its value (see Figure 5.4).

Info

In order for MIDI data to pass through Cubase, either the record enable or monitor enable button for the MIDI track must be active. Several MIDI tracks may be record enabled simultaneously allowing you to trigger and record several sounds at once.

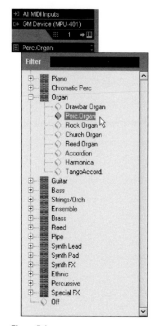

Figure 5.4
Selecting a program remotely by name, using the patch selector of the supplied GM MIDI device

Figure 5.5
Installing a MIDI device in the MIDI
Device manager

Using the patch selector for remote selection of sounds by name depends on whether the chosen device is supported in the MIDI Device Manager (Devices menu / MIDI Device manager). Click on 'Install Device' in the MIDI Device Manager for a list of supported MIDI devices. To install a device, click on the required device in the list (Figure 5.5). The device is now available in the output port menu of the MIDI track and when the device is selected a pop-up presets menu becomes available in the patch selector.

The presets for VST instruments are shown in the VST presets window or program list which opens when you click in the programs / patch selector field. The program lists for most VST instruments may be converted to the VST3 presets format allowing you to store the presets for all your instruments in the same location and thus build up your own centralised library of presets for use with Cubase. This allows you to search for sounds by name, category, character and so on.

Figure 5.6
Using the VST presets window to search
for bass sounds in the supplied Prologue
VSTi synthesizer

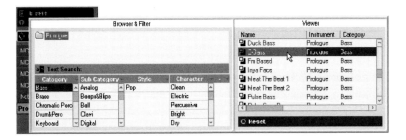

Set the left and right locators

Set the left and right locators in the ruler above the event display by clicking and dragging in the upper half of the ruler (a pencil tool appears). Set the left locator to bar 3.1.1.0 and the right locator to bar 7.1.1.0 (4 bars). It is assumed here that you have set you default ruler display to bars and beats. In this mode, the bar display figures refer to the time position in bars, beats, sixteenth notes and ticks.

Linear recording

Simple recording

Ordinary linear recording (meaning when you are NOT recording in cycle mode) is often better for simple recording tasks, long performances or for detailed punching in over specific segments. Linear recording behaviour depends upon the setting made in the linear recording mode menu on the Transport panel (mix, merge or replace) and the pre-roll, post-roll and punch button settings (see below). To activate recording, record enable the MIDI track and click on the record button (or press the '*' key on the numeric keypad). If you set up the program as outlined above you hear a two bar count after which recording begins on the chosen MIDI track at the left locator position.

Setting up the punch and pre-roll parameters

When punching in over an existing recording, it may be preferable to hear the music in the bars before the punch in point (rather than just a metronome precount). This allows you to play along with the music before you reach the punch in point, often resulting in a better take. To set this up in Cubase, proceed as follows:

- drag the left and right locators in the ruler to select the range in which you wish to record.
- activate the pre and post-roll buttons in the Transport panel and enter '1' (one bar) in each.
- activate the punch in and punch out buttons on the Transport panel (click on the buttons or use the 'I' and 'O' key commands on the computer keyboard).

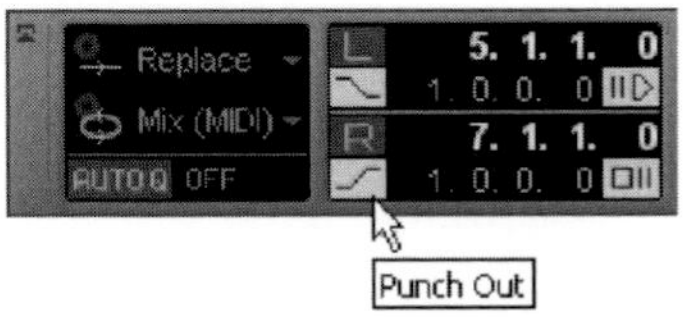

Figure 5.7
Setting up the Transport panel for punching in

- choose the appropriate mode in the linear record mode menu on the Transport panel. If you are punching in over a badly played section which you definitely wish to replace it might be appropriate to choose 'Replace' mode.
- activate the record enable button of the chosen MIDI track.

Selecting record automatically rolls the project cursor back one bar before starting playback. When the punch in point is reached Cubase automatically drops into record mode. Recording continues up to the punch out point. After the punch out point playback continues for a further one bar. Using a post-roll as well as a pre-roll helps you hear your take in context. In 'Replace' mode, all existing MIDI data in the recorded segment is replaced by your new performance.

Cycle recording

Preparing Cubase for Cycle recording

For cycle recording, add the following steps to those outlined above for linear MIDI recording:

- Select Project / Add Track / MIDI and enter a count of 3 in the dialogue to add three new MIDI tracks.
- Name the new tracks as 'drums', 'bass' and 'piano' or choose different names as you see fit.
- Choose appropriate MIDI input / output ports and MIDI channels for the three new tracks so that each track triggers the appropriate sound from the devices in your system when you activate its monitor or record enable button. Select the sound for each MIDI device either on the unit itself or remotely using the patch selector field.

Tip

If you are happy with the way the system is configured so far and often work with MIDI-only recordings you might like to save what we have achieved so far as a template. This could serve as a startup blank project whenever you start a new MIDI project. Select 'Save as template' in the File menu and choose a suitable name like 'MIDI startup', for example.

Activate the cycle button on the Transport panel. Cubase playback and recording now cycles between the left and right locators (between bars 3.1.1.0 and 7.1.1.0, as set above).

The advantages of recording in cycle mode

In cycle mode the punch in and out buttons can be largely ignored since the punch in button is auto-selected when Cubase is put into record mode and the punch out point (the position of the right locator) is never actually reached since Cubase cycles back to the left locator position. Recording is de-activated only when Cubase is stopped manually. When recording in cycle mode, Cubase automatically remains within the segment which is being recorded upon without any further effort, and any recorded material can be instantly monitored on the next lap of the cycle. Cycle recording in mix mode is particularly useful for continually adding to the material without dropping out of record and is convenient for building up a rhythm pattern.

MIDI cycle recording project 1 (Mix mode)

This project involves recording a drum part using the 'drums' MIDI track we created, above. Select 'Mix' in the cycle record mode selector. In mix mode the current MIDI recording is added to any existing data in the same part when recording in cycle mode. The idea in this project is to gradually add to the recording on each lap of the cycle without dropping out of record mode.

Start recording

Record enable the drums track. Click on the record button of the Transport panel (key command: '*' on the numeric keypad). A pre-count is heard according to what has been set in the metronome. When recording commences, the track header turns red and the project cursor starts to move. Anything played on your keyboard is now recorded into Cubase. Try recording something simple using a bass drum and snare. Cubase cycles between the left and right locators and you may add to the recording on each lap of the cycle.

Track switching

Once you are satisfied with what you recorded on the drums track, switch to the next track (the bass track) by pressing the down arrow key on the computer keyboard. Do this without dropping out of record. Record your bass part and then switch to the piano track, once again, without dropping out of record. Record your piano part and stop Cubase when all recording is complete. If necessary, you can go back and add further data to any of the tracks by switching between them using the up/down arrows of the computer keyboard (see Figure 5.8). When you are happy with your recording, don't forget to save it by selecting the save function in the File menu (Ctrl / Command + S).

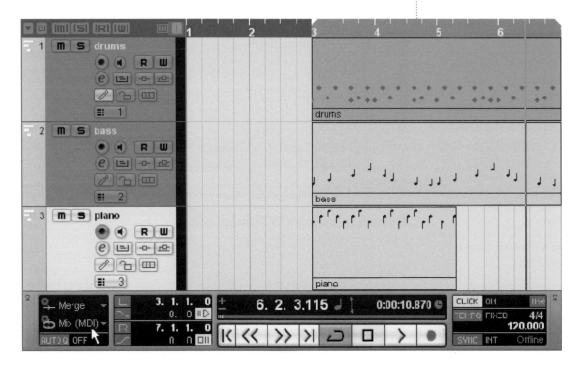

MIDI cycle recording project 2 (Overwrite mode)

Delete the events recorded in project 1, above. This time, select 'Overwrite' in the cycle record mode selector. In overwrite mode, the current MIDI input replaces any existing recordings in the same part and deletes any data which occurs after the drop-in point for each subsequent lap of the cycle.

Start recording

This time we are recording a single piano part. Record enable the piano track. Click on the record button of the Transport panel (key command: '*' on the numeric keypad). A pre-count is heard according to what has been set in the metronome. When recording commences, the track header turns red and the project cursor starts to move. Anything played on your keyboard (or other master instrument) is now recorded into Cubase. Try recording a fairly complex piano part.

Practice makes perfect

Your piano performance may be lacking the first time around the cycle. Do not drop out of record just start playing again on the next lap of the cycle. Your previous recording is replaced since you are in cycle record overwrite mode. All notes which come after your drop in point are replaced by the new performance. This allows you to keep practising the part until you play it 'perfectly'. When you get it right, your performance is already captured since you are still in record mode (see Figure 5.9). When you are happy with your recording, don't forget to save your work under a new name by selecting the 'save as' function in the File menu.

Figure 5.8
Cycle recording multiple MIDI parts in mix mode allows you to quickly build up a MIDI arrangement

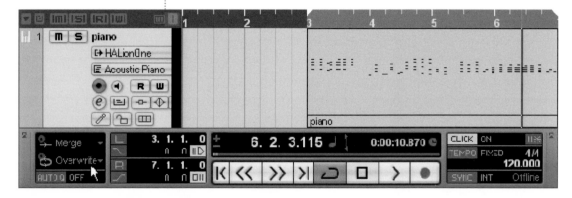

MIDI cycle recording project 3 (Stacked mode)

Delete the events recorded in the previous projects, above. This time, select 'Stacked' in the cycle record mode selector. In stacked mode, a new MIDI part is created for each lap of the cycle. The parts are automatically stacked on separate lanes within the vertical space of the MIDI track. Each of the previous takes is automatically muted as each new take commences.

Start recording

We are now recording a single piano part again. Record enable the piano track. Click on the record button of the Transport panel (key command: '*' on the numeric keypad). A pre-count is heard according to what has been set in the metronome. When recording commences, the track header turns red and the project cursor starts to move. Anything played on your keyboard (or other master instrument) is now recorded into Cubase. Try recording a complex piano part.

Relax while you play

This time you can feel really free to experiment since all your playing is automatically and conveniently captured in separate stacked parts, one for each lap of the cycle. These are also automatically numbered and arranged within the vertical space of the MIDI track (Figure 5.10). When recording is complete, editing the parts with the splice, mute and other tools allows you to assemble a 'perfect' take while still remaining in the Project window. If desired, you can merge all the wanted material into a single composite part

Figure 5.10
Cycle recording in stacked mode gives you maximum flexibility at the editing stage

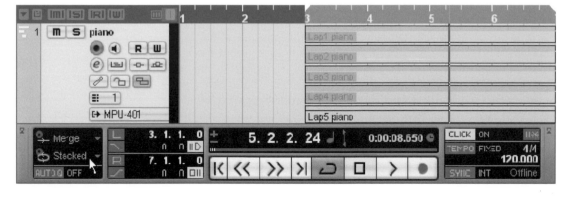

using Merge MIDI in Loop (MIDI menu). When you are happy with your recording (and editing), don't forget to save your work under a new name by selecting the 'save as' function in the File menu.

Combining cycle recording techniques

The techniques from the above three projects can be combined. How to record largely depends on what kind of recording you are making. For example, using cycle recording in mix mode is probably best suited to drum and percussion parts where you may wish to build up the rhythm on each lap of the cycle. Unless you are an excellent musician this same technique may not be so useful for recording your bass and piano parts. These might benefit more from cycle record in over-write mode. This gives you the opportunity to keep on repeating your part until you get a good take. Stacked mode probably gives you the most flexibility since it effortlessly organises your recording into neat, separate segments and leaves all your options open until you decide which takes to keep at the editing stage. Remember that you can freely switch between mix, overwrite and stacked modes on the fly without dropping out of record.

Retrospective record

When Cubase is in stop or play mode, any MIDI input is still recorded by the program, as long as one MIDI track is record enabled. This helps capture the magical performance you might produce when you are practising before starting to record or when you are playing along with an existing arrange-ment without recording. Retrospective record helps you avoid the 'if only I had recorded that!' syndrome which afflicts some recording sessions. Selecting Retrospective record from the Transport menu instantly creates a MIDI part beginning at the project cursor on the current record enabled track and this contains your recently played MIDI performance. If the MIDI input took place alongside an existing arrangement the data is synchronised with the other MIDI parts as if you had recorded it in the normal way. The amount of data which can be recorded by the Retrospective record function is chosen in File / Preferences / Record.

How do I include my MIDI recordings when I use Export/Audio Mixdown?

The problem

Cubase includes a virtual mixing console where both audio and MIDI tracks can be mixed and automated. When you have completed a combined MIDI + audio project and set up an ideal mix, it is possible to bounce the result to an audio file on hard disk using the Export / Audio mixdown function in the File menu. This is sometimes referred to as 'mixing in the box'. However, there is a problem: the MIDI tracks which trigger your external MIDI devices are NOT included in the mixdown! The Audio mixdown function operates upon the data found between the left and right locators for all audio tracks, Instrument tracks and MIDI tracks which trigger VST Instruments. However, it does NOT convert regular MIDI tracks which trigger external MIDI devices. The program has no way of knowing what audio signals these external devices are producing.

Info

See Chapter 12 for more details about Export/Audio mixdown.

The solution to the problem

The solution is to record the audio output of all external MIDI devices onto regular audio tracks before using Export / Audio mixdown. To achieve this you need to consider how the audio outputs of your MIDI devices are routed within your system. Most of us use an external mixing console to manage the audio signals from the MIDI network. If you followed the advice (above) of making a clear, logical diagram of your MIDI network and audio system with all the inputs and outputs clearly labelled, you can make good use of it here.

Assuming that the audio outputs of your MIDI devices are routed into the line inputs of your external mixing console, the following is what you need to do:

1   Set up the sound of each MIDI instrument in the external mixing console. If you intend to bounce the audio from the instruments to a stereo pair in Cubase then you should take some time setting up the mix. However, for the best results you are advised to record each instrument on a separate track as explained in the following points.
2   Route the audio output of the first instrument you wish to record to a group output of the external console. Connect the group output to the desired physical input of your audio hardware. (You will need two channels if recording in stereo).
3   In Cubase, create a new audio track and in the input routing menu choose the input bus into which you have routed the audio output of your MIDI device (via the group output of your external mixing console). Monitor enable the track and commence playback. Adjust the sound as desired and when satisfied record the audio signal.
4   Proceed in a similar manner to record the audio signals from each of your external MIDI devices onto separate audio tracks. If you have multiple input audio hardware then you may prefer to record all signals in a single pass.
5   When all the parts have been recorded onto regular audio tracks, mute all the original MIDI tracks in the Project window.
6   Set up your mix in the normal way, including the new audio tracks. Set the left and right locators to the start and end points of the music. Use Export / Audio mixdown to create an audio file on hard disk. The mix is now complete and includes all the audio signals from your MIDI devices.

Brief summary of MIDI recording techniques

Armed with the techniques outlined in this and previous chapters, you are now ready to tackle more elaborate MIDI recording projects. The recording projects outlined above are only exercises and must, of course, be adapted to suit your own needs. Whatever technique you choose, you can now quickly build up a number of MIDI tracks to form a musical arrangement in the Project window. To help clarify the basic process for MIDI recording Figure 5.11 presents the essential steps in the form of a flowchart. This describes what you might do when recording in a linear fashion on a single MIDI track.

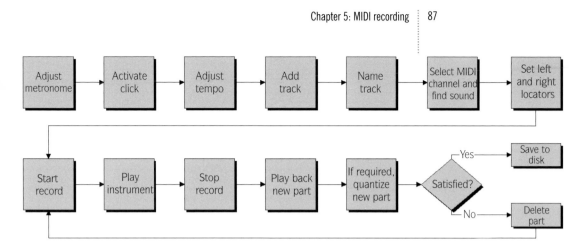

Figure 5.11
MIDI recording flowchart

In summary, the basic MIDI recording techniques include linear recording on a single MIDI track (or on a number of MIDI tracks simultaneously) and MIDI recording in cycle mode. When using Export / Audio mixdown to create a complete mix which includes all MIDI and audio tracks, all audio signals from external MIDI devices must first be recorded onto audio tracks.

You can achieve a lot in both the recording and editing sense while still remaining in the Project window, and you may be surprised how quickly you can build up an entire musical arrangement. However, there are times when you need to process and edit MIDI data in fine detail and this forms the subject matter of the next chapter.

Tip

Use the tools and techniques outlined in Chapter 4 to arrange and edit your MIDI parts in the Project window event display. Do not forget to save your work at regular intervals.

MIDI editing

This chapter explores the Key editor, Edit In-Place editor, List editor and Drum editor. These are for the detailed editing of the events found within MIDI parts. Coverage of the general MIDI editing functions and quantize functions found in the MIDI menu is also included.

General features of the MIDI editors

To open a MIDI editor, select a MIDI part and choose one of the editors from the MIDI menu. Each editor includes a toolbar, an infoline, a grid and a MIDI controller display. The notes (or events) are shown as graphical strips in the Key, List and Edit In-Place editors and as diamond-shaped symbols in the Drum editor. The Edit In-Place editor is similar to the Key editor but opens up in the Project window within the expanded vertical space of the chosen MIDI track. This has the advantage of allowing you to edit and line up MIDI events relative to the events on the other tracks in the Project window.

The grid is a series of horizontal and vertical guide lines which help you place notes at the correct pitch and at meaningful positions along the time line. This is particularly relevant when the snap button is activated, at which time the vertical lines of the grid become magnetic for all newly input or edited notes. To get a better idea of how the grid behaves try selecting different values in the quantize menu (when bars and beats is chosen as the display format in the ruler). The distance between the vertical grid lines is modified for each new value chosen. Deactivating the snap button switches off the magnetic behaviour of the grid lines, at which time notes may be freely inserted or dragged to any position along the time line.

The MIDI editor toolbar

All the MIDI editors feature a toolbar which varies slightly for each editor (Figure 6.1). The common features of the toolbars include the following (left to right):

Figure 6.1
MIDI editor toolbar (Key edit)

- solo editor button – for soloing the editor.
- acoustic feedback button – for automatic playback of selected and inserted notes via MIDI.
- info button – for showing or hiding the infoline.
- tool buttons – for selecting the various editing tools (see below).
- autoscroll button – to automatically scroll the display to follow the project cursor position.
- auto select controllers button – to automatically select all visible controller data within the range of the selected note(s). This helps when you need to move or copy notes and all their associated pitch bend and modulation data at once (for example). Now you need only edit the notes, and the controller data follows. For this to function correctly all target data must be visible in the controller lanes.
- show part borders button – activates flags which show the start and end position of the part currently being edited. This clarifies the display.
- edit active part only button – restricts all editing operation to the active part only.
- part list menu – provides a list of all selected parts or all parts in the track when you select more than one part or a whole track for editing. This allows you to quickly choose which part you wish to edit next. The display automatically scrolls to the start of each part you choose.
- insert velocity field – for selecting the default velocity for inserted notes.
- snap button – for switching on and off the magnetic action of the grid.
- snap type and quantize menu – for choosing how quantizing affects editing and data input, and for selecting the resolution of the grid.
- length quantize menu – for changing the length of existing notes when using length quantize from the MIDI menu and for choosing a default length for inserted notes.
- step input and MIDI input buttons – to allow the input of notes one at a time according to the current quantize resolution and to allow the modification of MIDI note and velocity values via MIDI.
- velocity colours menu – for selecting the manner in which colour is used for velocity in the controller display.

Tip

When editing parts which trigger VST Instruments it is possible to open the interface for the instrument directly from within a MIDI editor by activating the 'Edit VST instrument' button on the toolbar. The 'Edit VST Instrument' button is shown by selecting it in the pop-up toolbar menu (right click/Ctrl + click on the toolbar).

Info

The List editor toolbar features special mask and filter functions and has no infoline.

Infoline

When the infoline button is activated a horizontal information line appears between the grid and the toolbar (Figure 6.2). It displays the details of the currently selected note, including the start position, end position, length, pitch, velocity, channel, note-off velocity and articulation. Position and length information is displayed according to the time line format you have chosen in the ruler. The infoline is particularly useful for detailed editing since all fields can be directly edited using the mouse and computer keyboard. When more than one event is selected the infoline text is shown in yellow and contains the information relevant to the first of the selected events. Editing any of the yellow text values applies the changes proportionally. In this case, changing the velocity value from '75' to '80' adds five to the velocity of all selected events.

Pitch	Velocity	Off Velocity	Start	End	Length	Channel	Articulations
G4/79	90	64	3. 2. 2.110	3. 2. 3. 70	0. 0. 0. 80	3	None ▾

Alternatively, holding down Ctrl while changing the velocity applies the value in an absolute sense. This time, changing the velocity from '75' to '80' sets the velocity of all selected events to the absolute value of '80'.

The MIDI editor tools

To select a tool in any of the editors, click on one of the tool buttons in the toolbar or select a tool from the Quick menu (opened by right mouse clicking (PC) or Ctrl + clicking (Mac) in the grid). The tools are for the manipulation and editing of MIDI notes and Controller events and most of the tools listed here are relevant for all the MIDI editors. They include the following:

Object selection tool (pointer)

Similar to the Project window, the object selection tool (or pointer tool) is a general purpose tool for the selection, moving and copying of MIDI notes and events and for the manipulation of parameters anywhere in the MIDI editors. It is particularly useful for re-sizing in the Key editor where either the start or end of a note can be dragged to a new position (a double arrow appears when you position the pointer over the start or end points of the note). Unlike the Project window, the object selection tool for the MIDI editors is not a multi-function tool.

Draw tool

The draw tool is for inserting new events in the note grid or controller display. It may also be used for the modification of the length of an existing note by dragging the end point, and of the value of velocity and controller data in the controller display.

Erase tool

The erase tool is for deleting events by clicking on one event or a selected group of events. Pressing Alt while clicking with the erase tool deletes all following events in the Part.

Mute tool

The mute tool is for muting events. Click on events individually or drag a selection box over several to implement muting. Click on or drag over the muted events to un-mute them. A muted event is displayed in white.

Trim tool

The trim tool is for trimming the start or end points of notes. To trim the end of a note click on it at the required new end point. To trim the start of a note click on it while pressing Alt. The trim tool is particularly helpful for producing strumming effects by staggering the start points of the notes in a chord.

Split tool

The split tool is for splicing notes into two shorter notes. Notes are split at the mouse position and according to the current snap/quantize settings. Clicking on the note while pressing Alt produces multiple splits.

Glue tool

The glue tool is used to join together notes of the same pitch. Clicking on the note while pressing Alt joins all following notes in the part into one long note at the same pitch.

Zoom tool

The zoom tool is for zooming in and out of the grid display. To zoom in, select the zoom tool and click in the event display. To zoom out, click in the event display while pressing Alt. To zoom in to a specific area of the grid drag a box around the area of interest with the zoom tool. To step back through previously used zoom views click with the zoom tool while pressing Ctrl (PC) / Command (Mac).

Paint tool

The paint tool is a multi-function tool. Click on the button a second time to reveal the other options. The paint brush allows the free drawing of events on the note grid or in the controller display. The line, parabola, sine, triangle and square tools impose their respective shapes on inserted or edited events. When the snap button is activated, the position of notes and the size of the shapes imposed by the sine, triangle and square tools is regulated by the current quantize value.

Time warp tool

The time warp tool behaves in a similar manner to the time warp tool in the Project window. To operate correctly, the ruler must be set to bars and beats. Time warp operates within the active part in two modes: 'default' mode and 'musical events follow' mode. In the default mode, the events in the MIDI editor do not move when you drag the warp tool in the display. This might be used to match the tempo to MIDI material which was not played to a strict click. When the snap button is activated on the toolbar the time warp position snaps to the start and ends of note events. This is useful for lining up beat positions to note events. In 'musical events follow' mode, all MIDI events are moved as you drag the warp tool in the display. This is used to manipulate the tempo so that a musical passage fits within a given time frame or to match a MIDI event to a specific time cue.

To insert a tempo event click in the grid with the time warp tool. To delete a tempo event click on the event in the ruler while holding Shift. When you first drag or click in the grid with the warp tool, tempo events are automatically inserted at the start and end of the active part. This ensures that the tempo of material which occurs outside the active part is not changed. Before you use the time warp tool, tempo track mode must be selected in the Transport bar.

Drumstick tool

The drumstick tool is relevant only to the Drum editor. The Drum editor does not include a pencil tool in its toolbar. Instead, it is the drumstick tool which is used for event input and controller editing. The drumstick tool behaves slightly differently to the pencil tool in that clicking on an event a second time removes it from the grid and dragging horizontally inputs repeated notes at the current quantize setting (if the snap button is activated).

Info

When the snap button is activated and bars and beats is set as the time format in the ruler, all tool editing in the Key, List and Drum editors is magnetic to the settings in the quantize and length quantize menus. The vertical lines on the grid change their positions along the time line according to the quantize setting.

Step input and MIDI input buttons

The six step and MIDI input buttons are concerned with the input of notes one step at a time (step input) and the entering of note and velocity data via MIDI. The buttons function in two modes according to which of the step and MIDI input buttons has been activated.

With the step button activated, when you play a note on your MIDI keyboard it is recorded onto the grid one step at a time at the resolution of the quantize menu setting and with the note length at the length quantize menu setting. The input data is also modified according to which of the note, velocity on and velocity off buttons (the rightmost three buttons) you have selected in the toolbar. With the note button activated the pitch of the input notes follows the keys you play on your keyboard. With the note button de-activated the pitch of the input notes remains at C3/60. With the velocity on button activated the velocity of the input notes follows the velocity with which you play the notes on your keyboard. With the velocity button de-activated the velocity of the input notes matches that set in the insert velocity field. The velocity off button functions in a similar manner. A 'move insert mode' button allows you to insert notes into an existing sequence by pushing existing notes to the right.

With the MIDI input button activated, when you select an existing note on the grid and play a note on your MIDI keyboard, this imposes the received MIDI values onto the selected note according to which of the note, velocity on and velocity off buttons (the rightmost three buttons) you have selected in the toolbar. When the incoming MIDI values have been registered the editor moves on to the next note automatically. This allows you to re-record note and/or velocity data for an existing sequence in step-time.

General tips for the MIDI editors

The following tips are designed to help you get started in the MIDI editors.

- Once you have selected one note event in a MIDI editor, try using the left and right arrow keys on the computer keyboard to scroll through consecutive notes. This is often easier than using the mouse. In order to be able to hear each event as it is selected, activate the acoustic feedback button (loudspeaker symbol) in the toolbar. Use the up and down arrow keys to change the pitch of a selected note.
- Adopting a two hand approach speeds up tool selection and editing. Use the left hand to select the tools with the computer typewriter keys 1 to 9 (or F9 and F10 to step through the tools) and use the right hand for all mouse manipulations (vice versa for left handed users).
- To gain an initial understanding of the function of the grid, open a MIDI editor, make sure bars and beats is chosen as the display format in the ruler, activate the snap button and change the quantize menu to different values. For each new value selected in the quantize menu the distance between the vertical grid lines is modified. When the snap button is activated the grid becomes magnetic and any inserted notes are pulled onto the nearest vertical grid line. This also helps you get to

grips with the quantize functions. Selecting Over quantize from the MIDI menu pulls all recorded notes in the part onto the nearest vertical grid lines. You can see the effect of the quantizing action on the grid. Observing the effect of quantizing in a MIDI editor provides helpful visual feedback of what actually happens when you use the quantize functions and is a helpful for getting to know what quantize is all about.

- Clicking once in the ruler moves the project cursor to the position at which you clicked. Double clicking in the ruler starts playback from the point at which you clicked. Double clicking a second time stops playback and re-positions the project cursor to the point at which you clicked. This helps you navigate within your chosen MIDI editor.
- Use the G and H keys for horizontal zoom control in the grid display. At higher vertical zoom settings the MIDI note name / number appears inside the note strip.
- Click with the right mouse button (PC) / Ctrl + click (Mac) in the grid to open the Quick menu. This allows quick tool selection and provides rapid access to the menu items relevant to MIDI editing.
- Cubase benefits from unlimited undo / redo. Use Ctrl + Z (PC) / Command + Z (Mac) to undo an edit. Use Ctrl + Shift + Z (PC) / Command + Shift + Z (Mac) to redo an edit. To see the current edit history open the History dialogue (Edit menu). Move the blue line to step back and forth within the edit history. Note that the edit history is cleared when you close the project.

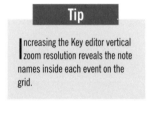

Tip

Increasing the Key editor vertical zoom resolution reveals the note names inside each event on the grid.

Key editor

The Key editor (Figure 6.3) is a piano roll style editor featuring time on the horizontal axis and pitch on the vertical axis. The main display area is the grid where notes are represented as graphical strips. There is a mini piano keyboard to the left of the display, which corresponds to the pitch, and a controller display below where velocity and various non-note events, such as

Figure 6.3
The Key editor

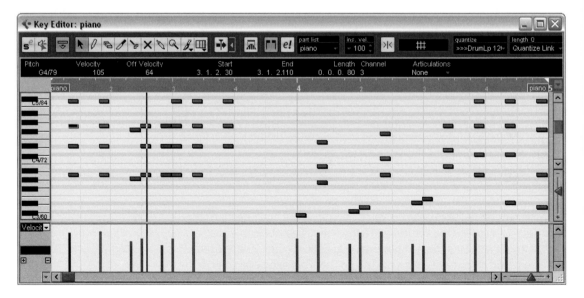

Pitch Bend and Modulation, are shown. Similar to the Project window and the other MIDI editors, there is a ruler which marks the time line in the chosen format and a toolbar and infoline (as outlined above).

To open the Key editor double-click on a MIDI part or press the Return key on the computer keyboard with a MIDI part selected. Alternatively, select 'Key editor' in the MIDI menu or press Ctrl (PC)/Command (Mac) + E on the computer keyboard (default key command). You can select more than one part from the same or different tracks and all notes in all parts are shown in the Key editor. However, the notes from only one part at a time are active and all other non-active notes are displayed in grey. Use the part list to select the active part and the 'show part borders' button to highlight the active part. Select the MIDI track alone with no parts selected to open the Key editor for all MIDI parts on the track.

Controller display

The Key editor features a controller display for velocity and non-note MIDI data such as pitch bend, aftertouch, program change, modulation, main volume, pan and articulations. By default, velocity is displayed when you first open the editor. To add a new lane click on the plus (+) box of an existing lane. You can save the current controller lane configuration using the controller lane presets menu. To change the type of event shown, click on the menu to the left of the controller lane to open a pop-up menu. If the type of data you wish to see is not present in the menu, click on Setup to open the Controller menu setup dialogue, and add the required data type to the menu using the left pointing arrow button.

Events are shown as vertical strips which are normally colour-coded according to their value (by default, blue for low values and red for high values). This is particularly useful for velocity since it gives an immediate idea of the intensity of the musical performance. The velocity colour is also applied to the note itself on the grid, which conveys the velocity status even if the controller display is hidden from view. By adding multiple controller lanes you can simultaneously display a number of different types of MIDI data. This is invaluable for getting a graphical overview of all the data for high precision editing.

Tip

When using the Key editor, try pressing 'P' on the computer keyboard to set the left and right locators to the start and end points of the selected part. Also activate cycle mode on the Transport panel, (key command: numeric keypad divide key [/]). Cubase now cycles within the selected part (between the left and right locators) ensuring that the project cursor does not disappear from view while you are in the Key editor.

Figure 6.4
The controller display allows multiple controller lanes to be shown

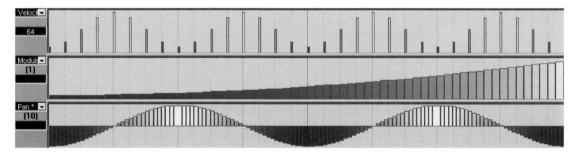

Key editor basic techniques

Most routine editing in the Key editor revolves around selecting, moving, copying, inserting, re-sizing and deleting notes and controller events using the tools. The draw tool is the standard tool for drawing new note events onto the grid. Notes are pulled onto the nearest vertical grid line when the snap button is activated. Their velocity is determined by the insert velocity value on the toolbar and, with single click inserts, their length is determined by the length quantize value. Clicking and dragging to the right with the pencil tool allows you to insert a note of a longer length. Clicking and dragging in the controller display with the pencil tool inserts new controller events. If there are events already in the controller display these are updated according to the new shape drawn by the pencil tool (Figure 6.5).

Figure 6.5
Inserting new notes and new controller events using the draw tool

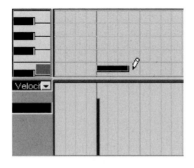
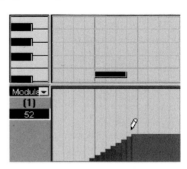

The object selection tool (pointer) would normally be used for the selection of notes on the grid and events in the controller display. The standard selection procedures as outlined in Chapter 4 also apply to the selection of events in the Key editor. The principal methods include dragging a box around a number of events or clicking on individual events. Selected notes may be moved by clicking on one of them and dragging to a new position. Holding Alt on the computer keyboard copies the notes instead (Figure 6.6).

Figure 6.6
Selecting and moving notes

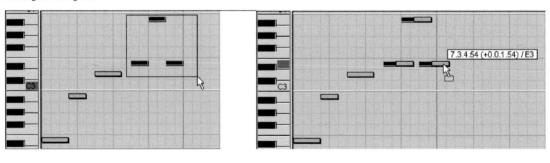

The object selection tool may be used for re-sizing notes by clicking and dragging on their start or end points. A double arrow appears when the tool is placed above the appropriate position (Figure 6.7).

Figure 6.7
Re-sizing notes using the pointer tool

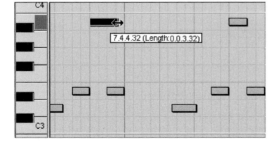
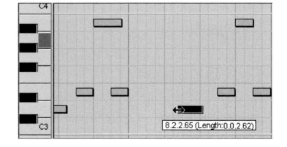

Deleting notes is achieved either by dragging over the notes with the erase tool or selecting the notes and pressing backspace on the computer keyboard. If your deletions are of an experimental kind, you may prefer to temporarily mute the notes using the mute tool.

Key editor close-ups

Editing a bass line

You have recorded a perfect bass line with a great feel but some notes are too long, some are too short and some overlap. The Key editor provides a solution as follows:

- Select the draw tool.
- Click and hold the draw tool near the end point of each offending note and drag the length to the desired duration.
- If the snap button is activated, the new length is snapped to the nearest vertical grid line. De-activating the snap button allows you to freely adjust the length of the note and may be a better option for this exercise.
- 'Delete overlaps' in the MIDI functions menu may also provide a partial solution to the problem.

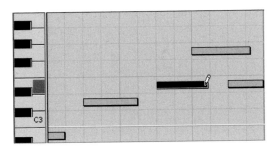

Figure 6.8
Editing the lengths of overlapping bass notes

Creating strumming effects with chords

You have successfully recorded a number of chords but would like to stagger start points of the notes to produce a strumming effect. To create the effect in the Key editor proceed as follows:

- Select the trim tool.
- Hold Alt on the computer keyboard and click on the start position of each note individually or drag across the start positions of all notes or a group of notes within the chord (a guide line is shown in the display).
- If you are seeking guitar-like strumming, a downward strum corresponds with the notes being staggered from the lower to the upper notes and an upward strum would be from the upper to the lower notes.
- Realistic strumming effects often involve staggering the notes in small groups within the chord. For example, a six-note guitar chord may sound more 'strummed' if you trim two separate groups of three notes (see Figure 6.9).

Figure 6.9
Trimming the notes within a chord to create a strumming effect

Editing note velocities

Certain high velocity notes within a sequence produce an unwanted percussive attack in the synthesizer sound you are using. To correct the problem proceed as follows:

- Select velocity in the Key editor controller display by clicking on the downward pointing arrow to the left of the Controller lane to open the pop-up controller selection menu. Normally, velocity is displayed by default when you first open the Key editor.

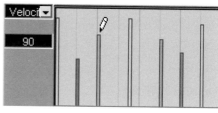

Figure 6.10
Changing velocity values using the draw tool

- The velocities of the recorded notes are now visible in the display as vertical strips.
- Select the draw tool and click and drag on the offending velocities to set them to appropriate new values.

Producing crescendos

If crescendos (or decrescendos) are required after the notes have been recorded then the controller display of the Key editor is one of the best places to create them. This technique is particularly useful for drum rolls and snare fills. Proceed as follows:

- Select velocity in the controller display.
- Select the paint/line tool and click and drag a line at the appropriate angle across the note velocities to which you wish to apply the crescendo.

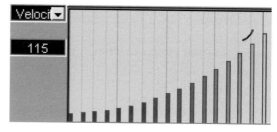

Figure 6.11
Producing a crescendo using the parabola shape of the paint tool

- When the mouse is released a velocity ramp matching the straight line appears.
- For a more exponential crescendo try using the parabola shape tool.
- This technique can be used on other types of data. For example, processing Main Volume controller events in this way allows you to create MIDI volume fades in and out.

Producing special effects with modulation

The Modulation Controller is often used with synth patches to produce real-time modulation of some aspect of the sound, such as increasing the brightness, modifying the cut-off frequency of the filter or adding more vibrato. Using the draw tool shapes, like sine and triangle, you can create special effects by drawing shapes in the controller display. Proceed as follows:

- Select modulation in the controller display. De-activate the snap button on the toolbar.

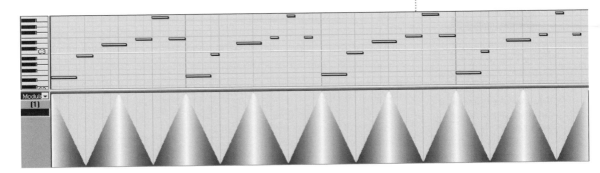

- Select the triangle shape draw tool and click and drag to the right from the upper left corner of the controller lane (when the value field should read 127) to the lower right corner (when the value field should read 0).
- When the mouse is released a triangular-shaped sequence of modulation events appears in the display.
- Try re-activating the snap button and choosing different quantize values, length quantize values and tool shapes (sine, triangle or square). The quantize value governs the period of the shapes while the length quantize values govern the density of the events. As a preliminary experiment try setting quantize to 1/4 note and length quantize to 1/128 triplet.

Figure 6.12
Drawing modulation shapes in the controller display for special effects

Multiple controller lanes for high-precision editing and special effects
If the filter section of the target synthesizer responds to Controllers 70-74, several controller lanes can be used simultaneously to set up tightly co-ordinated filtering effects. For example, this works with the supplied Monologue and Prologue VST instruments. Proceed as follows:

- Click on the plus (+) box to the left of an existing controller lane to create a new one. Open the number of controller lanes required.
- Select the controllers you intend to use in the pop-up controller selector menus to the left of the lanes. Try starting with three controller lanes showing controllers 70, 71 and 74.
- Select a draw tool and draw a shape in the display. Try any combination of the paintbrush, parabola, sine, triangle and square tools.

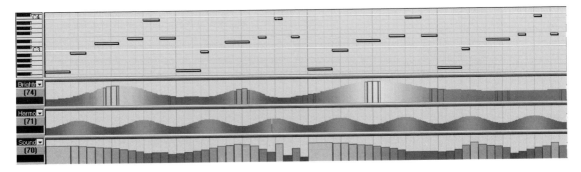

Figure 6.13a
Tightly co-ordinated editing in multiple controller lanes

Editing VST expression articulations

VST expression articulations allow you to add creative musical nuances to MIDI parts. Articulations include such things as accents and staccato applied to single notes, (known as attributes), and indications of loudness and playing style, (known as directions). To be able to use articulations, the target instrument on the Instrument or MIDI track must be compatible and the necessary VST expression map must be present in the system. Expression maps are activated using the expression map menu.

HalionOne is supplied with a number of VST expression track presets, designated by a 'VX' suffix. For a quick introduction to VST expression, add a new Instrument track using the HalionOne track preset named 'Acoustic Bass VX'. This already contains an expression map which triggers the appropriate samples in HalionOne. Record a test part on the track and then open the Key editor. Select 'Articulations' in the pop-up menu of a suitable controller lane. The acoustic bass features muted, open, flageolet and accent articulations. Use the pencil tool to insert articulation events in the articulation controller lane (see Figure 6.13b). The pencil tool also toggles an articulation event off by clicking on it a second time.

> **Info**
>
> A number of VST expression maps are supplied on the Cubase DVD in Additional Content / VST Expression / Expression Maps. These may be loaded using the load button of the VST Expression setup window.

Figure 6.13b

Adding articulation in a controller lane helps make your MIDI parts more musically expressive

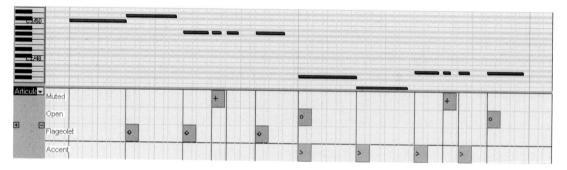

Edit In-Place

The Edit In-Place editor (Figure 6.14) is similar to the Key editor except that it is opened within the event display in the Project window. This means that you can look inside a MIDI part while still remaining in the Project window and, more

Figure 6.14
Edit In-Place editor

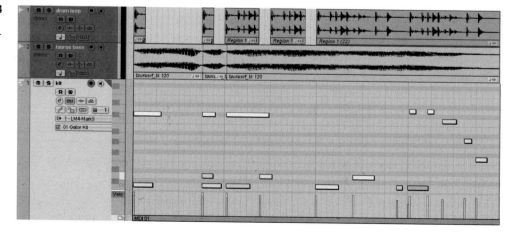

importantly, you can line up individual MIDI events to events on other tracks in the event display, or vice versa. For this purpose, try selecting 'Events' in the snap type menu. To open the Edit In-Place editor select a MIDI part, MIDI track or Instrument track and select 'Edit In-Place' from the MIDI menu, or press Ctrl / Command + Shift + I on the computer keyboard to toggle the editor on or off. Alternatively, try using the Edit In-Place button in the track list. If not already visible, activate it in the Track Control Settings dialogue, opened by clicking on the small downward pointing arrow at the top left of the track list.

The Edit-In Place editor opens within the vertical space of the selected track which expands to accommodate the grid. The vertical grid lines in the editor line up with the grid in the main part of the Project window. It is therefore a relatively easy task to line up MIDI events to other events along the time line. The other features of the editor include a controller display below the grid, a virtual keyboard to the left, and a toolbar above, (opened by clicking on the grey triangle found at the upper left side of the virtual keyboard).

Edit In-Place basic techniques

To zoom in vertically in the Edit In-Place editor, place the pointer in the left part of the virtual keyboard to the left of the grid so that a hand appears. Drag the hand to the left or right to zoom in and out. Drag the hand up or down to scroll the key range shown in the editor. To zoom in and out horizontally, use the standard Cubase zoom controls (by default, key commands G and H).

Clicking on the grey triangle in the upper left corner of the Edit In-Place editor opens a toolbar. The toolbar is a reduced version of the toolbar found in the other MIDI editors. Here you have access to the acoustic feedback button, solo editor button, part list, auto select controllers, insert velocity, length quantize, velocity colours and transpose parameters.

The snap and quantize behaviour is governed from the main Project window toolbar using the snap type and quantize type menus. (The grid type menu has no function in the Edit In-Place editor). Setting the snap type menu to 'Events' is particularly helpful for lining up MIDI events to other events on other tracks in the display or vice versa.

Edit In-Place close-ups

Snapping to events

As mentioned above, activating the snap button and selecting 'Events' in the snap menu is particularly useful in the Edit In-Place editor. For example, this makes it easy to line up a MIDI note with the start of an audio event, as shown in Figure 6.15.

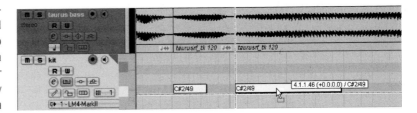

Figure 6.15
Lining up a MIDI crash cymbal (C#2) with the start of an audio event in the Edit In-Place editor

Moving audio events in relation to individual MIDI events is equally useful. For example, Figure 6.16 shows how you can 'punch a hole' in an audio event for the precise duration of a MIDI event. In this case, a gap is punched into an audio event (a drum loop) according to the position and length of a MIDI snare drum

Figure 6.16
Punching a gap into an audio event according to the position and length of a MIDI note (D1)

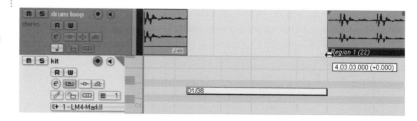

(D1). To achieve this the drum loop is split and the end of the resulting first event is dragged to the start of the MIDI note, while the start of the second event is dragged to the end of the MIDI note.

Selective moving and copying

Another advantage of the Edit In-Place editor is the ability to selectively move or copy specific MIDI events within a part along with other selected events in the general event display. For example, this would allow you to copy audio events along with just the MIDI notes which trigger a cymbal in a MIDI part, as shown in Figure 6.17. All non-selected MIDI notes are not copied or moved with the selection.

Figure 6.17
Selectively copying the cymbal crashes in a MIDI part along with some audio events

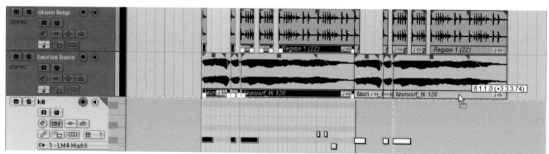

The List editor

Info

The List editor displays a simple time ordered list of the MIDI events. Unlike the Key editor, the vertical axis of the grid does not represent pitch. Changing the pitch in the List editor data 1 column therefore produces no visible change to the events in the grid. Time is shown on the horizontal axis of the grid.

The List editor (Figure 6.18) is a list-based editor where all data is presented in a list of time-consecutive events. It differs from the other editors in that all kinds of MIDI data, score and standard MIDI file events may be viewed and edited.

The List editor is opened from the MIDI menu or you may like to assign a Key command in File / Key Commands (try Ctrl/Command + Alt + L). Similar to the Key editor, the List editor features a grid and a toolbar containing a similar set of tools. However, the most important feature of the List editor is the list itself. There are a number of columns hidden behind the grid which can be revealed by moving the split point to the right of the screen. This reveals more details about the events in the list.

The columns contain information about each event including its type, start position, end position, length, data values 1, 2 and 3, MIDI channel and associated System Exclusive or text data in the comment column. For example, regular note events feature their pitch in the data 1 column followed by their velocity on in the data 2 column and velocity off in data 3. Controller events feature the controller name (or number) in the data 1 column followed

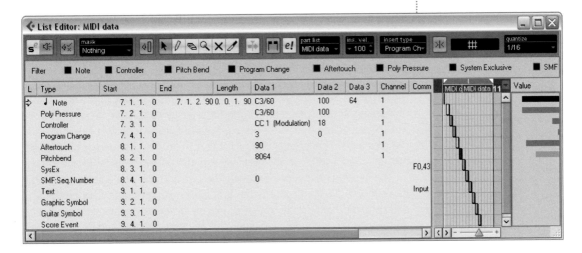

Figure 6.18
The List editor

by the value of the controller in the data 2 column. Most events have no entry in the comment column. However, the comment column for a System Exclusive event contains the System Exclusive message itself.

Features which are unique to the List editor include the Insert menu, the Mask menu, and the Filters. These are found in the toolbar.

The Insert menu

The Insert pop-up menu on the toolbar contains a list of event types. Any chosen event type may be inserted into the List by clicking with the draw tool on the grid. The event types include Note, Controller, Program Change, Aftertouch, Pitch Bend, Poly Pressure, SysEx, SMF and text.

The Mask menu and display filters

The Mask menu is used to force a display of one of the following:

1 all data of the same event type as the currently selected event
2 all data with the same event type and the same data 1 value as the currently selected event.
3 all data with the same MIDI channel as the currently selected event.

All other events are hidden from view. Alternatively, the events in the list may be filtered according to Logical editor presets.

The display filters are comprised of nine tick boxes, one for each of the main event types and for SMF and score events. The tick boxes are hidden or shown using the toolbar's 'Show filter view' button. When a box is ticked the corresponding event type is filtered out of the event list.

The Mask menu and display filters are among the most useful features of List edit. They can be used to clarify the list and to expose certain types of data for deletion or other editing.

List editor basic techniques

In the List editor, events may be edited by clicking on the column values and entering a new value with the computer keyboard (depends upon the value box setting in File / Preferences / Controls). Type a new value directly or use the up/down arrow keys to increment/decrement the value.

When the mouse pointer is moved into the grid area to the right of the list, it is automatically changed to a pencil tool. The horizontal bars in the display represent the data 2 values of events. These values may be changed graphically in the display in much the same way as in the controller display of the Key editor.

Clicking in the comment column for a System Exclusive event opens the MIDI Sysex editor. This is for editing System Exclusive data in fine detail and requires a good knowledge of SysEx theory in order to be successful. The user manual of your MIDI device normally lists the details of its SysEx messages.

The essential difference between the List and the Key editors is that the Key editor is directed towards the graphical editing of note data on the grid and controller data in the controller display, whereas the List editor is directed towards the more detailed editing of any type of event and its various values in the display list. As a general rule, the List editor is more useful for the editing of non-note events and helps when a more scientific approach is required. List edit is excellent for sorting events for analytical and troubleshooting purposes and might help you find undesirable events which are causing problems with your MIDI devices.

List editor close-ups

Editing System Exclusive messages
For the editing of System Exclusive messages proceed as follows:

- Click once in the comment column of the System Exclusive event in the list. The first part of the SysEx message is always visible in the comment column.
- The whole message is displayed in the MIDI Sysex editor which opens automatically. The data is shown in hexadecimal notation (Figure 6.19).
- Edit the data as desired and click on the OK button to keep the changes. A good knowledge of System Exclusive is required to make any meaningful changes.

Figure 6.19
Editing System Exclusive data

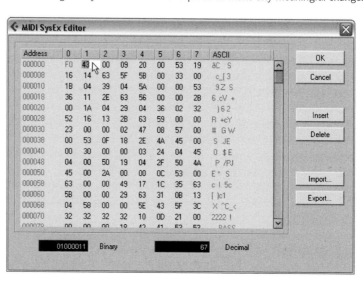

Finding unwanted Program Change messages

At some time in their use of the program, most Cubase users suffer from the problem of an unwanted or incorrect program change (or some other data type) embedded somewhere among the rest of the data. This is not always easy to find for deletion or editing. With the List editor filters the task is made easier. Proceed as follows:

• Select the track or part(s) containing the unwanted Program Change message.
• Activate the Show filter view button on the toolbar. Tick the filter boxes of all those data types you do not wish to see.
• The unwanted event(s) can now be found more easily among the remaining unfiltered data displayed in the list.

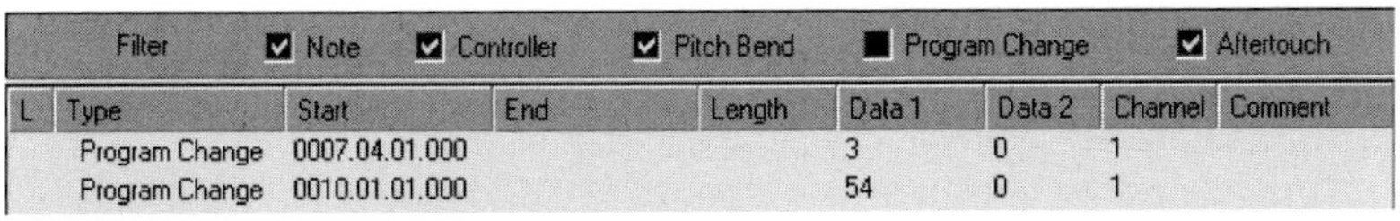

Filter	☑ Note	☑ Controller	☑ Pitch Bend	■ Program Change	☑ Aftertouch

L	Type	Start	End	Length	Data 1	Data 2	Channel	Comment
	Program Change	0007.04.01.000			3	0	1	
	Program Change	0010.01.01.000			54	0	1	

Figure 6.20
Exposing Program Change events using the List editor's filters

Inserting a Local Off Controller event

Most users set their master keyboard to Local Off for use with Cubase. This disconnects the musical keyboard from the sound-making circuitry of the instrument. Finding the Local Off control in the instrument itself is not always obvious and some instruments power up in Local On mode. To overcome these problems it is helpful to embed a Local Off message into a MIDI part which can be used within a default startup project to make sure that the master keyboard is always set to Local Off. To insert a Local Off event in List edit, proceed as follows:

• Create an empty MIDI part in the Project window, select it and open List edit.
• Select Controller in the Insert menu of the List edit toolbar.
• Select the draw tool and click once in the grid with the mouse at the beginning of the part. A new controller event with various default values is inserted into the list.
• Double-click in the data 1 column of the new event and enter the number '122' using the computer's numeric keypad (Controller 122 is the Local On / Off Controller).
• Double-click in the data 2 column and enter '0'. This is the off setting for Local Control. Should you need it '127' is the on setting.
• Make sure the MIDI track containing the part is transmitting to your master keyboard. When the newly created MIDI part is played, the Local Off message is sent to the keyboard and it is set to Local Off mode accordingly.

Figure 6.21
Creating a Local Off Controller message in List edit

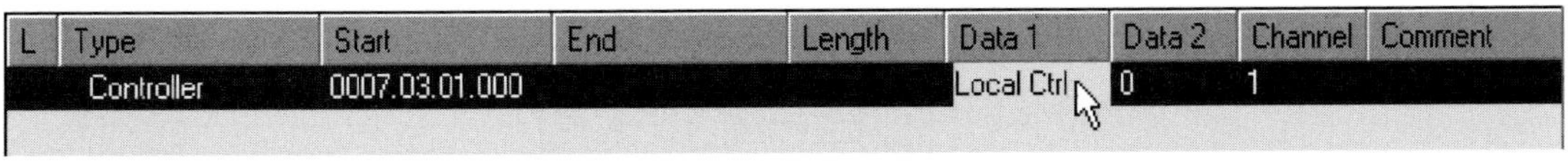

L	Type	Start	End	Length	Data 1	Data 2	Channel	Comment
	Controller	0007.03.01.000			Local Ctrl	0	1	

The Drum editor

The Drum editor is a drum machine style editor featuring time on the horizontal axis and pitch in the form of drum names on the vertical axis (Figure 6.22). Like the Key editor there is a grid but, this time, notes are represented by diamond-shaped symbols. The drum names are shown as a list to the left of the display and there is a toolbar above the grid and a controller display below, similar to those found in the Key editor. To open the Drum editor, select a MIDI part and then select 'Drum editor' from the MIDI menu. As the name implies, the Drum editor is designed for the editing of drum and percussion data. It operates in two modes: with a drum map or without a drum map. When a drum map is activated, more columns appear in the display and the editor features the names and note positions of specific drum setups, such as those found in external drum machines and modules or in a standard GM drum map. Without a drum map, the editor functions in a similar way to the Key editor.

Drum maps are assigned on a track-by-track basis and each track can be assigned a different drum map. Maps are chosen from the map menu in the Drum editor or in the Inspector for the track. When a map is assigned for a track in the Project window, the data display format switches to diamond shaped symbols for all parts on the track. New maps are added to the menu using the Drum Map Setup dialogue.

Figure 6.22
The Drum editor

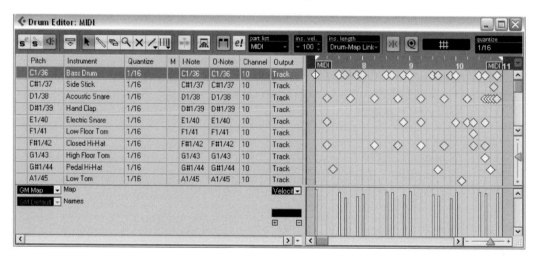

Drum editor columns

When a drum map has been assigned, pulling the split point to the right reveals a number of columns which are unique to the Drum editor. These include the following:

- Selection – a blank column for triggering or selecting each instrument with the mouse.
- Pitch – defines the base note for each instrument. This is a fixed value which cannot be modified and indicates the actual pitch which gets

recorded. There are 128 pitches available matching the 128 possible MIDI notes. The note in the pitch column often matches that found in the I-Note column but this may not always be the case.

- Instrument – for naming each instrument (drum) in the map.
- Quantize – for assigning an individual quantize value for each instrument which governs the resolution of any inserts or editing for the instrument on the grid.
- Mute – for muting individual instruments. Muting also occurs when you activate the 'solo instrument' button on the toolbar.
- I-Note (input note) – defines the pitch of the note you use to trigger each instrument. This is the source note you play on your master keyboard (or other controller instrument).
- O-Note (output note) – defines the pitch of the note which is transmitted from the MIDI output of Cubase when its corresponding input note is received. This is the note which is transmitted to the target MIDI device.
- Channel – for the selection of a MIDI channel for each instrument.
- Output – for the selection of a MIDI output port for each instrument. When set to 'track' the output for the instrument is transmitted via the MIDI port set for the track.

When a drum map has not been assigned, only the pitch, instrument and quantize columns are available. In this mode, you can still select the list of names and quantize values for the available maps using the Names menu (below the Map menu).

Setting up a Drum map

A Drum map is a set of 128 instrument slots each assigned to one of the 128 possible MIDI notes, and each with their corresponding name and values in the columns. Drum maps are assigned to MIDI tracks using the map menu which is found in the Drum editor or in the Inspector for the track. To set up a new map or save and load maps to / from disk, open the Drum Map Setup dialogue from the map menu (Figure 6.23).

Figure 6.23
The Drum Map Setup dialogue

	Pitch	Instrument	Quantize	M	I-Note	O-Note	Chanr	Output	Display Note	Head Symbol	V
	C1/36	Bass Drum	1/16		C1/36	C1/36	10	Track	F3/65	●	
	C#1/37	Side Stick	1/16		C#1/37	C#1/37	10	Track	C4/72	✦	
	D1/38	Acoustic Snare	1/16		D1/38	D1/38	10	Track	C4/72	●	
	D#1/39	Hand Clap	1/16		D#1/39	D#1/39	10	Track	C-2/0	●	
	E1/40	Electric Snare	1/16		E1/40	E1/40	10	Track	C4/72	●	
	F1/41	Low Floor Tom	1/16		F1/41	F1/41	10	Track	B3/71	∅	
	F#1/42	Closed Hi-Hat	1/16		F#1/42	F#1/42	10	Track	E4/76	×	
	G1/43	High Floor Tom	1/16		G1/43	G1/43	10	Track	D4/74	∅	
	G#1/44	Pedal Hi-Hat	1/16		G#1/44	G#1/44	10	Track	E4/76	×	
	A1/45	Low Tom	1/16		A1/45	A1/45	10	Track	C3/60	∅	
	A#1/46	Open Hi-Hat	1/16		A#1/46	A#1/46	10	Track	E4/76	⊛	
	B1/47	Low Middle Tom	1/16		B1/47	B1/47	10	Track	G3/67	∅	
	C2/48	High Middle Tom	1/16		C2/48	C2/48	10	Track	A3/69	∅	
	C#2/49	Crash Cymbal 1	1/16		C#2/49	C#2/49	10	Track	G4/79	⊛	
	D2/50	High Tom	1/16		D2/50	D2/50	10	Track	C4/72	∅	
	D#2/51	Ride Cymbal 1	1/16		D#2/51	D#2/51	10	Track	G4/79	×	
	E2/52	Chinese Cymbal	1/16		E2/52	E2/52	10	Track	G4/79	×	
	F2/53	Ride Bell	1/16		F2/53	F2/53	10	Track	G4/79	×	
	F#2/54	Tambourine	1/16		F#2/54	F#2/54	10	Track	C-2/0	●	

Drum Map Setup

Functions

Drum Maps
GM Map
jd800.drm
popdrumset1.drm
popdrumset2.drm
k1.drm
k4.drm
23rd century kit.drm
chaos kit.drm
cr-78 kit.drm
techno kit.drm
kv. 5.drm

■ Use Head Pairs
☐ Edit in Scores

Output
GM Device (MPU-401)

Close

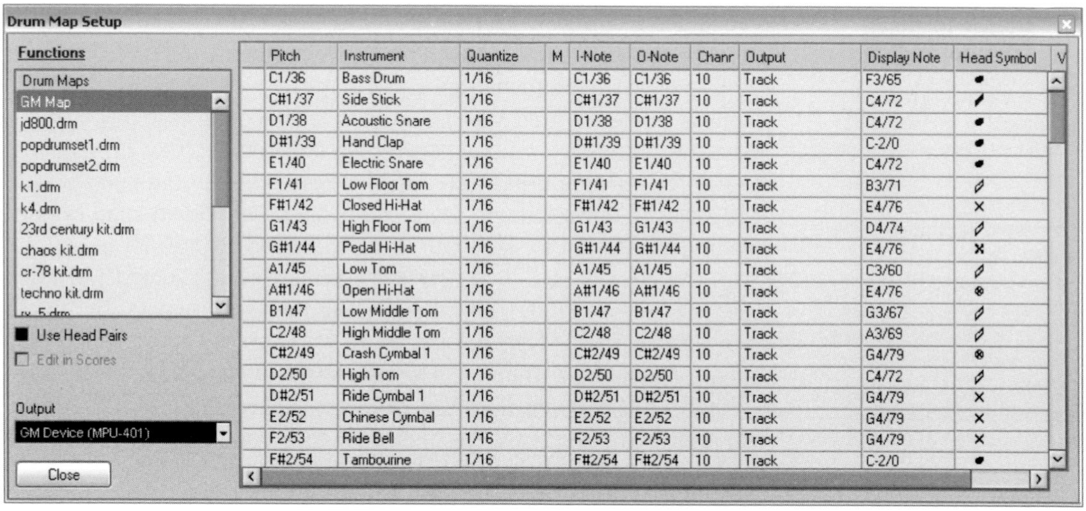

Even though changes can be made to the drum map while remaining in the Drum editor, the Drum Map Setup dialogue has everything you need for drum map editing purposes. You can create an empty new map or copy a new instance of an existing map using New Map and New Copy in the Functions menu. Still in the Functions menu, Save and Load allow you to save and load maps to/from disk and Remove allows you to delete the currently selected map from the list. Edit head pairs and Init Display Notes manage how drum parts are displayed in the Score editor.

Any value in the columns is edited by clicking on it and entering a new value with the computer keyboard or making a choice from a pop-up menu. Holding Ctrl (PC) / Command (Mac) while entering a value in the quantize, channel or output columns changes all instruments to the same value for that column.

In summary, the basic steps for setting up a drum map are as follows:

1   Create an empty new map or copy a new instance of an existing map using New Map or New Copy in the Functions menu. The new map appears in the list of drum maps.
2   Find the different instruments in the target drum kit by triggering the sounds via MIDI or by clicking in the selection column. Enter a suitable name for each instrument in the Instrument column.
3   Adjust the I-Note values to suit your playing style and key mapping preferences. Many musicians have become accustomed to the standard GM key positions (C1/36 for kick, D1/38 for snare and so on) but you can set up any configuration here.
4   Adjust the O-Note column values to match the target device(s). For elaborate drum programming your map may contain two or more target devices.
5   If required, adjust the MIDI channel and output port for each instrument.

Understanding the pitch, I-Note and O-Note columns

Using the Drum Map Setup window is generally straightforward but understanding the details of the pitch, I-Note and O-Note columns may require more effort. It makes things clearer to view the I-Note column as a map of where the sounds are being played on the keyboard and the O-Note column as a map of where the sounds are found in the target MIDI device. The pitch column is a series of fixed MIDI note values tagged on to each row, and it is always this pitch which actually gets recorded in Cubase. Now, imagine that you wish to set up a drum map which corresponds with the non-standard pitch values of the kick drum, snare and hi-hat sounds found in an external drum module (C0/24 for kick, D0/26 for snare and F#0/30 for hi-hat) but where you are still able to trigger these sounds from standard GM drum notes (C1/36 for kick, D1/38 for snare and F#/42 for hi-hat). This would mean adjusting the O-Note column values to match the non-standard note positions in the target drum module while keeping the I-note column values in standard GM positions (Figure 6.24.)

Imagine that you now wish to change the sound of the snare to one of the

Tip

To step through the drum sounds in a target device using the O-Note column, select the row which corresponds with the key you wish to use to trigger the sounds and double-click in the O-Note column. Use the up / down arrows on the computer keyboard to change the pitch in the O-Note column while triggering the sounds using your MIDI keyboard. Make sure the output port for the device is selected in the Output column.

Pitch	Instrument	Quantize	M	I-Note	O-Note	Chanr	Output
C1/36	Bass Drum	1/16		C1/36	C0/24	10	MPU-401
D1/38	Acoustic Snare	1/16		D1/38	D0/26	10	MPU-401
F#1/42	Closed Hi-Hat	1/16		F#1/42	F#0/30	10	MPU-401
A#1/46	Open Hi-Hat	1/16		A#1/46	A#0/34	10	Track

Figure 6.24
Adjusting the O-Note values to match the non-standard drum note positions of a target drum module

snares in the 'Snare Shop' preset of the HalionOne software sampler supplied with Cubase. Firstly, make sure that HalionOne is activated in the VST Instruments panel (opened from the devices menu or press F11 on the computer keyboard). Change the preset to 'Snare Shop'. To assign the snare

Pitch	Instrument	Quantize	M	I-Note	O-Note	Chanr	Output
C1/36	Bass Drum	1/16		C1/36	B0/35	10	1 - LM4-MarkII
D1/38	Acoustic Snare	1/16		D1/38	G#3/68	10	2 - HALionOne
F#1/42	Closed Hi-Hat	1/16		F#1/42	F#0/30	10	MPU-401
A#1/46	Open Hi-Hat	1/16		A#1/46	A#0/34	10	Track

Figure 6.25
Assigning the snare instrument to the HalionOne VST Instrument

instrument in the map to HalionOne, select HalionOne in the snare's output column. To locate your preferred snare sound adjust the O-Note value while triggering the sounds using your musical keyboard (Figure 6.25). Setting up multiple MIDI devices in this way might also mean that you need to change the MIDI channels in the channel column as well as the output ports for each of the sounds concerned.

To further clarify the function of the columns, the following is a brief summary of what happens to the MIDI data when you trigger your drum sounds via a drum map:

1 The incoming MIDI note finds its corresponding pitch in the I-Note column.
2 The note is instantaneously transposed to the value found in the pitch column on the same row (it is always this pitch value which gets recorded).
3 The outgoing MIDI note is instantaneously transposed to the value found in the O-Note column on the same row. The O-Note value is the final output note sent to the target MIDI device.

Drum editor basic techniques

The Drum editor features a drumstick tool which replaces the functions of the draw tool found in the other editors. The drumstick tool is used for inserting notes onto the grid. It differs from the draw tool in that it cannot be held and dragged on the grid to adjust the length of a note as it is being inserted. Instead the length is governed by the Insert Length setting on the toolbar. However, if you click and drag the drumstick horizontally along the grid, for one sound, a series of events is inserted at the resolution set by the quantize column for that sound (if global quantize is de-activated on the toolbar), or at the resolution set by the quantize value on the toolbar (if global quantize is activated on the toolbar). If the drumstick tool is clicked over an existing event, the event is deleted.

Tip

It is always the pitch column note which gets recorded in Cubase. Therefore, with a map containing O-Note data which does not match the pitch column data, the recorded notes only trigger the correct sounds when the correct drum map is active. There may be times when you no longer wish to use the drum map but wish to retain the recorded data suitably transposed to trigger the correct sounds (such as when you export your MIDI sequence as a Standard MIDI File). To achieve this, use O-Note Conversion in the MIDI menu.

The toolbar also features a 'solo instrument' button. This solos the currently selected instrument in the drum map. When the drum solo button is activated all instruments other than the one which is currently selected are muted in the mute column. This is excellent for soloing individual drum sounds for fine tuning in a mix.

Like the Key editor, the Drum editor features an Infoline, where existing events can be updated in terms of their position, length, pitch, velocity and channel. The Drum editor also has a controller display but it differs from the Key editor in that it shows the controller data for the currently selected instrument only. This is useful for creating velocity ramps for snare rolls, for example (see below).

Drum editor close ups

Inserting 1/16th note hi-hats

A common requirement for drum parts is the insertion of a hi-hat at regular 1/16th note intervals. To achieve this in the Drum editor, proceed as follows:
- Select an Insert Velocity and an Insert Length in the toolbar.
- Activate global quantize on the toolbar and set the quantize value to '1/16 note'. This governs the resolution of any inserted events. Alternatively, de-activate global quantize and set the quantize column value for the hi-hat instrument to '1/16 note'. When global quantize is de-activated the resolution for inserted events is governed by the values found in the quantize column.
- Select the drumstick tool and click and drag horizontally across the grid in the row corresponding to the closed hi-hat instrument. Drag for the desired number of bars. A series of events are inserted at the chosen resolution.

Figure 6.26
Inserting hi-hat events using the drumstick tool

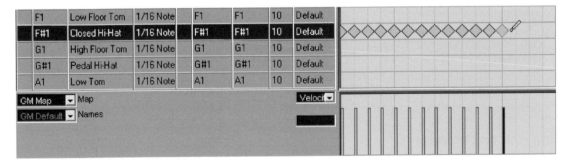

Creating crescendos for drum rolls and fills

The advantage of creating drum related crescendos in the Drum editor is that you can see the velocity data separately for each instrument in the Controller display. Proceed as follows:

- Select the instrument for which you wish to create a crescendo in the instrument list.
- Select velocity in the controller display.
- Select the line tool and click and drag a line at the appropriate angle

across the appropriate note velocities.
- When the mouse is released a velocity ramp matching the line appears.
- For a more exponential crescendo try using the parabola shape of the line tool.

Figure 6.27
Using the line tool to create a crescendo in the Drum editor's controller display

	A1	Low Tom	1/16 Note	A1	A1	10	Default
	C1	Bass Drum	1/16 Note	C1	C1	10	Default
	C#1	Side Stick	1/16 Note	C#1	C#1	10	Default
	D1	Acoustic Snare	1/16 Note	D1	D1	10	Default
	D#1	Hand Clap	1/16 Note	D#1	D#1	10	Default

GM Map ▼ Map
GM Default ▼ Names
Veloci ▼

Combining loop and solo

It is often helpful to replay a single drum sound repeatedly while you are adjusting its EQ and effects settings. This is particularly true of bass drum and snare sounds and could also apply to tom rolls when you are setting up pan positions. With the Drum editor this is a two stage process. Proceed as follows:

- In the Drum editor, select the events you want to hear soloed. This could be one event or the events from several bars. Click with the right mouse button (PC)/Ctrl + click (Mac) in the grid to open the Quick menu and select 'Loop selection' from the Transport section. Alternatively, select Shift + G (the default key command). Loop playback commences.

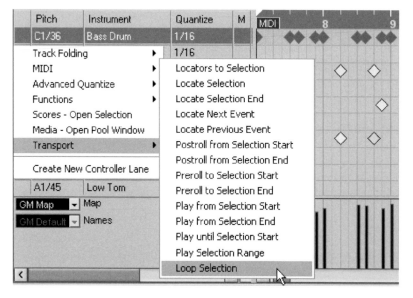

Figure 6.28
Select the events and activate 'Loop selection' from the Quick menu

Pitch	Instrument	Quantize	M
C1/36	Bass Drum	1/16	

1/16
Track Folding ▶
MIDI ▶
Advanced Quantize ▶
Functions ▶
Scores - Open Selection
Media - Open Pool Window
Transport ▶
Create New Controller Lane
A1/45   Low Tom

Locators to Selection
Locate Selection
Locate Selection End
Locate Next Event
Locate Previous Event
Postroll from Selection Start
Postroll from Selection End
Preroll to Selection Start
Preroll to Selection End
Play from Selection Start
Play from Selection End
Play until Selection Start
Play Selection Range
Loop Selection

GM Map ▼ Map
GM Default ▼ Names

Tip

As well as opening a single MIDI editor from the Project window, you can also open multiple editors on the screen and switch between them at will. Changes made in one editor are immediately reflected in the others. This is extremely useful for detailed work.

- Activate the solo editor and solo instrument buttons on the toolbar. Select the instrument you wish to hear.

Figure 6.29
Solo the instrument you wish to hear

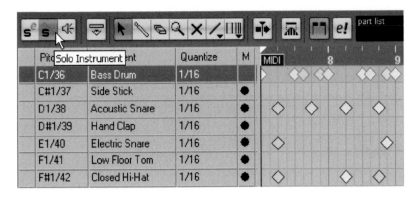

Smart moves

To help you remember the basic moves for using the MIDI editor tools, Table 6.1 summarises the main tool editing techniques. These are applicable to all the editors outlined in this chapter.

More about the MIDI menu

The MIDI menu contains a number of other important commands and a functions sub-menu. These complement the use of the main MIDI editors and help handle some of the common MIDI editing tasks with maximum speed and convenience.

Transpose

The transpose function opens a simple dialogue where you specify the amount by which you wish to transpose the currently selected part or notes. You can also specify an upper and lower barrier for the transposition which keeps the transposed notes within a chosen range of octaves. Transpose is good for making global transpositions of whole parts or a number of selected parts.

Merge MIDI in Loop

Merge MIDI in Loop merges all MIDI data between the left and right locators into a single new MIDI part on the currently selected track. If there is already a part on the destination track you can choose to merge this with the other data or erase it. Options are provided for including MIDI send and insert effects. Merge MIDI in Loop is the function to use when you wish to make your MIDI effects a permanent part of the data.

Freeze MIDI modifiers

Freeze MIDI modifiers makes all parameters in the MIDI Modifiers section of the Inspector a permanent part of the data.

Table 6.1 Smart moves for the MIDI editors

Tool	Keys held PC	Mac	Mouse action	Result
Object selection	-	-	click on event	selects event
	-	-	click on event and drag	moves event
	alt	alt	click on event and drag	copies event
	alt	alt	click and drag in grid	inputs note of length dragged
	-	-	drag the start/end point of note	re-sizes note
	-	-	click and drag in grid	opens rectangular selection box
	shift	shift	double click on note	selects all notes on same pitch
Draw	-	-	click on note end and drag	changes length of note
	-	-	click and drag in grid	inputs note of length dragged
	-	-	click and drag in controller display	inputs/changes values of events
Drumstick	-	-	click and drag horizontally in grid	inputs multiple notes at quantize resolution
Erase	-	-	click on event	deletes event
Mute	-	-	click on event	mutes event
Trim	-	-	click on note event	trims the start of the note
	alt	alt	click on note event	trims the end of the note
Zoom	-	-	click in grid	zooms in horizontally
	alt	alt	click in grid	zooms out horizontally
Line/parabola	-	-	click and drag in controller display	changes values in straight/curved lines
Paint	-	-	click and drag in grid	paints events freely on grid

Dissolve Part

Dissolve Part allows you to split the data in the chosen MIDI part(s) onto separate tracks according to either the channel or pitch of events. Channel is useful for splitting the multiple MIDI channel elements of a musical arrangement which have already been merged into a single part, such as a Type 0 Standard MIDI file. Pitch is excellent for splitting a drum or percussion part into its constituent instruments.

The MIDI functions

The MIDI functions are found in the Functions sub-menu of the MIDI menu. The MIDI functions are a convenient set of editing commands which may be used within the MIDI editors or directly on MIDI parts in the Project window. The functions include the following:

- Legato – increases the lengths of all selected notes to the start positions of the next note. Useful for pads and strings when you need smooth chord changes and a continuous sound.
- Fixed lengths – fixes the lengths of all selected notes to the same value as that chosen in the Quantize type selector of the toolbars (Project window or the editors).
- Delete doubles – deletes all doubled notes which occur on the same pitch and at exactly the same position. Always operates on whole MIDI parts. Delete doubles is useful for 'cleaning up' after you have been recording in cycle mode.
- Delete controllers – deletes all controller, aftertouch and pitch bend data from the currently selected part. Always operates on whole MIDI parts. Delete controllers is useful when you need to strip a MIDI part back down to its notes-only state.
- Delete notes – the Delete notes function is designed to find and delete low velocity and short ghost notes which were not intended as part of the performance. The Delete notes dialogue allows you to set thresholds for length and velocity, below which offending notes are deleted.
- Restrict polyphony – allows you to match the polyphony of your MIDI parts to the polyphony available in the target MIDI device. It functions by reducing the lengths of certain overlapping notes. This function may cause undesirable side effects and so should be used with care.
- Pedals to note length – finds all sustain pedal controller events (Controller 66) and changes the length of the notes concerned to match the on and off points of the pedal. After modifying the notes the sustain pedal events are deleted.
- Delete overlaps (mono) – adjusts the lengths of all overlapping notes which occur on the same pitch.
- Delete overlaps (poly) – adjusts the lengths of all overlapping notes in the part (regardless of pitch).
- Velocity – processes the velocity of the notes in a part according to a number of settings in a pop-up dialogue. You can add or subtract a fixed velocity, compress or expand the velocity according to a percentage, or restrict the velocity range between an upper and lower limit.
- Fixed velocity – sets all selected notes to the same velocity (as chosen in the Insert velocity field of the Key and Drum editors).
- Thin out data – reduces the density of recorded MIDI controller data. Helpful when large amounts of data are causing MIDI timing problems.
- Extract MIDI automation – converts all continuous controller data found in the MIDI part(s) into MIDI track automation data. After use, click near the lower left edge of the MIDI track to reveal the automation sub-tracks. To activate the automation, click on the automation read buttons (illuminated in green when active). Extract MIDI automation helps you get a clear overview of all your data in the Project window where it can be edited more conveniently.
- Reverse – reverses the playback order of the notes in the part.
- Merge tempo from tapping – uses the distance between the notes found in the selected MIDI part to calculate a tempo map. In the MIDI merge

options dialogue which appears when you use this function, you decide what timing resolution the notes in the part represent. This is most often used when you wish to create a tempo map which matches the tempo changes of an audio or MIDI performance which was created without a strictly regulated click track. To record the part which is to be used for the 'Merge tempo from tapping' function you simply 'tap' the MIDI note of your choice in time with the music (see chapter 18 for more details).

Quantize

What is quantize?

Quantize is a timing correction function applied either after a MIDI part has been recorded or at the same time as the recording is taking place (automatic quantize). It involves moving recorded events onto certain divisions of the bar according to a position-based grid. In Cubase, the resolution of these divisions is chosen in the quantize type menu on the toolbar. This imposes a grid of vertical lines across the event display which, when you activate the snap button on the toolbar, become 'magnetic' for the notes recorded nearby. Quantize was first devised as a purely corrective function but is now also used as a creative tool.

A simple corrective use of quantize might include moving all the hi-hats in a MIDI drum recording onto the nearest 1/16th note divisions of the bar. This is known as 'over quantize' or 'hard quantize'. A similar function involves moving events towards the nearest 1/16th note divisions according to a strength percentage. This is known as 'iterative quantize'. Over quantize and iterative quantize functions are found in the MIDI menu of Cubase.

Try using automatic quantize to hear an immediate example of how quantize affects the MIDI data. Activate the Auto Q button on the Transport panel and select 1/4 in the Quantize type menu in the Project window toolbar. Automatic quantize uses the over quantize function to automatically quantize your performance in real-time. Try recording a hi-hat part at 1/8 note intervals (for example). You will find it impossible to do so since all notes are forced onto the 1/4 note divisions of the bar. Set the Quantize type menu to 1/8 or switch off Auto Q and you can now record your part normally.

Quantize health risks

As you heard in the latter example, heavy use of the quantize functions is not always good for your musical health. It is not always desirable to have all the notes in all parts occurring on exact divisions of the beat. Too much quantize can result in music which is robotic and lifeless, so quantize should be used with care and attention to detail. Iterative quantize is often a better option than Over quantize since it retains some of the original feel of the musical performance. Of course, if your MIDI recording is performed extremely accurately it should not need any quantize at all.

Quantizing in the Project window

To quantize a MIDI part in the Project window, select it and choose a quantize value in the quantize type menu in the toolbar. Try 1/16 and select iterative quantize in the MIDI menu. Iterative Quantize tightens up parts that were loosely played but retains some of the feel of the original performance.

Where strictly metronomic timing is required try Over quantize instead. Quantize your part until it sounds musically correct. If desired, you can use Iterative quantize several times in succession. This progressively tightens up the part. You can undo any quantizing action using the main undo command in the Edit menu (Ctrl / Command+Z). This takes you back to the previous quantized state if you have implemented more than one quantizing action. You can go back to your original unquantized performance using MIDI / Advanced Quantize / Undo Quantize.

If you wish to make adjustments to the quantize effect, select 'Setup' from the Quantize type menu or select MIDI / Quantize Setup to open the Quantize Setup window. In Quantize Setup you can fine tune the quantize function with a range of control parameters. For example, this allows you to apply a swing factor to your performance or adjust the magnetic area within which the quantize function is sensitive. Clicking on the store button allows you to save your settings in the Quantize selector menu. Working directly out of the Quantize Setup window is a good way of becoming familiar with the quantize functions. Try ticking the Auto box to make quantize adjustments to a MIDI part 'on the fly'. For an obviously audible effect, try adjusting the swing slider to 100% with a grid setting of 1/8.

Quantizing in the MIDI Editors

In the MIDI editors, the quantize resolution is chosen in the quantize selector on the toolbar. This imposes a series of vertical lines across the display which you can actually see in the MIDI editors and, as already outlined, this is known as the grid. Try changing the quantize value in the toolbar and you will see the grid modified accordingly. Whenever you use a quantize function, the grid becomes 'magnetic' for the recorded notes in the part. Each note is pulled directly onto or towards the nearest vertical line. The MIDI editors provide excellent visual feedback of what is actually happening when you use the quantize functions. In Cubase, the quantize functions are available in two overall modes; grid quantize and groove quantize. Grid quantize mode is concerned with quantize templates based upon regular grid spacings between 1/128 and whole notes. Groove quantize mode is concerned with more complex quantizing templates which have been 'extracted' from audio and MIDI events. A groove, as the name suggests, is generally based upon the 'feel' of the music from which it is derived. But before we get into the details, let's start with the basics.

Basic quantize

Looking at the results of Over quantize and Iterative quantize graphically in the Key editor helps understand what the functions are doing to the data. Figure 6.30 shows the before-and-after case for the quantizing of an inaccurately played hi-hat to 1/16th note divisions of the bar, using Over quantize with quantize set to 1/16 on the toolbar. The first two beats of the bar are shown where each vertical line represents the 1/16th note divisions. The original part contains notes which occur at different points either side of the 1/16th note pulse. After quantization, all notes line up exactly to the grid.

Figure 6.31 shows what happens if we were to use Iterative quantize on the same hi-hat part. In this case, the corrected notes do not fall directly onto

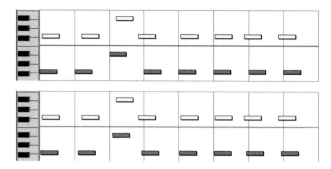

Figure 6.30
Using Over quantize to 'hard quantize' an inaccurately played hi-hat (upper grid) to exact 1/16th note divisions of the bar (lower grid)

Figure 6.31
Using Iterative quantize to quantize an inaccurately played hi-hat (upper grid) moves the notes towards the 1/16th note divisions of the bar (lower grid)

the 1/16th note divisions of the bar. Instead, they are moved slightly closer to the divisions, thus tightening things up while still retaining the original feel of the playing. This particular Iterative quantize function has a strength percentage of 50% which means that notes are moved towards the pulse by reducing the current distance from the 1/16th note grid lines by 50%. Unlike Over quantize, Iterative quantize can be used several times in succession, on each occasion moving the notes slightly closer to the chosen quantize resolution. Iterative quantize gives us a clue as to the nature of the more creative uses of the quantize functions.

Quantize Setup in detail

The Quantize Setup window allows you to adjust the quantize parameters and create/edit presets. It functions in 'grid quantize' or 'groove quantize' modes, depending upon how the quantize data is created.

Quantize Setup (Grid mode)

To open the Quantize Setup window in standard grid quantize mode (Figure 6.32), choose 1/16 from the Quantize type menu and select Quantize Setup in the MIDI menu. The Quantize Setup window in grid quantize mode includes the following parameters:

- Grid selector – a quantize selector menu containing a list of the possible note divisions of the bar between 1/128 and whole note values.
- Type selector – a quantize type menu with straight, triplet or dotted options.
- Swing slider – for adding a swing (shuffle) factor to the quantize function.
- Tuplet – for setting up complex quantizing functions based upon tuplet, triplet, quadruplet and more complex divisions of the bar.
- Magnetic area – determines a magnetic capture area within which notes are pulled onto or towards the grid. Notes outside the magnetic area are not affected by the quantizing action.
- Non-quantize – determines an area around each grid line within which notes will not be affected by the quantize function.

Info

Heavy use of Over quantize is not always good for your musical health. Iterative quantize is often a better option since it retains some of the feel of the original musical performance. When using Over quantize, try 'humanising' the effect by adding a few ticks in the Random Quantize setting of the Quantize Setup dialogue.

Figure 6.32
The Quantize Setup window in grid quantize mode

- Random quantize – adds a random number of ticks to the position of notes affected by the quantize function in order to humanise the correction effect (particularly useful for Over quantize).
- Iterative strength – regulates the strength of the Iterative quantize function in terms of a percentage. For example, a strength setting of 50% means that notes are moved towards the grid by reducing the note's current distance from the grid lines by 50%, each time the Iterative quantize function is used.
- Move controller – when Move controller is activated the quantize function also effects all pitch-bend, aftertouch, polyphonic pressure and continuous controller data found in the part.
- Auto – when auto is activated all changes made to the parameters are applied in real-time.
- Apply button – applies the edited quantize parameters.
- Presets section – allows the saving and loading of quantize presets and the removal of presets from the current list. These appear in the quantize type menu on the toolbar.

Adjusting any of the main parameters updates the Quantize Setup window's central display. This provides graphical feedback of the overall quantize template you have created and helps understand the function of each parameter as it is adjusted. The display shows one bar with blue lines indicating the positions of the quantize points.

Experimenting with grid quantize

Experimentation while listening to the results is one of the best ways of getting to know the quantize functions. For this purpose, it is recommended that you set up some key commands and work with the Quantize Setup window open on screen. Proceed as follows:

1 Open the Key commands window (File menu) and select MIDI in the categories list. Select the Iterative quantize command and assign the key combination 'Shift + Q'. Select the Undo quantize command and assign 'U'. Verify that Over quantize is assigned the 'Q' key (the default setting).
2 Select a MIDI part which contains notes which have not been recorded accurately (if necessary, create a special test part of badly played material)! Drum or rhythmic parts make good test material for the quantize functions.
3 While still in the Project window, open the Quick menu and select 'Loop selection'. You are now in cycle playback on the chosen MIDI part.
4 Open the Key or Drum editor and adjust the grid so that you can see the notes clearly on the screen.
5 Open the Quantize Setup window. You are now ready to start experimenting. Remember, it is important to be able to hear and see the results of your experiments.

The idea with this setup is to use the right hand with the mouse to manipulate the parameters in the Quantize Setup window and the left hand on the computer keyboard to initiate the quantize functions with the key commands. This two-handed approach is a valuable technique which can serve you well in all your quantizing operations.

Experiment 1

Check out the differences between Over quantize and Iterative quantize and learn how to use the key commands you created in step 1 above. Proceed as follows:

- In the Quantize Setup window, select 1/16 in the grid menu and 'straight' in the type menu.
- Press Q on the computer keyboard to apply Over quantize to the part. Press U to undo the quantizing. Listen carefully to the difference. The undo command restores the part to its original state before any quantizing was applied.
- Press Shift + Q (as set up in step 1, above) to apply Iterative quantizing to the part. Try applying this several times and note how inaccurately played notes gradually move closer to the grid lines. Adjust the iterative strength parameter in the Quantize Setup window to change the intensity of the iterative quantizing effect. Listen carefully to the results. Press U to undo the quantizing.
- Try experimenting with the grid and type menu settings in the Quantize Setup dialogue and check out the effect of adding swing using the Swing slider. Swing works well with rhythmic parts and you might like to try it on 1/16th note hi-hats.

Experiment 2

Check out the effect of the quantize settings in the Quantize Setup window in real-time as you adjust the parameters. Proceed as follows:

- Activate auto in the Quantize Setup window.
- Adjust the Random quantize parameter to 10 ticks.
- Move the magnetic area slider while listening to the part. Notice how the notes bob back and forth as you increase the magnetic area and also how they gradually move closer to their nearest grid lines. The small movements are due to the random quantize setting. Each time you move the magnetic area slider the part is quantized again (from its original unquantized state) using the new slider value and other values and, each time, applying a small random value to the quantized position. This technique applies the Over quantize function. Iterative quantize cannot be applied in this way.
- Experiment with the other parameters while listening to the results in real-time.

These experiments are designed to help you explore the quantize functions in grid mode and encourage an understanding of the more creative aspects of quantizing. If, while experimenting, you stumble upon a combination of settings which gives particularly pleasing results, be sure to save it using the Store button. You can always use it at a later stage in a more serious project.

Info

Swing occurs when every second note position on the quantize grid is pushed to the right. The more the notes are pushed, the more the music swings.

Info

You can undo / redo all MIDI editing using the undo / redo functions in the Edit menu or by pressing Ctrl+Z (undo) or Ctrl+Shift+Z (redo). You can also step back through your edits using the Edit history window (select History in the Edit menu). The edit history is cleared when you close the project.

Quantize setup (Groove mode)

What is groove quantize?

Groove quantize involves adjusting the timing and accent characteristics of musical material according to the natural groove or feel of a recorded musical performance (extracted from audio or MIDI recordings). While standard grid quantize processes material based upon regular note values (between 1/128 to whole notes), groove quantize processes material in a more irregular way. This irregularity usually involves a succession of events whose timings fall at slightly different points around the beat. This is comparable to the kind of timing nuances found in a real-world musical performance. Cubase allows us to extract such timing nuances from existing audio recordings or from MIDI parts and store the information as a groove template. Quantization using groove quantize thus allows the feel of one passage of music to be imposed upon another. You can also create a groove from scratch by adding or editing notes in a MIDI part and extracting the groove afterwards.

A groove can be quite simple, as in the case of a one bar 1/16th note shuffle groove or it can be a highly complex succession of timing events which vary over a number of bars. Groove quantize can be applied to whole arrangements or to selected elements, and different elements can be treated with different grooves.

Extracting a groove

There are two methods of creating your own groove quantize template, as follows:

1 To extract a groove from a MIDI part proceed as follows:

- Select a MIDI part in the event display. (No more than 16 bars. One, two or four bar patterns work well).
- Select 'Part to groove' in MIDI / Advanced Quantize.
- Open the Quantize type menu to reveal the newly added groove which appears last in the list with the same name as the part from which it was extracted.

2 To extract a groove from an audio event proceed as follows:

- Double-click on the audio event to open the Sample editor. Activate the Inspector and select the Definition section.
- If you are using a range selection, select the Range tool and select the appropriate range within the audio which corresponds with a precise number of bars and beats. Otherwise ignore this step.
- In the Definition section, select the desired resolution in the Grid menu (try 1/4, 1/8 or 1/16 note). Activate the Auto adjust button to calculate the tempo of the audio. The grid lines should line up with the main peaks in the waveform. Press the reset button and try again if you need to re-calculate.
- Open the Hitpoints section of the Inspector and drag the Sensitivity slider to the right until one hitpoint appears for each hit in the rhythm. Try selecting 1/4, 1/8 or 1/16 note in the Use menu. Audition the

audio between each consecutive pair of hitpoints to verify the results.
- In the Hitpoints section, click on the Make groove button to create the groove template.
- Open the Quantize type menu to reveal the newly added groove which appears last in the list with the same name as the audio event from which it was extracted.

Get into the groove

To explore the groove quantize functions of Cubase, open the Quantize Setup window (MIDI / Quantize setup) and switch to groove mode by choosing an existing groove quantize preset (Figure 6.33). If you cannot find an existing groove, create your own using one of the methods described above.

The Quantize Setup window in groove quantize mode includes the following parameters:

- Position, velocity and length sliders – these determine how much the position, velocity or length of the events in the groove template affect the target material (where 0% is no effect and 100% is maximum effect).
- Pre-quantize – allows the regular quantizing of material before it is groove quantized. This is helpful if Groove quantize produces undesirable results due to irregularities in the target part.
- Max. move in ticks – determines the maximum amount by which notes in the target are moved. Helpful for restricting the quantizing action within defined limits.
- Name and details field – gives the name of the original event / part from which the groove was extracted and details of the original tempo, time signature and event / part length. Knowing the original details can help judge whether the groove is likely to suit the target material.
- Presets menu – allows the storage and recall of quantize presets. These appear in the quantize type menu on the toolbar.
- Store and remove buttons – allows the storage of the current settings as a new preset or the deletion of the currently chosen preset. Removal involves a permanent deletion of the information and should therefore be used with care.
- Non-quantize – determines an area around each event in the groove within which notes in the target part are not affected by the quantizing action.
- Random quantize – adds a random number of ticks to the position of notes affected by the quantize function in order to vary the correction effect.
- Iterative strength – regulates the strength of the Iterative quantize function in terms of a percentage. For example, a strength setting of

Figure 6.33
The Quantize Setup window in groove quantize mode

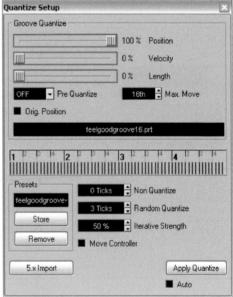

50% means that notes in the target part are moved towards the groove by reducing the note's current distance from the groove template events by 50%, each time the Iterative quantize function is used.

- Auto – when auto is activated all changes made to the parameters are applied in real-time.
- Apply quantize button – applies the quantize parameters using the Over quantize function.

Adjusting any of the main parameters updates the central graphical display of the Quantize Setup window. This provides visual feedback for the quantize template you are creating and helps understand the function of each parameter as it is adjusted. The display shows the number of bars in the groove and contains blue lines indicating the positions of the events in the groove template.

Advanced quantizing techniques

The quantizing tools of Cubase may be used purely for corrective purposes but, when used in a more creative manner, provide a powerful tool for injecting new life into your MIDI and audio recordings. The following outlines a number of advanced techniques and ideas for enhancing and experimenting with the feel of your tracks (relevant to both grid and groove modes).

Groove quantize can be used to match the timing characteristics of a MIDI part to an audio event by extracting the groove from the audio and applying the resulting groove template to the MIDI material. This is useful for making MIDI parts fit precisely alongside an existing audio arrangement. Much of the time, however, you might create a groove from an existing MIDI or audio event simply because you like the feel of the music. It is also possible to manufacture your own grooves by editing and manipulating the data in a MIDI part in the Key editor. You can then quickly create a groove template from this 'manufactured' MIDI part using 'Part to groove' (MIDI menu / Advanced). The latter technique is particularly relevant in the light of the various tips supplied below. These help understand what is going on 'inside' the groove. Quantize may be applied to both MIDI and audio material, as long as the target audio has been divided up into separate rhythmic components using Cubase's audio slicing functions.

Pushing a bass drum ahead of the beat produces a sense of urgency and delaying a snare to fall after the beat produces a lazy, laid back feel. Conversely, a late bass drum produces a relaxed effect and an early snare makes things sound tight and anticipated. Groove templates are best applied individually to separate bass drum and snare tracks to achieve the latter late / early effects. Experiment with your collection of grooves to hear which combinations work well together. Manipulation of the position of the snare in relation to the second and fourth beats can have a major effect on the groove of the whole song and making sure that the hi-hat part is not playing repetitions of exactly the same part throughout helps maintain the interest of the listener. To avoid exact repetitions of the same hi-hat part, use the Random quantize field in the Quantize Setup menu to introduce a slight variation in the quantizing action (try between 3 and 5 ticks). The hi-hat itself plays a major role in the character of the groove, especially when manipulating shuffle and swing feels. Shuffles are concerned with delaying every other note in a succession of regularly spaced note events. In Cubase the amount of swing can be controlled in fine detail using the swing slider in the Quantize Setup window (Grid mode). In a similar manner to the kick and snare, moving the hi-hat ahead of the beat produces a sense of urgency and moving it late produces a looser feel. You might also be concerned with rhythmic punctuations in the arrangement such as cymbal crashes and drum rolls. Moving crashes to occur ahead of the beat can produce excitement and moving them to be late produces a sense of expectation. Some styles of music rely on specific grooves with specific relationships between the kick, snare and hi-hat. For example, many shuffle grooves rely on a bass drum and snare which are quantized tightly to the beat while the hi-hat alone is quantized to the shuffle groove. Quantize is often best applied to specific parts of the arrangement rather than to the whole kit or rhythm section. For this reason, detailed quantizing works better when the constituent parts of the rhythm section are on separate tracks (particularly the kick, snare and hi-hat).

In real-world performances, the relative timing positions of the constituent parts of a drum rhythm are often in a constant state of change but the overall characteristics of the changes remain similar. In other words, the kick might always be played ahead of the beat, the snare might fluctuate on and around the beat and the hi-hat might always be behind the beat. It is also the case that the bass drum and snare are rarely played at precisely the same moment in each bar and all the instruments are in a constant state of subtle change in terms of accent. Approximating similar behaviour with both grid and groove quantize helps humanise and enliven the material. Try experimenting with the position, velocity and length sliders (groove mode) or the swing and magnetic sliders (grid mode) along with the random field in the Quantize Setup window to simulate similar behaviour in your MIDI parts. When applied to sliced audio events, similar slider manipulations can help you to mangle drum loops beyond recognition or to find a new, original feel for the rhythm. Once processing like this has been applied successfully, an A-B comparison usually reveals just how dull the original parts were sounding.

The use of quantize does not exist in isolation from other techniques such as tempo, accent and musical arrangement.

Tip

Generally, there is no one element which is responsible for the groove. Each instrument might emphasise different beats in the bar and the groove of each element might vary. You could have late bass drums on the first and third beats of the bar combined with early snares on the second and fourth. This makes things sound tight and tense.

Tip

For variations in the results, try experimenting with the position, velocity and length sliders and the random field in the Quantize Setup window.

Tip

Maintaining lots of space in the arrangement both in a musical and in a mix sense helps give all the instruments space to breathe. This allows the groove to shine through.

Audio recording

Chapter 3 outlined the basic audio recording process. This chapter provides more detailed information about audio recording, routing and the general handling of audio data. Although the main concern is audio recording within Cubase, it is also considered useful to include information about digital audio and recording techniques in general. Cubase does not exist in isolation from the rest of the sound recording world and it is essential to keep this in mind when using the software to record audio.

Digital audio

What is digital audio?
Audio recording in Cubase is of the digital variety. This means that the sounds you record are converted into a numerical representation of the signal using an analogue-to-digital (A/D) converter. These numbers are stored in a data retrieval system (normally your hard disk), and the sounds are reproduced by converting the numbers back into the analogue domain using a digital-to-analogue (D/A) converter. These converters are found on your audio hardware.

The quality of the audio is dependent on the general performance of the converters, the sample rate and the bit resolution. The sample rate is the number of times the analogue signal is measured (sampled) per second. The bit resolution, (also referred to as bit depth), is a measure of the accuracy of the system. The greater the number of bits the more levels of resolution are available to measure the audio signal. Popular bit resolutions include 8, 16, 20, 24 and 32-bit float. Regular audio CDs are 16-bit with a sample rate of 44.1 kHz.

Cubase normally operates in 16, 24 or 32-bit float resolutions with a sample rate choice of 11.25 to 96kHz. Theoretically, you can achieve very high quality recordings with the system. However, there are many other factors which affect the sound quality and paramount among these is how you actually make your recordings.

Some differences between analogue and digital recording
If you were recording on an analogue system your approach to sound recording might be slightly different to when using a digital system like Cubase. For example, when recording to a traditional analogue tape machine some sound

Info

The fundamental settings for a Cubase Project are made in the Project Setup window (see Chapter 3). Open Project Setup from the Project menu or use Shift + S. Most of the settings could be changed half-way through a project but the sample rate should be set once only before commencing. Most users operate at 24-bit resolution with a 44.1kHz sample rate. The emerging new professional standard (at the time of writing) is 24-bit/96KHz.

engineers may intentionally record with the VU meters slightly overloading on the highest peaks in the signal. Although, strictly speaking, the sound is distorting, the kind of harmonic distortion produced is not displeasing to the ear. In fact, pushing the levels in this way results in a natural compression effect and, some would say, adds a certain warmth to the sound. The VU meters tell us more about the average response of the signal rather than the peaks, and the 0VU point is more of a guide than an absolute maximum recording level.

The latter is not the case with digital audio. Digital audio systems use full-scale (FS) meters which fix the absolute maximum level you can record at 0dBFS, right at the top of the scale. There is no intended additional headroom above this maximum point. Signals exceeding 0dBFS simply produce unpleasant distortion. For this reason, when you record with Cubase you should ensure that no clipping occurs on the input bus.

The net result is that recording digitally sometimes results in recordings with a lower average level and less 'character' than may have been the case if you were recording the same sources onto analogue tape. The digital version may need more headroom to avoid distortion on the peaks in the signal whereas the analogue recording benefits from pushed levels and natural tape compression. Recording digitally at lower levels is sometimes problematic with 16-bit systems where there is limited dynamic range to capture the low level detail. The theoretical dynamic range of 16-bit is 96dB. However, capturing low-level detail is not an issue at higher bit depths like 24-bit and 32-bit float since these feature greatly improved dynamic range due to less quantising errors. The theoretical dynamic range of 24-bit is 144dB, which adds 48dB more at the lower end of the scale when compared to 16-bit. For this reason, you can safely record well below 0dBFS when using 24-bit, simultaneously obtaining greater headroom for signal peaks and better gain structure. For tracking purposes, levels might be set to produce between -10dBFS and -6dBFS on peaks with the average signal level hovering around -18dBFS.

Overall, the advantages of digital audio far outweigh the disadvantages. It suffers less from background noise and hiss, it has a better dynamic range than analogue, it can be conveniently stored on hard disk or other digital media, it can be easily processed in the digital domain using digital signal processing techniques, and exact copies of the original can be made with no loss of quality.

What bit resolution and sample rate should I use?

The short answer

The short answer is to use the highest bit resolution and sample rate your system can manage. For standard audio applications, 24-bit/44.1kHz is a good choice for most users. For greater fidelity assurance use 32-bit float/44.1kHz or 24-bit/96kHz.

The long answer

Although the short answer given above is adequate for the needs of many Cubase users, in reality the issues are slightly more complicated. Bit resolution (also known as bit depth) describes the range of values (quantising steps) available to measure the signal. There are 16,777,216 values for 24-bit and 65,536 values for 16-bit. Sample rate describes how many measurements of the signal are made per second. For example, 44.1kHz measures the signal 44,100 times per second.

The first thing to consider is the bit resolution and sample rate of the final media for which the recording is intended and then preferably work at a greater resolution within Cubase. If you are aiming to produce a standard audio CD then the final resolution is 16-bit/44.1kHz. However, the whole recording process benefits if you do all the initial work at a higher resolution, such as 24bit/44.1kHz or even 32-bit float/44.1kHz. You only apply dithering and truncate to 16-bit at the very last stage. This results in a significant improvement in the fidelity of the final audio signal. A final 16-bit audio signal produced in this way might have an apparent bit resolution of 18 or 19 bits which equates to a 12 to 18dB increase in dynamic range. Greater audible improvements are made by increasing the bit resolution rather than the sample rate, so it is best to concentrate on this first. The maximum possible resolution depends upon the resources of your host computer. Not all systems are capable of recording at high bit resolutions and sample rates. The whole idea with digital recording is to start with high resolution sources and maintain this high resolution for as long as possible until the final mastering stage, when dithering and truncation to 16-bit is usually applied.

The above advice suggests that if the sample rate of the destination media, such as a CD, is 44.1kHz then we should start out recording at 44.1kHz and maintain this sample rate throughout the whole process. This works as a rule of thumb. The objective here is to avoid the possibly detrimental effect of sample rate conversion. Working at a higher sample rate, such as 96kHz, and then converting to 44.1kHz at a later stage may result in more damage to the audio signal than if you had started out with 44.1kHz in the first place. This is especially true if you use sub-standard sample rate conversion. If you must use sample rate conversion, you are advised to use a high quality conversion plug-in such as Steinberg Wavelab's Crystal Resampler or similar to ensure optimum quality. Otherwise, play safe and set your Cubase project to the same sample rate as the final destination media (as suggested above).

It is also worth considering that you may in the future wish to release your music on one of the higher resolution audio formats such as DVD-A (Digital Versatile Disc – Audio) or SACD (Super Audio Compact Disc). DVD-A boasts a maximum resolution of 24-bit/96kHz and SACD uses an alternative high quality digital audio format known as DSD (Direct Stream Digital) which gives an equivalent performance. Working at 96kHz uses more computer resources but is likely to produce recordings with subtly improved transparency and detail. There is much debate on whether we can actually perceive the difference between 44.1 and 96kHz sample rates. 44.1 digital audio successfully produces signals up to 20kHz (the upper limit of human hearing) so, theoretically, we cannot improve matters any further by using a 96kHz sample rate, which raises the upper limit to around 48kHz (we cannot hear in this region). However, the upper threshold is not the factor which directly compromises the signal. It is rather the steep reconstruction filters in the 44.1 D/A conversion process which can be problematic. In any case, most professional mastering engineers claim they can hear the difference between 96 and 44.1kHz but most also admit that any improvement is subtle. Regardless of the debate, if your material is destined to be mastered in a professional mastering house they may well request the source files in 24-bit/96kHz format.

Info

24-bit vs 16-bit - in an ideal system, the maximum dynamic range is 144dB for 24-bit vs 96dB for 16-bit. 24-bit resolution results in less distortion during the quantisation process since there are more measurement values and thus smaller quantising steps (16,777,216 discrete steps for 24-bit vs 65,536 steps for 16-bit). However, an increase in bit depth does NOT result in an increase in level. 0dBFS remains at the same absolute level in both systems. The 48dB extra dynamic range for 24-bit is added at the lower end of the scale (the noise floor is lower due to smaller quantising errors in the digital conversion process). This means that you can leave more headroom when recording at 24-bit without fear of losing the low level detail in the signal.

Info

Avoid confusion between bit depth and sample rate. Bit depth is resolution-based and governs dynamic range. This determines the number of values available to measure the signal (quantising steps). The greater the bit depth the more measurement values available and the lower the noise floor (due to less quantising errors). Sample rate is frequency-based and governs the maximum frequency bandwidth of the system. This is the rate at which measurements of the signal are made. The faster the rate the higher the frequency which can be accurately reproduced. In Cubase, the bit depth and sample rate are set in the Project Setup window (Record Format and Sample Rate fields).

Buffer and storage considerations

Knowing the details of how digital audio is handled and stored inside your computer may help you get better results when recording and streamlining your system. Firstly, the source analogue signal is converted into digital information using the audio hardware's A/D converter. Once converted, the information is stored in a buffer (a temporary storage area). When the buffer is full, the system collects the data and stores it on your hard disk. This process happens repeatedly and very quickly. The actual speed depends upon the size of the buffer, the CPU power of the computer and the efficiency of the hard drive. The speed also contributes to the latency of the system (see below). You might like to try setting a smaller buffer size in your audio hardware driver software when you are recording. This suits recording since a smaller buffer size means less latency, and less latency means that you can monitor in real-time via Cubase with greater accuracy. However, a smaller buffer size also means that the drain on your CPU power is much greater and, in extreme cases, may cause other operational elements in the computer to slow down or fail. Therefore, when you are not recording (for example, when you are mixing), it may help to increase your buffer size slightly. This reduces your CPU overhead and allows you to use more plug-ins.

As for storage, most high performance hard drives can adequately handle the recording of digital audio. The audio files themselves are stored in the folder for the project as chosen when you first created it (by default, within a sub-directory named Audio). If you wish to verify the location of the project folder on the hard disk, open the Pool (Ctrl/Command + P) where the project folder is shown in the information line at the top of the window. For keeping track of how much space you have available, Cubase features a handy info line directly below the track list which shows the chosen sample rate and record format, and the remaining recording time in hours and minutes (Figure 7.1).

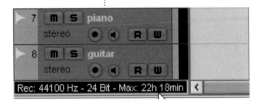

Figure 7.1
Keep track of the available recording time on your hard disk using the info line below the track list

Latency

Latency is the delay between the input and output of a digital audio system (expressed in samples or milliseconds). All digital audio systems take a small amount of time to respond to a user input and process the data through their hardware and software. This affects real-time performance. It not only imposes a slight delay between the audio input and output signals, it also affects the delay between the moment you move a channel fader on the screen and the moment you hear the audible result, and it imposes a slight delay between the moment you press a note on your MIDI keyboard and the moment you hear the sound from a VST Instrument. If the delay is too long then it becomes difficult to play accurately in real-time performance. So where does the latency come from? Latency is actually imposed by a combination of factors in the signal chain. Paramount among these are the audio buffers of the audio hardware. The audio buffer size can usually be adjusted and is often quoted in a control panel utility supplied with your audio hardware. Typical figures include 64, 128, 256 and 512 samples. These sample values can be converted to delay times in milliseconds by dividing the quoted figure by the sample rate you are using.

For example, at a sample rate of 44.1kHz:

$$64/44.1 = 1.45\text{ms}$$
$$128/44.1 = 2.9\text{ms}$$
$$256/44.1 = 5.8\text{ms}$$

and so on. Typically, you may also expect to add another 0.5ms to this figure for each of the A/D and D/A converters, and other elements in the signal chain may also add a small amount of delay. Thus, for a quoted buffer size of 128 samples you could expect a real-world latency of around 3.5 – 4ms each, for both the recording and playback parts of the signal chain. This equates to a total latency of around 7 – 8ms when monitoring in real-time via Cubase. (This latency only affects the monitoring of a real-time performance. Any tracks which are already recorded are not subject to the same latency issues).

It is a fact that real-world machines and electronic musical instruments also suffer from similar delays, and a delay of a few milliseconds is imposed each time you move further away from your monitoring loudspeakers (around

3ms per metre). Musicians naturally compensate for the delays they hear while playing in real-time, as long as the delay remains minimal and fairly constant. However, virtuoso performers, drummers and percussionists can pick up on even the slightest irregularities when monitoring during a live performance so the effect of latency must be minimised. To provide optimum real-time performance, professional audio hardware with a dedicated ASIO driver which can achieve overall latency times of less than 10ms is highly recommended.

Audio recording techniques

Recording vocals and acoustic instruments – microphone recording techniques

The first stage in making a recording of a vocalist or live instrumentalist is deciding where they are going to perform. The acoustic environment for the performance plays a major part in giving the recorded sound its particular characteristics. In a professional recording studio this environment is often an acoustically treated performance area which is isolated from the control room and the outside world. If you are lucky enough to have a similar facility as part of your Cubase system then so much the better.

The second stage is deciding which microphone to use and where to place it in relation to the vocalist or instrumentalist. The microphone is the very first stage in the recording path when you are recording live vocals, musical instruments and other real-world sources so, if you are serious about your recording, it is worth investing in a well-specified model. For good all-round performance and for the recording of vocals, large-diaphragm capacitor (condenser) microphones are a good choice. For acoustic instruments and drum kits the choice of microphone type widens enormously from small diaphragm pencil capacitor microphones to dynamic or ribbon models. Inexperienced sound recordists may have the impression that you can place any kind of microphone anywhere in front of the source and then start recording. Unfortunately, it is not quite as simple as this, since there are a multitude of different microphone models with different pickup patterns designed for different purposes and, even if you have chosen an appropriate model, a change of even a few centimetres in microphone position can affect the sound quality. It is wise, therefore, to experiment with the microphone position and, if you have several models, the microphone type. Dont be afraid to take a little time to get the sound right at the time of the actual recording. Occasionally, this might also involve applying EQ or compression. If you are recording vocals, a pop shield reduces the explosives, (the 'p' and 'b' sounds which cause pops and low frequency rumbles), and can simultaneously help set the ideal distance the vocalist should be from the microphone.

A third consideration is the use of a microphone pre-amp before the signal reaches your mixing console or Cubase, and this is certainly highly recommended. In general, you should try to limit the number of devices through which the signal has to pass before it arrives within Cubase so, when using a mic pre-amp, you would normally pass the signal directly from there into Cubase. The best mic pre-amps feature a superior signal path to many consoles and often provide high-quality compression and EQ controls.

Recording live sounds via microphones is generally more difficult than recording line level signals like synthesizers and samplers. This is because the sound signal is in a constant state of change and is likely to feature unpredictable peaks and lows in the amplitude. The level of difficulty is increased when you are using more than one microphone simultaneously, as in the case of recording a drum kit.

A high-quality microphone can radically improve the fidelity of the input signal. Models supplied by AKG, Audio Technica, Beyer, Blue, Brauner, Calrec, Coles, Electrovoice, DPA, Microtech Gefell, Neumann, Oktava, Rode, Royer, SE, Sennheiser, Shure and Sony are highly recommended.

Recording electric guitars, electric basses, synthesizers and samplers

The recording of electric guitars and basses presents a whole new set of potential problems to the sound recordist. Both instruments can be recorded using DI (Direct Injection) or microphone techniques or both simultaneously. You can also use a guitar or bass pre-amp which produces a convenient line level signal as output. This can be routed to the line inputs of your external mixer or directly into your audio hardware.

When placing microphones around a guitar speaker cabinet it is common practice to use two microphones, one placed close to the speaker and the other further back to pick up more of the room sound. A bass guitar cabinet is more likely to be recorded using a single microphone designed for lower frequencies and this signal is often mixed with a DI line signal from the bass amplifier or a DI box.

One of the problems when recording electric guitar and bass is that of noise interference. This manifests itself as a background buzz or hum which varies according to the relative positions of the guitar, amplifier and speakers. This is due to electromagnetic interference between the pickups of the guitar and the amplifier and speakers (or any other electronic equipment near to the guitar). Single-coil pickups are more prone to interference than humbucking pickups. Popular solutions include minimising the interference by experimenting with the relative positions of the guitar, amplifier and speakers and using gate and noise filtering processors after the recording has been made. CRT type computer monitors also cause significant hum when used near electric guitar instruments. The preferred solution for minimising this effect in a Cubase system, is to use an LCD/TFT flat-screen monitor. Otherwise, play your guitar at some distance from the computer equipment or, if you have the facilities, use a separate room for the guitar performance. Once again, the sound signal from these instruments is often unpredictable as there can be significant changes in level from one note (or chord) to the next due to the instrument's resonant behaviour and changes in the player's technique and playing intensity.

Synthesizers and samplers are easier to record since they are generally more predictable and, if they are controlled via the MIDI sequencer of Cubase, you can re-play the parts many times over until you are satisfied that you have set the optimum record level. They also have the convenience of line outputs which are easy to handle when routed into your external mixer or directly into your audio hardware. However, synthesizer and sampler

Info

For more recording tips, see 'Ten golden rules for recording and mixing' in Chapter 12.

sounds can often seem lifeless and lacking in character when compared to real acoustic instruments so care needs to be taken in how you record them. The use of effects and processing is a popular method of livening things up and some sound recordists will go as far as adding noise and distortion to the signal in order to give it more character. Subtle use of Cubase's supplied AmpSimulator or SoftClipper, Voxengo's TapeBus or PSP's Vintage Warmer produce good results for this kind of processing. Effects added in this way are often intended to be an integral part of the recorded sound. If you are not sure of what the final sound should be, it is better to add the effect at the mixing stage.

The magic formula for making great sounding recordings?

Sorry! There is no magic formula for making great sounding recordings, there are only guide lines. Despite enormous technological advances in all areas of the audio and recording industries and the availability of digital audio recording tools like Cubase, it remains impossible to devise a fixed set of rules which ensure a high-quality recording. One of the problems is that each individual has a different idea of what actually sounds good. Another is that recording equipment (such as microphones and loudspeakers) and sound itself behave differently according to the acoustic environment and temperature. And, of course, when recording a live musician, no two musical performances are ever exactly the same.

So, what are the guide lines? We've already touched upon some of them in this chapter and in Chapter 2 but one of the major requirements is to learn how to use your ears. These are actually the only tools you have to judge whether or not you are making what is, in your opinion, a great sounding recording. Once you've got your ears up and running, your task is to get the best possible sounding signal recorded into Cubase. This starts at source and may encompass a wider range of elements than just the sound itself. For example, is the vocalist singing in tune? Is the guitar in tune with the synthesizer you recorded on a previous session? Is everybody playing in time? Have you minimised any noise interference at source? Have you selected the best acoustic environment in which to make your microphone recording? Is the microphone placed in the optimum position relative to the source and the acoustic space? Once you have answered these and other questions relevant to preparing your session, you can then start to judge if you are achieving the sound quality you require in Cubase. It is important to capture a good performance and to get the right sound at the time of the recording; never expect to be able to fix it in the mix. Try to get the optimum signal level recorded whilst also avoiding distortion. When recording at 24-bit resolution, signal peaks at -6dBFS with an average level around -18dBFS is a good guide line. Unpredictable sound sources, like vocals, might benefit from compression. Take your time getting things right in the early stages of the recording process and never hesitate to experiment with microphone placement before resorting to EQ.

EQ might be used for creative effects but, at the recording stage, is best used in a corrective sense to filter out any low frequency rumbles, high frequency hiss or other interference which does not form part of the required

Tip

You cannot make judgements about sound without an accurate monitoring system in an acoustically balanced environment. One of the keys to making good recordings is accurate monitoring.

Tip

Using Cubase in cycle record mode might help you capture that once-only magical performance (see Audio recording in cycle mode below).

signal or to flatten out the frequency response of instruments recorded using close-miking techniques. For low frequency rumbles, many microphones incorporate low frequency roll-off filter switches and these might provide a better option than using EQ. When using a high or low pass filter to attenuate the low or high frequencies outside the spectral range of the required sound, great care must be taken to ensure that you do not shave off parts of the actual signal. You can sometimes safely reduce the top end (above around 10kHz) of such instruments as bass drums, bass guitars, bass synths, electric pianos and electric guitars. Similarly, you can sometimes safely roll off the low end (below 60Hz) of such instruments as vocals, violins, hi-hats and cymbals.

When using close-miking techniques, particularly on live drums, the lower frequencies are disproportionately boosted due to a phenomenon with cardioid or figure-of-eight pattern microphones known as the proximity effect. The proximity effect can be actively used to create a more intimate feel but, where it is not desired, a high-pass filter and / or low frequency shelving EQ (in the region below around 200Hz) might be used to adjust the spectrum for a more open sound. Another problem is over-emphasised harmonics in bass guitar, electric guitar, organ, drum and percussion performances due to resonances in the instrument itself or in the performance space. In this case, narrow band parametric EQ tuned to attenuate the unwanted harmonics often provides a solution.

The use of EQ in these contexts could be that found on your external console, pre-amp or on the input bus of the Mixer in Cubase. Bear in mind that the EQ sections of budget equipment often create more problems in the sound than they solve. Many experienced sound engineers prefer to use a minimum of EQ at the time of recording and there are some very good reasons for this. As soon as you switch in an EQ section you are routing the signal through another set of control circuits which can potentially degrade the signal. Degradation might be particularly apparent if you are using the EQ section of a budget mixing console. EQ also affects the phase of the frequency components within the signal and this can result in undesirable side effects and harshness. The guide line here is to get the sound as right as possible before it even enters your external console or mic pre-amp and, certainly, before it enters Cubase. EQ at the recording stage might be viewed as a last resort, when there is no other solution, but there are no hard and fast rules.

Last but not least, in all of the above recording techniques, monitor your sounds through high quality loudspeakers in an acoustically balanced room and avoid excessive monitoring levels.

This provides you with a very brief taste of what is involved in the wider recording process outside of the direct domain of Cubase. As you have probably realised, specific sound engineering skills are required if you intend to do a lot of audio recording using microphones. Microphone choice and placement is a big subject and it is beyond the scope of this book to cover it in detail.

Important

If you you are in doubt about any of these techniques, leave any corrective EQing to the mixing stage

Info

Readers who intend to use Cubase for vocal and live instrument recording and have no prior knowledge of sound recording are advised to seek more detailed information from specialist texts on the subject.

Audio routing in Cubase

A key element for understanding the operation of a traditional recording studio is a detailed knowledge of all the inputs and outputs of the mixing console and how all the other equipment is connected to it. In other words, you need to know where the audio signals are going to and where they are coming from, otherwise known as routing. Things are similar with Cubase. A clear understanding of how the signal travels from the source into your audio hardware, through Cubase, and finally back out again helps you grasp the details of the audio recording process. This seems like common sense but it is surprisingly easy to get confused when there are a large number of inputs and outputs in an audio system.

The input path

Figure 7.2 shows an example of the input path using a system with multiple input audio hardware. The signal is traced from its arrival at two of the physical inputs through to its destination as a stereo recording on one of Cubase's audio tracks. Looking at the signal path graphically allows you to stand back and think about what is actually taking place.

In this example, a stereo signal is connected to the line inputs of the audio hardware. It is first converted into digital form via the hardware's A/D converters. It then passes through the software audio mixer associated with the audio hardware. This is where settings which govern the operation of your audio hardware are made and, depending on the hardware in use, where the source level at the input of your audio hardware may be adjusted.

Next, the signal passes via the input section of the VST Connections window where the input ports of the audio hardware are connected to a chosen input bus. By default, at least one input bus is already present in the VST Connections window and this is normally connected to the first two audio inputs found in your audio hardware device. An input bus can be renamed in the Bus Name column and, although this is not essential, it helps clarify the source of the audio signal in other parts of the program. Intelligent labelling especially helps with multiple input/output hardware. Further input buses may be added by clicking on the Add bus button.

Now that the input bus is connected to a physical input, the input signal can be seen in the chosen input bus channel strip in the Mixer. Input buses appear to the left of all other channels in the Mixer. You can now visually monitor the level at source or the level being recorded to hard disk in the level meter of the input bus depending upon the global meter setting (Meter Input or Meter Post-fader). The input bus post-fader signal is what gets recorded to hard disk and the same signal is normally also routed to one or more audio channels for monitoring and recording purposes.

To hear the input bus post-fader signal, you must monitor enable an audio track / channel and set its input to the appropriate input bus (when monitoring via VST). The input bus is chosen in the Input Routing menu above the chosen audio channel. This opens a pop-up menu containing the available inputs, as activated in the VST Connections window. Normally, the chosen channel is also record enabled so that you can actually make your recording. Finally, when you make your recording it is represented as a waveform inside an audio event in the event display.

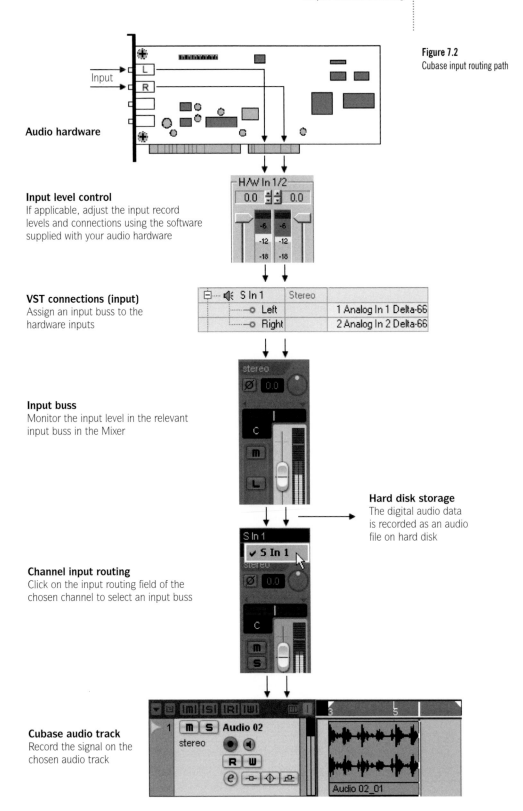

Figure 7.2
Cubase input routing path

Audio hardware

Input

Input level control
If applicable, adjust the input record
levels and connections using the software
supplied with your audio hardware

VST connections (input)
Assign an input buss to the
hardware inputs

Input buss
Monitor the input level in the relevant
input buss in the Mixer

Hard disk storage
The digital audio data
is recorded as an audio
file on hard disk

Channel input routing
Click on the input routing field of the
chosen channel to select an input buss

Cubase audio track
Record the signal on the
chosen audio track

The output path

Once recorded to hard disk, activating playback sends the signal back through the system to the outside world. Figure 7.3 shows the output routing path for three stereo and three mono audio tracks which are routed to four outputs of a multiple I/O audio device.

In Cubase, tracks are assigned as either mono or stereo when they are first added to the project using the Add track command (Project menu). A stereo track contains two audio signals, (the left and right channels of the stereo signal), and a mono track contains a single signal. By default, the signals recorded on any audio tracks arrive at the Mixer channels in the same order as they appear in the track list.

After arriving in the Mixer, the audio signals are routed to various destinations according to the settings in the output routing menus. In this case, synths and drum loop channels are routed to the Master stereo output bus and SFX 1, 2 and 3 to a Group channel. The Group channel is, in turn, routed to a second stereo output bus. The various signals are heard on the left or right of the stereo image according to each channel's pan control setting. Overall level changes and master insert effects may be applied in the output bus channel strips which appear to the right of all other channels in the Mixer. Finally, the master bus is routed to physical outputs 1 and 2 and Bus 2 is routed to physical outputs 3 and 4 of a multiple I/O audio hardware device in the output section of the VST Connections window. By default, at least one output bus is already assigned in the VST Connections window and this is normally routed to the first two audio outputs found in your audio hardware device. Further output buses are added by clicking on the Add bus button. After being converted back into the analogue domain via the D/A converters of the audio hardware, the composite audio signal arrives back in the real world where it can be amplified and monitored as required.

Key steps for routing an input signal onto an audio track

Despite having followed the audio recording tutorial in Chapter 3 and despite having fully understood the input and output routing setup within Cubase, the audio recording process may still remain difficult to grasp and retain. This is normal since there are quite a few parameters involved. For those readers who need further clarification, the following outlines the key steps for routing an input signal onto an audio track:

- Connect the audio signal to the appropriate physical input of the audio card or audio hardware device.
- Verify that the relevant input and output ports are active and visible in Devices / Device Setup / VST Audio System / << *name of your audio hardware driver* >>
- Connect the chosen audio hardware input port to an appropriate input bus in the VST Connections window.
- Verify that there is level activity in the meters of the chosen input bus in the Mixer.
- Adjust the input level using one or more of the following: the output gain of the audio source, the output gain of the send fader on your external

Project
window

Mixer
channels

Output
busses

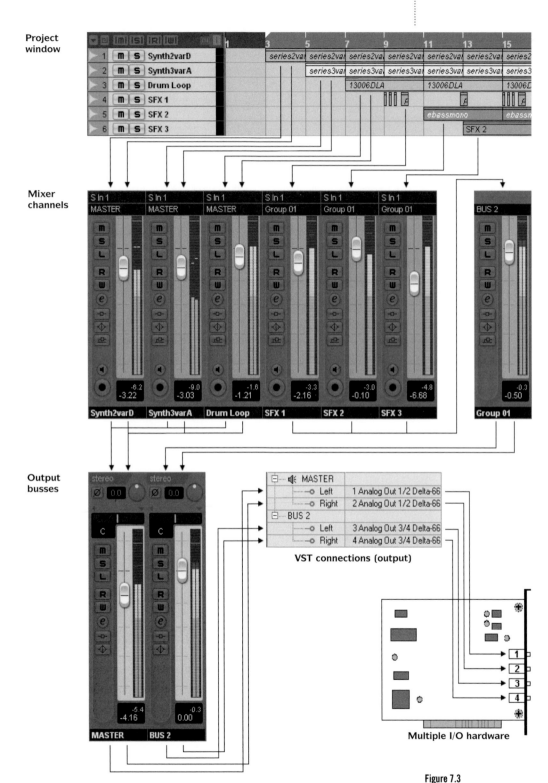

Figure 7.3
Cubase output routing path

mixing console through which the source is routed, the input level fader in the audio hardware's audio mixer (if available), or the input bus gain dial or fader controls.

- Add an audio track in the Project window and select the appropriate input bus by clicking on the input routing menu above the channel fader in the Mixer (or in the Inspector for the track).
- Activate the monitor button for the track. This allows you to hear and see the level of any input signal on the channel meters (assuming that you are monitoring the signal via Cubase). Activate the record enable button to make the channel ready for recording.
- Record the audio in the normal manner using the record button on the Transport panel.

Troubleshooting the recording process

If you have not yet managed to get an input signal showing in the meters or cannot hear your input signal, the following troubleshooting list may help solve the problem:

- Check that the source instrument or device which is supplying the sound signal is not faulty. Ensure that it is switched on / activated and check the audio cables for faulty connections.
- Check that there is not an impedance mismatch between the source signal and the input you have chosen on your audio card / device.
- Check that the audio card / device has been correctly installed and is operating outside of Cubase. Test the hardware for audio recording and playback functionality using a software application supplied with your operating system.
- Check that the audio card / device is connected in the VST Connections window (Device menu).
- It is easy to become confused about the left and right inputs of a stereo input device when recording mono sources and the multiple inputs of multiple I/O hardware. Make sure that the audio inputs are clearly labelled in the VST Connections window and that the correct input bus is selected on the chosen audio track.
- To hear and see the signal on the channel level meter of the chosen audio track make sure that the monitor button is activated (illuminated).

Monitoring in Cubase

The above troubleshooting steps solve the majority of problems with the setting up of the input routing of Cubase. However, you may also be encountering difficulties due to confusion about how best to monitor the signal (in both the visual and audio sense) and the manner in which Cubase behaves when you select an audio track.

Monitoring techniques
There are three basic audio monitoring techniques as follows:

Via an external mixer

If you have an external mixing console as part of your Cubase system then you may wish to monitor the signal directly from there before it arrives in the program. Most consoles allow you to do this. For this technique, choose Manual in Preferences / VST / Auto Monitoring (File menu) and do not acti-vate the monitoring button for the chosen audio channel. However, you need to manually activate the record enable button on the channel to make your audio recording. Using an external console allows zero latency monitoring while recording, so you can work with maximum accuracy when overdubbing.

Via the audio hardware using Direct Monitoring

Some ASIO 2.0 audio hardware drivers allow the use of Direct Monitoring. This allows the routing of the audio signal in the audio hardware to be controlled from within a music software application like Cubase. Direct Monitoring is activated in VST Audio System / << name of your audio hardware driver >> section of the Device setup window by ticking the Direct Monitoring option. If the option is greyed out it is not available with your audio hardware. Direct Monitoring re-directs the input signal from its usual path within the audio hardware so that you can hear it with minimum latency. With Direct Monitoring, you can still choose a monitoring mode in Preferences / VST / Auto Monitoring (While record enabled, While record running or Tapemachine style) and you can still use the record enable and monitor buttons but you cannot monitor the whole signal path which passes through Cubase (for example, you cannot hear the EQ and effects settings for the channel). Similar to the external console option above, direct monitoring allows minimal latency monitoring while recording, which suits timing-critical overdubs.

Via Cubase

In this mode, you monitor the audio after it has passed through the input and output stages of your audio hardware and Cubase. For this technique, choose either While record enabled, While record running or Tapemachine style in Preferences / VST / Auto Monitoring. (See below for a full explanation of these options). All three cases automatically activate the monitor button so that you can hear the input signal. The advantage of monitoring via Cubase is is that you can record a dry signal while monitoring it with added reverb or other processing (a popular technique when recording vocals). The disad-vantage is that the signal suffers from a slight delay (latency).

Record enable and monitor buttons

In order that there should remain no doubt as to the precise function of the record enable and monitor buttons, the following outlines the details:

- record enable button activated – activates record-ready status for the track (you can record on this track).
- record enable button de-activated – de-activates record-ready status for the track (you cannot record on this track).
- monitor button activated – activates monitoring of any incoming signal (you can hear the input signal and see its level on the meters).

Tip

To record multiple sources on several tracks, activate Preferences / Editing / Project & Mixer / Enable Record on Selected track and select the required number of tracks by clicking on each while holding the Shift key. In this way, each selected track is automatically record enabled. The number of simultaneous sources you are able to record depends upon how many physical inputs are present in your audio hardware.

- monitor button de-activated – activates monitoring of any signal already recorded on the track (you can hear and see the level of what has already been recorded).

Monitoring modes

The monitoring modes for Cubase are chosen in Preferences / VST / Auto Monitoring (Figure 7.4). These affect the behaviour of the monitor button relative to the record, playback and record enable status of Cubase (thus affecting how you monitor an incoming audio signal when recording). The monitoring modes include the following:

- Manual – the status of the monitor button for the channel is chosen entirely manually. This means that the monitor button is never automatically activated. This mode is suitable when you are monitoring via an external mixing console and do not wish to hear the signal via Cubase.
- While record enabled – the monitor button is automatically activated whenever the track is record enabled. This means that you are always listening to the incoming audio signal until you manually deactivate the record enable or the monitor button. This is suitable for regular track laying not involving manual drop-ins and for when you need to rehearse a part before pressing the record button. In this mode, you are monitoring via Cubase.
- While record running – the monitor button is only activated when Cubase is running in record mode. This means that you are always monitoring what is already recorded on the track unless you start recording. This is useful for manual drop-ins on a previously recorded track. In this mode, you are monitoring via Cubase.

Figure 7.4
Choose your audio monitoring mode in Preferences / VST / Auto Monitoring (File menu)

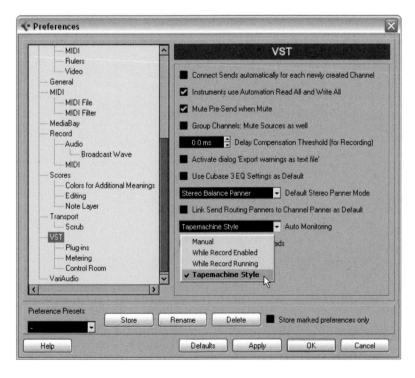

- Tapemachine style – the monitor button is automatically activated whenever the record button is activated, and remains active unless Cubase is running in playback mode, i.e. you monitor the incoming signal only when Cubase is in stop mode or running in record mode. This is a good general purpose mode and is useful for manual drop-ins on a previously recorded track.

Record modes for audio recording

The precise manner in which audio recording takes place is governed by the record mode section of the Transport panel. You are advised to become familiar with the record modes before commencing any serious recording projects. These affect both the linear and cycle recording behaviour of the program. The linear record modes determine what happens when a new audio recording 'overlaps' an existing event on the same track. The cycle record modes determine what happens when you record multiple takes over the same range in a continuous cycle when the Transport panel cycle button is activated. See 'Audio recording in cycle mode' below for more details. When audio events overlap you only hear the event which takes playback priority. The function of each record mode is outlined in the following table:

Record modes for audio recording

Linear record modes		Cycle record modes	
Mode	Overlap behaviour	Mode	Cycle behaviour
Normal	pastes new event on top	Mix	creates one region/event per lap
Merge	pastes new event on top	Overwrite	creates one region/event per lap
Replace	replaces existing event	Keep Last	keeps last complete lap in display
		Stacked	records laps in lanes

Tracks, channels and playback priority

Tracks and channels

In Cubase, tracks are listed vertically in the Project window. Audio tracks might contain any number of digital audio recordings represented as graphical events along the time line of the event display. When it is created, each audio track is automatically assigned its own audio channel and you can see these in the Mixer where, by default, they appear in the same order as they are found in the Project window. The tracks and channels in Cubase are not unlike those found in traditional multi-track recording setups where the tracks on a real world multitrack recorder are routed to the channels of a separate real world mixing console. The difference with Cubase is that the multitrack recorder and mixer are not physically separate and there can be literally hundreds of audio tracks with an almost infinitely wide mixing console to accommodate them! In fact, the Mixer automatically expands/contracts as you add/delete tracks in the Project window. The assignment of tracks to channels takes place invisibly, so in the routine recording process, you do not need to be concerned

Tip

For most applications it is best to activate 'Sync Project and Mixer selection' in Preferences / Editing / Project and Mixer. With this setting, all track selections in the Project window also select the corresponding channel in the Mixer and vice versa. This helps with workflow when jumping between the Project window and the Mixer.

with it. Cubase manages the available resources behind the scenes, leaving you to concentrate on the music and the recording, as you proceed with your session.

Playback priority

You can record several times on the same track over the same section but, with audio recording, the previously recorded material is never overwritten. The audio file which has been recorded on hard disk still exists, regardless of how you chop and change, cut and paste or otherwise manipulate events in the event display. The audio file is only ever deleted if you instruct Cubase expressly to do so. However, playback on the same audio track occurs according to a strict rule: an audio track can only play back one audio event at any one time. If events overlap, only one of them is heard. When working with multiple takes on the same track, use the To Front and Move to options in the Quick menu or Edit menu to choose which take you want to hear (Figure 7.5). You can also select takes using the drop down menu indicated by a small downward pointing arrow on the event.

Figure 7.5
Use the 'To Front' option in the Quick menu to choose the take you wish to hear

Mono or stereo

The mono or stereo configuration for audio tracks is chosen when you add a new track by selecting the Add Audio track command from the Project menu. In the Add Audio track dialogue which appears, you can also choose a multi-track or surround configuration (Figure 7.6). The chosen format is fixed at the time of creation and you cannot change the status later. However, it is possible to drag a stereo event onto a mono track (for example), at which time the stereo recording is played back in mono (you hear the left and right channels merged together). Equally, you can drag a mono event onto a stereo track, at which time you hear the same mono signal in both channels. Further mono/stereo manipulations are possible using Flip Stereo in the Audio Process menu.

Tip

To convert a stereo clip to mono, select the clip in the Pool, followed by Media / Convert files. In the Convert options pop-up, select Mono in the Channels sub-menu and 'New' in the Options sub-menu. To avoid losing the original stereo file, make a safety copy of the clip before using this technique.

Figure 7.6
Choose the configuration for the new audio track in the Add Audio Track dialogue

Audio recording strategies

Basic recording

If you followed the step-by-step audio recording procedure outlined in Chapter 3 you are already familiar with audio recording in Cubase. However, in this section we are concerned with practical techniques which streamline the process. Recording in a multitrack DAW tends to involve repetitive use of the same functions. However, the precise details vary according to the task at hand.

Preliminaries

Once the input bus is set up, recording is generally handled using the record track and Inspector in the Project window or using the audio channel for the track in the Mixer. It is assumed that you have already set the record levels on the input bus and that you have assigned the input bus in the input routing menu of the Audio track upon which you intend to record. The preliminary settings for the recording and overdubbing scenarios outlined below are as follows:

- Select 'Tapemachine style' in Preferences / VST / Auto Monitoring.
- Select 'Enable record on selected track' in Preferences / Editing / Project and Mixer. Selecting any track now automatically activates the record enable and monitor buttons allowing you to monitor the input signal in stop or record modes.
- Activate the Snap button in the toolbar. Set the Snap type menu to 'Grid' and the Grid type menu to 'Bar'. This will help move the project cursor to convenient bar positions before commencing recording.
- Select 'Normal' in the Transport panel Linear record mode menu.
- Activate 'Use pre-roll' and 'Metronome on' in the Transport menu. De-activate all other options.
- Verify that the cycle button is de-activated and enter one or two bars in the pre-roll amount field in the Transport panel.
- Verify that 'Metronome in Record' and 'Metronome in Play' are active in the Metronome Settings window.

Scenario 1 – Recording one long take

Here we are recording one long take of the musical performance of a live musician. It is assumed that any errors in the performance would be corrected at a later time, so this recording is continuous until the whole performance is complete. Proceed as follows:

1 In the Transport panel, de-activate the punch in and punch out buttons. Set up the correct tempo for the musical performance in the tempo field. Here, the musician is using the metronome of Cubase to keep in time.
2 Verify that the record enable button is active on the chosen record track.
3 Define the start point for your recording by clicking in the ruler to move the cursor to the bar of your choice.
4 Press the record button or '*' on the computer's numeric keypad. The

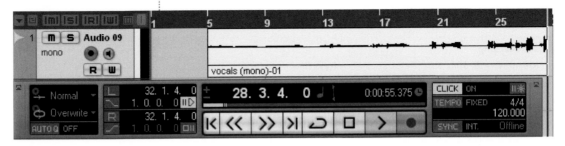

Figure 7.7
Recording one long vocal take

project cursor rolls back the number of bars you set in the pre-roll amount field. Playback commences with a metronome click so the musician can keep in time. Cubase drops into record mode at the bar you chose in step 3.

5   Record up to the end of the performance. If you experience a false start, delete the audio event and go back to step 4 to start again.

Scenario 2 – Dropping in to repair errors in a previous take

Automatic punch in and punch out

Automatically punching in and out of recording is a common requirement with multitrack recording systems. The technique is ideal for repairing imperfect passages, such as mistakes during a musical performance or clicks in the audio file.

The punch in and punch out buttons are found on the Transport panel. They work in conjunction with the left and right locators of the ruler. The left locator marks the punch in point and the right locator marks the punch out point. To implement automatic punch in and punch out, proceed as follows:

1   Set up the left and right locators to encompass the range you wish to record. Select and record enable the target track.
2   In the Transport panel, activate the punch in and punch out buttons.
3   Press '1' on the numeric keypad to set the project cursor to the left locator position (or rewind to some point before the left locator).
4   Start playback. The musician should play along with the music before the punch in point. When the project cursor reaches the left locator position, Cubase automatically starts recording (punch in).
5   Record the new take. Cubase automatically stops recording when the project cursor reaches the right locator position (punch out).

To hear your take in context you might like to activate the post roll button with a value of one or two bars in the post roll amount field. When you reach the punch out point playback now continues afterwards for the specified number of bars and beats, allowing you to verify the join between the new take and the previous recording.

Tip

To define a precise range for the punch in, listen to the recording and insert markers on the fly using the computer keyboard Insert key to mark the start and end points. Once defined, select the Range tool and double click between the two markers to select the range between them. Finally press 'P' on the computer keyboard to move the left and right locators to the marker positions. You are now ready to punch in over the defined range.

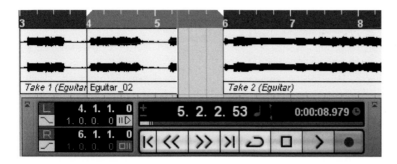

Figure 7.8
Using automatic punch in and out to record a guitar performance in bars 4 and 5

Manually dropping in on the fly

While automatic punch in and out is useful when you know exactly where you want to start recording, it is also useful to be able to punch into record mode at any moment on the currently selected (and record enabled) track. Such a situation might occur when your vocalist or other performer decides to produce a superb performance when you are monitoring a rehearsal but not actually recording. To drop in on the fly during playback without interrupting the flow of the music, click on the record button on the Transport panel or press the * key on the numeric keypad. To drop back out of record, click on the record button a second time. Cubase continues in playback mode.

Scenario 3 – Interrupting the take

Rather than complete one long take, as outlined above, you may prefer to interrupt the recording every time there is an error in the musical performance, rewind and continue recording from some point just before the error. Proceed as follows:

1. In the Transport panel, de-activate the punch in and punch out buttons.
2. Define the start point for your recording by clicking in the ruler to move the cursor to the bar of your choice. Press the record button or '*' on the computer's numeric keypad to start recording.
3. When there is an error press the spacebar twice, the first time to stop recording and the second time to roll back and commence playback.
4. Audition the take to find the position of the error. Stop playback at the error. Press Ctrl / Command + numeric keypad (–) to move the project cursor back one bar. This cursor position is the drop-in point for the next step.
5. Press the record button or '*' on the computer's numeric keypad to engage recording. There is a pre-roll during which the musician plays along with the previous take. Recording recommences at the drop in point as set in step 4. Go to step 3.

Figure 7.9
Recording takes in smaller sections

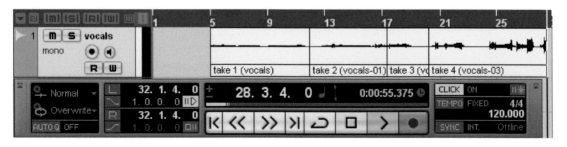

Scenario 4 – Recording takes in lanes

In the above scenarios you can, if desired, move to a new track for each take to avoid recording events on top of each other. However, by using 'Lanes fixed' mode you can record takes on separate lanes within the same track. This allows you to see multiple events in the display with greater clarity. Proceed as follows:

1   In the Transport panel, de-activate the punch in and punch out buttons.
2   Click on the Lane display type button and select 'Lanes fixed' from the pop-up menu.
3   Press the record button or '*' on the computer's numeric keypad to start recording.
4   Make a number of recordings over the same range using the techniques outlined in the above scenarios.
5   Each new take appears on a separate lane within the vertical space of the record track.

The most recent take appears in the lowest lane and playback priority is ordered from the lowest lane upwards. It is easy to see which parts of which events take playback priority since they are highlighted in green. The events may be edited directly in the event display which is convenient for assembling a composite take without ever leaving the Project window.

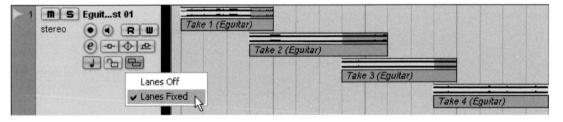

Figure 7.10
Selecting Lanes Fixed mode allows you to record takes onto separate lanes within the same track

Multitrack recording

For multitrack recording, it may be appropriate to open the Mixer on screen to see a number of channels simultaneously. This suits the simultaneous recording of several inputs on separate tracks. It also helps with overdubbing sessions where you may wish to change the mix of the backing tracks to suit the needs of a live performer. In these cases, open the Mixer in normal mode below the Project window (Figure 7.11).

Normal mode, (as opposed to extended mode), displays only the channel faders in the mixer and takes up less vertical space on the screen. It may also be useful to see the input and output buses. These are shown/hidden by clicking on the relevant icons in the panel to the left of the mixer channels. When recording multiple tracks, you need to record enable the appropriate number of tracks and make sure that the input routing menus are set to the appropriate input buses. The number of separate sources which can be recorded simultaneously depends on the number of active hardware inputs available on your system. Figure 7.6 shows an eight track recording taking

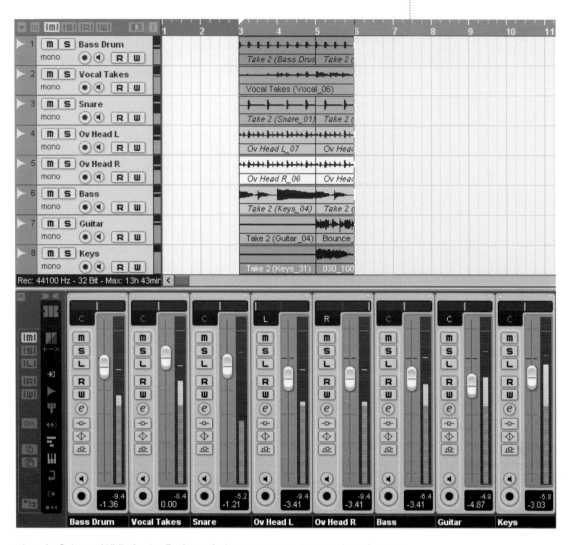

Figure 7.11
For multi-track recording, try opening the Mixer in normal mode below the Project window. This screenshot shows an eight track recording taking place in Cubase.

place in Cubase. While in the Project window, you can select tracks using the up/down arrow keys. While in the Mixer, you can select tracks using the left/right arrow keys. Several tracks/channels can be selected simultaneously by holding the Shift key while pressing the arrow keys. The Shift and arrow combinations provide a quick method of record enabling multiple tracks if you have activated 'Enable record on selected track' in Preferences / Editing / Project and Mixer.

Audio recording in cycle mode

Audio recording in cycle mode elevates the recording of multiple takes way beyond what you can achieve manually in linear recording mode. Cycle recording is implemented by activating the cycle button on the Transport panel before commencing the recording. Recording takes place in a continuous cycle between the left and right locators until you click on the stop button. This is an excellent technique for capturing a magical performance since you can leave Cubase in record mode while you perform the same segment of music over and over again. This is particularly useful for vocalists, who might be having difficulty with one particular section of a song or it might suit the recording of a guitar or saxophone solo where the musician would like to try a number of solos one after the other. You can later choose the best take or compile the best parts of a number of takes into a final composite version. You can even set up a cycle over the entire length of the song and perform the whole thing several times (assuming that you have the necessary hard disk space). Cubase makes all this very easy and benefits from an intuitive set of tools to select and edit the takes after recording has been completed.

Audio cycle recording behaviour varies according to two main factors: the Audio cycle record mode chosen in Preferences / Record / Audio Cycle Record Mode and the Cycle record mode chosen in the Transport panel. All the options record one long audio file which is automatically divided up to match the length of each take.

Audio cycle record mode (Preferences)

The Audio cycle record mode in Preferences governs the audio aspects of the cycle recording process. There are three options, which operate as follows:

- Create regions – regions are sections within audio clips. When Create regions is selected, one region is automatically created for each lap of the cycle and each region is automatically named with a sequential take number. When recording has been completed a single event appears between the left and right locators containing the last take. Other takes can be selected from the Set to Region option in the Quick menu. This is the default setting for Cycle record mode. See Chapter 8 for more details about regions.
- Create events – a separate audio event is created for each lap of the cycle. When you have finished recording, the events appear on top of each other between the left and right locators. You can select takes by using the To Front option in the Quick menu. Create events has the advantage that all the events are immediately available in the event display and if the material is not too complicated you can quickly edit the events to assemble a composite take while still remaining in the Project window.
- Create events and regions – creates both events and regions simultaneously which gives you the choice of using either regions or events for the manipulation of your multiple takes.

Cycle record mode (Transport panel)

Clicking on the cycle record mode selector in the Transport panel opens a menu with a number of options which determine the manner in which recordings are made when in Cycle mode. The modes function as follows:

- Mix and Overwrite modes – in these modes the Audio cycle record mode, as outlined above, is taken into consideration. If Create regions is chosen a single event (containing the last take/region) remains in the display after recording is completed. If Create events has been chosen separate events for each lap of the cycle appear in the same range on the audio track (pasted on top of each other).

- Keep Last – in this mode the Audio cycle record mode is not taken into consideration. Regions are created for each lap of the cycle but only the last complete lap in the cycle is kept as an audio event. Other takes can still be selected from the Set to Region option in the Quick menu.
- Stacked – in this mode, the Audio cycle recording mode is NOT taken into consideration. An audio event for each lap of the cycle appears on its own lane within the vertical space of the audio track. The most recent take appears in the lowest lane and playback priority is ordered from the lowest lane upwards. It is easy to see which parts of which events take playback priority since they are highlighted in green. The events may be edited directly in the event display which is convenient for assembling a composite take without ever leaving the Project window.
- Stacked 2 (No mute) – the same as stacked mode except that no muting of events takes place.

Practical audio recording projects in cycle mode

For the following cycle recording projects, set up Cubase as outlined in Preliminaries, above, but in addition activate 'Start record at left locator' in the Transport menu.

Audio cycle recording project 1 (Keep Last mode)

To record multiple takes in 'Keep Last' cycle record mode, proceed as follows:

1 Click on the cycle record mode selector in the Transport panel and select Keep Last from the pop-up menu.
2 Set the left and right locators to the appropriate range within your musical arrangement.
3 Activate the cycle button on the Transport panel (press / on the numeric keypad).
4 Select the target record track and make sure it is record enabled.
5 Press the record button or '*' on the computer's numeric keypad to start recording.
6 Record the performance as many times as you wish. On each lap of the cycle a new region is automatically created, suitably named with a sequential take number. Only the last complete take is kept as an audio event in the event display (Figure 7.12).

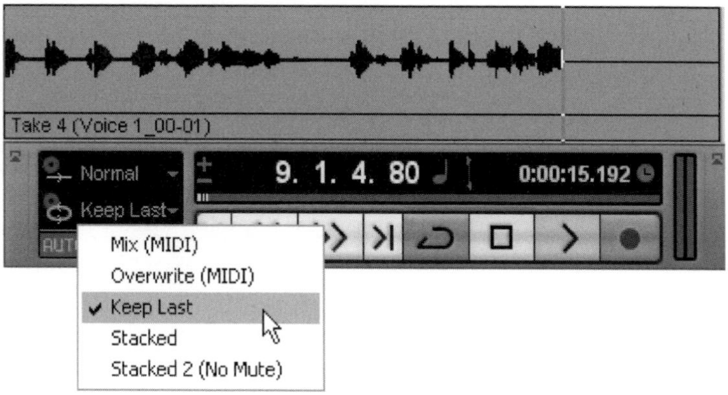

Figure 7.12
Recording a vocal line in Keep Last cycle record mode. Here, the fourth lap of the cycle is shown.

Keep Last mode allows you to record the musical performance repeatedly over the same range until you get a good take. When you think you have succeeded you stop recording and it is only the good take which remains in the event display. However, should you need to, you can still select any previous take using the Set to Region option in the Quick menu.

Figure 7.13
Use the Set to Region field in the Quick menu to select a previous take

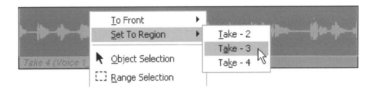

Audio cycle recording project 2 (Stacked mode)

To record multiple takes in 'Stacked' cycle record mode, proceed as follows:

1 Click on the cycle record mode selector in the Transport panel and select Stacked from the pop-up menu.
2 Set the left and right locators to the appropriate segment of your musical arrangement.
3 Activate the cycle button on the Transport panel (press / on the numeric keypad).
4 Select the target record track and make sure it is record enabled. In order to be able to see the stacked lanes in the vertical space of the audio track try expanding its vertical size by clicking and dragging on the lower limit of the track in the track list.
5 Press the record button or '*' on the computer's numeric keypad to start recording.
6 Record the performance as many times as you wish. On each lap of the cycle a new event is automatically created, suitably named with a sequential take number and automatically arranged on lanes within the vertical space of the track (Figure 7.14).

Figure 7.14
Recording a vocal line in Stacked cycle record mode. Events are stacked onto separate lanes.

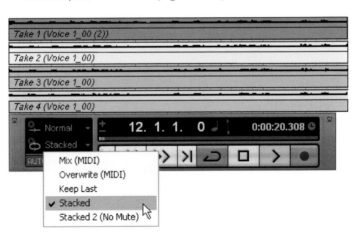

Stacked mode allows you to record your musical performance repeatedly over the same range and display the resulting takes as separate events within the vertical space of the record track. This means you can immediately carry out detailed editing of the events using the standard tools while still remaining in the Project window (to assemble, for example, a perfect composite take). Playback priority works from the lowest lane upwards and those parts of the events which take priority are highlighted in green.

Audio events, audio clips and audio files

The concepts of audio events, audio clips and audio files need to be fully understood to appreciate exactly how Cubase handles audio data. Luckily, you do not need to be aware of these details for routine audio recording and editing but knowledge of what is going on behind the scenes can help when you are troubleshooting or when you are involved at a deeper editing level.

Whenever you make an audio recording, there are three things which occur in Cubase as follows:

1 an audio file containing the actual audio recording is created on the hard disk.
2 an audio clip which points to this audio data is created in the Pool.
3 an audio event which points to the clip is created in the event display of the Project window.

These three elements are shown in Figure 7.15. This shows the state of affairs just after you have made an audio recording in Cubase. The details of Figure 7.15 can be explained in three steps as follows:

Info

See Chapter 10 for more details about the Pool.

Figure 7.15
An audio event points to its corresponding audio clip which, in turn, points to its corresponding audio file on hard disk

AUDIO FILE

X File_00.wav

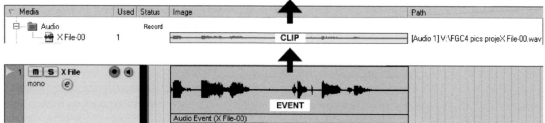

1 an audio file called X File_00 is created on the hard disk in the Audio folder of a project called ProjectX. The audio file takes its name from the name of the audio track at the time of recording.
2 an audio clip, also called X File_00, is created in the Pool and, at this stage, this audio clip provides a reference to, or points to, the whole audio file stored on hard disk. Like the audio file, the audio clip also takes its name from the name of the audio track at the time of recording.
3 an audio event is created in the event display which provides a reference to, or points to, the audio clip (at this stage it points to the whole audio clip).

Info

An audio file and its corresponding audio clip always begin with the same basic name, but the overall name may change after certain kinds of editing operations. If you change the name of the audio clip, the basic name of the audio file on disk is changed accordingly.

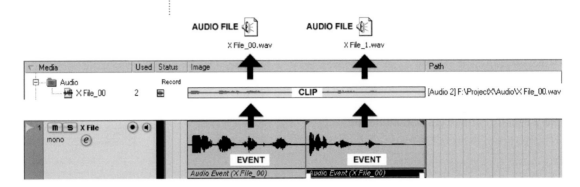

Figure 7.16
The relationship between the events, clip and audio files after splitting and processing an event

Let's imagine that we are only interested in the second half of the recorded audio event. We decide to split it in two and fade out the second half using the split tool and the fade out function (Audio / Process sub-menu). The result of the editing is shown in Figure 7.16. You could happily go on splitting and processing your events without too much concern about the number of audio files and clips you are creating behind the scenes. You can undo your processing in the normal way, using Ctrl/Command + Z. You can even undo it at a later date using Cubase's Offline Process History (Audio menu).

Let's take a look at the details of Figure 7.16. When you split the event, you produced two events which point to the same audio clip. The first event points to the first half of the clip and the second event points to the second half of the clip. Before you applied the processing, the clip was still pointing to the whole of the audio file. However, when you applied the processing, something unexpected happened. Rather than change the original audio file, a completely new audio file was created (X File_1) and stored in an Edits subdirectory on disk. Finally, you have two events which point to the same clip and a clip which points to two different audio files. The audio clip knows at which moment it should start pointing to the second audio file.

You may ask why Steinberg designed this part of the software like this. The main reason is that you always preserve your original recording on the hard disk in an unchanged state. This is re-assuring and means that, if things go wrong, you can always go back to it. Another reason is that when you process an audio file several times, each process is stored in a separate edit file. This allows the use of the Offline Process History to go back to a clean version of a guitar recording, one month after you applied compression, distortion and reverb to it (for example).

The following provides a summary of the above information:

- audio events are what you see in the event display and provide the means by which you visualise your audio recordings. Audio events appear at various points in time within your project and feature a start time and an end time. The placement and size of events can be edited at any time after recording has been completed. Audio events point to the whole of, or part of, an element in the Pool known as a clip. Each audio event points to a single clip – it cannot be associated with more than one.
- an audio clip is an element which points to an audio file on the hard disk. An audio clip provides an interface between the audio events in the event

display and the audio files on the hard disk. It decides which section of which audio file gets accessed by which audio event.

- an audio file is the raw audio material stored on hard disk. There are two categories of audio files; those containing the original data as captured at the time of the original recording (stored in the Audio sub-directory), and those containing edited audio data as created when audio processing is applied (stored in the Edits sub-directory).

Info

All audio files created by audio and plug-in processing are stored in the Edits sub-directory of the main project folder.

Audio editing

This chapter describes audio editing techniques in general and provides detailed coverage of the Audio Part editor and the Sample editor. Topics include the audio event Infoline, the audio menu options, time stretching, fades and crossfades, hitpoints, groove template creation, audio looping, audio warping and pitch correction.

The Audio Part editor is for the editing of audio events grouped inside an audio part. It is often more convenient to edit audio events in groups rather than as separate events. Manipulations of data in the Audio Part editor involve splicing, trimming and moving events in much the same way as takes place in the Project window. This editor also features special functions for editing events which have been recorded in Cycle Record mode, and for editing audio slices. Editing in the Audio Part editor is non-destructive. This means that the actual audio file on hard disk is not altered by any editing actions.

The Sample editor allows you to view and edit your audio data in fine detail at the sample level. Here, you are working with the actual waveform of the audio data in terms of defining regions, calculating hitpoints, cutting, copying and pasting, and performing other detailed audio processing. Editing is non-destructive in the sense that you can always go back to a previous version of the edited file using the Offline Process History (Audio menu) and, for as long as you are working in the same continuous session, you can use the Undo command (Edit menu).

Audio event editing in the Project window

This section describes a number of event-based editing techniques in the Project window. For general tool-based audio editing see Chapter 4.

Using the Audio event Infoline

An Infoline appears above the display when you activate the info button on the toolbar in either the Project window or the Audio Part editor. This displays various parameters for the currently selected audio event or for the first of a multiple event selection (Figure 8.1). A parameter may be edited directly by double-clicking in its value field and entering a new value using the computer keyboard, or you can drag the value up or down if you have activated 'Increment / Decrement on Left click and drag' in File / Preferences / Editing / Controls / Value Box. In this case, the changes are sensitive to the current snap resolution when the Snap button is activated.

File	Description	Start	End	Length	Offset	Snap	Fade In	Fade Out	Volume	Mute	Lock	Transpose	Finetune
Trumpet	Take 2	3. 1. 1. 0	5. 2. 3.105	2. 1. 2.105	0. 0. 0. 0	3. 1. 1. 0	0. 0. 0. 0	0. 0. 0. 0	0.00 dB	-	-	-1	-5

Figure 8.1
The Infoline for an audio event

When more than one event is selected the infoline text is shown in yellow and contains the information relevant to the first of the selected events. Editing any of the yellow text values applies the changes relatively to all selected events. For example, changing the start position moves the start position of all the currently selected events but maintains their relative positions. However, if you wish to apply the same absolute start position to all the selected events hold down Ctrl while making the change. In this case, the start times of all selected events snap instantly to the same position. Note that applying the same file name in the File field to a number of audio files is NOT possible since all audio files must retain a separate and unique name. However, it is possible to enter an absolute name for all descriptions in the Description field.

Other useful manipulations on the Infoline include the following:

- Edit the name of the audio file and clip associated with the audio event by entering a new name in the File field. Similarly, a new description may be entered in the Description field. The description appears first in the audio event followed by the name of the audio file in brackets.
- Edit the start, end and length fields to precise numerical values in (you guessed it!) the start, end and length fields. This is applicable when you know the precise point at which you want the event to start or end, or the precise length. When bars and beats are shown in the ruler, these values are displayed in bars, beats, sixteenth notes and ticks (each sixteenth note contains 120 ticks).
- The offset for an audio event allows you to slide the audio back and forth in time without changing the position of the event which contains it. The contents may also be moved by dragging within the event while pressing Ctrl + Alt. This helps when you want to manually line up audio content such as drum hits to specific beats in the bar. If the audio event already plays the whole clip, the offset value cannot be adjusted.
- The Snap point value provides another way of moving an audio event to a new position in the display. This is an absolute value corresponding to a point on the ruler and does not move the position of the Snap point within the event.
- The volume field provides a numerical method of setting the volume of the event, providing +24dB of boost or infinite attenuation. The volume is normally adjusted by moving the blue volume handle in the centre of the event.
- The fade in and fade out fields provide quick numerical methods of adjusting the fade in and out characteristics of the event. The fade characteristics are normally adjusted using the blue fade handles at each end of the event (see Chapter 4 for details).
- The Mute field offers a quick method of muting the current selection.
- The Lock field allows you to lock the position, size and other characteristics of an audio event such as volume changes, fades and audio processing. This protects audio events against accidental damage and changes when a project is near to completion.

- Transpose allows you to apply real-time pitch shifting to the selected audio event(s) in the range -24 to +24 semitones. This could be used if you change the key at a later date after having completed the recording. The pitch shifting remains reasonably transparent if the pitch change is between -3 to +3 semitones. If you are sure the pitch change is permanent, you may achieve better results by using 'Freeze timestretch and transpose' in the Audio / Realtime processing sub-menu and choosing one of the MPEX algorithms.
- Finetune is similar to Transpose but allows pitch change between -49 and +50 cents (1 cent = 100th of a semitone). This is helpful for retuning instruments or for creating effects. For example, phasing and ADT effects may be created by copying an event onto a spare track and detuning it by a small amount (try between -2 and -40 cents).

Important

Changing the name in the File field of the Infoline changes the name of the clip in the Pool and the name of the actual audio file on hard disk. This is significant if you are working with a file from an audio library since you may change the name of the file on hard disk without really wanting to. Other applications in your system which accessed the same file may then have difficulty finding it. To avoid this, try activating 'Copy Files to Working directory' in File / Preferences / Editing / Audio / On Import audio files / Use Settings.

Audio menu options

There are a number of excellent audio editing tools in the Audio menu of Cubase. These are accessed via the Audio menu itself, via key commands or via the audio section of the Quick menu. Editing is generally directed to one or more selected audio events or parts.

Events to Part

It is often helpful to group a number of audio events into a single audio part so they can be moved around and edited as a single block. To achieve this, drag a selection box around the desired audio events and select 'Events to Part' in the Audio menu or Quick menu. This is particularly useful when events overlap or are pasted on top of each other since, once they are contained within an audio part, they can be viewed and edited with greater precision in the Audio Part editor, where the events are displayed on separate lanes.

Dissolve Part

Dissolve Part provides the opposite function to Events to Part, above. Here, the individual audio events are taken back out of the part and displayed in the event display in the normal way. This may be required when you need to make detailed changes to the musical structure in the Project window.

Bounce selection

Bounce selection creates a single new audio file and clip from the currently selected audio events or range selection and, if chosen, a single new audio event which replaces the original events or parts. All auto-fades, fades and crossfades are included in the bounce. Real-time effects are not included. For multiple selections over several tracks, the function operates on a track-by-track basis. Audio events, (and the associated audio files and clips), created with Bounce are named according to the source track name.

Bounce Selection may also be used to bounce the current range selection in the Sample editor to a new file and clip. In this case, a second instance of the Sample editor is automatically opened containing the bounced audio. When using Bounce Selection in the Project window or Audio Part editor, a dialogue appears asking if you wish to replace the currently selected material (Figure 8.2). If you click on Replace the original selected audio events or parts are replaced with a single audio event. If you click on No, the events are not replaced. In both cases, a new audio file is created on the hard disk and a new audio clip is created in the Pool. The original audio files and clips associated with the events from which the bounce was made are not deleted or modified in any way.

Figure 8.2
Bounce Selection Replace Events dialogue

Detect silence

Detect silence (Audio / Advanced sub-menu) allows you to process your audio material based upon a variable threshold for silence within the chosen audio event. As well as finding the silence itself, the Detect Silence function is equally good at finding the wanted non-silent passages within your audio material. The following sections outline two scenarios where the Detect silence function is particularly helpful:

Scenario 1

Electric guitar recordings frequently suffer from unwanted noise and interference between the wanted parts of the performance. Detect Silence provides a way of quickly and automatically removing the unwanted noise, without resorting to noise gates or manual editing. Proceed as follows:

- Select the audio event containing the electric guitar and select Detect Silence in the Audio menu. As a starting point, set the parameters to the values shown in Figure 8.3.
- Set the Open Threshold parameter to around –18dB. This governs the threshold for opening the gate to allow the wanted part of the signal through.
- Set the Close Threshold parameter to around –20dB. This governs the threshold for closing the gate to block the unwanted part of the signal (i.e. that part of the audio to be treated as silence).
- Set Minimum Time Open to around 50ms. This holds the gate open for the prescribed length of time after the Open threshold level has been reached to avoid the gate opening and closing too many times during passages featuring quick staccato notes or similar attributes.
- Set the Minimum Time Closed to around 50ms. This holds the gate firmly shut for the prescribed length of time after the Close threshold level has been reached and is usually set to a relatively small value to avoid cutting out any wanted material.
- Set the pre and post-roll parameters to around 50ms and 70ms respectively. These add an offset before and after opening and closing

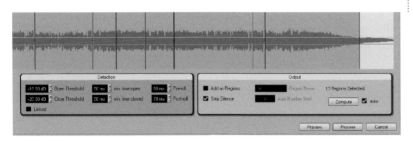

Figure 8.3
Finding the unwanted noise between the wanted parts of an electric guitar performance in the Detect Silence dialogue

the gate to make sure you do not lose any of the attack or decay in the wanted parts of the audio.

- Activate Strip Silence and de-activate Add as Regions.
- Click on the Compute button followed by the Process button.
- Close the dialogue to go back to the Project window where your original audio event has now been automatically split into a number of separate events. All those sections containing the noise are removed from the performance (Figure 8.4).

Tip

To group all events created by Detect Silence into a single audio part use 'Events to Part' (Audio menu).

Figure 8.4
A cleaner electric guitar performance in the Project window after treatment using Detect Silence

Scenario 2

Drum loop libraries on CD often feature tracks containing a series of consecutive loops with silence in between each loop. Detect Silence allows you to automatically detect and highlight such loops by defining them as regions. To achieve this, proceed as follows:

- Import the audio track(s) from CD using File / Import / Audio CD.
- Select the audio event containing the drum loops and then select Detect Silence in the Audio menu.
- Adjust the main parameters to similar values to the electric guitar example outlined above but use open and close thresholds of around -30dB, activate Add as Regions, and de-activate Strip Silence.
- If you want your regions to start tightly cut to the first beat of each loop, try a value of 0ms for the pre-roll setting.
- Enter a generic name into the Regions Name field.
- Click on the Compute button followed by the Process button. Close the dialogue to go back to the Project window (Figure 8.5).

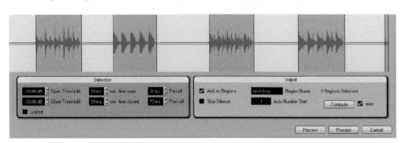

Figure 8.5
Finding the relevant audio for the creation of automatic regions in the Detect Silence dialogue

Figure 8.6
The resulting regions in the Sample editor

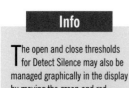

Info

The open and close thresholds for Detect Silence may also be managed graphically in the display by moving the green and red handles. The green handle corresponds with the open threshold and the red handle corresponds with the close threshold.

In this case, rather than stripping the silence we are automatically marking the areas of interest within the audio material. Double-click on the audio event to open the Sample editor. Activate the Show Regions button. The regions you created in the Detect Silence dialogue are now visible in the list and can be selected, played and edited as desired (Figure 8.6).

Time stretching

Time stretching involves changing the length of the chosen audio material without changing the pitch. The use of the term 'time stretch' is slightly misleading since you can both stretch and compress the length of the target audio. Time stretching is applied in two ways in Cubase: using the Time Stretch option in the Audio / Process sub-menu (outlined in Chapter 9) or using the Object selection tool in time stretch mode. The following outlines the use of the Object selection tool in time stretch mode to time stretch an audio event containing a drum loop.

The time stretch algorithms

Time stretch is available as the third function of the Object selection tool. It is implemented when you resize the audio event by dragging the start or end points. However, the actual time stretch algorithm used for the operation is chosen in File / Preferences / Editing / Audio (Figure 8.7).

There are two algorithms available; MPEX and Realtime. There are various advantages and disadvantages to each algorithm so it is worth experimenting to achieve the best results.

- MPEX – MPEX is a proprietary time stretch algorithm designed by Prosoniq. MPEX stands for 'Minimum Perceived Loss Time Compression / Expansion'. This sometimes gives better results when you want your sound to stay true to the character of the original. It is recommended for vocals, instrumental solos, drum loops and mixes. Set the quality menu to Preview or Mix Fast when previewing, or to one of the other settings according to the type of material you are time stretching. Poly Musical is the default high quality setting which works well with drum loops, mixes and most other material. Solo Musical is recommended for vocals and instrumental solos. If these fail to produce acceptable results, try Poly Fast or Poly Complex.
- Realtime – uses the same time stretch algorithm as that which is used for

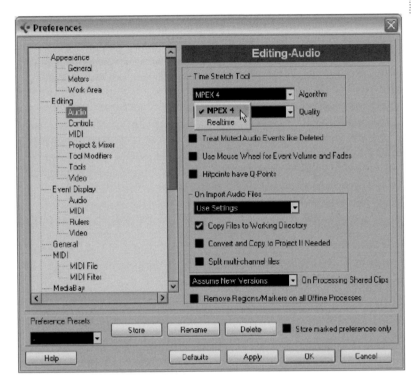

Figure 8.7
Select the time stretch algorithm in the
Preferences dialogue

the audio warp functions. This is a good all-round alternative to MPEX. Events subject to Realtime stretching are displayed with a small double-arrow in the lower right corner. The quality of the results can be modified by changing the warping algorithm in the algorithm menu of the Sample editor toolbar.

Time stretching a drum loop

It is assumed here that you are inserting a drum loop into a Project which already has a fixed tempo which you do not wish to modify. To make the chosen loop fit the tempo using the Object selection tool in time stretch mode, proceed as follows:

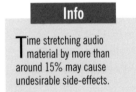

Info

Time stretching audio material by more than around 15% may cause undesirable side-effects.

- Import your chosen drum loop and place it in the Project window event display. Make sure that it loops for a precise number of bars (in its own original tempo). Popular lengths are one, two and four bars (Figure 8.8).
- Activate the Snap button and set the Grid type menu to 'Bar'. Move the drum loop audio event to its intended start position in the musical arrangement.
- Choose the MPEX algorithm in File / Preferences / Editing / Audio. Select Poly Musical in the quality menu.

Figure 8.8
A one bar drum loop in the event display

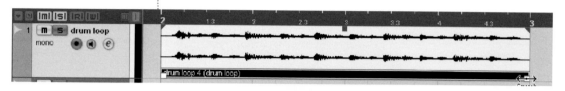

Figure 8.9
The one bar drum loop after time stretching

• Select the Object selection tool in time stretch mode and drag the end point of the event to the nearest bar division in the event display. The audio is automatically time stretched according to the chosen algorithm when you release the mouse (Figure 8.9). The drum loop now plays in time with the current fixed tempo.

Fades and crossfades

There are many different ways in which fades and crossfades can help when you are editing audio. Simple graphical fade techniques using the fade handles of an audio event have already been described in 'Using the tools' in Chapter 4. The following sections outline some of the other techniques and the uses of the various fade dialogues.

Auto fade

Splitting audio events in the Project window or Audio Part editor sometimes results in digital clicks. This most often occurs when the edits are not at zero crossing points in the waveform and may be troublesome at the start or end of an event, when one event is placed immediately after another. One solution is the Auto fade function. Auto fade imposes a short automatic fade-in, fade-out or crossfade for the events in the Project window, to avoid clicks and encourage glitch-free transitions between adjacent audio events. This can be set up globally or on a track-by-track basis. A global setting might result in unnecessary drain on the CPU power of the computer since not all tracks need auto fades. A global setting may also cause undesirable loss of attack transients without you really noticing. You are therefore advised to implement auto fades only on single tracks and only when they are needed.

The global Auto fade dialogue is opened by selecting 'Auto Fades Settings' in the Project menu. Since you are being advised here not to use a global setting, leave the parameters in the global dialogue inactive (i.e. do not tick any of the Auto fade in, Auto fade out or Auto crossfade boxes). The Auto fade dialogues for each track are opened from the track list Quick menu or by clicking on the Auto fade button in the track Inspector (Figure 8.10). The track version of the dialogue is identical to the global version except that it features a 'Use Project settings' tick box. When working on a track-by-track basis, de-activate this tick box since you are setting up the parameters for one track only.

The Auto fade dialogue allows you to set the characteristics of the fade curves by clicking on any of the preset curve buttons or set up custom shapes by dragging directly in the curve displays. Set the length parameter to suit the material being processed. To activate the auto fading tick the desired Auto fade in, Auto fade out or Auto crossfade box and click on OK.

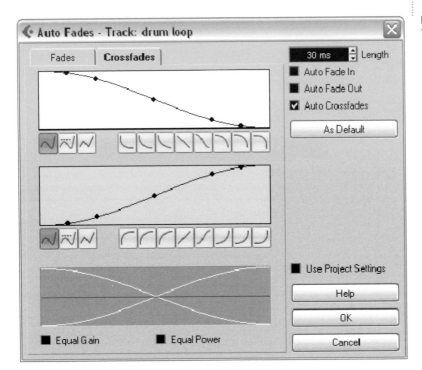

Figure 8.10
The track Auto fade dialogue

Fade in and Fade out dialogues

When you have set up a fade in or a fade out using the blue fade handles at the start and end of an audio event the characteristics of the fade can be modified by double-clicking above the fade line. This opens a fade in or fade out dialogue (Figure 8.11). The Fade out dialogue is simply the inverse of the Fade in dialogue shown here.

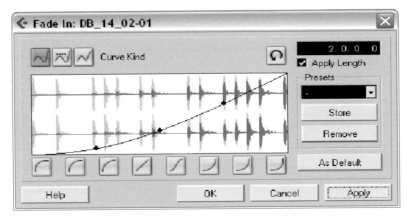

Figure 8.11
The Fade in dialogue

The fade in and fade out dialogues allow you to modify the characteristics of the fade curve by clicking on a preset curve button or you can set up custom shapes by dragging handles directly in the curve display. Spline, damped spline and linear curve characteristics are available together with a length option which allows you to re-adjust the length of the fade from within the dialogue. A restore button allows you to reset the dialogue to the default settings. The same fade may be applied to multiple events by making a multiple selection before opening the Fade dialogue.

Fades set up using the blue handles are not applied to the audio clip itself. This means that a number of events which refer to the same audio clip can each have an independent fade curve. This differs from the fades which are applied using the Fade in and Fade out functions of the Process menu, which apply the fade to the audio clip itself (described in Chapter 9).

Info

Regular spline mode radically affects the shape of the neighbouring parts of the curve as you drag the curve handle within the display and sets up a naturally balanced curve. Damped spline mode only has a minimal effect on the neighbouring area and sets up a curve which is more linear. Damped spline mode is therefore easier to control when dragging handles in the display.

Adjust fades to range

As an alternative to dragging the handles in the event to create fades, Cubase provides another more elegant means of achieving similar results. This involves the use of the Range selection tool as follows:

- Select the Range selection tool in either the Project window or the Audio Part editor.
- Select a range over the start of your chosen audio event corresponding with the length of fade in you want to apply. Select 'Adjust fades to Range' in the Audio menu or press 'A' on the computer keyboard to create an instant fade in (Figure 8.12).

Figure 8.12
Using the Range selection tool with 'Adjust fades to Range' to apply a fade in to an audio event

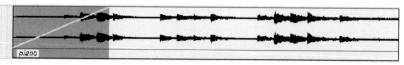

- Select a range over the end of your chosen audio event corresponding to the length of fade out you want to apply. Select 'Adjust fades to Range' in the Audio menu or press 'A' on the computer keyboard to create an instant fade out (Figure 8.13).

Figure 8.13
Using the Range selection tool with 'Adjust fades to Range' to apply a fade out to an audio event

- Alternatively, select a range over the central area of your chosen audio event. Select 'Adjust fades to Range' in the Audio menu or press 'A' on the computer keyboard. A fade in and a fade out are simultaneously applied on either side of the selected area (Figure 8.14).

Figure 8.14
Using the Range selection tool with 'Adjust fades to Range' to simultaneously apply a fade in and a fade out to an audio event

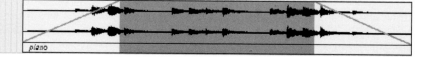

- To automatically open the fade in or fade out dialogues (or both) select 'Adjust fades to Range' or press the 'A' key command a second time in any of the above techniques.

Crossfading

Crossfades can be applied between audio events in the Project window if they are on the same track and they overlap. When they do not overlap a cross-fade might still be applied if the audio clips they are referenced to overlap. In this case, the events are resized so that the crossfade can be created. If the audio events do not overlap and the whole of the audio clip is referenced by the audio event, no crossfade can be created. Things are similar in the Audio Part editor except that the events are viewed on separate lanes, which makes it slightly easier to set up the crossfades, (see Audio Part editor basics, below).

Tip

To reduce lip noise and interference in vocal takes set the crossfade dialogue so it produces a bowl shaped curve like that shown in Figure 9.2. Set the length to suit the target material and save as the default. Next, mark all points of interference 'on the fly' using Edit / Split at cursor. Lastly, select the split events and select Audio / Crossfade (X).

Let's consider setting up a crossfade between two takes of an 8 bar saxophone melody. Take One is good until an error in bar 5. Take Two plays successfully from bar 4 to the end of the melody in bar 8. We need to create a crossfade somewhere in bar 4. To achieve this in the Project window, proceed as follows:

- Select the zoom tool and draw a selection box around the two takes, in this case over the length of the eight bars of the melody (Figure 8.15).

Figure 8.15
Zoom in to the area of interest

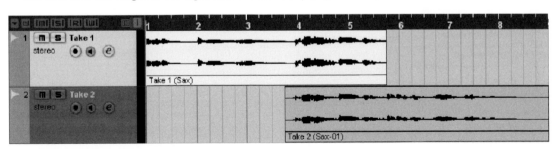

- Activate the Snap button, select Grid in the Snap type menu, select Use Quantize in the Grid type menu, and select 1/8 Note in the Quantize type menu. This helps you when you arrange your overlap (you may often need a smaller resolution). Find a point in bar 4 where the two takes are playing the same note in the same manner. Resize Take One so that it ends (in this case) 1/8 note after this point. Resize Take Two so that it starts 1/8 note before this point (Figure 8.16). You now have a 1/8 note overlap.

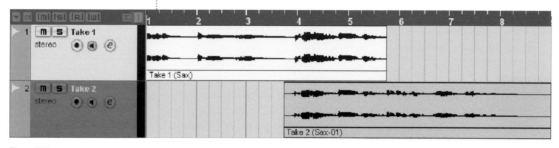

Figure 8.16
Resize the events so that they overlap

- Hold down the Ctrl key on the computer keyboard to limit horizontal movement and drag Take Two on top of Take One (Figure 8.17).

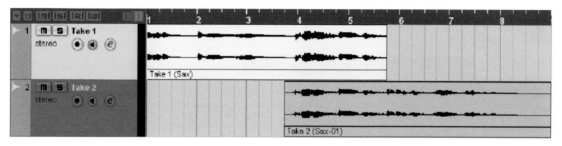

Figure 8.17
Drag one event on top of the other

- Press X on the computer keyboard. The crossfade is automatically created using the current default crossfade settings (Figure 8.18). To adjust the characteristics of the crossfade, press X a second time or double-click on the crossfade area to open the crossfade dialogue.

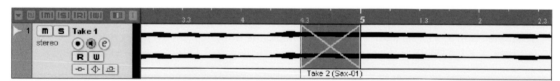

Figure 8.18
Press X to create a crossfade

The Crossfade dialogue

The Crossfade dialogue (Figure 8.19) is opened by double-clicking on the crossfade area. Alternatively, select the events containing the crossfade and press X on the computer keyboard. Several crossfades may be modified in the Crossfade dialogue simultaneously by selecting all the events containing the crossfades.

Figure 8.19
The Crossfade dialogue

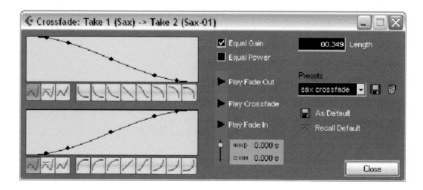

The Crossfade dialogue features fade out curve and fade in curve displays. You can audition the signal using the Play Fade out and Play Fade in buttons. The resulting crossfade is auditioned using the Play Crossfade button. Eight preset curves are available for each of the fade in and fade out curves with a choice of spline, damped spline or linear characteristics. The fade curves can also be edited manually by clicking and dragging directly in the curve displays.

Activating the Equal Power option ensures that the crossfade contains equal acoustical energy throughout the course of the crossfade. In other words, the perceived loudness remains constant. In this mode, the curve displays have only a single editable point which is moved horizontally in the display. Equal Power mode might have been applicable to the saxophone crossfading exercise outlined above. However, a successful result relies upon the incoming and the outgoing signals having very similar characteristics.

Many crossfading tasks benefit more from Equal Gain which ensures that the summed amplitude of the two curves remains constant throughout the crossfade. This is suitable for a wide range of crossfading tasks where you want the fade in curve to automatically mirror the fade out curve for effortless, constant-gain crossfades.

The right panel of the Crossfade dialogue features a length field where you can adjust the length of the crossfade, and default settings where you can save the current configuration as the default crossfade for future operations, or recall the existing default. A Preset menu provides storage and recall of your own presets.

The Audio Part editor

To open the Audio Part editor select an audio part and press Ctrl + E (PC) / Command + E (Mac) on the computer keyboard or double-click on the part (Figure 8.20). The editor features time on the horizontal axis and tracks and lanes on the vertical axis. Single or multiple parts on one or more tracks can be selected for editing. When events within the part overlap, each is shown on a different lane within the track height. Events can be freely dragged between tracks and lanes. Playback priority is enforced from the bottom lane up. Lanes are particularly useful for editing multiple takes on the same track,

> **Tip**
>
> To change the time format of the length parameter of the Crossfade or Fade dialogues change the primary time format of the Transport bar.

> **Tip**
>
> To remove fades and crossfades, select the events or range containing the fades and then select 'Remove Fades' in the Audio menu.

Figure 8.20
The Audio Part editor

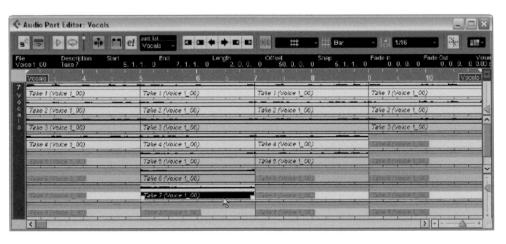

as occurs during cycle recording, or for tidying up after you have been dropping in manually. The toolbar at the top of the window contains a similar tool set to the Project window except that the glue tool is not present, and the scrub and play tools are on separate buttons. The operation of all other tools is similar to those found in the Project window (see 'The Project window tools' in Chapter 4 for more details). There is the usual show / hide infoline button, a solo button, and the scroll bars and zoom controls at the lower and right edges of the window.

Snap points

When the vertical zoom is set to a sufficient factor, the Audio Part editor reveals a snap point within the currently selected event. By default, this is found at the start of each event (Figure 8.21).

Figure 8.21
The Snap point of a selected audio event in the Audio Part editor

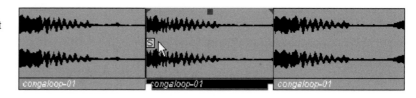

The snap point is marked by an 'S' handle attached to a vertical line and this may be dragged to any point within the event. When the Snap button is active, the snap point becomes a magnetic anchor which governs how an event lines up to the nearest time division as defined in the snap and grid type menus. Thus, you can find a musically significant moment within the event, such as the first downbeat in the bar or the precise hit point of a bass drum, and use this when you move or quantize the events, or line up one event with other events in the display.

Info

In the Project window, the snap point of an audio event is modified using 'Snap point to cursor' (Audio menu). When it is not at its default position at the start of the event the snap point is visible as a vertical blue line.

Audio Part editor auditioning tools

The Audio Part editor features a similar toolbox to that found in the Project window and is thus already familiar to the majority of users. The auditioning functions are particularly helpful here. The play and scrub tools allow you to quickly audition any audio passage by clicking upon or dragging within events. The local audition and loop buttons provide local playback of the material currently in the editor. Playback takes place over the current event or range selection. When no selection is made, the whole audio part is played. Pressing the loop button activates the audition button simultaneously, and loop playback continues until you de-activate the audition button.

Using the auditioning tools switches the signal routing to bypass any effects or EQ on the audio channel and allows you to set an exclusive auditioning level using the audition mini-fader on the toolbar. All this helps with detailed audio editing where effects and EQ might otherwise mask the result. If you wish to hear the audio through the channel in the normal way, engage standard play in the Transport panel ('Enter' on the computer keyboard).

Tip

To quickly switch between and audition the contents of any event , track or lane in the Audio Part editor click on an event with the Play tool (loudspeaker icon).

Audio Part editor basics

Editing audio events in the Audio Part editor is similar to editing events in the Project window (see 'Using the tools' in Chapter 4 for more details). The following outlines editing techniques which are specific to the Audio Part editor.

Similar to the other editors within Cubase, setting the left and right locators around the target part may help with navigation. To achieve this, select the part and press 'P' on the computer keyboard or press Shift + G to engage cycle playback. This helps keep the Project cursor visible within the editor. Once inside the Audio Part editor, you may prefer to use the local play, cycle and audition tools rather than the main Transport functions. When you have selected multiple parts for editing, use the part list menu on the toolbar to switch between parts. Activating the 'Show Part Borders' button helps clarify the display.

Creating a sound effect

This section outlines how to create a sound effect using a cymbal crash. This helps understand the basics and reveals some of the creative uses of the editor. The objective is to split the crash into a number of segments and then re-order them in overlapped succession on different lanes within the Audio Part editor. Proceed as follows:

- Record a cymbal crash in the Project window or drag and drop an existing cymbal file onto an audio track. Edit the cymbal crash event so that it has a duration of four bars. With the event selected, open the Quick menu and select 'Events to Part' in the Audio section (Figure 8.22). This creates an audio part which contains the audio event.

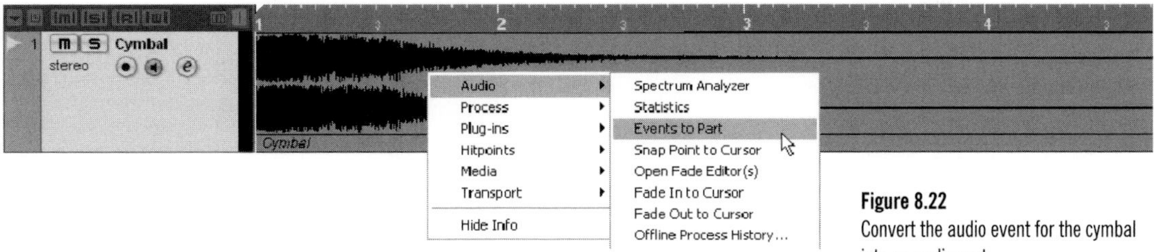

Info

See 'Creative audio editing techniques' later in this chapter for more about the Audio Part editor.

Figure 8.22
Convert the audio event for the cymbal into an audio part

- Double-click on the new audio part to open the Audio Part editor. Select the Split tool in the toolbar and divide the cymbal crash into four 1 bar events (Figure 8.23).

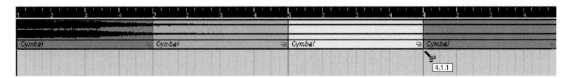

- Select the Object selection tool (pointer) and drag the third bar of the cymbal onto the second lane at position 1.4.1, as indicated by the tool when the event is dragged (Figure 8.24). To help place the events accurately activate the Snap button and choose 'Beat' in the Grid type menu.

Figure 8.23
Split the cymbal into four 1 bar events in the Audio Part editor

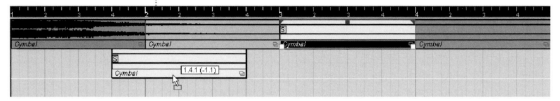

Figure 8.24
Drag the third bar of the cymbal onto the second lane at position 1.4.1

- Drag the second bar of the cymbal onto the third lane at position 2.3.1 (Figure 8.25).

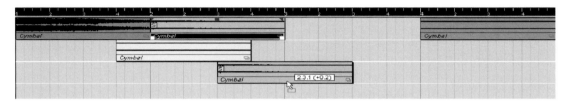

Figure 8.25
Drag the second bar of the cymbal onto the third lane at position 2.3.1

- Finally, drag the first bar of the cymbal onto the fourth lane at position 3.2.1 and drag the fourth bar of the cymbal to position 1.1.1 on the first lane (Figure 8.26). If you find this procedure confusing just remember that all you have done is split your original cymbal into four parts and then re-assembled them in reverse order with one beat overlaps.

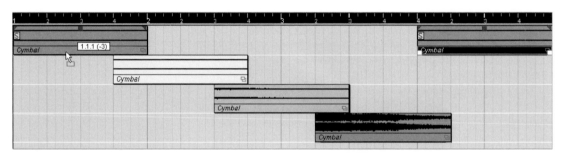

Figure 8.26
Drag the first bar of the cymbal to position 3.2.1 and the fourth bar of the cymbal to position 1.1.1

Figure 8.27
Select all the events and press 'X' on the computer keyboard to complete the effect

- Resize the event on the fourth lane so that your events span four bars. Commence playback to hear the new order of events. The result is a hybrid reverse cymbal effect. To complete the effect, select all the events (Ctrl + A / Command + A) and press 'X' on the computer keyboard. This automatically creates crossfades between the events giving smooth transitions between each part of the cymbal (Figure 8.27).

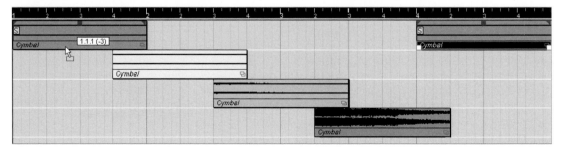

If you choose the right kind of cymbal for this exercise you should get a pleasing result. Overlapping and crossfading is a popular technique for creating smooth transitions between events, and splitting and moving events around like this is something that occurs frequently in the Audio Part editor. This is indeed what you do when creating composite versions of vocals or other multiple take material. The technique also helps create unique sonic transformations when applied to sustained notes from two different instruments or when mixing and matching sounds within drum loops.

Editing miscellaneous takes

When you have recorded different versions of the same material on several different tracks or when you have recorded a number of takes on the same track as a result of dropping in or punch recording, it is easier to edit the material in the Audio Part editor. Proceed as follows:

- Drag a selection box around the events you wish to edit. These may be on the same track or on different tracks.
- Select 'Events to Part' in the Audio menu (or use the Quick menu).
- Double-click on one of the parts to open the Audio Part editor or press Ctrl / Command + E.
- In the Audio Part editor, parts which were on different tracks in the Project window each appear in their own horizontal track in the editor. For multiple recordings which took place on the same track, each take appears in its own lane within the vertical space of its respective track (stacked).
- Use the part list menu to switch between tracks. Alternatively, use the Play tool to switch between and audition the contents of each track or lane.
- The events may be edited using similar techniques to those outlined in 'Creating a composite recording in the Audio Part editor', below.

The Sample editor

To open the Sample editor select an audio event and press Ctrl + E (PC) / Command + E (Mac) on the computer keyboard or double-click on the event (Figure 8.28). Alternatively, double-click on an audio clip in the Pool. The

Figure 8.28
The Sample editor

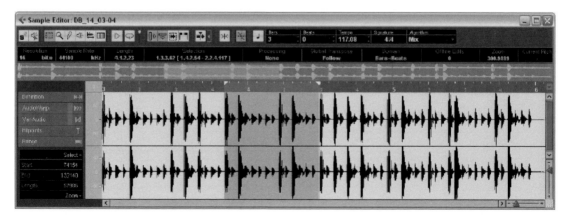

Tip

To change the amplitude units of the vertical axis between percentage or decibels right click (PC) / Control click (Mac) in the scale to the left of the waveform display.

Sample editor window features a toolbar and info section at the top and an Inspector to the left. The contents of the toolbar may be modified by right-clicking / control clicking in the toolbar and making a selection from the pop-up menu. Below the toolbar there is the thumbnail view which shows the whole of the clip associated with the selected audio data. The main display area shows the waveform of the currently selected material with time on the horizontal axis and amplitude on the vertical axis. The display varies according to which tool or function is chosen.

Editing in the Sample editor is, not surprisingly, optimised for working at the sample level. Samples are the atoms of digital audio; they are the smallest particles of audio you can manipulate in Cubase. In the Sample editor, you can see these atoms strung together if you view your audio data at maximum resolution (Figure 8.29). When you make a selection in the waveform display using the Range selection tool, the length, start and end are shown in the selection display on the toolbar in the chosen time format. This allows you to edit material with surgical precision. However, this does not mean that you need to be permanently concerned with the microscopic details of your audio material while working in the Sample editor; much of the time you can work in an intuitive fashion, using what you hear as the main basis for your editing decisions.

Figure 8.29
A waveform at maximum resolution in the Sample editor

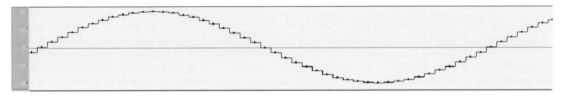

The Sample editor features its own set of tools, many of which are similar in operation to those found in the Project window (see Chapter 4 for more details). These include from left to right:

Range selection tool

For manually selecting specific areas of the waveform by clicking and dragging in the main display area. Range selections are magnetic to the zero crossing points in the waveform when the 'Snap to zero crossing' button is activated. When this button is de-activated range selections are made freestyle with single sample resolution.

Zoom tool

For zooming in and out in the main display area. The Zoom tool is particularly useful in the Sample editor for zooming in to specific details in the waveform.

Draw tool

For detailed manual re-drawing of the waveform at high resolution. This is designed for detailed repair work such as removing digital clicks and is only available when the zoom resolution is lower than 1.

Play tool

For auditioning the audio material by clicking on the waveform in the display. Playback commences from the position at which you clicked and continues for as long as you hold the mouse button. The playback zone is shown in blue.

Scrub tool

For auditioning the audio material by dragging over the waveform. This plays the audio according to the speed and direction you drag, much like rocking the tape back and forth over the playback heads of a tape machine.

Time warp tool

Similar to its function in the Project window and other editors, the time warp tool is for dragging a bar position to a time position. However, it takes on particular significance in the Sample editor for precisely lining up the tempo to audio material. This can be achieved manually by visually dragging tempo events to specific peaks in the waveform. Alternatively, tempo events can be dragged to hitpoints. If the snap button is active, dragged tempo events snap to the nearest hitpoints. This might be used to line up the beats in the bar to each beat as indicated by the hitpoints calculated for a drum loop.

Holding Shift while clicking in the Sample editor display inserts a tempo event. Holding Shift while clicking on a tempo event in the ruler deletes the event. Tempo track mode must be selected in the Transport bar in order to use the time warp tool (time warp does not function in fixed tempo mode). For more details on the use of the time warp tool see Chapter 19.

Sample editor play and loop buttons

The Sample editor features its own play and loop buttons for local playback of the audio. Playback occurs over the audio event or the whole clip according to the status of the Show Audio event button. If you have made a range selection playback is focused on this instead. Pressing the loop button allows playback in a continuous loop. Alternatively, try Shift + G for loop playback of the current range selection or Alt + spacebar to play the range selection once.

Together with the play and scrub tools, these functions provide a convenient method of auditioning in the Sample editor. Their use switches the signal routing to bypass any effects or EQ on the audio channel and allows you to set an exclusive auditioning level using the audition mini-fader on the toolbar. This helps with detailed editing where effects and EQ might otherwise mask the result. If you wish to hear the audio through the channel in the normal way, engage standard play in the Transport panel ('Enter' on the computer keyboard).

Sample editor Autoscroll and Snap to zero crossing buttons

As elsewhere in Cubase, when the autoscroll button is activated the display automatically follows the position of the Project cursor. Use the 'F' key to enable / disable autoscroll. When the Snap to zero crossing button is activated all range selection, cutting, copying and pasting, and hitpoint editing snaps to the nearest zero crossing point in the audio waveform. Zero crossing points are where there are the least amounts of energy in the audio signal. Editing here reduces the occurrence of audible clicks and makes for a good join when one section of audio is joined to another.

Sample editor view options

A number of buttons on the toolbar affect what you see in the Sample editor. These include:

- the Show Inspector button – when the Show Inspector button is activated the Sample editor Inspector appears to the left of the main display. The Inspector gives you convenient access to all the audio warping, musical mode, pitch correction, hitpoint and other advanced audio processing functions (see below for details).

- the show info button – this shows / hides the infoline which displays various details about the audio clip in the editor such as its resolution, sample rate, length and so on. This is purely for information as none of the parameters may be directly edited on the infoline.

- the Show audio event button – this enables / disables the view and flags of the audio event associated with the waveform. This button is not present if you have opened the Sample editor via an audio clip in the Pool.

- the Show regions button – this shows / hides the Regions list which appears to the right of the main display. Regions are areas within your audio material marked as sections of interest or relevance, much like you might highlight sections of interest within the text of a book. They can be created automatically when recording audio in cycle mode or they can be created manually in the Sample editor (see 'Creating and handling regions in the Sample editor', below).

The Sample editor Inspector tabs

The Sample editor Inspector appears to the left when you activate the Show Inspector button on the toolbar. The Inspector features a number of tabs (sections) which help you edit the audio more conveniently. A number of the functions found here are unique to the Inspector while others are duplicates of functions found in the main menus. The Inspector tabs include the following:

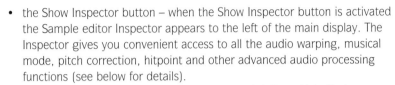

Definition – here you define how a bars and beats grid lines up with the audio waveform. When the tempo of the audio is unknown the auto adjust button automatically matches the grid to the waveform and attempts to calculate the tempo of the audio. Manual adjust allows you to drag the beats on the grid to the main peaks in the waveform. This helps when you want to match the rhythmic pulse of the audio to the tempo of Cubase in fine detail, especially for audio with an irregular beat. In simple cases of audio loops with a regular pulse, Cubase can usually calculate the tempo automatically in which case activating Musical mode may be all you need to produce tempo-synchronised playback. The reset button allows you to clear the grid and start again.

Audio Warp – here you manage various parameters for the warping of audio. Activating Musical mode produces tempo-synchronised playback of loops and similar material. Musical mode locks the tempo grid of the audio to the tempo of Cubase, thereby stretching or compressing the audio in real-time. To freely warp the audio activate the Free Warp button. Shift-click or click and drag in the display to create and edit warp tabs. Free warp can be used independently of Musical mode or in combination with it. The quantize setting governs the resolution of the warp tabs which appear in the display in Musical or Free warp mode. A swing parameter allows you to apply a swing feel to the audio. To specify the time stretch algorithm for audio warping use the algorithm field in the musical information section of the toolbar.

VariAudio – this is for the editing of individual pitches within monophonic vocal recordings and other similar material. VariAudio divides the target audio into segments according to an analysis of its pitch and timing characteristics. The segments are equivalent to notes as found in a piano roll style editor like the Key editor. The pitch, length and timing of these segments can be edited in order to correct tuning and timing irregularities in the musical performance.

Hitpoints – this section is for hitpoint calculation and editing. Hitpoints are used to mark the dominant peaks within the audio waveform which usually correspond with the rhythmic pulse of the material. They are created by dragging the Sensitivity slider. The higher the setting of the slider the more hitpoints are created. The hitpoints may be edited by activating the Edit hitpoints button. Hitpoints help match audio to tempo. They also allow you to create audio slices and groove templates or add events, regions and markers according to hitpoint positions. Hitpoint editing and hitpoints in general are described in more detail below.

Range – provides quick access to a number of common range selection and zoom functions and displays the current selection start, end and length in samples. This helps you select the area of interest within the waveform and zoom in and out.

Process – provides quick access to a number of common audio processing commands such as cut, copy, paste, bounce and insert silence. Also from here you can make all real-time processing a permanent part of the data using the Flatten command, edit the current selection using the on-board processing functions and plug-ins, or select the audio process history, statistics or spectrum analyser.

Regions

Regions are areas within your audio material marked as sections of interest or relevance, like highlighted or underlined sections of interest within the text of a book. They can be created automatically when recording audio in cycle mode or they can be created manually in the Sample editor. Click on the Show Regions button to reveal the Regions list to the right of the main display (Figure 8.30). You can create a new region at any time by selecting a range within the waveform and clicking on the Add button above the Regions

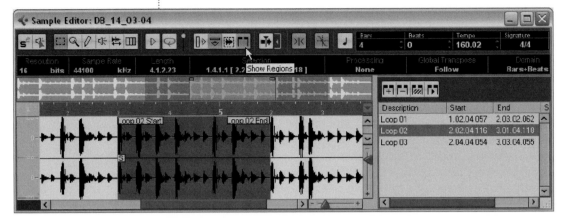

Figure 8.30
Activate the Show regions button to
reveal the Regions list in the Sample
editor

list. Regions may be played, selected or removed using the corresponding
buttons above the list. The start and end points of each region can be directly edited in the corresponding columns. New audio events can be created
from any region by Ctrl / Command dragging directly from the selected area
in the waveform display or by dragging from the Regions list onto a track in
the Project window.

Snap points

When the Show Audio event button is activated, a vertical line with an 'S'
handle known as the Snap point is shown in the waveform display. The Snap
point is usually set to a musically significant moment within the audio and,
when the Snap button is activated in the Project window, is used to snap the
event to the current snap resolution. The Sample editor allows you to freely
drag the snap point to any position within the waveform and if you also activate the scrub tool you can hear the audio as you drag it. This helps place
the Snap point with great precision. Alternatively, set the Snap point to the
position of the cursor by selecting Audio / Snap point to Cursor.

Navigating in the Sample editor

Navigating and auditioning in the Sample editor

Before opening the Sample editor, set the left and right locators around the
target event by selecting it and pressing 'P' on the computer keyboard. This
highlights the location of the event along the time line in the Sample editor
and helps with navigation. Double-click on the event to open the Sample editor. Once inside the editor, you have the choice to use the main Transport
controls or the local play, loop and audition controls for playback.

Helpful key commands

At first sight, navigating within the Sample editor may seem confusing. The following key commands help clarify and speed up some of the basic operations:

- Zooming – use Shift + F to zoom to the whole clip associated with the
  event, Shift + E to zoom to the event itself, and Alt + S to zoom to the
  current range selection.

- Playback – use Shift + G to loop the current range selection or Alt + Spacebar to play the range selection once. Alternatively, try activating File / Preferences / Transport / Playback toggle triggers local preview. This allows you to use the Spacebar to audition in the Sample editor.

The thumbnail view

The thumbnail view above the main display is helpful for navigating and zooming within the clip. This is similar to the Overview display in the Project window. The current horizontal section of the waveform you can see in the main display is marked by a corresponding pale blue box in the thumbnail view. You can drag the selection box to different positions within the clip and it can be resized by dragging the start or end points.

Sample editor basics

Copy and paste

One of the best ways to get to know the Sample editor is to experiment with a test audio recording. For this it is suggested that you make a recording of the spoken letters 'VST'. The objective is to test various editing techniques and re-order the letters using the copy and paste functions. Proceed as follows:

- Take a microphone and record the spoken letters 'VST' onto an audio track in the Project window. To get a clear and well-defined recording pronounce the letters in a slow, deliberate fashion. Double-click on the resulting audio event to open the Sample editor. You can see the three letters as three distinct shapes in the waveform as shown in Figure 8.31.

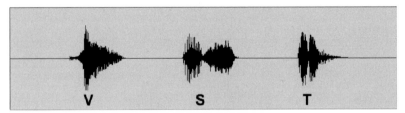

Figure 8.31
Test recording of the spoken letters 'VST'

- Reveal the audio event by activating the 'Show Audio event' button. The start, end and snap point handles are shown. Activate the 'Snap to zero crossing' button. This helps ensure click-free editing when you copy and paste in the Sample editor.

Figure 8.32
The audio event tabs are revealed when you click on the Show Audio event button

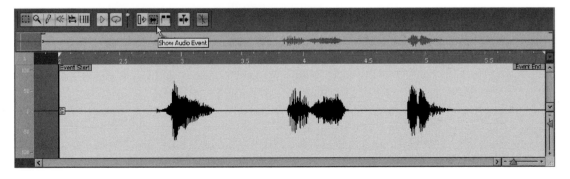

- Audition the audio event by clicking on the play button in the toolbar. Adjust the playback level using the audition mini-fader on the toolbar.
- Select the Range selection tool and drag across the display area. Select the letter 'S' in your audio recording. The selection area is shaded in turquoise(see Figure 8.33).

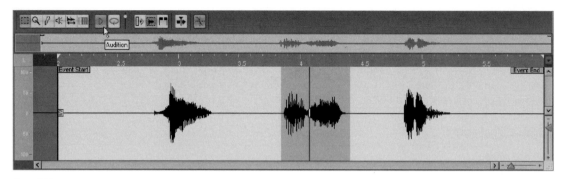

Figure 8.33
Select and play the 'S' of your 'VST' test recording

- Press Alt + Spacebar on the computer keyboard to play the 'S' sound once. Press Shift + G on the computer keyboard to play the 'S' sound in a continuous loop.
- While still in loop playback, try adjusting the start and end positions of the range selection by dragging the start or end points (a double arrow appears). Each time you release the mouse button, playback re-commences from the start of the range selection. This technique is useful for finding the correct start point of a drum loop (Figure 8.34).

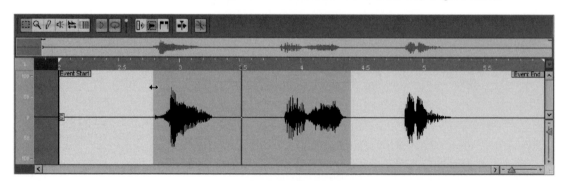

Figure 8.34
Try adjusting the start and end position of the range selection while in loop playback

Tip

Multiple Sample editors may be opened simultaneously when you are working on several clips at the same time. This is useful for copying, pasting and merging audio between different clips.

- Now, select 'V' (the first peak in the waveform) by dragging the mouse in the display (Figure 8.35). Copy the selection by pressing Ctrl + C / Command + C.

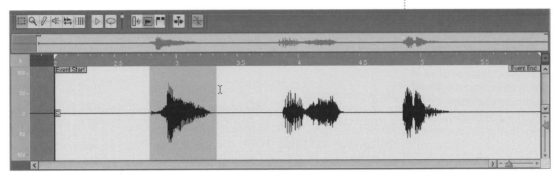

- Click once on the point just after the 'T' (the third peak in the waveform). Press Ctrl + V / Command + V on the computer keyboard to paste the 'V' just after the 'T' (Figure 8.36). When the range selection is at a single sample value, the contents of the clipboard are inserted at the current range selector position (shown by a vertical line). When the range selection is greater than a single sample, the segment encompassed by the range selection is overwritten by the contents of the clipboard.

Figure 8.35
Select and copy 'V'

- Select the last two peaks in the waveform and audition the selection. The result is the required spoken letters: 'TV' (Figure 8.37).

Figure 8.36
Paste 'V' just after the 'T' at the end of the waveform

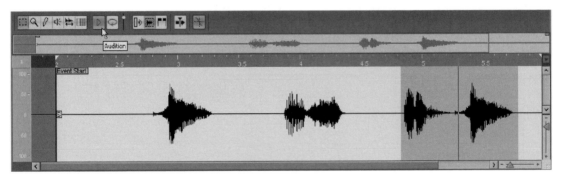

If you are happy with the edit, you could delete the first two peaks in the waveform, the original 'V' and 'S', by selecting them and pressing backspace

Figure 8.37
Audition 'TV'

Tip

To merge the current contents of the clipboard with the existing audio in the Sample editor use the Merge Clipboard function in the Process menu (see 'Merge Clipboard' in Chapter 9).

on the computer keyboard. Alternatively, select the new 'TV' section and activate the Show Regions button. Click on the add button above the regions list and name the new region as 'TV'. If desired, Ctrl + drag the region onto the Project window to create a new audio event.

Digital click removal

Audio files occasionally suffer from digital clicks and other interference. The Sample editor allows you to manually repair the damage by zooming in to the click at high magnification and re-drawing the waveform. The following outlines the basic procedure:

- To open the Sample editor double-click on the audio event which contains the unwanted click. The offending click may be already visible in the display as a brief spike in the waveform, similar to Figure 8.38. Many kinds of interference are not so obvious and could be more difficult to find.

Figure 8.38
Open the sample editor and find the click in the waveform

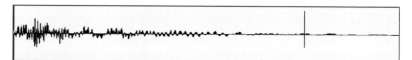

- Locate the mouse in the ruler at the position of the click and drag down to zoom in (activate 'Zoom while Locating in Time Scale' in File / Preferences / Transport). Zoom in until a factor of lower than 1 is indicated on the infoline (Figure 8.39). At less than 1 the waveform is shown as a line rather than as a filled shape.

Figure 8.39
Zoom in to the click

- The offending click is now clearly visible in the display. Select the draw tool and manually redraw the waveform over the appropriate range (Figure 8.40). Draw the new line very carefully, attempting to match the characteristics of the surrounding waveform.

Figure 8.40
Select the Pencil tool and manually redraw the waveform

Tip

If you are having difficulty finding your click, scroll through the waveform at a medium to high zoom factor and look out for a small segment of the waveform which has different visual characteristics to the surrounding audio.

An alternative to manually redrawing is to select a short segment of the surrounding audio and to paste this over the click. The Sample editor Inspector helps with this procedure. To achieve a successful result, without changing the length of the audio clip, proceed as follows:

- Activate the Show Inspector and the Snap to zero crossing buttons on the toolbar. Select samples in the Sample editor ruler.
- Working at high magnification, select the precise range of the click using the Range selection tool. Select Edit / Event or Range as Region in the

Inspector Process section. Make a mental note of the length of the selection in samples, as shown in the selection field of the infoline.

- Search for a suitable adjacent area of the waveform using the Range selection tool. Select an area whose length is the same as, or greater than, the number of samples in the region for the click (as defined in step 2).
- When you have found a suitable area, copy it using Ctrl / Command + C.
- Select the region created in step 2 and click on the Select Region button above the Regions list. This selects the range of the region.
- Select Process / Merge Clipboard in the Inspector Process section. In the Merge Clipboard dialogue which appears set the Sources mix slider to 100% copy and click on the Process button. This overwrites the click.

Creative audio editing techniques

Creating a composite recording in the Audio Part editor

The recording of a live performer sometimes requires several takes before a satisfactory result is achieved. Rather than stop Cubase after each take, it is often more convenient to record continuously in cycle mode. In cycle mode, the audio is recorded as one long audio file automatically divided into separate takes, one for each lap of the cycle. This process is outlined in 'Audio recording in cycle mode' in Chapter 7.

A multi-take recording of this kind may be conveniently edited in the Audio Part editor where the audio is automatically divided into separate regions and stacked onto separate lanes. Each lane represents the recording from one lap of the cycle and is named with a sequential take number. A 'perfect' composite recording can be assembled from the different takes by splitting, resizing and muting the material. This process is sometimes referred to as compositing or 'comping'. To create your own composite recording, proceed as follows:

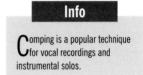

Info

Comping is a popular technique for vocal recordings and instrumental solos.

- Select the raw audio event(s) recorded in cycle mode in the Project window and then select 'Audio / Events to Part' from the Quick menu. Choose 'Regions' if the 'Create Part using Regions?' dialogue appears. This creates a multi-lane audio part which is suitable for editing in the Audio Part editor. Press 'P' on the computer keyboard to set the left and right locators to the start and end of the part. Double-click on the part to open the Audio Part editor (Figure 8.41).

Figure 8.41
A multiple take recording in the Audio Part editor featuring four takes

- First, you may wish to audition the material to establish which takes you prefer. Only one take can be played at any one time and the lowest lane gets playback priority. Try using the Mute tool working from the lowest lane upwards to progressively mute those takes you do not wish to hear (Figure 8.42).

Figure 8.42
Use the Mute tool when auditioning the material, working from the lowest lane upwards

- To make the task easier, it may be appropriate to colour code the different lanes and to divide all the takes into one or two bar events using the Split tool (Figure 8.43). Alternatively, try splitting the material according to the range of each musical phrase. To start with, try working with the Snap button activated and the resolution set to bars or beats. To avoid clicks at the split points, activate the 'Snap to Zero crossing' button. De-activate the button after editing is complete to avoid affecting subsequent editing tasks.

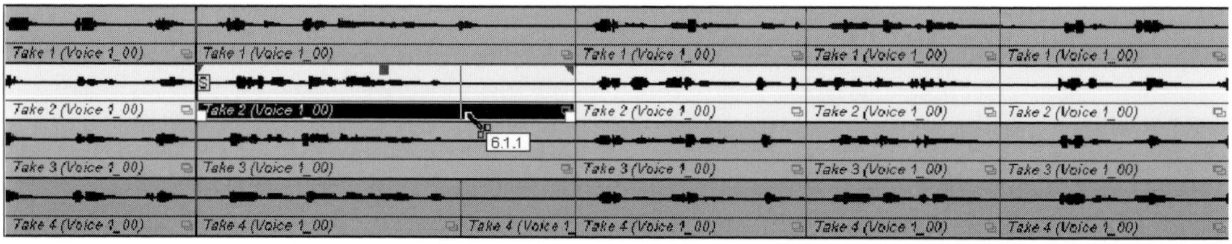

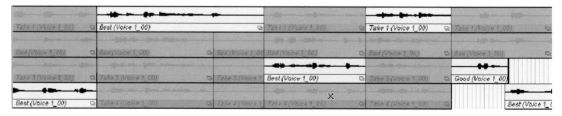

Figure 8.43
Use the Split tool to divide the takes into their constituent musical phrases or bars

- Assemble a basic composite version of the performance by muting those events you do not wish to hear. For clarity, rename the best takes and the bad takes in the description field of the Infoline for each event (Figure 8.44). Use Shift + G to loop around the currently selected event range.

Figure 8.44
Mute those events you do not wish to hear and, if desired, name the best performances

- For detailed composite take editing (especially vocal performances), you may need to audition very short sections of the material, such as when editing single words in a vocal line. In these cases, it is best to work at

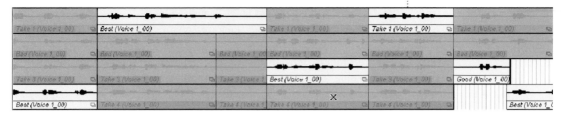

higher zoom factors with the Snap button de-activated (Figure 8.45).

- So far, you have been attempting to chain together all the very best parts of the material, ensuring that there are no dramatic signal level changes and no audible interference as you pass from one event to another. When the edited events produce the desired composite version, you may be able to improve matters further by setting up crossfades between all adjacent events. To achieve this, delete all muted events, select the remaining events by pressing Ctrl + A on the computer keyboard, and create the crossfades by pressing 'X' (Figure 8.46).

Figure 8.45
Work at higher zoom factor with the Snap button de-activated for detailed editing

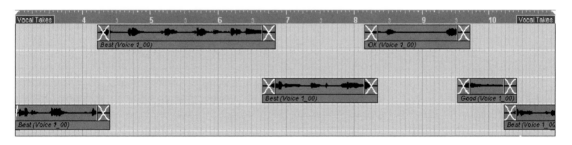

- If there are overlaps between the events, the crossfades have the duration of the respective overlaps. If there is no overlap between adjacent events, the events are automatically lengthened according to the default length setting in the Crossfade dialogue. If events are not adjacent, no automatic crossfade is created. The crossfade curves may be individually or globally adjusted in the Crossfade dialogue (see 'Fades and Crossfades', above). The ideal crossfade length depends very much on the effect you are trying to produce. For example, if you are aiming for seamless joins on vocal lines try a length of 30ms with a spline-shaped curve with or without Equal Gain, as shown in Figure 8.47.

Figure 8.46
Delete all muted events and apply crossfades for smoothing the joins between the remaining events, (the lengths of the crossfades in this screenshot have been artificially lengthened – in reality they may be much shorter)

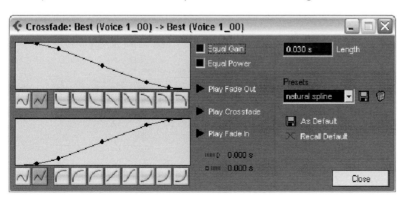

Figure 8.47
Try these settings in the Crossfade dialogue for seamless joins between vocal takes

Creating and handling regions in the Sample editor

Regions are areas within your audio material marked as sections of interest or relevance. They provide useful signposts to specific passages within your audio recordings. They are created, viewed and edited within the Sample editor but may also be created automatically when recording audio in cycle mode or when using Detect Silence. Here, we take a look at how regions are handled in the Sample editor. Let's imagine that you have made a recording of some speech from the media, some part of which you intend to use as a quotation, or as an effect within your music. Regions help you make your choice more easily. Proceed as follows:

- Double-click on the audio event which contains the speech to open the Sample editor. Activate the Show Regions button to open the Regions display (Figure 8.48).

Figure 8.48
Open the Sample editor and activate the Show Regions button

- Activate the local audition and loop buttons on the Sample editor toolbar. Playback commences from the start of the audio event (Figure 8.49). Listen to the audio and select an area of interest with the Range selection tool. Since you are in local playback and loop mode the cursor jumps to the range you have selected and continues to loop around the selected area.

Figure 8.49
Activate the local audition and loop buttons

- Select a word, a phrase or a whole sentence within the audio. Fine tune the range selection by dragging the start or end points. When you are satisfied, click on the Add Region button above the Regions list and enter a name for the region. You might use the first word of each speech snippet as the region name (Figure 8.50).

Figure 8.50
Select, add and name a region

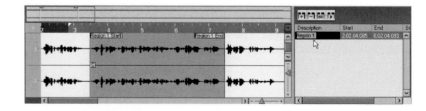

- Select the next area of interest in the audio material and add and name another region. You are still in local playback and loop mode so, each time you make a new selection, the cursor automatically loops within it. Continue in the same manner until you have marked all areas of interest. You now have a list of regions (Figure 8.51).

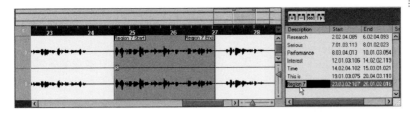

Figure 8.51
Select, add and name other regions to form a list of regions

- Stop playback by de-activating the Audition button. Do not deactivate the loop button. You can now audition a region in the audio clip by selecting any Region in the Regions list and clicking on the Region list Play button (Figure 8.52). Playback loops around the selected region. Audition any other region in the list by selecting it without dropping out of playback.

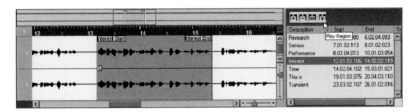

Figure 8.52
Audition each region by selecting it in the list and activating the Region list Play button

- The regions are shown in a time-ordered list but, of course, you can audition them in any order you like. Effectively, you can now jump to any point of interest with greater ease and, by naming each region descriptively, you have created convenient signposts which help you navigate within the audio material. When you have made a decision about which region you intend to use, fine tune its start and end points as desired and drag and drop it from the Regions list into the Project window (Figure 8.53).

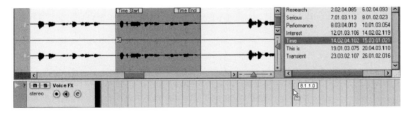

Figure 8.53
Drag and drop the chosen region from the Regions list into the Project window

Creating and editing hitpoints in the Sample editor

What are hitpoints?

Hitpoints are special markers calculated within an audio clip at the locations of the main peaks in the signal. A signal peak is a point in the waveform where there is rapid amplitude gain, otherwise known as an attack transient. These points normally correspond with the main performance hits in the signal and can be seen as mountain-like peaks in the waveform display. They might correspond with each note played by a musical instrument, each word sung by a vocalist, or the main percussive hits in a drum or percussion performance. By placing markers at these points we capture the rhythmic pulse and divide the performance into its constituent parts. In Cubase, a segment of audio found between a pair of hitpoints is known as an audio slice. A common objective, especially when slicing drum and percussion loops, is to finish up with a single sound or drum hit between each consecutive pair of hitpoints.

Calculating Hitpoints

Figure 8.54
The Sample editor Inspector Hitpoints section

To calculate hitpoints select the Hitpoints tab in the Sample editor Inspector and drag the sensitivity slider to the right. Hitpoints are calculated for the current range selection, or the whole clip if no range selection has been made. Thereafter, these hitpoints remain attached to the clip. Hitpoints are shown or hidden by toggling the Hitpoints section open or closed. Hitpoints may be re-calculated at any time by clicking on the Hitpoint section's Remove All button and resetting the sensitivity slider. Alternatively, use the commands in the Audio / Hitpoints sub-menu. You may wish to re-calculate when you have made a new range selection or are not satisfied with your hitpoint editing. The number of displayed hitpoints depends upon the sensitivity slider position and the setting in the Use menu. The sensitivity slider displays more hitpoints the more you move it to the right. When the Use menu is set to 'All', all the calculated hitpoints are active and visible. When the Use menu is set to one of the note values (1/4, 1/8, 1/16, 1/32 or metric bias) only those hitpoints which are near to the chosen note resolution are taken into account. Hitpoints may also be entered manually by activating the Edit hitpoints button and clicking in the display while holding Alt.

Editing hitpoints

Hitpoint editing is only possible when the Edit hitpoints button is active. Editing is used in combination with the hitpoint sensitivity slider to finish up with the desired number of hitpoints at the appropriate positions in the waveform. When the Edit hitpoints button is active, the pointer assumes a number of different functions according to where you place it in the display. These are as follows:

- Play – when moved between two hitpoints the pointer changes to a speaker symbol allowing you to audition the audio between the two points. This is used to verify the accuracy and suitability of the calculated hitpoints.
- Insert – moving the pointer to the central area of the display while holding Alt allows you to manually insert a hitpoint (a pencil symbol is shown).
- Move – locating the pointer on a hitpoint handle in the upper part of the display allows you to drag the hitpoint to a new location (the hitpoint is highlighted in green).
- Disable – locating the pointer on a hitpoint handle in the upper part of the display while holding Alt allows you to disable the hitpoint (the hitpoint is highlighted in green and a disable cross appears). Disabling is useful when your chosen sensitivity setting has calculated correctly positioned hitpoints throughout most of the waveform except for a small

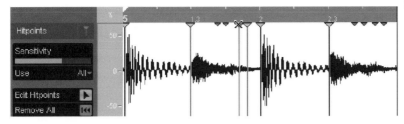

Figure 8.55
Disabling erroneous hitpoints in Edit hitpoints mode

number of erroneous hitpoints. Disabling the offending hitpoints provides a quick and convenient solution (see Figure 8.55). If required, disabled hitpoints can be re-enabled by clicking on the hitpoint handle a second time. (Note: you cannot disable a manually inserted hitpoint).

- Lock – clicking once on the hitpoint handle locks the hitpoint (at which time it is shown in dark blue). Locking a hitpoint ensures that it is not affected by further manipulations of the hitpoint sensitivity slider. This is useful when you wish to choose a specific selection of hitpoints which are at the correct positions in the waveform and then remove the rest by lowering the sensitivity slider. Any locked hitpoints remain in the display regardless of how much you reduce the sensitivity (see Figure 8.56).

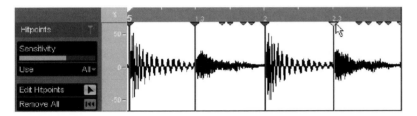

Figure 8.56
Lock the best hitpoints and then remove all other hitpoints by lowering the hitpoint sensitivity slider

- Delete – to delete a hitpoint, drag it out of the Sample editor.

Creating a groove template from hitpoints

As outlined above, hitpoints mark those points in the audio waveform where there is rapid amplitude gain (attack transients). In the case of drum and percussion loops, these points correspond with the rhythmic pulse of the material. Since, by calculating the hitpoints, we have effectively created a rhythmic template of the performance, why not extract this data for use in other parts of Cubase? This is indeed what you can do using the Sample editor Inspector's Definition and Hitpoints sections. To create your own groove quantize template proceed as follows:

- Double-click on the target audio event to open the Sample editor. Activate the Inspector and select the Definition section.
- If you are using a range selection, select the Range tool and select the appropriate range within the audio which corresponds with a precise number of bars and beats. Otherwise ignore this step. See 'Editing a loop in the Sample editor' below for details of how to find the range you need.
- In the Definition section, select the desired resolution in the Grid menu (try 1/4, 1/8 or 1/16 note). Activate the Auto adjust button to calculate the tempo of the audio. The grid lines should line up with the main peaks

Figure 8.57
Adjust the hitpoint sensitivity slider to match the hitpoints to the main hits in the rhythm

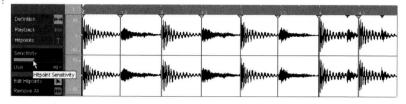

in the waveform. Press the reset button and try again if you need to re-calculate.

- Open the Hitpoints section of the Inspector and drag the Sensitivity slider to the right until one hitpoint appears for each hit in the rhythm (Figure 8.57). Try selecting 1/4, 1/8 or 1/16 note in the Use menu. Audition the audio between each consecutive pair of hitpoints to verify the results.
- In the Hitpoints section, click on the Make groove button to create the groove template (Figure 8.58).
- Open the Quantize type menu to reveal the newly added groove which appears last in the list with the same name as the audio event from which it was extracted (Figure 8.59).

Figure 8.58
Click on the Make Groove button to create the groove template

Figure 8.59 (right)
The new groove quantize preset appears in the Quantize type menu

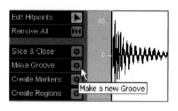

Info

It is possible to create a groove template by selecting a tightly edited audio event and then selecting Audio / Hitpoints / Create Groove Quantize from Hitpoints. You will need to enter the original tempo of the audio into a pop-up box. While this is quick, it is not as accurate as the more detailed technique outlined here.

Tip

One of the most useful functions when working with loops is 'Loop selection', found in the Transport menu or activated using Shift + G. Loop Selection engages cycle playback over the current event or range selection and functions in the Project window, Audio Part editor or Sample editor.

Working with loops

Editing a loop in the Sample editor

This section outlines how to edit the length of a drum or percussion recording in the Sample editor to create a loop. Proceed as follows:

- Double-click on the audio event which contains the drum or percussion material to open the Sample editor. Use the Range selection tool to mark the approximate range of the prospective loop.
- De-activate the autoscroll button. Activate the local audition and loop buttons (or press Shift + G). Playback loops around the selected area.
- Select the Region button and add the selection to the region list. This serves as a backup of your rough loop if you should lose your selection at a later point in this process.
- Tune the length of the loop by dragging the start or end points of the selected region. The Range selection tool changes into a double arrow whenever you place it over the start or end points of the selection. Each time you set a new position for either the start or end, playback recommences from the start of the loop. This helps you set the start to the exact downbeat and fine tune the length to a precise number of bars. Try activating the Snap to zero crossing button to avoid clicks.
- For sample-accurate editing double-click in the start or end fields of the

Inspector's Range section and use the up / down arrow keys on the
computer keyboard to change the values one sample at a time.
- Once you are happy with the loop, mark it as a new region using the Add
Region button and name it appropriately.
- To create a new event for the loop, select the new region in the Region
list and drag it onto the Project window event display. Alternatively,
press Ctrl / Command and drag from the range selection in the waveform
display.

Tip

If you are working at high magnification and have accidentally lost the start point of your range selection,
proceed as follows: stop playback, activate autoscroll, and press L to locate the start of the selection.
Now de-activate autoscroll and press Shift + G to recommence loop playback without losing the start
point.

Audio slicing a loop in the Sample editor

Slicing the audio

As outlined elsewhere, hitpoints allow you to find the main rhythmic components in your audio material. In Cubase, each section marked by a pair of hitpoints is known as an audio slice. Audio events can be automatically divided
up into audio slices using the Slice and Close button in the Hitpoints section
of the Sample editor Inspector or by selecting Audio / Hitpoints / Create audio
slices from hitpoints. In the case of drum loops, each audio slice usually contains a single sound or hit on each beat or fraction of a beat in the loop. The
events contained within the resulting sliced part automatically follow any
changes in tempo without changing the pitch of the sound and without the
side-effects of time stretching. This results in more natural sounding loops
when you adjust them away from their original tempos and allows you to
freely use tempo changes throughout the project. To create audio slices from
a drum loop, proceed as follows:

Info

Cubase supports the import of
REX files giving users access
to a rich source of ready-made
audio sliced material as supplied
by third party sound library
developers.

- Select the audio event which contains the target loop and double-click
on it to open the Sample editor. Select the intended loop using the
Range selection the start and end points. Make sure the start point corresponds precisely with the downbeat of the first beat of the loop and
adjust the end point so the loop plays back over the required number of
beats (Figure 8.60). Ignore this first step if you are using a library drum
loop which is already tightly edited and whose corresponding clip fills the
whole event. In this case you need not make a range selection.

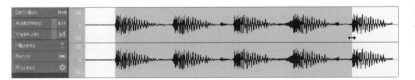

Figure 8.60
Adjust the loop so that it plays for the
required number of beats

- Open the Definition section of the Sample editor Inspector. Select the desired resolution in the Grid menu (try 1/8 note). Activate the Auto adjust button.

- Open the Hitpoints section of the Sample editor Inspector and drag the sensitivity slider to the right until one hitpoint appears for each hit in the rhythm (Figure 8.61).

Figure 8.61
Adjust the hitpoint sensitivity slider to match the hitpoints to the main hits in the rhythm

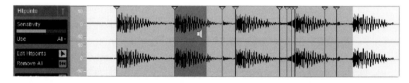

- Audition the audio between each pair of hitpoints to verify the results (Figure 8.62). The audio slice turns blue as it is played. Attempt to produce audio slices where one sound or hit is present in each slice. For greater accuracy when using a range selection, you may need to re-adjust the range start point to the position of the first hitpoint. If this is the case, re-activate the Auto adjust button in the Definition section to re-adjust the grid. You may get better results by using a greater number of hitpoints than expected, thus dividing the audio into smaller slices. The more accurate the audio slices, the more accurate will be the handling of the result when played back at different tempos. You cannot always rely upon the accuracy of the automatically generated hitpoints.

Tip

or click-free slices try manually dragging hitpoints to the nearest zero crossing point with the snap to zero crossing point button activated. For this technique it is best to work at high magnification factors.

Figure 8.62
Audition each audio slice by clicking between each pair of hitpoints in Edit hitpoints mode

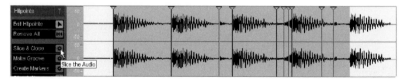

- When you are satisfied with the settings, click on the Slice and Close button in the Hitpoints section to create the audio slices (Figure 8.63).

Figure 8.63
Click on the Slice and Close button to create the audio slices

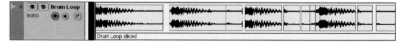

- As soon as you click on the Slice and Close button, the Sample editor is automatically closed and the original audio event in the Project window is replaced by an audio part which contains the new audio slices (Figure 8.64). The timing of the slices in the new audio part are automatically adjusted to match the current tempo of the project. When you change the tempo the sliced part follows.

Figure 8.64
A new audio part containing the audio slices is created in the Project window

For detailed audio slice editing, double-click on the sliced part to open the Audio Part editor. Activate cycle playback to audition the part. Without stopping playback you can double-click on any problem slice to re-open the Sample editor. De-activate autoscroll in the Sample editor. This helps you focus on the selected problem slice and you can now drag the hitpoint at the start of the slice to a new position to change its timing or ensure a clean attack. After any editing, and while still in playback, click on the Slice and Close button again to re-calculate the slices. You can re-calculate the audio slices in this manner as many times as you wish. The new settings are immediately taken into account in the sliced part. All this can be achieved without dropping out of playback, allowing you to quickly verify the results. For fine tuning and avoiding clicks try activating the snap to zero crossing button. Placing your hitpoints at zero crossing points may help optimise the timing precision and the crispness of the attack segments of your slices.

Tip

To assign sliced audio to the supplied Groove Agent One pads, select all slices in the Audio Part editor and drag onto a pad. Hold down shift and release the mouse to drop the slices to consecutive pads. To create a corresponding MIDI part with the original timing of the slices, drag from the exchange pad (double arrow) into the Project window.

Closing the gap

If you change the tempo of Cubase by a relatively small amount, the timing changes of sliced data within audio parts remain fairly transparent. However, reducing the tempo by more than a few beats-per-minute results in gaps between the audio slices. Figure 8.65 shows the audio slices for a drum loop where the project has been set to the original tempo of the loop, at 120bpm.

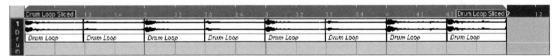

Figure 8.65
Audio slices for a drum loop set to its original tempo of 120bpm

When the tempo is reduced to 110bpm gaps appear between the audio slices which interfere with the successful playback of the loop (Figure 8.66).

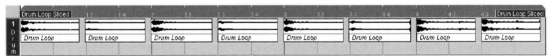

Figure 8.66
Gaps between the slices when the tempo is reduced to 110bpm

To cure the problem, select the part in the Project window, or press Ctrl + A to select all the events in the Audio Part editor, and select 'Close Gaps' in the Audio menu. This applies time stretching to each slice in order to close all the gaps (Figure 8.67).

Figure 8.67
Close the gaps using the 'Close Gaps' function

The Close Gaps function should be used only when you are sure that there will be no more tempo changes. If at a later date you decide that you wish to change the tempo again, you must revert to the original unstretched audio material.

Increasing the tempo by more than a few beats-per-minute compresses the sliced events more tightly together creating overlaps which sometimes result in clicks. To cure the clicks try setting up auto fades in the Auto fades dialogue for the track. Try activating the fade out option with a 5ms to 10ms fade time.

Changing the feel

It is sometimes appropriate to change the timing of the audio slices using quantize. This can result in a loop with a tighter feel or a completely new groove. For audio slices which have been divided into 1/8 note segments try the following:

- Double-click on the audio part containing the audio slices to open the Audio Part editor.
- Select all the slices by pressing Ctrl + A on the computer keyboard.
- Open the Quantize setup dialogue from the Quantize type menu. Set 1/8 notes in Grid and Straight in Type with a swing factor of between 50% and 100%.
- Click on the Apply Quantize button.

The events in the Audio Part editor are moved according to the quantize settings. If you like the results, try using the Close Gaps function to produce a smoother effect. This technique is sometimes effective if you need to mangle your loops beyond recognition but is highly dependent upon the nature of the target material.

> ### Tip
>
> For loop mangling try importing some REX files. First, line them up in the Project window so they play over the same range. Next select all the parts and open the Audio Part editor. In the editor, select all the slices and mute them. Finally, commence loop playback and selectively unmute the slices of your choice to create a new composite loop.

Matching the feel of an audio bass line to a MIDI kick drum

When an audio event is divided into its rhythmic components it becomes possible to process its timing according to the feel of other events or parts. For example, you could impose the timing characteristics of a MIDI kick drum onto an audio bass line, resulting in tightly synchronised kick and bass. To achieve this proceed as follows:

- Select all audio events on the audio bass instrument track.
- Press Ctrl + E to open multiple Sample editors for all audio clips associated with the selected events.
- Working on each clip in turn in the Sample editor Inspector hitpoints

section, use the sensitivity slider to calculate hitpoints at each and every bass note and then select Create events. The objective is to split events into separate shorter events each containing a single bass note. Close the Sample editor window for each clip in turn when the processing is complete.

- Select the MIDI kick drum track and activate the In Place editor for the track using the In Place editor button in the track header.
- Activate the Snap button and select 'Events' in the project window snap type menu.
- Manually drag the relevant bass note events to their nearest kick drum notes in the Project window. With the In Place editor open and 'Events' selected in the snap type menu, the bass events are now sensitive to the positions of the MIDI kick drum notes.
- Work though the whole arrangement to line up the relevant bass note events to their nearest MIDI kick drum notes.

Audio Warping in the Sample editor

Why do we need audio warping?

Most of us record our audio material synchronised to the current tempo of the project, usually by playing in time with the metronome click, and most audio material of a musical nature has some kind of inherent rhythm which can be defined as a tempo, expressed in beats-per-minute. However, what happens if you later decide to change the tempo of the project? or use a tempo ramp which gradually increases or decreases? And what happens if your audio contains unwanted tempo fluctuations? In these cases, the rhythmic pulse of the audio would no longer match the tempo of Cubase. The audio warping functions help overcome these problems. Audio warping may be applied to specific segments of the material when you need to match tempo-fluctuating audio to the bars and beats of the grid, or it may be applied in a special mode known as Musical mode which matches whole clips to tempo.

Info

Cubase recognises the tempo definition information contained within Acid format Wave files. These files are therefore immediately ready for Musical mode and automatically adjust to the current tempo when they are imported.

Matching tempo fluctuating audio to bars and beats using audio warp

Audio warping involves stretching or compressing the audio between chosen anchor points in the waveform. These anchor points are known as warp tabs and they appear as markers in the ruler and waveform display. Warp tabs may be created manually by activating the Free warp button in the Audio warp section of the Sample editor Inspector and clicking in the display, or they may be generated from hitpoints using Audio / Realtime processing / Create Warp tabs from hitpoints. Warp tabs may be dragged to specific bar or beat divisions along the time line thereby time stretching or compressing a segment of the audio. This allows you to correct a sloppy performance or change the feel of the audio. When you stretch or compress the audio in this way, fixed warp tabs are inserted at the start and end of the audio event. Your audio becomes rather like a curtain attached simultaneously at both ends of a curtain rail. You can stretch or compress the curtain in between for lesser or greater folds in the fabric!

Tip

Audio warping is not a good technique for correcting the timing of multiple drum tracks since you can easily suffer undesirable phasing effects between tracks. For this task ordinary cut and drag editing in the Project window or Audio Part editor may be a better choice.

1 Matching audio to bars and beats using Free warp

Free warp helps when you need to correct the timing of a rhythmic recording which was not played accurately or a drum loop with undesirable tempo changes,. This suits relatively short audio clips. The technique assumes that the rhythmic recording or loop is already close to the desired tempo. Proceed as follows:

- Double-click on the event containing the target drum loop to open the Sample editor.
- Click on the Audio warp tab and select Free warp. Activate the snap button and select the Mix warping algorithm on the toolbar.
- Zoom in to each peak in the waveform display in turn (or if preferred to the peaks which are on each beat of the bar) and verify if the start of the peak lines up with the nearest bar or beat division in the ruler. If it is inaccurate, click in the display to create a warp tab at the position of the peak and drag it to the nearest bar or beat (Figure 8.68). When the snap button is active the warp tab snaps to the chosen beat division when you drag near to it. For each warp tab you drag, time stretching is engaged over a short segment in order to match the audio to the grid.

Figure 8.68
Click in the display in Free warp mode to create a warp tab at the position of the peak and drag it to the nearest beat

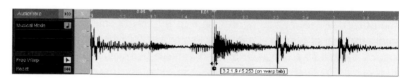

- Continue in a similar manner throughout the remaining audio and close the Sample editor when complete. The audio event is now shown with a double arrow in the lower right corner which means audio warping is engaged for this event (Figure 8.69).

Figure 8.69
Audio events containing warped audio are shown with a double arrow in the lower right corner

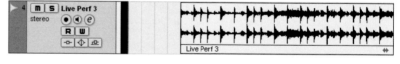

- Activate the metronome click and engage cycle playback. The audio now plays in perfect time with the click.

Tip

To delete a Warp tab, press Shift and click on the tab (an eraser is shown). To show / hide Warp tabs click on the Free warp button in the Sample editor Inspector Audio warp section.

2 Matching audio to bars and beats by creating warp tabs from hitpoints

A more detailed and precise technique for correcting audio with unwanted tempo fluctuations involves calculating hitpoints for the clip and then creating warp tabs from these. This avoids scrolling through long passages and creating warp tabs one at a time. Proceed as follows:

- Double-click on the audio event which contains the target audio to open the Sample editor.
- In the Hitpoints section of the Sample editor Inspector, adjust the hitpoint sensitivity slider and edit the hitpoints until you have one hitpoint on each significant peak in the waveform (Figure 8.70).

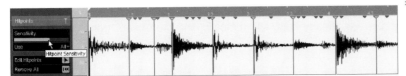

Figure 8.70
The resulting hitpoints placed on the most significant peaks in the waveform (the first bar is shown)

- Select Audio / Realtime processing / Create warp tabs from hitpoints. Warp tabs are generated at the positions of the hitpoints. Select the Audio warp section of the Sample editor Inspector and activate the Free warp button to reveal the warp tabs (Figure 8.71). The number next to each tab indicates the time-stretch status of each segment where less than 1.0 means time compression, more than 1.0 means time stretch, and exactly 1.0 means no audio warping is implemented.

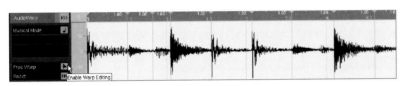

Figure 8.71
Warp tabs created from hitpoints. The warp tabs and their values are shown in the ruler

- Activate the snap button and select the Mix warping algorithm on the toolbar. To match the audio to the bars and beats, drag the appropriate warp tabs to the nearest beat divisions (Figure 8.72). Make sure that 'on warp tab' appears in the pop-up box before you drag each tab. With the snap button active the drag action snaps to the nearest beat divisions. It may not be necessary to drag all of the warp tabs. Alternatively, try selecting Quantize audio to automatically straighten up the audio to the bars and beats (Audio / Realtime processing / Quantize audio).

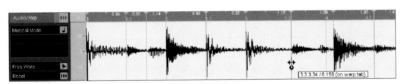

Figure 8.72
Dragging warp tabs to the nearest beat. Notice how the first few tabs now line up precisely with the beat divisions

- When processing is complete close the Sample editor. The audio event is now shown with a double arrow in the lower right corner which means audio warping is engaged for this event.
- Activate the metronome click and engage cycle playback. The audio now plays in perfect time with the click.

Tip

To undo audio warping click on the reset button in the Sample editor Inspector Audio warp section. To make audio warping a permanent part of the audio click on the Flatten button in the Sample editor Inspector Process section.

Matching audio to tempo using Musical mode

Musical mode offers you a fuss-free way of locking audio to tempo. It is especially suited to drum loops and other rhythmic material with a regular beat. It defines the internal tempo of an audio clip, matches this to the grid and applies real-time time stretching to ensure the clip follows the current tempo of Cubase. This liberates your creativity since you can now freely try out tempo changes and use lots of different audio loops of any tempo, without worrying about how you are going to make everything fit together. The following techniques help you get started with musical mode.

1 Matching audio to tempo for a drum loop of known bpm

When you already know the tempo of the drum loop, (for example, when using loops from a sample library), proceed as follows:

- Double-click on the event containing the target drum loop to open the Sample editor and then proceed with one of the following steps.
- If the clip is already tightly edited to an exact number of bars and beats Cubase may have already automatically calculated the correct tempo for the loop. In this case all you need do is activate Musical mode. The loop now follows the tempo of Cubase.
- If the clip is not tightly edited to an exact number of bars and beats but begins on the first down beat of the bar, enter the known tempo in the tempo field and then activate Musical mode. The loop now follows the tempo of Cubase.
- After activating Musical mode, you may need to drag the end point of the event to the nearest bar division in the Project window to ensure playback over a whole number of bars.

Figure 8.73
For a drum loop of known bpm, enter the tempo and activate Musical mode

2 Matching audio to tempo for a drum loop of unknown bpm

- Double-click on the event containing the target drum loop to open the Sample editor.
- Select the first bar of the loop using the Range selection tool and engage loop playback (Shift + G). If necessary, adjust the start and end points of the range selection to ensure a precise one bar loop. Verify that the loop begins on the first down beat of the bar.
- In the Definition section, click on the Auto adjust button. The internal tempo of the audio clip is calculated according to your one bar selection. Activate Musical mode.
- The loop now follows the tempo of Cubase

Figure 8.74
For a drum loop of unknown bpm, define the first bar of the loop and activate auto adjust followed by Musical mode

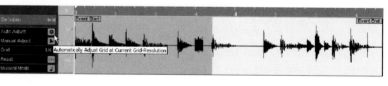

3 Matching audio to tempo using combined Musical mode and manual warp

This technique uses a combination of Musical mode and manual warping to match a loop with tempo fluctuations precisely to the individual beats of the grid. First, follow one of the techniques outlined above (option 1 or 2) to match the audio to tempo using Musical mode. With Musical mode active, your loop is now globally in time with the current tempo of Cubase. However, it is assumed here that there are still minor tempo fluctuations within the audio performance which you do not require. To remove these fluctuations, proceed as follows:

- While still in the Sample editor, click on the Definition tab, select 1/8 in the grid resolution menu and activate Manual adjust. This imposes a grid over the audio at 1/8 note intervals, indicated by vertical lines. The intention here is to align the audio at 1/8 note resolution.

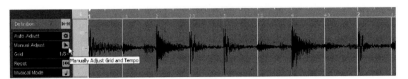

Figure 8.75
Activate Manual adjust to impose a grid over the audio

- Zoom in to the start of the audio and ensure that it begins precisely on the first down beat of the bar. The snap point and grid start should both be found at this point.
- Adjust the view to a zoom factor of around 33 using the G and H keys. Scroll through the audio using the right arrow of the horizontal scroll bar in order to find the markers which correspond to the start of each bar. These are shown as slightly thicker vertical lines. If any do not line up with the nearest peak in the waveform, click in the display and manually drag the marker to the peak. The mouse pointer changes to a double-arrow symbol and the marker is highlighted when you navigate near to it.

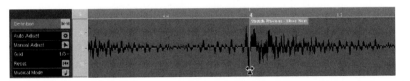

Figure 8.76
Scroll through the audio and line up the start of each bar marker to the nearest peak in the waveform

- Now go back to the start of the loop and scroll though the waveform again but this time adjusting any of the beat position markers which do not match their peaks in the waveform. The beat positions are shown as thin vertical lines.

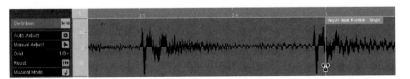

Figure 8.77
Scroll through the audio a second time and line up the beat markers to the nearest peaks in the waveform

- Once editing is complete close the Sample editor. The loop now follows the tempo of Cubase and all tempo fluctuations within the loop are straightened out to match the bars and beats.

VariAudio

VariAudio is a specialised section within the Sample editor for the editing of individual pitches within monophonic vocal recordings and other similar material. VariAudio divides the target audio into segments according to an analysis of its pitch and timing characteristics. The segments are equivalent to notes as found in a piano roll style editor like the Key editor. The pitch, length and timing of these segments can be edited in order to correct tuning and timing irregularities within a musical performance.

Tip

Try assigning Key commands to Shuttle Play 2x and Shuttle Reverse 2x. When you activate autoscroll these commands help you quickly scroll back and forth within the Sample editor display and within audio events in the Project window.

Selection and analysis

To get started with VariAudio proceed as follows:

- Double click on the target audio event to open the Sample editor.
- Select the VariAudio tab in the Sample editor inspector.
- Click on the Pitch & Warp or the Segments button. Either option analyses the audio, after which segments are superimposed over the usual waveform display. Each segment represents a separate pitch within the audio material.
- Assuming the analysis is accurate, you can edit the pitch by dragging segments up or down in Pitch & Warp mode.

Editing in detail

Segment editing varies according to whether you have activated the Segments or Pitch & Warp button. Segments mode is where you match the segments to the notes within the audio by adjusting their length and position. Pitch & Warp mode is where you change the pitch and timing of the audio. The following sections outline the details.

Segments mode

In Segments mode the segments are shown with a hashed background. In this mode you can adjust the length of the segments by dragging the start and end points, or you can split, glue, move or delete them. This helps you match the segments more closely to the audio material and compensates for inaccuracies in the initial analysis. The more accurate the segments the more transparent the pitch and timing manipulations.

The length and position of each segment normally corresponds with a single note event within the audio. Where this is not the case move the start or end points using the background waveform as a guide. The start and end anchors are shown as small double arrows when you move the mouse near the start or end points of the segment (Figure 8.78). Each segment normally ends where the next one begins. Once again, move the start or end points to butt segments together. If you need to change the position of the segment without affecting its length use the move anchor located at the upper mid section of the segment.

Figure 8.78
Move the start or end points to match the segment more accurately to the notes within the audio

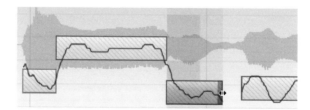

The audio analysis may occasionally produce a segment which spans two or more notes, in which case it may be necessary to split the segment into two or more separate segments. To split a segment move the mouse pointer to the lower part of the segment until you see the scissors tool appear and click at the appropriate point (Figure 8.79).

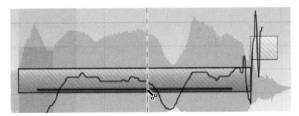

Figure 8.79
Splitting a segment which spans two notes

Similar to the latter case, the audio analysis may occasionally produce two segments for a single note, in which case it may be necessary to glue the segments together. To glue one segment to the next hold down Alt while clicking on the segment (Figure 8.80).

Tip

To quickly toggle between Pitch & Warp and Segments mode press the tab key on the computer keyboard.

Figure 8.80
Glueing two segments which span a single note

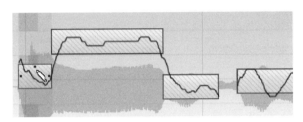

Pitch & Warp mode

In Pitch & Warp mode the segments are shown with a plain background. In this mode you change the pitch and timing of the audio. To change the pitch hover the mouse over a segment until the hand symbol appears and drag the segment up or down. When you change the pitch in this manner a virtual keyboard appears in the background to help you find the desired pitch (Figure 8.81). By default, the pitch snaps to semitone steps. To freely move the pitch without snap hold down the Shift key while dragging.

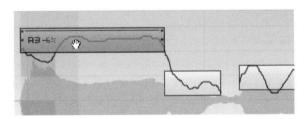

Figure 8.81
Drag segments up or down in the display to change the pitch

To change the timing drag the start or end of the segment. This inserts warp tabs around the segment and the audio is warped according to where you drag the tab along the time line (Figure 8.82).

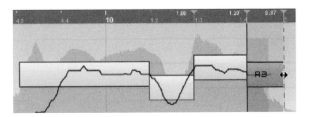

Figure 8.82
Dragging the start or end of a segment in Pitch & Warp mode warps the timing of the audio

Pitch quantize

The pitch quantize slider allows you to correct the pitch of the currently selected segment (or segments) to the nearest semitone. The higher you set the slider, the closer the segment is moved to the absolute pitch value (Figure 8.83). If the chosen segment is already at an exact semitone pitch value the pitch quantize slider has no effect.

Figure 8.83
Move the pitch quantize slider to correct the pitch

Straightening and tilting pitch modulation

Each segment is endowed with micro pitch information indicated by a curve within the segment. Micro pitch governs such things as vibrato, portamento, and any other other form of pitch modulation. Manipulating pitch modulation helps you change some of the key expressive elements within a musical performance.

The Straighten pitch slider allows you to straighten out the pitch modulation curve. The higher you set the slider the lesser the modulation (Figure 8.84). For example, this helps you straighten out vibrato where it is not desirable, or render the pitch of a sung note more stable.

Figure 8.84
Move the Straighten Pitch slider to straighten out pitch modulation such as vibrato

Micro pitch information is also responsible for the tuning inflections sometimes found at the start and end of notes. Using a technique known as tilting you can modify existing inflections or create your own. In Pitch & Warp mode, moving the mouse pointer to the top of a segment allows you to mark an anchor point around which you can tilt the micro pitch data up or down. Once you have marked the anchor point you can tilt the pitch modulation by dragging up or down at the upper left or right corners of the segment (Figure 8.85).

Figure 8.85
Tilting the pitch modulation to produce a pitch inflection at the end of a note

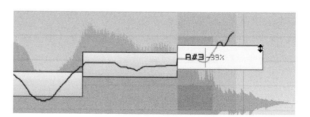

Extracting MIDI

It is possible to extract VariAudio pitch information as MIDI notes with or without pitch bend using Functions / Extract MIDI in the Inspector. You usually get a better match when you include the pitch bend data and when the segments are tightly edited. Using this function you can sing a melody into Cubase and then transcribe it into a MIDI part to trigger a synth or sampler.

Info

You can undo / redo all audio editing using the undo / redo functions in the Edit menu or by pressing Ctrl + Z (undo) or Ctrl + Shift + Z (redo). You can also step back through your edits using the Edit history window (select 'History' in the Edit menu). The edit history is cleared when you close the project.

Audio processing

This chapter describes the audio processing functions found in the Process sub-menu of the Audio menu. The audio processing functions are for off-line processing only. Off-line processing is that which does not occur in real-time and implies some kind of permanent change to the stored audio files.

The audio processing functions act upon audio data on the hard disk but due to the manner in which Cubase has been designed, two types of undo functions are available. Firstly, the normal undo/redo commands in the Edit menu are available while your project is running. Secondly, after you close the project, almost all audio editing can be modified or removed at a later date using the Offline Process History dialogue (Audio menu). This means that you can use offline audio processing with an unprecedented amount of freedom since you can always go back to the original versions of your audio files.

The processing options

Figure 9.1 shows the audio processing options in the Process menu. You can also process your audio in a similar manner using the audio plug-in effects in the Plug-ins menu (these are usually used for real-time processing and are described in Chapter 13). The basic operation of the majority of the audio processing functions is fairly easy but it is not quite so obvious how and why you might use them. The 'how and why' forms the subject matter of this chapter.

What gets affected

The processing functions may be applied to audio events, audio clips or range selections. With audio clips, the processing is applied to the whole clip. With audio events, only that part of the associated audio clip which is referenced by the event gets processed. With range selections, only that part of the associated audio clip which is referenced by the range gets processed. With multiple event selections, all audio events have the same process applied in equal amounts. For example, if you select two consecutive events and apply fade out processing, the fade does not occur over the whole length of the two events but within each single event.

| Envelope |
| Fade In |
| Fade Out |
| Gain |
| Merge Clipboard |
| Noise Gate |
| Normalize |
| Phase Reverse |
| Pitch Shift |
| Remove DC Offset |
| Resample |
| Reverse |
| Silence |
| Stereo Flip |
| Time Stretch |

Figure 9.1
The functions in the Process menu

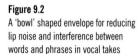

Info

Processing audio events in the Project window is useful but detailed work benefits from working within the Sample editor. The processes are conveniently available in the Process section of the Sample editor inspector. You would normally select a specific range using the Range selection tool before applying the processing.

Common buttons in the audio processing dialogues

Most of the audio processing functions feature a dialogue window which opens when they are selected. Each window has a number of common buttons and menus available. These include, in all windows, the Preview, Process and Cancel buttons and, in the envelope and fade dialogues, the presets menu and Store and Remove buttons. The Preview button allows you to hear the result of the processing before it is actually applied. When in Preview mode, the audio is played back in a continuous loop and you can hear the effect of any changes you make to the parameters in the dialogue on the next lap of the cycle. Some parameter changes re-start the audio instantaneously. All this is very useful for experimenting. The Process button processes the target audio when you are satisfied with the settings you have made. The Cancel button allows you to leave the dialogue without applying any processing. The presets menu and buttons allow you to store (or remove) your own presets. Some dialogues have More and Less buttons for showing or hiding a number of additional parameters.

The Process functions

Envelope

The Envelope function (Figure 9.2) applies an amplitude envelope to the selected audio. Spline, damped spline or linear curves are available or you can create your own shapes by clicking and dragging on the curve, whereupon a new breakpoint is added. The breakpoint handles may be dragged to any position within the display and are deleted by dragging them outside of the window. There are always at least three breakpoints in the display; one at the start, one at the end and one somewhere in between. The uppermost limit of the display represents unity gain so that a straight line drawn at the top of the display results in no change in amplitude in the target audio.

The Envelope function is good for applying multiple breakpoint envelopes to audio files in a number of creative and corrective applications. For example, unwanted breaths or syllables which are too loud within a vocal performance can be tamed by carefully reducing the level at the offending points in the waveform. For such correction, select each offending part of the waveform in the Sample editor and apply your chosen envelope to each in turn. If you are deleting unwanted breathing and lip noise between vocal lines or within speech, a 'bowl' shaped envelope produces more natural results than applying silence (Figure 9.2).

Figure 9.2
A 'bowl' shaped envelope for reducing lip noise and interference between words and phrases in vocal takes

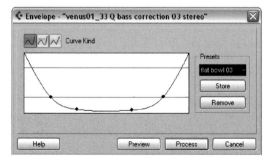

Fade in and Fade out

The Fade in and Fade out dialogues provide an alternative method of applying fades when you do not wish to use the usual blue fade handles within the audio events. The advantage of using the blue handles is that a number of audio events which refer to the same audio clip can each have an independent fade curve. Conversely, fades set up from the Process menu are applied directly to the audio clip. This is advantageous when you require global fade settings which are applied to all events which refer to the same section of an audio clip.

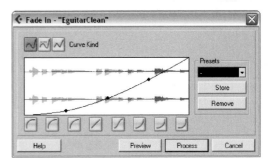

Figure 9.3
Fade in dialogue

The Fade in and Fade out functions open similar dialogue windows, except that one has the inverse fade characteristics of the other (Figure 9.3). The fade dialogues allow you to set the characteristics of the fade curves by clicking on any of the eight preset curve buttons or you can set up custom shapes by dragging handles directly in the curve display. The curve of the Fade in dialogue always starts in the lower left corner of the display and finishes in the upper right corner (the inverse is true for the Fade out dialogue). Spline, damped spline and linear curve characteristics are available and you can save and recall your own presets.

The Fade functions are sometimes useful for applying very short fades (5-10ms) at the beginning or end of an audio file to mask sharp transients or digital clicks. This would normally be achieved at a high zoom factor in the Sample editor and results in an audio file which starts and ends more smoothly. Fades out and in are also helpful when used together with the Silence function (outlined below) since fades to and from digital silence are often better than brutally cutting to silence in one move.

Gain

The Gain function (Figure 9.4) allows you to add gain or attenuate the amplitude level of the target audio between -50dB and +20dB. The parameters include a main gain slider and pre and post crossfade sliders. As you move the slider, the percentage increase in level is shown as well as the amount of increase/decrease in dBs.

When in preview mode, any audio clipping is indicated in the text line below the main gain slider. This is excellent for warning you of marginal clipping which may otherwise go unnoticed. The pre and post crossfade sliders allow you to apply the gain change gradually either at the start or end of the target audio. A Pre-Crossfade setting indicates that the gain change should start gradually from the onset of the target audio selection and should only reach its full effect at the time specified in the Pre-Crossfade field. A Post- Crossfade setting indicates that the gain change should gradually be removed, starting at the time specified in the Post-Crossfade field before the end of the audio selection.

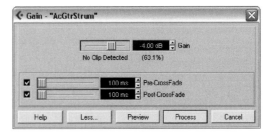

Figure 9.4
Gain dialogue

The Gain function is a powerful level management tool which might be applied to recordings with problematic level changes, such as a vocalist who

Tip

When using the Process functions for editing in fine detail in the Sample editor, always work with the Snap to zero crossing button activated. This avoids clicks and glitches between the processed and unprocessed parts of the audio clip.

is occasionally singing either too close or too far away from the microphone or for cutting down sudden extreme peaks or resonances in the audio material. It is also a useful alternative for manually reducing background noise and interference in vocal and lead guitar parts. For detailed editing, it is a good idea to work with the Gain function in the Sample editor (with the Snap to Zero crossing button activated).

Merge Clipboard

Merge Clipboard (Figure 9.5) allows you to merge the contents of the clipboard with the currently selected range when working in the Sample editor. Merge Clipboard is only available if you have used Cut or Copy in the Sample editor (i.e. when the clipboard contains audio data) and no merge operation is possible unless you have made a range selection. The merge operation begins at the start point of the range selection and continues to the end of the selection or until the end of the clipboard contents, whichever comes first.

Figure 9.5
Merge Clipboard dialogue

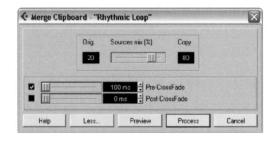

The Merge Clipboard dialogue features a percentage slider where you can select the percentage level of the original audio (the current selection) and the copied audio (the audio data in the clipboard), and pre and post fade options for the merging operation. The pre and post options allow you to merge the clipboard gradually either at the start or end of the target audio. A Pre-Crossfade setting indicates that the clipboard should be merged gradually from the onset of the target audio selection and should only reach its full effect at the time specified in the Pre-Crossfade field. A Post-Crossfade setting indicates that merged audio should gradually be removed, starting at the time specified in the Post-Crossfade field before the end of the audio selection.

Merging audio is good for creating sound effects and hybrid instrument, drum and percussion sounds. For example, by merging the audio from a number of different snare drums you can create your own hybrid snare sound. In this context, it is worth experimenting with the pre and post crossfade options of the Merge Clipboard dialogue in combination with the percentage slider, where you might effectively retain the attack of the original instrument and merge the decay of the clipboard. The same technique could be applied to create your own hybrid bass drum sound. This is particularly applicable to working with audio slices in hitpoint mode where it is easier to copy and merge between different slices. When copying and merging between different audio clips try working with two or more Sample editor windows open simultaneously.

Tip

To merge the attack of one drum sound with the decay of another, try setting the Merge Clipboard percentage slider to '100% copy' and adjust the pre crossfade to between 50 and 100 ms. Activate the pre-crossfade tick box. This mixes the attack of the original with the decay of the copied sound currently in the clipboard.

Noise Gate

A noise gate is an automatic amplitude level control device which radically attenuates the level of the target signal whenever it falls below a certain threshold. This is commonly used to filter out unwanted background noise and interference in the inactive parts of musical performances. Noise gates are very often implemented as real-time devices but the Noise Gate function in the Process menu allows you to process your audio in a more permanent and detailed fashion. The Noise Gate dialogue (Figure 9.6) features the common parameters associated with noise gating.

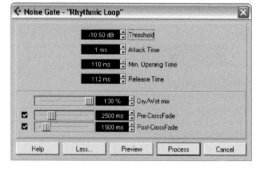

Figure 9.6
Noise Gate dialogue

The Threshold parameter sets the level at which the gate begins to close. When the input signal falls below the threshold, the target signal is attenuated (cut). The Attack determines the speed with which the noise gate opens to allow the signal through when the level rises above the threshold. The Minimum Opening Time sets a fixed time for which the gate is held open once the threshold has been exceeded. This allows you to impose a time for which the gate is sure to stay open in material featuring radical level changes and avoids chattering effects (rapid opening and closing of the gate). The Release Time determines how fast the signal is attenuated when it falls below the threshold. The Dry/Wet mix slider determines the mix between the original signal and the gated signal. The Pre and Post Crossfade options allow you to impose the gating action gradually either at the start or end of the target audio. A Pre-Crossfade setting indicates that the gating action should occur gradually from the onset of the target audio selection and should only reach its full effect at the time specified in the Pre-Crossfade field. A Post-Crossfade setting indicates that the gating effect should gradually be removed, starting at the time specified in the Post-Crossfade field before the end of the audio selection.

The Noise Gate function is a useful alternative to the supplied Gate and VST Dynamics plug-ins. For the gating of background noise, try setting the Attack, Minimum Opening and Release times to 1ms, 100ms and 100ms respectively and then find the best threshold level for your target material. Fine tune the parameters to suit the sound and the gating effect you require. For creative effects, Noise Gate is good for extremely tight gating where you only allow the extreme peaks to pass through. Try settings of 1ms, 140ms and 70ms for Attack, Minimum Opening and Release and set the threshold quite high (around -13dB). Fade this effect in or out using the Pre and Post Crossfade parameters. This works particularly well with drum loops and rhythm material. Figure 9.6 shows the settings used for an eight second drum loop where a tight gating effect is gradually imposed over the first 2.5 secs, remains at its maximum for around 4 secs and is then gradually reduced over the remaining 1.5 secs.

Normalize

Normalisation allows you to increase (or sometimes decrease) the overall amplitude of an audio file according to a specified maximum level. The process functions by finding the current maximum peak in the chosen audio and

Figure 9.7
Normalize dialogue

establishing how many dBs it is below the new maximum level you have chosen. The whole signal is then boosted by this number of dBs.

The Normalize dialogue (Figure 9.7) features just one main slider: the maximum level parameter. This is where you choose the new required maximum level for the selected audio material. The processing can also be applied gradually at the start or end of the selection using the Pre and Post Crossfade options. A Pre-Crossfade setting indicates that normalisation occurs gradually from the onset of the target audio selection and only reaches its full effect at the time specified in the Pre-Crossfade field. A Post-Crossfade setting indicates that normalisation should gradually be removed, starting at the time specified in the Post-Crossfade field before the end of the audio selection.

The maximum level possible is 0dB but it is advisable to normalise to slightly below the theoretical maximum, especially for pre-mastering applications (try -0.3dB). Normalisation is sometimes used to boost the level of audio files which were recorded at too low a level. While this can help make up for a poorly recorded signal you should be aware that the noise floor is also boosted by the same number of dBs, thus emphasising any hiss or background noise. Normalisation should therefore not be used as a routine 'quick fix' for poor recording techniques. The best remedy for sounds recorded at too low a level is to record them again at a higher level.

Normalisation might also be used to boost the signal to its absolute maximum before transferring mixed material to CD. This is common for rock, pop and dance material. However, if you are intending to boost the loudness of the target audio, normalisation is not the best option. Normalisation does *not* boost signals according to their perceived loudness but according to the highest amplitude peak in the selected material. This means that normalising finished tracks to the same maximum level does not necessarily result in tracks which have the same perceived loudness. Perceived loudness is mainly governed by the average signal level of the material and not the extreme peaks. Loudness maximisers, multi-band compressors and other kinds of processing are often a better choice for finished tracks.

Normalize should preferably not be used several times on the same audio file since this can result in degradation of the signal. Also bear in mind that normalisation should not be necessary at all if your audio has already been recorded or mixed at an optimum level.

Phase Reverse

The Phase Reverse function inverts the phase of the selection. This turns the waveform upside down since all positive elements in the signal (those above the zero amplitude line) become negative, and all negative elements in the signal (those below the zero amplitude line) become positive. This is clearly seen if you use Phase Reverse on a small test selection at a high zoom factor in the Sample editor.

Many mixing consoles, including Cubase's own mixer, feature a phase reversal button on each channel which produces a similar result. One reason for reversing the phase of a signal is when it forms the left or right channel of a stereo image which has been recorded out of phase. With one of the signals out of phase the stereo image lacks clarity and there may also be a loss of bass frequencies. The situation becomes even worse if you try to mix the two out of phase channels into a mono signal. This can result in some of the frequencies disappearing altogether.

If you suspect that a stereo file is out of phase try applying Phase Reverse to one of the channels and then compare the result to the original. When applied to a mono selection, Phase Reverse has no configurable parameters and so does not feature a dialogue window. When applied to a stereo selection Phase Reverse features a dialogue window and phase reversal can be applied to both channels, or to the left or right channel using the 'Phase Reverse on' menu (Figure 9.8).

Figure 9.8
Phase Reverse dialogue

Pitch shift

The Pitch Shift function allows the detailed modification of the pitch of the target audio with or without changing its length. It features two pages: a regular Transpose page and an Envelope page, opened by clicking on the corresponding tabs at the top of the dialogue. The Pitch Shift function is used for corrective pitch manipulation, the creation of basic harmonies and the creation of sound effects.

Transpose page

The Transpose page (Figure 9.9) features a virtual keyboard and three parameter sections; Pitch Shift Settings, Pitch Shift Base and Pitch Shift Mode.

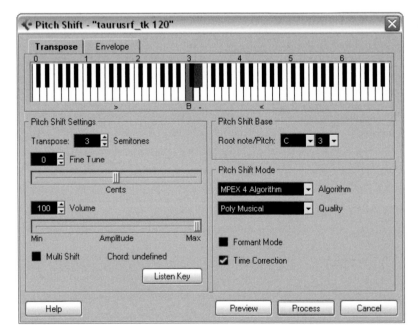

Figure 9.9
The Transpose Page of the Pitch Shift dialogue

The virtual keyboard display

The virtual keyboard offers a visual overview of the pitch shift settings. A red marker shows the position of the base pitch which provides a reference point from which to implement pitch shift operations. A blue marker indicates the amount of pitch shift relative to the base pitch. When the Multi Shift box is ticked there may be a number of blue markers in the display forming a chord for creating harmonies. The position of the blue marker(s) may be modified by clicking directly on the virtual keyboard, at which time guide tones are heard at the respective pitches so that you can hear the musical interval. If you wish to hear the blue marker pitch again, click on the Listen Key button. The position of the red marker (the base pitch) may be modified by clicking directly on the virtual keyboard while pressing Alt.

Pitch Shift Settings

This section allows you to set a pitch shift amount using a course value of between –16 and +16 semitones and a fine tuning value between –200 and +200 cents. There is also an amplitude slider for regulating the amplitude of the resulting pitch shifted audio. Activating Multi Shift mode allows you to specify a number of simultaneous pitch shifted notes by clicking on the virtual keyboard. A different amplitude may be set for each note in the chord. To include the base note in the result, click on the red marker in the virtual keyboard so that it turns blue. Clicking on the Listen Chord button allows you to hear the resulting harmony in the form of a chord.

Pitch Shift Base

This changes the position of the base pitch (the red marker) using note and octave values.

Pitch Shift Mode

This section displays the name of the pitch shift algorithm, six quality modes, and formant and time correction options.

- MPEX algorithm - MPEX is a proprietary pitch shift and time stretch algorithm designed by Prosoniq. The quality menu is only available when time correction is activated. Set the quality menu to Preview or Mix Fast when previewing, or to one of the other settings according to the type of material you are time stretching. Poly Musical is the default high quality setting which works well with drum loops, mixes and most other material. Solo Musical is recommended for vocals and instrumental solos. If these fail to produce acceptable results, try Poly Fast or Poly Complex.
- Formant mode – when activated, formant mode optimises the processing for vocal material and helps avoid some of the worst side effects of pitch shifting. For processing most other kinds of audio material, formant mode should be de-activated.
- Time correction – when time correction is activated, pitch shifting does not affect the length of the resulting audio. When time correction is deactivated, pitch shifting changes the length of the audio, resulting in an effect similar to changing the playback speed of a tape recorder.

Envelope page

The Envelope page (Figure 9.10) features a waveform display with a user configurable tuning curve and two parameter sections: Pitch Shift Settings and Pitch Shift Mode.

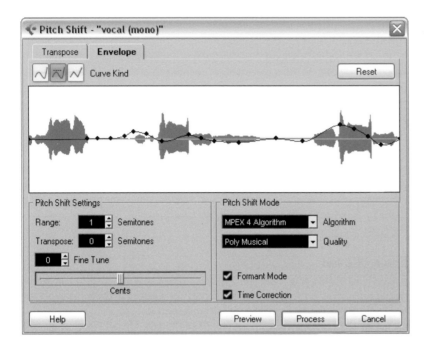

Figure 9.10
The Envelope page of the Pitch Shift dialogue

Waveform display

The waveform display features the waveform of the target audio and a user configurable tuning envelope. The horizontal centre line in the display represents zero pitch shift. The shape of the curve is changed by clicking directly in the waveform display, at which time a handle appears at the corresponding point along the curve. The handle is dragged to a new position to change the shape of the curve. When the curve rises above the centre line the pitch rises and when the curve falls below the centre line the pitch descends. To delete a handle drag it outside of the display. The currently selected handle is shown in red. Spline, damped spline and linear curve shapes are available.

Pitch Shift Settings

The Pitch Shift Settings feature Range, Transpose and Fine Tune parameters. Range determines the pitch range, represented vertically in the display, between −16 and +16 semitones. Transpose allows you to transpose the currently selected handle numerically as opposed to graphically in one semitone steps. Fine Tune provides numerical transposition of the currently selected handle in one cent steps.

Pitch Shift Mode

This section is identical to that found in the regular Transpose page (see 'Pitch Shift Mode' in the Transpose section, above, for a full explanation).

Tip

To create the effect of reducing the audio playback speed on a tape recorder, split and select the last bar of the target audio. Open the Pitch shift function in Envelope mode. De-activate time correction, use linear mode and set the range to 6 semitones. Drag the existing rightmost handle to the lower right corner of the display. After processing, split the resulting event in half and re-process the second half in the same manner with the range set to 9 semitones. Re-process the resulting event of the latter process again in the same manner with the range set to 15 semitones.

Pitch Shift summary

Using Pitch Shift in Envelope mode is excellent for manually re-tuning a melody which a vocalist has sung out of tune, and other kinds of corrective pitch manipulation. It is also good for the creation of sound effects when the time correction function is de-activated. In this context, try increasing the pitch range of the display and use spline-shaped curves for smooth pitch and speed changes.

Pitch shifting may produce undesirable side-effects, the most common of which is a 'chipmunk' effect when vocals or speech are pitch shifted upwards. Equally, when shifted downwards the human voice can take on an 'alien' character and may become unintelligible. The MPEX Solo Musical setting with Formant mode activated are usually the best settings for the human voice. However, some undesirable side-effects are inevitable if you are pitch shifting vocal sounds by more than 3-4 semitones.

The values you finally choose for any pitch shifting depends upon the audio characteristics of the material being processed and the desired effect. For example, if you are producing sound effects, you may be searching for the very audio artefacts which somebody who is transposing a vocal recording is attempting to avoid.

Remove DC Offset

A DC offset occurs when there is too much direct current (DC) in the signal. In extreme cases, a DC offset manifests itself as a waveform which is not visually centred around the zero axis in the waveform display. This is usually due to mismatches between audio equipment at the time of recording. A DC offset is problematic since it affects where the zero crossing points in the waveform appear and interferes which certain kinds of processing.

The Remove DC Offset function eliminates the DC offset. It is normally applied to whole clips or whole audio files since a DC offset is invariably present throughout an entire recording. If you wish to check a clip for DC offset, select it in the Pool and then select Statistics in the Audio menu.

Remove DC Offset has no dialogue window.

Resample

The Resample function changes the sample rate of the selected audio. Changing the sample rate affects the pitch and length. The Resample interface features two fields where you can either set a new sample rate directly or change the sample rate in terms of a percentage. The original sample rate of the selected audio is shown at the top of the dialogue. You can change the sample rate directly by double clicking in the 'New rate' field and entering a new value. Alternatively, you can change the percentage value in the 'Difference' field.

Resample allows the changing of the pitch and length over an extremely wide range providing a percentage range of between -99% and +1000%. Negative percentages speed up the sound, making the length shorter and the pitch higher. Positive percentages slow down the sound, making the length longer and the pitch lower. A value of 0% means that the audio is at its original sample rate (i.e. no change), a value of 100% is twice the sample rate, and a value of 1000% is eleven times the sample rate. -50% is half the original sample rate. Using the more extreme settings results in audio played back at ultra slow or ultra fast speeds. Resample is always worth a try for the creation of special effects and is a valuable alternative to the Pitch Shift and Time Stretch functions.

Figure 9.11
Resample dialogue

Reverse

The Reverse function simply reverses the selection. In other words, after processing, you can play the audio backwards. Great! But what could we use this for? Reversing certain kinds of audio material produces a kind of crescendo, similar to a drum roll. Favourite material for this kind of effect includes snare drum hits, (preferably with a reverb tail), and cymbals. Reversals on any kind of audio material can sometimes produce startling results which are good for sound effects, and shorter reversed segments can often find a place in a rhythmic pattern. See 'Combination Processing' below for an example of how to use the Reverse function in combination with other processing.

The Reverse function has no dialogue window.

Silence

The Silence function overwrites the current selection with complete silence. This is most often useful when working in fine detail in the Sample editor. Much of the time you might clean up audio events in the Project window by dragging the start and end points to mask the unwanted material but, for high precision silencing of multiple sections, it is easier to edit in the Sample editor. In the latter case, activate the Sample editor's Snap to Zero crossing button to avoid digital clicks.

Brutally removing all unwanted noises in a vocal recording with the Silence function alone is rarely a satisfactory solution. Sudden changes between background ambience and absolute digital silence stick out like a sore thumb and in many cases the silence actually emphasises the background noise. The Silence function is therefore best used in combination with the Fade functions (outlined above) to fade down to the silence and fade back in to the wanted material after the silence. Alternatively, use real-time noise gating or the Noise Gate function.

The Silence function has no dialogue window.

Stereo Flip

The Stereo Flip function is for various kinds of stereo processing and therefore works with stereo files only. The Stereo Flip dialogue (Figure 9.12) features a mode selection menu and Pre and Post Crossfade parameters.

Stereo Flip includes a number of modes for processing stereo material. These include the following:

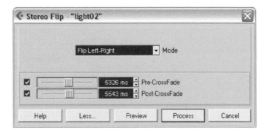

Figure 9.12
Stereo flip dialogue

- Flip Left-Right – reverses the stereo image by copying the left channel to the right channel and the right channel to the left channel.
- Left to Stereo – copies the left channel to the right channel.

- Right to Stereo – copies the right channel to the left channel.
- Merge – merges the left and right channels into both channels, producing a mono result.
- Subtract – subtracts the left channel information from the right, and the right channel information from the left, thereby attenuating all audio in the centre of the stereo image.

The processing can be applied gradually at the start or end of the selection using the Pre and Post Crossfade options. A Pre-Crossfade setting indicates that the change in the stereo image occurs gradually from the onset of the target audio selection and only reaches its full effect at the time specified. A Post-Crossfade setting indicates that the stereo processing should gradually be removed, starting at the time specified in the Post-Crossfade field before the end of the audio selection.

Stereo Flip has a number of uses for the processing of stereo material. The most obvious is for the correction of a recording where the left and right sides of the stereo image were inadvertently reversed. The second, third and fourth options in the mode menu all provide ways of creating a monophonic result where both channels contain the same signal. This strengthens the centre of the stereo image. In contrast, Subtract attenuates the centre of the stereo image and is therefore useful for taking out the voice from a stereo recording, for karaoke style purposes. Using the Pre and Post Crossfade options allows you to gradually fade in or fade out the stereo manipulation, and when used with Flip Left Right mode produces stereo sweeping effects between the left and right channels.

Time Stretch

Time stretching allows the changing of the length of the chosen audio material without changing the pitch. The use of the term 'time stretch' is slightly misleading since you can both stretch and compress the length of the target audio.

Although time stretching may be applied quickly by resizing events using the time stretch function of the Object selection tool in the Project window, using the Time Stretch function in the Process menu (Figure 9.13) allows optimum use of the time stretch algorithms, the adjustment of the length in

Figure 9.13
Time Stretch dialogue

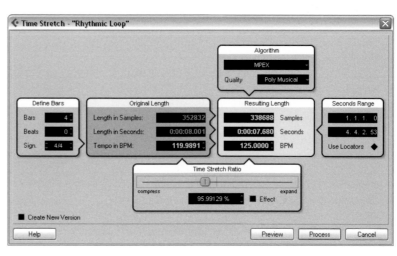

terms of tempo and gives a wider range of options. The Time Stretch function is the preferred choice when you are processing important material and want to be sure of producing the best possible result.

The Time Stretch dialogue (Figure 9.13) features a number of sections where you set various parameters which govern the time stretching operation.

Original Length and Define Bars sections

The Original Length section is where you see the details of the target audio in terms of its current length in samples and seconds. If you know the number of bars and time signature of the target selection, you can enter this in the Define Bars section. This information is used to define the tempo. This allows you to time stretch according to tempo rather than time, by changing the BPM field in the Resulting Length section.

Time Stretch Ratio and Range sections

These sections allow you to set up time stretching according to a ratio or according to a defined bar range. You may also use the current range of the left and right locators by activating 'Use Locators'. The compress / expand slider shows the amount of compression or expansion as a percentage ratio. It can be adjusted directly by moving the slider handle. When the Effect box is unticked, compress / expand values between 75 and 125% are available. This is the standard mode when you want to minimise the side-effects of time stretching. When the Effect box is ticked, compress / expand values between 10 and 1000% are available in Real-time mode and between 50 and 200% are available in MPEX mode. The compress / expand slider and range settings are mutually inter-dependent and modifying one always modifies the other.

Resulting Length section

The Resulting Length section shows you the length of the time stretched audio which results from the current settings in the other sections. The length is shown in samples, seconds and BPM. The values may also be directly modified, which in turn modifies the Range and Time Stretch Ratio sections.

The Algorithm section

The Algorithm section determines which time stretch algorithm is used for the operation. There are two algorithms available as follows:

- MPEX – MPEX is a proprietary time stretch algorithm designed by Prosoniq. MPEX stands for 'Minimum Perceived Loss Time Compression / Expansion'. This sometimes gives better results when you want your sound to stay true to the character of the original. It is recommended for vocals, instrumental solos, drum loops and mixes. Set the quality menu to Preview or Mix Fast when previewing, or to one of the other settings according to the type of material you are time stretching. Poly Musical is the default high quality setting which works well with drum loops, mixes and most other material. Solo Musical is recommended for vocals and instrumental solos. If these fail to produce acceptable results, try Poly Fast or Poly Complex.

- Realtime – uses the same time stretch algorithm as that which is used for the audio warp functions. Variations in the quality of the algorithm are chosen in the Presets menu. This is a good all-round alternative to MPEX.

Using time stretch

Time stretch can be used to great effect for establishing new tempos for drum loops. Like pitch shifting, time stretching is also excellent for creating sound effects. When audio material is time stretched, Cubase must build the audio data required to make the file longer. Depending on the type of material being processed, this may not always sound entirely natural. A similar problem occurs when the audio material is time compressed. In general, stretching or shrinking a file by more than about 15% begins to produce undesirable audio artefacts.

When working with drum loops, the loop should already have been edited so that its duration fits a specific number of bars. The number of bars, or the tempo (if known), is entered in the Original Length or Range sections. You may then enter a new tempo for the loop in the BPM field of the Resulting Length section. Alternatively, you can set up a specific range into which you want the time stretched loop to fit by dragging a left/right locator range in the ruler and clicking the 'Use Locators' button in the Range section.

For sound effects, try using more extreme time expansion and compression percentages. This is best achieved in the Time Stretch Ratio section using the compress / expand slider with the effect box ticked. Use the Realtime algorithm in Advanced mode and set grain size to 222, overlap to 50% and variance to 100% in the Advanced Warp Settings dialogue. Good source material for this includes vocals, speech, percussion and real-world sounds such as birdsong, animal calls, running water, sea waves and atmospherics.

Combination processing

One single processing function is not always enough to bring about the desired result, especially when working in a creative context. The following describes a technique for creating a backward reverb effect.

Backward reverb (or echo) is popular for the production of surreal ambient effects, particularly with guitar and vocals. It is achieved by playing the audio backwards and adding reverb or echo to the reversed sound. After adding the effect, the audio is then played in its normal direction. The result is a backward reverb or echo occurring before each peak within the audio. This produces the aforementioned surreal ambient effect. The effect is created in Cubase using the Reverse function and the supplied plug-in effects. Proceed as follows:

Figure 9.14
Select an audio event containing a drum loop or other rhythmic material

- Select the audio material you wish to process. For this exercise, it is best to work with an audio event in the Project window (Figure 9.14). Try using a drum loop or other rhythmic material.

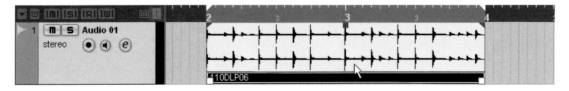

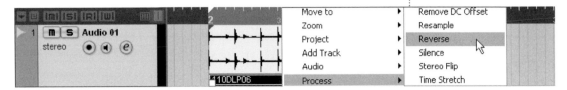

- Select the Reverse function in the Process menu. The selected audio event now plays backwards (Figure 9.15).
- Select RoomWorks from the Audio / Plug-ins sub-menu. Here you are applying the reverb as an offline process rather than as a real-time effect (Figure 9.16).

Figure 9.15
Reverse the audio using the Reverse function

- In the RoomWorks interface, select 'FX Auxiliary Verb' in the preset menu. Click on the 'More' button and adjust the wet / dry mix to 100%and 0% respectively. Activate the Tail parameter and enter a reverb tail of 1000ms (Figure 9.17). Click on the Preview button to audition the result and when you are satisfied click on the Process button.

Figure 9.16
Select RoomWorks from the Plug-ins submenu

- Apply the Reverse function to the audio event a second time. The original audio now plays back in its normal direction but the reverb effect is reversed and placed in front of the peaks in the waveform. This produces the surreal effect described above (Figure 9.18).

Figure 9.17
Adjust the parameters in the Roomworks interface to add reverb to the selection

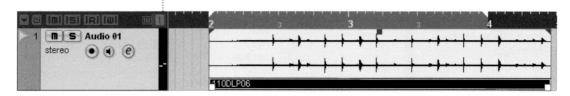

Figure 9.18
Reverse the audio event a second time

- At this point the start point of the drum loop is not on the first downbeat of the bar since the reversed reverb tail is now found in front of the first beat. To make it easier to place the audio event accurately in the event display, drag the Snap point to the first beat of the bar in the Sample editor (Figure 9.19).

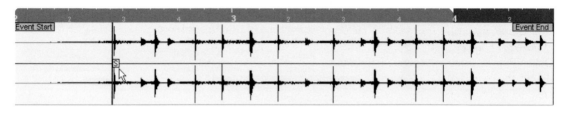

Figure 9.19
Adjust the Snap point of the audio event in the Sample editor

- Moving the audio event in the Project window with the Snap type menu set to 'grid' and the Grid type menu set to 'bar', places the audio event accurately in the event display with the reversed reverb tail occurring before the first beat of the bar (Figure 9.20).

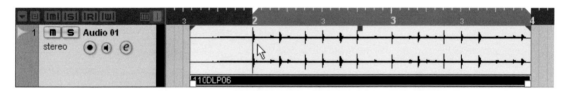

Figure 9.20
Move the audio event to the desired position with the Snap resolution set to 'bar'.

This kind of processing is valuable to those searching for new sound effects and, used in a subtle fashion, becomes a valuable addition to the range of effects you can produce with Cubase. Try the same procedure with any of the other reverb or delay plug-ins in your system.

Offline Process History

The Offline Process History dialogue (Figure 9.21) allows you to undo audio processing at a later date after the session is closed. This means that you can go back and remove the compression, noise gating, reverb and any other offline processing applied to an audio clip many weeks, months (or even years!) after you first applied it. This is assuming that your audio data remains intact at the same location on the hard disk.

You can always go back to the original version of your audio files. However, you may not always be able to modify, replace or remove each processing step individually. The exceptions include operations which change the length of the audio clip, such as time stretch or cut and paste editing. Such a function could only be individually modified or removed if it was the last

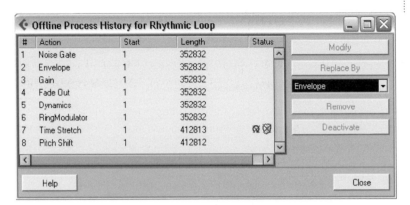

Figure 9.21
The Offline Process History dialogue

editing operation which took place. Functions which cannot be modified or removed are indicated by an icon with a cross in the Status column of the Offline Process History dialogue. For example, the Time Stretch operation in the list shown in Figure 9.21 cannot be individually removed unless the Pitch Shift operation which comes after it is removed first.

The Offline Process History dialogue features a list of all the offline processes which were applied to the current audio selection. You can select any of the processes in the list by clicking on it and the process may then be removed, replaced or modified using the Remove, Replace and Modify buttons (except for the cases outlined above). The Modify button is particularly useful since it opens the dialogue window for the corresponding audio process and recalls the exact settings. Modification is then a matter of tweaking the existing settings. In this context, the Offline Process History dialogue can be used as an interface for fine tuning the overall result of a complex multiple audio processing procedure.

The Pool

The Pool is designed for the management of the current project's audio and video clips and their associated files on hard disk. Each project has its own single instance of the Pool. Here, you can carry out clip-based editing and organisational tasks and keep track of which clips are currently in use and which file on hard disk is referenced by each clip. It includes functions for importing, auditioning, renaming, copying and deleting clips and files, and finding out which events in the Project window are referenced to the currently selected clip. Conversely, you can find out which clips in the Pool are referenced by the currently selected event. The Pool is also where you import data from audio CDs and prepare you projects for archiving. The essential thing to bear in mind when you open the Pool is that you are moving one step closer to the raw data on hard disk.

The Pool in detail

The Pool window

The Pool (Figure 10.1) is opened by selecting Open Pool Window from the Media menu or by pressing the Open Pool button on the Project window toolbar (default key command: Ctrl / Command + P).

Figure 10.1
The Pool

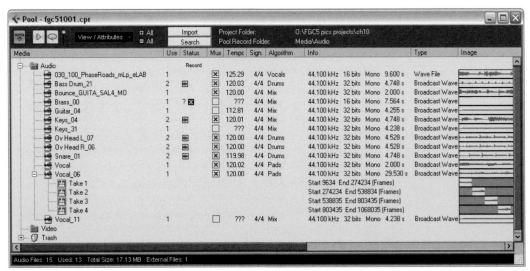

Figure 10.2
The Pool View menu

The Pool displays a list of all the audio and video clips contained within the current project. The clips are stored within the audio and video folders. There is also a trash folder which serves as an interim storage area for disused clips before permanent removal from the project or from the hard disk. The audio, video and trash folders are permanent fixtures and cannot be deleted. Any number of sub folders can be arranged within the audio, video and trash folders.

The Pool columns

The clip list in the Pool features a number of columns. Each column is hidden or shown using the View menu (Figure 10.2). The columns display a wide range of information about the media used in the project, as follows:

- Media – shows the names of the clips in the Pool. The clips are stored within the Audio, Video and Trash folders. A plus (+) sign next to a clip means that it contains regions. Click on the plus sign to reveal the regions.
- Used – shows the number of times that the clip is referenced within the project. A blank space in this column means that the clip is not currently used.
- Status – indicates the record and file status of clips and the position of the current record folder using various symbols as follows:
- The Record symbol indicates the current record folder for the project (by default the audio folder). The Pool allows you to create additional folders inside the audio folder using Create Folder (Media menu). You may designate any one of these as the record folder using Set Pool Record Folder (Media menu). Subsequent recordings are stored within the chosen folder.
- The audio wave symbol indicates that the clip has been processed in some way.
- The question mark indicates that the clip is referenced by the project but the file associated with it could not be found on the hard disk (known as a missing file). This occurs if you delete, move or name a file outside of Cubase or change a file common to more than one project.
- The X symbol indicates that the clip is referenced to an audio file which is stored outside of the project audio folder.
- The R symbol indicates that the clip has been recorded at some time during the current session. This provides a quick means of finding recently recorded clips.
- Musical mode – shows the musical mode status of each clip. Musical mode may be manually activated here by clicking in the corresponding check box.
- Tempo – shows the internal tempo of the audio clip if already defined. If no tempo has been defined, '???' is displayed in the column. The defined tempo is used to calculate the appropriate time stretch factor for those clips set to Musical mode.
- Signature – shows the time signature of the audio clip. This may be edited here or in the Sample editor.

- Info – displays the sample rate, bit depth, stereo / mono status and duration of audio clips, and the frame rate, number of frames and duration of video clips. For regions, the start and end time is displayed in samples.
- Type – indicates the type of audio or video file referenced by the clip.
- Date – shows the date and time the audio file was modified.
- Origin Time – indicates the original time position at which the clip was recorded. This is helpful when you use Insert into Project / At Origin (Media menu) since it inserts the clip at the same time position as when it was originally recorded. Broadcast Wave files already have a time position embedded in the file header data and this appears in the Origin Time column. Imported Broadcast Wave files recorded in other applications can therefore be assembled in Cubase at their original time positions. To edit the origin time click on the value.
- Image – displays a waveform of the clip. Click anywhere in the waveform box to audition the clip. Local playback begins from the position at which you click and continues to the end of the clip.
- Path – shows the location on hard disk of the file referenced by the clip.
- Reel name – a parameter which may be included when you import an OMF file (Open Media Framework Interchange), intended to provide a reference to the original tape or media from which the audio file was taken.

> ### Tip
>
> Click on the title strip of the columns to sort the Pool data by name, duration, type, date, file location and so on. For example, try sorting the clips by date to find the most recently recorded files. Try also using the Optimize Width option in the View menu to clarify the column display.

The Pool toolbar

The Pool toolbar features Info, Play and Loop buttons. These allow you to show / hide the Infoline below the clip list, audition the currently selected clip or region, or audition the currently selected clip or region in loop mode. The View menu allows you to choose which columns are displayed in the list and the All plus (+) and minus (-) boxes allow you to open or close all folders. There is an Import button for importing audio and video clips directly into the Pool and a Search button for searching for audio files on your system (see below). The toolbar also displays the path of the current project folder and the currently chosen Pool record folder.

Figure 10.3
The Pool toolbar

The Pool Infoline

The Pool Infoline is shown or hidden using the Info button on the toolbar. The Infoline displays how many audio files are present, how many are used, the size of the files in Megabytes and the number of files located outside of the Project folder. While basic, this gives an instant overview of the file status and approximate hard disk space used in the project. For example, this may help you decide if you need to remove some or all of the unused media in an ongoing project which involves the auditioning of a wide range of audio files, many of which are never used in the final version.

Figure 10.4
The Pool Infoline

Audio Files: 15   Used: 13   Total Size: 17.13 MB   External Files: 1

The Pool Search function

Clicking on the Search button in the toolbar opens a search window in the lower half of the Pool. The search function behaves in a similar manner to the search functions available in any standard operating system. You enter a file name or extension in the search field, and add a wild card ('*') where appropriate. For example, to find all those wave files which contain 'snare' somewhere in their name, enter *snare*.wav (see Figure 10.5).

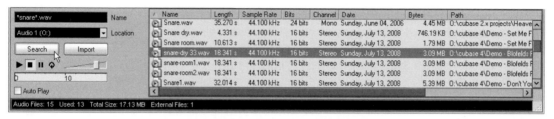

Figure 10.5
Using the Pool Search function to find a snare drum

Getting to know the Pool and Media menu

This section outlines the key functions of the Pool and Media menu. (Note: the Media browsers are covered in Chapter 11).

Importing clips

Import Medium

To import audio or video clips, click on the Import button on the Pool toolbar (Figure 10.6). This opens an Import Medium dialogue where you can select one or more files of the supported types from your hard disk or other storage media. Click on Open to import the chosen file(s). An import options dialogue may appear according to your settings in File / Preferences / Editing / Audio / On import audio files. Here, it is recommended you select 'Copy files to working directory' so that imported files are always copied to the working directory. You can then work freely with them in the current project without fear of interfering with work in other projects or applications.

Figure 10.6
Click on the Import button to import audio or video files into the Pool

Import Audio CD

The Import Audio CD function supports import of audio CD tracks from any CD / DVD drive connected to the system. This is useful when working with sample and drum loop libraries. The 'Import From Audio CD' dialogue allows you to audition each CD track before importing and select a name and folder for the file(s). To import from an audio CD proceed as follows:

- Insert an audio CD into the appropriate optical drive of your computer. Select Import Audio CD in the Media menu to open the 'Import From Audio CD' dialogue (Figure 10.7). If it is not already open the Pool is automatically opened in the background.
- Select the appropriate drive in the menu at the top of the dialogue. To audition the CD tracks select a track in the track list using the computer keyboard up / down arrow keys and click on the play tracks button (Figure 10.8). If required, define a specific section of a track by dragging

the markers in the play progress meter. In this case, only the defined section is auditioned, and only the defined section is imported when you proceed with the import operation.

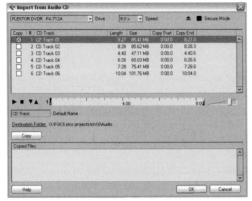

Figure 10.7
Open the 'Import From Audio CD' dialogue

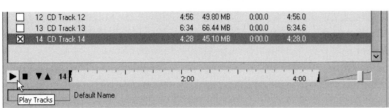

Figure 10.8
Audition the CD tracks using the local play functions

- Activate the check box for all those tracks you wish to subject to the import process. To select more than one track use the Shift or Ctrl modifier keys.
- The default record folder for the import operation is the working audio folder for the current project. If required, choose an alternative folder using the Destination Folder button. Enter a generic name for the file(s) in the Default Name field (Figure 10.9).

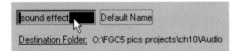

Figure 10.9
Enter a generic name for the chosen audio CD tracks in the default name field

- If required, activate Secure Mode to ensure a more accurate reading of the CD (this takes more time). Click on the copy button to import the audio data. A percentage meter registers the progress of the import operation (Figure 10.10).

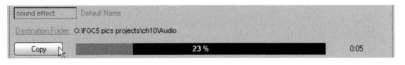

Figure 10.10
Click on the copy button to import the audio CD tracks

- When the import operation is complete click on the OK button to close the Import From Audio CD dialogue. The imported tracks are shown in the Pool if you imported to the audio folder of the current project (Figure 10.11).

Figure 10.11
The imported CD tracks in the Pool

Info

Cubase allows the importing of audio media in the following file formats: Wave (.wav), AIFC and AIFF (.aif), REX (.rex), REX 2 (rx2), Sound Designer II (.sd2), Wave 64 (.w64), MPEG Layer 3 (.mp3), MPEG Layer 2 (.mp2), MPEG (.mpeg), Ogg Vorbis (.ogg), and Windows Media Audio (.wma). For video media, Cubase supports the following file formats: Quick Time Video (.mov and .qt), AVI Video (.avi), and MPEG video (.mpg).

Auditioning clips

A clip or region is auditioned by selecting it and pressing the play button on the toolbar. Loop playback is achieved by activating the loop button. Alternatively, click on the waveform image in the Image column (Figure 10.12).

Figure 10.12
Audition a clip by clicking on the waveform image

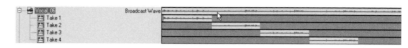

Renaming clips

Clips are renamed by clicking once on the currently selected clip name. Enter a new name into the name field in the standard fashion (Figure 10.13). The renaming of clips should be approached with caution since re-naming a clip also re-names the referenced audio file on hard disk. This is especially hazardous if you are renaming clips which reference audio files located outside of the project working directory (those marked with the X symbol in the Status column).

Figure 10.13
Approach renaming of clips with caution since this also renames the associated file on hard disk

Copying clips

Clips are copied by selecting New Version in the Media menu (Figure 10.14). This makes a copy of the currently selected clip but does not create a new audio file for the clip (i.e. the clip references the same audio file as the original clip). An incremental number is added to the copy to differentiate it from the original.

Figure 10.14
Select New Version in the Media menu to copy a clip

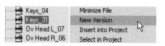

Dragging and dropping clips

Clips may be freely dragged from the Pool and dropped directly into the Project window. When using drag and drop, an event is created for the clip on the track at the position at which you release the mouse button. A blue marker line and position box show the current drop position before you release. To use this technique, proceed as follows:

- Place the Pool in a position where it does not entirely obscure the Project window event display.
- Click on the chosen clip icon (to the left of the clip name) and drag. A dotted rectangle representing the clip appears.
- Drag the clip into the Project window event display.
- Release the mouse button at the appropriate position. A new event is created which is referenced to the dragged clip. The event is inserted at the position at which the mouse button is released and is moved to the nearest beat according to the current snap value (if the snap button is activated).

As well as dragging clips out of the Pool, audio and video files can be dragged directly into the Pool from the computer desktop, from the file browsing software of the operating system, or from the Media bay. These are useful alternatives to the regular import functions.

Deleting clips

There are three ways to delete clips as follows:

- Deletion from the Pool only. This removes the clip from the Pool but does not remove the referenced file from the hard disk.
- Deletion from the Pool and from the hard disk. This removes the clip from the Pool and also permanently deletes the referenced file from the hard disk.
- Deletion by removing unused media (using the 'Remove Unused Media' function in the Media menu). This removes unused media from the Pool, or from both the Pool and the hard disk.

Deleting from the Pool only

To delete a clip from the Pool only proceed as follows:

- Select the clip in the Pool and press Backspace or Delete on the computer keyboard (or select Delete from the Edit menu).
- If the clip is used, a warning dialogue appears (Figure 10.15). Click on Remove to remove all occurrences of the clip from the event display.
- After clicking on Remove, a further dialogue appears giving a choice of removing the clip from the Pool or moving the clip into the Trash folder. Select 'Remove from Pool' to remove the clip from the Pool only (Figure 10.16). The clip is deleted from the Pool but the associated file on hard disk remains.

Info

Newly recorded audio events which are deleted from the Project window without saving in the current session are automatically placed in the Trash folder.

Figure 10.15 (left)
Clip is used warning dialogue

Figure 10.16 (right)
Select 'Remove from Pool' to remove the clip from the Pool only

Deleting from the Pool and from the hard disk

To delete a clip from the Pool and from the hard disk proceed as follows:

- Select the clip in the Pool and press Backspace or Delete on the computer keyboard (or select Delete from the Edit menu).
- If the clip is used, a warning dialogue appears (Figure 10.15, above). Click on Remove to remove all occurrences of the clip from the event display.
- After clicking on Remove, a further dialogue appears giving a choice of removing the clip from the Pool or moving the clip into the Trash folder. Select Trash (Figure 10.17). This moves the clip into the Trash folder. The Trash folder is an intermediary storage area before the final deletion

Info

Clips may be dragged directly from the Audio and Video folders into the Trash folder if they are not currently in use. Conversely, any clip may be dragged from the Trash folder into the Audio and Video folders.

Figure 10.17 (left)
Select 'Trash' to move the clip into the Trash folder

Figure 10.18 (right)
Select 'Empty Trash' in the Media menu and then Erase in the final Warning dialogue to permanently delete clips and their associated files on hard disk (Caution: this operation cannot be undone!)

of the clip and its referenced file on hard disk. Clips may be stored there indefinitely and you can restore a clip at any time by dragging it from the Trash folder into the other media folders.

- To finally delete clips and their associated files on hard disk, select Empty Trash (Media menu). This opens a final warning dialogue giving you the choice to Erase or Remove from the Pool (Figure 10.18). Choosing Remove from the Pool removes the clips in the Trash folder from the Pool but does not erase the associated files on hard disk. Choosing Erase permanently deletes all clips currently stored in the Trash folder and also permanently deletes their associated files on hard disk! Caution: This operation cannot be undone! Proceed in a similar manner to delete single clips and files but first open the Trash folder, select a single clip and press Backspace or Delete.

Important

Deleting clips in Cubase is deliberately NOT simplistically easy. This protects against accidental permanent deletion of clips and their associated files on hard disk. The Trash folder gives you the option of keeping absolutely all the files associated with a project right up until the last moment – it is a kind of 'safety buffer' between keeping and finally deleting the files on disk. Use Empty Trash only when you are 100% sure that you no longer need the files contained therein.

Removing Unused Media

To remove all unused clips from the project proceed as follows:

- Select 'Remove Unused Media' from the Media menu.
- In the dialogue which appears, select 'Remove from Pool' if you wish to remove the clips from the Pool only but retain the referenced files on hard disk. Select 'Trash' if it is your intention to remove the clips from the Pool and permanently delete the referenced files on the hard disk.
- All unused media is removed from the Pool according to the choice you have made in the previous step.

Removing all the unused clips from a project is an operation you might undertake when the Pool has become cluttered with a large number of unused clips after lengthy experimentation or the auditioning of miscellaneous material. If you regularly audition audio material from a number of different locations outside the working directory of the current project then you should, above all, not use the Trash folder when using 'Remove Unused Media'. In the latter case, select 'Remove from Pool' to remove the clips from the Pool only.

Finding events, clips and missing files

Find the events referring to the currently selected clip in the Pool

To find all events which refer to a clip, select the clip in the Pool and select 'Select in Project' from the Media menu. This immediately selects all those events in the Project window which refer to the clip. This also operates with multiple selections.

Find the clip referenced by the currently selected event in the Project window

To find the clip referenced by an event, select the event in the Project window and select 'Find Selected in Pool' from the Audio menu. If it is not already open, the Pool window is automatically opened with the corresponding clip selected.

Finding missing files

Whenever you open a Project which references files which have been moved, renamed or otherwise changed either outside of Cubase or as a result of manipulations in another Project, a 'Resolve Missing Files' dialogue appears. This allows you to locate or search for the missing files immediately or, if you close the dialogue, you can search for the files at a later time using 'Find Missing Files' in the Media menu. This opens the same 'Resolve Missing Files' dialogue (Figure 10.19).

Figure 10.19
Use the 'Resolve Missing Files' dialogue upon opening the Project, or at a later stage, to find missing files

The Resolve Missing Files dialogue features the following options:

- Locate – allows you to manually search for the file on your system. This is suitable when you have some idea of where the file is located and how it was renamed or otherwise changed.
- Folder – allows the selection of a specific folder in which to locate the missing file using the Locate button. This is suitable when you know the likely folder location of the missing file.
- Search – opens a search window where you can specify a file name and search location for the missing file. An asterisk (*) may be used as a wild card for generic search operations. For example, the search operation shown in Figure 10.20, searches for all wave audio files which contain "Vocal" in the first five letters of the file name. Once a file has been accepted, by clicking on the Accept button, Cubase attempts to find all other missing files in the same folder as the accepted file.

Figure 10.20
'Search for File' window for searching for missing files

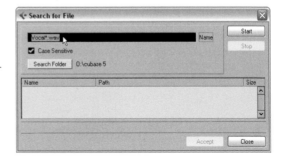

Avoiding missing file problems

There may be occasions when you cannot find the missing files. The consequences of this depend very much upon the importance of the files which are
missing. Unfortunately, if an important file has gone missing and remains
missing despite your best efforts to find it, then there is no real way to re-
create it other than to re-record from scratch. The good news is that if you
follow strict procedures for recording, saving, backing up and clip and file
management then you should never suffer from any missing files at all. The
three essential steps to avoid missing files are as follows:

- Always copy any media to the working directory of the project when
  importing.
- Never permanently delete clips and their associated files for media which
  is located outside of the working directory of the project.
- Never move, rename or delete the project audio files in another
  application or using the file management tools of your operating system.

Other precautionary measures include using an external application to make
an archive backup of the entire project either to a second hard drive or to
removable media such as CD or DVD, or saving to a new folder while remaining in Cubase using 'Back up Project' (File menu). See 'Archiving your project' and 'Backing up your project', below.

If you suffer from missing files as a result of a mistake or when you have
intentionally permanently deleted a number of files but the clips are still
located within the project, you may wish to delete them. To achieve this,
select 'Remove Missing Files' from the Media menu.

The only types of missing audio files which are recoverable are edit files. If
an edit file is missing and marked as reconstructible in the Status column of
the Pool, then it is possible to recreate the file by selecting 'Reconstruct' in
the Media menu.

Editing and processing clips

Clips may be processed directly using the Process or Plug-in options in the
Audio menu. Audio processing in the Pool is best achieved using the Quick
menu (Right click / Ctrl click) with the clip selected. The Quick menu gives
direct access to all the available off-line audio processing options in your system in the lower part of the menu display (Figure 10.21). When using audio
processing at the clip level, processing is applied to the whole clip unless otherwise specified in the dialogue of the processing option itself.

Audio clips may be edited in detail by opening them in the Sample editor.

Figure 10.21

Use the Quick menu for rapid access to
the audio processing options in your
system

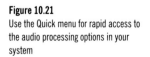

To achieve this, double click on
the clip icon to the left of the
clip name in the Pool or select
the clip and press Ctrl + E /
Command + E. When the
Sample editor is opened using
a clip, there is no Show Event
button available on the toolbar.

Minimising and freezing clips

Minimize File

'Minimize File' (Media menu) permanently deletes all unused sections of the currently selected clip(s). This is useful when you want to minimise the amount of disk space which is taken up by a project (for example, prior to archiving). The operation involves permanent deletion of audio data on hard disk and the clearing of the entire edit history for the clip. For these reasons, the Minimize File function should be used with great caution.

Freeze Edits

'Freeze Edits' (Audio menu) allows you to make all audio processing and applied effects a permanent part of the data. If there are several clips which refer to the same audio file you must choose the new version option in the dialogue box which appears, in order to proceed with the Freeze Edits function. If the target clip is a single edit version and no other clips refer to the same audio file, the dialogue box gives you the option of replacing the original clip or creating a new one. If you are 100% sure that you will never need to revert to a previous edited version of the clip, select Replace. Using the Freeze Edits function 'Replace' option is useful when you want to reduce the amount of disk space which is taken up by a project. Like 'Minimize File' above, the operation involves permanent deletion of audio data on hard disk and the clearing of the edit history for the clip. It should therefore be approached with great caution. If in doubt, always create a new version and leave the original intact.

Backing up your project

As a safety precaution it is wise to occasionally save a back up of the current project to a new location. This is achieved using 'Back up Project' in the File menu. This saves a copy of the project to a different folder. To make a back up proceed as follows:

- Select 'Back up Project' in the File menu. This opens a Set Project Folder dialogue. Select an existing folder or make a new one (Figure 10.22). The folder must be empty.

> **Caution**
>
> Minimize files and freeze edits operations cannot be undone!

Figure 10.22
Choose the back up project folder in the Set Project Folder dialogue

Figure 10.23
Make the appropriate selections in the
Back up Project Options dialogue

- Click on the OK button to open the Back up Project Options dialogue (Figure 10.23). Here, you can specify the name for the project and choose to minimise all audio files, freeze all edited files, remove all unused files and to not back up video files. These options are useful for reducing the overall size of the back up when hard disk space is an issue. There is also a check box to keep the current project active after the back up process is complete. If you do not activate this check box the back up project becomes the active project.

Archiving your project

Caution

Archiving which involves deletion of data from the hard disk should be approached with extreme caution.

Archiving is usually understood to mean making a final version of a fully completed project and copying this onto removable media for long term storage. For maximum safety, experts recommend archiving each project to two or three physically different locations. If desired, when archiving has been successfully completed the original project can be deleted from the working hard disk, thus freeing up space for new projects.

Archiving is usually a two stage process which involves, firstly, optimising the size and contents of the completed project using the 'Prepare Archive' function (Media menu) and, secondly, transferring this optimised version to removable storage media such as CD or DVD, or to a spare internal or external hard disk. 'Prepare Archive' checks for missing files, verifies that all files referenced by the clips in the Pool are contained within the working folder of the project, and gives you the option to use Freeze edits to make all audio processing a permanent part of the data. This gives you a complete version of the project with all files contained within the working project folder. Thus, when you copy the project folder to the archive location you can be sure that all the necessary files are included. To prepare a project for archiving proceed as follows:

Create Folder
Empty Trash
Remove Unused Media
Prepare Archive...
Set Pool Record Folder

Figure 10.24
Select 'Prepare Archive' in the Media menu

- Open the Pool and select 'Prepare Archive' in the Media menu (Figure 10.24).
- If there are any missing files in the project a dialogue appears giving you the option to find them (Figure 10.25). Selecting Find opens the 'Resolve Missing Files' dialogue. Selecting Cancel abandons the Prepare Archive operation. A project which contains missing files is not considered suitable for archiving purposes. If the missing files cannot be

found anywhere on your system then, in order to proceed further with the Prepare Archive procedure, you must remove the missing files using the 'Remove Missing Files' function.

- When there are no missing files, the Prepare Archive process moves on to the next stage. Another dialogue appears giving you the option to make edits permanent (Figure 10.26). This allows you to make all audio processing and applied effects a permanent part of the data and operates in a similar manner to the Freeze Edits function (Audio menu). Selecting 'Permanent' freezes all processed clips in the project and involves permanent changes to the audio data on hard disk (see 'Minimising and Freezing', above, for more details). The Permanent button should therefore be used with caution. Selecting 'No' performs no freeze operations on the clips in the Pool.
- After completion of the previous step, Prepare Archive ensures that all audio files referenced by the clips in the Pool are contained within the working folder of the project. Any files which are located outside of the project folder are copied to the working directory. If your project references external video files you also get the opportunity to copy these to the working directory. Upon completion, the project is considered ready for archiving (Figure 10.27).
- Copy the overall Project folder to your chosen storage medium using the file handling software of your operating system.

Figure 10.25
Missing Files warning dialogue

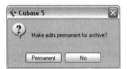

Figure 10.26
Prepare Archive 'Make edits permanent' dialogue

Figure 10.27
The Pool is ready for archiving

Who is responsible?

The above outlines just one archiving method. Bear in mind that this is not the only way of archiving your work. The above procedure should not be understood as a completely foolproof way of archiving your projects since archiving requirements can vary enormously. The above procedure should therefore be viewed as a rough guide. This text assumes no responsibility for decisions made about whether or how you reduce the size of your audio files, whether you delete any audio files, or any other decision made with regard to the safety of your data. These decisions remain the sole responsibility of the reader.

Importing and exporting the Pool

The Pool is usually saved as an integral part of the project but it can also be imported and exported independently. This might be useful if you need to include a number of audio files from another project in the current project or if you need to import / export the Pool from / to Steinberg Nuendo, which recognises the same Pool file format. When a Pool file is imported, the clips contained therein are added to those currently in the Pool. For the clips contained in an imported Pool to be correctly referenced to the files on hard disk, the files themselves must be located in their original folders as indicated by the path names. To import or export the Pool, select Import Pool or Export Pool from the Media menu. Pool files are given the extension '.npl'.

Tip

Successful archiving of your Cubase projects relies upon a thorough and complete understanding of the Pool and all the functions in the Media menu. Before embarking on serious archiving tasks, re-read this chapter thoroughly and consult the Cubase user documentation.

Tip

Before exporting the Pool, create a special folder using Create Folder (Media menu) and drag all the clips into it. When you later import the Pool into another Cubase or Nuendo project all the clips are neatly packaged in their own folder and are easier to find among any clips already in the current Pool.

VST Sound and the Media browsers

VST Sound is a generic media management system. It provides a common link between your sounds, loops and presets and helps you organise all your media within a centralised database. The core element of VST Sound is the Media Bay, a browser window for the management of all your Cubase-related files and presets. The Media Bay is available in two other forms known as the Loop browser and the Sound browser. These three browsers provide advanced media management tools for viewing, searching, tagging and auditioning the relevant files on your system. However, the VST Sound concept reaches out further than the browser windows, especially with the management of presets. Above all, it helps you to choose sounds rather than plug-ins when working with software and hardware instruments, and it helps you to organise all your effects presets into a single universal library. Recall of presets is allowed wherever you see the diamond-shaped VST Sound symbol and, due to the tagging system, you can do such things as search for all bass sounds within your entire preset library when adding an instrument track, or show only the piano sounds for the supplied HalionOne sampler.

The Media browsers

The Media menu includes the Media Bay, Loop browser and Sound browser. These are really different versions of the the same generic browser but each is streamlined for a specific task.

Media Bay

The Media Bay is the default browser for universal media management tasks and is pre-configured to show all sections of the browser and all file types (Figure 11.1). The Media Bay features four main sections: the browser, the viewer, the scope section and the tag editor.

The browser section

The browser shows all the searchable locations in your system when you select the Full tab or it shows only the current folder selection when you select the Focus tab. When you first select a folder, the Media Bay scans its contents and displays the results in the viewer section. Folders currently being scanned are shown in red. When scanning is complete they are shown in light blue. If scanning is interrupted they are shown in orange. Folders

Figure 11.1
The Media Bay

which have not yet been scanned are shown in yellow. Activating the Deep Results button above the media list displays all relevant files in the selected folder and in all the sub-folders found therein. Activating 'Rescan on select' automatically re-scans a folder each time you select it. This is best left de-activated until you know you have made significant changes to the media stored on the hard disk.

The viewer

The viewer is the centre of activities in the Media Bay and includes the media list and a filter section. The filters exist in Details and Category modes. In Details mode you can select tag categories in the tag pop-up menu and then fix a search condition and criteria to the chosen tag. It is possible to activate multiple tags and conditions by clicking on the '+' symbol which appears to the right of the

Figure 11.2
Details audio file search in the Media Bay

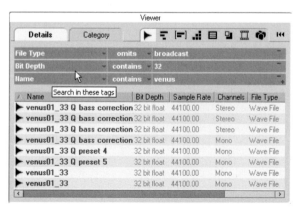

search criteria. The conditions include 'contains', 'omits', 'equals' and so on. For example, to search for all non-Broadcast Wave 32-bit audio files containing 'venus' in the file name, select the 'Show audio files' button above the viewer and set up three tag conditions as shown in Figure 11.2.

Category search is particularly suited to searching for sound presets. For example, to search for multiple snare sound presets in the supplied HalionOne sampler activate the 'Show VST plug-in presets' button above the viewer, select Instrument, Category and Sub-category columns and activate 'HalionOne', 'Drum&Perc', and 'Snare Drum' respectively, as shown in Figure 11.3.

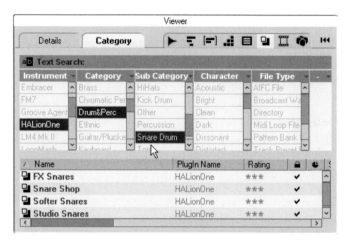

Figure 11.3
Looking for snare sounds using a Category plug-in preset search in the Media Bay

Of course, a detailed search based upon tags is only as good as the precision with which the files in your system are tagged in the first place. Luckily, the media supplied with Cubase is already tagged since manually tagging files can be a lengthy process. When browsing for audio files, systems which contain very large numbers of files may benefit from de-activating Deep Results in the Browser section, so that you are viewing files in the chosen folder only.

The scope section

The scope section allows you to interact with the file selected in the viewer. When an audio file is selected the waveform is displayed with play, stop, pause and cycle buttons. You can now audition the audio file from here (Figure 11.4).

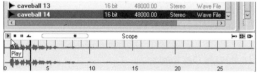

Figure 11.4
Auditioning an audio file in the scope section

When a MIDI file is selected a miniature bars and beats display is shown with play and stop buttons and a MIDI output port selector. You can now play the MIDI file. When a VST instrument sound preset is selected 'MIDI input', 'Choose MIDI file' and 'Play' buttons appear. Here, you can audition the cho-

Info

The total number of files displayed in the viewer may be adjusted in Preferences / Media Bay.

Figure 11.5
Auditioning Prologue chromatic percussion sounds using MIDI file playback in the scope section

sen sound by activating the MIDI input button and playing your MIDI keyboard or you can load a MIDI file and activate the Play button to automatically audition sounds using the chosen MIDI file. The latter is particularly useful when stepping through sounds since the MIDI file is re-triggered from the start each time you change sound, allowing you to audition effortlessly (Figure 11.5).

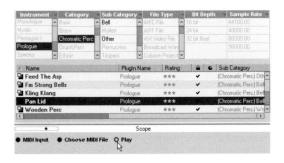

The tag editor

Media files such as audio, video, mp3 and other types have so-called metadata information stored in the header of the file. This provides additional information about the file such as the length, size, bit depth and sample rate for audio files or the artist, album, bit rate and genre for mp3 files. Cubase provides additional tags which may be included in the metatata of your media files to help identify, manage, search and sort them. The tag editor is where you can edit and view the metadata of the selected file and the values of any additional tags you have attached to your media. Here you have the choice to view the managed tags only, by selecting the 'Managed' tab. These include those tags you have activated for the tag editor in the Manage tags dialogue, (i.e. those you consider relevant for this file type). Or, you can view all the tags and metadata for the file by selecting the 'All' tab. Here you see regular attributes such as name, date created, media type, bit depth, sample rate, plug-in category, plug-in name, size and so on, as well as the additional tags provided by Cubase.

Figure 11.6
Managed tags for a Prologue bass sound preset

The Manage tags window

The Manage tags window (Figure 11.7) is opened by clicking on the Manage tags button in the Media Bay. Here you decide which tags are displayed in the viewer columns, the viewer filter and the tag editor, for each file type. You can also create your own user tags.

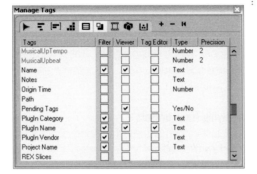

Figure 11.7
The Manage tags window

Loop browser

The Loop browser is intended for loop-based music and is pre-configured to show only audio files and MIDI loops. The scope section features a 'play in project context' icon which allows you to audition loops at the current project tempo. Used in combination with the scope section cycle and auto play functions, you can now automatically audition loops in context as you select them. This helps you quickly find the loops you need for the current project.

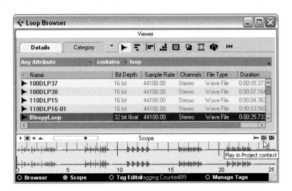

Figure 11.8
Auditioning loops at the current project tempo in the Loop browser

Tip

A MIDI loop is created from a part on an Instrument track using File / Export / MIDI loop. It contains the MIDI data, VST instrument settings and track data.

Sound browser

The Sound browser is pre-configured to show only track presets and VST presets. This is a good option when you are searching for synth sounds, plug-in effects or track presets. It is probably among the best options when making global searches by category for instrument sounds (see Figure 11.9 for an example).

Figure 11.9
Searching for bright, chromatic, percussive bell sounds in the Sound browser

Using VST Sound within Cubase

VST Sound helps you get to your media quickly and accurately at various locations within the program. These locations are indicated by a diamond-shaped VST Sound logo. The following sections outline the practical uses of VST Sound within Cubase.

Applying Track presets

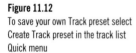

Figure 11.10
Apply Track preset field in the Inspector

The Inspector features the Apply Track preset field (Figure 11.10). Apply Track preset allows you to apply the channel settings of an audio, MIDI, instrument or multiple track preset to the currently selected track. This may include any combination of the insert effects, EQ, volume, gain, phase, VST instrument preset, MIDI Modifiers, MIDI Input Transformer, and MIDI output routing parameters (depending upon the track type).

Clicking on Apply Track preset opens a presets browser from where you can select a Track preset, or sound if you are using an Instrument track (Figure 11.11). When the presets browser is open use only the spacebar for auditioning purposes and the reset button to revert to the original settings. Close the browser only when you are satisfied with the new settings since closing applies the settings permanently.

Figure 11.11
Apply Track preset browser

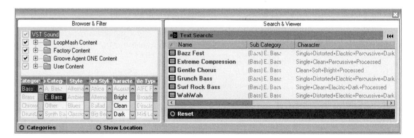

Creating Track presets

Whenever you have set up a track for a particularly useful purpose or the combination of EQ and insert effects is particularly pleasing you can save the settings as a Track preset for future use on other tracks. To achieve this right-click on the track in the track list and select Create Track preset in the Quick

Figure 11.12
To save your own Track preset select Create Track preset in the track list Quick menu

menu. This opens the Save Track preset dialogue where you can name and tag your new preset (Figure 11.12).

Loading and saving plug-in presets

Plug-in effects and VST instruments feature a Load / Save presets field. Clicking directly within the field opens a mini-browser which is fixed in position over the plug-in's GUI and is for load-only purposes. Clicking on the VST Sound logo and selecting the load or save functions opens a separate mini-browser. When loading, the browser is set to automatically look in the correct location for those presets which are relevant to the chosen plug-in. When using the save function, a Save preset dialogue appears where you can name and tag your new preset.

Extracting the sound from a Track preset

Instrument tracks allow you to extract the sound from a Track preset by clicking on the VST Sound symbol below the VST instrument name in the Inspector. This is useful when you wish to use the sound only and not the other settings which were saved as part of the Track preset.

Using Inserts and EQ section presets

The Inserts and EQ sections of the Inspector or Channel settings window include functions for the loading and saving of presets or the recall of settings contained within Track presets. This is good for transferring insert and EQ combinations between different tracks and projects. Click on the VST Sound symbol to the left of the Inserts or EQ bypass buttons to open the Inserts or EQ presets management menu (Figure 11.15).

Browsing Track presets when adding a new track

When adding audio, MIDI or instrument tracks you can click on the Browse presets button in the Add track dialogue to open the viewer for the Track presets relevant to the chosen track type. The browser for Instrument tracks allows you to audition the chosen Track preset before you actually create the track, by activating the MIDI input button and playing your MIDI keyboard (Figure 11.16).

Figure 11.13
Use the Load or Save preset functions in the plug-in GUI for management of plug-in effects and VSTi sound presets

Figure 11.14
Selecting 'Extract sound from Track preset' in the Inspector for Instrument tracks

Figure 11.15
To open the EQ preset menu click on the VST Sound icon on the EQ tab in the Inspector

Figure 11.16
Auditioning Track presets via MIDI before adding an Instrument track

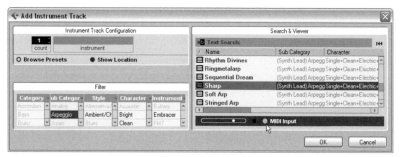

Mixing and EQ

Mixing in Cubase involves similar tools to those found in a traditional recording studio. The program features a virtual mixing console known as the Mixer, which includes EQ controls, auxiliary sends, insert points and automation. A virtual effects rack is supplied as standard offering various EQ, reverb, dynamics, delay, modulation, filter, distortion and other effects. You can mix both audio and MIDI tracks in the same virtual console.

If you are completely new to the field and have just started mixing, you should perhaps not be surprised to find that it is not as easy as it sounds. The quality of the recordings we hear every day on the radio or television and on commercial CD releases is taken for granted but when you attempt to achieve similar results it soon becomes clear that there are an enormous number of parameters involved. Mixing is a combination of art and science and it may take years of experience and training to master the various techniques. This is not to suggest that it is impossible to achieve a good result without any prior experience, but it certainly requires patience, perseverance and the extensive use of, sometimes the most under-valued tool in your arsenal, your ears! If you do not know how to listen then you do not know how to mix.

We have already touched upon the basics of recording, routing and processing in previous chapters. This chapter proceeds to the deeper level of how you mix all your tracks together into a composite whole. It explores the Mixer and the main functions relevant to mixing and EQ. It provides specific mixing guidelines and mixing techniques to help you get a better mix, and it features in-depth EQ coverage to help you get the most out of the mixer EQ section. Real-time audio effects are outlined in a separate chapter.

Mixing in theory

What is mixing?

Mixing is the stage at which the various elements of your recording endeavours come to fruition. The sounds you have carefully recorded are blended together, and reverb, EQ, compression and other effects and processing are applied where needed, in order to give the music a polished, unified and finished sound. Unfortunately, it is also the point at which a collection of well recorded tracks can be destroyed by a poor mix!

In practical terms, mixing involves setting all the levels of a multi-track recording in order to achieve a well-balanced stereo (or surround) result. Balance is the key word for mixing. The stereo image is carefully balanced so that it is not weighted too heavily to the left or right and certain instruments are mixed more forward or back in the mix, producing a sense of depth and focus. A good mix is not too boomy at the bass end, nor too harsh in the upper frequencies. Despite careful attention at the track laying stage, some sounds may still need corrective EQ, and EQ may be used to carefully blend or highlight sounds or for other creative purposes. The mix often includes reverb and other effects, which must be carefully mixed with the source sounds. Certain tracks also benefit from additional processing like compression or noise gating, and the whole mix might be processed through a loudness maximiser or compressor / limiter to modify the final level and dynamics of the signal.

The role of mixing in music production

In the recording studio, the mixing stage is sometimes viewed as an entirely separate activity. However, mixing cannot be completely separated from the rest of the music production process. Before mixing there is the recording stage and after mixing there is the mastering stage.

Each stage in the sound recording chain contributes to the final result and great care must be taken when the signal is actually captured. Mistakes made during the track laying stage are also apparent when you come to do the mix, probably more so. Likewise, if your mix is to later undergo a mastering stage care must be taken not to apply too much compression or limiting.

In popular music, the producer / engineer is often building the mix from the very first recording. As each musician adds their part, the sound image of the final mix gradually takes shape. Alternatively, in classical music, the sound image relies on the use of strategically placed microphones in, hopefully, an ideal acoustic recording environment. The mix is already largely decided at the moment of recording and any mixing which occurs is rather different from that which takes place with multi-track recordings in popular music.

When recording MIDI tracks you are probably more concerned with the quality of the performance rather than the quality of the sound. The sound can always be changed at a later stage by changing the sound program on the MIDI device. However, beware of changing the sound at the mixing stage as this might mask or negatively affect other elements in the mix.

Ten golden rules for recording and mixing

To help create a better mix with a Cubase system, remember the following guidelines:

1 Do not make a recording which sounds bad and then expect to 'fix it in the mix'. It is better to have a recording which already sounds good and then you can 'improve it in the mix'.
2 When recording with a microphone, choose the best model for the application and place it carefully relative to the source and acoustic environment.

3 Record at an optimum level whilst also avoiding distortion. Leave sufficient headroom for any transient peaks in the source signal.
4 Be aware of the acoustic environment in which you are recording and mixing. Where necessary, use acoustic treatment to dampen undesirable reflections.
5 Monitor all recordings and the mix through good quality studio monitors placed in the best position in your listening environment.
6 Do not over-use EQ in your mix. Cutting frequencies is often preferable to boosting. EQ is best viewed as a way to correct, or creatively change, well-recorded sounds and balance and blend the instruments in the mix.
7 Do not over-use processing and effects in your mix. This applies especially to reverb and compression. Before using any effect always have a clear objective in mind.
8 Pan sounds to appropriate positions across the stereo image and attempt to achieve some depth in the sound field. For example, in popular music, the lead vocal, kick drum and snare drum are usually panned centre with the lead vocal mixed forward, whereas the backing vocals are usually panned wide and placed back in the mix.
9 Do not abuse your ears by monitoring at abnormally loud sound levels. Take plenty of breaks during the mixing session to maximise clarity of thought and minimise ear fatigue.
10 As far as possible, know every aspect of Cubase and the peripheral equipment in your recording setup.

These 'rules' exist only as a guide and, where appropriate, the rules can be broken. There are not always pre-set methods of achieving the desired results and some of the most important developments in music production have occurred as a result of creative experimentation.

Tip

A good mix depends as much on what you take out as what you put in.

The Mixer

In Cubase, the Mixer takes centre stage in the mixing process and, just like a real-world mixing console, it is important to know all of its functions to get the best results.

The Mixer is laid out like a conventional console with a series of vertical modules, each of which controls an Audio, MIDI, Group, Instrument, FX or Rewire channel (Figure 12.1). To the left and right of the central channel area there are the input and output buses, responsible for routing signals into and out of the program. The various channels are linked to their corresponding tracks in the Project window and, by default, the order of the channels follows the order of the tracks displayed in the track list. Channels are shown when the corresponding tracks are present in the Project window or when a VST instrument, FX or Rewire device is activated within the system. Group, VSTi, FX and Rewire channels are always shown to the right of the Audio, MIDI and Instrument channels. To open the Mixer, select 'Mixer' in the Device menu or press F3 on the computer keyboard.

The Mixer is displayed in normal or extended mode (click on the arrows in the Common panel to change the view). In normal mode, you see all the basic channel parameters including volume, pan, mute, solo, read, write, edit channel settings, EQ bypass, effects bypass, monitor enable and record enable. In extended mode, the vertical height of the mixer is expanded to display additional channel elements such as insert, send and EQ panels, or meters and surround panners. The extended view is helpful when you are adjusting the EQ for a number of channels at the same time or when you are setting up multiple sends or insert effects.

Figure 12.1
The Mixer

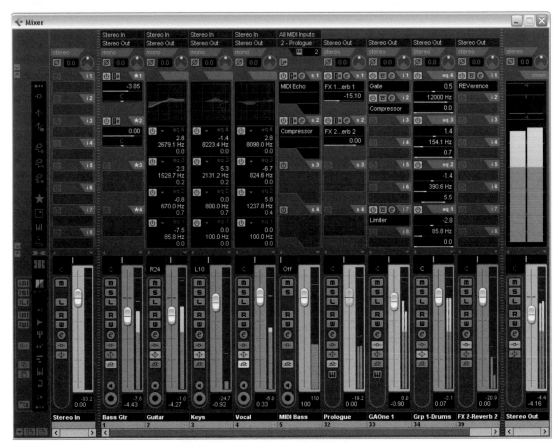

Manipulating the Mixer controls is largely mouse-based unless you have an external physical control surface. The main parameters are adjusted as follows:

- Click and drag on the faders and pan controls to change their values. Hold Ctrl / Command and click once on a fader to reset the fader to 0dB. Hold Ctrl / Command and click once on a pan control to reset the pan to the centre position. Hold Shift to make fine fader level and pan adjustments.
- When a channel EQ is active, the EQ state button is illuminated in green. Click once on an active EQ state button to disable the EQ, at which time it is illuminated in yellow.

- When a channel Insert or Send is active, the Insert or Send state buttons are illuminated in blue. Click once on an active Insert or Send state button to disable all insert or send effects for the channel, at which time it is illuminated in yellow.
- Click on the edit button ('e') to open the Channel Settings window where you can adjust EQ, manage effects and all other parameters for the channel.
- Click on the mute button ('M') to mute the channel, at which time the mute button is illuminated in yellow.
- Click on the solo button ('S') to solo the channel, at which time the solo button is illuminated in red and all other channels are muted.

Common panel

The left-most panel of the mixer is known as the Common panel (Figure 12.2). This is used to manage the settings of the Mixer on a global level. Changes made here affect all, or specific types, of mixer channels. The upper-most buttons of the Common panel (those in the extended part of the Mixer) allow you to quickly change the extended view between insert, EQ, send, studio send, surround panner, large scale meters or channel overview. The Common panel is particularly useful when you wish to, for example, instantly de-activate all the mute or solo buttons after complex muting and soloing operations and helps ensure that you are reading all the available channel automation in the mix when you activate the global Read button. The channel type show / hide buttons help you view only those channel types you really need to see. Clicking on the 'All targets narrow' icon allows you to see around thirty channel faders on a 17 inch monitor. This is great for getting an overview of your mix. Also

Figure 12.2
The Common panel

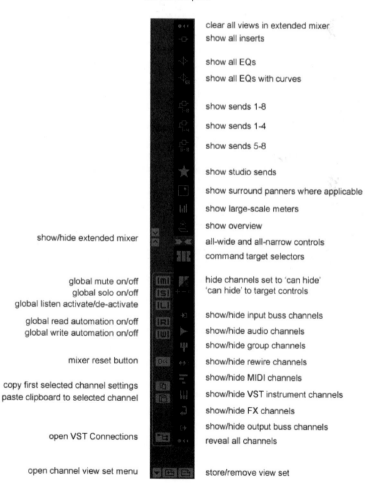

clear all views in extended mixer
show all inserts

show all EQs
show all EQs with curves

show sends 1-8
show sends 1-4
show sends 5-8

show studio sends
show surround panners where applicable
show large-scale meters
show overview
all-wide and all-narrow controls
command target selectors

hide channels set to 'can hide'
'can hide' to target controls

show/hide input buss channels
show/hide audio channels
show/hide group channels
show/hide rewire channels
show/hide MIDI channels
show/hide VST instrument channels
show/hide FX channels
show/hide output buss channels
reveal all channels

store/remove view set

show/hide extended mixer

global mute on/off
global solo on/off
global listen activate/de-activate

global read automation on/off
global write automation on/off

mixer reset button

copy first selected channel settings
paste clipboard to selected channel

open VST Connections

open channel view set menu

Tip

When using the Mixer, it is not always convenient if channels are automatically record enabled when selected. To disable automatic record enabling, open Preferences / Editing and disable 'Enable Record on Selected Track'.

check out the 'Hide channels set to Can Hide' option which hides all those channels which have 'Can Hide' activated. The current Mixer view may be saved as a preset using the Store View Set button.

Audio channels

The number of possible Audio channels in Cubase is virtually unlimited and depends upon the processing power of the host computer. The Mixer expands automatically according to how many tracks you add. An Audio channel can be mono, stereo or surround / multiple, depending on the configuration you choose when the track is first created. All channel formats feature a single channel fader and a single set of function buttons. The only difference with stereo and multiple channels is that they include dual or multiple meters (and a surround panner where applicable). Apart from these minor differences, each Audio channel contains the same set of parameters and these are outlined in Figure 12.3.

Figure 12.3
Audio channel control functions

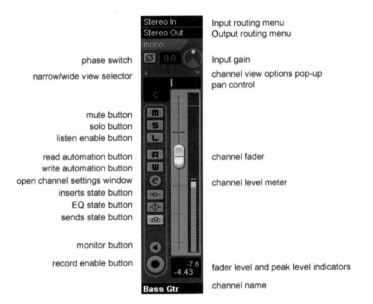

Tip

Right-click on the panner of a stereo audio channel to select between dual, combined or balance panners. The balance panner is the default panner control for stereo channels.

MIDI channels

Like Audio channels, the number of MIDI channels in Cubase is also virtually unlimited and depends upon the processing power of the host computer and the polyphony limitations of your peripheral MIDI devices. Once again, the Mixer expands according to how many MIDI tracks you add. MIDI channels behave in much the same way as their audio counterparts except that when you move the channel fader you are sending MIDI Volume messages and when you move the pan control you are sending MIDI Pan messages to the receiving MIDI device. MIDI channels feature mute, solo, read, write, edit channel settings, bypass, record and monitor enable buttons which behave similarly to Audio channels. It is important to bear in mind that when you move the controls on a MIDI channel you affect MIDI data only, you are not directly controlling the audio itself. As mentioned elsewhere in this book,

MIDI is not audio, it is a set of digital instructions (see Chapter 5 for full details about MIDI theory). MIDI channels control external MIDI devices, onboard VST Instruments or Rewire devices. Each MIDI channel contains the same set of parameters and these are outlined in Figure 12.4.

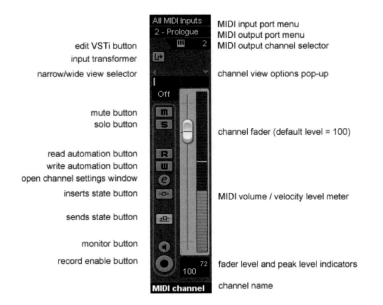

edit VSTi button
input transformer
narrow/wide view selector

mute button
solo button

read automation button
write automation button
open channel settings window
inserts state button

sends state button

monitor button
record enable button

MIDI input port menu
MIDI output port menu
MIDI output channel selector

channel view options pop-up

channel fader (default level = 100)

MIDI volume / velocity level meter

fader level and peak level indicators

channel name

Figure 12.4
MIDI channel control functions

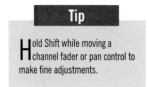

Tip

Hold Shift while moving a channel fader or pan control to make fine adjustments.

Instrument channels

Instrument channels control the audio output of VST instruments assigned to Instrument tracks and feature the same function set as Audio channels except for the addition of an edit VST instrument button. Instrument tracks are a hybrid track type for the recording and playback of MIDI data which exclusively triggers a single VST Instrument. An Instrument track provides one MIDI input and one stereo audio output, linking a MIDI-based track in the Project window to a VST instrument-based channel in the Mixer.

FX channels

FX channels are specialised container channels for the send effects within a project. Each FX channel might be viewed as an effects device, as found in the effects rack of a traditional recording studio. An FX channel normally contains at least one effect assigned as an insert, usually chosen at the time the FX channel is added to the project, and. is designed to process signals routed from the auxiliary sends of other audio-based channels. For more elaborate send processing, several effects may be assigned in series in the insert slots of the FX channel. Traditionally, effects used as send effects have their wet / dry mix set to fully wet (100% wet). In this configuration, the FX channel produces only the wet signal, while the channel from which the send signal is being routed produces only the dry signal. The fader of the FX channel acts as the return level for the effect.

Tip

Group channels can be used to quickly create stems of the main elements within your mix. Stems are separate audio files of these elements. To create stems in Cubase, assign the chosen Group channels as the input sources for an appropriate number of empty Audio channels. Record enable these Audio channels and press the Transport record button to record all the stems in one pass.

Tip

Open the graphical user interface for a VST Instrument from the Mixer by clicking on the VSTi edit button in an Instrument or VST Instrument channel.

Group, VST Instrument and Rewire channels

Group, VST Instrument and Rewire channels are the other channel types which may be present in the Mixer. Group channels are added using the usual Add track function but VST Instrument and Rewire channels are present when the relevant device is active within the system. All these channel types handle audio signals.

Group channels are bus channels (mono, stereo or multiple) to which any number of regular audio-based channels may be routed. The function buttons and general operation of Group channels are similar to regular audio channels, with the exception of the record enable and monitor buttons which are not present. Other audio-based channels are routed to a Group by selecting a Group output in the output routing menu. If required, Group channels themselves may be routed to other Group channels.

Groups are useful for dividing a mix into separate sub-mixes. For example, if you are mixing four channels of backing vocals and want to apply the same compression, EQ and reverberation to all of them, it is easier to mix them to a Group first and apply the treatment from there. This minimises the CPU load. Likewise, once you have established a drum mix, it is easier to balance its level with the rest of the mix by sending it to a Group. In both cases, it is also easier to arrange the stereo pan position of each voice / instrument by soloing the Group to listen to it in isolation. Instrument types suitable for grouping include drums, percussion, vocals, pads, strings, brass and so on.

VST Instrument channels are also shown in the Mixer. In order to be displayed a VST instrument must first be activated in the VST Instruments panel. To open the VST Instruments panel select Devices / VST Instruments or press F11 on the computer keyboard. To activate an instrument click in one of the panel slots and make a selection from the pop-up menu. The general operation of VST Instrument channels is similar to regular audio channels, with the exception of the record enable and monitor buttons which are not present. VST Instrument channels feature an additional edit button below the regular buttons which opens the GUI for the instrument.

Rewire channels are displayed in the Mixer when a Rewire channel is activated in the Rewire panel for the device (Devices menu). Rewire allows the real-time streaming of digital audio into Cubase from such things as software synthesizers, drum modules and other sequencers. The function buttons and general operation of Rewire channels are similar to regular Audio channels, with the exception of the record enable and monitor buttons which are not present.

Channel controls

The channel insert, EQ and send controls are adjusted in a number of locations, including in the extended section of the Mixer and in the Channel Settings window. The channel controls may also be adjusted in the Inspector (see Chapter 4 for details).

1 Adjusting the controls in the extended section of the Mixer

The insert / send assignments and EQ configuration can be immediately viewed and edited on any channel by activating the extended Mixer. The channel must be in wide mode in order to view the extended channel strip. You can choose what to view in each channel's pop-up options menu (Figure 12.5) or globally for all channels by clicking on the appropriate symbol in the Common panel.

Inserts in the extended Mixer

Audio insert effects are activated in the inserts section for each channel. Insert effects are assigned by clicking in one of the insert effects slots and choosing an effect from the pop-up menu (Figure 12.6). There are a total of eight insert effects slots. Insert effects are arranged in series i.e. the signal passes through each effect in turn. The output of each effect provides the input for the next effect in the following slot. However, inserts 1-6 are pre-fader and inserts 7-8 are post-fader. The post-fader inserts are intended for processing which is best applied after the channel fader, such as limiting for peak level control. To move the contents of any insert slot to another, drag from the source insert slot number and release over the target slot. Hold Alt to copy rather than move. This allows you to freely change the order of effects and copy effects between channels.

Figure 12.5
Choose what to view in the extended part of the Mixer using the channel's pop-up options menu

Figure 12.6
Assigning an Audio channel insert effect

Sends in the extended Mixer

Eight auxiliary send controls in the extended Mixer allow you to send the channel signal to effects, effects side chains, groups or output buses. Before a destination is available in the send menu it must first be active. For example, to activate a standard send effect first create an FX channel using Project / Add track / FX channel. You may then assign a send control to the effect by selecting it from the pop-up menu which appears when you click on the send effect slot. To send the channel signal to the effect, increase the corresponding send mini-fader level (Figure 12.7). Send effect signals are added to the original signal in parallel. The relative levels of the original (dry) and effected (wet) signals may be adjusted to achieve the desired result.

Figure 12.7
Setting the level of an Audio channel auxiliary send

EQ in the extended Mixer

The EQ for audio channels may be adjusted in the extended part of the Mixer using the built-in 4-band EQ sections. These are arranged in a similar manner to a real-world mixing console. EQ is outlined in more detail below.

MIDI effects in the extended Mixer

The MIDI insert and send effects sections of the extended Mixer are implemented in a similar manner to the Audio effects sections. Clicking once in any

Figure 12.8

Assigning insert and send effects on MIDI channels is handled in a similar manner to Audio channel effects

of the insert or send effects fields in the MIDI insert or send sections opens a pop-up menu from which you can choose one of the available MIDI effects (Figure 12.8). Here, you are affecting MIDI data and not audio signals, but the logical structure remains very similar to the audio equivalent. There are four insert effect and four send effect slots.

2 Adjusting the controls in the Channel Settings windows

For detailed management of all the controls of a single channel, Cubase provides the Channel Settings window. To open the Channel Settings window click on the channel edit button ('e'). The main advantages of the Channel Settings window is that you can see all of the parameters simultaneously and, for audio-based channels, the EQ section features an EQ curve display where you can make adjustments graphically. You can also customise the Channel settings window to show only what you really need to see.

Audio channel Settings

For Audio, Instrument, Group, FX, VSTi and Rewire channels, the Channel Settings window (Figure 12.9) features a duplicate of the channel fader, insert effects, EQ section, send effects section and all other parameters associated with the channel. This is ideal for detailed work. The channel fader, insert and send sections function in similar manner to the main Mixer. The EQ section features an EQ curve display in which you can quickly create custom curves, and a useful EQ presets menu (see the 'EQ' section, below, for more details).

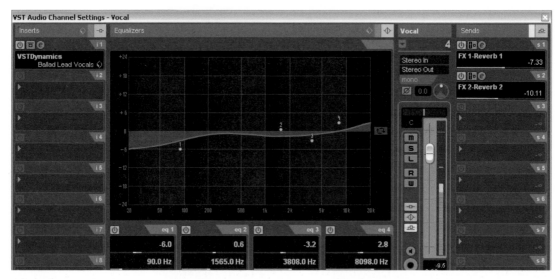

Figure 12.9

Audio channel settings window

MIDI Channel Settings

Similar to the Audio Channel Settings window, the MIDI Channel Settings window features a duplicate of the channel fader, MIDI insert effects, MIDI send effects and all other MIDI channel parameters. And similar to the Audio Channel Settings window, the main advantage of the MIDI Channel Settings window is that you can see multiple parameters simultaneously. All parame-

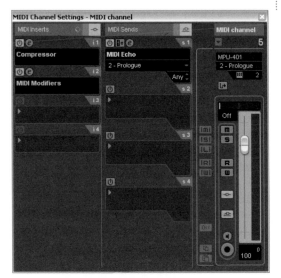

Figure 12.10
MIDI Channel Settings window

ters function in a similar manner to the main Mixer window.

Input and output buses

The main input and output buses appear to the left (input) and right (output) of the regular channels in the Mixer (Figure 12.11). Input busesprovide control of any incoming signals from the audio hardware inputs while output busesprovide control of outgoing signals being routed to the audio hardware outputs. The manner in which the input and output busesare connected to the audio hardware is managed in the VST Connections window. The input and output busesmay be mono, stereo or multiple channel format. Input busesare used primarily for the recording of input signals (see Chapter 3 for details of setting up an input bus for recording). The remainder of this section is concerned with the use of output buses.

By default, the regular audio-based channels are routed to the first stereo output bus which, in turn, is usually assigned to the first pair of stereo out-

Figure 12.11
The input and output buses to the left and right of the regular Mixer channels

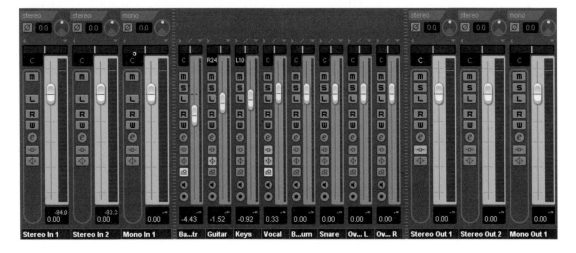

Figure 12.12
Main mix bus with
inserts section set up
for a stereo mix

Figure 12.12
Main mix bus with
inserts section set up
for a stereo mix

puts in the audio hardware. The output routing for a channel is chosen in the output routing menu in the upper section of the Mixer. When mixing to stereo most of the output routing menus of the regular channels are set to the same stereo master output bus (sometimes referred to as the main mix bus). In this manner, the channel fader on the main mix bus provides the master fader for the whole mix (Figure 12.12).

By activating the extended Mixer you can see the inserts section for the stereo master output bus. Here, you can activate effects and processing which affect the whole mix. The output bus insert effects routing is similar to that of regular channels where the signal passes through each effect in the slots in descending order. However, output bus inserts are normally intended for processors which are suitable for a final stereo mix or mastering project. This includes such things as limiters, compressors, loudness maximisers, noise reduction processors and denoisers. Inserts 1-6 are pre-fader and inserts 7-8 are post-fader. The post-fader inserts are intended for processing which is best applied at the very end of the signal chain after the master fader, such as limiting and dithering.

Multiple bus and surround configurations

Users with multiple I/O hardware may configure their system for surround sound or other multiple input / output configurations. Multiple channel surround buses or a number of extra buses may be added to the system in the VST Connections window. I/O buses added in the VST Connections window appear in the Mixer to the left (for input buses) and to the right (for output buses) of the regular audio, MIDI and other channel types.

Input buses are mainly used for recording purposes and are outlined in chapters 2 and 3. Output bus assignments might involve surround configurations, where a single bus is all that is needed to control a 5.1 surround output, or multiple output configurations where additional mono or stereo buses are used to route signals to other parts of your audio system (see Figure 12.13).

Once activated, additional output buses are available in other parts of the system. For example, any Audio channel can be assigned to any of the available output buses in the output routing menu of the channel.

Figure 12.13
After having been
activated in the VST
Connections window,
additional output buses
appear in the Mixer to
the right of the regular
channels

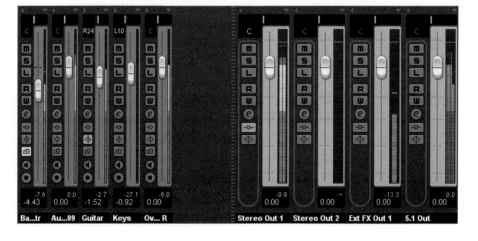

EQ

EQ is an abbreviation for 'equalisation'. This involves increasing or decreasing the levels of different frequency bands within a sound signal for corrective or creative purposes. Essentially, EQ combines the actions of various types of filters but, whereas filters are normally concerned with removing frequencies, EQ involves both reducing and boosting frequencies within the signal. One of the most popular implementations of EQ is known as parametric EQ. This allows you to select a frequency band within the spectrum, adjust the width of this frequency band and increase or decrease its level. Cubase provides a built-in EQ section with four modules per channel which can be set to various types of parametric and shelving EQ or low and high pass filtering. The modules are viewed and adjusted in the extended part of the Mixer, in the Channel Settings window, or in the Inspector.

EQ in the Mixer window

In the Mixer, the layout of the EQ controls resembles that of a classic real-world console. Here, you have the choice of viewing the parameters as mini-faders or as controls with a curve display (Figure 12.14). The advantage of viewing the EQ section in the extended Mixer is that you can adjust the EQ for a number of related tracks simultaneously and you maintain a good overview of your EQ settings. This is similar to how you might work with a real-world console.

EQ in the Channel Settings window

To open the Channel Settings window for a channel, click on the channel edit button ('e'). The Channel Settings window shows the EQ section as four modules with an EQ curve display in the central area of the window (Figure 12.15). The EQ curve display provides visual feedback of the EQ settings. Frequency is shown on the horizontal axis and gain on the vertical axis.

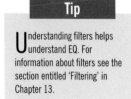

Tip

Understanding filters helps understand EQ. For information about filters see the section entitled 'Filtering' in Chapter 13.

Figure 12.14
Mixer EQ sections displayed with a curve display and with mini-faders

Figure 12.15
The EQ section in the Channel Settings window

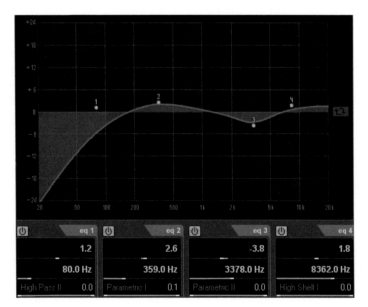

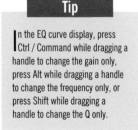

Tip

In the EQ curve display, press Ctrl / Command while dragging a handle to change the gain only, press Alt while dragging a handle to change the frequency only, or press Shift while dragging a handle to change the Q only.

Clicking in the display activates a numbered handle and its corresponding module. The handle can be freely dragged to any position and allows the adjustment of frequency and gain simultaneously. Double-clicking on a handle deletes it and de-activates its corresponding module. Moving the handles in the EQ curve display while listening to the result in real-time is a great way of intuitively adjusting the EQ. This is the main advantage of adjusting EQ in the Channel Settings window.

EQ details

EQ controls

To help you understand the EQ section in more detail, Figure 12.16 shows the functions of one EQ module in isolation.

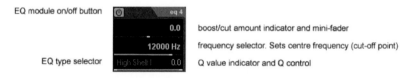

Figure 12.16
EQ control functions

EQ module on/off button

boost/cut amount indicator and mini-fader

frequency selector. Sets centre frequency (cut-off point)

EQ type selector

Q value indicator and Q control

EQ Modules 1 and 4 may be set to parametric, shelving, high-pass or low-pass types. EQ modules 2 and 3 may be set to two parametric types only. The different types of EQ are chosen in the type menu for each band and include the following:

• Parametric 1–2 – standard parametric EQ providing centre frequency, bandwidth and level boost or cut parameters. Two types of response curve are provided.
• Low shelf 1–4 – a low shelving filter providing overall low frequency boost or cut below the selected frequency cut-off point. Four contrasting response curves are provided.
• High-pass 1–2 – a high pass cut-off filter where all frequencies below the selected frequency cut-off point are significantly reduced and all those above pass through unchanged. Two contrasting response curves are provided.
• High shelf 1–4 – a high shelving filter, providing overall high frequency boost or cut above the selected frequency cut-off point. The opposite of the low shelf filter. Four contrasting response curves are provided.
• Low-pass 1–2 – a low pass cut-off filter where all frequencies above the selected frequency cut-off point are significantly reduced and all those below pass through unchanged. The opposite of high-pass mode. Two contrasting response curves are provided.

The EQ section, as displayed in the Channel Settings window, features two other useful parameters as follows:

• Preset management menu – for the storage and recall of EQ presets.
• Invert equaliser button – for inverting the EQ curve. This is useful for finding an unwanted frequency range by first boosting it so that you are certain you have found it and then cutting it by selecting the invert button.

Parametric EQ in theory

This section quickly outlines the theory behind parametric EQ. This is of value to those who are new to EQ'ing. The essential pre-requisites for a parametric EQ are a gain control, a centre frequency selector and a Q control. The frequency selector allows you to tune the EQ to the frequency band you wish to process and the Q control governs the width of this band, (otherwise known as the bandwidth). The gain control provides the means to boost or cut the chosen frequencies. Figure 12.17 shows a graphical view of these main controls.

Parametric EQ in practice

Now, bearing the theory in mind, let's conduct an experiment with a single Cubase EQ module. Try the following:

- Activate a single EQ module while playing a complex signal through the chosen Audio channel (try a rhythm guitar or a drum performance).
- Select parametric II mode.
- Set the gain control to -24dB to radically cut the chosen frequencies.
- Set the Q control to 6.0.
- Slowly sweep the frequency selector from the maximum to the minimum position

Figure 12.17
Parametric EQ controls

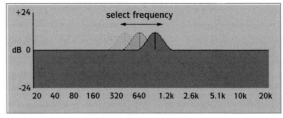

Frequency control

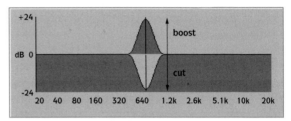

Gain control

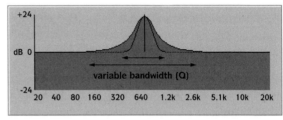

Q control

As you sweep the frequency selector listen to the change in the sound as the cut frequency band sweeps down through the spectrum. The effect is particularly apparent between 100Hz and 6kHz. As you reach the lower part of the frequency range the sound becomes more treble biased as the bass and lower-mid frequencies are reduced in level. Using a more moderate version of this technique you can, for example, find and correct the problem frequencies in a sound which was recorded with too much lower middle or too much bass. Try the same experiment with the Q control set to different values.

EQ Summary

The built-in EQ section provides a convenient means of shaping your sounds for both corrective and creative purposes. The inclusion of parametric EQ, shelving EQ and high and low pass cut-off filters means that the EQ section matches the performance of that found on many real-world mixing consoles. The preset menu is particularly welcome since any EQ configuration can be saved for later recall and instant comparisons can be made between different settings. (For more about EQ and filters see Chapter 13).

Tip

To make A/B comparisons between the equalised and unequalised signal, click on the channel EQ state button (green = EQ enabled, yellow = EQ disabled).

Info

EQ is an important tool in any mix but if your sounds are already well recorded you shouldn't need to use much EQ to get the desired result. Using EQ in the mix should be more about blending sounds together rather than correcting poor recordings.

The anatomy of sounds

This section highlights the important frequency ranges for a number of popular musical instruments in the form of EQ anatomy charts. This is a bit like dissecting and looking inside each sound. Each chart outlines where in the spectrum of each instrument you might cut or boost and the effect this is likely to have.

How to use the EQ anatomy charts

The first thing to bear in mind before using the following EQ anatomy charts is that you cannot adjust a chosen frequency band if there is no activity in this band within the recorded signal. For example, you cannot enhance the so-called 'air' of a vocal track between 14kHz and 20kHz if this frequency range is not present in the recording. All you add is hiss! Similarly, you cannot easily boost the 80Hz bass region of a kick drum if it was originally recorded with a microphone which did not capture this frequency. Also bear in mind that you cannot make accurate EQ adjustments if your monitoring equipment or headphones are not capable of accurately reproducing the whole of the audible frequency range.

Each EQ anatomy chart displays multiple zone EQ curves. The upper curve shows the key areas within the frequency spectrum where the chosen instrument may be boosted while the lower curve shows the key areas where it may be cut. The effect of boosting or cutting is indicated for each zone. The amount of boost or cut is a rough (and conservative) estimate and may vary considerably for each treated sound. Similarly, the centre frequency and bandwidth for each zone may also vary. There are no hard and fast rules. Where appropriate, suitable high-pass or low-pass filter settings are indicated by the lower curve. Occasionally, low or high shelving filters might better suit the EQing task rather than multiple parametric curves. For reference purposes, the lower part of the display features an unequalised FFT spectral analysis of a typical instrument in each category.

Above all, the curves shown in the charts are NOT intended as overall EQ settings which you would want to re-create in their entirety. They show individual frequency bands each of which is useful for the specific effect indicated. The EQ anatomy curves were created using typical acoustic instrument sounds in each category. The accuracy of the curves cannot be guaranteed for all sounds in the same category since the tone colour and spectral components of sounds vary enormously. Mixing cannot be reduced to the sonic equivalent of painting by numbers. The charts are therefore suitable as rough guides. They help you quickly tune in to the salient elements of your sounds, but you may well need to fine tune the settings to achieve the desired result and you must at all times use your ears and your own judgement.

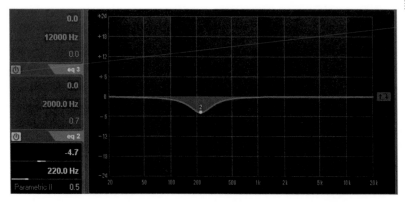

Figure 12.18
Curing a boomy kick drum in the
Channel settings EQ curve display

Depending upon the nature of your creative or corrective task, you might need to use only one part of the curve or several. For a boomy kick drum, try a moderate broad band cut centred around 200-300Hz, (as indicated in the EQ anatomy kick drum chart in Figure 12.20, below). This corrective EQ setting is easily created by dragging a handle to the appropriate position in the Channel Settings EQ curve display and setting an appropriate Q value (Figure 12.18). Alternatively, click on the frequency field and type in the centre frequency. Then adjust the gain and Q by ear using the mini faders.

For a cold, piercing vocal, try a little broad-band boost centred around 250-300Hz and a subtle cut centred around 1.5kHz or perhaps a sharper cut at around 3.5kHz, (as indicated in the EQ anatomy vocals chart in Figure 12.31). This is easily created by dragging handles to the appropriate positions in the Channel Settings EQ curve display and setting the appropriate Q values (Figure 12.19). Alternatively, click on the frequency fields and type in the centre frequencies. Then adjust the gains and Q controls by ear using the mini faders.

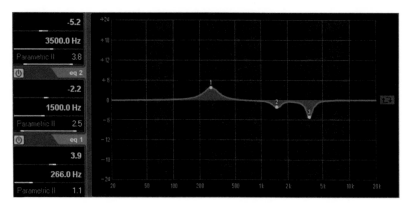

Figure 12.19
Correcting a cold, piercing vocal in the
Channel settings EQ curve display

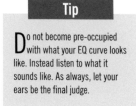

Tip

Do not become pre-occupied with what your EQ curve looks like. Instead listen to what it sounds like. As always, let your ears be the final judge.

EQ anatomy charts

Figures 12.20 to 12.31 show the EQ anatomy charts for a selection of popular musical instruments and vocals. These were created using an apulSoft apQualizr high precision equalizer plug-in but the curves are easily translated into the built-in EQ or Studio EQ plug-in of Cubase.

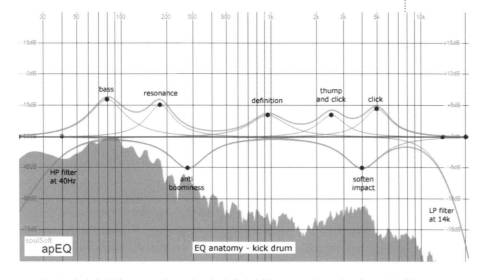

Figure 12.20

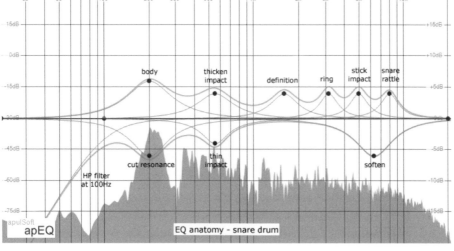

Figure 12.21

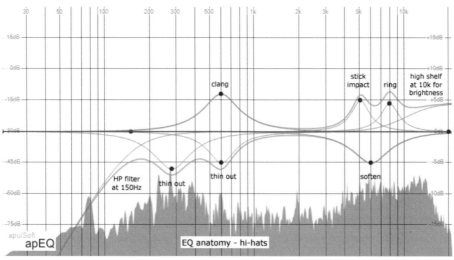

Figure 12.22

Figure 12.23

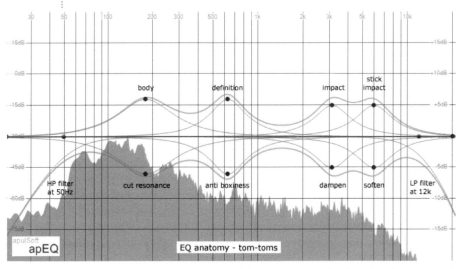

Figure 12.24

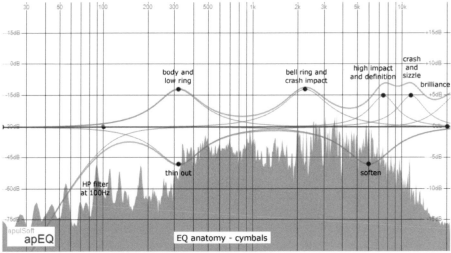

Figure 12.25

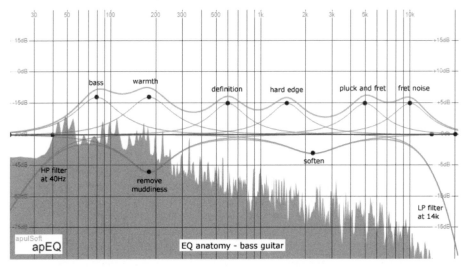

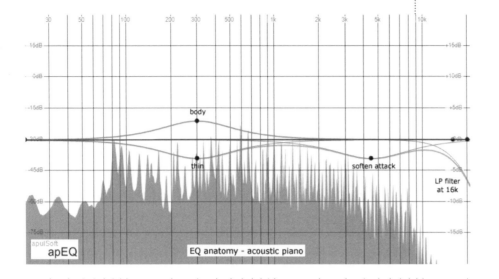

Figure 12.26

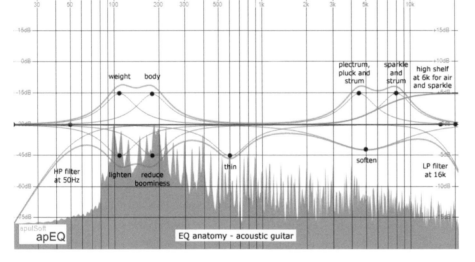

Figure 12.27

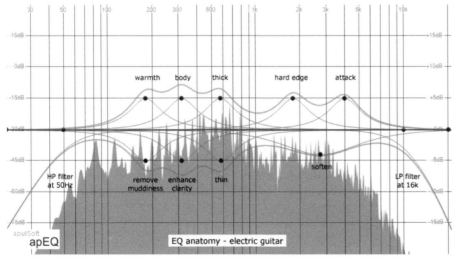

Figure 12.28

Figure 12.29

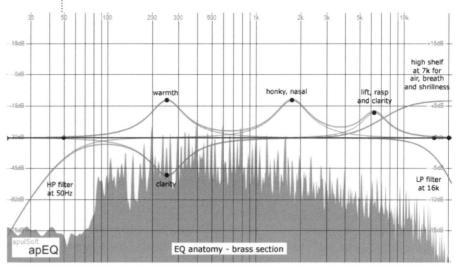

Figure 12.30

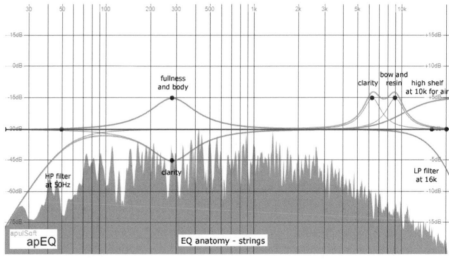

Figure 12.31

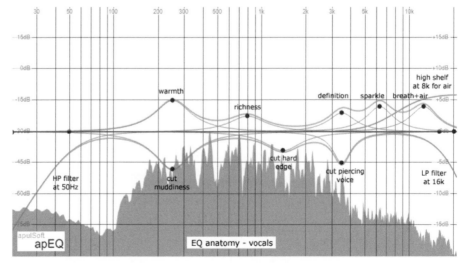

Mixing decisions

No matter how many mixer channels or how many effects and processors you have, you still have to actually do the mix. Above all, this involves listening very carefully and making a large number of decisions based upon what you hear. The following section focuses on the key elements of your mix and helps you make the right decisions.

Info

For more details about real-time effects and processors see Chapter 13.

Mixing tips

The ten golden rules for recording and mixing (above) help with some of the basic decisions involved in the recording and mixing process but here are some additional tips to help you create a better mix:

- Mixing the drum kit and bass first is just one way of laying the foundations for the rest of the mix but this is by no means the only way. Many engineers start with the lead vocal or whatever else they judge to be the most important tracks.
- In popular music the lead vocal is normally mixed more 'up-front' than the other sounds in the mix and is often treated with reverberation. The correct balance of the dry (original) and wet (reverberant) signals of the vocal sound and their balance with the rest of the mix is crucial, as is the choice of reverb settings.
- The lead vocal, kick drum, snare drum and bass instrument work well when panned to the centre of the stereo image. In contrast, backing vocals, hi-hat, tom-toms and cymbals are usually panned to the left and right of centre.
- The drum kit should not be panned excessively wide as this can give the odd impression that the drummer has very long arms!
- The vocal or other lead instrument may be difficult to hear because it is being masked by the frequencies of other instruments. Rather than boosting the sound you wish to hear, try instead cutting some of the frequencies of other instruments which operate in the same range. For vocals, try cutting the accompanying instruments between 2kHz and 4kHz and slightly boosting the vocal itself in the same range. To add still more presence to the vocal try a subtle boost at around 3.5kHz.
- Some instrumental and vocal performances produce wildly fluctuating signal levels. These are difficult to mix since sometimes they are too loud and sometimes too soft. Applying mild compression can help control this type of unmanageable signal. The problem can also be resolved by riding the faders as part of a manual or automated mix. Yet another technique involves splitting the problem track into a number of separate subtracks and treating each with different compression and fader settings (commonly known as multing).
- The perceived distance, location and depth of a sound are determined by its relative level, its high frequency content and the delay / reverberant characteristics which surround it (especially the early reflections). Cutting the high frequency content and adding subtle early reflections (or delay) can move a sound 'back' in the mix. Reducing the level of the direct sound and adding a slight amount of reverberation can increase the perceived distance still further. Careful use of short delays (less than 40ms) on monophonic sources

helps give them depth and directional focus.

- For depth enhancement, avoid surrounding all your sources with excessive reverb. Inevitably, this results in a cloudy, unfocused mix.

- If the mix sounds muddy attempt to clarify the definition of the main instruments by slightly boosting their most prominent frequencies. However, beware of boosting multiple instruments at the same frequency range. Instead, attempt to differentiate the sounds by giving each instrument its own EQ space.

- A mix may also sound muddy due to a confused and boomy bass end. In this case, try some broad band cut on the bass instruments centred between 200 and 250Hz. Bear in mind that bass sounds are often mixed dry (no reverb) since this enhances bass clarity.

- If the mix is sounding harsh, identify which instruments are producing this harshness and cut the offending frequencies. Upper frequency hard edge usually occurs somewhere between 1kHz and 3kHz so try cutting in this range. Many instruments can be softened by applying a broad band cut centred between 3kHz and 4kHz. To add more warmth, try a moderate broad band boost centred around 200Hz on selected instruments.

- Sounds to which you have applied corrective or creative EQ may sound good within the mix but unnatural when listened to in isolation. This is normal. If it sounds right in the mix then it is right. It is standard practice to subtly adjust the EQ for instruments occupying the same frequency range in order to avoid masking.

- Be aware of the internal spectral balance within each sound. Boosting or cutting in one frequency range affects other frequency ranges. For example, boosting bass frequencies may dull the sound while cutting bass may brighten it. The primary frequency change has a secondary effect. This gives you more than one way to achieve the same result.

- Broad bandwidths tend to give more natural results than narrow bandwidths when boosting frequencies with parametric EQ. Narrow bandwidths are better tolerated when cutting frequencies.

- Always listen to the original sound before you apply EQ. Only apply EQ if it is absolutely necessary. When EQ has been applied, always recheck the equalised sound against the unequalised sound (using the EQ state button) and check both versions with the other tracks in the mix. If the EQ has not improved the mix do not use it.

- Your mix may benefit from bus compression and / or overall limiting. Typically, bus compression is placed over the main mixer output and its purpose is to help glue the elements of your mix together. This usually requires gentle low ratio and soft knee settings. Limiting is normally inserted last in the chain where its primary purpose is to avoid digital clipping. Typically, this involves fast attack and high threshold settings which affect only the highest peaks in the signal. Compression and limiting at the mixing stage should not be too radical if your mix is to undergo a later mastering stage.

- Do not try to achieve a mix by continually raising levels and boosting EQ frequencies since not only will it sound like an aural battlefield, you will also quickly run out of headroom on the master fader.

- As you proceed with the mix try to keep a focus on the overall sound image you wish to create. Many engineers listen to one or more mixes of established artists, before and during the mix session, as a point of comparison with their own mix. However, it may not be appropriate to precisely match this sound if your mix is to undergo a later mastering session since a completed commercial release may have been agressively mastered.

- Judging the mix accurately after having worked on it for some time is not always easy. Some engineers recommend listening to the mix from outside the mixing room with the door open. This technique often shows up faults with the mix which were not obvious when you were in front of the speakers. Strange but true!

- As well as performing the mix in one take, do not be afraid to also try recording the mix in separate sections. These can be edited together at a later stage.

- If your mix is to undergo further editing and processing at a later mastering stage, do not apply noise-shaped dither and truncate to 16-bit at the mixdown stage. Instead, mix to a high-resolution format such as 32-bit float or 24-bit. Noise-shaped dither is applied later as the last step in the mastering session prior to truncation. Global fades in and out are also best left to the mastering session.

- When you have completed the mix, try listening to it on different audio systems such as a regular home hi-fi system, a walkman or a car hi-fi system. Try also listening to the mix on high quality headphones. If it sounds like you intended on all systems then you have probably created a good mix.

The above tips help with a number of issues which may be encountered during the course of a mixing session but only knowledge, experience and practice will produce the 'perfect' mix.

Mixing strategies

Designing your own mixing layout in Cubase

The first thing you might like to do before proceeding with a mix is to set up the working environment of Cubase so that it is optimised for mixing tasks. This is rather like a traditional recording studio when the engineer resets all the faders, dials and buttons on the console before proceeding with mixing.

Figure 12.32 shows a single screen layout optimised for mixing. A reduced Project window forms part of the layout, where the Marker track has been made larger than the other tracks. The Marker track helps you find your way around the musical arrangement and is especially useful if you have set up cycle markers. Mixers 2 and 3 are displayed next to the Project window, configured to show the FX and Group channels respectively. This provides quick access to the send effects return levels and group levels. The main Mixer is shown in extended mode for access to multiple EQs, inserts and sends, and large-scale meters on the main mix output channel. The ASIO

> **Tip**
>
> A good mix depends as much on the musical performance and arrangement as on the sound itself. It is a renowned fact that poorly arranged music is more difficult to mix.

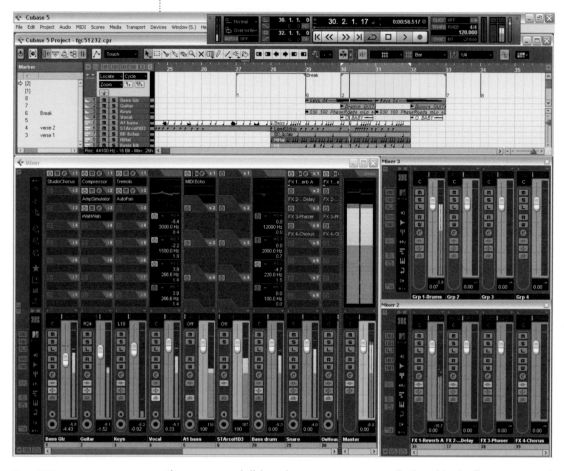

Figure 12.32
Cubase mixing layout

time usage and disk cache usage meters are displayed in the Transport panel for monitoring the system load. This helps when using large numbers of real-time effects where ideally the ASIO load should not average much higher than 50 – 60%. If your mixing layout goes beyond the limits of your screen this is not a big disadvantage since you can always use the main scroll bars to quickly move around. Equally, you can scroll through the channels in the Mixer using the Mixer window scroll bar when there are too many channels to fit in your Mixer window width. Alternatively, use the left / right arrow keys on the computer keyboard to scroll / select the channels.

Once you have set up a satisfactory layout you can save it as a Workspace (Window / Workspaces / New workspace). Your mix environment may now be recalled at any time from the Organise workspaces dialogue (Alt + Pad 0) or using a key command (by default, Alt + Pad 1 to Pad 9).

Using Group channels

Group channels are useful for creating stems of the main elements within your mix, such as drums, bass, vocals, guitars, pads, strings, brass, wood-wind, dialogue, sound effects and so on. Stems are separate audio files of these main elements. To create stems in Cubase, firstly route the source

Audio channels according to their instrument type to separate Group channels. Next, assign the Group channels as the inputs for an appropriate number of new empty Audio channels. Name these new channels appropriately
and set their outputs to 'no bus' to avoid high levels on the stereo output
bus. Finally, record enable the new Audio channels and press the transport
record button to record all the stems in one pass. Stems are commonly used
in the film and television industries.

Group channels also provide an alternative for send effects (instead of the
usual FX channels) or for unorthodox routing configurations. For example, for
parallel compression you could send the channel signal to a Group channel which
contains a compressor as an insert. The source channel provides the source signal level and the Group channel provides the parallel compression level.

Useful solo functions

When you solo an audio-based channel with an active auxiliary send routed
to an FX channel, the FX channel is also automatically sooled. This is helpful
when you wish to listen to a soloed track complete with any effects which
have been applied to it. If, however, you wish to hear the channel dry, then
click on the mute button of the FX channel before activating solo. Any other
channels you want to listen to when activating a solo button can be 'protected' from the soloing action using the solo defeat function. To activate solo
defeat, hold Alt and click on the solo button of the chosen channel. Now
when you activate the solo button of another channel, the 'solo defeated'
channel is not muted. To de-activate the solo defeat function, hold Alt and
click on the solo button of the 'solo defeated' channel a second time.

Routing signals to side chains

The Mixer allows you to send audio-based channel signals to any active side
chain via the auxiliary sends. Before the side chain input is available to the
send control, the side chain button must first be activated in the relevant
audio effect. For example, activating the side chain button of the supplied
Compressor audio effect allows it to be used for ducking. Typically, ducking
involves the reduction in the level of a music track according to the presence
of a voice-over track (speech), as is often heard on music radio stations. To
route a channel signal in this manner, proceed as follows:

Send 1
routed to
Compressor
side chain

- Create or open a project which includes a music track and a voice-over
  track.
- Activate the Compressor audio effect in an insert slot of the music track.
- Activate the side chain button in the Compressor plug-in.
- Select the Compressor side chain input in a send slot of the voice-over
  track.
- Activate the side chain send slot and set an appropriate send level.
- Try the Compressor settings in Figure 12.32b. Try ratios between 2 and
  8 : 1.

Figure 12.32b
The Mixer sends allow you to route the
audio signal of one channel to the side
chain input of an audio effect on another
channel for corrective or creative
processing

Using the Mixer context menu

To open the Mixer context menu right click / command click anywhere on the Mixer display (Figure 12.33). This is a multi-purpose menu for managing the Mixer view, command targets, hide status, channel link, channel add, save / load channel settings, and for meter management. The options function as follows:

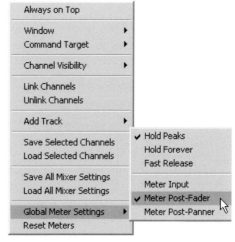

Figure 12.33
The Mixer context menu

- Window – allows you to show or hide the extended and routing views of the Mixer.
- Command target – the settings here govern which channels are subject to 'set target channels to can hide' and 'all targets wide' or 'all targets narrow' commands.
- Channel visibility – allows you to set or clear the 'can hide' status on the target channels.
- Link / Unlink channels – links two or more channels together so that moving the fader, mute, solo, monitor or record enable controls on one of the linked channels also moves the same controls on all the other linked channels. To link channels, select two or more channels in the Mixer by holding the Shift key on the computer keyboard (alternatively for consecutive channel selections use the left / right arrow keys while holding Shift on the computer keyboard). Select Link Channels in the Mixer context menu to implement the link. Link Channels is immediately useful for grouping channels together for common tasks, such as muting the backing vocals in a mix, lowering the volume of linked string channels while maintaining their relative levels, or soloing all the drum tracks.

- Save / Load Selected channels – saves or loads the current settings of the selected channel(s). All parameters are saved or loaded. When loading a multiple channel file, only the currently selected channels are affected. For example, if you selected six channels when you saved the file then, to load all six channels, you must manually select six channels when you load the file. Good for copying settings between multiple tracks in the same mix or in an alternative version of the same project.
- Save / Load all Mixer settings – saves or loads all the current parameter settings for all channels in the Mixer, including the input and output buses. This is like taking a global snapshot of the whole Mixer. Good for re-initialising the Mixer to your preferred settings prior to commencing a mix or for copying mixes between different versions of the same project.

This function does not add channels when there are less channels in the destination Mixer than in the saved file.

- Global Meter Settings – features a number of options for changing the behaviour of the meters. When 'Hold Peaks' is activated a horizontal line at the peak level of the signal remains in the display for a short time. The hold time may be modified in File / Preferences / VST. When 'Hold Forever' is activated the highest peak in the signal is held permanently in the meter display, which is helpful for finding the maximum peak within any audio passage. When 'Fast release' is de-activated, the meters react slightly more slowly to changes in the signal allowing you to perceive the average peak level. When 'Fast Release' is activated, the meters behave like fast digital peak meters and react extremely quickly to show all the peaks in the signal. This is good for recording highly dynamic signals where you may wish to monitor the transient peaks more clearly in order to avoid distortion. The 'Meter Input', 'Meter Post-Fader' and 'Meter Post-Panner' settings allow you to see the level at different points in the signal chain. In Meter Input mode, you are viewing the meter level of the source audio as recorded on hard disk if you are looking at an audio-based channel or of the incoming audio signal if you are looking at an input channel. Meter Input mode is normally used when recording. In Meter Post-Fader mode, you are viewing the level of the signal after it has passed via the channel fader. In Meter Post-Panner mode you are viewing the level of the signal after it has passed via the channel fader and the pan control. Post-Panner mode is relevant to stereo signals only. The pan position you choose is now reflected in the channel meter. Some sound engineers claim that this is more intuitive and logical to use.
- Reset Meters – resets all meters simultaneously. Helpful if you are measuring levels over a specific passage or checking for clipping.

Other useful Mixer techniques

Other useful Mixer techniques include the following:

- Various key commands help with the operation of the Mixer. Use the left / right arrow keys on the computer keyboard to select the channels. Hold Shift while pressing the left / right arrow keys to make multiple channel selections. Use the up / down arrow keys to change the fader level of the currently selected channel or a number of selected channels. Use 'M' to mute and 'S' to solo the currently selected channel or a number of selected channels.
- Automatic record enabling of channels upon selection is not convenient for most mixing purposes. To disable automatic record enabling upon channel selection, open File / Preferences / Editing / Project & Mixer and disable 'Enable Record on Selected Track'.
- The settings of one channel can be copied to another using standard copy and paste techniques. Pressing Ctrl / Command + C on the computer keyboard copies the settings of the currently selected channel to the clipboard. Ctrl / Command + V pastes the contents of the

Tip

For instant A / B comparisons between the output of two channels, activate the mute button on just one of the channels and select both. Press 'M' on the computer keyboard to instantly toggle auditioning from one channel to the other.

clipboard to the curently selected channel. Settings may be copied from one Project window to another.

• During mixing you are likely to concentrate on specific passages using Cubase in cycle playback mode. To make this easier, try setting up a number of cycle markers in the Marker track. Hold Ctrl / Command and drag with the pointer in the Marker track to insert a cycle marker over the selected range. To move the left and right locators to the start and end of a cycle marker range, open the cycle marker pop-up menu and make a selection from the list. Alternatively, press Shift + G to start immediate loop playback around the currently selected cycle marker.

• The pre-fader button in the Send effect slots is used to change the routing configuration to the effects. When the pre-fader button is in its default deactivated state (the post fader setting), the channel fader affects both the channel level and the send level. When the pre-fader button is activated (the pre-fader setting), the channel fader affects the channel level as usual but no longer affects the send level. The send level is now controlled by the send slot mini-fader only. A pre-fader setting is good for creative sound effects. For example, to create an autopan effect where you hear the effects signal only, send the channel signal to the AutoPan plug-in, activate the send pre-fader button and reduce the channel fader to its minimum. You now hear only the effects signal. Or try setting up a pre-fader send to a reverb effect and then slowly fade out the dry signal to leave the reverberant signal only. This creates the illusion of the sound disappearing into the distance.

Mixer routing

It is helpful to remember the basic routing order as the signal passes through an audio-based channel. This is as follows:

1 phase switch
2 input gain
3 inserts 1-6
4 EQ
5 pre-fader aux send
6 channel fader
7 inserts 7-8
8 post-fader aux send
9 pan

To help further clarify your mixing tasks, Figure 12.34 shows a flowchart of the signal as it passes through an audio channel and a master stereo output bus and the order in which the effects and EQ are applied.

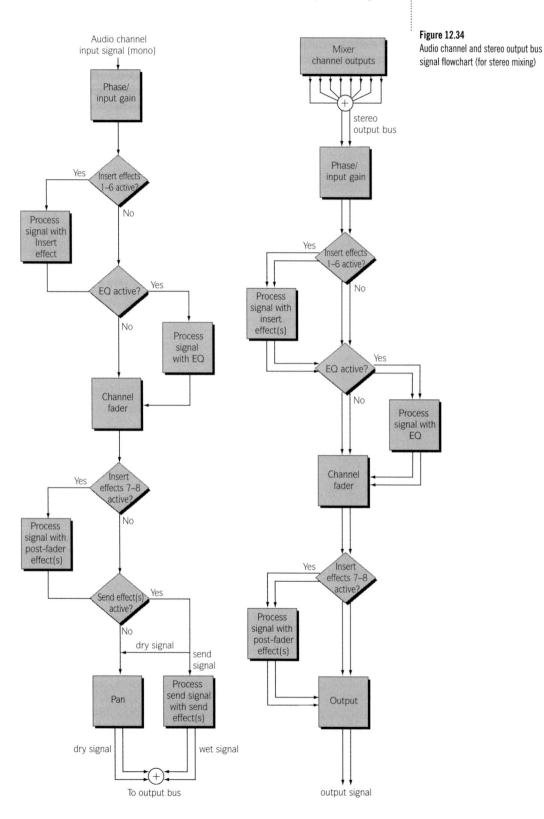

Figure 12.34
Audio channel and stereo output bus
signal flowchart (for stereo mixing)

Mixing down

The final mix

The final mix involves mixing down the multi-track audio into a stereo or multi-channel / surround format. Depending on your preferences and overall system resources, this can occur using a variety of techniques. The main choices are as follows:

- Mixing down via an external console or summing mixer. Here, the signals from the tracks in Cubase are routed to the external mixer via the multiple digital or analogue outputs of your audio hardware. The final mix takes place using a combination of the controls within Cubase and those of the external device. The mix is transferred in real-time to an external storage medium, such as analogue tape or hard disk recorder, or may be passed back into Cubase for recording on the hard disk of the host computer.
- Mixing down to external media using the virtual Mixer in Cubase. In this case, the final mix takes place entirely within Cubase. The mix is transferred to the final medium via the analogue or digital outputs of your audio hardware. This technique suits mixing down to analogue tape or external hard disk recorder and offers the possibility of an automated mix within Cubase if your external console does not feature automation.
- Mixing down to an audio file using the virtual Mixer in Cubase and the Export / Audio Mixdown function. The resulting audio file is stored on the hard disk of the host computer. This is known as 'mixing in the box'. In this case, the final mix takes place entirely within Cubase. The mix is transferred directly to the hard disk as an audio file in the format specified in the Export / Audio Mixdown dialogue. This allows you to produce high-resolution audio files suitable for later transfer to CD or other media (see below for details of the Export / Audio Mixdown function).

The third option tends to be the most popular choice among Cubase users since it is convenient and helps maintain the quality of the audio. Some users argue that passing through a high quality external summing mixer, as outlined in option 1, can improve the sound of the mix. In all cases, if your mix is to undergo further editing and processing at a later mastering stage, do not apply dithering and do not truncate to 16-bits at the mixing stage. Instead, choose a high-resolution audio format in the Export / Audio Mixdown dialogue, such as 32 or 24-bit/44.1, and mix down without dithering. Global fades in and out are also best left to the mastering session. However, if no mastering stage is envisaged and you wish to produce a final audio file which is suitable for burning onto an audio CD, use dithering and choose 16-bit/44.1kHz in the Export / Audio Mixdown dialogue

Integrating the MIDI tracks in your final mix

If you are using option 1, as outlined above, the audio signals from your external MIDI devices may be integrated into the final mix by routing them to the external mixer. The audio signals need not be recorded within Cubase.

However, if you are using Export / Audio Mixdown to export your final mix as an audio file (opton 3), all MIDI tracks which are triggering external MIDI devices are not included in the mix. Cubase has no way of knowing what audio signals your external units are producing. The solution is to bounce the audio outputs of your external MIDI devices onto regular audio tracks before proceeding with the final mix. This technique is fully explained in the section entitled 'How do I include my MIDI recordings when I use Export / Audio Mixdown?' in Chapter 5.

Export / Audio Mixdown

Mixdown basics

Export / Audio Mixdown allows you to create a stereo (or surround format) audio file of the whole mix. It also allows you to create an audio file from any passage and any track within your project and features channel batch export functions for exporting multiple channels to separate files.

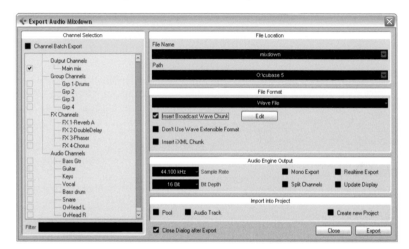

Figure 12.35
The Export / Audio Mixdown dialogue

To open the Audio mixdown dialogue select Export / Audio Mixdown in the File menu (Figure 12.35). Export / Audio Mixdown operates on all non-muted audio-based channels between the left and right locators. The basic procedure for mixing down is as follows:

• Move the left and right locators to the start and end points of the passage in the project you wish to mix down. This could be a few bars or the whole length of the project. Mute all tracks which you do not wish to include in the mix.
• Carefully audition the selected passage to make sure the mix sounds exactly as required.
• Open the Export / Audio Mixdown dialogue and select the file format, number of channels, bit depth and sample rate for the destination file. Wave is the standard audio file format used in PC systems and AIFF is the standard in Mac systems. For internet and website applications, the MPEG1 Layer 3 format is available.

- If you intend to mix down to a final stereo file to be used for the creation of an audio CD, 16-bit/44.1kHz are the correct settings. If it is a final audio file to which no further processing is to be applied, you would also need to apply dithering when truncating the bit depth (reducing the bit-depth from 32 or 24-bit to 16-bit). Dithering is applied in slots 7 or 8 of the main mix output channel.
- If your mix is to undergo further editing and processing at a later mastering stage, do not apply noise shaped dither and truncate to 16-bit at the mixdown stage. Instead, mix to a high-resolution format, such as 32-bit float or 24-bit. Dithering is applied later, as the last step in the mastering session, prior to truncation.
- Choose the channel you wish to mix down in the channel selection pane on the left. For mixing down a whole stereo mix, select the main stereo output channel to which all the channels in the Mixer are routed (the main mix channel).
- Activate 'Pool' or 'Audio track' in the 'Import into project' section if you wish to import the resulting audio file after it has been created.
- Select a name and path for the new file and, after verifying that you have made the correct settings in the dialogue, click on the Export button.

Info

If an External FX plug-in is active within the project, Export / Audio Mixdown is always conducted in real-time export mode. This is necessary in order to capture the real-time output of the external effects device.

Info

If your DAW system features a CD-R drive, you can burn a sequence of 16-bit/44.1kHz stereo audio files to an audio CD using an audio CD burning application.

In the above procedure, make sure you set the left and right locators to appropriate positions. When placing the right locator, it is preferable to leave a gap of one or two bars after the audio tracks have finished to take into account any reverberation tail or other effects which may spill over beyond the end point of the music.

Channel batch export

To use the channel batch export function activate the channel batch export check box at top left of the Export / Audio Mixdown dialogue. This changes the channel selection view to allow selection of multiple channels or channel types and changes the filename field to a prefix. To export multiple channels to separate audio files choose the channels in the channel selection view, choose a prefix name, path and file format, and click on the export button. All selected channels between the left and right locators are automatically exported as separate audio files. The file names take the following format:

prefix; channel number; channel type; channel name.

Thus, a batch export using the prefix 'export' for three audio tracks on channels 1, 2 and 3 named piano, guitar and vocal results in the following file names:

export – 01 – Audio – piano
export – 02 – Audio – guitar
export – 03 – Audio – vocal

The purpose of your mixdown

It is preferable to have a clear idea of the purpose of your mixdown before commencing since this helps choose the correct settings and audio format. Your mixdown might be a rough mix, or batch exported files for use in other projects or other software. In the latter cases, the audio format can vary enormously according to the task at hand. Other possibilities include audio CD demos, finished master files or files intended for mastering at a later stage. Properly dithered 16-bit/44.1 stereo audio files are what you need for an audio CD demo or final master file. Non-dithered 32-bit float or 24-bit high-resolution formats are usually what you need if your mix is to undergo further editing and processing at a later mastering stage.

Other possibilities for exporting audio include the creation of:

- MP3 files for multimedia applications
- Multiple-channel interleaved files
- Split stereo or split multi-channel files
- Mono files

If you encounter difficulties when using Export / Audio Mixdown, try activating 'Real Time Export' in the output section. This takes longer but may provide a solution. Also make sure that none of your tracks have their monitor buttons activated, as this blocks transfer of the channel data during the export process.

Info

Mastering is often better handled in a specialised mastering and CD burning application like Steinberg Wavelab or Bias Peak.

Tip

Export Audio Mixdown is useful for bouncing several tracks and their effects into a single mono or stereo audio file to free up space in the project and on the hard disk. This also helps conserve processing power.

Mixer moves

To help you in your various mixing tasks, Table 12.1 shows a number of useful key commands and practical mixer moves:

Table 12.1 Mixer moves

Key selected		Mouse action	Result
PC	Mac		
F2	F2	-	opens the Transport panel
F3	F3	-	opens the Mixer
F4	F4	-	opens VST Connections window
F11	F11	-	opens VST Instruments panel
F12	F12	-	opens VST Performance meter
M	M	-	mutes selected channel(s)
S	S	-	solos selected channel(s)
ctrl	cmnd	click once on fader	resets fader to 0dB
ctrl	cmnd	click once on pan control	resets pan position to centre
Shift	Shift	move fader or pan control	changes setting in fine amounts
-	-	click on channel headroom indicator	resets headroom indicator
-	-	double-click on channel strip name	opens channel name entry pop-up
L/R arrow	L/R arrow		selects next consecutive channel
U/D arrow	U/D arrow		changes volume fader level of selected channel

The Control Room Mixer

The Control Room Mixer is a specialised mixer for managing control room monitoring, studio performance area monitoring, headphone mixes, talkback, external equipment interfacing and general signal distribution within your studio environment. The manner in which you use it depends upon what equipment is included in your setup and how many inputs and outputs are included on your audio hardware. For example, at its most basic level you can use it to regulate the listening volume of your main control room monitors. In a more elaborate setup, you could create separate mixes for up to four separate studio destinations, distribute the metronome click among these destinations, patch in up to six different external machines such as CD players, hard disk recorders and so on, activate multiple, stereo or mono downmix configurations and switch between main and nearfield monitors in the control room.

Setting up the studio connections

Before you can use the Control Room Mixer you need to set up the inputs and outputs of your audio hardware in the Studio section of the VST Connections window. It is best not to use the same inputs and outputs here that you use for the main Mixer inputs and outputs, as this may lead to confusion. To assign a studio bus, click on the Add Channel button. Assign the device and outputs for each bus in the Audio Device and Device Port columns. Figure 12.36 shows an elaborate configuration for connecting talkback microphone, CD player, two studio sends, control room headphones and main or nearfield monitor connections. This setup only suits multiple I/O audio hardware but shows the wide ranging applications of the Control Room Mixer.

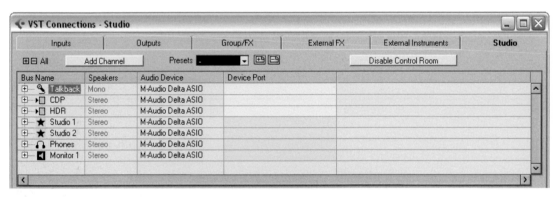

Figure 12.36
VST Connections studio setup

The Control Room Mixer window

When you have assigned the required studio buses in the VST Connections window, open the Control Room Mixer from the Devices menu. Figure 12.37 shows the Control Room Mixer set up in a multiple I/O configuration as described above.

Figure 12.37
The Control Room Mixer window

Main functions and controls

The Control Room Mixer can be viewed in extended or reduced mode. The extended view shows either meters or inserts. Click on the Show Meters / Inserts icon to change the view. The configuration in Figure 12.37 features, from left to right, external equipment inputs, the studio send channels, the control room headphones channel, the control room level channel, the common panel with talkback, dim and listen functions, and the monitor channel.

You can select a source signal for each of the channels using the various buttons above the level faders. The external equipment bus allows you to select one source using the numbered buttons. The setup shown here allows you to choose either a CD player or hard disk recorder. The studio sends include external, auxiliary or main mix as sources, while the control room headphones or main level channels allow you to choose between all possible choices: external, main mix, studio 1 auxiliary or studio 2 auxiliary. The control room headphones channel is intended for headphone monitoring in the control room and not as a headphone mix for musicians in the performance area. The talk button engages the talkback mic. This is routed to all those studio sends with their talkback enable buttons activated. The dim button reduces the level in the control room.

The Listen functions

The Control Room Mixer Listen functions allow you to listen to individual channels or any combination of channels in the main Mixer by engaging the Listen enable button of either the Headphone or Control Room channels. This is extremely useful for exclusive monitoring of, for example, a vocal recording as it is taking place. It is equally useful for monitoring different instruments or groups of instruments in isolation when making a multi-track recording. To set up which channels to monitor, go to the main Mixer and

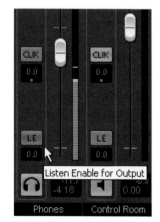

Figure 12.38
Using the Listen enable button in the Control Room Mixer

activate the listen buttons ('L' buttons) of the desired channels. In the Control Room Mixer, you can monitor the chosen channels in after-fader listen or pre-fader listen modes by activating or de-activating the AFL/PFL button. When you need to set up a different combination of listen enabled channels, you can disable the current listen selection by clicking on the 'De-activate All Listen' button in the Control Room Mixer.

Setting up the studio sends

The mix in each studio send channel is set up using the auxiliary studio sends in the main mixer. To set up your own studio send mix, open the main mixer in extended mode and select studio sends in the pop-up menus of the appropriate channels (or select the studio sends icon in the Common panel). Each studio send slot features a mini-fader, pan control and pre-fader button (Figure 12.39). Only those sends which are activated in VST Connections are available here. Activate and adjust the levels of the studio sends on the required channels while monitoring the appropriate studio send channel in the Control Room Mixer.

Figure 12.39
Set up the mix for each studio send channel in the studio sends section of the main Mixer

Patching in external equipment

The Control Room Mixer makes it easy to patch in external equipment like CD players, mini-disc players or hard disk recorders. All you do is connect your external equipment to the appropriate inputs of your audio hardware and then assign these to the external inputs in the studio section of the VST Connections window. Once connected and assigned, you can select any one of these in the Control Room Mixer left-most channel using the numbered buttons. Opening the Control Room Mixer in extended mode reveals an input gain dial for regulating the level. This is useful for matching the relative levels when comparing your own mix in Cubase to a commercially released CD.

Using the Control Room Mixer to manage your control room monitors

For studios with separate full range and nearfield control room monitors (or more complicated systems), the Control Room Mixer allows you to effortlessly switch between them. To configure your setup, assign the required number of monitor buses to the appropriate outputs in the studio section of the VST Connections window. You can now choose which monitors you are listening to by switching between the monitor selection buttons in the lower section of the monitor channel (the right-most channel strip).

Tip

Use the down-mix preset buttons in the Control Room Mixer monitor channel to quickly compare stereo and mono playback of the current mix.

Audio effects

Cubase is supplied with a wide range of audio effects and processors. These are found in the Plug-ins sub-menu of the Audio menu or in the pop-up menus of the audio-based channel insert slots and are designed principally for real-time processing. Real-time processing is that which takes place at the same time as the music is playing, as opposed to the off-line processing available in the Process menu, which takes place when you are not in playback mode. However, to maximise the flexibility of the program, all plug-in effects may also be applied as off-line processes.

Plug-in audio effects and processing devices may be loaded in the effects panels of Cubase when you need them. They do not usually function as stand-alone programs and, therefore, always require a host (like Cubase) in which to run. As well as the plug-ins supplied with the program, you can add additional Steinberg and third party developer plug-ins.

Because of its open-ended nature, the plug-in concept offers possibilities beyond the normal confines of the core program. Plug-ins open up whole new worlds of audio processing to the Cubase user and endow the program with a large degree of expandability and flexibility within a single software environment. This allows users to build their own virtual studio according to their budget, their system resources, and the kind of project they are working on.

Plug-in formats and standards

Plug-ins are supplied in a number of different formats such as AU, Direct X, RTAS, and VST, each of which suits the host program in which they are intended to run. The format relevant to Cubase is the popular VST plug-in standard which runs under Windows and Mac OS X. VST plug-ins run in all VST compatible applications including, of course, Cubase. However, the plug-ins supplied with Cubase are designed to run in Cubase alone and cannot be used in other programs.

A VST plug-in normally features a graphical user interface (GUI). This is where you manipulate the control parameters for the device and save and load presets. Most plug-ins are software-only but a small number are supplied as hybrid software / hardware units. This usually means that the GUI appears within Cubase like a normal VST plug-in but the audio processing takes place within the associated hardware. This is advantageous since it reduces the load on the CPU of the host computer.

Audio effects in theory

In the quest for instant results, the theoretical aspects of audio signal processing are often forgotten. However, taking some time to understand the theory can help you achieve better results. This section, therefore, covers the theoretical aspects of the main effects and processing techniques you are likely to encounter in your use of Cubase.

Audio effects and audio processing refer to a number of methods by which you can modify an audio signal for creative or corrective purposes. Effects are generally those techniques which modify the sound for creative purposes and often involve adding elements to the signal (such as reverb, delay and chorus). Processing tends to mean the modification of signals for corrective purposes and often involves subtracting elements from the signal (such as compression, gating and filtering). However, these too can be used for creative effects. For the sake of convenience, 'audio effects' as used in this text is taken to mean all types of audio effects and audio processing. The essential thing to remember is that all effects and processing involve the modification of the original sound in some way.

Audio effects can be divided into a number of sub-categories like delay, distortion, dynamics, filtering, modulation and reverb. The theoretical aspects of these are outlined in the following sections.

Delay

The concept of delay is easily understood by the majority of users but, nowadays, surrounded by ever more exotic effects, it tends to be under-valued.

Delay is the replication of a signal which occurs at a set time after the original. When the delayed signal is clearly distinguishable from the original, this is classed as a particular type of delay known as echo. Delay effects often involve repeating echoes, produced by adding an amount of feedback to the delay circuit. Delay is also an essential element when producing modulation effects like chorus and flanging and plays a part in reverb devices where a pre-delay controls the length of time between the original sound and the onset of the reverberation effect.

Info

In 1951, Helmut Haas discovered that the ear perceives delays of less than 30–40ms as part of the direct sound and this became known as the Haas effect. Haas also found that short delays help the ear locate the direction of the original source. The careful use of short delays across the stereo sound field therefore helps place mono sources at specific positions within the stereo image and adds depth and focus to the mix.

Delay and echo are terms which essentially refer to the same thing but, strictly speaking, an echo is a sound reflection separated from the original sound by more than 30ms. Before 30ms the ear perceives the reflections as part of the original sound and the whole sound is fused into one. After 30ms the ear begins to differentiate the original and the delayed signal. This is important to remember since it can help you achieve the desired effect when programming the delay devices supplied with Cubase.

Delay devices feature a relatively simple set of controls which usually include the following parameters:

- Delay time – sets the time delay for the replication of the signal, usually measured in milliseconds.
- Feedback – determines the proportion of the delay which is fed back to the input, thereby controlling the number of repeats for the delay line.
- Pan – pans the delayed signal to different positions in the stereo image (in a stereo delay device).
- Mix – controls the mix of the original (dry) signal and the effects (wet) signal.

Bearing in mind the 30ms threshold, ADT effects (Automatic Double Tracking) are created using delay times of around 30 to 60ms with no, or very little, feedback. ADT simulates the effect of doubling the sound, since the ear perceives the delayed signal as a separate event but the delay time is not great enough for it to become detached from the original sound. As you increase the delay time beyond 50-60ms and increase the feedback, other kinds of effects, such as slap-back echo, are possible. Here we begin to clearly differentiate the original and the delayed signal. If you also manipulate the stereo imagery by delaying one channel by a different amount to the other you can create pseudo-stereo effects. As you increase the delay time still further, special effects such as ping pong echoes and multiple echo effects become possible. Ping pong is the term applied to an echo which bounces a number of times between each channel of the stereo image. With longer delay times, all kinds of special effects can be created and, in Cubase, the timing of the echoes can be tuned to the tempo of the music using the tempo sync features.

If needed, you can also work out the delay times for any given tempo with a calculator, using the following equation:

delay (in seconds) = (240 / current tempo) / note value

where note value equals four for a quarter note, eight for an eighth note, sixteen for a sixteenth note and so on.

Distortion

Distortion is the adding of extra frequencies to a sound signal using a non-linear audio process. This results in a change in the waveform. Distortion can be of the unwanted type, such as that encountered when you record at too high a level, or it can be of the wanted type, such as the warm characteristics of tube amplifiers or mildly over driven analogue tape. Distortion of the wanted type usually involves the adding of extra harmonics based upon the most prominent frequency components in the original signal. Distortion is referred to by a number of different names including saturation, overdrive and fuzz.

Distortion effects range from subtle simulated tape saturation and mild distortion to extreme overdrive. Simulated tape saturation effects often use only small amounts of low order odd harmonic distortion (especially third harmonic distortion) and apply this distortion to the loudest peaks in the signal. Tube simulations or overdrive type effects use combinations of both odd and even numbered harmonics added in greater amounts to the signal, where lower-order harmonics (second, third, fourth and fifth) produce a musical

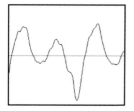 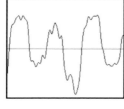 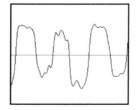 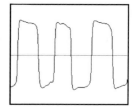

Figure 13.1
The effect of changing the amplifier tube settings in AmpSimulator's 'Studio Clean 1' preset. A clean guitar signal (left) is treated with 1 tube, 2 tube and 3 tube amplifier settings, progressively distorting the signal into a more square shaped waveform.

thickening of the sound and the addition of higher-order harmonics produces more metallic results.

Since distortion often involves an obvious change in the waveform of the signal, it is useful to view exactly how in a graphical representation. The results vary widely between different distortion effects. Some distort the signal into triangular-like or sawtooth-like wave shapes while others produce square wave characteristics. Figure 13.1 shows how the amplifier tube settings of the supplied AmpSimulator plug-in progressively distort the waveform into a square-like shape, suggesting the addition of predominantly odd harmonics for this particular effect.

Dynamics

Dynamics processing involves the automatic control of the level of the signal in various ways and includes the techniques of compression, limiting, expansion and gating.

With classic compression, loud parts become quieter and quiet parts become louder; compression converts a large dynamic range into a smaller dynamic range. With expansion, loud parts become louder and quiet parts become quieter; expansion converts a small dynamic range into a larger dynamic range. Compressors and expanders are automatic gain control devices. Compressors start to reduce the gain of an audio signal when the level rises above a set threshold and expanders reduce the gain as the level falls below a set threshold.

The amount of compression or expansion is usually described in terms of a ratio, (e.g. 2:1, 10:1 20:1, infinity:1). When an infinitely high ratio of compression is applied to an input signal, the output does not increase above the threshold no matter how much level is applied at the input. This is a particular type of compression known as limiting. When an infinitely high ratio of expansion is applied to an input signal, the output reduces to zero as soon as the input drops below the threshold. This is a particular type of expansion known as gating, (also known as noise gating). Therefore, compression and limiting can be grouped into the same category, and expansion and gating can be grouped into another.

Compression and limiting

There are a number of standard controls common to compressor / limiter devices which are included in various combinations depending upon the design. The main parameters include the following:

- Threshold – sets the level at which compression begins to occur. When the input signal rises above the threshold, the output signal from the device is attenuated (reduced in level) according to the ratio set with the ratio control.

- Ratio – varies the amount of gain reduction. A ratio of 2:1 indicates that for every 2dB the input rises above the threshold there is only a 1dB increase in the output. A ratio of 10:1 indicates that for every 10dB the input rises above the threshold there is only a 1dB increase in the output and so on. A ratio of 1:1 indicates that there is no change in gain between the input and output levels.
- Attack time – determines the rate at which the compressor attenuates the output level after the threshold has been exceeded.
- Release time – determines the rate at which the compressor returns to its normal output gain after the input signal has fallen below the threshold level.
- Makeup gain – since compression often involves an overall reduction in output level a makeup control is provided to increase the level after compression.

Compressor / limiters also generally feature soft-knee or hard-knee parameters. Soft-knee is when compression begins gradually a number of dB's below the threshold, whereas hard-knee is when the compression begins more suddenly at the threshold level. Soft-knee compression tends to sound more natural and transparent to the listener whereas hard-knee compression produces a more audible effect.

The relationship between the input level, output level and ratio is best viewed in diagrammatic form as in Figure 13.2. The various compressor graphical displays in Cubase resemble this same format. Figure 13.2 shows the threshold set at −20dB. When the ratio is set at 2:1, an input level exceeding the threshold by 10dB results in a 5dB attenuation in the output level. When the ratio is set at infinity:1 the output level remains at −20dB no matter how high the input level rises above the threshold.

Compressors are often used to increase the average signal level in an attempt to make sounds seem louder. They are also used for evening out the level of overly dynamic signals so they can be managed more easily in the mix. The settings vary widely depending upon the input signal and the effect you are attempting to achieve. Consider the following examples:

Figure 13.2
Compressor / limiter input and output levels for different ratios

- For classic downward compression which evens out the dynamics try a threshold of around 10–15dB below the maximum peaks in the signal and a ratio between 2:1 and 8:1. Set the makeup gain to bring the output back up to the required level.
- For bus compression (compression of a mix or group signal) try a threshold around 30-50dB below the maximum peaks and a gentle ratio of less than 2:1 combined with a soft knee setting.

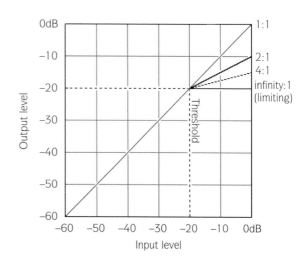

- To add punch and definition to bass guitar or lead guitar try attack and release times of around 40–60ms, ratios between 5:1 and 15:1 and a hard knee setting. Setting a relatively slow attack time allows the initial impact of each note to pass through unhindered before the compression takes effect. This maintains the original attack characteristics while still compressing the body of each note , adding punch and allowing the sound to cut through in the mix.

Tip

Deliberately setting both the attack and release time of a compressor very fast (less than 1-2ms), together with a threshold set for the peaks in the signal, can produce desirable distortion in the individual cycles of the waveform. Try ratios between 2:1 and 6:1. Used in a subtle manner, this can simulate the effect of tape saturation, adding warmth to the signal.

- For rock vocals try a moderately fast attack time of around 5-15ms combined with a release of around 100ms, ratios between 3:1 and 6:1, and a soft knee setting. In this case, a moderately fast attack time keeps wildly fluctuating attack levels under control..
- To increase the body of a drum sound try a relatively fast attack time combined with a fast release time of around 30ms or less. Conversely, to emphasise the actual hit of the drum try a moderately slow attack time combined with a slow release time.

In most cases the threshold would be set first until you see activity in the gain reduction meter corresponding with that part of the signal which needs processing. You would then tune the attack, release and ratio controls to achieve the desired effect. Unless you are attempting to create a deliberately audible effect, the parameters must be set carefully in order to avoid the following undesirables:

- Undesirable level reduction of a whole mix or group when compression is triggered by one dominant instrument (commonly known as hole punching).
- Undesirable increase in the background noise and interference when boosting the level of a signal with makeup gain. This can often be resolved by gating the signal prior to compression.
- Undesirable audible pumping or breathing due to too short or too long a release time.
- Undesirable excessive compression where the natural dynamics within the signal are lost.

Compressors and limiters are often found in the same device but the applications of pure limiting are different from those of compression. Limiters are generally used to stop a signal passing above a set threshold, no matter how loud the input becomes. This is known as 'brickwall' limiting. Limiting devices are characterised by very fast attack times, so that fast transients can be detected and corrected very quickly. The threshold for limiting is normally set quite high to ensure attenuation of only the transient peaks while the rest of the signal passes through unaffected.

Expansion and gating

Expansion and gating are the opposites of compression and limiting. The characteristics are best viewed in diagrammatic form (see Figure 13.3).

Although expanders have their uses, most of this section concentrates on the use of one particular kind of expander, commonly known as the noise gate. A noise gate is a very high ratio expander. If the input signal falls below the threshold the output is radically attenuated. This is extremely useful for eliminating the unwanted noise and interference which may be present in between the wanted sections of a musical performance. Figure 13.3 shows the behaviour of an expander / noise gate whose threshold has been set at −20dB.

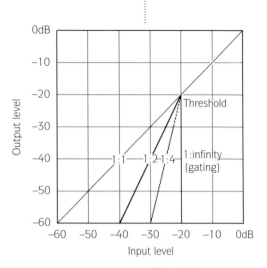

Figure 13.3
Expander / gate input and output levels for different ratios

Typically, expander / noise gates feature the following control parameters:

- Threshold – sets the level at which expansion begins to occur or the gate begins to close. When the input signal falls below the threshold, the output signal is attenuated according to the ratio set with the ratio control.
- Ratio – varies the amount of gain change. A ratio of 1:2 indicates that for every 1dB the input falls below the threshold there is a 2dB decrease in the output. A ratio of 1:infinity indicates that as soon as the input falls below the threshold the output is radically attenuated (i.e. the signal is gated). Classic gating devices feature fixed infinite ratios with no ratio controls. Instead, the gating action is regulated with a threshold (as above) and sometimes a floor or gain control which determines by how many dB the signal is attenuated when it falls below the threshold.
- Attack time – determines the rate at which the expander / noise gate opens (to allow the signal through) when the signal rises above the threshold.
- Release time – determines the rate of attenuation when the signal has fallen below the threshold.
- Hold time – controls the length of time for which the level of the signal is guaranteed to be held before attenuation occurs.
- Gain / floor – more advanced devices may include a gain or floor control which governs the overall gain of the expansion curve or defines the residual signal level after expansion or gating.

The attack control of a noise gate is normally endowed with a very fast attack time in order to cope with sounds which have rapid attack transients such as drum and percussion sounds. This ensures that the first part of the sound opens the gate quickly enough so that it passes through unhindered. However, sounds with slower attack characteristics benefit from slower noise gate attack times in order to avoid the audible click which can sometimes occur when the gate is opened abruptly. The hold time is used to determine how long the gate remains open and, once it starts to close, the release time determines the rate at which the signal fades away.

As well as their usual noise elimination function, noise gates can also be used creatively to modify the envelope of the signal. For example, special effects can be created by intentionally slowing down the attack portion of a sound using a slow attack setting, or the body of the sound can be attenuated with a fast release time to produce staccato effects.

Info

Frequency-conscious gating, as implemented in the Gate and VST Dynamics plug-ins, helps gate live drum recordings suffering from leakage between microphones. This technique involves filtering the side-chain signal which triggers the gate so that it emphasises only the frequency range of the wanted instrument. For example, tuning the filter to the frequency bandwidth of the bass drum makes the gate sensitive to the bass drum alone. This means that the gate only opens when the bass drum is playing and any leakage into the bass drum mic from the snare and hi-hats is minimised.

Filtering

A filter is a device which attenuates one or more chosen frequency bands within a sound while allowing the others to pass through unchanged. In the same way as a coffee filter filters the larger particles of coffee from the source coffee mixture, or an air filter filters the larger particles of air-born dust from the air, a sound filter filters various sound particles (harmonics) from the raw source sound which passes through it. Various types of sound filter are available but the essential idea of all sound filters is that of a device which modifies the harmonic structure of the treated sound.

The filter type determines what kind of filtering action takes place on the source signal. The main filter types include low pass, high-pass, band pass and band-reject. Each filter features a cut-off frequency. This determines the frequency at which the filter begins to have an effect. In the case of a low-pass filter those frequencies below the cut-off point are allowed to pass through unchanged while those above are significantly reduced. The cut-off point of a low-pass filter therefore regulates the overall brightness of the tone. Resonance is another attribute of most filters and this is also referred to as Q or emphasis. This modifies the frequencies around the cut-off point, regulating the sharpness or resonant character of the tone. Other aspects of filter design include filter slope characteristics, phase response and the implementation of envelope generators to control the action of the cut-off frequency.

Filter types

The four basic types of filter are low-pass, high-pass, band-pass and band-reject. Variations and combinations of these are known by different names such as notch filtering and parametric EQ. The use of filters in the pure sense implies the cutting of frequencies, whereas EQ implies the cutting and the boosting of the chosen frequencies. Understanding the action of the four basic filter types can lead to a better understanding of EQ and is the first step in becoming familiar with filtering in general.

Filter types are generally recognised by their amplitude response. This is shown on a graph of amplitude against frequency (see Figures 13.4 to 13.7, below).

Each filter type is characterised by one part of the frequency spectrum which is allowed to pass through, known as the pass band, and another part of the spectrum which is significantly reduced, known as the stop band. The point at which the filtering action begins, (when the amplitude response passes from the pass band to the stop band), is known as the cut-off frequency (or cut-off point). There is always a transitional area between the pass band and the stop band. The rule for defining the exact point for the cut-off frequency is generally accepted as that point where the signal has fallen 3dB below the level of the pass band. Therefore, it is true to say that a significant number of frequencies below (or above) the cut-off point will have already been attenuated before the cut-off point itself is reached.

Low-pass

A low-pass filter allows those frequencies below the cut-off point to pass through with little change while those above are significantly reduced.

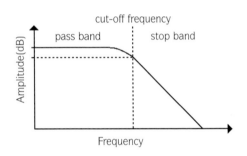

Figure 13.4
Amplitude response of a low-pass filter

High-pass

A high-pass filter significantly reduces those frequencies below the cut-off point while those above are allowed to pass through with little change (the opposite of the low-pass filter).

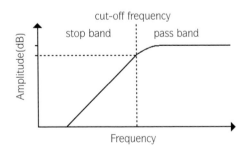

Figure 13.5
Amplitude response of a high-pass filter

Band-pass

A band-pass filter allows a band of frequencies to pass through between two cut-off points while significantly reducing frequencies both above and below the pass band. The mid-point of the amplitude response curve is referred to

Figure 13.6
Amplitude response of a band-pass filter

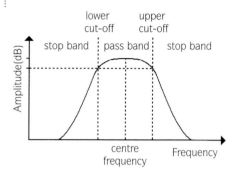

as the centre frequency and the frequency range between the lower and upper cut-off points is known as the bandwidth.

Band-reject

A band-reject filter attenuates (rejects) a band of frequencies between two cut-off points while allowing the rest of the signal to pass through with little change (the opposite of the band-pass filter). The mid-point of the amplitude response curve is referred to as the centre frequency and the frequency range between the lower and upper cut-off points is known as the bandwidth.

Figure 13.7
Amplitude response of a band-reject filter

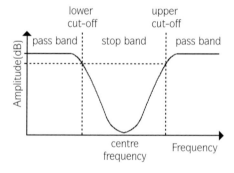

In its most basic form, a low-pass filter (for example) is regulated using a single parameter, the cut-off frequency. This governs the point at which the upper frequencies in the sound begin to be attenuated, thereby controlling how the spectrum is modified. However, this attenuation takes place according to a slope as the filter passes between the pass band and the stop band. This slope describes the rate at which the upper frequencies are attenuated and is generally measured in terms of dBs per octave. The slope varies according to the manner in which the filter has been designed. In voltage-controlled circuitry, the rate is governed, among other things, by the number of resistors and capacitors used in the circuit. A simple passive filter with one resistor and one capacitor in the circuit is known as an RC filter and this has an attenuation slope of 6dB per octave. Other common rates include 12dB per octave, 18dB per octave and 24dB per octave. These slopes can be plotted graphically in terms of relative attenuation against frequency.

Filter resonance (emphasis)

Resonance can be defined as the frequency or frequencies at which an object vibrates in sympathy with itself or with external vibrational phenomena. Filters too can be endowed with this kind of behaviour. Passive RC filters have no resonant frequencies and simply filter the source according to their amplitude and phase response. However, active filters may be designed to produce a boost in the response around the cut-off frequency. Some filtering plug-ins include a parameter which is used to regulate the amount of resonance (see StepFilter and Tonic). The parameter is commonly referred to as resonance, emphasis or Q. Figure 13.8 shows what happens to a low-pass filter amplitude response for low, high and maximum resonance values.

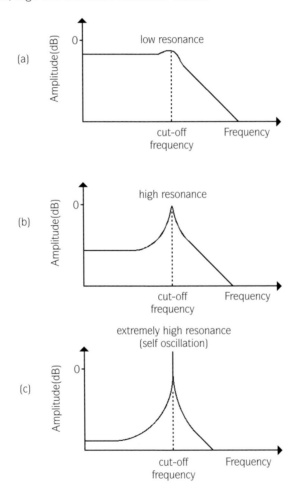

Figure 13.8
The effect of resonance on a low-pass filter amplitude response

When the resonance control parameter is set to low or medium positions the bandwidth of the emphasised frequencies is quite wide and they are only boosted by a small amount (Figure 13.8a). For higher resonance values the bandwidth of the emphasised frequencies is quite narrow and they are boosted by a large amount (Figure 13.8b). As the resonance is increased the lower frequencies are progressively attenuated. At maximum resonance the lower and upper frequencies virtually disappear from the filtered signal leaving a single harmonic which oscillates at the cut-off frequency (Figure 13.8c). In the latter case, an amount of the source signal normally still passes through.

The effect of resonance can be summarised as follows: resonance results in the emphasising of a narrow band of frequencies (harmonics) located around the cut-off point. This narrow band can be moved around within the frequency spectrum by changing the frequency of the cut-off point. This results in effects which are particularly pleasing to the ear. At extreme resonance values, when the filter enters a state of self-oscillation (as in Figure 13.8c), special effects and pitched tones can be produced.

Using filters

The resonant low-pass filter has, more than any other filter type, been responsible for some classic subtractive synthesis effects and is excellent for producing the filter sweeps commonly used in dance music. The supplied Step Filter plug-in allows the simultaneous changing of both the cut-off frequency and the resonance in synchronisation with the current tempo of the project. Setting up a medium to high resonance level and then sweeping the cut-off frequency up and down has been used in innumerable synth patches and dance tracks.

In addition to sweeping effects, filters may be used to produce pseudo-stereo effects, comb-filter effects, wah-wah effects and such things as AM radio and telephone simulations. In a corrective sense, filters are particularly useful for hum and hiss removal and band-limiting. Filters are, of course, essential to all EQ.

Modulation

Modulation encompasses a wide range of effects including chorus, flanging, and phasing, and the slightly lesser known techniques of amplitude modulation, frequency modulation and ring modulation. Modulation is the modification of the characteristics of one signal using a second signal. The modulating signal could be an LFO (a low frequency oscillator) or some other kind of signal somewhere in the audible range. For example, simple modulation effects include vibrato and tremolo. Vibrato is a form of frequency modulation where the frequency (or pitch) of the target signal is modulated by an LFO. Tremolo is a form of amplitude modulation where the amplitude level of the target signal is modulated by an LFO.

Chorus, flanging and phasing

Although the classic modulation effects like chorus, flanging and phasing are easily recognisable, the ways in which they are produced in modern effects devices is not so obvious.

Chorus is an effect produced by passing a signal through one or more delay lines and modulating the delay time(s) with an LFO. The result is mixed with the original signal. The modulation of the delay times produces phase cancellation effects and changes in the perceived pitch and timing, creating the illusion of an ensemble of sound sources. Comparatively short delay times

---

Info

For the more advanced uses of filters and EQ, check out the PSP Neon Linear phase parametric EQ and the Apulsoft apEQ plug-ins.

Info

The effect known as 'wah-wah' is created by sweeping a bandpass filter up and down in the frequency domain. This is easily created in Cubase using the supplied Wah Wah plug-in.

are used. It was first conceived as a means of attempting to make a solo musical performance sound like more than one performer.

Flanging is a similar effect created by mixing a delayed version of a signal with the original and modulating the delay time with an LFO whilst also applying an amount of feedback. Comparatively short delay times are used. This produces phase cancellation effects which are heard as a comb filter effect sweeping up and down within the frequency spectrum.

Phasing is created by mixing a phase-shifted version of a signal with the original and modulating the phase shifting with an LFO whilst also applying an amount of feedback. Similar to flanging, phasing is also perceived as a comb filter effect weeping up and down within the frequency spectrum, but the swept frequency bands are not always harmonically related to the source signal.

Amplitude modulation, frequency modulation and ring modulation

Amplitude modulation, frequency modulation and ring modulation tend towards more esoteric effects and are implemented in sound synthesis, as well as sound effects devices.

Amplitude Modulation is achieved by modulating the amplitude of one audio signal by another signal where both signals are in the audible range. Using simple sine waves for the modulator produces a signal containing the target signal and two side-bands which are the sum and difference frequencies of the target signal and the modulating signal. Applying amplitude modulation where the modulating signal is an LFO produces tremolo effects. When the modulator is not an LFO (i.e. when it is in the audible range), the result tends towards densely packed inharmonic frequencies added to the signal.

Frequency modulation is probably better known for its uses in sound synthesis. In FM, the frequency of one signal is modulated by another. Applying frequency modulation where the modulating signal is an LFO produces vibrato effects. When the modulator is not an LFO (i.e. when it is in the audible range), multiple frequencies known as side-bands are added to the signal.

Ring modulation is a special kind of amplitude modulation where the target signal and the modulating signal are multiplied to produce the sum and difference of their frequencies in the output. Unlike amplitude and frequency modulation, the original frequency of the source signal is not present in the output. Typically, this produces 'alien' effects for speech and metallic tones for pitched sounds.

Info

Cubase is supplied with a wide range of modulation effects including auto-pan, chorus, flanging, phasing, tremolo, vibrato and others.

Reverb

Reverb is an abbreviation for reverberation. Reverberation is an effect produced by a multiple series of echoes occurring after the original sound in an acoustic space. It is characterised by three distinct phases, as shown in Figure 13.9. Reverberation is found in virtually every acoustic space and its characteristics vary enormously depending on the size of the space and the kinds of materials and objects found therein.

Figure 13.9 approximates what takes place in a real reverberant space. Firstly, the original sound arrives directly from the source to the listener's ear. After a short pause the first reflections from the surfaces of the room (or

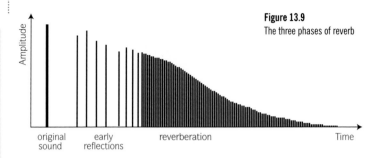

Figure 13.9
The three phases of reverb

(Axes: Amplitude vs Time; labels: original sound, early reflections, reverberation)

Info

The early reflections within reverberation are crucial in giving the treated sound a sense of depth and focus, and clarify the location of the direct sound. Careful manipulation of early reflections can enhance the clarity, shape and depth of sounds within the mix.

other acoustic space) are heard; these are known as early reflections. This is followed by a complex mass of multiple reflections as the reflected sounds continue to bounce off the various surfaces. The amplitude of these multiple reflections decays exponentially to form what is commonly known as the reverb tail. In real reverberant spaces (especially in large ones), the upper frequencies decay at a faster rate than the rest of the signal.

The aim with virtual reverb plug-ins is to re-create the same kind of behaviour. However, the first thing you may notice when comparing different devices is that reverb units are not all created equal. Convincing reverberation remains difficult to replicate artificially and requires a large amount of processing power to achieve the best results. Among the best attempts are those using convolution techniques. Convolution uses impulse responses from real reverberant spaces thus producing highly convincing results.

Info

For reverb, Cubase is supplied with the Reverence convolution reverb and Roomworks.

Other

There are a multitude of other effects which do not necessarily fit neatly into any particular category. These include such devices as the supplied Grungelizer plug-in which adds crackle, noise and distortion to your signals, and Bitcrusher which adds distortion to signals by truncating the bit resolution.

Other miscellaneous effects and processing techniques include bass maximisation, click and hum removal, harmonic excitement, loudness maximisation, pitch processing, psychoacoustic enhancement, spatial processing, stereo enhancement, sonic optimisation, tape saturation emulation, and vocoding.

Setting up audio effects in Cubase

Info

The precise routing order for a signal passing through an Audio channel runs as follows:
1 phase switch
2 input gain
3 inserts 1–6
4 EQ
5 pre-fader aux send
6 channel fader
7 inserts 7–8
8 post-fader aux send
9 pan

In Cubase, real-time audio effects may be assigned as insert effects or send effects. There are no strict rules about which effects are assigned to which kind of effects slots but not all effects are suitable for use as insert effects, and reverb effects are almost always assigned as send effects. The effects routing structure of the Mixer is similar to that found in a classic real world console (see Info box).

Insert effects

Insert effects are assigned by clicking in any of the Insert effects slots of an audio-based channel or an input / output channel, at which time a pop-up menu appears containing the plug-ins available in your system (Figure 13.10).

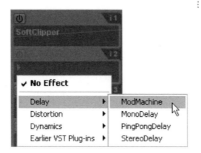

Figure 13.10
Assigning an effect in an Insert effects slot

Insert effect assignments are unique for each channel and each time you activate an insert effect you also activate an additional instance of the chosen plug-in effect. This uses processing power so, while insert effects are invaluable, they tend to use more system resources than send effects. Each channel in the Mixer has a total of eight insert slots. Effects are assigned to the insert slots in the extended channel strips in the Mixer, in the Channel Settings window or in the Inspector. The order of effects can be freely modified by dragging and dropping between slots.

With insert effects, the signal passes directly through the effects in series in descending order (see Figure 13.11). Inserts 1-6 are pre-fader, meaning that the audio signal is routed directly to the effects and has not yet passed via the channel fader.

After having passed through one or more of insert effects slots 1-6, the output from the effect(s) is routed via the EQ section (if active), channel fader, inserts 7 and 8, and pan control to the chosen output bus. Inserts 7 and 8 are special case post-fader slots which are suitable for processing which benefits from coming after the channel fader, such as limiting. Slots 7 and 8 are particularly useful when used in an output channel for final limiting, loudness maximisation or dithering during a mix or mastering session.

In general, insert effects are best suited to processing like compression, distortion, EQ, expansion, filtering, limiting and noise gating. Chorus, flanging and phasing also work well as insert effects.

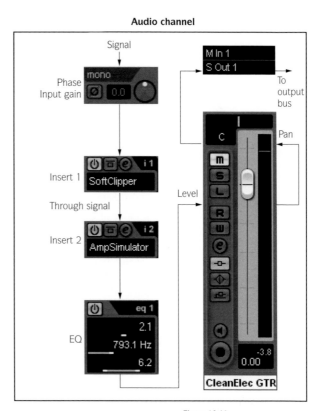

Audio channel

Figure 13.11
The routing configuration for Insert effects (slots 1-6)

Tip

To open all insert plug-in interfaces for any audio based channel simultaneously hold Ctrl + Alt + Shift and click on the Edit Channel Settings button.

Info

The number of effects which are used within a project is restricted only by the processing power of your computer. Sophisticated high-end plug-ins use substantial amounts of CPU power and using a large number of these simultaneously could slow down system performance. Open the VST Performance window (Devices menu) to monitor the current load on your CPU. Aim for no more than 50 – 60% average load on the ASIO meter.

Send effects

Send effects are managed using FX channels. The effect is actually assigned as an insert effect on the FX channel, which may at first seem confusing. The first thing to do when setting up a send effect is to add an FX channel to the project. This is achieved in the same way as for other channel types by using the Add function (Project menu). The Add FX channel dialogue allows you to choose an effect for the new FX channel (Figure 13.12). The effect for the channel may be changed at a later time, or other effects may be added, in the remaining Insert slots of the FX channel.

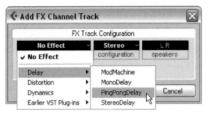

Figure 13.12
Choosing an effect for an FX channel in the Add FX channel dialogue

Once an FX channel is activated in the project, you can send signals to it for processing from the auxiliary send slots of any audio-based channel. Send effects are assigned by clicking in any of the send slots for the channel, at which time a pop-up menu appears containing the FX channels and other routing destinations (Figure 13.13). The send level is regulated using the mini-fader of the effects slot. Send effects can be chosen on as many audio-based channels as required, in any order, and with unique send levels for each slot. This saves on processing power since, for example, any number of audio channel sends can use the same reverb effect which you have activated only once in a single FX channel.

Each channel in the Mixer has a total of eight send slots. The send slots are assigned in the extended channel strip in the Mixer, in the Channel Settings window or in the Inspector. The routing configuration for send effects is similar to a traditional mixing console. Figure 13.14 traces the signal as it is split between the dry and wet signal paths in a typical post-fader send configuration. The dry signal passes through the pan control of the channel strip, as usual, and is routed to the chosen output bus. The send signal is routed post-fader via the send level and the send effect to the chosen output bus. This wet signal joins the dry signal in the mix. The FX channel fader controls the level of the effect.

With FX channels, the effect (or wet) signal is added in parallel to the dry signal in the mix via the FX channel fader, which is usually routed to the same output bus as the dry signal. A suitable mix between the dry and wet signals is achieved by carefully balancing the fader level of the source channel with the fader level of the FX channel. Under normal circumstances, the mix control in the user interface of the effect in the FX channel is set to 100% wet. This ensures that the FX channel governs only the wet signal and the source channel governs only the dry signal.

Each send is routed either pre or post-fader. If it is pre-fader, the signal is routed to the FX channel before it arrives at the channel fader. In this case,

Figure 13.13
Assigning a send effect in a send effects slotslot

Audio channel

FX channel

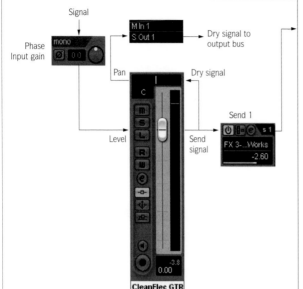

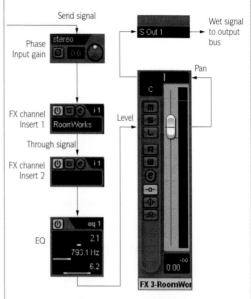

the channel fader level does not influence the send level. If it is post-fader, the signal passes via the channel fader before it is routed to the FX channel. In this case, the channel fader level influences the send level. Post-fader is the default setting.

You may wonder how the pre-fader switch might be useful. Practical uses include occasions when the channel fader has been set rather low and does not provide enough signal for the effect send. In this case the pre-fader signal provides more level. The pre-fader switch also allows you to fade out a signal in the mix without also fading any effect applied to it. This can be used for special mixing techniques like fading out a sound which has pre-fader reverb added to it. The result gives the impression that the sound is disappearing into the distance as the dry signal fades away whilst the reverberation signal remains. In general, send effects are best suited to reverb, delay, chorus, flanging and phasing.

Figure 13.14
Typical routing configuration for send effects

Info

The number of effects which are used within a project is restricted only by the processing power of your computer. High-end plug-ins use substantial amounts of CPU power and using a large number of these simultaneously could slow down system performance. Open the VST Performance window (Devices menu) to monitor the current load on your CPU. Aim for no more than 50 – 60% average load on the ASIO meter.

Common GUI functions for audio effects

The graphical user interface (GUI) for any of the currently active effects can be opened by clicking on the edit button of the slot corresponding to the effect. The edit buttons are labelled with a lower case 'e' and are found in all channel effects slots in the Mixer, in the Channel Settings window and in the

Inspector. All GUIs for the effects open in a separate window similar to that shown in Figure 13.15.

Basic GUI functions

The GUI parameters common to most effects include an On button, automation read and write buttons, presets management functions and, where appropriate, an output and/or mix control. An effect is activated by clicking the On button, at which time it is illuminated in blue. Clicking on the presets field opens the presets browser which automatically searches for the presets relevant to the chosen effect. If desired, the presets browser may be resized to show only the list of presets in the viewer, as shown in Figure 13.16. There are also load and save presets functions which open the browser at a separate location within your screen space.

Figure 13.15
The graphical user interface for the supplied Flanger effect

Figure 13.16
Opening the presets browser

Figure 13.17
Use the mix dial to set the proportion of wet and dry signal

The output control is for setting an appropriate level for the output of the effects device. This varies according to the application. The mix dial determines the mix between the wet and dry signal which passes to the output (Figure 13.17). When used as a send effect, the mix dial is normally best set to 100% wet and, when used as an insert effect the wet and dry signals might be provisionally set to equal proportions.

The general rule is that most visible parameters can be manipulated in some way by clicking and dragging with the mouse or using the mouse wheel. All parameter changes made as part of a mix can be automated by activating the read and write buttons found next to the On button.

Tempo sync controls

Where applicable, the supplied effects feature tempo sync controls. These allow the synchronisation of various parameters (such as LFOs and delay times) to the current tempo of Cubase. Activating the tempo sync button changes the relevant control to note values instead of numerical values (Figure 13.18).

Figure 13.18
In tempo sync mode control values are shown as note values instead of numerical values

The note values determine the division of the bar which Cubase uses for synchronisation purposes. For example, setting a value of 1/8 where a delay time is concerned produces repeated delays at 1/8 note intervals, or setting a value of 1/1 where an LFO controlling auto pan is concerned produces a panning effect which occurs once in each bar.

Side chain buttons

Where appropriate, the supplied VST3 plug-ins feature side chain buttons at the top of the GUI next to the automation read and write buttons. This concerns a number of delay, dynamics and modulation effects. An active side chain disengages the source signal which normally feeds the side chain and instead allows you to send a second signal to control some element within the effect. When activated, the side chain inputs become available in the auxiliary sends of audio channels or, if preferred, you can send a signal directly to the side chain using the output routing menu for the channel.

Side chains may be used in a wide range of creative and corrective audio processing techniques. For example, activating the side chain for a delay effect allows you to mute the delay when the side chain signal rises above a fixed threshold. When used with a compressor effect you could apply compression to a bass guitar according to the presence of a kick drum signal in the side chain, or apply ducking to a musical signal according to the presence of a voice-over signal . When used with a gate effect you could rhythmically open and close the gate on a sustained synth pad according to a percussive signal in the side chain. For modulation, you could control the LFO of a chorus effect according to the amplitude envelope of the side chain signal. There are many possibilities.

Audio effects in practice

There now follow descriptions and practical uses of a selection of the VST3 audio effects supplied with the program. A number of alternatives from other developers are recommended particularly in the important categories of EQ, dynamics and reverb. These are chosen for features and sonic characteristics which significantly enrich and complement the supplied VST3 collection. All plug-ins are covered in a similar order to that of the plug-ins pop-up menu and are arranged in similar categories.

Delay effects

Delay – supplied plug-ins
Cubase is supplied with MonoDelay, PingPongDelay and StereoDelay for standard delay effects such as ADT, slapback, ping pong and echo effects. For more advanced delay effects, ModMachine combines the modulation of delay time, filter frequency and filter Q to allow the creation of some unique filtered chorus and delay effects.

MonoDelay for ADT and slapback echo effects
ADT (Automatic Double Tracking) involves mixing the source signal with a delayed copy using delay times of around 30-60ms. This is good for thickening or enlivening the source and particularly suits vocals, guitars and saxophones. MonoDelay is suitable for simple delay effects of this type. In addi-

Figure 13.18b
Use the side chain button for a wide range of creative effects

tion to the standard delay parameters MonoDelay features filtering which helps separate the delayed signal from the source (when required). For example, adjusting MonoDelay to the settings shown in Figure 13.19 produces a filtered 'shadow' which sits behind the original signal and tends to lift the sound. The 'Lo' roll-off filter reduces frequencies below 480Hz while the 'Hi' roll-off filter reduces frequencies above 10kHz in the delay signal path. This combined with a 40ms delay and minimal feedback produces the desired ADT effect.

Slapback echo relies upon similar principles to ADT but usually increases the delay time to beyond 60ms. Figure 13.20 shows an example where the delay time is extended to 125ms with a narrower frequency band for the filtering.

Figure 13.19 (left)
MonoDelay ADT effect

Figure 13.20 (right)
MonoDelay slapback echo effect

ModMachine

ModMachine is capable of producing esoteric filtered delay and chorus effects, but to get to know the parameters it is best to first use it in a simple capacity. To this end, try setting up ModMachine for a chorus effect which uses no filter modulation, as shown in Figure 13.21. This uses a minimal delay time with subtle delay time modulation, medium modulation width and no feedback. To modify this setup for a classic delay effect, try increasing the delay time to 125ms, increase the feedback to around 40 and decrease the mix to around 20. Even though this setup uses no filter modulation, the filter remains in the signal path after the delay feedback loop and just before the output (output mode). To hear the delay effect you should select highpass as the filter type to allow the signal through.

Figure 13.21
ModMachine chorus effect with no filter modulation

The filter controls of ModMachine are arranged in two sections. The upper section manages the filter frequency while the lower section manages the filter Q. When the speed dials are set to zero and the sync buttons are de-activated, the Lo and Hi parameters become inactive. In this mode, the filter becomes a static filter where the frequency dial governs the centre frequency and the Q-Factor dial governs the resonance. Figure 13.22 shows ModMachine set up in this manner with the filter placed in the feedback loop (loop mode) and set to lowpass. In this configuration, there is no filter modulation but the filter has a dampening effect on the delayed signal as it passes through the feedback loop. This is helpful for emulating the dampening effect of analogue tape delay units where the delay signal progressively loses more high frequencies each time the tape loop passes over the playback heads. Also try this setup with longer delay times and modify the mix dial as desired.

For filter modulation, start with the overall settings shown in Figure 13.22 and modify the filter sections to match the settings shown in Figure 13.23. Select the output position and bandpass type for the filter and try increasing the delay time to around 1000ms and the mix to around 30%. Here the

Figure 13.22
ModMachine filtered delay effect with
the filter placed in the feedback loop

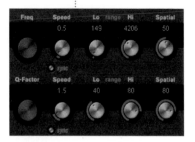

Figure 13.23
ModMachine filter modulation settings
designed for the filter placed at the
output in bandpass mode

bandpass filter centre frequency modulates between the Lo and Hi values
while the filter Q simultaneously modulates between its Lo and Hi values. The
spatial parameters distribute the delay effects around the stereo image.

Delay – alternatives

There are a wide range of delay alternatives available. Notable among these
are Native Instruments Reaktor Echomania and Fusion Reflections; Native
Instruments Spektral Delay; PSP Audioware 608 Multi Delay, PSP42 and
PSP84; Steinberg Karlette; and Waves Supertap. If you are already an owner
of Reaktor and are looking for delay effects with a difference, Echomania and
Fusion Reflections are well worth exploring. Fusion Reflections combines chorus and delay with delay modulation, stereo spread and diffusion controls.
Echomania combines delay and EQ with delay modulation, EQ modulation
and distortion. Steinberg Karlette is an earlier plug-in which emulates a tape
loop echo unit. This is a multi-tap device featuring four delay lines with traditional delay time, dampening, pan, feedback and sync controls. Waves
Supertap is a high-precision multi-tap device combining up to six delay lines
with delay modulation and EQ controls.

> **Tip**
>
> To appreciate the full range of
> third party developer VST plug-
> ins available in any category,
> search the KVR Audio website on
> the internet at www.kvraudio.com

PSP84

PSP Audioware developed the PSP84 delay plug-in as a more elaborate version of their Lexicon PSP42, which is an emulation of the legendary Lexicon
PCM42 hardware delay unit. The PSP84 (Figure 13.24) features two inde-

Figure 13.24
PSP84 delay unit. An ideal alternative to
Cubase's supplied delay plug-ins.

pendent delay lines with channel link button, wet signal and feedback loop phase inversion buttons, pan controls, switchable low pass, band pass or high pass resonant filter, and modulation of delay times and filter cut-off frequency. In addition, there is tape saturation emulation and vintage spring or plate reverberation. All this adds up to a delay unit of exceptional character, warmth and creative potential.

Delay times up to 5secs per channel are available and times may be set in milliseconds or, for tempo sync operation, in note values. The delay and feedback inversion buttons are helpful for deep flanging and pseudo stereo effects. The filter may be placed at the input, in the delay feedback loop or in the wet signal path just before the output. When placed in the feedback loop, progressively greater high frequency dampening of the feedback signal can be achieved to emulate the dampening action of traditional tape loop echo units. Modulation of the filter cut-off frequency combined with low delay times produces warm chorus and flanging. Setting the filter to input mode while modulating the cut-off frequency in band pass mode produces excellent auto wah-wah effects. The LFO modulation may be set in frequency values or synchronised to the tempo of Cubase. The reverb section takes its feed from either the wet signal alone or the combined wet and dry output mix, and makes a valuable addition to the vintage sound.

The PSP84 is excellent for tracking and mixing and is particularly suited to guitar and vocal effects and drum loop mangling. Its effects arsenal spans traditional echo and delay to sumptuous chorus and flanging. The unit can sound crystal clean, glowingly warm or analogue dirty and when required can produce totally wacky, weird and wonderful effects and soundscapes. Despite its power PSP84 remains easy to use, combining intuitive parameter manipulation with an intelligent user interface.

If you need a simpler version with the same sound character try PSP84's little brother, the Lexicon PSP42. Alternatively, PSP supply the powerful PSP 608MD multi-tap delay, featuring up to 8 delay lines.

Distortion effects

Distortion – supplied plug-ins

There are two distortion plug-ins supplied with Cubase: AmpSimulator and SoftClipper.

AmpSimulator

AmpSimulator simulates the warmth and distortion associated with guitar amplifiers, ranging from mild distortion through to extreme overload. The heart of the plug-in is in the Amplifier and Cabinet menus. These define the essential character of the

Figure 13.25
AmpSimulator

distortion. The amplifier models include: Clean, American Clean, Jazz and Tube settings for moderate distortion; Lead settings for smooth lead guitar; and Crunch and Modern settings for extreme overdrive. The character of each may be subtly modified by the cabinet setting and the sound of the cabinet itself may be filtered using the Lo and Hi damping controls. Finally, the Drive dial governs the amount of distortion and the Low, Mid And High tone controls and Presence dial allow you to fine tune the overall result. AmpSimulator is designed mainly for guitar processing but also has its uses for enlivening synth sounds.

SoftClipper

SoftClipper is a relatively simple device featuring separate second and third harmonic controls. These allow the harmonics to be added to the signal in varying proportions. This suits the simulation of mild tube distortion and tape saturation where adding very subtle distortion enhances detail and warmth. The saturation effect may be emphasised by increasing the input above 0dB. Try the settings in Figure 13.26 to give guitar and other sounds a subtle high frequency edge.

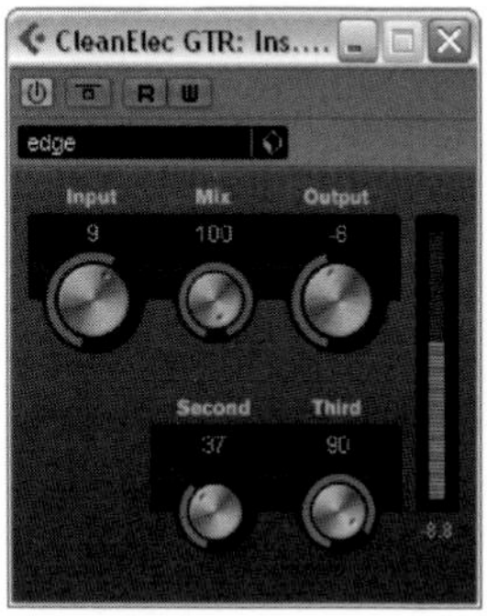

Distortion – alternatives

Notable distortion plug-in alternatives include IK Multimedia Amplitube, Native Instruments Guitar Rig, Softtube Vintage Amp Room and Steinberg Quadrafuzz. Quadrafuzz is outlined in the section entitled 'Additional Effects', below.

Figure 13.26
SoftClipper

Dynamics effects

Dynamics – supplied plug-ins

Cubase is well-stocked with dynamics processors including Compressor, EnvelopeShaper, Expander, Gate, Limiter, Maximizer, MultiCompressor, VintageCompressor and VST Dynamics. However, using any dynamics processor requires a good understanding of the parameters and an in-depth knowledge of how the settings are likely to affect the target signal.

Having a clear idea of the difference between peak and average levels in music helps understand what gets affected when you manipulate dynamics. Peak levels are brief transients which register momentarily on a peak level meter at the highest positions and average level is the energy contained within the main body of the signal. The energy in each transient peak is very small in isolation but in greater numbers contributes to the impact and clarity of the sound. However, it is the average level which gives the main indication of the perceived loudness of the signal. Dynamics processing can therefore be set to control only the highest transient peaks or it can be set to act upon the main body of the music where most of the energy is found. The former may have little or no initial effect on the perceived loudness whereas the latter is likely to radically affect the perceived loudness and shape of the signal. Of course, compressors and expanders can be set to act at any given threshold between the high and low points in the signal.

Dynamics processing, therefore, is concerned with manipulations of the peak and average levels within audio signals, for example: to control transient

peaks (peak limiting), to gently reduce the loudest sections (classic downward compression), to enhance the lower level details of the music (low or
mid-level upward compression), to increase the level of the loudest sections
(upward expansion) or to reduce low-level sections in the signal (downward
expansion / gating). Much of this can be achieved with the supplied dynamics plug-ins.

Peak limiting with Limiter

Classic peak limiting involves setting a 'brick wall' level above which the loudest peaks in the input signal do not pass to the output, no matter how high
they rise above the threshold. In Limiter, this brick wall is set with the output
parameter. In Figure 13.27 the output is set to -0.3dBFS to ensure no transient clipping when limiting a mix. When used in this capacity, Limiter is best
inserted as a post-fader effect in slots 7 or 8 of the main stereo output bus.

Limiter is pre-set to a very fast attack time so that transient peaks are
brought under control instantaneously. The input parameter allows you to
boost the input to achieve loudness maximisation effects and the release
parameter governs the time it takes to return to a normal level after gain
reduction. For the most natural results, set this to auto (program dependent
release).

Classic downward compression with Compressor

Classic downward compression pushes down the rising attack energy in the signal while emphasising the release. This fattens the sound and brings out detail
but may also dull the high frequency content. Classic settings normally produce
a gentle curve like the one shown in Figure 13.28 which features a 4 : 1 ratio
with a soft knee setting. Try starting with the attack at 50ms and release at
100ms and adjust to taste. In contrast to the limiting settings outlined above,
here we are starting to lower the threshold into the body of the signal. Set shorter attack times if you wish to squash more transients and adjust the release time
to avoid pumping effects. Appropriate settings are highly dependent upon the
characteristics of the input signal and the desired result.

Figure 13.27
Limiter set for limiting transient peaks to
-0.3dBFS

Figure 13.28
Classic downward compression using
the supplied Compressor plug-in

Info

As well as controlling the wanted parts of the signal, compression may also result in an increase in the
level of some of the unwanted parts of the signal, such as interference or headphone spill between sung
vocal lines. To avoid this effect, try using expansion / gating to reduce the level of the interference prior to
compression.

Mid-level upward compression with Compressor

Mid-level upward compression uses a comparatively low threshold, a subtle ratio and sufficient makeup gain to push up the lower and mid-level detail in the signal. The louder parts of the signal remain unchanged. For this kind of processing, try the Compressor plug-in settings shown in Figure 13.29. This uses a gentle 1.3 : 1 ratio with the threshold at -45dB and 6dB of makeup gain. A fairly fast attack at 4ms and a hard knee setting keeps the input signal under control. Try a soft knee setting for a more natural effect. These settings bring out the inner detail of a recording and increase the density of the sound. Try this on strummed acoustic guitar and you should hear the rhythmic and percussive elements emphasised. For a slightly more exaggerated effect try decreasing the threshold still further to around -56dB, combined with a 1.68 : 1 ratio, 20ms attack and around 13dB of makeup gain.

Figure 13.29
Mid-level upward compression

Info

By activating its side chain button, Compressor may be set up for ducking. Ducking typically involves reducing the level of a music track whenever the speech on a voice-over track is present. Gain reduction of the music track begins when the voice-over signal routed to the side chain exceeds the threshold. The amount of gain reduction is regulated by the compression ratio. Try ratios between 2 and 8 : 1.

Parallel compression with Compressor

Parallel compression may be used for subtle compression techniques where quiet signals are transparently boosted relative to loud signals or for intentionally audible effects where compression artefacts are emphasised while still maintaining the dynamics of the original signal. Try the following setup for transparent parallel compression using Compressor. This uses a group channel and an audio channel:

- Add a group channel and select the audio channel of the source signal to be treated with parallel compression
- On the source audio channel send the output to the main stereo output faders and set up an auxiliary send to the group channel. On the send slot, activate the pre-fader button and set the level to unity gain.
- Activate Compressor as an insert effect on the group channel.
- Set Compressor as follows: threshold -56, ratio 2.0, makeup zero (no auto), attack 2.8, hold 0, release 400, analysis 80, live button active.
- As a starting point, set the group channel fader to -2dB.

In this configuration the source audio channel provides the uncompressed signal and the group channel provides the compressed signal. In louder passages the parallel compression effect is proportionally less than in quiet passages. Thus, there is little effect on loud passages whereas quiet passages are boosted in level. This results in very transparent compression. Adjust the relative levels of the source audio channel and the group channel for the desired amount of compression.

Classic noise gating with Gate

Gating involves a radical drop in output level once the input falls below a set threshold. To reduce background noise, the threshold is set just above the noise level. Figure 13.30 shows the Gate plug-in set up for classic noise gating. Here the threshold is set at -35dB but this must be adjusted according to the noise level in the signal you are gating. Careful adjustment of the attack, release and hold parameters ensures a natural transition between the gated and ungated signal. Try starting with an attack of 2ms and a release of 250ms. A fairly fast attack ensures that the gate opens fast enough when the wanted part of the signal rises above the threshold. A long release ensures a gradual attenuation when the gate closes in order to avoid unnatural radical cuts between the signal and absolute silence. For this setup, the side-chain filter is switched out.

Figure 13.30
Gate set up for classic noise gating

Tip

To change the ratios and thresholds of the compressor / expander plug-ins drag the handles directly in the curve display.

Frequency conscious gating with Gate

A popular technique in live drum recording is the gating of individual instruments within the kit to reduce leakage between microphones. For example, the sounds of the cymbals and the bass drum often leak into the snare drum microphone and vice versa. 'Frequency conscious' gating may provide a solution to this problem. The essential idea is the setting up of a gate which is tuned to open only when the frequencies of the wanted instrument are present. The technique can be extended to any occasion when you need to separate a wanted sound from background interference. In the Gate plug-in, this is achieved using the side-chain filter.

Tip

Drums and percussion which vary greatly in dynamics may prove difficult to treat with frequency conscious or any other kind of gating. In these cases, gentle downward expansion may be more appropriate than hard gating.

Figure 13.31 shows the Gate plug-in set up for frequency conscious gating of a bass drum. This uses the side-chain filter set to band pass mode with a very narrow Q. The frequency is tuned to the dominant band in the bass drum which, in this example, is 73Hz. You can find this by ear by engaging

Figure 13.31 (left)
Frequency conscious bass drum gate

Figure 13.32 (right)
Frequency conscious snare drum gate

the side-chain filter monitor button while in playback. A very fast 0.1ms attack ensures the capture of the click of the bass drum and a medium fast release of 73ms with a hold of 25ms captures the body. The analysis is set to the peaks of the incoming signal and the Live button is de-activated to engage the default look-ahead behaviour of the gate. The threshold setting must be precisely adjusted to allow only the bass drum to pass through. Also see the supplied 'Isolate BD' presets which use the side-chain filter in the more orthodox low pass mode.

Similarly, Figure 13.32 shows the Gate plug-in set up for the frequency conscious gating of a snare drum. The side-chain filter is set to band pass mode and the centre frequency is tuned to the impact of the snare with a fairly wide Q setting. The attack, release and hold settings are similar to those for the bass drum example, above. The threshold setting must be precisely adjusted to allow only the snare drum to pass through.

Info

Frequency conscious gating of drums presents few problems if the parameters are set up very carefully. However, make sure that you are not losing the initial transients in the attack phase of the sound. It is this part of the signal which endows drums with their impact and clarity. When attacks are set too slow or thresholds are set too high the initial impact is easily lost.

Punch with VintageCompressor

The supplied VintageCompressor simulates the action of older style classic compressors (such as the UREI 1176LN hardware unit). Here, you regulate the amount of compression by pushing up the input until you see gain reduction taking place in the gain reduction meter. Gain reduction starts when the input signal reaches around +6dB. Once you have applied input gain you must normally apply a corresponding amount of cut with the output control to bring the signal back down to a reasonable level. The attack and release controls operate in a similar manner to the Compressor plug-in described above. Activating the punch button ensures that the attack of the compressed sound cuts through regardless of how short an attack time you set. This is good for adding punch to drums, bass and percussive instruments. Try the settings in Figure 13.33 to add punch to a snare or a whole drum kit.

Figure 13.3
Try these VintageCompressor settings on a snare or a whole drum kit

Dynamics – alternatives

There is a wide range of dynamics plug-in alternatives. High on the list are the Abbey Road EMI TG12413 Limiter, Blue Cat Dynamics, Flux Solera and Pure series, IK Multimedia T-Racks Vintage compressor, Izotope Ozone mastering suite, Melda Production MDynamics and MultiBandDynamics, PSP Master Compressor, PSP Old Timer, PSP Vintage Warmer, PSP Xenon Limiter, Sonalksis SV-719 gate, Sonnox Oxford Dynamics and Oxford Limiter, SSL LMC-1, TC Powercore Brick Wall Limiter, Universal Audio UAD 1176LN, URS Classic Compressors, Voxengo Crunchessor, and Waves C1 Compressor / Gate.

Abbey Road TG12413 Limiter

The Abbey Road EMI TG12413 Limiter (Figure 13.34a) provides authentic vintage-style compression and limiting based upon the original EMI limiters of the EMI TG12345 and TG12413 consoles used at Abbey Road Studios in the late 60s and early 70s. These consoles were used to record classic albums such as the Beatles' Abbey Road and Pink Floyd's Dark Side of the Moon. The TG12413 includes two modules: the 1969 for an authentic emulation of the original TG12345 hardware, and the 2005 based upon the hardware reissue TG1 Limiter supplied by Chandler Limited. Both modules provide transparent control of transients while also adding warmth and character thanks to the simulation of the original diode-based gain reduction circuit. These plug-ins are remarkable for their fuss-free GUIs which include just four control parameters. The apparent simplicity of the interface belies the range of processing possibilities. The TG12413 is full of character, can flatter almost any audio signal and where appropriate can produce extreme and intentionally audible compression effects.

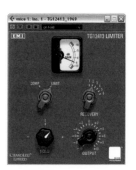

Figure 13.34a
The EMI TG12413 1969 version, providing high-quality vintage compression and limiting within a fuss free interface

Blue Cat Dynamics

The Blue Cat Dynamics plug-in (Figure 13.34b) is a dynamics processor featuring compressor, limiter, expander, gate and waveshaper functions. The interface includes an upper curve for compression and limiting, and a lower curve for expansion and gating, each with their own threshold, ratio and knee controls. This allows you to create custom dynamic control curves combining compression and expansion functions simultaneously. The effect of the set-

Figure 13.34b
Blue Cat Dynamics

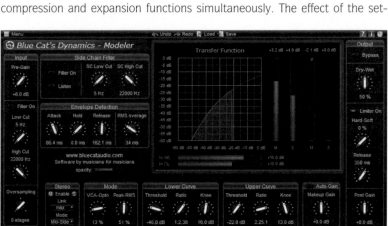

tings are reflected in the transfer function display which shows the shape of the curve and the real-time behaviour of the signal being processed. There are input and output meters and gain change meters which turn red when compressing and green when expanding. The detection mode for the plug-in is freely variable between opto and VCA behaviour where opto produces a smooth, musical response and VCA produces a more snappy, aggressive response. A side chain filter allows you to set up frequency conscious gating and compression. A useful brickwall limiter is provided last in the chain which can be regulated for hard or soft knee limiting, or when the release time is set to zero for hard or soft saturation / clipping. A dry / wet control allows you to mix the source signal with the compressed signal which makes it easy to set up parallel compression. To avoid aliasing and improve the audio quality for critical applications the plug-in includes 2x and 4x oversampling settings. In the stereo version the input can be switched between normal left / right and mid / side operation allowing creative and corrective manipulation of the stereo image. Blue Cat Dynamics also supports real-time gain control of an audio track via MIDI control change messages using Dynamics and their own Gain plug-in. The appearance of the GUI may be freely modified using skins. With sufficient knowledge you can create your own skins but a good selection is supplied as standard, each streamlined to a specific function of Dynamics. Happily, the GUI also includes undo / redo buttons which are so seldom included in plug-ins of this type and yet are so useful. Overall, Dynamics is an extremely flexible dynamics processor providing the majority of commonly used dynamics functions within a single unit.

PSP Old Timer

Old Timer is a simple compressor designed to be easy to use with minimal controls and yet providing a wide range of very musical sounding compression effects. The controls feature a seven step ratio selector with ratios from a gentle 1.2 : 1 up to 10 : 1, a time control which sets a fast attack / release at low values and slow attack / release at high levels, and a compressor control which increases the amount of compression the higher you set it. The actual amount of compression available varies between around 8dB for a 1.2 : 1 ratio and 30dB for 10 : 1. A global switch provides a valve setting for emulation of tube compression or a clear setting for clean, transparent compression. For optimal transparency the gain reduction meter would normally be active between -4 and -8dB. Old Timer excels at smooth, gentle compression and is suitable for single tracks or might occasionally serve as a bus compressor. It is good at gluing sounds together, levelling and emphasising inner detail

Figure 13.34c
PSP Audioware Old Timer

Info

For dynamics processing also check out Melda Production MDynamics. MDynamics Sidechain allows side chain triggering by inserting it on an LRC + lfe Group channel. An audio channel sent to this group and panned right on the surround panner forms the main signal (surround panner in y-mirror mode). An auxiliary send routed to this group from a second audio channel feeds the side chain. Set the Group channel input gain to +9.5dB and route it to the main stereo out. Activate the secondary side chain input of the MDynamics Sidechain plug-in.

Info

For full coverage of the Mixer built-in EQ see Chapter 12.

EQ effects

EQ – supplied plug-ins

In addition to the built-in EQ of the Mixer, Cubase is supplied with the StudioEQ, GEQ-10 and GEQ-30 plug-ins. StudioEQ operates in a similar manner to the built-in EQ (see Chapter 12 for details). The GEQ-10 and GEQ-30 are 10 band and 30 band graphic EQ units.

GEQ30 graphic equaliser

The GEQ30 plug-in (Figure 13.35) is a 30 band graphic equaliser with 12dB of cut or boost in thirty third-octave frequency bands. The disadvantage of graphic EQs is their inability to change the centre frequency for each band. However, like its hardware counterparts the GEQ30 is very easy to set up. For example, it is quick and easy to find problem resonances within a sound and reduce them, and by clicking on one slider and then dragging across the GUI you can quickly set the levels of all frequency bands. Moreover, once you have set up an EQ curve you can modify the overall depth of the effect using the Range dial. The character of the EQ may be further modified using the filter response menu. Here, you can choose between a true response and various resonant modes for the filter bands. It is worth trying Resonant mode where applying gain to any band also applies an amount of cut to the adjacent bands, or the musical sounding Classic mode where the resonance is decreased as the gain is increased and vice versa. Overall, the GEQ-30 and its little brother, the GEQ-10, make a refreshing change to the usual parametric EQs to which we have become so accustomed.

13.35
GEQ-30 graphic EQ

EQ – alternatives

It is worth having a number of EQ plug-ins from different developers in your collection. Each tends to impose a slightly different character on the treated sound and having a choice helps you find the most suitable EQ for each equalisation task. Among those worth exploring are ApulSoft apEQ, Eiosis Air EQ, Flux Epure, IK Multimedia T-Racks Linear Phase EQ, Kjaerhus GEQ7 Golden EQ, PSP MasterQ, PSP Neon, PSP SQuad EQ, Sonalksis SV-517 equaliser, Sonnox Oxford EQ, TC Electronic Assimilator, UAD Cambridge EQ, UAD Neve 1073 EQ, Waves Linear Phase EQ and Waves Renaissance EQ.

Eiosis Air EQ

Eiosis Air EQ challenges traditional approaches to plug-in EQing. Most obvious is the absence of an EQ curve display. This avoids visual distractions and encourages you to listen to the sound in more detail. You may also choose to hide all frequency, gain, and Q indicators, and generally re-configure the interface to your own preferences.

Air EQ includes 7 bands of EQ plus the 'air' EQ control itself. The main bands feature low and high pass filters in the lowest and uppermost positions with five parametric EQs in between. The lowest and highest of the latter may be switched between parametric or low / high shelving filters. The special 'air' band is designed to breath life into uninteresting sounds and add brightness and character without harshness. The supplied presets bank features combinations of EQ bands set up for specific instruments and tasks. Most presets feature each band labelled according to task rather than frequency with names such as density, presence, clarity, body, string noise, click and so on. This encourages intuitive use of the controls and helps you to quickly tune in to the desired part of the spectrum. Air EQ excels at boosting mid and upper frequencies and is good for sweetening and enlivening vocals and acoustic guitars. This plug-in uses very little CPU power and has zero latency, so it is especially suitable for tracking and mixing in Cubase.

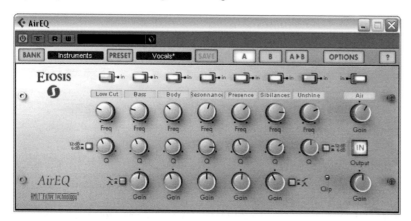

Figure 13.36a
Eiosis Air EQ is especially suitable for tracking and mixing in Cubase

Figure 13.36b
Sonnox Oxford EQ. High precision EQ for mixing and mastering

Sonnox Oxford EQ

Among the EQ alternatives, the Sonnox Oxford EQ plug-in remains one of the most desirable (Figure 13.36b). The Oxford EQ is based upon the EQ section of the renowned OXFR3 console. The controls feature: variable slope high and low pass filters; low and high EQ switchable between shelving and parametric control; and low-mid, mid and high-mid parametric EQ. The overall characteristics may be modified using a four-position EQ type selector featuring: 1) clinical style EQ emulating the SSL 4000 series; 2) unsymmetrical boost / cut EQ curves suited to drums and percussion; 3) musical style EQ similar to Neve and SSL G series consoles; and 4) soft and gentle EQ for mastering and other applications.

ApulSoft apQualizr high precision equaliser / analyser

ApQualizr is a high precision equaliser featuring graphical editing of multiple filters on top of a large real-time FFT analysis display (Figure 13.36c). Filters are inserted by clicking in empty space in the display. Peaking EQ, high and low pass, high and low shelf, and band-reject and band-pass filters are available. Up to 63 filters may be inserted and a whopping 40dB of boost or cut is available on the dB scale. Frequency, gain and Q settings are adjusted in the dialogue for each filter or by dragging the filter within the display. When desired a stacking function produces steeper and more resonant filter curves for the high / low pass and shelving filters. This combination of controls results in a device capable of both very extreme intentionally audible EQ effects and very subtle transparent correction. The real-time FFT display features resolution settings of 4, 8, 16 or 32k for progressively more detailed FFT analysis. The timing of the visual display is perfectly synchronised to the audio signal being processed thus helping you make the connection between the spectral analysis on screen and what you are hearing. When used in stereo the FFT analysis can produce a colour coded display where the left channel is green, the right channel is red and the combined stereo signal is shown in blue. Other features include high magnification zoom functions, 64-bit internal precision, 2x or 4x oversampling for more accurate filtering of high frequencies, and left / right or mid / side stereo modes.

ApQualizr provides extremely flexible EQing and FFT analysis. The range and accuracy of its parameters go beyond the limits of most other similar devices. It is particularly useful for transparent corrective EQing and analytical work. Unlike most other devices in this category it includes band-reject and band-pass filter types. Using its band-reject filter you can precisely target and invisibly remove very narrow frequency bands. It is also one of the few EQ plug-ins which includes real-time FFT analysis and a filter curve within the same display. This really helps tune in to the spectral details of the signal being processed.

Figure 13.36c
ApulSoft apQualizr high precision equaliser and real-time spectrum analyser

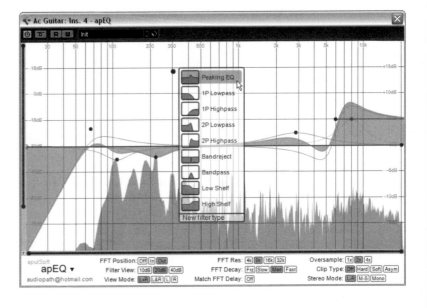

Filter effects

Filter – supplied plug-ins

ToneBooster

ToneBooster is a basic filter with centre frequency (tone), gain and width controls. It operates in either peak or bandpass mode. This is similar to a parametric EQ except that the gain control does not allow you to attenuate the level. Peak mode allows you to boost a single band within the signal which can produce resonance effects when the width is set quite narrow. Bandpass mode allows only those frequencies within the chosen bandwidth to pass through. This allows you to band limit sounds to specific frequency ranges which is occasionally useful for guitar, pad and synth sounds.

WahWah

As the name suggests, the WahWah plug-in is specialised in the production of wah wah effects. Wah wah is created by sweeping a peak or bandpass filter up and down within the frequency spectrum. In WahWah the sweeping effect is created using the pedal control. This mimics the action of a real wah wah pedal. The low and high frequencies, bandwidth and gain change resulting from moving the pedal are regulated using the respective Lo and Hi controls. To get started, try selecting the 'Warm Wah' preset and then choose one of the following techniques for recording your pedal manipulations:

- Select 'automation' in the menu below the pedal dial and activate the Write automation button of the plug-in. Commence playback and move the pedal dial as desired using the mouse. Stop playback when you have completed your automation recording. De-activate the Write button and activate the Read button. Commence playback again to hear the results.
- Or alternatively, select 'modulation' in the menu below the pedal dial and select the WahWah plug-in as the output on a spare MIDI track. Record enable the chosen MIDI track. The pedal dial may now be controlled via the modulation wheel of your MIDI keyboard. Commence recording and move the pedal dial as desired. Replay the passage after recording to hear the results. You may need to edit the MIDI modulation data in one of the MIDI editors. Redrawing the curve with greater resolution gives a smoother wah wah effect.

Figure 13.37
ToneBooster

Figure 13.38
WahWah plug-in and pedal automation curve in the project window

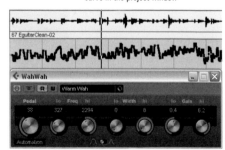

Filter – alternatives

There is a wide range of filter plug-in alternatives available including Native Instruments Reaktor Analogic Filter, Ohm Force Predatohm, PSP Nitro and Steinberg Metalizer, StepFilter and Tonic. See 'Additional Effects' below for descriptions of Metalizer and StepFilter.

Modulation effects

Modulation – supplied plug-ins

The supplied modulation effects are wide ranging and versatile. They are often the first choice for adding movement and excitement to sounds and are always worth trying in combination with other effects. Almost all the plug-ins in the modulation range may be synchronised to the tempo of Cubase. Modulation effects are popular for guitar, bass, strings, organ and electric piano, and help thicken or sweeten almost anything in the mix. However, like most other effects they are best when not overused. There now follows more detailed descriptions of the Cloner and StudioChorus plug-ins.

Cloner

Cloner produces up to four copies of the input signal (known as voices) each of which can be delayed or detuned. The delay and detune sliders govern the relative proportions of delay and detune for each voice while the overall delay and detune depth is governed by the global delay and detune dials. The global delay and detune dial values may be 'humanised', meaning that subtle variations are introduced into the settings. The overall effect is spread across the stereo image using the spatial control. Cloner produces particularly clean and rich chorus effects which are difficult to match with traditional chorus devices. It is recommended for guitar, bass and voice doubling effects. Try the settings shown in Figure 13.39 for a voice doubling effect.

Figure 13.39
Cloner

StudioChorus

StudioChorus features two chorus units arranged in series, each with rate, width, spatial, mix, delay and low and high frequency roll-off filters. The delay control sets the basic delay value, rate governs the rate of an LFO which modulates the delay time, and width governs the depth of the effect. The LFO may be set to a sine or triangular wave and the rate may be synced to the tempo of Cubase. Cascading two units in series allows for the creation of some very rich chorus effects. Try the settings in Figure 13.40 for bass guitar.

Figure 13.40
StudioChorus

Modulation – alternatives

Modulation plug-in alternatives include Audio Ease Deep Phase Nine, Ohm Force Mobilohm, Universal Audio UAD-1 Dimension D, Voxengo Vintage Modulator, Waves MetaFlanger, and many others. The UAD-1 Dimension D, for example, is an emulation of the original Roland Dimension D, a unique device with only four control buttons which may be activated in various combinations to produce warm and characterful chorus.

Other effects

Others – supplied plug-ins

Cubase provides Octaver and Tuner in the Others category. Octaver features only three controls: direct level, and octave 1 and 2 dials. The octave dials provide transposed copies of the input, one and two octaves down in pitch. Octaver might provide a solution when you wish to thicken synth sequences or simulate a bass line using a guitar.

Figure 13.41
A software guitar tuner

Tuner is a pitch monitoring device which analyses the input and gives a reading of its pitch in terms of note value, frequency and octave. Deviations from the centre pitch position are measured in cents. This plug-in is intended as a software replacement for a guitar tuner and is therefore useful for tuning guitars and any other stringed instrument. The string is in tune when the two arrows are in the centre position pointing at the pitch value and the cent value equals zero.

Others – alternatives

Plug-ins which fit into the 'others' category are often hybrid effects which combine techniques from more conventional processing to produce something unique. Such is the case with Noveltech's Character and Vocal Enhancer plug-ins which run on the TC Powercore system. These allow you to capture the identity of a sound and then enhance this identity to make it stand out in the mix. Another hybrid effect worth checking out is Glitch by dblue, a real-time audio effects step sequencer featuring nine adjustable effects with stereo panning and filters.

Also in the 'others' category are restoration and tape saturation emulation. For restoration, Bias Soundsoap, Steinberg De-noiser, Steinberg De-clicker and Waves Xnoise come high on the list, and if you have the budget, the Cedar Audio restoration tools give excellent results. Tape saturation emulation is of great value to digital audio since it can add character and warmth when a digital recording sounds cold and lifeless. Tape saturation emulation has proved difficult to reproduce digitally. Among the finest efforts are the DUY DaD Tape simulator, PSP Vintage Warmer, RSO Extreme Punch 2 analogue tape emulator and Voxengo AnalogFlux Tape Bus.

PSP Vintage Warmer

Vintage Warmer combines compression, limiting, and tape saturation emulation. It may be used as a single or multiband compressor, or as a brick-wall limiter, so it is equally at home in the dynamics category. Its overload characteristics produce warm saturation reminiscent of analogue tape. This can help remedy the problems of Cubase users suffering from cold, brittle or characterless digital recordings.

Figure 13.42
PSP Vintage Warmer

The heart of the device (Figure 13.42) is in the drive, knee and speed dials. Drive regulates the amount of input gain, allowing you to boost or attenuate the signal passing to the compressor / limiter. Knee sets up the characteristics of the compressor / limiter where low settings produce hard knee limiting effects while higher settings produce fast soft knee compression. Knee dial settings around 50% are often the best for tape saturation emulation. The speed dial produces slower attack / release behaviour at low settings and faster attack / release behaviour at higher settings. The other controls include a release multiplier dial which modifies the release time established with the speed dial according to a multiplication factor, a ceiling control which sets the peak level above which the output signal is not allowed to pass, and low / high shelving EQ (single band mode) or three-band pre-limiter level adjustment (multiband mode). Vintage style VU / PPM meters and toggle switches for single-band / multiband, stereo / mono and stereo link on / off modes complete the picture.

Vintage Warmer works equally well on individual tracks, whole mixes or as a mastering effect. To become familiar with its operation, try moving the controls in broad strokes at first, and then back off the effect until it is just noticeable. The knee dial can have a dramatic effect on the density, punch and impact of the sound. Take care to not overdo the effect.

Voxengo AnalogFlux Tape Bus

Voxengo's AnalogFlux series of plug-ins are all about emulating analogue warmth and one of the best in the collection is Tape Bus which emulates analogue tape. Seven tape impulses are provided, each of which imposes a different tape-style colouration upon the signal. Other controls include record gain, low and high EQ, a saturation curve dial for regulating the harmonic content of the saturation, and frequency and gain dials for the pre-emphasis

Figure 13.43
Voxengo AnalogFlux Tape Bus

high-shelf filter. Push the record gain up to achieve more saturation. The distortion meter between the Out and Curve controls gives an indication of how much saturation is taking place. Try the settings in Figure 13.43 to enliven dull-sounding drum kits and loops.

Pitch Shift

Pitch Shift – supplied plug-in

Pitch Correct

Pitch Correct is a real-time pitch correction plug-in for monophonic audio recordings like vocals, saxophone, trumpet or guitar which were sung or played out of tune. The effect may be subtle in corrective applications or intentionally audible when producing pitch based sound effects.

The plug-in features a relatively simple GUI with seven parameters. These operate as follows:

- Speed – determines the speed of the pitch change where higher values produce a more audible effect. 100 produces the classic 'Cher' effect.
- Tolerance – governs the depth of the effect.
- Transpose – allows real-time transpose of the pitch of the incoming signal between -24 and +24 semitones.
- Scale source – governs the scale to which the pitch is corrected. This can be a chromatic or internal scale of your choice, or the pitch can be made to follow MIDI notes.
- Shift – transposes the formant characteristics.
- Optimize – optimises the formant behaviour for general purpose use, or for male or female vocals.
- Preservation – when activated the natural formants of vocals are preserved during pitch correction. When de-activated the formants are transposed resulting in less natural sounding vocals but good for sound effects.

Pitch Correct is normally used as an insert effect. The speed and tolerance parameters govern the essential intensity and depth of the pitch change. Lower values produce transparent pitch shifting while higher values produce intentionally audible sound effects. Try the settings in Figure 13.44 for gentle, transparent pitch correction of vocals. Alternatively, for the 'Cher' effect

Figure 13.44
Pitch Correct set up for transparent real-time pitch correction

try: Speed 100, Tolerance 0, Transpose 0, Scale source: internal scale of your choice, Shift 0, Optimise General, Preservation On. For a monotone synthetic effect try: Speed 90, Tolerance 10, Transpose 0, Scale source: MIDI Note, Shift 0, Optimise Female, Preservation On. To use the latter effect, add a MIDI track, activate its monitor enable button and set its output routing to Pitch Correct. Play the notes of your choice on your MIDI keyboard during playback of the audio track where Pitch Correct is inserted.

Reverb effects

Reverb – supplied plug-ins

A number of reverb plug-ins are supplied with Cubase including Reverence, Roomworks and Roomworks SE. Reverence is a high-end convolution reverb and Roomworks is a room simulator.

Reverence

Reverence is a convolution reverberation device for the simulation of concert halls, rooms and other acoustic spaces (Figure 13.45). It produces rich, authentic reverberation. The GUI controls include pre-delay, time scaling, size, level, ER tail split, ER tail mix, three band EQ, wet / dry mix balance and output level. Where required, the controls allow you to quickly modify the basic effect, especially the time scaling and size parameters which can change a small space into a large one or vice versa, and the ER tail mix which can isolate the early reflections making the treated signal sound closer and more dry. The main central display area shows a waveform or spectrogram of the impulse response, or provides information about the currently selected IR such as the name, number of channels and length. The secondary display shows an EQ curve or one or more pictures of the acoustic space where the IR was recorded. The EQ section features high and low shelving filters and a parametric EQ which allow you to highlight or dampen the sound of the reverb thereby simulating the reflective or absorptive characteristics of a natural acoustic space. A reverse function allows you to reverse the IR for sound effects and auto gain normalises the IR for a more constant level between different presets. A trim slider allows you to trim the the start or end of the IR which is good for producing gated reverb effects.

Figure 13.45
Reverence

Reverence presets are loaded in the normal manner via the standard presets menu. Each preset may contain up to 36 preset assignments stored on the program matrix buttons. The IRs of presets assigned in this manner are pre-loaded into RAM memory thus facilitating faster load times and smooth crossfades between presets when automating a mix. Hence, the matrix buttons are also known as automation presets.

To store a preset onto a program matrix button, click once on an empty button. A white frame flashes around the button. Click on the browse button to open the presets menu. Select a preset and close the dialogue. The white frame stops flashing and the button background is now displayed in blue. The preset is now assigned to the button and its IR is loaded in RAM memory. In this manner, multiple presets may be assigned to the buttons and the overall configuration may be saved as a preset. To recall a preset assignment double-click on the relevant program matrix button.

You can use the import button to import your own IR files and, if desired, any pictures associated with the acoustic space. The associated picture files must be located at the same level as the IR file and must be jpg, gif or png formats.

Info

Early versions of Reverence suffer from a problem when saving presets from imported IRs. To save a preset which uses an IR you have imported do not use the main Save preset function. Instead, first click on the store button to the right of the program matrix and choose a name in the pop-up menu. After this operation, save the preset a second time in the normal manner using the main Save Preset function.

Reverence is supplied with a good range of presets including concert halls, churches, theatres and studio spaces. In addition, a wide choice of impulse response files are available for download on the internet which can be imported into Reverence to expand your presets library. Reverence would normally be used as a Send effect with the mix control set fully wet (100).

Roomworks

Roomworks is a reverberation device for the simulation of rooms and acoustic spaces (Figure 13.46). The interface includes low and high shelf input filters, pre-delay, reverb, size, diffusion, width and low and high frequency damping filters.

Figure 13.46
Roomworks

Roomworks' pre and post reverb filtering are the keys to adjusting the character of the reverb. After setting up the predelay, time, size and diffusion parameters to achieve a basic sound, the input filtering and damping sections allow you to change the tone colour between bright and heavily dampened effects. The overall shape of the results can be still further modified using the controls in the envelope section.

The unit is supplied with a good range of presets. It works well with drums and can place snares and overall kits in a variety of reverberant spaces with convincing ease. It excels at producing small and medium sized room simulations. Roomworks would normally be used as a Send effect with the wet only button activated to provide a 100% wet signal from the unit.

Reverb – alternatives

Reverb is an essential effect in any studio setup and many Cubase users seek out units from other developers. The possibilities include hardware units, convolution software plug-ins, or algorithmic software plug-ins (non-convolution). Hardware units have the advantage of greater DSP power for the complex processing needed to simulate reverb and this takes place without use of the CPU in the host computer. Software convolution reverb plug-ins use impulse responses taken from real acoustic spaces or reverb devices and produce very convincing results. Algorithmic software reverb plug-ins use similar processing techniques to conventional hardware units. Both of the latter techniques use the host CPU for all processing, which might be disadvantageous if you have limited CPU power.

Of particular note in the software category are 2C Audio Aether, Audio Ease Altiverb, Sir Convolution reverb, Sonnox Oxford Reverb, Universal Audio UAD Plate 140 and Voxengo Pristine Space Convolution Processor. There now follow descriptions of Audio Ease Altiverb and Voxengo Pristine Space.

Audio Ease Altiverb

Altiverb is renowned as the industry standard convolution reverb plug-in. The GUI is laid out like a classic rackmount unit with a centrally placed display showing either an impulse response browser, a waterfall diagram or a waveform diagram. Its main control parameters include reverb length, room size, wet / dry mix, damping, early reflections, reverb tail, stage position and EQ.

Audio Ease encourage you to think of Altiverb as an echo chamber where the input to the unit passes through one or two speakers placed in the chamber and the output is produced via microphones which pick up the reverberation in the chamber. This set up is indeed how most of the impulse responses are recorded and Altiverb allows you to view a diagram of the placement of the speakers and microphones within the chosen acoustic space. Furthermore, you can modify the position of the speakers relative to the microphones using the stage position controls, thus producing a corresponding modification in the reverberation. In addition to all this, a virtual reality movie, photographs and detailed recording information are provided for each acoustic space which help you gain a real appreciation of the kind of space in which you are placing your material.

The essential strength of Altiverb is its vast library of impulse responses

Figure 13.47
Audio Ease Altiverb. Probably the
ultimate convolution reverb

and the precision with which they are recorded. The library features a wide range of cathedrals, churches, halls, small rooms, scoring stages, and stadiums as well as vintage reverb device and abstract sound design impulses. The locations range from the Mechanics Hall, Worcester, USA to the Antwerp Sports Stadium, Belgium to the Vienna Konzerthaus Mozart Hall, Austria to the Sydney Opera House, Australia, so you can literally travel the world of reverberation.

Like all convolution reverb plug-ins, using Altiverb may result in slightly more load on the CPU of the host computer, when compared to an average plug-in. It may also take a few seconds to read the impulse response cache file each time you activate it. Overall, Altiverb offers access to a whole new world of reverberation treasures and could justifiably be described as the ultimate convolution reverb plug-in. It is particularly suitable for those seeking convincing emulation of the reverberant behaviour of real acoustic spaces. In Cubase, it is best used as a send effect.

Voxengo Pristine Space

Voxengo Pristine Space is an 8-channel convolution reverb processor. Its multi-channel capability means that you can implement simultaneous multiple reverb effects. For example, this allows you to mix the early reflection part of one impulse response with the reverb tail of another, or simulate the effect of overhead mics and ambient room mics for an acoustic drum kit using two different impulses. For sound design and special effects, you can arrange a number of reverb effects in series.

Pristine Space provides control curves for the time-based modification of volume, stereo width, pan position, high and low pass filtering and overall EQ. This is achieved using multiple breakpoint envelopes in a graphical display. Offset, length, delay, gain and reverse controls are provided for each impulse response. The eight channels are normally arranged in four stereo pairs. Preset configurations are supplied for true stereo reverb insert, true

Figure 13.48
Voxengo Pristine Space

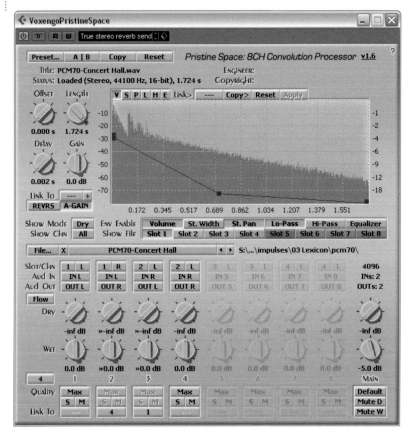

stereo reverb send, 2-step 2-channel serial insert and so on, which helps you quickly set up the device for use as an insert or send effect in Cubase. The impulse responses are loaded into one of eight slots and each slot is colour-coded, which helps clarify what you are editing when working with multiple reverbs.

Pristine Space is particularly good for experimental work and sound design. It is not supplied with its own library of impulse responses. Instead, it relies upon the free IR files available for download on the internet or you can design your own using Voxengo's Impulse Modeller plug-in. When compared to an average plug-in Pristine Space may result in slightly more load on the CPU,. It is best activated in a single instance as a send effect.

Additional effects

A number of legacy effects are installed alongside the VST3 plug-in collection and you may also use plug-ins from previous versions of Cubase if they are still present on your hard disk. Three of the best from the earlier range of plug-ins are Metalizer, Quadrafuzz and StepFilter.

Metalizer

Metalizer is a variable band-pass filtering device with tempo or time based frequency band modulation. This produces a range of effects from flange-like sounds and wah-wah to extreme notch filtering effects. The heart of Metalizer is the sharpness dial. This governs the essential quality of the effect and the higher its setting the narrower the band-pass filter, as shown in the graphical display. The tone and feedback dials affect the high frequency and resonant content of the effect and this is reflected in the display by the density and brightness of the waveform inside the filter curve. Switching in the filter band modulation allows time or tempo-based modulation of the filtered frequency band up and down the frequency axis for the production of classic wah-wah and other swept filter effects. Clicking and dragging directly in the graphical display allows simultaneous control of the sharpness and tone parameters. Metalizer is good for wah-wah and special filtering effects. It works best on harmonically rich sound sources like strings, distortion guitars and complex synth sounds.

QuadraFuzz

QuadraFuzz is a multiband distortion device providing level control in four frequency bands both before and after distortion. This was originally a hardware circuit designed by Craig Anderton. The original concept has been expanded by Spectral Design to provide control over the width of the frequency bands before distortion. The edit window is where you need to go if you want to create your own effects. Like many distortion devices, you need to maintain a balance between the input and output stages since applying radical distortion can create radical level changes. Try using the solo button while making changes in the frequency band selector display to help judge more accurately the result of each change. Distortion is applied to the signal according to the choice of transfer function (Shape button). A transfer function governs the relationship between the amplitude of the input and output signal which pass through it. Changing the shape of this function produces various types of distortion in the output signal. The shapes you see on each button give a rough indication of the characteristics of the chosen transfer function. The lower the button you select the more harmonics are added to the signal. Harmonic distortion is added only to those parts of the signal you choose using the frequency selectors, and how much distortion applied to each band depends on the levels you set. QuadraFuzz is well suited to the production of all types of fuzz guitar effects but it is also excellent for synth sounds and for subtly highlighting or completely mangling drum and percussion sounds. It might also be used for adding subtle warmth and character to certain frequencies within a mix.

StepFilter

StepFilter is versatile step-based and static filter device suitable for rhythmic, tempo-linked and traditional filtering effects. The first thing to try with StepFilter is to play a drum loop in cycle playback mode and check out the various patterns in the Examples preset. Try changing the tempo sync value to 1/8, 1/16 and 1/32 notes with pattern 1 selected. Next, listen to the effect of changing the base cut-off and base resonance dials. Be careful with your speakers and your ears! At high resonance levels this can produce piercing ringing effects. Now move on to the cut-off and resonance displays themselves. Simply drag the mouse in the displays to set up your own patterns. The cut-off and resonance values of the two displays are stepped through simultaneously. If you want just straight filtering, de-activate the sync button. At this point in time, all step sequencing functions are de-activated. However, the first markers in each of the cut-off and resonance displays remain active as do the base dials and the filter type slider. StepFilter is good for filtering effects on dance tracks and works well with drum loops.

Powered plug-ins

There are a number of so-called powered plug-ins available which are a good choice for those who wish to use high-end plug-ins without unnecessary load on the CPU of the host computer. These take the form of software plug-ins which appear within Cubase in the usual manner combined with a hardware component like a rackmount unit or PCI / PC Express card. The hardware takes care of most of the digital signal processing, thus relieving the host CPU of the burden and simultaneously doubling as a copy protection device. Included in this category are the UAD powered plug-ins, which run on a dedicated PCI or PCI Express card and the TC Electronics Powercore system which is run using a PCI card or an external unit connected by Firewire. Similarly, the SSL Duende system features a rackmount unit connected to the host computer via a Firewire cable providing up to 32 channels of high-end SSL EQ and dynamics processing.

Integrating external hardware effects units

While the supplied plug-in effects are good, processing such as reverb is still often best handled using an external hardware unit. To make the use of external devices a relatively painless process, Cubase includes an External FX plug-in module which allows you to integrate hardware effects into the Mixer and use them in the same way as an internal plug-in. This is possible only if you have audio hardware with multiple inputs and outputs, since you need to route the effects signal in and out of Cubase via additional buses, separate from the main input / output buses. To integrate an external send effect, proceed as follows:

- Open the VST Connections window (Devices menu or press F4) and select the External FX tab. Click on the Add External FX button and in the dialogue which appears select the I/O configuration for the device and enter an appropriate name. If desired you can use the 'Associate MIDI device' button to link a MIDI device panel with your external unit. This device panel then gets used as the GUI for the external unit whenever you click on the insert slot edit button (see the user documentation for more details about MIDI devices). Click on OK to add the External FX bus and in the VST Connections window activate the input and output ports to which you are connecting the external unit. Leave the delay, send gain and return gain columns at their default zero settings (Figure 13.49).

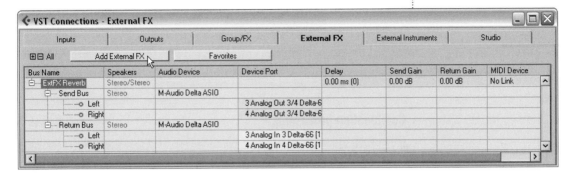

- Connect your external effects device to the physical inputs and outputs associated with the new External FX bus.
- In the Mixer, add a new FX channel (Project / Add track / FX channel). In the pop-up dialogue which appears adjust the configuration to match the number of channels on the external unit (usually mono or stereo). Select the External plug-ins sub-menu and choose the appropriate external effect from the list (Figure 13.50). You have now created a send effect which routes the send and return signals to / from the external device.
- When the external FX channel is created or when you later click on the edit button for the effect, the External FX interface appears on the screen (Figure 13.51). Here you can adjust the send and return levels and enter a time for delay compensation if your external unit introduces latency into the signal path during playback. To help find out the exact time required, the interface features a 'ping' button. This sends a short pulse to your external unit and measures the time it takes to come back via the return line. When measuring the latency in this way, temporarily reduce all delay parameters in your external unit to zero or use a bypass button to avoid measuring the delay in the effect rather than the latency in the signal path.

Figure 13.49
Set up the external FX bus in the VST Connections window

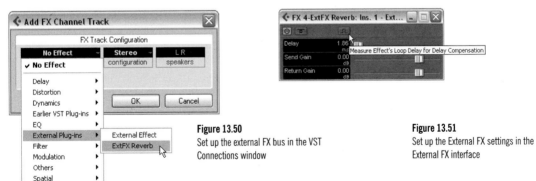

Figure 13.50
Set up the external FX bus in the VST Connections window

Figure 13.51
Set up the External FX settings in the External FX interface

- You can now send a signal to the external hardware effect in exactly the same way as you would to an internal software effect. Choose an audio-based track to which you wish to apply the effect and open its send panel. Activate the external effect in one of the send slots. Adjust the send level using the mini-fader in the send slot.

Info

Unlike conventional plug-ins, only one instance of each external hardware effect may be activated in the Mixer. For this reason, the integration of external hardware devices is best suited to effects like reverb, which can be set up as a single-instance auxiliary send on an FX channel, or mastering processing which can be set up as a single-instance insert on the main stereo output bus.

Combination processing

If you have enough processing power you can set up creative effects by using more than one plug-in in the insert slots. Try the following combinations:

- Compression followed by overdrive distortion (typically used by guitarists to achieve more sustain).
- Compression followed by filtering.
- Delay followed by chorus/flange.
- Distortion followed by chorus/flange.
- Phasing followed by wah wah.
- Tremolo followed by autopan.
- Reverb followed by phasing.
- Filtering followed by delay.

Experimentation can yield some surprisingly good effects and if you are feeling really adventurous try using combinations of three or four effects. In addition to using insert effects, you could also simultaneously incorporate one or more send effects.

Plug-in information

To see an overview of all the plug-ins installed in your system, select 'Plugin Information' from the Devices menu. This opens the Plug-in Information window (Figure 13.52) which displays a list of plug-ins according to the tab selected at the top of the window. For VST plug-ins, the various columns show information about the category, version number, latency, number of inputs / outputs and so on, for each device. The left-most column allows you to de-activate those plug-ins you never use by unchecking the tick box. This de-activates the plug-in within Cubase but it remains installed on your computer. You can re-activate it later if you need to.

Info

While a very large plug-in collection may give you more choice, it may also bury you in a labyrinth of indecision when you are recording and mixing. It is better to have a relatively small number of 'go to' plug-ins. These are the ones you keep going back to because they get the job done.

Plug-in Information

| VST PlugIns | MIDI PlugIns | Audio-Codec PlugIns | Program PlugIns | Project Import-Export PlugIns |

[Update] [VST 2.x Plug-in Paths] [Update Plug-in Information]

A	In	Name	Vendor	File	Path	Category	I/O	Version	SDK	Latency	S
✓	-	Reaktor5 FX 2x8	Native Instruments Software Synth	Reaktor5 FX 2x8.dll	C:\Program Files\Steinberg\VstPlugins\ Native Instruments	SpatialFx	Stereo / 7.1 Cine	5.1.5.0	VST 2.4	0	
✓	-	Reaktor5 Surround	Native Instruments Software Synth	Reaktor5 Surround.dll	C:\Program Files\Steinberg\VstPlugins\ Native Instruments	FxISurround		5.1.5.0	VST 2.4		
✓	-	Kontakt2_8out	Native Instruments Software Synth	Kontakt2_8out.dll	C:\Program Files\Steinberg\VstPlugins\ Native Instruments	Instrument		2.0.2.0	VST 2.3		
✓	-	Reaktor4 FX	Native Instruments Software Synth	Reaktor4 FX.dll	C:\Program Files\Steinberg\VstPlugins\ Native Instruments	Fx	Stereo / Stereo	4.1.3.0	VST 2.3	0	
✓	-	Reaktor5 FX	Native Instruments Software Synth	Reaktor5 FX.dll	C:\Program Files\Steinberg\VstPlugins\ Native Instruments	Fx	Stereo / Stereo	5.1.5.0	VST 2.4	0	
✓	-	Kontakt2_16out	Native Instruments Software Synth	Kontakt2_16out.dll	C:\Program Files\Steinberg\VstPlugins\ Native Instruments	Instrument		2.0.2.0	VST 2.3		
✓	-	PSP 608	PSPaudioware.com	PSP 608.dll	C:\Program Files\Steinberg\VstPlugins\ PSPaudioware	Fx	Stereo / Stereo	1.0.0.0	VST 2.3	0	
✓	-	PSP 84	PSPaudioware.com	PSP 84.dll	C:\Program Files\Steinberg\VstPlugins\ PSPaudioware	Fx	Stereo / Stereo	1.0.0.0	VST 2.4	0	
✓	-	PSP MasterComp	PSPaudioware.com	PSP MasterComp.dll	C:\Program Files\Steinberg\VstPlugins\ PSPaudioware	FxIMastering	LRC+Lfe / Stereo	1.0.0.0	VST 2.4	1660	
✓	-	PSP Xenon	PSPaudioware.com	PSP Xenon.dll	C:\Program Files\Steinberg\VstPlugins\ PSPaudioware	FxIMastering	Stereo / Stereo	1.0.0.0	VST 2.4	159	
✓	-	PSP Neon HR	PSPaudioware.com	PSP Neon HR.dll	C:\Program Files\Steinberg\VstPlugins\ PSPaudioware	FxIMastering	Stereo / Stereo	1.0.0.0	VST 2.4	24638	
✓	-	Lexicon PSP42	PSPaudioware.com	Lexicon PSP42.dll	C:\Program Files\Steinberg\VstPlugins\ PSPaudioware	Fx	Stereo / Stereo	1.0.0.0	VST 2.4	0	
✓	-	PSP VintageMeter	PSPaudioware.com	PSP VintageMeter.dll	C:\Program Files\Steinberg\VstPlugins\ PSPaudioware	Fx	Stereo / Stereo	1.0.0.0	VST 2.2	0	
✓	-	PSP Neon	PSPaudioware.com	PSP Neon.dll	C:\Program Files\Steinberg\VstPlugins\ PSPaudioware	FxIMastering		1.0.0.0	VST 2.4		
✓	-	PSP VintageWarmer2	PSPaudioware.com s.c.	PSP VintageWarmer2.dll	C:\Program Files\Steinberg\VstPlugins\ PSPaudioware	FxIMastering	Stereo / Stereo	1.0.0.0	VST 2.4	2175	
✓	-	PSP MasterQ	PSPaudioware.com s.c.	PSP MasterQ.dll	C:\Program Files\Steinberg\VstPlugins\ PSPaudioware	FxIMastering		1.0.0.0	VST 2.4		
✓	-	PSP VintageWarmer	PSPaudioware.com s.c.	PSP VintageWarmer.dll	C:\Program Files\Steinberg\VstPlugins\ PSPaudioware	FxIMastering	Stereo / Stereo	1.0.0.0	VST 2.4	511	
✓	-	Pentagon I	rgcAudio Software	Pentagon I.dll	C:\Program Files\Steinberg\VstPlugins	Instrument		1.0.0.0	VST 2.2		
✓	-	XCHANTER	rurik leffanta	XCHANTER.DLL	C:\Program Files\Steinberg\VstPlugins	Instrument		1.0.0.0	VST 2.0		
✓	-	SSL LMC-1	Solid State Logic Ltd.	SSL LMC-1.dll	C:\Program Files\Steinberg\VstPlugins\ Solid State Logic\L	Fx	Stereo / Stereo	1.1.0.0	VST 2.3	0	
✓	-	Oxford Inflator Native	Sony Oxford	Oxford Inflator Native.dll	C:\Program Files\Steinberg\VstPlugins\ Sonnox Oxford	Fx		1.5.0.1	VST 2.4		
✓	-	Oxford EQ Native	Sony Oxford	Oxford EQ Native.dll	C:\Program Files\Steinberg\VstPlugins\ Sonnox Oxford	Fx	Stereo / Stereo	1.6.0.1	VST 2.4	0	
✓	-	Oxford Dynamics Native	Sony Oxford	Oxford Dynamics Native.dll	C:\Program Files\Steinberg\VstPlugins\ Sonnox Oxford	Fx	Stereo / Stereo	1.3.0.1	VST 2.4	20	
✓	-	Oxford Limiter Native	Sony Oxford	Oxford Limiter Native.dll	C:\Program Files\Steinberg\VstPlugins\ Sonnox Oxford	FxIMastering	Stereo / Stereo	1.1.0.1	VST 2.4	104	
✓	-	Oxford TransMod Native	Sony Oxford	Oxford TransMod Native.dll	C:\Program Files\Steinberg\VstPlugins\ Sonnox Oxford	Fx		1.3.0.1	VST 2.4		
✓	-	Oxford Reverb Native	Sony Oxford	Oxford Reverb Native.dll	C:\Program Files\Steinberg\VstPlugins\ Sonnox Oxford	Fx	Stereo / Stereo	1.0.0.0	VST 2.4	0	
✓	-	AmpSimulator	Steinberg Media Technologies	Cubase Plug-in Set.vst3	C:\Program Files\Steinberg\Cubase 5\VST3	FxIDistortion	Stereo / Stereo	2.0.2.215	VST 3.0.1	0	
✓	-	Vibrato	Steinberg Media Technologies	Cubase Plug-in Set.vst3	C:\Program Files\Steinberg\Cubase 5\VST3	FxIModulation		2.0.2.215	VST 3.0.1		
✓	-	UV22HR	Steinberg Media Technologies	Cubase Plug-in Set.vst3	C:\Program Files\Steinberg\Cubase 5\VST3	Fx	Stereo / Stereo	2.0.2.215	VST 3.0.1	0	
✓	-	Tuner	Steinberg Media Technologies	Cubase Plug-in Set.vst3	C:\Program Files\Steinberg\Cubase 5\VST3	Fx	Stereo / Stereo	2.0.2.215	VST 3.0.1	0	
✓	-	Tremolo	Steinberg Media Technologies	Cubase Plug-in Set.vst3	C:\Program Files\Steinberg\Cubase 5\VST3	FxIModulation	Stereo / Stereo	2.0.2.215	VST 3.0.1	0	
✓	-	Gate	Steinberg Media Technologies	Cubase Plug-in Set.vst3	C:\Program Files\Steinberg\Cubase 5\VST3	FxIDynamics	Stereo / Stereo	2.0.2.215	VST 3.0.1	88	

Figure 13.52
Plug-in Information window

Mastering

What is mastering and what is a master?

'Mastering' is a final editing and processing stage which comes after mixing. Officially, this stage is referred to as pre-mastering, since it takes place before the real master (the glass master) is produced at the CD duplication factory. For most of us, mastering is understood to mean the same as pre-mastering. Here, you might adjust the final sound quality using any combination of EQ, filtering, compression, expansion, loudness maximisation, stereo processing, harmonic excitation, dithering or other processes, and you might also adjust the order, spacing, lengths and levels for a group of mixes intended as the tracks for a CD.

In broad terms, a 'master' is a final high quality recording from which copies can be made. This could be a master produced within Cubase, or the master produced after a final mastering stage in other software or in a professional mastering house. A master may also be referred to as a pre-master.

For commercial releases, the mastering stage often takes place under the direction of a highly experienced professional mastering engineer. While professional mastering of your mixes is likely to give better quality results, doing it yourself and producing your own factory-ready CD master is certainly possible (CD duplication plants readily accept masters in red-book audio CD format).

Info

Mastering is the final stage in a chain of processes which contribute to the production of a finished musical work or recording project. These processes include: composition, arrangement, performance, recording, mixing and mastering.

Mastering decisions

The way you approach mastering is highly dependent upon the nature of your project and your personal preferences, but assembling the tracks for a CD master would normally involve the following steps:

- General editing decisions such as removing clicks, topping and tailing and adjusting track lengths
- Deciding the track order and the spacing between tracks
- Expansion / compression, equalisation and other sound processing decisions
- Fading, levelling and limiting decisions
- Dithering and truncating the bit-depth to 16-bit
- CD track indexing and burning of the final Red Book audio CD

Info

Many professional mastering houses master to DDP (Disc Description Protocol) on Exabyte tape. This helps optimise results since DDP is not subject to the same error rate and handling difficulties as CDR.

The mastering stage may be the first time that you hear your group of finished mixes one after the other and at this point you may hear some surprising differences in the sound quality and perceived loudness of each track. These are the kinds of elements which need correction during the mastering session in order to finish up with a homogeneous set of tracks. However, the way you use sound processing in a recording at the mastering stage is significantly different to the way in which you use it on individual instruments at the mixing stage. For example, emphasising the snare using EQ may also affect the vocal and emphasising the kick drum may also affect the bass guitar. The sound processing settings for mastering are therefore likely to be far less radical. In this context, it is vitally important that you use an accurate monitoring system in an acoustically balanced listening space, otherwise the subtle changes of the mastering process cannot be heard correctly.

If your mixes are already sounding exactly the way you wish then further modification with mastering processing may not be necessary at all. In this case, the remaining mastering decisions would involve the track order and spacings, dithering and truncating to 16-bit, and indexing and burning the CD.

Mastering in Cubase

Although it may be preferable to use a specialised program for mastering (such as Steinberg Wavelab or Bias Peak), almost all of the mastering steps suggested above can be applied within Cubase. The one exception is the final step of creating track indexes and burning the CD. Cubase is not designed for the detailed preparation of the track list for a CD and integrated CD burning is not included. For some suggestions about how to approach CD burning, see 'Burning the CD', below.

The remainder of this section details how to set up Cubase for a mastering session and suggests some mastering plug-in chains for the insert slots of the stereo master output bus.

Creating a mastering template

Cubase is supplied with a mastering template but it is a good idea to create your own personalised version which you can use to start each mastering session. This streamlines the project for the usual mastering operations. Try the following:

- Select 'New Project' in the File menu and create a new empty project using the 'Empty' option in the Project assistant dialogue.
- In the Project Setup dialogue (Project menu), enter a suitable length for the project in the Length field. If you expect to work with the standard audio CD format you might like to enter the normal audio CD duration of 74 minutes. Select 'seconds' in the Display format field. Enter the appropriate sample rate and record format in the respective fields.
- If you generally use the Control Room Mixer for monitoring, open this in extended mode, configured to show only the main control room monitoring channel with the large-scale meters displayed in the extended section. This provides a clearly visible stereo level meter and mono / stereo compatibility switching using the cycle downmix preset selection

---

Info

To measure the average loudness of each CD track, select the CD track event and use the Statistics function in the Audio menu. Compare the average RMS power levels for each CD track, (the lower-most values in the Statistics window).

Figure 14.1
Stereo mastering template in Cubase

button. Place the Control Room Mixer to the right of a suitably sized Project window as shown in Figure 14.1.

- Add two stereo audio tracks in the Project window. Name the first track 'CD tracks' and the second 'Editing' (for example). The first track is for your CD tracks and the second is for rough editing purposes. This is assuming that you intend to pass all the CD tracks through the same mastering processing of the stereo master output bus. However, if it is your intention to apply separate real-time processing on each CD track then you may need to put each song on a different audio track in the Project window. Alternatively, you could automate the processing. Add the Marker track for navigation purposes.

- Resize all tracks as appropriate and select seconds in the Project window ruler. Activate the overview button to help with zooming and navigating within your mastering project. Try setting the Snap mode to Shuffle. In Shuffle mode, all events on a track are tightly snapped one against the other and the order may be changed by dragging one event in between two others. This is excellent for quickly re-ordering CD tracks.

- For spacing, try preparing empty audio events of various lengths (1, 2 and 3 secs, for example) and store these on the rough editing track. In shuffle mode these can be inserted between two CD tracks at any time by holding Alt and dragging a copy of the event to the desired join between two tracks. A green insert marker is displayed.

- Click on the edit button of either of the audio tracks to open the Channel settings window. Arrange the Channel settings window below the Project window as shown in Figure 14.1. Customise the view to show inserts, EQ and fader.
- In the 'Choose edit channel' menu of the Channel settings window select the main stereo output bus. Set up your chain of mastering plug-ins in the insert slots. You might like to activate the Limiter and UV22HR in slots 7 and 8. For CD mastering set the UV22HR to 16-bit / Lo / Autoblack. If desired, add other processors in the remaining slots.
- Arrange the Transport panel and the GUIs for your plug-ins in the remaining screen space. Activate the large-scale time display and VST performance windows from the Device menu. A large-scale time display is easier to see and the VST performance window helps you keep an eye on the current CPU overhead.
- Save the project as a template using 'Save as template' (File menu). Enter a name such as 'stereo mastering' in the pop-up dialogue and click on OK to save the project in the Project Templates folder. Next time you select New Project (File menu) the new mastering template is available in the template list.

Typical mastering plug-in processing chains

Figure 14.2
High quality mastering plug-in chain

The processing chains shown below might typically be found in the insert slots of the stereo master output bus during a mastering session. While it is possible to use various of the supplied plug-ins for mastering purposes, mastering quality EQ, compression and limiting normally requires high precision plug-ins designed specifically for the purpose. Therefore, some of the plug-ins shown in these examples are from alternative plug-in developers. To get started with mastering try the following processing chains:

1 High quality mastering

This following constitutes a high-quality mastering chain featuring linear phase equalisation, expansion / compression, loudness maximisation, limiting, and dithering (Figure 14.2). Alternatives from the plug-ins supplied with Cubase are shown in brackets.

- Slot 1: PSP Audioware Neon HR EQ (or the supplied Studio EQ)
- Slot 2: Sonnox Oxford Dynamics (or the supplied MultibandCompressor)
- Slot 7: PSP Audioware Xenon (or the supplied Limiter in slot 7 and UV22HR in slot 8)

2 Classic mastering chain for adding warmth and character

A digital mix suffering from a cold, brittle quality might benefit from the analogue-like characteristics of the PSP Neon HR Linear Phase EQ. PSP Vintage Warmer or Voxengo Tape Bus may help add warmth to the signal (Figure

14.3). Overall, this chain includes equalisation, compression, tape saturation emulation and limiting. If you are using the supplied Limiter plug-in, make sure you are limiting only the peaks in the signal. In this case, there is normally only occasional activity in the gain reduction meter.

- Slot 1: PSP Neon HR EQ (or the supplied Studio EQ)
- Slot 2: VintageCompressor
- Slot 3: Voxengo Tape Bus (or the supplied SoftClipper)
- Slot 7: PSP Vintage Warmer (or the supplied Limiter)
- Slot 8: Apogee UV22 HR dithering

Figure 14.3
Mastering plug-in chain for warmth and character

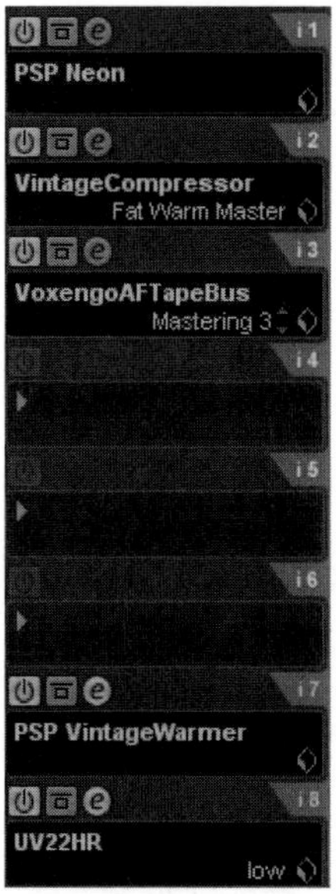

All stages in these mastering chains are optional and individual plug-ins can be bypassed using their respective bypass buttons. Depending upon the desired result, the order of the EQ and compressor plug-ins may be reversed, and tape saturation may sound better as the first process in the chain. Unless you wish to impose radical changes upon your mixes for creative effect, the settings for most mastering processors must be set with great subtlety and precision. Be aware of undesirable interaction between the processes. If the mix is already sounding exactly as you want to hear it, then it may not need any mastering processing at all (except for dithering).

Mastering processing settings

This section outlines the kinds of settings you might need when using a mastering effects chain featuring EQ, dynamics and limiter plug-ins. The settings are likely to be far less radical than those used for tracking and mixing. The details outlined here should be viewed only as a rough guide since settings vary widely dependent upon the precise characteristics of the signal being processed. Due to the often specialist requirements of mastering, reference is made to various high-end plug-ins from other developers.

EQ settings for mastering

Flattering the mix with Studio EQ

A dull mix may need to be flattered at the mastering stage either to reinforce a weak bass end or to bring out the detail and air in the upper frequencies, or both. A common reason for a dull mix is too much activity in the mid frequencies. This tends to mask the other frequencies in the signal and may also result in harshness. Correcting these issues might involve slightly boosting the lower and upper frequencies whilst also attenuating the mid frequency band (or it may require just one of these measures). The target low frequency band is usually that below around 150Hz. Boosting here should always be approached with great subtlety since too much bass just adds boominess. The air frequencies are in the region between 15kHz to 20 kHz but beware of boosting too much as this may give the impression that your mix is now sounding thin. Attenuating the mid frequencies often involves a wide and extremely subtle curve somewhere between 1 and 6kHz. Beware of cutting the frequencies too much as this can seriously upset the balance. Any adjustments to the all-important mid frequencies should always be kept to an abso-

Info

The examples used in this section are available for download from the PC Publishing website at:

www.pc-publishing.com

Figure 14.4
Subtle curve for flattering the mix in the supplied Studio EQ plug-in

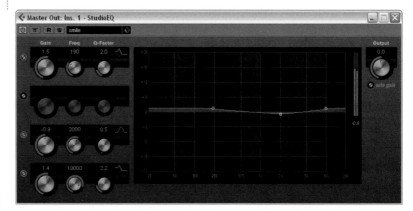

lute minimum. These measures sometimes produce an EQ curve which resembles a smile, hence this kind of EQ is sometimes referred to as a 'smile curve'. Try the settings shown in Figure 14.4.

Adding warmth with PSP Neon

One undesirable side-effect inherent in EQ plug-ins is phase shifting between the different frequency bands. This results in loss of clarity and harshness. Since digital mixes sometimes suffer from a cold, brittle quality to the sound, the last thing you want to do is process the signal with an EQ which adds still more harshness. Linear phase EQ devices provide a solution. One outstanding example in this category is PSP Audioware's Neon Linear Phase EQ. This produces warm, analogue-like results. Even if you impose a fairly radical EQ curve, any undesirable side effects are likely to be minimal in linear phase mode. The high resolution version of the plug-in features the proprietary FAT mode (Frequency Authentication Technique) which ensures a smooth high frequency response. To warm up your mix, try matching the PSP Neon curve to that shown in Figure 14.5 (bands one

Figure 14.5
PSP Neon HR Linear Phase EQ for warm, transparent, analogue-like EQ control

to five only are active). This resembles the smile curve shown above but is a more radical curve designed to add warmth and air to a harsh, congested mix. Flatten the curve slightly if the settings are too radical for your own mix.

Dynamics settings for mastering

Wideband dynamics

Wideband dynamics processing may be used in mastering to add subtle punch and percussive impact, to help bring out inner detail, or to give more body and density to a recording. It is also helpful for parallel compression and upward expansion. Classic parallel compression involves combining the unprocessed and compressed signals in a manner which transparently raises the level in soft passages but has little effect in loud passages. It may also help re-inject natural dynamics by adding the unprocessed signal to the compressed signal. Upward expansion (sometimes referred to as decompression) helps restore dynamic life into a recording which has been overly compressed.

Mastering applications often require very gentle ratios. To add coherence and density to a recording with devices like Flux Solera, Melda Production MDynamics, PSP Master Compressor, Sonnox Oxford Dynamics, or the supplied plug-ins, try very gentle ratios between 1.01 and 1.5 : 1 with thresholds between -30 and -50dBFS. Gentle control can also be achieved with slightly higher ratios between 1.1 and 3 : 1 with a higher threshold between -3 and -10dBFS. Try starting with an attack of around 100ms and a release of 250ms and then adjust to taste. Set the makeup gain to compensate for any loss of level. To emphasise percussive impact, try the supplied Compressor plug-in with the following settings: - threshold: around -25dB, ratio: 1.3 : 1, soft knee: active, attack: 100ms, release: auto, and makeup gain: +1dB. Try following this with the Limiter plug-in with its threshold set to -0.5dB and auto release active. This ensures transient peak control.

When set up carefully compression can be applied in a fairly transparent manner. However, undesirable side-effects include blurring of the transients and a loss of depth. In addition, the lower frequencies in a composite signal tend to dominate the attack and release of the compression. This may result in the bass line dictating the dynamic changes in the upper frequencies. A still worse effect of this is 'hole punching' where sudden low frequency energy may severely reduce the level of the rest of the signal, producing a virtual drop-out in the perceived loudness.

Punch and density with Melda Production MDynamics

Using wideband dynamics for mastering requires an accurate, flexible device with a clean, transparent signal path. Parameters with very wide value ranges and exceptional resolution also help manage the subtleties of mastering settings.

Figure 14.6
MDynamics from Melda Production
featuring custom curve shaping and high
precision control for clean, accurate
dynamics processing

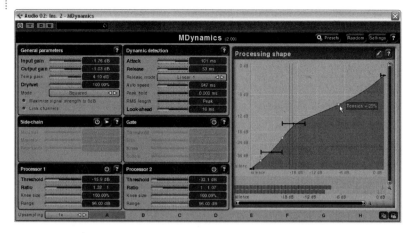

MDynamics (Figure 14.6) from Melda Production fulfils the latter requirements. This is a wideband device featuring two compressor / expander processors, a dedicated gate and a side chain filtering section. Expander / compressor ratios between 1 : 3 and infinity : 1 are available in small resolution
steps. The thresholds for these and the dedicated gate go all the way down
to -80dBFS. The dynamic detection includes wide ranging attack (0 to
1000ms) and release (1 - 5000ms), auto release, peak hold time, peak / rms
response choice and look ahead processing. The input and output level settings offer +/- 24dB gain with two decimal place accuracy. The jewel in the
crown is the transfer curve display which is based upon the Melda Production
Envelope System (MES). The shape of the curve is normally controlled by the
main processor parameters but when you activate the power shape button
the display switches to a different mode where you can modify the curve
shape using various handles and drag points. Power shape mode inherits the
current curve. This means you can set up a basic curve using the main controls and then fine tune it using power shaping. High resolution zooming is
available by pressing Alt and dragging a box around the area of interest. In
addition, MDynamics operates with zero latency and features 1x to 4x up
sampling to improve sound quality at lower sampling rates. It can also hold
multiple presets using the tab buttons along the lower edge of the window
which is helpful for comparing settings. For parallel compression and other
effects, a dry / wet mix control allows you to mix the original signal with the
compressed signal.

Info

MDynamics may be set to one of three modes: Logarithmic, Squared and Linear. Logarithmic produces
classic dynamic processing where a signal exceeding the threshold by 10dB at a compression ratio of
2 : 1 produces 5dB attenuation in output level. In this same scenario, Squared mode produces slightly
greater output attenuation of 6.4dB and Linear mode produces a still greater value of 7.5dB. Thus, Squared
and Linear modes produce progressively more compression or expansion.

MDynamics is good for upward expansion, parallel compression and
adding punch and density. For example, to add punch and emphasise percussive impact in rhythmic material try setting Processor 1 for gentle com-

pression at 1.32 : 1 with a threshold of -15dB and Processor 2 for gentle expansion at 1 : 1.07 with a threshold of around -32dB. This produces a gentle upward expansion curve which is tamed by the compression as it goes higher up the scale. Set the attack to 100ms and the release to 53ms with auto release active in Linear 1 mode. Set RMS length to peak and look-ahead to 16ms. While listening to the signal adjust the Temp gain control so that the input signal peaks are dancing over the apex of the curve, as shown by the line representing the input signal in the curve display (see Figure 14.6). Try Logarithmic or Squared modes. The idea is to catch the rising percussive transients and emphasise them. You may need to reduce the output gain by one or more dBs. To emphasise the effect increase both the expansion and compression ratios. This exaggerates the curve. Also try adjusting the range controls of Processors 1 and 2 to modify the shape of the curve. Alternatively activate custom power shaping and drag the handles on the curve while listening to the audio. Using this kind of curve you can also tune the side chain to one of the instruments in the mix, such as the snare drum for example, to obtain a slight lift in its level.

For parallel compression, insert MDynamics as a post fader effect in slot 7 or 8 of the audio channel containing the recording to be processed. Set Processor 1 to -56dB threshold with a ratio of 2 : 1 and a 100% soft knee. Select an attack of 2.8ms and a release of 400ms with an rms length of 49ms. Add 15dB of output gain and set the dry / wet mix to 50%. Select logarithmic mode. These settings provide highly transparent parallel compression which can add body and density to a recording and provide subtle lift to low level detail. Adjust the dry / wet mix to modify the effect.

Multiband compression

Multiband compressors may help overcome some of the undesirable effects of wideband compression. Multiband compressors split the input signal into a number of frequency bands so that you can apply dynamic processing to one band without affecting the other frequencies in the recording, or apply different types of dynamic processing to each band. Mastering techniques often benefit from splitting the signal into only two bands to avoid the detrimental effects of phase shifting between the bands and interference with the internal balance of the recording.

While multiband compression is very powerful it is also more difficult to use and can easily ruin a good recording if set up incorrectly.

> **Tip**
>
> Use a hard-knee setting for a more obvious punchy effect, but take care that you do not over emphasise any unwanted pumping side effects. Use a soft knee setting for smoother punch and density.

> **Info**
>
> Any processing which affects the crucial mid-band frequencies in the mix (between around 250Hz and 6kHz) should be approached with subtlety and caution, since it is easy to disturb the natural internal balance of the main instruments if you use radical or inappropriate settings.

> **Info**
>
> A multiband compression device could equally be described as a dynamic multiband equaliser. Mixes might benefit more from normal, classic equalisation when static correction or enhancement is needed on specific frequencies throughout the whole musical passage. Multiband compression is more appropriate for boosting the lack of bass in a quiet passage or reducing the harsh high frequencies in a loud passage.

Using Multiband Compressor for frequency selective dynamics processing

This example uses the supplied Multiband Compressor to increase the level of a kick drum which was mixed too low and reduce the high frequency level of a vocal which becomes harsh during loudly sung passages. Ordinary EQ or wideband compression are not ideal for this task. Using multiband compression, you can locate the frequency range of the problem instrument or voice and expand or compress to emphasise or de-emphasise the sound as required. Assuming that the above two problems are occurring in the same mix, proceed as follows:

- Activate the Multiband Compressor in an appropriate insert slot in the master output channel.
- In the user interface, load the preset named 'Reset'. Activate the bypass buttons of the second and fourth frequency bands.
- In the upper part of the display, adjust the upper split point of the low frequency band to around 100 to 120Hz and the split points of the third frequency band to give a range of 6kHz to 12kHz (see Figure 14.7).
- Adjust the compression settings of the low frequency band to ratio: 1.3, attack: 50, and release: 208 (or auto). Boost the makeup gain of the lower frequency band to +5dB. Lower the threshold to where the kick drum is currently living in the mix. You should now see some corresponding activity in the gain reduction meter. Listen carefully. You are attempting to emphasise the low frequency pulse of the kick drum. Try narrowing the frequency band if the processing affects the other bass instruments too much. The net effect is more kick drum presence without processing the other frequency ranges in the mix.
- Now adjust the compression settings of the third frequency band to ratio: 4, attack: 5, and release: auto. Adjust the threshold while listening to the mix. Here you are applying downward compression near the threshold

Figure 14.7

Multiband Compressor settings to simultaneously emphasise a kick drum and tame a harsh vocal

where the vocal becomes harsh during the loud passages. Whenever the vocal becomes loud and harsh the upper frequencies are compressed downwards, hopefully without undesirable side-effects on the other instruments in the mix.

Note how we have achieved the above effects without processing the mid band and the upper band. This is helpful, since the mid band is responsible for the main body of a mix, including the natural internal balance of the vocals, snare and dominant instruments. If the mid-band is already sounding right it is best not to touch it. The upper band is responsible for the 'air' in the mix and this may also be best left untouched.

Difficult multiband dynamics tasks may require specialist plug-ins. Where greater accuracy and flexibility is required you could try products from other developers such as: Melda Production MultiBandDynamics, Nomad Factory A.M.T. Multi Max, Sonalksis CQ1 multiband dynamics processor, or Wave Arts Multi Dynamics.

Limiting and loudness maximisation settings for mastering

Limiting is generally used to manage the highest peaks in the signal. The threshold for limiting is usually set quite high, and attack times are typically set extremely fast to ensure brief transients are kept under control. For maximum transparency and preservation of the natural dynamics of the signal, peak gain reduction of no more than around 6dB is recommended. After this the effect starts to draw attention to itself. By controlling the peaks and simultaneously applying gain to the overall signal, a significant increase in the average level can be achieved, resulting in greater perceived loudness. This is commonly known as loudness maximisation. The trick with loudness maximisation is to increase the perceived loudness while also preserving the natural dynamics within the signal. Extreme loudness maximisation results in various distortions in the signal but may suit club and hard rock mixes.

Advanced limiting with Sonnox Oxford Limiter

Peak control and loudness maximisation without excessive loss of transient and dynamic detail is the primary purpose of the Sonnox Oxford Limiter (Figure 14.8). The Oxford Limiter features a two-stage processing design. The first stage is a pre-process section where gain envelope compensation and compression is applied. The second stage includes peak overshoot control and enhancement. The threshold for dynamic gain control action is fixed at 0dBr. However, gain envelope compensation begins below the threshold, reducing exponentially to insignificant at lower levels. Up to 18dB of gain may be applied to increase the effect of the processing using the input gain fader. The pre-process section is unusual for its inclusion of a variable attack parameter. Setting the attack to relatively slow values allows peak transients to pass through the first stage and escape the effects of hard limiting. Any sample overshoots in these peaks may subsequently be controlled in the second stage by engaging Safe mode or setting the enhancement control to 100%. The latter ensure zero sample overloads in the output. This whole process allows you to avoid the harshness associated with fast limiting. The

Figure 14.8
Typical Sonnox Oxford Limiter CD
mastering setup

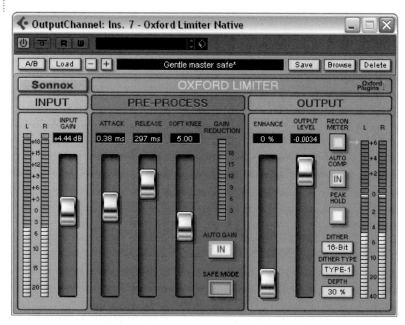

enhancement fader may be used to maximise the signal still further and any potential inter-sample peak reconstruction errors which could occur during D/A conversion may be corrected using the auto-compensation function. Used carefully, the Oxford Limiter can match the levels of your own productions to those of commercial releases. For mastering within Cubase, it is best placed in the last plug-in slot (slot 8) on the stereo master bus (i.e. after the main faders).

Limiting and dithering with PSP Xenon

Where ultimate transparency and pristine audio quality is required the PSP Xenon is an excellent choice (Figure 14.9). This features 64-bit precision throughout its internal signal path and operates at sample rates up to 192kHz. It features two processing stages. In the first stage, a transient control governs how much of the transients pass through and a release control affects the perceived loudness. In the second stage, three transient buttons govern brick wall limiting behaviour using lookahead processing and Finite Impulse Response envelope detectors. Other features include: an Oversample button which oversamples the limiter envelope detector to avoid inter-sample peak reconstruction errors in the D/A converter; a Leveller parameter which applies gradual gain reduction to loud passages before limiting for natural dynamic changes between quiet and loud passages; and a Link dial which governs how much the stereo image is affected by the processing. In the latter case, 0% allows greater loudness at the expense of potential stereo image fluctuations, and 100% ensures the greatest stability in the stereo image at the expense of less perceived loudness. Xenon uses TPDF generated noise for dithering with three styles of noise shaping following the izophonic curves of the human hearing system. Excellent meters featuring standard peak and K system designs (K-12, K-14, K-20) complete the

Figure 14.9
PSP Audioware Xenon for limiting and
loudness maximisation, featuring high
precision metering with K-system
options

picture. Xenon is suitable for all kinds of audio material. It preserves internal detail and stereo image, and minimises transient smearing. For mastering within Cubase, it is best placed in the last plug-in slot (slot 8) on the stereo master bus (i.e. after the main faders).

Using the supplied limiting and dithering plug-ins
Cubase is supplied with the Limiter and UV22HR plug-ins for limiting and dithering. For mastering purposes these are best placed in the 7th and 8th slots of the stereo master bus inserts (both after the main faders). Make sure there is only occasional activity in the gain reduction meters of the Limiter plug-in since this indicates that you are limiting only the extreme peaks in the signal. When using the Limiter plug-in for mastering, DO NOT push the final output level to the absolute maximum 0dBFS point. An out ceiling of between -3dB and -0.3dB is more appropriate. This helps avoid potential inter-sample peak reconstruction errors which may occur during D/A conversion.

Dithering

What is dithering?
A reduction in the bit depth of a digital audio signal means that you are now expressing the audio with shorter wordlength samples. This results in a slight loss in the definition of low level signals, since reducing the wordlength means that you have had to throw away some of the least significant bits. Without processing, this manifests itself as a particular kind of low level non-linear distortion known as quantisation noise. Dithering involves adding a low level controlled noise to the signal which takes into account the least significant bits before they are discarded. This converts the low-level distortion into

Info

Loudness maximisation and limiting are normally placed after the master output bus faders. In Cubase, this means slots 7 or 8.

Info

Mastering constitutes a whole separate branch of audio processing in its own right and cannot be covered fully in this text. Those seeking more in-depth coverage are advised to consult specialist books on the subject (see Recommended Reading at the back of this book).

a more friendly linear noise or 'hiss' and preserves some of the integrity of the original signal. Using a process known as noise shaping, the more friendly noise is re-distributed to parts of the audio spectrum where it is less obvious to the ear. The net result is enhanced clarity and spaciousness.

Dithering is most often applied at the point just before you convert a high resolution file (such as 24-bit) to a lower resolution file (such as 16-bit). For CD mastering purposes in Cubase, this is normally when you are producing the final 16-bit master audio file using Export / Audio Mixdown.

When to use dithering in Cubase

All internal audio processing in Cubase is performed at 32-bit float resolution, so if you are using the Export / Audio Mixdown function to create an audio file of lesser resolution then you may need to use dithering. To be exact, dithering should be applied in the following cases:

- When using the Export / Audio Mixdown function to create a final master audio file of any bit depth less than 32-bit float (i.e. 24-bit, 16-bit or 8-bit).
- When mixing down to external media where the bit depth is less than 32-bit float.
- When truncating the bit depth from 32-bit float to 24-bit as an interim process, some experts recommend using dither without noise shaping and preferably TPDF dither, although Steinberg consider this to be rather a matter of taste than necessity. At the mixing stage, if it is your intention to perform a final mastering stage at a later date, mix down without dither to a high resolution file. Apply noise-shaped dither only as the last step before truncation during the mastering session.

Loading a dithering plug-in

Cubase is supplied with the Apogee UV22 HR dithering plug-in which supports dithering to all the popular bit resolutions. Dithering is always applied after the master faders. This means loading the UV22 HR in insert slots 7 or 8 of the main stereo output channel as follows:

- Open the extended Mixer and activate the inserts panel on the main stereo output channel.
- Click in the name field of slot 8 and select 'UV22 HR' from the effects pop-up menu.
- Upon selecting the UV22 HR plug-in, the graphical user interface is opened automatically (Figure 14.10).

Figure 14.10
The Apogee UV22 HR plug-in

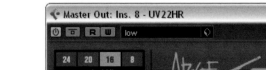

Apogee UV22 HR dithering functions

The UV22 HR dithering plug-in incorporates an advanced dithering algorithm developed by Apogee featuring the following parameters:

- hi – applies a standard normal level of dither which suits most signals.
- lo – applies a lower level of dither noise to the signal.
- auto black – when activated, the dither noise is muted when there are silent passages in the signal.
- output bits – specifies the bit resolution of the output. This should be matched to the resolution of the destination medium. The choice is between 8, 16, 20 and 24-bit.

Using dithering

As with any processing, you should use your ears to decide if the dithering settings you have chosen give the best result. However, given that dithering is intentionally an extremely subtle kind of processing, it may be difficult to perceive the results. To get a feel for what dithering can do for you, try a test procedure of producing an audio mixdown file (File / Export / Audio Mixdown) at a resolution of 8-bits both with and without dithering. Preferably, use an audio file which includes some low level material. Listen to the difference between the two files. Now try the same experiment with 16-bit files. The most important thing to remember when you use dithering is that the output bit depth should be matched to the bit-resolution of the exported file.

Important

Noise-shaped dithering is normally a once-only operation performed as the very last step in the mastering process. It is best not to re-apply noise shaped dither to audio that has already been subject to this process. If you intend to conduct a final mastering stage in a specialised mastering application (or in Cubase) do not apply noise shaped dither at the mixing stage. Instead, mix down to a high resolution file without dither (24-bit or 32-bit float). At the mastering stage, import this file into the mastering application and apply noise-shaped dither as the very last process just before truncation to produce the final 16-bit master audio file.

For CD mastering, try setting the Apogee UV22 HR plug-in to lo / 16-bit with auto black on. If you are instead using the PSP Xenon Limiter, try noise shape type C / 16-bit with autoblack on. Both of these are good general purpose settings for CD mastering.

Recommended order of use of plug-ins for mastering

Placing plug-ins in a chain may result in undesirable interaction between the different processes. The following is a suggested order for some of the common pre-mastering processing steps to avoid problems and to arrive at a final version of the recording which is suitable for duplication or manufacture:

- De-essing
- Equalisation
- Dynamics

- Harmonic excitement
- Reverberation
- Stereo imaging / MS processing
- Sample rate conversion (e.g. down sampling from 88.2kHz to 44.1kHz)
- Limiting / level maximisation
- Dithering
- Truncation (e.g. reduction of the bit depth from 24-bit to 16-bit)

This list is certainly not the only way of ordering the processes. For example, depending on the application, the order of equalisation and dynamics might be reversed. Compressing after EQ produces a smoother result but may undo some of the settings of the EQ if the threshold is set inappropriately. EQing after compression allows you to adjust the EQ parameters with more clarity, knowing that EQ changes are not changing the action of the compressor. Limiting is often placed after sample rate conversion since the conversion process can result in slight level increases. As for dithering and bit reduction, take care that you do not confuse these processes with sample rate conversion! The most important rule for dithering is that it is normally a once-only final step just before bit reduction.

Downsampling issues

Using Cubase for downsampling (using the 'Sample Rate' field in the Export Audio Mixdown dialogue) is not advisable if limiting and dithering are at the end of your mastering chain, since this places sample rate conversion AFTER limiting and dithering. It may be better to do the downsampling in one pass WITHOUT limiting, dithering and truncation, and then re-import the down-sampled audio file for these final stages in a second pass. If your project is destined to be duplicated on CD, try starting off with the standard CD sample rate of 44.1kHz and maintain this sample rate throughout the project. In this way you do not subject your file to the possible damage caused by poor quality sample rate conversion.

The quality of the sample rate conversion when using Export Audio Mixdown may not be sufficient for all applications. For the best quality you are advised to use a dedicated sample rate conversion plug-in like the Voxengo r8brain Pro at the appropriate position within the chain. Alternatively, do the final stages of your mastering processing in an external editor like Wavelab, which features a high quality sample rate conversion plug-in known as the Crystal Resampler.

Quality control

Overusing plug-in effects can damage the pristine quality of your digital recordings, especially if you are working with 16-bit files. Almost all audio processing (even simple gain changes) increases the wordlength of the audio. After editing or processing, a 16-bit signal might be expressed in 32-bit float resolution. If you were to save this processed signal as a 16-bit audio file, bit reduction and loss of low level detail results. Do this once and the effect is

---

Info

Not all of the mastering processes shown here are covered by the supplied plug-ins. Although Cubase may be used for mastering, Steinberg Wavelab, Bias Peak (or similar) are preferable for dedicated mastering and CD burning tasks.

minimal. Do it a number of times to a number of signals and the cumulative effect results in loss of transparency and detail.

To help maintain quality, start with high resolution sources (e.g. 24-bit/44.1kHz, 24-bit/88.2 or 24-bit/96kHz) and maintain this high resolution for as long as possible throughout the project. Avoid printing effects one at a time to the same audio file. Multiple effects processing is best applied in a single pass. Where possible, keep effects in real-time until the final mix. Unfortunately, the latter is not possible when you are using the off-line processing in the Processing menu. Use only high quality plug-ins which preferably have a 64-bit internal resolution. If it is your intention to carry out a final mastering stage in Cubase or other software, do not truncate the bit-depth or use noise-shaped dither at the mixing stage. Instead, mix to a high resolution file without noise-shaped dither (32-bit float or 24-bit). Avoid applying noise-shaped dither more than once in the same project.

These steps help you get a better result when you finally arrive at the mastering stage. With mastering you are aiming to squeeze the final 10% of quality from your completed stereo mix but remember; if a mix is already sounding correct it may need no further processing other than sample rate conversion, dithering and truncation to 16-bit. One of the skills of mastering engineers is knowing just how much processing is required and when to leave a mix alone.

> **Info**
>
> The full details of truncation, dithering and downsampling are beyond the scope of this text. Those readers needing more in depth coverage are advised to consult specialist texts or to search the internet.

Burning the CD

As outlined above, Cubase does not include integrated track indexing and CD burning functions. You must therefore conduct the final burning and organisation of the CD in other software (e.g. Steinberg Wavelab, Bias Peak, Ahead Software Nero, Roxio Easy CD Creator, Roxio Jam and others). The chosen software must be capable of burning the final CD in the standard Red Book audio CD format.

> **Info**
>
> Red Book refers to the technical specifications which govern the correct creation and manufacture of an audio CD, as defined by Sony and Philips. An actual copy of the Red Book is usually only available to CD manufacturing plants. Other CD types have similar colour coded books which govern their creation, such as Yellow Book for CD-ROM, Green Book for CD-i, Orange Book for write-once CD-R, White Book for video CD and Blue Book for CD-Extra.

The first dilemna is deciding exactly how you are going to mix down the final 16-bit audio; as one long audio file containing all the tracks, or as separate files, one for each track on the CD. This decision is largely dictated by the capabilities of your chosen CD editing and burning software. Some applications allow you to split a single audio file into a number of tracks, others require each track as a separate file. In both cases, if you have carefully spaced your tracks in Cubase you will need to duplicate this in the burning software. One approach is to make a careful note of the intended pauses between each track and enter these manually. Most CD burning software allows you to adjust the pauses. However, bear in mind that the data on audio CDs is divided up into frames, where there are 75 frames per second and each frame contains 588 stereo samples. On an audio CD you can only ever start a CD track at the beginning of a frame. This can lead to subtle problems when adjusting start times and pauses between tracks. Normally, small amounts of silence are inserted to ensure that track starts and ends do not get cut off when the CD is played. Luckily, most CD burning software takes care of these finer points automatically, as long as the timing requirements of your CD remain relatively simple (if in doubt stick to spacings of whole seconds).

Once the track list and suitable pauses have been entered you should carefully audition the material once more to make sure that it sounds as intended. When you proceed to the actual burning of the CD, ALWAYS use disc-at-once mode since this ensures that the CD is recorded in one pass without interruption (as opposed to track-at-once which results in the writing laser being turned off between each track). Also, experts recommend the use of 2x or 4x burning speed to minimise writing errors.

If you intend to produce a production master CD yourself, bear in mind that the CD writing process is prone to error, especially if you use a poor quality CD recorder and poor quality media. To avoid errors, always use a high quality CD recorder and the best media. Also, work in a clean, dust-free atmosphere and never touch the surface of the master compact disc. If you are duplicating your own audio CDs for demo purposes, it is still worth working within strict guidelines to avoid problems.

MIDI effects

Cubase includes a range of real-time MIDI effects. These are found in the Send and Insert panels of each MIDI channel. The modification of MIDI data has traditionally been an off-line editing process but, with MIDI effects, the emphasis has changed. Like their audio counterparts, MIDI effects are plug-in modules which can be added to the effects panels of MIDI channels when you need them.

The difference between MIDI effects and audio effects

The MIDI effects structure and routing are similar to that found with audio effects but with the following very important differences:

- MIDI effects are for the real-time processing of MIDI data. They do not process audio signals.
- Unlike an audio send effect, a MIDI Send effect cannot be globally used by all MIDI tracks. Each MIDI send effect is unique to the track to which it is assigned. MIDI send effects have no send level control.
- Since you are processing a sequence of digital instructions rather than an audio signal, the results of certain effects may not be directly comparable to their audio counterparts.

Setting up MIDI effects in Cubase

Real-time MIDI effects may be assigned as insert or send effects. There are no strict rules about which effects are assigned to which kind of effects slots. However, the routing configuration for inserts and sends is different and thus may have a radical effect on the results. For example, a MIDI Send configuration allows you to route the send data to a different MIDI device to the source which is helpful for creative applications.

MIDI Insert effects

MIDI Insert effects are assigned in the MIDI Inserts panel of a MIDI or Instrument track. The MIDI Inserts panel is opened in the expanded Mixer, in the MIDI Channel Settings window or in the Inspector (Figure 15.1). Each MIDI or Instrument track has a total of four MIDI Insert slots. Click on an Insert effect field to open the MIDI effects pop-up menu.

Figure 15.1
MIDI Insert effects are assigned using the Insert slots in the Insert panel of a MIDI or Instrument channel

With MIDI Insert effects, the MIDI data passes through the effects in series (see Figure 15.2). When more than one insert effect is activated, the signal passes through each in turn, in descending order. Thus with multiple Insert effects, the data received by each effect is that which is output by the preceding effect in the panel. Depending on the effects used, the final output may not resemble the original input data at all. The destination MIDI device is that which is assigned for the MIDI track.

MIDI Insert effects are suited to almost all MIDI effects.

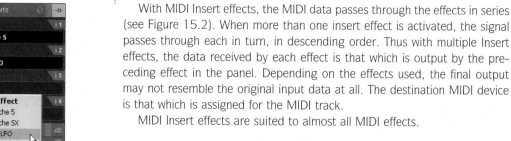
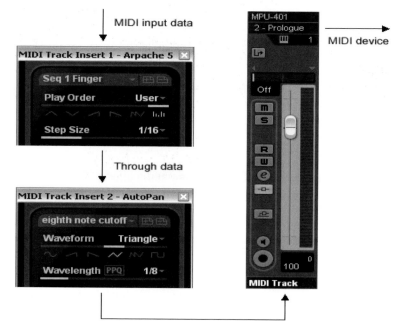

Figure 15.2
The routing configuration for MIDI Insert effects

MIDI Send effects

MIDI Send effects are assigned in the MIDI Send panel of a MIDI track. Instrument tracks do not include MIDI Send effects. The MIDI Sends panel is opened in the expanded Mixer, in the MIDI Channel Settings window or in the Inspector (Figure 15.3). Each MIDI track has a total of four MIDI Send slots. Click on a Send effect field to open the MIDI effects pop-up menu.

With MIDI Send effects, the MIDI data is routed to the chosen MIDI output port for the track as usual and a copy of the data is also sent in parallel to the MIDI effect. The data produced by the effect is routed to the MIDI output port chosen in the Send effects slot which may differ from that of the track (Figure 15.4). Thus, the send effect destination device and sound may be different to those of the MIDI track.

One advantage of routing the send data to a different device to the track is to avoid MIDI data cancellation and phasing problems when the effect data and track data coincide. Such a case may occur with the MIDI Echo effect. If such phenomena become problematic, try routing the send effect data on a separate MIDI channel assigned to the same sound or, in the case of VST

Info

Unlike audio Send effects, each assigned MIDI Send effect is unique to the MIDI track and there is no assignment of MIDI Send effects in a globally available MIDI Send effects panel.

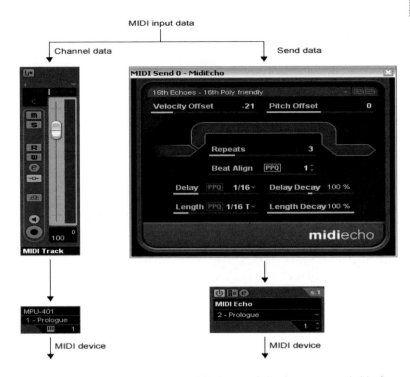

MIDI input data

Channel data

Send data

Figure 15.3 (above)
MIDI Send effects are assigned using the Send slots in the Send panel of a MIDI channel

Figure 15.4 (left)
The routing configuration for MIDI Send effects

instruments, try activating a second instance of the instrument. Aside from solving problems, using the Send effects to route the MIDI data to a completely different device and sound patch is valuable for creative purposes. In addition, MIDI Send effects feature a pre / post button. When this is de-activated the MIDI Send effects are processed after the MIDI Modifiers and MIDI Insert effects for the track. When the pre / post button is active the MIDI data feed to the send effects occurs before passing through the MIDI modifiers and Insert effects for the track. Also note that MIDI send effects remain active even if you disconnect the MIDI output port of the host track which can help when experimenting.

MIDI Send effects allow more complex routing configurations and are thus helpful for difficult processing tasks and creative applications.

Tip

Combining MIDI send effects with MIDI Insert effects is a fruitful avenue of exploration for creating sequenced echoes, arpeggios and sound effects.

Common GUI functions for MIDI effects

The graphical user interface (GUI) for any of the currently active MIDI effects can be opened by clicking on the edit button of the slot corresponding to the effect. The edit buttons are labelled with a lower case 'e' and are found in all effects slots in the Mixer, in the MIDI Channel Settings window and in the Inspector. Most GUIs for the MIDI effects open in a separate window similar to that shown in Figure 15.5. When opened from the Inspector, some of the effects open within the Inspector itself. If required, you can force these kind of effects to open in a separate window by pressing Alt while making an effects selection.

Figure 15.5
The graphical user interface for the MIDI Auto LFO effect

Most MIDI effects include a Presets menu which is opened by clicking on the Presets field near the top of the GUI (Figure 15.6). You can add your own presets by clicking on the plus (+) folder symbol next to the Presets menu and you can delete the currently chosen preset by clicking on the minus (-) folder symbol. Any stored presets are globally available to all projects.

Many of the MIDI effects feature dual action value fields which can be set according to note or PPQ values (Figure 15.7). Note values help set the parameters to fixed divisions of the bar for tempo driven echoes and modulations, while PPQ mode helps with small increments and irregular timing effects.

Figure 15.6
Use the Presets menu to store and recall MIDI effects presets

Figure 15.7
Make adjustments in the MIDI effect value fields using note values (left) or PPQ values (right)

The supplied MIDI effects

There now follow descriptions of a number of the supplied MIDI effects. Please consult the user documentation for full details of all other MIDI effects.

Arpache 5

Arpache 5 is an arpeggiator MIDI plug-in (Figure 15.8). Typically, an arpeggiator is a device which automatically steps through the notes in a held chord in a repeated sequential order. Arpache 5 achieves a similar effect by transforming MIDI input data. The parameters allow the creation of standard arpeggios, random arpeggios and arpeggios which follow a user-specified note order.

Figure 15.8
Arpache 5

Arpache 5 features the following parameters:

- Play Order section – determines the playback order for the arpeggio. The options include normal up / down, inverted down / up, up only, down only, random and user modes. The user mode allows you to set the playback order according to the settings in the play order display in the lower section of the GUI..
- Step size – determines the arpeggio playback speed according to a note value.
- Length – regulates the length of each playback note according to a note value.
- Key Range – determines the pitch range of the playback in semitones starting from the lowest input note. For example, a setting of 12 ensures that all arpeggiated notes are within the same octave (12 semitones) and

any higher notes are transposed down. A setting of 24 allows the arpeggio to be automatically transposed in as many octaves as are available within the range.

- Thru – when activated, all notes arriving at the input of the arpeggiator are passed through to the output. When de-activated, the input notes are not passed through to the output. For standard arpeggio behaviour, thru would be de-activated.
- Play Order display – when User is selected in the Play Order section the playback order is determined according to the settings in the play order slots which represent each step in the arpeggio in incremental time position order. The numbers you choose for each field specify which note from the input chord is allocated to each step in the arpeggio, counting from the lowest note in the chord. For the correct behaviour, always fill the slots consecutively starting from the left.

User guide

To set up Arpache 5 for standard arpeggiator purposes proceed as follows:

- Select a MIDI track and activate the monitor button so that you can play live through the track.
- Set the output port of the MIDI track to an appropriate MIDI device. Select a suitable sound. Try using the supplied Prologue VST Instrument set to the 'Classic Ana' preset.
- Activate the Arpache 5 MIDI plug-in as an Insert effect on the chosen MIDI track.
- In the Arpache 5 interface, activate the Normal play mode, set Step size to 1/8, Length to 1/32 and Key Range to 11.
- Hold down a three note chord comprising C3, E3 and G3 (or any other three note chord). These settings produce an arpeggio which steps through the notes in the held chord in ascending and descending order, at a speed corresponding to 1/8th note intervals at the current project tempo. Each playback note has a 1/32nd note duration.
- Try changing the Key Range to 12. This causes the lowest note to step up an octave on each cycle of the arpeggio. Try changing the speed by setting the Quantize value to 16.
- Try activating the random mode to produce a randomised playback order.
- Check out the effect of the other Play order buttons and try setting up your own custom play order by activating user mode and entering values into the Play Order slots (values of 1, 2, 1, 3, 1, 2, 2, 1 give good results with three note chords).

Auto LFO

Auto LFO is a modulation device for MIDI Controller data (Figure 15.9). It allows the continuous modulation of any chosen Controller between a specified value range. Auto LFO is suitable for producing automatic MIDI panning effects by modulating MIDI Controller 10 or for automated tempo driven modulations of the cut-off and resonance parameters of a synthesizer by

Figure 15.9
Auto LFO

modulating MIDI Controllers 71 and 74. Simultaneous modulation of several controllers may be achieved by inserting two or more Auto LFOs in sequence in the MIDI inserts.

Auto LFO features the following parameters:

- Waveform – determines the modulation waveforms applied to the chosen MIDI Controller. The depth of these waveforms is scaled according to the Value Range (below). Six waveforms are available.
- Wavelength – determines the speed of one modulation cycle. For example, if you set this to a 1/4 note, a modulation cycle is repeated once every quarter note. The wavelength can be set to note values or to ticks when PPQ is activated.
- Controller Type – allocates the target MIDI Controller to which the modulation effect is to be applied. Pan (Controller 10), Sound Variation (Controller 70), timbre / harmonic (Controller 71) and brightness (Controller 74) are possible targets but the suitability of each controller depends upon the MIDI implementation in the target device.
- Density – controls the density of the MIDI controller events which are used to describe the modulation effect. A high setting results in a smoother curve. However, it is not always best to set the density at the highest level since producing a large number of Controller events may occasionally cause MIDI transmission problems.
- Value Range – determines the lower and upper value limits for the waveform thereby regulating the range of the modulation effect.

User guide

Auto LFO can be used for a wide range of automated modulation effects. To set up automated modulation of the cut-off parameter of the supplied Monologue VST instrument, proceed as follows:

- Add an instrument track and set its instrument to the supplied Monologue virtual analogue synthesizer. Open the GUI and select the 'BandFifths' preset.
- Record a simple test sequence of notes over a length of 4 bars or use an existing 4 bar MIDI recording. Here, the 4 bar length is important since it is the length of time over which the cut-off parameter is to be modulated.
- Activate the Auto LFO MIDI plug-in as an Insert effect on the chosen Instrument track.
- In the Auto LFO interface, select the sine waveform, enter a wavelength of a 1/2 note in the Wavelength field, set Density to medium and set the Controller type to Brightness (Controller 74). Set a minimum value of 5 and a maximum of 55. With a wavelength of a 1/2 note the modulation cycle has a duration of half a bar.
- Commence playback and listen to the effect of the modulation in the Monologue VST instrument. To see the action of the modulation open the Monologue interface by clicking on the edit instrument button and observe the cut-off dial. If everything is functioning correctly you should

see the dial moving back and forth every half a bar.
- Try changing the speed by setting the Wavelength value to 7860 (4 bars) combined with a ramp waveform.

Beat Designer

Beat Designer is a step-based drum pattern creation tool (Figure 15.10). It can be activated as an insert on any MIDI or Instrument track. The interface includes a list of drum names in the left column, a central pattern grid, and lane offset and swing controls to the right. Four numbered pattern banks are available below the main display each of which contains twelve patterns stored on the keys of a one-octave virtual keyboard. The instruments list corresponds with the currently loaded drum map of the host track but if no drum map is loaded the list shows the standard GM drum names. The horizontal time display is divided into up to 64 equal steps where the length of each step may be regulated between 1/128th and 1/2 notes. The length of the pattern varies according to the settings where sixteen 1/16th note steps gives a length of one bar, thirty two 1/16th note steps gives a length of two bars, and so on. For playback purposes Beat Designer is slaved to the main transport so the playback speed varies according to the current tempo.

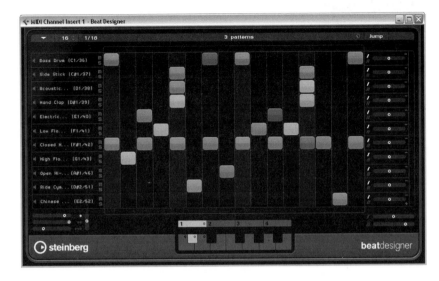

Figure 15.10
Beat Designer

Beat Designer is purely an interface and makes no sound on its own. In order to trigger sounds the MIDI or Instrument track must contain a valid target device in the output routing menu. Beat Designer marries well with the supplied Groove Agent ONE virtual drum machine but may be used with any VST instrument.

Setting up

To get started with Beat Designer proceed as follows:

- Select Project / Add track and add an Instrument track. In the pop-up Add dialogue select Groove Agent ONE in the instrument field.
- Open the Groove Agent ONE interface and select the 'Maple Kit CD' preset from the Load preset menu. This contains a simple kit which is already mapped to the standard GM drum note positions so it will be immediately compatible with the standard map in Beat Designer. Close the Groove Agent One interface.

Figure 15.11
Arrange the instruments list like this

- Select the new Instrument track and in the Inspector for the track click on the MIDI inserts tab. Click in the empty field of the first slot and select Beat Designer from the pop-up menu.
- The Beat Designer GUI is automatically opened on the screen. To verify that the current instruments in the list are triggering Groove Agent ONE click on the preview buttons to the left of the instrument names. You should hear the drum sounds.
- By default eight instrument lanes are shown but add two more lanes by clicking on the + sign of the last lane near the lower right corner of the window.
- When you click on the names in the list you can select a new instrument for each lane from the pop-up menu. Arrange the list so it shows ten instruments in the same order and with the same names as Figure 15.11

You now have a working kit ready and you can begin creating a pattern.

Creating and editing patterns

Let's create one basic rhythm pattern and a tom-tom fill pattern as follows:

- Leave the step resolution at 1/16 notes and the number of steps at 16 (the default settings). Commence playback on the transport panel.
- Select an empty key on the virtual keyboard below the display.
- Click in the bass drum lane on the steps where you want to insert bass drum events. Drag the pointer vertically on an inserted event to change the velocity. To delete an event click on it a second time.
- Proceed similarly with the snare drum and hi-hats to create the pattern of your choice or try approximating the pattern shown in Figure 15.12
- Now, select another empty key on the virtual keyboard below the display and proceed in a similar manner to create a classic downward moving tom-tom fill using the four tom-toms in the instrument list.
- After creating the fill try adjusting the lane offsets for the 2nd, 3rd and 4th toms to 0.60, 0.70 and 0.40 using the lane offset sliders to the right of the grid (as shown in Figure 15.13). This slows the events down in the middle thereby adding some feel to the pattern. The fill shown here also features a bass drum with a lane offset of 0.30 and a splash cymbal at the start.
- Save the patterns as a pattern bank preset using the VST Sound 'Save Preset' function in Beat Designer. This saves the pattern and the Instrument track data including all VST Instrument settings. A pattern bank preset is a special case track preset. You can use the 'Apply Track Preset' VST Sound function to recall the pattern bank and the relevant VST instrument to a track in the Project window.

> **Tip**
>
> To move a lane up or down in the instrument list click and drag in empty space in the lane header.

> **Tip**
>
> To change the velocity of all events on a lane hold Shift while dragging vertically on one of the events.

Figure 15.12
Try approximating this pattern at 120bpm

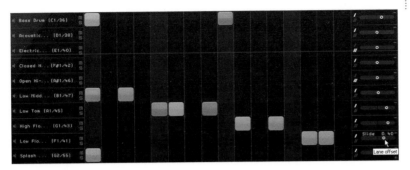

Playing patterns

Once you have created your patterns you can select them on the fly during
playback by clicking on the keys of the virtual keyboard, by live triggering via
MIDI, or via recorded MIDI notes on the host track in the Project window.
Playback behaviour varies according to the status of the 'Jump' and 'Now'
buttons as follows:

- Jump activated / Now de-activated – pattern selection by clicking on the
  virtual keyboard or by live or recorded MIDI trigger waits until the end of
  the current pattern before being executed.
- Jump activated / Now activated – pattern selection by recorded MIDI
  events on the host track triggers the new pattern immediately and from
  the start point, regardless of the current pattern playback position.
  Pattern selection by clicking on the virtual keyboard or by live MIDI
  trigger behaves in the same manner as point 1 above.
- Jump de-activated – manual pattern selection with the mouse is
  executed immediately and incoming MIDI notes no longer trigger pattern
  switching. The Now button is not available in this mode.

Arranging patterns in the Project window

To create a full arrangement you can chain your patterns together in the
Project window by recording either the MIDI triggers or the MIDI data onto
the host track. To use MIDI triggers to chain patterns together, activate the
Jump button and use one of the following:

- Drag from the sub-bank button of Beat Designer onto a MIDI or
  Instrument track to create MIDI parts containing the MIDI trigger notes
  corresponding to the patterns in the sub-bank. These are inserted on the
  track starting at the point where you release the mouse. You can now
  use the parts to trigger the corresponding patterns and they can be
  copied and arranged on the track as desired.
- Drag from a single pattern key of Beat Designer onto a MIDI or
  Instrument track to create a single MIDI part containing the
  corresponding single MIDI trigger note. This is inserted on the track at
  the point where you release the mouse. You can now use the part to
  trigger the corresponding pattern.

If you do not wish to use MIDI triggers to chain your patterns together but instead wish to copy the actual MIDI data of your patterns, de-activate the jump button and drag from the sub-bank button or pattern key similar to the above steps. This time all of the MIDI data from each pattern is written direct-ly into a MIDI part and you can now edit and arrange the data in the usual manner on the MIDI or Instrument track.

Loading pattern bank presets

Although Beat Designer pattern banks may be loaded using the Load Presets menu found in the Beat Designer GUI, searching for and auditioning pattern banks which contain the associated VST instrument reference are best han-dled in the Media Bay (at the time of writing). Open the Media Bay from the Media menu, activate the browser and scope sections, select VST Sound in the browser, and select only the pattern bank icon at the top of the viewer section. You are now presented with a list of the available pattern banks. Make a selection from the list and use the play, stop, autoplay and audition level controls in the scope section to manage playback behaviour. When you have found a preset you wish to load double-click on it. This adds a track in the Project window containing Beat Designer as a MIDI insert. If the pattern bank contains only pattern data with no reference to a VST instrument a MIDI track is created. If the pattern bank contains a reference to a VST instrument an Instrument track is created.

Experimenting with preset patterns

Experimenting with the supplied presets is a good way of getting to know Beat Designer. In the Media Bay, double-click on the pattern bank preset named 'Afrique Latino 133bpm' to create a corresponding Instrument track in the Project window. Close the Media Bay after the track has been created and click on the edit button of the Beat Designer MIDI insert slot to open the GUI. Commence playback and select the pattern on key G1 / 43 (see Figure 15.14). Notice the single dot on the first event on the cowbell lane. This is a flam. Flams are created by clicking in the lower part of the event to enter one, two or three dots for three different flam behaviours. The level and timing of the flams is set up with the controls in the lower left corner of Beat Designer. Try changing the flam characteristics of the first cowbell event. Also take the opportunity to experiment with the swing controls. Two different swing val-

Figure 15.14

Experimenting with the patterns in the supplied presets helps you get to know Beat Designer

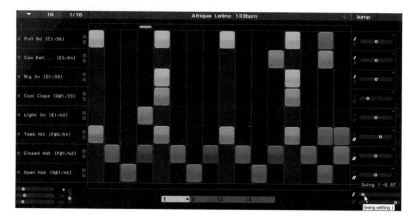

ues can be applied using the swing selectors in the lanes and the swing sliders at the lower right of the GUI. In this same pattern try activating swing type
2 on lanes 6, 7, and 8 and adjust the swing 2 slider to both negative and
positive values during playback. You may be surprised just how much this can
affect the groove of the pattern. Taking this further try de-activating swing
types 1 and 2 on tracks 4 and 5 (claps and light snare) and now apply swing
to the pattern using a combination of swing sliders 1 and 2. The effect upon
the groove is still more radical.

MIDI Echo

MIDI Echo (Figure 15.15) produces delay and chorus effects. The parameters of MIDI Echo function as follows:

- Velocity Offset – determines a velocity amount which is added to or
  subtracted from each echo repeat to simulate crescendo or echo fade
  effects.
- Pitch Offset – determines a pitch amount in semitones which is added to
  or subtracted from each echo repeat, thereby changing the pitch of each
  consecutive echo to produce ascending or descending pitch sequences.
- Repeats – determines the number of echo repeats for each incoming
  MIDI note.
- Beat Align – determines how the first echo is quantized, expressed in
  ticks or note values. This has no effect when you use MIDI Echo for
  playing live. However, the parameter produces confusing results since
  there is a difference in response between live playing and recorded MIDI
  parts. Try setting this to 1 to minimise the latter problem.
- Delay – determines the speed of the echoes relative to the current
  tempo, expressed in ticks or note values.
- Delay Decay – adds or subtracts a number of ticks to each successive
  echo repeat to produce accelerated or decelerated echo effects. A setting
  of 100 produces no change. A setting or less than 100 produces echoes
  which speed up. A setting or more than 100 produces echoes which slow
  down.
- Length – determines the
  length of the echoed
  events, expressed in
  ticks or note values.
  When set to its lowest
  value the echoes are the
  same length as the
  original note.
- Length Decay –
  regulates the length of
  each successive echo
  repeat where higher
  values result in longer
  notes.

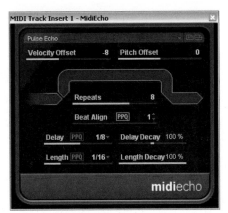

Figure 15.15
MIDI Echo

User guide

For the initial testing of MIDI Echo, try using a simple MIDI part triggering a piano sound so you can hear the results clearly. Use the settings in Figure 15.15 as a starting point or try the supplied presets.

MIDI Monitor

MIDI Monitor (Figure 15.16) is a real-time MIDI message analysis plug-in. It is normally used as an insert effect to monitor the details of the MIDI data stream of the chosen track. To display the MIDI data, you activate the Record Events button at top left. MIDI input data is shown in the data list in the lower half of the GUI. The input section buttons allow you to display live input or playback events, or both. You can filter the input data to show any combination of the main MIDI message types (note on / off, controller, aftertouch, pitch bend and so on). The storage buffer for MIDI Monitor can be switched between small, medium and large storage sizes and the data in the list may be exported as a simple text file for detailed analysis in an external text editor. To clear the data list you click on the clear list icon (cross symbol). MIDI Monitor helps find problem MIDI messages such as unwanted program change and system exclusive messages and helps analyse any situation where MIDI communication is faulty or erratic.

Figure 15.16
MIDI Monitor

Step Designer

Step Designer is a monophonic MIDI step sequencer (Figure 15.17). MIDI note data is generated by drawing events in the upper half of the grid which displays time on the horizontal axis and pitch on the vertical axis (1 octave at a time). Velocity values, gate times and two MIDI controllers may be controlled for each note by dragging the corresponding value sliders in the lower half of the display. The horizontal time display is divided into 32 equal steps the length of which can be regulated between 1/128th and 1/2 notes. For playback purposes, Step Designer is slaved to the main transport so the playback speed varies according to the current tempo and the length of the steps.

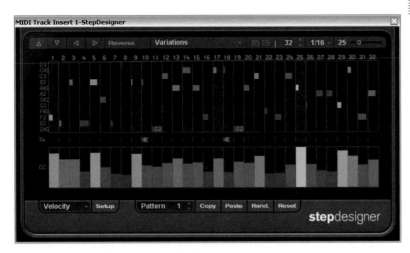

Figure 15.17
Step Designer

Step Designer features control panels above and below the main display which include the following parameters:

- Shift octave buttons – move the pitch of the pattern up or down in octaves.
- Shift step buttons – scroll the notes to the left or right. Notes which are pushed off the end of the pattern are wrapped around to the opposite end of the sequence. This is helpful for creating pattern variations and changing the feel.
- Reverse – reverses the note order of the pattern.
- Presets menu – allows the storage and recall of presets. A preset is a collection of up to 200 different patterns.
- Number of steps – determines the overall length of the pattern between 1 and 32 steps.
- Step size – determines the length of each of the 32 steps in the sequence in terms of a note value between 1/128th and 1/2 notes.
- Swing – imposes a swing feel upon the current pattern, where every second note position on the grid is pushed to the right (so that it falls slightly later). A higher percentage produces more swing.
- Controllers section – provides a selection menu which determines what data is visible in the lower half of the display. The Setup button opens a dialogue where you can select which two MIDI controllers are to be targeted by Step Designer (this is globally set for the current instance of Step Designer and cannot be individually set for each pattern).
- Pattern – determines the current pattern number (up to 200 may be held in memory).
- Copy and paste buttons – these are used to copy and paste the data from one pattern to another. This is helpful for creating variations of the same pattern.
- Random and reset buttons – the Random button generates a random sequence of notes in the currently displayed octave which replace any existing notes in the current pattern. The Reset button clears the current pattern and all associated controller data in the current pattern.

User guide

To generate your own pattern in Step Designer proceed as follows:

- Assign Step Designer as an Insert effect on a MIDI track.
- Allocate the MIDI output port of the track to a suitable MIDI device and sound patch. For this exercise, try using the supplied Monologue VST Instrument set to the 'Acid Bass' preset.
- Select a length for the pattern in the length field. The default 16 step setting is suitable for experimentation.
- Select the quantize value for each step in the Quantize field. Once again, the default 1/16 note setting is suitable for experimentation.
- Click and drag the mouse left to right across the note event display. A series of note events are inserted as small graphical rectangular blocks. This is a quick manner of entering note data. Alternatively, to enter a pre-defined series of notes click at the appropriate pitch position for each step.
- Click and drag the mouse across the velocity display in the lower half of the window. The velocity values are adjusted according to the position of the mouse. This is a quick manner of entering velocity data. Alternatively, try dragging the velocity levels for each step individually.
- Commence playback. The Step Designer pattern plays back in a continuous loop synchronised to the current project tempo.
- During playback, try editing the notes and velocity data.
- Click on the Controllers menu and select the Gate option. Edit the gate times of the notes in the lower part of the display. The gate times affect the lengths of the notes in the pattern.
- Click on the setup button and select the Harmonic and Brightness controllers in the controllers menu (controllers 71 and 74). Edit the Harmonic and Brightness values in the lower part of the display. This produces real-time changes of the cut-off and resonance parameters in the Monologue VSTi. Open the Monologue interface to observe the movement of the parameters.
- Click on the setup button to assign other controllers to Step Designer. Experiment with the value settings of the chosen controllers.

Other techniques

To get more out of Step Designer try the following techniques:

- To slide the octave up or down, click and drag vertically on the note list to the left of the note display. Moving notes in the current pattern out of the display results in a note name appearing, indicating the presence of notes in other octaves. This is helpful for keeping track of the notes in multi-octave patterns.
- To tie any note to the preceding note, click on any of the tie indicators found in the strip between the upper and lower sections of the interface. Ties can be implemented on any number of successive steps in the pattern and the tied note always takes on the pitch of the note to which it is attached. Changing the pitch of tied notes moves all tied steps simultaneously.

Tip

To trigger pattern changes via MIDI, activate Step Designer as an insert effect and monitor enable (or record enable) the track. You can now change patterns using the keys on your musical keyboard where C1 / 36 selects pattern 1, C#1 / 37 selects pattern 2 and so on. For automated pattern changes, record the appropriate MIDI notes.

Info

For more elaborate arrangements, try running two or more Step Designers simultaneously on different MIDI tracks triggering different sounds.

Transformer

Transformer is a real-time MIDI data conversion tool (Figure 15.18). It operates in a similar manner to the Logical Editor except that it cannot act upon the length and position of the data. It transforms data without permanently changing the source. You can delete, transform or insert data based upon user-configurable filters. The filter is defined in the upper part of the window and the action which should take place upon the filtered data is defined in the lower part of the window.

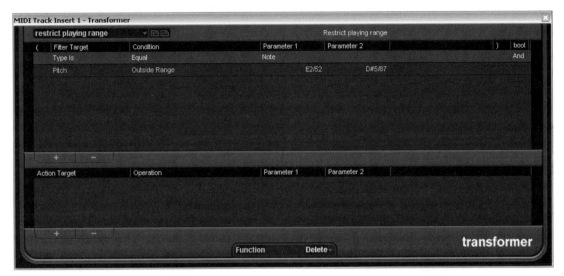

Figure 15.18
Transformer

User Guide

Simple configurations within Transformer may be expressed in plain English, such as 'if the incoming MIDI message type is an Aftertouch message delete it'. This translates into the Transformer window as follows:

- In the upper Filter section, set the Filter target to 'Type', set the condition to 'Equal' and Parameter 1 to 'Aftertouch'.
- Ignore the Action section.
- Select Delete in the function menu.

This results in the real-time deletion of all aftertouch messages from the incoming MIDI data.

Taking a look in the pop-up menus of the various columns reveals that more elaborate filtering and transformations are possible. Try loading some of the presets to see how the more complex functions are set up. You may also like to consider the following examples.

Setting a filter to restrict the input range for a chosen instrument

For restricting the MIDI input to the playing range of a trumpet, for example, proceed as follows:

- In the upper Filter section, set the Filter target column to 'Type', the

Condition column to 'Equal' and the Parameter 1 column to 'Note'.
- Click on the Add Line button. Set the Filter target column to 'Value 1' (Pitch), the Condition column to 'Outside Range' and the Parameter 1 and 2 columns to 'E2 (52)' and 'D#5 (87)'.
- Select Delete in the function menu.

The result is the real-time deletion (or filtering) of any notes outside the chosen range. This kind of filter is excellent for keeping within the natural note range of an instrument, if a sense of realism is what your music needs.

Changing pitch bend into pan data

To set a transformation which changes pitch bend into pan data proceed as follows:

- In the upper Filter section, set the Filter target column to 'Type', the Condition column to 'Equal' and the Parameter 1 column to 'Pitch bend'.
- In the lower Action section, add two lines using the Add Line button. For the first line, set the Action target column to 'Type', the Operation column to 'Set to fixed value' and the Parameter 1 column to 'Controller'. For the second line, set the Action target column to 'Value 1', the Operation column to 'Set to fixed value' and the Parameter 1 column to '10' (Pan Controller number).
- Select Transform in the function menu.

The result is the real-time transformation of pitch bend messages into pan data. This is good for the real-time application of pan data using your master synth pitch wheel.

Many more configurations are possible and, by adding more data lines in each section, complex filters and transformations can be designed. Any efforts made with Transformer will serve you well when you use the main Logical editor

How do I make the MIDI effects a permanent part of the data?

The data produced by the MIDI effects can be made a permanent part of the data using 'Merge MIDI in Loop' in the MIDI menu (Figure 15.19).

Merge MIDI in Loop merges all non-muted MIDI events between the left and right locators in a new MIDI part which is created on the currently selected MIDI track. If there is already MIDI data on the destination track you can choose to overwrite it or merge all the data. To use Merge MIDI in Loop proceed as follows:

- Adjust the left and right locators to encompass the MIDI passage you wish to merge.
- Mute all those MIDI tracks you do not wish to include in the merge operation, or if you are working on a single track you could use its solo button.
- Select a destination MIDI track.

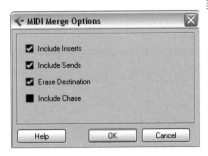

Figure 15.19
Merge MIDI in Loop dialogue

- Select Merge MIDI in Loop from the MIDI menu.
- Activate the Include Inserts and / or Include Sends options to include the desired MIDI effects.
- Activate the Erase Destination option if you wish to erase the current MIDI part on the destination track and replace it with the merged data. For example, this would be the case if you were working on a single MIDI part and wished to make its MIDI effects a permanent part of the data. Erasing the destination avoids double notes.
- De-activate the Erase Destination option if you do NOT wish to erase the current MIDI part on the destination track and wish to merge all the chosen data with it. In this case, you are merging the data with itself which may result in double notes.

Automation

Mix automation is considered a standard requirement in professional recording studios. It gives the producer, sound engineer or musician more scope to produce the best possible mix and provides instant recall of a mix which was performed on a previous occasion. Typically, automation involves the real-time recording of fader and control movements but may equally be achieved via the graphical editing of automation curves. The automation may be overdubbed or edited as many times as necessary in order to achieve the desired result. Cubase includes similar features and allows automation of all mixer controls, all plug-in effect controls, and all VST instrument controls.

Basic automation

Basic automation can be recorded in Cubase using two methods:

1 Activating the Write buttons and recording the movements of the controls in real-time.
2 Opening an automation track in the event display and drawing an automation curve.

Recording automation in real-time

Automation read and write buttons are found on every channel strip in the Mixer and duplicated in the track list and in the Inspector. They are also found at the top of each plug-in GUI window. To help manage reading and writing automation Cubase provides an automation panel. This is opened by clicking on the automation panel button in the Project window toolbar (Figure 16.1).

Recording automation is independent of the the main Transport panel record functions. All you need do is activate the write buttons on the appropriate channels and engage play. All control manipulations on the write

Figure 16.1
The automation panel

enabled channels are recorded in real-time.

Before recording automation, create a new project or open an existing test project. Make sure you have two or three audio tracks recorded in the project. Set up Cubase to cycle over a suitable passage. Leave one or two empty bars at the start. This is useful for any automation settings you may wish to implement before the music starts. Organise your layout so you can see both the Mixer and the Project windows simultaneously. Open the automation panel and drag it to a suitable screen position. To start recording automation, proceed as follows:

- Select Touch Fader mode in the automation panel.
- Activate the Write button of one of the Audio channels in the Mixer (Figure 16.2). This also automatically activates the Read button for the channel. Active Read and Write buttons are illuminated in green and red respectively. Alternatively, activate the global Write button in the automation panel.
- Start playback in Cycle mode and move the fader of the Audio track you Write enabled (Figure 16.3).

Figure 16.2
Activate the Write button for an Audio channel

Figure 16.3
Move the fader while in playback mode

- Stop moving the fader after the first cycle. On subsequent laps of the cycle, the fader moves according to the manipulations you made on the first lap of the cycle.
- To see the volume automation you have just recorded, activate the 'Used Only' button and click on the Volume button in the 'Show Used' column of the automation panel (Figure 16.4). This opens the corresponding automation track for the relevant track in the Project window event display. The automation is displayed as a curve linked together by small black handles known as automation events. automation tracks may also be opened by clicking on the lower left corner of the audio track, at which time the show / hide automation arrow appears.
- Try re-recording the volume automation again on the same track. Notice how the automation sub-track track turns red each time you touch the fader. In

touch mode, recording is only engaged when you move the fader or when you click and hold the fader.

- It may not always be convenient to re-record the fader movements while the fader is also moving according to the automation which has already been recorded. To temporarily suspend reading, activate the 'Suspend Read' button in the automation panel (Figure 16.5).

Figure 16.4 (left)
To see the volume automation, activate 'Used Only' and click on the Volume button in the automation panel

Figure 16.5 (right)
Activate the Suspend Read button in the automation panel to temporarily suspend reading

Drawing an automation curve

It is sometimes more appropriate to draw an automation curve in the event display rather than moving controls in real-time. Such a case might occur if you wanted to produce a carefully controlled panning effect. For example, to pan one of your sounds from the left to right over a precisely defined passage within the mix, proceed as follows:

- In the track list right click on the track to which you wish to apply a pan effect. Select 'Show Automation' from the pop-up menu (Figure 16.6).
- By default, the Volume automation track appears. Click in the automation track name field and select 'Standard Panner - Pan Left - Right' from the pop-up menu (Figure 16.7).
- Activate the Read button for the pan automation track in the track list. Select 'Beat' in the Grid Quantize menu and select the Line tool from the Project window toolbar. Draw a line at the appropriate position in the event display to produce the pan effect of your choice (Figure 16.8). Alternatively, use the Draw tool to freely draw any curve shape.
- Activate playback to hear the result. Adjust and experiment with the curve as required.
- Try using the other tools in the toolbar and different Grid Quantize menu settings to create different shaped automation curves (Figure 16.9).

The automation track pop-up menu does not show all the available automation parameters simultaneously. To select other automation data, select the 'More' option. The 'More' option opens the Add Parameter dialogue from where you can select the automation parameter of your choice.

Figure 16.6 (above)
Select 'Show Automation' from the Track list pop-up menu on the chosen track

Figure 16.7 (below)
Select the standard panner from the automation track pop-up menu

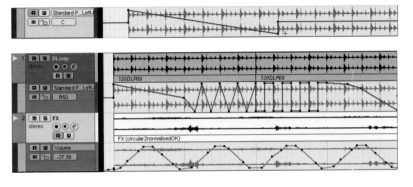

Figure 16.8 (left)
Using the Line tool to draw a pan automation curve in the standard panner automation track

Figure 16.9
Try the other tools to create different shaped automation curves

Figure 16.10
Automation modes in the Project window toolbar

Automation modes

Cubase provides the following automation modes as chosen in the Project window toolbar or in the automation panel:

- Touch – automation starts to be written when you click on a control during playback and continues until you release the mouse button. This is the standard automation mode for recording movements in real-time.
- Autolatch – automation starts to be written when you click on a control during playback. The last set value for the control continues to be written until you stop playback or de-activate the Write button. In this mode, the release of the mouse button does not switch off the automation.
- X-Over – automation starts to be written as soon as you click on a control during playback. The last set value for the control continues to be written until the new automation curve crosses a point on the existing curve (or until you stop playback or de-activate the Write button). In this mode, the release of the mouse button does not switch off the automation. Good for writing fades up to a set level on the existing curve.
- Trim mode – automation starts to be written when you click on a control during playback and continues until you release the mouse button. When trim mode is selected, the faders of channels with their Write buttons activated are temporarily reset to the mid position. When you write the automation, the changes affect the existing curve relative to the movements of the fader above or below the mid-point. More importantly, Trim mode can be used to change the automation between the left and right locators when Cubase is in stop mode. Proceed as follows: find the automation you wish to trim in the automation tracks in the event display, set the left and right locators around the events, select Trim mode, activate Write on the appropriate channel and then move the channel fader up or down.

Why use automation?

Automated mixing is one of a number of tools (albeit a rather special tool) that you can use to get a better mix. The decision to use it or not is a function of the artistic and technical imperatives of the project. One of the things to avoid is using automation just because it happens to be available. This might produce a mix with lots of intricate automation but you may lose the focus of what kind of mix the music really needs.

If you do not have an external control surface and rely entirely upon your computer keyboard and mouse, simultaneous control of multiple parameters in a complex mix is difficult. In this case, automation becomes more of a necessity rather than a luxury. One of the key areas where automation excels is when riding faders to achieve a better balance between tracks. A classic case is when riding the fader for the lead vocal channel to maximise intelligibility throughout the course of the mix. This can avoid using too much compression. Equally useful is the drawing of corrective automation curves to gate spill between drum mics or the background noise between the phrases of vocal lines. This is usually more precise than conventional real-time gating. Automation is equally useful for creating filter sweep effects in VST instruments, or dynamic sound effects by automating the movements of the controls of plug-in effects. Automation might also involve jumping from one static mix configuration to another rather than smooth, continuous changes.

Any dynamic mixer control change may be a candidate for automation but, of course, your mix may not need any automation at all. It may simply require a small number of manual changes at specific points in the mix. This is perfectly acceptable since it is not a crime to not use automation!

Automation in practice

Keeping the voice on top

Vocal intelligibility is extremely important in popular music or any project involving the human voice, but in many mixes and performances the voice may be too loud at one moment and too soft the next. While compression can help keep an overly dynamic signal in check there is almost always a point in the mix where it either jumps out too far in front or disappears behind the other instruments. After repeated listening to the same passage you can get a feel for where the vocal is sounding wrong and it is usually an intuitive act to correct the issues by riding the fader for the channel in real-time. By using automation you can record your fader movements any number of times until you get it just right.

In Cubase, this kind of automation is best recorded in Touch mode. It may also help to work in cycle playback mode and record the automation over comparatively short sections. Figure 16.11 shows a vocal track which has been subject to volume automation. The quiet sections are boosted in level according to the automation curve.

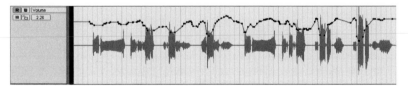

Figure 16.11
A vocal track and associated volume automation track after recording automation

Variations on this technique may be applied to any type of track with a similar problem. You can also adapt the procedure to dynamic EQ changes or dynamic control of reverberation and other plug-in effects.

Editing the automation

After recording automation in real-time it may need editing in fine detail and, as outlined above, the editing tools also allow you to draw automation curves from scratch.

Editing techniques

As you can see, automation data is displayed as small black handles along the length of the automation curve and it is these which govern the shape of the curve. These handles are known as automation events and similar to other event types they may be edited using the standard mouse and tool techniques of the Project window. The following are some of the most useful techniques:

- Select one or more automation events by dragging a box around the relevant area in the automation track using the Object selection tool. Alternatively, step through the events using the left / right arrows on the computer keyboard. Selected automation events are displayed in red.
- Delete one or more automation events by selecting them and pressing the backspace or delete keys on the computer keyboard. Alternatively, use the Eraser tool.
- Copy a group of automation events using Ctrl + C. Paste the copied events by moving the Project cursor to another position in the automation track and pressing Ctrl + V. The copied events overwrite the chosen section starting at the Project cursor position. Alternatively, use the Range Selection tool to move the events to a new position (or copy by pressing Alt).
- Click on any automation event and drag it to a new position to change the shape of the curve. Movements snap to the current snap resolution.
- Write a single new automation event by clicking once on an event-free part of the automation line.
- Write new automation events by dragging any of the draw tools (pencil, line, parabola and so on) in an automation track.

Tip

To adjust the resolution of the automation data, use the Reduction level parameter in the automation panel.

Correcting irregularities

Recording real-time automation in the Mixer may result in erratic irregularities in the automation curves. It may therefore be appropriate to fine tune the results for a smoother effect. To smooth an automation curve, proceed as follows:

- Zoom in to the relevant automation track so that you can see the individual automation events clearly (Figure 16.12). Set up the left and right locators and activate playback in cycle mode. In this way, you can make all edits 'on the fly' and hear the results on the next lap of the cycle.
- In this example, we delete the first group of pan automation events and move one of the handles to the left pan position at the very beginning of bar 7 (Figure 16.13). Activate the Snap button to help place the event. The left pan position corresponds with the uppermost position in the automation curve.
- Thin out the events between bars 7 and 8 and move the event located at the beginning of bar 9 to the centre pan position. Create a suitable curve between the event at bar 7 and the event at bar 9 (Figure 16.14). This gives you a smooth pan from the left to the centre pan positions over two bars.

You may like to tidy up other automation events in a similar manner. However, it may not be appropriate to make all automation scientifically correct. Leaving some of the rough edges may be what gives your mix its char-

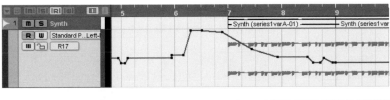

Figure 16.12
Automation events before editing

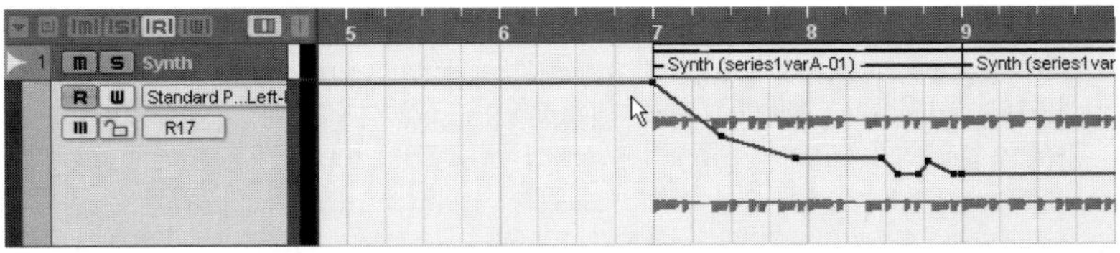

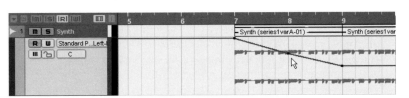

Figure 16.13
Delete the first group of pan automation events and move one of the handles to the extreme left pan position at the beginning of bar 7

Figure 16.14
The resulting smooth pan over two bars

acter. Above all, avoid the habit of working visually. The aim is not to produce a visually perfect event display but to produce a good sounding mix! Always listen very carefully as you make each change and preferably work in cycle playback mode. If the automation sounds best 'rough and ready' then leave it that way.

Moving and copying automation

Moving or copying automation events in the Project window event display are common requirements. Moving is useful for those occasions when the timing of individual events or a group of events is not quite right. Copying saves time when you have a number of repetitive sections of automation. If 'Automation Follows Events' is enabled (Edit menu), automation events are automatically attached to regular Audio and MIDI events and copied or moved with them. Here, we look at how automation events are copied and moved independently.

Three methods of independently moving groups of automation events are as follows:

- Select the Object selection tool and drag a selection box around the group of automation events. Press Ctrl / Command + X to cut the events. Place the cursor at the position at which you wish to paste the automation events. Press Ctrl / Command + V to paste the events.
- Select the Range selection tool and drag in the appropriate automation track(s) to select the area of interest. Once selected, click in the shaded area (at which time a hand appears) and drag the selection to a new location.
- Select the Object selection tool and drag a selection box around the group of automation events. Click on any one of the selected events and drag the whole group horizontally backwards or forwards along the track. The horizontal movement is magnetic to the current snap resolution and you can only drag the group as far as the next event in the automation track.

Two methods of independently copying groups of automation events are as follows:

- Select the Object selection tool and drag a selection box around the group of automation events. Press Ctrl / Command + C to copy the events. Place the cursor at the position at which you wish to paste the copied automation events. Press Ctrl / Command + V to paste the events.
- Select the Range selection tool and drag in the appropriate automation track(s) to select the area of interest. Once selected, press Alt on the computer keyboard, click in the shaded area (at which time a hand appears) and drag a copy of the selection to a new location.

Automation follows events

If you enable 'Automation follows events' in the Edit menu, any automation data found in the same range is automatically attached to regular Audio and MIDI events when they are moved or copied. This provides one of the easiest methods of moving and repeating automation data. An example is shown in Figure 16.15.

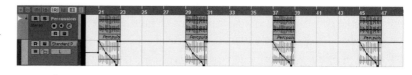

Figure 16.15
With 'Automation follows events' enabled, copying a percussion event four times produces four instances of the same automated pan effect

Using automation to clean up recordings

Editing the volume automation curve of a track to reduce the gain in passages containing hiss, hum, breaths, and spill is an excellent, and often preferable, alternative to using a noise gate. This technique is especially suited to cleaning up vocal recordings. It involves firstly isolating the vocal phrases by selecting the surrounding unwanted passages and bringing them down in level, followed by zooming in and editing the automation curves in detail. Proceed as follows:

Stage 1

1 Open the Volume automation track for the audio track which needs to be cleaned up (Figure 16.16).

Figure 16.16
Open the Volume automation track for the track which needs to be cleaned up

2 In the Project window toolbar, select the Line tool and de-activate the Snap button.

Tip

When moving automation handles, activate the Project window infoline. The infoline displays the start time and value of the event as you drag it. This helps place the events with greater precision. Alternatively, click directly on the value field in the infoline to activate a slider which may be used to change the value of the event.

3 Drag the Line tool over the range of the passage before the vocal begins at the lowest vertical height on the Volume automation track. Use the waveform as a visual guide for where you need to drag (Figure 16.17).

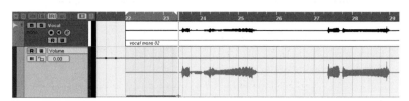

Figure 16.17
Drag the Line tool over the passage before the vocal begins

4 The automation Read button is automatically activated and four automation events are written to describe the new curve (Figure 16.18).

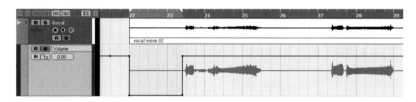

Figure 16.18
Four automation events are written to describe the new curve

5 Next drag the Line tool over the range of the gap between the first and second phrase in a similar manner to step 3 above, to create a second attenuated section (Figure 16.19).

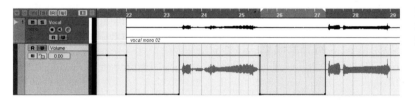

Figure 16.19
Using the same technique, attenuate the level of the next gap between phrases

6 Work through the track in a similar manner to reduce the level of all the unwanted interference between the vocal phrases (Figure 16.20).

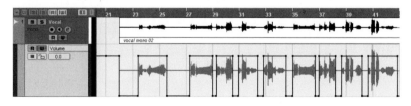

Figure 16.20
Process the whole vocal track so that all gaps between phrases are taken down in level

Stage 2

1 Commence playback from the start of the track to hear what you have achieved so far. To hear the details it may be best to solo the track.
2 Where required zoom in and fine tune (or redraw) the curve using the editing techniques described above (Figure 16.21).

Figure 16.21
Where required, edit the curve in fine detail to achieve the desired result

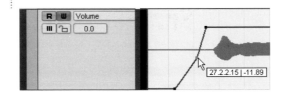

3 Work through the track methodically until you are satisfied with the the new clean version of the material.

Things to listen for during this procedure are the breaths before and after vocal phrases which you may have cut too tight or left too loud. Avoid taking out absolutely all the breaths, particularly those just before the onset of each phrase, as this can make the performance sound unnatural.

You can also use this technique for reducing sibilance and plosives in vocal recordings, cleaning up brass and acoustic instrument performances, cleaning up spill between drum mics, and for reducing amplifier hum and interference in electric guitar parts. While it is often beneficial to clean up some of the dirt on your tracks you should take care not to suck out all the life and character of the musical performance.

Creative automation effects

As an alternative to the conventional mix management and cleaning up approaches, it is worth trying automation for creative effects such as gated stuttering and chopping of the audio, or for auto panning. To create these effects, write the volume or pan automation using one of the draw shape tools, as found in the Project window tool bar. Try the triangle or sine shape tools at a quantize resolution of 1/16th notes with the snap button active (Figure 16.22).

Figure 16.22
Try using the shape tools on automation tracks for creative effects such as gated chopping and auto panning

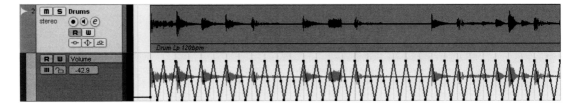

Surround sound

Surround sound implies the use of a multiple channel sound diffusion system where there are speakers behind and to each side of the listener, as well as in front. Most surround sound configurations have their historical foundations in the film industry, which began using multichannel formats as long ago as the early 1950s. Early implementations involved a number of channels to the front of the listener and one to the rear, known as the effects channel. Early 70mm wide-screen cinemas featured five channels across the cinema screen and a surround channel which fed multiple speakers to the rear and sides of the auditorium. As wide-screen cinema fell out of fashion the need for a large number of channels across the front became obsolete. In the 1970s Dolby Laboratories encouraged the use of a surround sound system based upon three main screen channels (left, centre and right), with two low frequency bass extension channels and one surround channel to the rear. The centre channel was traditionally used for dialogue. The company also developed a 70mm format featuring a stereo surround channel. This was the forerunner of the 5.1 channel Dolby Digital Surround format.

At this point, you may well ask why Cubase should need to be equipped with surround sound when this is largely the domain of the film industry. The answer lies in the fact that, in recent times, there has been a convergence of the film sound, television sound and record industries such that they no longer work in isolation, and surround sound has become an accepted common standard among all three. In addition, surround systems are finding their way into more and more homes and the DVD-Audio disc aims to bring multichannel surround sound to the general consumer market (possibly eventually replacing standard audio CDs). Surround mixes are already a common occurrence in the audio industry. Cubase is ready to help you create your surround mix if you should need to.

Demystifying surround sound

Surround sound has been championed by two organisations: Dolby Laboratories and DTS (Digital Theatre Systems). One of the main differences between the two systems is that the audio data stream for Dolby Surround is stored on the film-strip itself (between the sprocket holes) whereas the audio data for DTS is stored on a separate laser disc. The audio encoding algorithms for both methods involve data compression techniques and both sys-

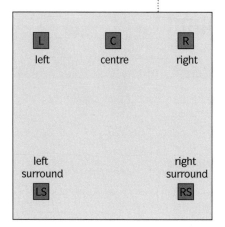

Figure 17.1
3/2 system for surround sound

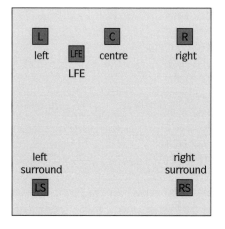

Figure 17.2
5.1 channel surround sound

tems are already available on many DVDs and music CDs. Both use the same kind of multiple channel sound formats in order to be compatible with the current hardware installed in cinema auditoriums.

The popular 5.1 channel surround configuration is a special implementation of the standard surround setup known as 3/2. The standard 3/2 configuration forms the essential reference system for surround sound. It features a left, centre and right channel in front of the listener and left surround and right surround channels to the rear (Figure 17.1).

Figure 17.1 shows the five speakers of a basic surround setup. '3/2' simply means three channels to the front and two to the rear. The front centre channel has its origins in the film industry where it is used for dialogue. 5.1 channel surround adds an additional specialised channel to the basic 3/2 system known as the LFE channel (Low Frequency Effects channel). This is the '.1' in the '5.1' name (Figure 17.2). There are many derivations of this in other surround configurations like 3/2/1, 5/2/1, 6.1 and 7.1. In all these cases, the '1' refers to an LFE channel. The other numbers refer to the number of full-band-width speakers featured in the surround system and, in the first two cases, how they are distributed between the front and rear parts of the listening space.

In the film industry, the LFE channel traditionally handles sub bass frequencies between 20Hz to around 80Hz. This is used for material which will not compromise the end result if the program is reproduced on a system which cannot handle the low frequencies or does not feature an LFE channel. In may ways, the LFE channel is intended as an optional effects channel and is not considered as an essential element which must be used in order to conform to the 5.1 (or similar) standard.

Once a surround mix has been created it has to be encoded to conform to the chosen surround format. This is achieved using special software and hardware (not included in Cubase). For example, to create media suitable for playback in 5.1 channel Dolby Digital format, the multiple audio files created by a surround mix must be converted into a data stream known as AC-3. At the time of playback, the AC-3 data is decoded into the intended playback format using multi-channel audio playback hardware featuring Dolby Digital decoding. In fact, the AC-3 data stream may be decoded for mono, stereo or 5.1 channel surround playback and so represents an adaptable format.

Common surround sound formats

The common surround formats include the following:

- Dolby Stereo (Dolby Surround) – Dolby Stereo is a four channel surround format developed in the 1970s for the film industry featuring left, centre, right and monophonic surround channel (of limited bandwidth). This is sometimes referred to as LCRS. In the early days of home theatre, it was possible to decode the left, right and surround channel information using early Dolby Surround decoders.

- Dolby Pro Logic – early 'home-theatre' Dolby Surround decoders could not derive a centre channel. The introduction of the Dolby Pro Logic format allowed the decoding of the centre channel and helped create a sound quality equivalent to cinema auditoriums in the home theatre environment. Dolby Pro Logic II improved matters further since it was capable of producing five channel surround (left, centre, right, left surround, right surround) from Dolby Surround encoded material, and also enhanced surround reproduction from any other un-encoded stereo signal. The surround channels for Pro Logic II featured full bandwidth reproduction.

- 5.1 channel digital surround – a digital surround format featuring five discrete full bandwidth channels and one limited bandwidth low frequency effects (LFE) channel. These are arranged as left, centre, right, in front of the listener and left surround, right surround to the rear. Traditionally the low frequency effects channel is located between the left and centre channels in front of the listener (see Figure 17.2). 5.1 channel digital surround sound is implemented by two organisations, Dolby Laboratories and DTS (Digital Theatre Systems).

- Dolby Digital 5.1 – the Dolby implementation of 5.1 channel surround sound. This involves conversion of the six discrete audio channels into a digital data stream known as AC-3. The AC-3 data stream is later decoded using proprietary Dolby decoding equipment. Dolby Digital is the most popular surround format for DVD (Digital Versatile Disc).

- DTS – a similar 5.1 surround system to Dolby Digital. In the film industry, the DTS audio data stream is stored on a separate laser disc whereas the Dolby audio data stream is stored on the film-strip itself. When used on DVD the DTS digital data stream is recorded on the medium itself. The DTS system uses slightly less compression and some experts claim that it has a superior sound quality.

- 6.1 channel digital surround – a surround format similar to Dolby Digital 5.1 but with an additional centre surround channel to the rear. 6.1 formats include Dolby Digital EX and DTS ES.

- 7.1 channel digital surround – a surround format similar to Dolby Digital 5.1 but with additional left and right side speakers or, in the case of the proprietary SDDS 7.1 format (Sony Digital Dynamic Sound), left centre and right centre front channels to handle wide screen cinema.

Setting up the surround features in Cubase

General Setup

For full surround reproduction the Cubase user needs audio hardware connected to the host computer which is capable of producing the number of audio outputs required for the chosen surround format. For example, standard 3/2 would require five audio outputs and 5.1 channel surround would require six. Of course, the sound reproduction system would also need to feature multiple speakers and amplifiers to match the number of channels of the chosen format.

Figure 17.3
The Add output bus dialogue allows you
to add an output bus in your chosen
surround format

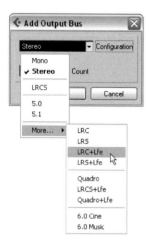

Creating a surround output bus

You configure the output of Cubase for surround sound by creating a surround output bus in the outputs section of the VST Connections window,
selected from the Devices menu. Proceed as follows:

- Open the VST Connections window and click on the outputs tab.
- Click on the Add button to open the Add bus dialogue. The choice of
  formats provided in the Configuration menu includes mono, stereo,
  LRCS, standard 3/2 (5.0), 5.1 surround and various other
  left/right/centre/surround/LFE permutations and quadraphonic (Quadro)
  formats (Figure 17.3). Most of these are described above. Quadro allows
  the setting up of mixes based upon the four channel quadraphonic
  format devised for vinyl records in the early 1970s.
- Select a surround format from the Configuration menu. Since it is such a
  popular format many readers may choose the 5.1 surround format. Once
  chosen, the details of the new surround bus are displayed in the VST
  Connections window (Figure 17.4). Make sure that the channels are
  routed to the appropriate output ports of your audio hardware.
- When you create a new surround bus, a surround output channel strip is
  added in the Mixer (Figure 17.5). The meters follow the order of the
  channels as listed in the VST Connections window (from left to right).

Figure 17.4 (right)
5.1 surround bus in the VST Connections
window

Figure 17.5 (below)
5.1 surround output bus channel in the
Mixer

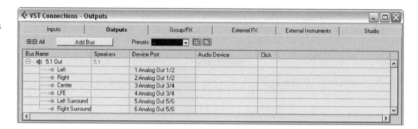

At this point, any audio-based channels routed to the surround bus may be
mixed in surround, using the surround panner. The surround panner is available only when a surround bus is chosen in the output routing menu.

Using surround channels

Regular audio tracks are normally in mono or stereo format but when they
are added to the Project they can also be assigned as surround channels in
the Add track dialogue. A surround channel is appropriate for playback of
multichannel interleaved files. Libraries of 5.1 surround files of this type are
commonly available or you can create your own.

Surround format channels are also applicable to software samplers which
include 5.1 surround support, such as Steinberg's Halion or Native
Instruments' Kontakt. In the case of Kontakt, a number of its outputs may be
configured in Cubase for 5.1 use. These appear in the Mixer in the normal
way as VSTi channels, and may be mixed to 5.1 as desired. Kontakt is supplied with a range of surround presets in its library (see Figure 17.6).

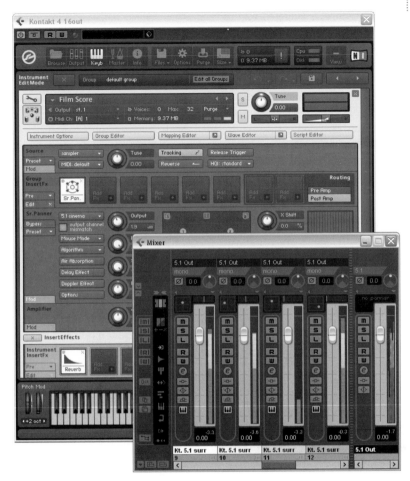

Figure 17.6
Native Instruments Kontakt sampler configured for surround sound in Cubase

Figure 17.7 (below)
Select the surround output bus in the Mixer channel output routing pop-up menu

Mixing surround sound

To mix in surround sound you need to route all channels in the Mixer to the surround output bus. This is selected in the output routing pop-up menu in the upper section of the channel strip (Figure 17.7).

Alternatively, you can route a channel signal directly to any of the surround outputs using the other routing options in the menu. When a surround output is chosen for regular audio-based channels, a miniature surround panner replaces the normal pan control in the Mixer channel strip. This allows you to graphically place the sound within the surround soundfield. The current position is indicated by a blue marker. You can move the position of the marker by dragging it within the display. A slightly larger version of the surround panner is available in the extended part of the Mixer (Figure 17.8).

Using the surround panner plug-in

For more elaborate control of the surround pan position, double click on the surround panner control in the channel strip. This opens the more detailed surround panner interface (Figure 17.9). The surround panner interface displays a representation of the speaker configuration for the chosen surround format. The level

Figure 17.8
The SurroundPan controls in the Mixer channel strip

Figure 17.8
The SurroundPan controls in the Mixer channel strip

Figure 17.9
The surround panner interface

of each channel is indicated next to each virtual speaker where 0dB represents the full power of the source audio signal. The level is also indicated graphically by thick blue lines which appear at each virtual speaker. The relative levels of the channels are controlled by dragging a ball within the display, at which time the blue lines change length and the indicated levels are modified accordingly. Any of the channels can be switched off by Alt-clicking on the speaker icon. Modifier keys facilitate the moving of the ball as follows:

- Hold Ctrl / Command + Shift while dragging in the display to restrict movement to the x axis (horizontal) only.
- Hold Ctrl / Command while dragging in the display to restrict movement to the y axis (vertical) only.
- Hold Alt while dragging in the display to restrict movement to the diagonal between the top left and lower right corners.
- Hold Ctrl / Command + Alt while dragging in the display to restrict movement to the diagonal between the lower left and top right corners.

The lower part of the interface features the following:

- Mode menu – this governs the manner in which the speakers are distributed around the listening position. Standard and Position modes produce aligned front speakers as found in a cinema auditorium and Angle mode implements speakers which are equi-distant from the listening position. The default setting is Standard mode.
- Mono / stereo pop-up – determines the manner in which the single mono marker or dual stereo markers move around the display. This is particularly relevant for stereo signals where the movement of the right channel marker is mirrored on the x axis or the y axis, or both simultaneously. 'Mono Mix' is the default setting for mono channels and 'Y-Mirror' is the default for stereo channels. The left and right channels of a stereo signal routed through a surround panner set to Mono Mix are added together before entering the plug-in. A mono signal routed through a surround panner set to a stereo mode is split into two channels before entering the plug-in.
- Centre level dial – determines the percentage by which the centre channel provides the centre image where 100% results in full use of the centre channel, (in which case the left and right front channels are reduced in level when the marker is in the central vertical area), and 0% results in zero use of the centre channel, (in which case the left and right front channels are raised in level when the marker is in the central vertical area). When the centre channel has been reduced to 0% the left / right front channels behave like a regular stereo setup where the centre sound is produced by the in-phase signals of the left and right source signals.
- LFE dial – determines the amount of the source signal which should be routed to the LFE channel. This is relevant only when the surround configuration includes an LFE channel (as in 5.1 surround).
- Divergence dials – control the differentiation of the distribution of the source signal between the different channels where levels higher than 0% result in a less exclusive distribution. i.e. the higher the percentage on the dial the less differentiation between the corresponding channels.

VST Instruments

This chapter outlines the installation and basic use of VST Instruments within Cubase and describes some of the VST Instruments supplied with the program.

What are VST Instruments?

VST is an abbreviation for 'Virtual Studio Technology' or 'Virtual Studio' and was introduced by Steinberg in 1996 for their Cubase VST sequencer. VST Instrument is an abbreviation for 'Virtual Studio Instrument' and the term is often shortened still further to read 'VSTi'. VST compatible audio effects and processing units come in the form of plug-ins which can be added to the host software when required. VST 2.0 technology took this concept one stage further by introducing a special kind of plug-in which allowed the transmitting and receiving of MIDI data as well as audio. This encouraged the development of more sophisticated regular plug-ins but, more importantly, inspired the development of software synthesis and sampling instruments which can operate within the convenient environment of the host software. These became known as VST Instruments.

A VST Instrument could be a software synthesizer or sampler, a software drum module or some other virtual sound-making device and, once activated inside the host software, it can be played via MIDI using an external MIDI keyboard or triggered from an existing MIDI or Instrument track. In many respects, VST Instruments behave in the same way as their real-world counterparts, the only major difference being that they reside within the RAM memory of your computer.

Installing VST Instruments

A good range of VST Instruments are automatically installed when you first install Cubase. There are also a wide range of VST Instruments available from third party developers. These must be installed separately following the supplied installation instructions. Cubase should already be running successfully on the computer before you install the VST Instrument. You can normally choose to install into the Cubase VstPlugins folder or into the shared VstPlugins folder. When you next launch Cubase, the newly installed VST Instrument is added to the list of available instruments within the software. To find out what is currently installed, select Devices / Plug-in Information.

Activating VST Instruments

A VST Instrument is activated by selecting it in the Add dialogue when you add an Instrument track, or it is activated in the VST Instruments panel.

Adding an Instrument track

To add an Instrument track select Project / Add track / Instrument. In the Add dialogue select the VST Instrument in the instrument menu (Figure 18.1). An Instrument track provides one MIDI input and one stereo audio output, linking a MIDI-based track in the Project window to the chosen VST Instrument. You can now use this track to play the VST Instrument via MIDI in the normal manner. VST Instruments activated in this way always feature a single stereo audio output.

Figure 18.1
Selecting a VST Instrument in the Instrument track Add dialogue

Figure 18.2 (right)
VST Instruments panel

Activating in the VST Instruments panel

To open the VST Instruments panel select Devices / VST Instruments (Figure 18.2). To activate an instrument in the VST Instrument panel click on a panel slot and make a selection from the pop-up menu (Figure 18.3). VST Instruments activated here are triggered via conventional MIDI tracks and when first activated you may be asked if you wish to create a MIDI track assigned to the instrument, (depending upon the settings in Preferences / VST / Plug-ins). By default, a single stereo output is activated for the instrument but, for those instruments with multiple outputs, you can activate any combination of outputs in the output routing menu. A corresponding number of VST Instrument channels are created in the Mixer to regulate the volume, pan position, EQ and routing of the audio outputs from the instrument.

Figure 18.3
Click on a VST Instrument panel slot to open the pop-up selection menu

To open the GUI for the VST Instrument click on the edit button (lower case 'e') in the VST Instrument slot (Figure 18.4). The GUI may open automatically when you first activate the instrument (depending upon your settings in Preferences / VST / Plug-ins).

In order to play the VST Instrument, assign the output port of a MIDI track to the instrument, if not already assigned when you first activated it (Figure 18.5). With the record or monitor buttons of the MIDI track enabled, you can now play the VST Instrument live from a MIDI keyboard, or record and play back your performance as desired.

Figure 18.4
Click on the Edit button to open the interface for the VSTi

Figure 18.5
Assign a MIDI track to a VST Instrument in the output routing menu

VST Instrument automation

Automation of VST Instrument parameters is achieved by activating the Write button in the GUI window of the instrument and recording the movements of the controls in real-time (Figure 18.6). The automation is written in normal playback mode; activating the record button on the Transport panel is not necessary. To play back the automation, activate the Read button in the GUI window of the VST Instrument.

Figure 18.6
To record the movements of the controls, activate the Write button in the GUI window of the VST Instrument

Alternatively, you can manually draw automation curves in the VST Instrument automation sub-tracks in the Project window. When you first activate a VST Instrument, one or more VSTi tracks and a VSTi device track appear in the Project window. The VSTi tracks and associated sub-tracks handle regular automation like volume, pan, EQ and so on, while the VSTi device track and associated sub-tracks handle automation specific to the VST Instrument. The sub-tracks may be used to edit any automation already recorded or to create automation data from scratch using the draw tools (Figure 18.7).

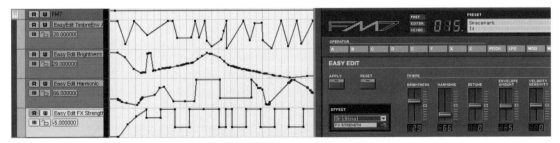

VST Instrument automation is convenient for producing filter sweeps and sound effects and can add an extra dimension to synthesizer parts. For example, try using the draw tools to create shapes which modulate the filter cut-

Figure 18.7
Create or edit VST Instrument automation in the automation sub-tracks in the Project window

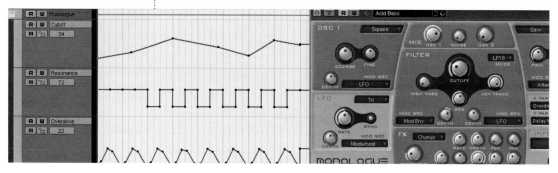

Figure 18.8
Modulating the cut-off, resonance and drive controls of the supplied Monologue synth using automation curves

off, resonance and drive controls of the supplied Monologue synthesizer (Figure 18.8).

System requirements and performance issues

VST Instruments require a VST 2.0 (or later) host application like Steinberg Cubase and most run on both the PC and Mac computer platforms. There are a number of computer hardware factors which affect the performance and playability of a VST Instrument. Paramount among these are CPU speed, the amount of RAM memory and audio hardware latency.

Software synthesis, software sampling and software effects processing are CPU-intensive activities. The number of voices available for any software instrument is, therefore, directly related to the amount of CPU power available. The drain on CPU power varies according to the number of notes being played simultaneously and according to the complexity of the tone being produced by the instrument. Many software samplers and sample-based drum machines require substantial amounts of RAM in order to run smoothly.

Latency

Latency is the delay between the input and output of a digital audio system (expressed in samples or milliseconds). All digital audio systems take a small amount of time to respond to a user input and process the data through their hardware and software. This affects real-time performance with VST Instruments since it imposes a slight delay between the moment you press a note on your MIDI keyboard and the moment you hear the sound from the instrument. If the delay is too long then it becomes impossible to play in real-time. (Real-world electronic musical instruments also suffer from a similar delay). For real-time performance, the audio hardware should preferably be capable of latency times of less than 10ms. Achieving this requires a good quality audio card / hardware with a high performance ASIO driver. (See relevant internet sites and software / hardware developer documentation for precise details of ASIO drivers and hardware system recommendations).

Info

Most performance based problems with VST Instruments are likely to be related to any combination of your computer's CPU power, RAM memory, audio hardware driver, chosen buffer size and A/D and D/A converters. To ensure the best performance, high speed CPUs, large amounts of RAM, and professional audio cards / hardware with dedicated ASIO drivers are highly recommended.

Maximising system resources

If you run out of CPU power or RAM due to a large number of VST Instruments within the same project there are two methods by which you can free up some system resources: 1) convert the VST Instruments audio output into regular audio files or 2) freeze the VST Instruments.

Converting VST Instrument audio output into regular audio files

The audio from Instrument tracks and VST Instrument channels can be directly converted into audio files for use on regular audio tracks using Export / Audio Mixdown (File menu). This allows export of all non-muted Instrument track and VST Instrument channel audio output between the left and right locators to one or more audio files. Use channel batch export mode for multiple channel export to separate files. To preserve audio quality select 32-bit float for the bit depth.

Instrument Freeze

An alternative to the above technique is to use the freeze buttons available in the VST Instrument panel or in the Inspector for Instrument tracks. These allow you to freeze the performance of a VST Instrument so that playback takes place from a ghost audio track rather than being calculated in real-time. To freeze an instrument, proceed as follows:

- Make sure that the VST Instrument performance plays back exactly as required, including automation if any has been recorded.
- Open the VST Instruments panel from the Devices menu (press F11 on the computer keyboard) or select an Instrument track.
- Click on the freeze button (Figure 18.9).

Figure 18.9
Freezing a VST Instrument

- In the Freeze instrument options dialogue which appears, you can choose to freeze the instrument only, in which case any pre-fader insert effects on the VST Instrument channels are not frozen with the instrument, or you can choose to freeze both the instrument and all pre-fader insert effects. Tail size allows you to set a tail time for any echo or reverberation effects. 'Unload instrument when frozen' helps free up still more computer resources by unloading the VST Instrument after the freeze operation. This is welcome for RAM-hungry software samplers.

The resulting ghost audio file is stored in a new freeze folder, located in the project folder. All Instrument tracks, MIDI tracks, VST Instrument device tracks and events relevant to the frozen instrument are now greyed out and cannot be edited. However, the audio output still remains active on the relevant channels as if you are still triggering the VST Instrument in the normal way. Frozen VST Instruments can at any time be un-frozen by clicking on the corresponding Freeze button a second time.

Exploring the supplied VST Instruments

There now follow descriptions of a selection of the VST Instruments supplied with the program.

Prologue

Prologue (Figure 18.10) is a virtual analogue synthesizer featuring three oscillators, eight filter types, four ADSR envelope generators, LFO modulation, frequency modulation, ring modulation and built-in effects.

To start tweaking the parameters of Prologue, you might like to begin with a suitable basic preset like 'Brett Bass'. This uses all three oscillators, each with sawtooth selected as the source waveform. Movement is provided by detuning oscillators 2 and 3 and character is injected by using moderate amounts of drive, soft distortion and chorus effects. This preset includes classic filter settings with the cutoff at around 8k and a small amount of resonance. The cutoff frequency is modulated by the LFO set to a slow 0.346. This produces the slow sweeping effect you can hear during the sustain part of the sound.

Let's try editing the Brett Bass preset to hear some of the sonic possibilities of Prologue. For example, try reducing all oscillator levels to zero and set the ring modulator control to its maximum level. This is the classic setting for ring modulation. Set the waveform of oscillator 2 to one of the vocal vowel sources (A, E, I, O or U). Audition the sound to hear how the tone acquires

Figure 18.10
The Prologue synthesizer

the voice-like characteristics of the chosen oscillator 2 waveform. Ring modulation multiplies the frequencies of oscillators 1 and 2 to produce their sum and difference frequencies. Ring modulation is commonly used to produce metallic and bell-like tones.

Now reset Prologue to the original Brett Bass preset. In the oscillator 2 section, select the sine waveform, activate frequency modulation, set fine tune to 1.0050 and ratio to 11. Reduce the drive control to zero and the filter cut-off frequency to around 5k. De-activate distortion in the EFX section and reduce the cut-off modulation depth to zero in the LFO section. Audition the sound to hear how it has been transformed into an organ-like tone.

Do not forget to try the pitchbend range and maximum number of voices parameters in the upper left and right corners, and the portamento and legato controls to the left. Prologue also features a wide range of source waveforms including standard sawtooth, parabolic, square, triangle and sine waves along with over fifty variations in formant, vocal, partial, resonant pulse, slope and negative slope categories. The four envelope generators, two LFOs, external modulation, velocity, aftertouch and key pitch tracking may be assigned to a large number of destinations. All this, together with the the distortion, delay and modulation effects, adds up to an analogue-style synthesizer of great flexibility and potential.

Prologue is supplied with over 200 presets which are well stocked with synth bass, lead and pad sounds.

Monologue

Monologue (Figure 18.11) is a monophonic virtual analogue synthesizer featuring two oscillators, a filter with six filter types, modulation and amplitude ADSR envelopes, LFO and effects.

Figure 18.11
Try setting Monologue to these simple settings as a starting point for programming your own sounds

To get to know the possibilities try the following simple exercise:

- Select square waves for oscillators 1 and 2 and set all their controls to zero and their mix levels to 0dB. Set the noise control to off. Set the modulation sources of oscillators 1 and 2 to LFO and mod wheel respectively.
- In the filter section, select LP12 mode and set the cutoff to 74 and resonance to 31. Set the high pass and key track controls to zero. Set the left modulation source to 'mod env' and set the depth to -60%.
- In the LFO section, set the source wave to triangle, the rate to 10.98Hz, the depth to 100% and the modulation source to mod wheel.
- In the FX section, set the overdrive and effects mix controls to zero.
- Set the mod envelope ADSR to 48, 53, 0, 0 and the amp envelope ADSR to 0, 46, 0, 0.
- Finally, set pitch bend to 2 and random pitch to 6.3. Your patch should now look the same as Figure 18.11

Auditioning this patch reveals a short, simple sound. We have stripped down the sonic possibilities to the bare essentials. We can now clearly hear the effect of any further parameter changes. In all of the following experiments, audition the sound while manipulating the controls. Start by increasing the PWM control of oscillator 2. Try also increasing the modulation depth and experimenting with the effect using the modulation wheel of your keyboard. The sound is immediately richer and more interesting. Next, try changing the left filter modulation depth control. This transforms the sound between resonant and bright characteristics. Now try adding some overdrive, chorus or delay to inject more life into the sound. When you have found something which sounds promising, try adjusting the filter cutoff and resonance simultaneously by moving the handle in the x-y controller. Carefully tune the mod envelope attack to give more bite to the start of the sound and increase the decay and release of the amp envelope to give more body and duration. Finally, try increasing the oscillator 1 modulation depth to hear the effect of the LFO as you move the modulation wheel of your keyboard. If you discover an inspiring patch, don't forget to save it.

Monologue is designed specifically for creating monophonic bass, lead and sequenced synth tones. Take a listen to the supplied presets for further examples and ideas.

HalionOne

HalionOne (Figure 18.12) is a sample player specialised in the playback of the supplied HSB (Halion Sound Bank) format samples.

HalionOne features a comparatively simple GUI showing the name of the currently loaded preset and eight control parameters. The controls vary according to the type of preset selected but, for most sounds, include cutoff, resonance, DCA envelope, DCF filter; and reverb, delay, chorus or flange parameters. If desired, you can bypass the on-board effects by clicking on the effects LED. More uncommon parameters are included where appropriate, such as the glide control in the 'Touch of Teebee' preset or the talkbox con-

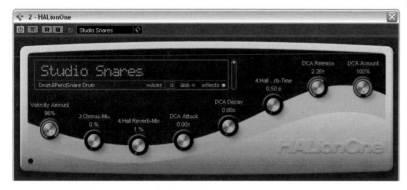

Figure 18.12
HalionOne sample player

trol in the 'Talking Lead' preset. An efficiency mini-fader allows you to lessen the CPU load for processor-hungry presets. This might be required for a pre-set like 'Atmosphere', which quickly drains computer resources by allocating six voices to each note played. Lowering efficiency reduces the audio quali-ty, but all bounces and exports to audio remain at maximum resolution.

The strength of HalionOne lies in the range and quality of its presets. Over 600 HalionOne presets are supplied with Cubase and these include good selections in all the usual categories of bass, brass, drums and percussion, plucked, organ, piano, sound effects, strings, synth leads and pads.

Groove Agent ONE

Groove Agent ONE (Figure 18.13) is a virtual drum machine inspired by the renowned Akai MPC hardware units. The GUI is dominated by 16 virtual drum trigger pads which can be switched between any of eight banks giving a total of 128 pads. The name of the assigned MIDI note and sample is shown for each pad. A pad bank is recalled using the numbered buttons above the pad display. When there are samples present within a bank its cor-responding numbered button is highlighted in red. You can trigger sounds via MIDI or by clicking on a pad. The higher up the pad you click the greater

Figure 18.13
Groove Agent ONE

Tip

To mute a pad, hold Shift and click on it.

the velocity of the triggered event. Triggering a sound highlights the corresponding pad and selects the instrument for editing in the virtual LCD display to the left of the pads. This shows information about the instrument and allows you to edit various pad parameters using the rotary dials and pad edit buttons. For example, you can allocate a pad to any one of 16 stereo output channels. Multi-channel operation allows you to apply EQ and effects separately to each sound which helps create a better mix.

Sample management and editing

To create your own Groove Agent ONE setup, you can drag and drop any audio sample from the Media Bay, Project window, Sample editor or Audio Part editor onto a free pad. You can also drag multiple samples onto a single pad (up to eight) to create layers or by pressing Shift while dragging you can distribute the samples among multiple pads. Pad names and MIDI note assignments may be modified by right-clicking on the names or notes. Samples may be dragged from one pad to another empty pad or if there is already a sample present on the target pad the samples are exchanged. A global reset button in the top right corner allows you to clear all current pad assignments from Groove Agent ONE. For safety purposes, the reset button is always locked. Hold Shift while clicking on it to unlock it for a few seconds in order to conduct a reset. Caution! This function definitively clears all sample data from Groove Agent ONE!

It is best to precisely edit the starts, ends and lengths of samples in the Sample editor or in an external audio editor before dragging onto the pads since you cannot edit these elements once inside Groove Agent ONE and you cannot later drag the samples from the pads to other parts of the program. However, you can edit a wide range of performance based parameters and apply filtering with which you can radically alter the playback characteristics of your own samples or of the supplied presets. When editing it is best to use a MIDI keyboard to trigger the sounds and the mouse or other controller to tweak the parameters. For this configuration activate the MIDI input icon at the top right of the edit window. Adjust the tuning using the coarse and fine controls in the Voice section. Here you can also modify the trigger mode between one shot and key hold, establish mute groups for elements such as closed and open hi-hats and set up the output routing. A filter section provides low pass, high pass and band pass filters. Check out the 'Tribal House Kit' to hear how high pass filters have been used to give a sharp edge to the samples. Finally, the Amplifier section allows you to modify the volume, panning, envelope and velocity sensitivity.

Saving and loading presets

When you have created your own setup in Groove Agent ONE you can save it as a VST Sound preset in the normal way using the Save preset function. A wide range of presets is supplied with the program encompassing many different musical styles. These are recalled using the VST Sound Load presets function.

Alternatively, you can use the import button to import the mapping data from Akai MPC exchange format files (.pgm file extension). Note that this imports the mapping data only.

Recalling as a track preset

Groove Agent ONE marries well with the Beat Designer MIDI plug-in where Beat Designer provides a sequencing front-end for creating patterns and triggering the samples. A Beat Designer pattern and associated Groove Agent ONE setup on an Instrument track may be saved together as a pattern bank preset. Total recall of the pattern and associated Groove Agent ONE sounds is achieved by adding an Instrument track from a pattern bank preset which was saved in this manner. To do this more easily, browse and audition the pattern bank presets in the Media Bay. When you find a suitable preset, double-click on it to automatically create an Instrument track.

Combining Groove Agent ONE with audio slicing

Using drag and drop techniques, the audio slices from a sliced audio part may be mapped onto separate pads in Groove Agent ONE and a corresponding MIDI part which matches the original groove may be created in the Project window. To achieve this, proceed as follows:

- Select a suitable audio loop and open it in the Sample editor.
- Select the hitpoints tab and click on the Slice and Close button (see Chapter 8 for more details about audio slicing). A sliced audio part is created in the Project window.
- Activate Groove Agent ONE in the VST Instruments panel (Devices / VST Instruments) and ensure the GUI is visible on screen.
- Drag and drop the sliced audio part to an empty pad in Groove Agent ONE (Figure 18.14). The slices are automatically assigned to multiple pads and the Exchange section MIDI export pad (double arrow) is highlighted.
- Drag from the MIDI export pad to a MIDI track in the Project window. A MIDI part is created containing the notes to trigger the samples in Groove Agent ONE and corresponding with the original groove of the audio slices (Figure 18.15).

Now that you have the correct trigger notes within a MIDI part with the groove accurately captured it is possible to edit the MIDI data in various ways to reconstruct a new loop. For example, you can reverse, mute, delete or add notes, apply quantize, split and re-order the MIDI event or subject the data to Logical Editor operations. Try the Logical Editor settings in Figure 18.16. This retains the original loop data on the main beats but changes the other pitches randomly between C1/36 and C3/60. It also makes minor changes to the velocity and may be used repeatedly until you find a loop you like. You may need to adjust the settings to suit the pitch range of your own loop. Try combining

Info

For more information about using Groove Agent ONE with Beat Designer see Chapter 15.

Tip

If you program a drum loop (or similar) within a MIDI part on an Instrument track, you may like to save this as a MIDI Loop by selecting the part and using File / Export / MIDI Loop. MIDI Loops contain all MIDI data and the Instrument track / VST instrument settings. They are helpful for exchanging loops between different projects.

Figure 8.14
Assign the audio slices to multiple pads in Groove Agent ONE using drag and drop

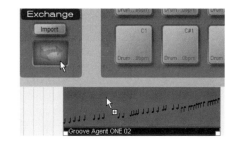

Figure 18.15
Drag from the MIDI export pad to the event display in the Project window to create a MIDI part for the audio slices

Figure 18.16
The Logical editor can help you create a
new loop from audio slices

this with quantizing. To modify the loop still further try replacing the samples by dragging new audio to the pads in Groove Agent ONE. You may be surprised how quickly you can create a new loop.

Info

Using the basic technique described here, Groove Agent One may be used as a drum replacement tool. For this purpose it is easier to edit the exported MIDI part of the drum performance so that a single pitch triggers the kicks and a single pitch triggers the snares. This makes it easier to replace the kick and snare by dragging new samples onto just the two relevant pads.

LoopMash

LoopMash (Figure 18.17) is a loop reconstruction tool for combining, modifying and remixing audio files based upon their tempo, rhythmic components and spectral content. One of the loaded audio files is designated as the master and the essential rhythmic groove which drives LoopMash is taken from this. Various slices of the other files replace the audio of the master based upon how similar they are to it and how the parameters are set up within the interface. In essence, you feed a combination of audio files into the input and you get a new audio loop at the output!

The GUI comprises eight tracks upon which you can place your chosen audio files. Files can be dragged directly onto the interface from the Project window, Media Bay or Sample editor. When a file is first imported it is analysed and the audio is divided into 1/8 note slices. These slices are indicated on the horizontal axis of the interface which allows a total of 4 bars. Only the first four bars are used for audio files which are greater than this length. To the left of the tracks there are similarity sliders which control playback behaviour. Below the tracks there are twelve pads. On each of these you can store an eight track configuration and all associated parameter settings (known as a 'scene'). Alternatively, in edit mode the lower section displays a number of global editing parameters.

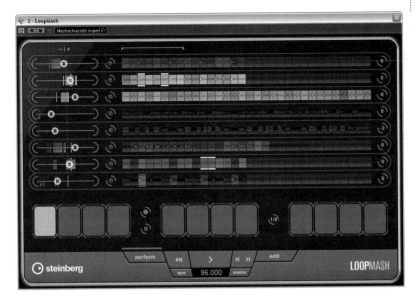

Figure 18.17
Deleting doubled notes

> **Tip**
>
> While experimenting with LoopMash is is easy to stumble across a great sounding loop. It is also easy to lose the best settings when you fine tune the loop, so it pays to save your work as a preset at regular intervals.

Exploring the controls

The results you hear from LoopMash are dominated by two elements: 1) the track you choose as the master and 2) the settings of the similarity sliders to the left of the tracks. The master track, chosen by clicking on the master button for a track, dictates the essential rhythmic characteristics of the output. The similarity sliders govern which tracks are more likely to have their slices used. The more you move a similarity slider to the right the more slices from the corresponding track are selected for playback. Tracks with higher playback priority are displayed more brightly.

The master track also dictates the position of the similarity threshold, a thin vertical thin line in the similarity slider display. When LoopMash playback is active a number of vertical lines 'dance' within each slider. These lines indicate the degree of similarity of the slices on the track to those of the current playback slice on the master track. The higher the lines dance the more likely they will be chosen for playback. Tracks whose lines dance higher than the similarity threshold set by the master track are far more likely to be chosen (Figure 18.18).

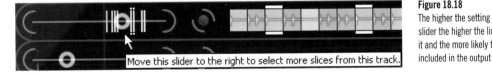

Move this slider to the right to select more slices from this track.

Figure 18.18
The higher the setting of the similarity slider the higher the lines dance around it and the more likely the slices are to be included in the output

Other important controls include the transpose parameters to the right of each track allowing real-time transposition between -12 and +12 semitones and the loop length slider above the track display which helps select the best passage for looping. The parameters in the edit section also have a significant impact upon the results, particularly the Number of Voices and Slice Selection Offset settings (Figure 18.19). Number of Voices sets the global polyphony of LoopMash between one and four voices thus restricting the

Figure 18.19
The edit section of LoopMash

number of slices which can be played simultaneously. Slice Selection Offset selects progressively more dissimilar slices the higher you set it thus deflecting emphasis away from the master track towards more variation and abstract results. Also provided in the edit section are: Voices per Track which sets the number of voices for each track and gives more variety in the output when set to low values; a random value for randomising the selection of slices; a slice quantize parameter which progressively quantizes slices to the 1/8 note grid rather than the master track the more you move it to the right; a staccato control which progressively shortens the durations of the slices the more you move it to the right; a slice timestretch option which applies real-time stretching to the slices to compensate for gaps and irregularities; and finally a dry / wet mix slider which governs the mix between the original audio of the master loop and the output of LoopMash.

The current settings may be saved as a scene by selecting the orange save button and clicking on a pad. A pad can be cleared by selecting the orange cross and clicking on a pad. (Caution: saving scenes and clearing pad memories cannot be undone).

Tip

Even a very small change in the position of one of the sliders in LoopMash can have a significant impact upon the audio output. Delicate manipulation of the controls in small steps rather than broad strokes may therefore help find just the right combination of settings.

Info

You can record scene changes within a project by recording MIDI notes onto a track or by recording automation.

Exploring the performance possibilities

When the sync button is activated playback from LoopMash is synchronised to the current project tempo and when the sync button is de-activated it is synchronised to its own local tempo. To slave playback to the project transport panel you must activate the sync button and the local play button of LoopMash. You can jump between scenes manually on the fly by clicking on the pads or you can trigger scene changes via MIDI where notes C1 / 36 to B1 / 47 correspond with the twelve pads, C2 / 48 and D2 / 50 start and stop playback, and E2 / 52 and F2 / 53 activate and de-activate sync. Jump behaviour is governed by the Jump Interval setting. For example, when this is set to '1: Next bar' scene changes always wait until the end of the current bar before taking place. To manually step through each 1/8 note segment in the loop click on the step buttons to the right of the play button. This is helpful for analysing exactly which audio slices are being triggered at each step. To audition individual slices click on the slice in the track display.

Exploring the presets

LoopMash is supplied with a range of presets which are loaded in the normal manner from the VST Sound Load Preset menu. Exploring the presets by tweaking the controls and listening to the results helps get to know the effect of each parameter. Try loading the preset entitled 'Don't Stop the Mash 89' and proceed as follows:

- After loading the preset, select the Perform button to show the pad display. Select the first pad on the left (pad scene 1), de-select sync and press the play button. LoopMash commences playback.
- This scene features the master track only on track 1 which is a two bar drum loop. Moving the similarity slider for the track makes no difference at this stage since there are no suitable active alternatives for the slices. Thus, what you hear is sequential playback of the slices which matches the original loop.
- While still in playback select the edit view and note that all the parameters for this scene are set to their default values. The number of voices for LoopMash has been set to one voice only.
- Set the jump interval to 1 (located between pads eight and nine). This means that jumping between scenes will always wait for the end of a whole bar. Select scene 2. The scene flashes while waiting for the end of the current bar. When scene 2 becomes active you can hear that a bass is added on track 2.
- Select the edit view again and note that number of voices for LoopMash has now been set to two voices. Set it to one voice and listen to the result. With one voice polyphony the bass becomes dominant since its similarity slider has been set quite high. Put the number of voices back to two and check out the effect of raising the Slice Selection Offset to the second notch. The bass line becomes more interesting. You may also notice a tighter feel if you raise the Slice Quantize slider to maximum and the Staccato slider to around 25%.
- Go back to the perform view and select scene 3. A rhythm guitar is added and the polyphony has now been raised to three voices.
- Now try scene 4. This introduces more emphasis on the rhythm guitar by raising its similarity slider and cutting out the bass track. The Slice Selection Offset is increased to ensure some variation in the slice choice.
- Scene 5 changes the master track to track 4 which features a female vocal. As a variation, try reducing the master track 4 similarity slider to zero, raise track 1 to its maximum and track 2 to around 25%. In the edit view set the random slider to its maximum value. Notice how the master track still drives the rhythm even when its similarity slider is set to zero.
- Try exploring the other scenes in a similar way and check out the other available presets.

Tip

Try activating the eight outputs for LoopMash to give you eight channels in the Mixer. This allows you to manage track levels and add effects and EQ separately to achieve a better mix. In this configuration, de-activate the stereo output of LoopMash and route the eight mixer tracks via a group channel to retain control of the overall level.

Combining Cubase with applications from other developers

You can significantly increase the creative potential of Cubase by combining it with some of the more elaborate applications and VST Instruments supplied by other developers, especially those featuring modular synthesis environments and sampling. This is particularly relevant for those using Cubase for electronic music composition, orchestral composition and arranging, and sound effects creation. Favourites include Propellerhead Reason software synthesis studio, Native Instruments Reaktor sound studio, Native Instruments Kontakt software sampler and Applied Acoustics Systems Tassman physical modelling synthesizer. Reason is easily integrated into Cubase using the Rewire protocol, while the others may be integrated as standard VST Instruments. These applications provide much more than ordinary software musical instruments. They are often complete studio, synthesis, sampling, sequencing and sound processing environments in their own right.

Figure 18.20
Kontakt. Among the best software sampler choices for Cubase users

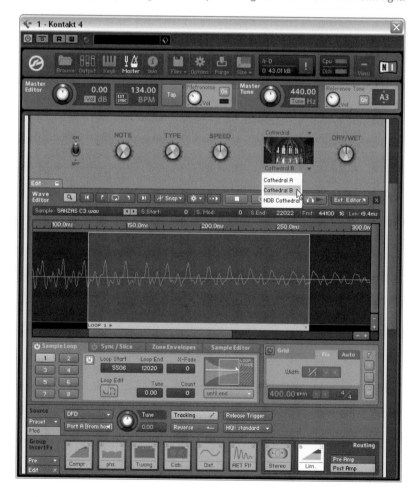

Reason provides analogue synthesizers, samplers, drum machines and effects together with sequencing, mixing and patching features, all within an intuitive virtual rack environment. Kontakt (Figure 18.20) is a powerful soft-

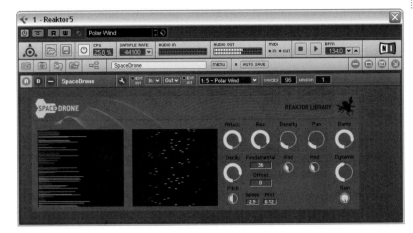

Figure 18.21
Reaktor's Space Drone synthesizer in
action in Cubase

ware sampler in an elegant and easy-to-use GUI, supplied complete with its own on-board convolution reverb and an outstanding library, the cornerstone of which is a special version of the Vienna Symphonic Orchestra sample collection. Tassman provides a modular environment where you can build your own musical instruments based upon physical modelling. This allows the creation of truly authentic acoustic instruments and unusual hybrid instruments. Reaktor is the ultimate modular sound studio, allowing you to build your own instruments and effects and providing a vast library of synthesizers, samplers, effects, drum machines and sequencers (Figure 18.21). All these applications integrate well into the Cubase software environment.

Summary

VST Instruments provide a convenient means of accessing high quality sound sources within the software environment of Cubase. All that is required to trigger the sounds is one external keyboard connected to your computer via MIDI and a low latency audio card. This arrangement helps avoid elaborate external MIDI networks with complex MIDI cabling issues, and saves physical space in your recording studio. In addition, VST Instruments do not develop electronic faults and are not subject to the usual wear and tear suffered by real-world instruments. Unlike MIDI tracks which trigger external MIDI devices, MIDI tracks which trigger VST Instruments can be converted directly into audio data.

There is an extremely wide range of VST Instruments supplied by different developers and representing a vast array of instrument types and synthesis techniques. One of the best internet resources for finding out what is available is the KVR Audio website at www.kvraudio.com.

Info

One of the best internet resources for finding out what is available is the KVR Audio website at www.kvraudio.com.

Tempo and time signatures

Tempo and time signatures are managed in the Tempo and Signature tracks in the Project window or in the Tempo Track editor. The advantage of using the tracks in the Project window is that you can see your tempo curve or time signatures lined up with the other events in the display which makes it easier to draw tempo curves and edit the events in context. The Tempo Track editor may be a better choice for detailed work since it offers more editing parameters.

Tempo control exists in two modes: Fixed tempo mode and Tempo track mode. These operate as follows:

- Fixed tempo mode – is when the tempo button in the Transport panel is de-activated. In this mode, the tempo follows the single fixed tempo shown in the Transport panel.
- Tempo track mode – is when the tempo button in the Transport panel is activated. In this mode, the tempo varies according to the tempo curve in the Tempo Track.

Time signature events are always active regardless of the tempo mode.

Tempo and Signature track details

The Tempo Track is for creating and editing tempo changes. In both the Tempo track in the project window and the Tempo track editor, tempo events are shown as small square handles along the length of a curve. The positions of these handles determine the shape of the curve which in turn governs the tempo when tempo track mode is activated. The shape of the curve is modified by dragging existing handles to new locations or drawing new events. The shape of the curve is also governed by the curve type selection where jump mode produces instantaneous tempo changes at each tempo event position, and ramp mode produces smooth, graduated curves between events. There can be only one Tempo track in each project but the tempo data may be created and edited in either the Tempo Track editor or in the Tempo track in the Project window.

In the project window, time signature events are displayed as small flags in the Signature track. In the Tempo track editor they are shown in the time signature strip below the ruler. All time signature settings are active in both fixed and tempo track modes.

Info

When the Tempo Track is active, all MIDI and audio tracks which are set to Musical Timebase follow the tempo changes in the Tempo Track. To follow the tempo successfully unmatched audio material must be in Musical mode or in the form of sliced audio parts.

The Tempo Track editor

The Tempo Track editor is opened by selecting Tempo Track from the Project menu, or by pressing Ctrl / Command + T on the computer keyboard (Figure 19.1). The editor is dominated by the tempo display area which shows tempo in beats-per-minute (bpm) on the vertical axis and time in the chosen time format on the horizontal axis.

Figure 19.1
The Tempo Track editor

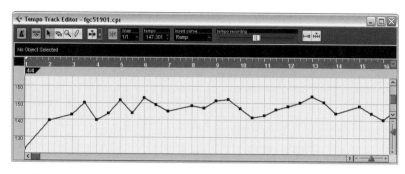

The Tempo Track editor toolbar

The Tempo Track editor toolbar features the following:

Figure 19.2
The Tempo Track editor toolbar

- Activate Tempo track button - to activate or de-activate the tempo track.
- Show info button - to show or hide the infoline.
- Object selection, Eraser, Zoom and Draw tools – the Object selection tool is for selecting events by clicking on individual events or dragging a selection box around several. Selected events are shown in red. Selections may be dragged to a new position, or edited on the infoline. The Eraser is used to delete unwanted events. The Zoom tool allows you to zoom in to the tempo curve for detailed editing. The Draw tool is used to draw a new tempo curve or add a new time signature.
- Autoscroll – when activated the display follows the position of the project cursor. When de-activated the display remains static.
- Snap button and snap menu – govern the snap resolution when inserting or moving events in the display. When the snap button is activated and bars and beats is chosen in the ruler, events are placed according to the resolution chosen in the snap menu. When the ruler shows other time formats events are placed according to the visible vertical grid lines. When snap is de-activated, events may be freely inserted or moved with no regard for bar or time positions.
- Tempo field – shows the current tempo.
- Insert Curve field - governs the curve type for newly inserted tempo events.
- Tempo recording slider – allows the recording of tempo events in playback mode. This is helpful for creating tempo ramps in real-time while listening to MIDI-based music.

- Process tempo button - opens the Process tempo dialogue where you can define a new duration or end time for the tempo events between the left and right locators. This is good for sound to picture projects where you may wish to match bar ranges or bar positions to specific time ranges and time code addresses.
- Process bars button - opens the Process bars dialogue where you can insert, delete or replace time between the left and right locators. This provides an alternative to the insert and delete time functions in the Edit / Range sub-menu and takes time signatures into consideration.

The Tempo and Signature tracks in the project window

The Tempo and Signature tracks may be shown in the project window event display using the Add track function in the Project menu (Figure 19.3). These appear in the track list in a similar manner to the other track types and offer the advantage of tempo and signature event alignment according to the positions of other events in the display.

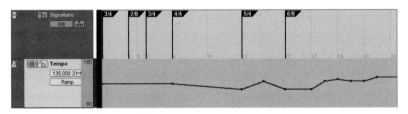

Figure 19.3
The Tempo and Signature tracks in the Project window event display

   To draw a new tempo curve, enter new time signatures and for general editing, use the Project window toolbox. The relevant tools include the object selection, range, eraser, zoom and pencil tools. These function in a similar manner to when editing other event types. Use the pencil tool, or press Alt and click with the object selection tool, to draw a new curve or enter a new time signature.

   To modify the vertical tempo range of the Tempo track, double-click on the lower or upper tempo limit in the track header and enter a new value using the computer keyboard. Here, you can also see the current tempo and adjust the curve type for newly inserted tempo events.

Editing tempo curves and time signatures

Creating a tempo curve

To create a test tempo curve in either the Tempo track editor or the Tempo track in the project window, proceed as follows:

- Activate tempo track mode in the Transport panel.
- Activate the Snap button and select 'Ramp' in the Insert Curve field.
- Select the Draw tool and click and drag in the tempo display to create your own test curve (Figure 19.4).

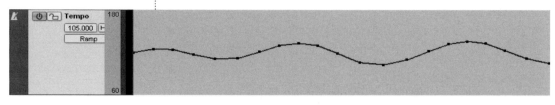

Figure 19.4
A test tempo curve

To change the curve type, select a group of tempo events and then select 'Jump' in the type field on the infoline. The shape of the curve is modified accordingly (Figure 19.5). Where required, jump and ramp characteristics can exist within the same curve.

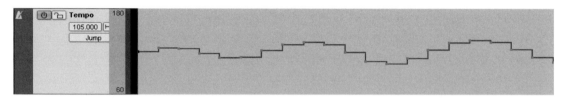

Figure 19.5
Changing the curve type to Jump mode

To move one or more tempo events, make a selection using the object selection tool and drag the event(s) to the desired location. If you do this on the Tempo track in the Project window and activate snap to events, dragged tempo events snap to the other events in the display (Figure 19.6).

Figure 19.6
Dragging tempo events in the Project window event display with snap to events active allows you to line up tempo events to sp0ecific events in the arrangement

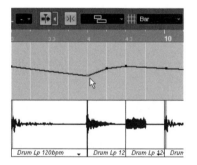

Figure 19.7 (above)
Change the tempo of the currently selected event using the value field on the infoline

Tip

To set up a simple linear tempo ramp click on the curve with the object selection tool once at the start and once at the end of the intended passage for the ramp. Drag either of the two resulting tempo events up or down to create the ramp.

To edit the value of a single event, select the event and move the mouse wheel while hovering over the value for the event on the infoline (Figure 19.7). Alternatively, double-click on the value and enter a new figure using the computer keyboard.

Info

When inserting or moving tempo events, the resolution of the tempo values depends upon the vertical zoom setting, where low zoom factors allow only whole integer tempo value changes and high zoom factors allow changes in smaller steps.

Figure 19.8
To insert a time signature event, click in the time signature strip with the draw tool

Inserting and editing time signature events

To insert a time signature event select the draw tool and click at the appropriate time position in the time signature strip (Figure 19.8). Alternatively, press Alt and click in the time signature strip with the Object Selection tool. Time signature events are always placed on the first beat of the bar.

To edit a time signature event, select the event and move the mouse wheel while hovering over the small up / down arrows on either side of the signature on the infoline (Figure 19.9). Alternatively, double-click on the time signature and enter a new value directly using the computer keyboard.

Figure 19.9
To change the currently selected time signature use the small up / down arrows in the time signature field on the infoline

Info

By selecting 'Increment / Decrement on Left click and drag' in Preferences / Editing / Controls / Value Box, you can change the values on the infoline by dragging the mouse directly in the value field. Alternatively, use the mouse wheel.

Time display format in the ruler

The display characteristics of the ruler can be changed between linear bars and beats and linear time using the options in the lower section of the pop-up ruler options menu. This is opened by clicking on the arrow button to the right of the ruler (Figure 19.10).

Bars and beats linear mode (also referred to as tempo linear mode) is selected by default when you edit the Tempo Track. Bars and beats linear results in a display where each bar in the ruler is represented by the same horizontal distance, regardless of any tempo changes (Figure 19.11).

In contrast, Time Linear mode results in a display where the distance between each bar in the ruler becomes greater as the tempo is decreased (Figure 19.12).

Figure 19.10
Click on the arrow button to the right of the ruler to open the pop-up time display menu

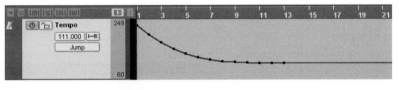

Figure 19.11
The Tempo Track display in 'Bars+Beats Linear' mode

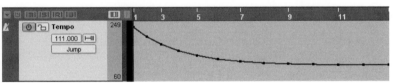

Figure 19.12
The same curve in 'Time Linear' mode

Why use tempo changes?

The tempo of most music created using live musicians varies either subtly or dramatically. These variations add to the liveliness and feel of the performance, and almost all great musical performances involve tempo changes. It is therefore sometimes beneficial to emulate this behaviour within Cubase.

There are no hard and fast rules about exactly how tempo changes should be applied. General guidelines for song forms include increasing the tempo on all the choruses and going back to the original tempo for the verses. More subtle manipulations might include wider tempo variations in the early stages of the music and lesser tempo variations as the song progresses, giving the impression of a group of musicians settling into the groove. Hook lines might benefit from slight tempo increases to generate excitement.

Matching the tempo to a musical performance

Tempo matching using Merge MIDI from tapping and hitpoints

There are several techniques for matching the tempo of Cubase to that of an audio recording of a real-world live musical performance. Among the most practical is to use the 'Merge tempo from tapping' function. This adjusts the tempo according to a sequence of MIDI notes you have recorded in time with the music. Alternatively, you can adjust the tempo using the Time warp tool. The following is a two-stage process which uses a combination of both these techniques. Proceed as follows:

Stage 1
- Activate Tempo track mode on the Transport panel and add the Tempo track in the event display.
- Import the recording of the musical performance onto an audio track. Activate Linear time base (shown by a clock symbol) on the chosen audio track (Figure 19.13). It may help to line up the downbeat of the first bar to a bar start grid line in the event display.

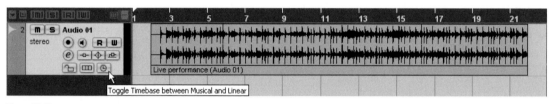

Figure 19.13
Activate Linear time base on the chosen Audio track

- Add a MIDI track. Activate Linear time base and record enable the track (Figure 19.14).

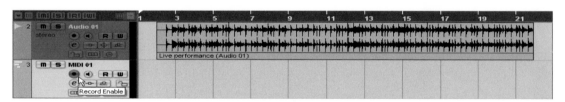

Figure 19.14
Record enable a MIDI track and set it to Linear time base

- De-activate the metronome click. and enable record on the MIDI track. Engage recording and tap on the MIDI keyboard in time with the audio material. Try using a hi-hat or rimshot sound at quarter note intervals and start on the first downbeat of the first bar (Figure 19.15).

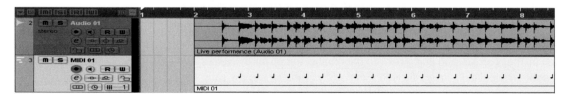

Figure 19.15
MIDI events recorded in time with the music at quarter note intervals

- Audition the recorded MIDI events and make sure their positions correspond to the timing of the audio material. If necessary, edit the positions of the MIDI events in the Key editor (with the Snap button de-activated).

- Select the recorded MIDI part and select MIDI / Functions / Merge tempo from tapping. Select the desired resolution. In this case, quarter notes are selected. Activate 'Begin at Bar Start' (Figure 19.16).
- Click on OK in the 'Merge tempo from tapping' dialogue. Tempo events are inserted on the Tempo track according to the positions of the MIDI notes. Mute the MIDI track and play back the performance with the metronome click activated. The tempo of the click now matches the musical performance (Figure 19.17).

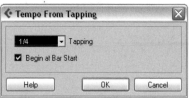

Figure 19.16
Choose the resolution for the tempo events in the 'Merge tempo from tapping' dialogue

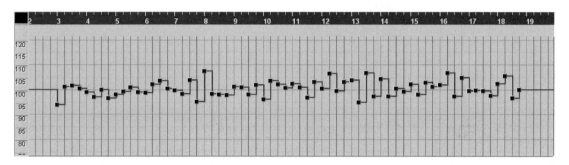

Figure 19.17
The resulting tempo events in the Tempo track editor. In this case, the tempo fluctuates around 100bpm

If your MIDI notes were recorded with sufficient accuracy, the first stage of this process may be all you need to establish an accurate tempo map of the musical performance. However, if you need still greater accuracy try completing the second stage outlined below.

Stage 2

- Add the Marker track in the Project window and set it to linear time base.
- Double-click on the audio event to open the Sample editor.
- Open the Hitpoint section of the Sample editor Inspector and adjust the sensitivity slider to calculate hitpoints for the audio material (Figure 19.18).

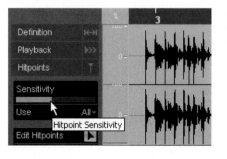

Figure 19.18
Adjust the sensitivity slider in the Hitpoint section of the Sample editor Inspector to create hitpoints

- Adjust the sensitivity slider so that hitpoints appear on the main hits in the material. Verify the audio segments by clicking between each pair of hitpoints with the Edit hitpoints button activated. The objective is to avoid the creation of too many hitpoints, especially those placed closely

together, whilst also attempting to finish up with one hitpoint at each
quarter note position. You may need to edit the hitpoints manually. The
result when aiming for hitpoints at quarter note intervals resembles
Figure 19.19. Do not be too concerned if there are not hitpoints at
absolutely all quarter note positions since you are seeking a good guide
and not absolute perfection.

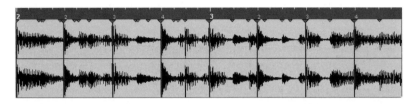

Figure 19.19
Hitpoints created in the Sample editor
for the main hits in the musical
performance

- Select Audio / Hitpoints / Create markers from hitpoints. This creates
  markers in the Marker track at the positions of the hitpoints. Go back to the
  Project window to view the markers in the Marker track (Figure 19.20).

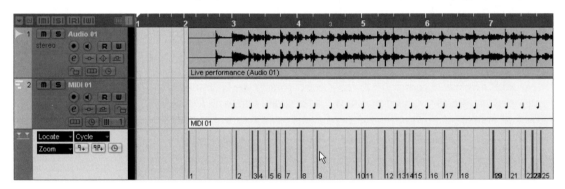

Figure 19.20
Markers in the Marker track (created
from the Hitpoints)

- Select the Time warp tool (in the default Warp grid mode). At this time
  the tempo events produced in stage 1 (above) appear in the ruler
  (Figure 19.21).

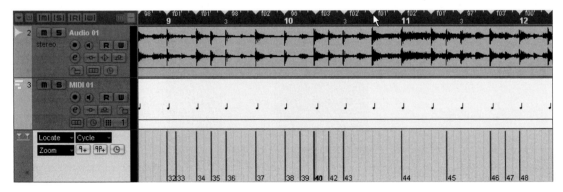

Figure 19.21
With the Time warp tool selected, the
existing tempo events appear in the ruler

- In the Project window toolbar, activate the Snap button and set the Snap
  type menu to events. With snap to events active, the marker events
  become 'magnetic'.

- A short vertical line appears whenever you place the Time warp tool in the event display at the same position as an existing tempo event (those visible in the ruler). Click and drag from this position to snap the corresponding tempo event to the nearest 'magnetic' marker, (Figure 19.22). If there is no marker at the position, you may need to drag the tempo event manually with the Snap button de-activated. In this case, line up the tempo event visually to just before the peak in the waveform which corresponds to the 'hit' of the beat.

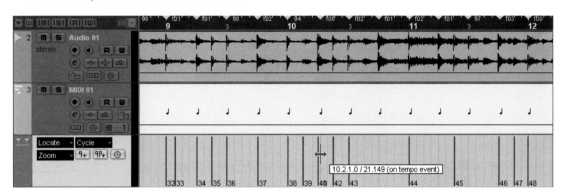

Figure 19.22
Drag the tempo events to the nearest markers in the event display

- Work through the tempo events in a similar fashion, lining them up with the nearest marker events. If the tempo events appear to be dragged too far off the tempo, the marker concerned may be inaccurate. Seek out the best position for each event while auditioning the material. Some tempo events may already be in the correct position.

The techniques outlined in this second stage help you refine the data created in stage 1 to produce an extremely accurate tempo map. Creating hitpoints and converting them to markers in the event display effectively provides you with rhythmic anchor points upon which you can 'hang' you tempo events.

Tempo matching using the Beat Calculator

The Beat Calculator (Figure 19.23) is designed to match the tempo of Cubase to that of an audio event. To match the tempo of Cubase to an audio event, proceed as follows:

- Edit the target audio event to fit a precise number of bars and beats. Alternatively, import a ready-made audio loop or similar material.
- Select the event and open the Beat Calculator from the Project menu.
- In the beats field, enter the number of beats which corresponds with the length of the event.
- Click on 'At Tempo Track Start' or 'At selection start' as desired. A tempo event is inserted at the appropriate position in the Tempo Track..
- Audition the event alongside the metronome click to verify that it matches the newly calculated tempo.

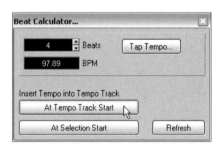

Figure 19.23
The Beat Calculator

Synchronisation

Synchronisation refers to the technique of running two or more devices in perfect time with each other. This is required in Cubase systems which include external devices such as video tape recorders, tape machines, hard disk recorders, sequencers and drum machines. The devices must be connected together in some way so that they are all 'aware' of their time positions relative to the other units in the system. This is achieved using a time encoded signal (time code). Digital systems may also require the use of word clock or some other clock reference signal. One of the units in the system is chosen as the master device and the others are chosen as slaves. The master device generates the reference code for the system and the other units synchronise themselves to this. Precisely how this is achieved depends upon the application. Positional synchronisation techniques may be divided into two main categories: bar-based synchronisation and time-based synchronisation.

Bar-based synchronisation

This involves sending MIDI Clock between units which keeps them synchronised in terms of bar position and tempo. This is an older, entirely MIDI based technique which is recommended only when there is no other solution. A typical use includes the synchronisation of external sequencers and drum machines which do not feature MTC (MIDI Time Code).

MIDI Clock includes a clock message transmitted 24 times per quarter note and Start, Stop and Continue messages. Song Position Pointer (SPP) messages are invariably also included in the transmitted data. The receiving device responds according to the Start, Stop and Continue messages and calculates the tempo at which it should be running by measuring the time between each MIDI Clock message. The additional Song Position Pointer messages are used for calculating the current position within the song. This allows fast forward and rewind operations and the possibility of starting at any point within the music. (Before Song Position Pointers, synchronisation could only be achieved by commencing playback from the start of the song).

Time-based synchronisation

This involves the use of 'time-stamped' code which provides an absolute time-based reference for synchronisation purposes. This comes in the form of SMPTE or EBU time code and MIDI time code (MTC). Time-based synchronisation using SMPTE, EBU or MIDI time code is preferable to bar-referenced synchronisation since it is more accurate and is tempo-independent.

Time code has its origins in the film industry where the time stamped information was measured in terms of a number representing hours, minutes, seconds and frames. The resolution of the code was determined by its frame rate (e.g. 24 frames-per-second) and this was originally how many film frames passed through the camera per second. This kind of time code has been adopted for audio purposes and is now widely used in various forms throughout the audio industry.

SMPTE is an abbreviation for the Society of Motion Picture and Television Engineers and time code is often referred to by this name, (pronounced 'simptee'), since this organisation was the first to establish a time code standard. However, strictly speaking SMPTE time code is only one standard, as used in the USA. The other is EBU Time Code as used in Europe (established by the European Broadcasting Union).

The different types of time code can be identified by the manner in which they are stored and transmitted and by their frame rates. Time code is transmitted as Longitudinal Time Code (LTC), Vertical Interval Time Code (VITC) or MIDI Time Code (MTC) and these are defined as follows:

- Longitudinal Time Code (LTC) – the code is recorded as a stream of audio pulses on an audio track. LTC is commonly used for audio work and video productions.
- Vertical Interval Time Code (VITC) – this code is embedded within the video picture and is popular for video editing.
- MIDI Time Code (MTC) – this is a special kind of time code with a slightly lower resolution than LTC which is transmitted via MIDI.

Time code varies in the number of frames per second for the encoded signal. This is known as the frame rate and could be one of the following:

24 fps – traditional 35mm film rate.
25 fps – European standard for audio and PAL video (EBU).
30 fps – USA standard for audio work (30 Non-Drop, SMPTE time code).
30 dfps – NTSC broadcast format.
29.97 fps – NTSC colour television and video non-drop frame format (29.97 Non-Drop).
29.97 dfps – NTSC colour television and video drop frame format (29.97 Drop).

The basic format for all time code is hours : minutes : seconds : frames. When greater accuracy is required, the frame is divided into 80 sub-frames. For audio work, it is normal practice to use 25 fps in Europe and 30 fps in the USA. LTC and MTC time code at the latter frame rates are the types of time code with which you are most likely to come into contact in audio work.

Synchronisation in digital systems

The problems

Under normal circumstances, when Cubase is not slaved to an external device, both the MIDI and audio data are locked to the same clock (the digital audio hardware's internal clock). However, when Cubase is slaved to an external device using time code alone (MTC), the positional reference of the program is governed by the incoming time code, while the clock reference for the audio data is still locked to the internal audio clock. Due to variations in tape speed and/or audio clock speeds, this can result in timing drift between the audio recorded in Cubase and the audio recorded in the external unit and/or the MIDI data. The problem may manifest itself as a loss of clarity or as phasiness in the sound quality.

The solutions

Word Clock

A popular solution to the problem outlined above is the use of word clock. One unit is chosen as the single master time code and word clock source (sometimes also the unit where A/D conversion takes place), and all other units are slaved to this device. Word clock keeps the sample rates of digital audio hardware in synchronisation by using a clock which is referenced to the transferred data bits, normally at the same rate as the sample rate chosen for the digital audio system. Using word clock requires audio hardware equipped with word clock connectors. Many digital audio signals, such as S/PDIF, AES3 and ADAT, are self-clocking since the clock reference is embedded within the signal. With these interfaces, lock can therefore be achieved without the use of word clock. However, locking to word clock is likely to provide better jitter-free performance.

ASIO Positioning Protocol (APP)

APP is designed to ensure sample accurate positioning between suitably equipped devices. It requires audio hardware with an ASIO 2.0 driver which includes APP functionality, and the ability to read positional information in the external device (see the electronic documentation and the Steinberg website for more details about APP).

Synchronising without Word Clock

It is worth bearing in mind that some of the synchronisation problems outlined above are relevant to those systems where Cubase is slaved to an external device. You may encounter less problems if you are running a system where Cubase is always the master device. Equally, if you are synchronising Cubase to devices whose timing clocks are very stable, such as another computer or a hard disk recorder, then you may encounter minimal problems if you synchronise using time code without a reference clock. However, the fact remains that a system synchronising digital devices without a reference clock (such as word clock) cannot guarantee accurate long-term synchronisation. The longer the audio recording, the more apparent becomes the timing drift.

If you intend to set up your system without Word Clock, it may help if you use time code which was generated from your audio hardware. For this and other purposes, Cubase is supplied with a SMPTE generator plug-in (outlined in the next section).

The SMPTE Generator plug-in

Cubase is supplied with a SMPTE Generator plug-in (Figure 20.1). This can be used as an insert effect on any audio track. The audio track is routed to the appropriate output of your audio hardware and recorded onto the intended time code track of the external device. The generation of the time code may be linked to the project ruler by activating the link button. In this case, time code generation begins from the location of the project cursor when you activate playback. The frame rate matches the frame rate set in the Project Setup window (Project menu). Otherwise, deactivate the Link button and press the Generate button. This generates time code at the chosen frame rate beginning from the specified start time.

As well as providing a convenient time code source, the SMPTE Generator is also helpful for becoming familiar with the various different types of time code. However, be careful when routing the time code through your audio system. Reduce the volume level before pressing the generate button to avoid damage to your speakers or to your ears!!

Figure 20.1
The SMPTE Generator plug-in

Setting up synchronisation in Cubase

It is important to have a basic understanding of the different types of time code, as outlined in the above sections, since you may come into contact with them in the peripheral equipment which you connect to your audio system. However, internally, Cubase recognises only MIDI Time Code (MTC), ASIO Positioning Protocol (APP) or VST System Link as time code sources. The practical synchronisation of Cubase to external audio hardware, like tape recorders or hard disk recorders, often implies the use of a hardware synchronisation device (synchroniser) which converts LTC time code into MTC. For professional applications, the synchroniser would also provide word clock for the system. A typical synchronisation setup of this type is shown in Figure 20.2.

Synchronisation in Cubase is managed in the Synchronisation Setup dialogue opened from the Transport menu (Figure 20.3). This is used to select the time code source, the MIDI Machine Control status, the drop out and lock behaviour, and the MIDI input and output ports for MIDI Machine Control in/out, MTC in/out and MIDI Clock out.

When Cubase behaves as the slave to an external device using MTC, you need to set the appropriate MIDI Input for the time code, a start time which Cubase uses as the beginning of the project (in the Project Setup dialogue Start field), and activate the Sync button on the Transport panel (press 'T' on

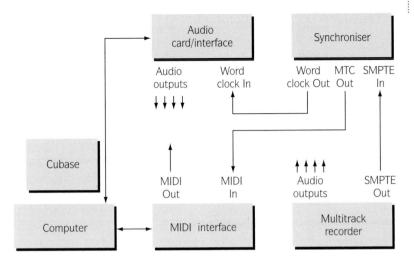

Figure 20.3
The Synchronisation Setup dialogue

the computer keyboard). In this configuration, Cubase commences playback in synchronisation with the external device when it receives time code with the same or a greater value than the set start time.

Practical synchronisation in Cubase

Cubase as the master device using MIDI clock

Cubase cannot be slaved to an external device using MIDI Clock since it does not recognise incoming MIDI Clock messages. Due to the technical limitations of MIDI Clock, it is not considered a suitable format for providing master timing control of Cubase. However, Cubase can generate MIDI Clock and therefore behave as the master device for external devices which recognise the data. MIDI Clock is suitable for the synchronisation of external sequencers and drum machines. To set up synchronisation using MIDI Clock, proceed as follows:

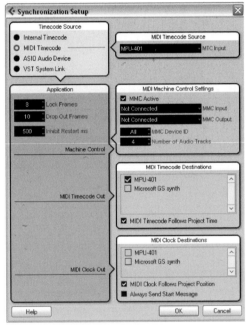

- Connect a MIDI cable between the appropriate physical MIDI output port of your MIDI interface and the MIDI input of the drum machine or external sequencer.
- Enable the reception of MIDI Clock data in the external MIDI device.
- Open the Synchronisation Setup dialogue in Cubase by selecting 'Sync Setup' in the Transport menu (Figure 20.4).
- In the Synchronisation setup dialogue, activate the appropriate MIDI port in the 'MIDI clock destinations' section (Figure 20.5).
- Click on OK to leave the dialogue. Press play in Cubase to send the MIDI Clock messages. The receiving device runs synchronised to Cubase.

MIDI Clock may also be the solution if you are recording the MIDI data from a non-MTC equipped drum machine or sequencer into Cubase. In this case,

Figure 20.4 (left)
Select Sync Setup in the Transport menu

Figure 20.5 (right)
Activate the appropriate MIDI port in the Sync Setup 'MIDI clock destinations' section

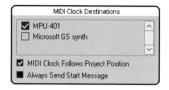

configure Cubase in the same manner as above, but also connect a second MIDI cable from the MIDI out of the external device to a MIDI input port of your MIDI interface. In this setup, MIDI Clocks are transmitted via the MIDI output of Cubase to the slaved device and the MIDI note data from the external unit is sent back to Cubase via the second MIDI cable. Activating record in Cubase records the incoming data onto a record enabled MIDI track.

Cubase as the master device using MIDI time code

Using Cubase as the master device is a popular solution when synchronising external multitrack machines and video recorders and, in many circumstances, is a better solution than using it as the slave. Proceed as follows:

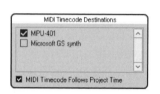

Figure 20.6
Select the appropriate MIDI output port for the MTC in the 'MIDI time code destinations' section

- Connect a MIDI cable between the appropriate MIDI output port of your MIDI interface and the MIDI input of the external device.
- Enable the reception of MTC in the external device.
- Set Cubase and the external device to the same frame rate. In Cubase, set the frame rate in the Project setup window (Project menu). For most situations you would choose 25fps or 30fps.
- Set the start time for Cubase in the Project setup window (Project menu). Also set an appropriate start time in the external unit.
- In the Sync Setup dialogue, activate the appropriate MIDI port in the 'MIDI time code destinations' section (Figure 20.6).
- Click on OK to leave the Sync Setup dialogue. Press play in Cubase to send MTC. The receiving device plays back synchronised to Cubase.

Cubase as the slave device using MIDI time code

As outlined above, MTC is a particular kind of time code which can be transmitted through an ordinary MIDI cable. MTC supports 24, 25, 30 and 30 drop frame formats. The device which sends the MTC to Cubase could be a synchroniser which converts SMPTE time code into MTC or, perhaps, another sequencer. A synchroniser is often used to provide an interface between a multitrack tape or hard disk recorder and a computer based sequencer, like Cubase, and this forms the main subject matter of this section.

Before synchronisation can occur with the multitrack recorder, one of the tracks must be striped with time code (although some devices produce their own time code signal without using a track). After striping, this code is routed to the time code input of the synchroniser which drives the rest of the system. In this example, the synchroniser converts the SMPTE time code into MTC, which is routed to the computer and Cubase via a MIDI cable connected to the MIDI interface.

To set up Cubase with a multitrack recorder and a synchroniser which converts SMPTE time code to MIDI time code, proceed as follows:

- If required, stripe a track of the multitrack recorder with time code. For this task you could use Cubase's SMPTE Generator plug-in (as described above).
- Ensure that your synchroniser is correctly connected to the multitrack recorder (normally time code output of the multitrack recorder connected to the

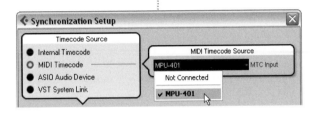

time code input of the synchroniser) and that the MTC out from the synchroniser is connected to the MIDI In of your MIDI interface.
- If you are using word clock, ensure that the word clock output from the synchroniser is connected to the word clock input of the audio card / audio hardware device.

Figure 20.7
Set the time code source to MIDI time code and select the MIDI port for the incoming MTC in the Synchronisation Setup dialogue

- In the Synchronisation Setup dialogue, set time code Source to MIDI time code. Select the MIDI port for the incoming MTC in the 'MIDI time code source' input pop-up menu (Figure 20.7).
- Select the appropriate start time, frame rate and display offset (if required) in the Project Setup dialogue (Figure 20.8).
- Click on the Sync button in the Transport panel to activate synchronisation (or press T on the computer keyboard).
- Cubase is now ready to slave to any incoming MTC. Rewind the multitrack recorder to before the start time of the project and commence playback. When Cubase receives time code on or after the project start time, Cubase begins playback, in synchronisation with the multitrack recorder.

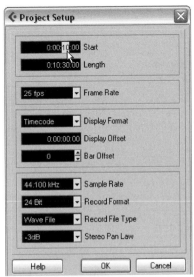

Cubase automatically chases and locks to each new position selected on the external device. In the Synchronisation Setup dialogue, the Drop Out and Lock Time options dictate the speed with which Cubase reacts to the incoming code, as follows:

Figure 20.8
Select the start time, frame rate and display offset in the Project Setup dialogue

- Lock Time specifies the number of correct frames of time code required before Cubase locks to it.
- Drop Out Time specifies the number of incorrect frames (or drop outs) which are tolerated before Cubase abandons synchronisation.

Synchronising Cubase with a tape recorder using MIDI Machine Control (MMC)

MIDI Machine Code (MMC) is a special part of the MIDI protocol which specifies MIDI messages for the control of such things as tape transports. The implementation of MMC in Cubase allows you to set up remote control of the transport functions of external devices using the Transport panel.

The use of MMC is a two-way process involving both MMC messages and MTC. It requires both the MIDI input and MIDI output of the tape recorder to be connected to Cubase. MMC messages are transmitted from the MIDI output of Cubase to the MIDI input of the tape recorder, which controls the transport and other functions. The tape recorder transmits MTC to the MIDI input of Cubase and this locks the two machines in synchronisation. The process requires the recording of time code onto one track of the tape recorder which is converted into MTC during playback.

To set up your system and the Synchronisation Setup dialogue for use with a tape machine which supports MMC, proceed as follows:

- Ensure that the MIDI in and out cables are correctly connected between the tape recorder and Cubase and that time code has been recorded onto one track of the tape. Set up the tape recorder for MMC operation.
- In the Synchronisation Setup dialogue, set the time code source to MIDI time code. Select the MIDI port for the incoming MTC in the MIDI time code source 'MTC Input' pop-up.
- Activate 'MMC Active' in the MIDI Machine Control section. Select the MMC input and output ports and the number of audio tracks on the external device (Figure 20.9).

Figure 20.9
Typical synchronisation setup settings for MMC operation

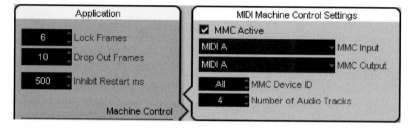

- Select the appropriate start time, frame rate and display offset (if required) in the Project Setup dialogue (Project menu).
- Activate the Sync button on the Transport panel.
- Press the play button on the tape recorder and play the tape for a short section to allow Cubase to lock to the current time code position.
- Stop the tape and activate playback in Cubase. If all is well, the tape rolls back to just before the current time position in Cubase and commences playback. After a second or two Cubase commences playback in sync with the tape recorder. Thereafter, all Cubase transport buttons, including play, stop, fast forward and rewind, control the transport of the tape recorder.

Production tips and power tools

This chapter outlines a number of tips, techniques, macro commands and workspaces which help you on your way to becoming a Cubase power user. The emphasis here is on speed and efficiency, so if improving your productivity and workflow is a priority then this chapter is essential reading. The topics covered explore some of the lesser known aspects of Cubase as well as finding new ways of using common functions.

100 speed tips

The following is a comprehensive list of tips for enhancing speed and getting the best out of Cubase. The text is divided into a number of logical categories to help you find the tip you need.

Saving and file handling

1   Select Ctrl / Command + Alt + S to save the project with an incremental number automatically appended to the file name. This function is valuable for making regular saves of the latest version of your work as the project progresses. If things go wrong in the current version you can always revert to an earlier version.
2   Always re-name your audio tracks before starting to record. Cubase uses the track name for the name of the audio file which is written to the hard disk and by using meaningful names, rather than the default 'Audio 1', 'Audio 2' and so on, the files are easier to recognise if you need to find them individually at a later stage. A take number is chronologically appended to the file name for each new recording on the same track.
3   To avoid missing file problems and confusion store each Cubase project in its own separate folder. The program is designed with the idea of storing each project file and all its associated audio, edit and image files within a single overall folder. You can have several versions of the same project within the same folder but storing completely different projects within the same folder is to be avoided.

Navigation and zooming

4   To navigate quickly between different sections of your music without dropping out of playback, activate play and hold the numeric keypad '+' key to fast forward, or the '-' key to rewind. Release the key to

instantly go back into normal playback mode. Hold Shift to increase the wind speed.

5   To use drag zooming in the ruler without affecting playback or the cursor position, hold the Shift key while dragging.

6   To quickly modify the left / right locator positions, click in the ruler while pressing Ctrl to set the left locator and while pressing Alt to set the right locator.

7   To lock the view on the start of a range selection when editing at high magnification in the Sample editor, proceed as follows: stop playback, activate autoscroll, and press L to locate the start of the selection. De-activate autoscroll before re-commencing playback. The view now remains locked to the start point.

8   The Zoom tool is often the best choice for basic zooming tasks. Click once to zoom in and double click to zoom out.

9   To achieve a full horizontal and vertical view of all events in the project, hold Shift and click once with the zoom tool in the event display.

10   To zoom in to a specific range, make a range selection using the Range selection tool followed by 'Zoom to selection'. Use 'Undo zoom' to go back to the previous zoom setting. Assign key commands to 'Zoom to selection' and 'Undo zoom' (try 'Z' and 'Alt + Z').

Event editing

11   Click in empty space in the Project window with the right mouse button to open the context sensitive Quick menu. Hold down a modifier key (Ctrl, Command, Shift or Alt) to open a pop-up toolbox instead. To reverse the Quick menu / pop-up toolbox functionality, select 'Pop-up toolbox on right click' in Preferences / Editing / Tools.

12   To repeat a number of consecutive events in the Project window select Repeat in the Edit menu (Ctrl / Command + K) and enter the number of repeats required in the pop-up dialogue. Alternatively, select the object selection tool and point at the lower right corner of the event while pressing Alt (until the pencil symbol appears). Drag to the right to repeat the events. The number of repeats is shown in a pop-up box.

13   To create a crossfade between two audio events, drag one audio event so that it slightly overlaps another. Press the 'X' key on the computer keyboard. A default crossfade is created. Double click on the crossfade area to modify the crossfade curve characteristics.

14   To cut and paste range selections within events with automatic splits and re-alignment of following events, use the range selection tool with delete time, cut time and paste time (Edit menu / Range). Delete time deletes the range selection and moves all following events leftwards to close the gap. Cut time is similar but also copies the deleted range to the clipboard. Paste time copies the clipboard at the start point of the range selection and moves all following events rightwards to make room for the pasted data.

15   To select all events on the currently selected track, use 'select all events' from the track list Quick menu.

16   To rename all events on a track to the same name, use any modifier key

+ Return to enter a new name for the track. Alternatively, select several events and change the name on the infoline.

17 Before opening the main editors, press 'P' followed by the numeric keypad divide key to set the left and right locators and cycle playback to the current selection. This helps keep the cursor visible within the edit window.

18 To split all selected events at the same point, select a number of events in the Project window and click on any one with the split tool. Alternatively, use the 'split at cursor' and 'split loop' commands in the edit menu.

19 As an alternative to the split tool for splitting events, press Alt and click with the object selection tool.

20 To delete all events on a track which come after the horizontal position at which you click, press Alt and click with the erase tool.

21 To create empty audio or MIDI parts in the Project window, press Alt and drag with the object selection tool. Alternatively, drag with the draw tool or double click between the left and right locators.

22 To nudge a selected event back or forward in time in the event display, use Ctrl + left arrow and Ctrl + right arrow (default key commands). The nudge resolution is determined by the current ruler setting and the grid settings in the Project window toolbar.

23 To automatically close gaps between adjacent events when modifying their lengths, activate the snap button and select Shuffle mode in the snap type menu.

24 To find the length of any range, or group of events, activate the snap button and choose Events in the snap type menu. Select the range tool and drag across the required range (the range snaps to the start or end of events). The length of the selection is shown in the length field of the infoline in the same time format as that chosen in the ruler.

Markers

25 To add standard markers, click on the add marker button found in the track list section of the Marker track or press the insert key on the computer keyboard. Standard markers are placed at the current location of the project cursor. Alternatively, add markers freely anywhere in the Marker track using the draw tool or during playback using the insert key.

26 To add cycle markers, press Alt + C on the computer keyboard. This adds a cycle marker over the current range of the left and right locators.

27 For instant cycle marker playback, select a cycle marker and press Shift + G. This places the left and right locators at the start and end of the cycle marker and automatically commences playback in cycle mode.

28 Double-click in a cycle marker in the Marker track with the range selection tool to globally select the cycle marker range for all tracks in the project.

29 When you have created hitpoints in the Sample editor you can generate markers at the hitpoint positions by selecting Create Markers in the Sample editor inspector. This is helpful for lining up tempo events to audio hits using the time warp tool in the Project window.

30   In order to clarify the Marker track display in the Inspector, you may find it preferable to see the description column next to the marker ID number. To achieve this, change the position of the description column by dragging the column header to the left in the Inspector.

Key commands

31   Key commands do not exist for workspaces numbered above 9. If you prefer to avoid the mouse for activating higher numbered workspaces, use Alt + Pad 0 to open the 'Organise workspace' dialogue. Once open, use the up / down arrows to navigate the list of workspaces. Press return to activate the currently selected workspace. Press Alt + F4 to close the dialogue.

32   Assign key commands to Calculate hitpoints and Remove hitpoints in the Key commands dialogue. Try 'K' and 'Shift + K'. These are useful for instant hitpoint creation and removal in the Sample editor.

33   Try reversing the default key commands for 'Zoom to Selection' (Alt + S) and 'Project Setup' (Shift + S). This helps navigate within the Sample editor, where you can now use Shift + F to zoom to the whole clip, Shift + E to zoom to the event, Shift + S to zoom to the current selection, and Shift + G to loop around the current selection. In other words, all the common zoom and loop key commands now use the Shift modifier key. This is easier to remember and easier to use.

34   Assign Key commands to Shuttle Play 2x and Shuttle Reverse 2x. Try the '.' and ',' keys (full stop and comma). In combination with autoscroll these commands help you quickly scroll back and forth within the Sample editor display and within audio events in the Project window.

35   If you frequently need to manually activate / de-activate the monitor button for channels / tracks, assign a key command to the monitor command in the Key Commands dialogue. Try 'Ctrl + Shift + M'.

MIDI

36   When activating MIDI effects in the Inspector, the parameters of certain devices open within the Inspector itself. If this is not convenient, you can force the effect to open in a separate window by pressing Alt while making the selection.

37   To quickly select all notes of the same pitch in the Key editor, hold down Ctrl / Command and click on the relevant key in the virtual keyboard to the left of the main display.

38   The presets menu for VSTi and external MIDI devices is good for auditioning sounds on the fly. Step through the sounds in the list using the up / down arrow keys on the computer keyboard. Also try filtering presets by category or name to help find the desired sound.

39   Use the 'Edit VST instrument' button on the toolbar of the MIDI editors to quickly open the user interface for a VST instrument while working in the editor. If the Edit VST instrument button is not visible on the toolbar, select it from the toolbar pop-up menu which appears when you click on the toolbar with the right mouse button.

40   If you want to export a MIDI sequence as a Standard MIDI File and the track concerned uses a drum map, use 'O-Note Conversion' (MIDI

menu) to transpose the notes before exporting. This ensures that the correct sounds are triggered.

41 To 'humanise' the effect of Over quantize, try adding a few ticks in the Random Quantize setting of the Quantize Setup dialogue.

42 If you find yourself involved in MIDI editing tasks which seem laboriously repetitive and time-consuming, remember the Logical editor. This editor often provides one-step solutions for mouse click intensive editing and may even help avoid repetitive strain injury!!

43 To reveal the note names inside each event on the grid in the Key editor, increase the vertical zoom resolution.

44 To insert a series of notes at the same pitch in the Key editor, select the paint tool and drag it across the grid while pressing Ctrl / Command. To control the insert resolution, activate the snap button and select the desired quantize value in the Quantize type menu. Set the Length Q menu to 'Quantize Link'. Alternatively, press Alt and move the object selection tool (pointer) near to the end of an existing note and then drag across the grid. The chosen note is repeated over the range you drag.

45 If you have programmed a drum loop (or similar) within a MIDI part on an Instrument track, you can save this as a MIDI Loop by selecting the part and using File / Export / MIDI Loop. MIDI Loops contain all MIDI data and the Instrument track / VST instrument settings. They are helpful for exchanging loops between different projects.

46 Click on the Edit In-Place button above the track list to toggle on and off the Edit In-Place editor for the currently selected MIDI tracks. Alternatively, use the default key command: Ctrl / Command + Shift + I.

Audio editing

47 To remove fades and crossfades, select the events containing the fades using the Object selection tool or select the range containing the fades using the range selection tool, and then select 'Remove Fades' in the Audio menu.

48 The Snap point of an audio event in the Project window is visible as a vertical blue line (when it is not in its default position at the start of the event). In the Project window, the Snap point may be modified using 'Snap point to cursor' (Audio menu). The Snap point is also adjustable in the Sample editor.

49 Try opening multiple Sample editors when you are working on several clips at the same time. This is useful for copying, pasting and merging audio between different clips.

50 To merge the current contents of the clipboard with the existing audio in the Sample editor use the Merge Clipboard function in the Process menu.

51 To avoid clicks when splitting events, try activating the 'Snap to Zero crossing' button in the Project window toolbar. You may wish to de-activate the button after editing is complete, to avoid unwanted side-effects in other editing operations.

52 When using the Process functions for editing in fine detail in the Sample editor, always work with the snap to zero crossing button activated. This avoids clicks and glitches between the processed and unprocessed parts of the audio clip.

53 To make the tempo of Cubase fit the length of an audio event
    containing a drum loop, you need to know its length in beats. Select the
    drum loop event, enter the beat length into the Beat Calculator (Project
    menu) and click on 'At Tempo Track Start'. This changes the tempo of
    Cubase to that of the loop. This assumes that the length of the loop has
    already been edited to match a precise number of bars and beats.

54 In the Audio Part editor, use the Play tool (loudspeaker icon) with the
    'Edit active part only' button de-activated, to quickly switch between
    and audition the contents of each event, track or lane.

55 To avoid clicks between audio slices after increasing the tempo, set up
    auto fades in the Auto fades dialogue for the track. Tick 'auto
    crossfades' and de-select 'use project settings'. Try between 15ms and
    30ms for the crossfade. Alternatively, try activating the fade in and fade
    out options with a 5ms to 10ms fade time.

56 To merge the attack of one drum sound with the decay of another
    proceed as follows: open the Sample editor, select a drum sound using
    the range selection tool and copy the sound to the clipboard. Select a
    second drum sound with which you wish to merge the copied sound and
    define the appropriate range in the Sample editor. Open the Merge
    Clipboard dialogue (Audio / Process menu). Set the percentage slider to
    '100% copy' and adjust the pre-crossfade to between 50 and 100ms.
    Activate the pre-crossfade tick box. Fine tune the settings while in
    Preview mode. When satisfied click on the Process button.

57 To mix and match sound slices between different drum loops, open a
    number of synchronised sliced loops or Rex files simultaneously in the
    Audio Part editor. Use the mute and other tools on the different events
    to create new rhythms and arrangements.

58 To drag and drop a range selection directly from the Sample editor into
    the Project window, hold Ctrl on the computer keyboard, click in the
    highlighted selection and drag into the event display.

59 To remove unwanted noise in between words or phrases in vocal takes
    or speech, try using a combination of 'Split at cursor' (Alt+X) and the
    Crossfade function (X). Adjust the settings in the Crossfade dialogue to
    resemble a bowl-shaped envelope. Use 'Split at cursor' to split the
    audio event whenever you hear unwanted noise and interference. When
    you have worked through enough audio, select all the newly split events
    and select Crossfade (X) to implement crossfades at all the split points.
    Fine tune the crossfade settings where necessary.

60 To tile two or more Sample editors on the screen, select the audio
    events to be edited and select Window / Minimize All, followed by
    Return, followed by Window / Tile horizontally. When you are finished
    editing, close the editor windows and select Window / Restore All.

Mixer

61 When using the Mixer to create a mix it is not convenient if channels
    are always automatically record enabled when selected. To disable
    automatic record enabling, open Preferences / Editing / Project & Mixer
    and disable 'Enable Record on Selected Track'.

62 To open the user interface for a VST Instrument directly from the Mixer, click on the 'Edit VST instrument' button in the VST Instrument channel strip.

63 To change a fader level for a single channel in a group of linked channels in the Mixer, hold Alt on the computer keyboard while making the change.

64 When dragging a handle in the built-in EQ curve display, press Ctrl to change the gain only, press Alt to change the frequency only, and press Shift to change the Q only.

65 To make A / B comparisons between the equalised and unequalised signal, click on the channel's EQs state button (green = EQ enabled, yellow = EQ disabled).

66 Try activating File / Preferences / Editing / Sync project and mixer selection. In this mode, the contents of an open Channel Settings window automatically follows your track or mixer channel selection. This is useful for keeping track of all the channel settings when switching between tracks / channels.

67 Any combination of channels in the Mixer can be temporarily hidden by activating the 'Can Hide' option found in each channel's pop-up menu. Show or hide the chosen channels using the 'Hide channels set to Can Hide' icon in the left panel.

68 To open a pop-up menu of the assigned effects right click on an active Inserts state or Sends state button of any audio based channel. Make a selection from the menu to open the GUI for each effect.

69 To open all insert plug-in interfaces for any audio based channel hold Ctrl + Alt + Shift and click on the Edit Channel Settings button.

70 Creative effects can be achieved by using more than one effect in the insert slots. Try the following: compressor followed by fuzz, fuzz followed by chorus, echo followed by flange, chorus followed by flange, tremolo followed by autopan, reverb followed by phasing, filtering followed by delay.

71 To make fine adjustments in the Mixer, hold Shift while moving a channel fader or pan control.

72 Assign a key command to 'Mixer - Section: Extended'. Try F5 or F9. This gives you instant toggling of the the extended Mixer without using the arrows in the Mixer common panel.

73 To regulate the overall level of an audio based channel after automation has been applied, use the channel input gain control or, for two or more automated channels, change the output routings to a Group and apply overall level changes using the Group channel fader.

74 To apply master bus reverb or delay which continues after the master fader has been fully attenuated, (for example, on fade outs when mixing or mastering), insert the reverb or delay effect in insert slots 7 or 8 of the master bus (i.e. post fader).

75 To set multiple tracks / channels to the same input or output bus, select the required tracks / channels and change the input or output menu selection of any one while holding Shift + Alt.

Automation

76 To change the recording resolution for automation data, adjust the automation reduction level in the automation panel.

77 When moving automation handles, activate the Project window infoline. The infoline displays the start time and value of the event as you drag it. This helps place the events with greater precision. Alternatively, click directly on the value field in the infoline to change the value of the event.

78 A good way of viewing the behaviour of the different automation modes is to write the automation while viewing the corresponding sub-track in the Project window event display. Each time you click on a control when the Write button is active, the corresponding track header in the track list turns red to indicate that automation is being recorded.

79 To clarify the display of automation data in the Project window, activate 'Show Track colours' at the top of the track list and use the pop-up track colour selector for each automation sub-track to choose an appropriate colour.

Import / Export

80 The Import sub-menu of the File menu helps you import audio, video or standard MIDI files directly into the event display at the current project cursor position. The Import Medium function in the Media menu helps you search for any file type recognised by Cubase and import this into the Pool only. Both methods support multiple file import.

81 Before mixing down using Export / Audio Mixdown, check that all track monitor buttons are de-activated. Audio-based tracks with their monitor buttons active are NOT included in the audio mixdown. This can easily occur when using 'Tapemachine Style' or 'While Record Enabled' monitor modes since record enabled tracks automatically activate their monitor buttons when in stop mode.

82 When using Export / Audio Mixdown, make sure that any reverberation tail which occurs after the audio tracks is preserved by adding two or more bars of safety margin to the right locator position.

83 To copy tracks between projects, use Export / Selected Tracks, and Import / Track archive (File menu).

Pool

84 To find the current maximum peak amplitude and the average loudness of an audio clip, select the clip in the Pool and then select Statistics from the Audio menu. The resulting Statistics window shows the maximum peak amplitude (Peak Amplitude), which means the single highest peak found in the selection, and the average RMS power (Average), which means the average loudness of the signal.

85 Before exporting the Pool, create a special folder using Create Folder (Pool menu) and drag all the clips into it. When you later import the Pool into another Cubase or Nuendo project all the clips are neatly packaged in their own folder and are, thus, easier to find among any clips already in the current Pool.

86 To view more details about Broadcast Wave files in the Pool, click in the Info column for the file to reveal a pop-up info box.

87 To find out the total size taken up by the audio files in a project, activate the Show info button in the Pool (see the Total Size field).

88 To sort the audio files used in a project alphabetically or by type, date or path, click on the relevant column header in the Pool.

Miscellaneous

89 Try setting Preferences / Editing / Controls / Value Box to 'Increment / Decrement on Left Click and Drag'. This means that by clicking on a value field and dragging the mouse position vertically you can instantly change values in a fast, fuss-free way. The technique works well when adjusting the start, end, volume, fade in, fade out or transpose values for a selected event in the Project window Infoline. It is also good for adjusting length, pitch, velocity and channel data in the Key and Drum editor Infolines, and for changing the tempo (in fixed mode).

90 To quickly change the project tempo press Shift + T on the computer keyboard followed by the up or down arrows. Alternatively, use the mouse wheel.

91 While in the Project window, you can select tracks using the up / down arrow keys. While in the Mixer, you can select tracks using the left / right arrow keys. Several tracks / channels can be selected simultaneously by holding the Shift key while pressing the arrow keys. By default, selecting also record enables the tracks and the Shift + arrow combinations therefore provide a quick method of record enabling multiple tracks.

92 Ctrl / Command click on the click, tempo and sync buttons to open the Metronome, Tempo and Sync Setup windows respectively.

93 To name all parts dragged onto a track according to the track name, activate 'Parts get track names' in Preferences / Editing. This is useful for copying parts between instruments in MIDI orchestral projects, where you might use a template with the tracks already named according to the instruments in the orchestra.

94 To implement tempo changes over a specific range without affecting the rest of the tempo in the project, proceed as follows: 1) As a guide, set up the left and right locators around the desired range in the ruler. 2) Select the Time warp tool in normal mode. 3) Hold Shift and click at the left and right locator positions to enter tempo events at the start and end of the selected range. Tempo changes may now be freely added within the selected range without affecting the rest of the tempo structure of the project.

95 For instant loop playback of the currently selected event in the event display, press Shift + G (Transport menu / Loop selection).

96 To set up a loop within an event, activate the Independent Track Loop button available in the Audio Part editor and MIDI editors. During playback, the chosen range loops throughout the length of the event. This is helpful for finding new loop-based arrangements. Closing the editor cancels the looping effect.

97 It is best to activate 'Copy Files to Working Directory' in Preferences / Editing / Audio / On Import Audio Files as your default setting. This means that all imported audio is always copied to the working directory

and the original source audio files are not used. This avoids missing files and accidental modification of audio files used in other projects.

98 To save different Project startup settings as templates, select 'Save as template' in the File menu and choose a suitable name in the 'Save as template' dialogue. The template is now available in the templates list whenever you select 'New project' in the File menu. Templates are useful for creating startup projects optimised for 24 track audio, 16 track MIDI, 2 track mastering and so on, or for pre-configuring the system for use with advanced software samplers and synthesizers like Kontakt and Reaktor.

99 Experts recommend using two hard disk drives with Cubase; one for the system and program files and the other for the project and audio files. This maximises performance and makes it easier to maintain the audio disk. For large capacity hard disks it is preferable to create several smaller-sized partitions since this allows easier defragmentation and management of data.

100 Back up your data. Although hard disk failure is not a common occurrence, backing up your data is essential if you wish to avoid the potentially disastrous situation of losing all your files. Popular back-up media include: spare internal hard drives, hard drives in removable caddies, USB keys, CD and DVD.

Info

If any of the tips outlined here are particularly useful to you, copy them into Cubase's notepad (Project menu) along with your own tips / notes and save this as part of your default project. That way, your favourite tips and info are always available when you start up a new project.

Macro magic

The macro section of many Cubase setups often remains empty because, while users are aware that macros can be enormously powerful, few have the time or the patience to create their own. This section shows you how and also provides you with a time-saving startup library of powerful ready-made macros.

What are macros?
Macros are user-configurable 'super functions' made up of a number of basic functions strung together in a logical sequence. They are very powerful since a large number of moves can be reduced to a single key command. Functions that you use one after the other repetitively can now be selected at lightning fast speed via a macro command, resulting in dramatically increased efficiency and productivity. Macros are managed in the Key commands window.

Key commands window
The Key commands window is opened by selecting File / Key commands. The macro section is toggled on and off in the lower half of the display by clicking on the Show / Hide macros button (Figure 21.1). If you are new to macros there may be no macros in the list when you first go there. New empty macros are created by clicking on the New macro button. A command is added to the new macro by selecting a function from the upper half of the window and clicking on the Add command button. You can keep on adding functions to the macro to create an elaborate sequence of commands. Once created, a key command may be assigned to the macro in the macro section

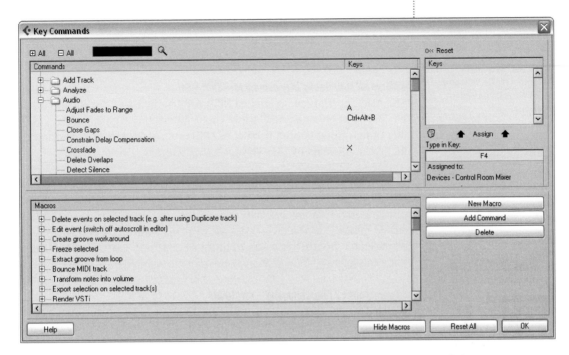

Figure 21.1
Key commands window featuring the macros section in the lower half of the display

in the upper half of the window. This means that the macro can now be activated with a single keystroke.

Macro library

The following is a list of both simple and advanced macros designed to enhance your use of Cubase and to teach you how to create your own macros by example. Each entry features the macro name, the suggested key command, the list of functions which make up the macro, and a brief description of what the macro does and how it can be used.

1 Bounce audio track [Key command – Shift+F1]

Designed to select all events on the currently selected audio track and bounce them all into one single audio event which overwrites all the original events in the event display. (This creates a new file on the hard disk and a new clip in the Pool, regardless of what you choose in the Replace dialogue which appears).

Macro 1

Edit – Select All on Tracks
Audio – Bounce

2 Bounce all audio tracks [Key command – Shift+F2]

This macro bounces all audio tracks into events of the same length, based upon the range of the overall project. This is particularly useful when you need to export multitrack audio material into another audio application which does not recognise regular global file exchange formats. You can maintain the relative positions of the audio events simply by starting all files at the same time position.

Macro 2

Tool – Range tool
Edit – Select all
Audio – Bounce
Tool – Select tool
Navigate – Up
Navigate – Down

3 Merge MIDI track [Key command – Shift+F3]

This macro merges all MIDI parts on the currently selected MIDI track and

Macro 3

Edit – Solo
Edit – Select All on Tracks
Transport – Locators to Selection
MIDI – Merge MIDI in Loop
Edit – Solo

Macro 4

Edit – Select All
Transport – Locators to Selection
Add Track – MIDI
MIDI – Merge MIDI in Loop

Macro 5

Edit – Lock
Edit – Select All on Tracks
Edit – Delete
Edit – Select All on Tracks
Edit – Unlock

Macro 6

Transport – Locate Selection
Edit – Duplicate
Transport – Locators to Selection
Transport – Set Left Locator
Edit – Left selection side to cursor
Zoom – Zoom Full

Macro 7

Transport – Locate Selection
Edit – Duplicate
Edit – Duplicate
Edit – Duplicate
Transport – Locators to Selection
Transport – Set Left Locator
Edit – Left selection side to cursor
Zoom – Zoom Full

bounces them all into one single MIDI part. Overwriting the original parts in the event display depends upon your choice in the 'Erase destination' option in the MIDI Merge options dialogue which appears.

4 Merge all MIDI tracks [Key command – Shift+F4]

This macro merges all non-muted MIDI parts in the event display into a single MIDI part on a new MIDI track. Useful for creating type 0 standard MIDI files or for mixing down a number of MIDI drum parts into a single composite part. It assumes that the pointer tool is selected.

5 Crop selection [Key command – typewriter '=']

This macro uses the lock command to shield the current selection from the delete command and its action is similar to an image crop function as found in image editing software. All you do is select one or more events on the currently selected track and execute this macro to delete all other non-selected events on the track. It is intended for operation on the currently selected track only.

6 Dupli zoom x 2 [Key command – Ctrl+F2]

Doubles the number of instances of the current range selection, automatically zooms in to the currently used area of the event display and reselects the duplicated section. It is designed to be used after having made a selection with the range selection tool (double-click on an event, for example) and may be repeated as required (by pressing the assigned key command a number of times). Repeating the macro results in useful musical numbers. For example, selecting an event with the range selection tool and pressing Ctrl / Command+F2 (the suggested key command) gives two duplicates, pressing it twice in succession gives four duplicates, pressing it three times gives eight duplicates, pressing it four times gives sixteen duplicates... and so on. The number of duplicates for each selection of the macro is always doubled. This is particularly useful when working with drum loops. If required, the zoom command may be left out of the macro. Note that all the events between the left and right locators are reselected. This allows you to use the macro for 'multiplication' rather than 'addition'. For a meaningful result, always use the range selection tool with this macro.

7 Dupli zoom x 4 [Key command – Ctrl+F4]

Quadruples the number of instances of the current range selection, automatically zooms in to the currently used area of the event display and re-selects the duplicated section. It is designed to be used after having made a selection with the range selection tool (double-click on an event, for example) and may be repeated as required (by pressing the assigned key command a number of times). Repeating the macro results in useful musical numbers. For example, selecting an event with the range selection tool and pressing Ctrl / Command + F4 (the suggested key command) gives four duplicates, pressing it twice in succession gives sixteen duplicates, pressing it three times in succession gives sixty four duplicates... and so on. The number of duplicates for each selection of the macro is always quadrupled. This is useful when working with drum loops and you can build up a large number of duplicates very quickly. If required, the zoom command may be left out of the macro. Note that all the events between the left and right locators are reselected. This allows you to use the macro for 'multiplication' rather than 'addition'. For a meaningful result, always use the range selection tool with this macro.

8 Dupli zoom + 3 [Key command – Ctrl+F3]

A simpler macro than the 'dupli zoom' multiplication macros outlined above. This simply 'adds' three duplicates to the current selection and zooms in to the used area of the display. It may be used repetitively but it always adds three duplicates and so does not always produce a musically meaningful number of events. It provides an alternative to the standard repeat command selected by pressing Ctrl / Command + K. Other similar macros could be designed for other musically useful numbers of repeats. If required, the zoom command may be left out of the macro.

9 Open focused editor [Key command – W]

Sets the left and right locators to the currently selected event, opens the relevant editor, zooms in and selects the range of the event. This macro automatically organises your event selection ready for editing purposes and functions well with all event types. For a more stable view, switch off autoscroll.

10 Events to audio part and edit [Key command – Ctrl+Alt+E]

Puts the currently selected audio events into an audio part and opens the Audio Part editor. Simple but very useful. Ideal for editing multiple audio takes which have been recorded in cycle recording mode.

11 Punch range setup [Key command – Ctrl+#]

This macro prepares Cubase for the 'Punch range record' macro outlined below (Macro 12). It assumes that no punch buttons have already been activated on the Transport panel and requires the preparation of suitable workspace and zoom presets. The zoom presets menu is found to the left of the horizontal zoom slider in the lower right corner of the Project window. The workspace presets menu is found as a sub-menu in the Window menu. The action of the macro runs as follows: 1) The Transport panel punch out button is activated. 2) A workspace, containing settings for a suitably sized Project window with a visible Transport panel, is selected. 3) A zoom preset set for a 10-15 second horizontal view (or some other suitable zoom setting) is selected. 4) A second zoom preset set to a four row vertical track size is selected. 5) The range tool is selected ready to make a selection for the punch in.

12 Punch range record [Key command – #]

Designed to make punch-in recording easier, this macro gives a two bar pre roll before your chosen range selection and automatically punches in and out of record mode at the start and end points. Although it is not essential, the procedure works better if you have already prepared the way using the 'Punch range setup' macro, outlined above. In any case, before starting to punch record using this macro, ensure that the cycle, punch in and pre-roll buttons are de-activated on the Transport panel and that the punch out button is activated. Select any section of your music using the range selection tool. You are now ready to start punch recording. This macro works even

Macro 8

Transport – Locate Selection
Edit – Duplicate
Edit – Duplicate
Edit – Duplicate
Transport – Locators to Selection
Transport – Set Left Locator
Zoom – Zoom Full

Macro 9

Transport - Locators to Selection
Edit - Open
Zoom - Zoom to Locators
Edit - Select in Loop
Zoom - Zoom to Selection
Edit - Select None
Zoom - Zoom to Locators

Macro 10

Audio – Events to Part
Transport – Locators to Selection
Edit – Open
Zoom – Zoom Full

Macro 11

Transport – AutoPunch Out
Workspaces – Workspace 2
Zoom – Zoom Preset 2
Zoom – Zoom Tracks 4 Rows
Tool – Range Tool

Macro 12

Transport – AutoPunch In
Transport – Locators to Selection
Transport – To Left Locator
Transport – Step Back Bar
Transport – Step Back Bar
Transport – Start

when a range over several tracks is selected, at which time simultaneous recording on all tracks takes place. You are also free to record on both audio and MIDI tracks at the same time. You would most often use the range selection tool to govern where recording takes place but the macro also works when you select events with the object selection tool. Overall, this macro is excellent for all kinds of detailed punch in work and, if necessary, makes it easy to punch in over the same section a large number of times. If you need a post-roll after the recorded section, activate the post-roll button and enter a post roll value in the Transport panel. This macro works best with 'Enable record on selected track' active (Preferences / Editing / Project & Mixer) and with 'Tapemachine style' selected (Preferences / VST).

Macro 13

Transport – Set Marker 9
Transport – To Left Locator
Transport – Step Back Bar
Transport – Step Back Bar
Transport – Play until Next Marker

13 Punch range playback [Key command – ']

This macro makes it easy to audition what you have just recorded with the above punch range record macro (Macro 12). It sets marker 9 at the current position of the cursor (which would normally be found placed just after the recording), rewinds to the start of the recorded section, steps back two bars and then plays back the passage up to marker 9. The macro may be used repetitively but for successful operation you should allow playback to reach marker 9 before recommencing.

Macro 14

Transport – Locators to Selection
Navigate – Right
Transport – To Right Locator
Edit – Cut
Edit – Paste

14 Reshuffle [Key command – Alt+R]

Shuffles the next event back to the end point of the current event selection. This macro always works on the next event to the right of the current selection and may be used repetitively. For a successful result, you must also select the track concerned. The outcome is the closing of all the gaps between events so that they appear consecutively on the track. Good for pulling events back together after editing which changes their lengths.

Macro 15

Transport - Stop
Transport - Locators to selection
Transport - Locate selection
Edit - Cut
Transport - Record

15 Retake [Key command – Ctrl+pad *]

This macro is designed primarily to be used just after recording a bad take and allows an instant re-take over the same range with a single key command. It operates on the currently selected track and functions by deleting the previously recorded event and then re-recording over the same range. It also operates by selecting any audio event over which you wish to re-record. It functions best when not in cycle mode and with pre-roll, post-roll and punch out activated. It has no effect if no event is selected.

Workspaces

What are workspaces?

Workspaces are complete window layouts which may be stored or recalled at any time, allowing you to quickly adapt your working environment to the task at hand. They come in two varieties:

1 Workspaces

'Workspaces' contain the layout and contents of the windows stored at various moments within the active project. They may be recalled within the active project only and are not globally available to other projects. A workspace includes window sizes, window positions, track sizes, horizontal zoom resolutions, horizontal and vertical scroll positions, ruler time settings, tool selection, mixer configuration, Transport panel configuration and so on. Essentially, most of what you can see on the screen at any given moment may be saved as a workspace (similar to taking a snapshot).

2 Workspace presets

Once created, regular workspaces may also be stored as presets known as 'Workspace presets'. These are globally available to all projects. Workspace presets store the main windows only and do not include all the details within each window. However, they have the advantage of being globally available to all projects and are useful for setting up generic window layouts for primary tasks such as recording, editing and mixing.

Organize workspaces dialogue

Workspaces are managed using the 'Organize Workspaces' dialogue which is opened by selecting Window / Workspaces / Organize, or pressing Alt + Pad 0 (Figure 21.2). This displays the list of available workspaces in the current project to the left, and the list of globally available workspace presets to the right.

There is always at least one active workspace which is indicated by a grey selection bar in the list, even if you have not yet created any workspaces in the current project. In the latter case, the default active workspace appears named as 'Main' in the list. New workspaces may be created at any time by clicking on the 'new' button. The stored data is based upon the positions and contents of the currently open windows in the project. When you create a new workspace you are obliged to name it in the list.

You can activate any existing workspace by double-clicking in its number column (#) or by selecting it and clicking on the activate button. A workspace may be locked by clicking in its box in the locked column, which keeps the selected workspace in its original form regardless of how you change the windows in the project. This means that you always go back to the original stored workspace each time you select it. To store a workspace as a preset which is

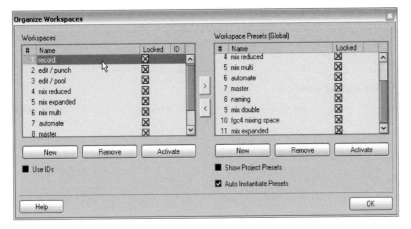

Figure 21.2
Organize workspaces dialogue

available globally to all projects, move it from the left column into the right column using the arrow buttons between the two lists. If required, workspace presets on the right may be moved back to the left workspace list in a similar manner. Activating 'Auto instantiate presets' automatically copies global workspace presets into the list on the left, if there are not already workspaces created for the current project. This is useful when creating new projects. Activating 'Use IDs' allows you to re-number the workspaces in the ID column regardless of their position in the list. This is helpful when recalling specific workspaces using key commands (Alt + Pad 1-9) since the keypad numbers now refer to the ID numbers and not the list numbers.

Handling workspaces and workspace key commands

Handling workspaces requires a little practice. The first rule to keep in mind is that you are always working within the active workspace. Secondly, this active workspace can either be locked or unlocked. If it is locked, you are not actually changing what is stored in the workspace if you adjust the current window layout. However, if it is unlocked, the contents are immediately changed if you make any adjustments. A very good and easy tip for keeping an eye on your workspace status is to observe the number in brackets next to the Window menu. The number within the brackets specifies the currently active workspace, and the presence or non-presence of a full-stop next to the number denotes its lock status. For example, '(1)' means that the active workspace is number 1 and it is unlocked, whereas (1.) means that the active workspace is number 1 and it is locked.

The Organize workspaces dialogue is helpful for the overall management of workspaces but the default key commands are often better when creating and using workspaces during the heat of a recording session. The relevant key commands can be found next to the menu items in the workspaces sub-menu (Figure 21.3).

The basic sequence of events to create a workspace using the key commands runs as follows:

1 Set up the windows in the project as desired.
2 Press Alt + Pad / to create a new workspace. Enter a name into the pop-up dialogue.
3 Press Alt + Pad . to lock the workspace.
4 Press Alt + Pad 1-9 to recall the workspaces you create.
5 Press Alt + Pad . a second time to unlock the workspace if you need to update it.

Workspaces for workflow

Like macros, workspaces help improve your workflow. This section explains how by describing the creation of workspaces for recording, editing and mixing.

A workspace for recording

A workspace for recording normally requires the Project window and the Transport panel with perhaps a reduced Mixer and Pool (Figure 21.4).

The workspace shown here includes a reduced Project window with the

Figure 21.3
Workspaces sub-menu showing the default key commands

Figure 21.4
A workspace for recording. Here, the first take of the recording session is under way.

Mixer open below it and the Transport panel open above. To grasp the logic of this workspace we need to consider the recording process itself. Here, it is assumed that you need to record an external source, such as a live musical performance via a microphone. The first thing you need to verify in Cubase is the level of the input signal. Hence, this workspace features the Mixer with the input channels visible so you can monitor the input and adjust input levels as you proceed with the recording session. The input / output menus are visible on all channels to help set the input and output routing. The output channels are visible so you can monitor and adjust the overall output level. The Transport panel includes the performance meter, record mode, locators, main transport, and master sections. The tracks are set to a vertical size of 2 rows allowing you a view of the record and monitor buttons and of the events as they get recorded. The Inspector, Infoline and Overview switches are de-activated but you may prefer to open the Inspector for certain detailed recording operations. The open Pool window and Remaining record time display in the corner help you keep an eye on the audio clips as they get recorded and how much disk space remains.

A workspace for event editing

A workspace for event editing often includes the Project window maximised to show the greatest amount of event display possible (see Figure 21.5). A suitable track row size of four rows is chosen to get a good view of the events, the Infoline is activated to display information about each event as it is select-

Figure 21.5
A workspace for editing where the event display is made as large as possible

ed, and the Overview helps you navigate and zoom within the whole project. An open Inspector might be helpful if you are selecting presets or changing MIDI channel parameters. The Transport panel is also shown and features the Marker section to help with navigation, the jog wheel for detailed lining up of the cursor position, and the master level control to adjust the overall level while editing.

A workspace for mixing

A workspace suitable for mixing might include the extended Mixer with a Project window reduced to its minimum vertical height (Figure 21.6). The screen width shown here allows around fifteen mixer channels to be displayed in wide mode. The input and output channels have been hidden to allow a greater number of regular channels to be displayed simultaneously. The Project window features an enlarged Marker track to help navigate within the project and regular tracks with their row size reduced to the minimum. When the Marker track is selected, the markers are also shown in list form in the open Inspector to the left. To help still further with navigation the Transport panel is reduced to just the locator and marker sections, providing buttons for moving the cursor to the left and right locator positions, or to the first fifteen markers. The time display helps when Cubase is linked to other machines via time code and the performance meters help you keep an eye on the CPU load.

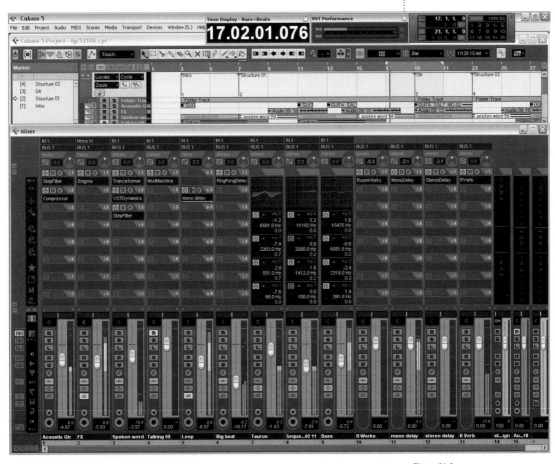

Figure 21.6
A workspace for mixing, featuring the
extended Mixer dominating the screen
space

What's so good about workspaces?

Any one of the above workspaces might be useful but the real advantage of workspaces is being able to switch instantaneously between them at any stage during the evolution of a project. This is very liberating. Rather than approaching your workflow in standard 'do all the recording, do all the editing and then mix it' fashion, you can now effortlessly jump between different streamlined environments. Of course, the advantages do not end there. You can store a workspace at any moment throughout the development of your project and go back to that particular view at any time in the future. Furthermore, you can create workspaces suitable for all kinds of other everyday Cubase tasks, such as tiling multiple editors; opening multiple insert effect interfaces; organising reduced, extended and multiple Mixer layouts; tiling a large-scale Pool window alongside the Project Browser; and so on. The possibilities are endless.

Info

Large orchestral arrangements often call for working on specific groups of instruments on multiple tracks. Rather than scrolling up and down in the Project window to find the required instruments, just store a number of workspaces with the appropriate vertical scroll positions. You can now switch instantly between the different project views.

Project Logical editor

The Project Logical editor (Figure 21.7) is helpful for global track and event editing tasks, such as track and event renaming, global selections based upon names or media type, and track operations (see the supplied presets for some examples). It is opened from the Edit menu and features a similar layout to the Logical editor for MIDI data.

Figure 21.7 shows a preset for pre pending the words 'Good take' to all selected events or parts. This helps quickly rename the best takes as you proceed with a recording session.

Figure 21.7
The Project Logical editor

Other possibilities include the following:

Figure 21.8
Moving events one tick at a time

When you assign a key command to this function it provides a fuss-free solution for moving events back and forth by one tick. To move events backwards, assign the subtract function in the action operation column.

Figure 21.9
Highlighting events in yellow

In this case, the name entered in the Parameter 1 column of the action section must match one of the colour names as defined in the project Colour selector Event colours list.

Recommended reading

Knowledge of sound recording, microphones, mixing, MIDI, sampling, sequencing, digital audio and acoustics can help you get better results with Cubase. There are a wide range of books available on these subjects. The following list should help you get started:

Anderton, Craig 'MIDI for Musicians', (Amsco Publications, 1995), 120pp.

Borwick, John 'Microphones – Technology and Technique', (Oxford: Focal Press, 1990), 241pp.

Borwick, John ed. 'Sound Recording Practice', (Oxford: Oxford University Press, 1996), 616pp.

Buick, Peter and Lennard, Vic 'Music Technology Reference Book', (PC Publishing, 1995), 160pp.

Clackett, Dave 'Handbook of MIDI Sequencing', (PC Publishing, 1996), 244pp.

De Furia, Steve and Scacciaferro, Joe 'The Sampling Book', (Omnibus Press, 2002), 152pp.

Eargle, John 'The Microphone Book', (Focal Press, 2004), 368pp.

Everest, F. Alton 'The Master Handbook of Acoustics', (New York: TAB Books, 1994), 452pp.

Gibson, David 'The Art of Mixing', (Music Sales Limited, 1997), 127pp.

Harris, John 'Recording the Guitar', (PC Publishing, 1997), 156pp.

Howard, David M. and Angus, James 'Acoustics and Psychoacoustics', (Oxford: Focal Press, 2nd edition, 2001), 416pp.

Huber, David Miles 'The MIDI Manual', (SAMS, 1991), 268pp.

Huber and Runstein 'Modern Recording Techniques', (Oxford: Focal Press,1997), 496pp.

Katz, Bob 'Mastering Audio: The Art and the Science', (Focal Press, 2002), 319pp.

Kirk, Ross and Hunt, Andy 'Digital Sound Processing for Music and Multimedia', (Oxford: Focal Press, 1999), 352pp.

Lehrman, Paul 'Midi for the Professional', (Music Sales Corp., 1993), 239pp.

Massey, Howard 'Behind the Glass', (Backbeat UK, 2000), 224pp

Mellor, David 'Recording Techniques for Small Studios' (PC Publishing, 1993), 208pp.

Millward, Simon 'Sound Synthesis with VST Instruments', (PC Publishing, 2002), 277pp.

Moylan, William 'Understanding and Crafting the Mix: The Art of Recording', (Focal Press, 2007), 424pp.

Ortiz, Joe and Pauly 'Beat It! (MIDI drum programming)', (PC Publishing, 1997), 114pp.

Owsinski, Bobby 'The Mixing Engineer's Handbook', (Music Sales Limited, 1999), 234pp.

Poyser, Debbie, Johnson, Derek and Jones, Hollin 'Fast Guide to Propellerhead Reason', (PC Publishing, 2007), 474pp

Rona, Jeffrey and Wilkinson, Scott (Editor) 'The Midi Companion', (Hal Leonard Publishing Corp, 1994), 96pp.

Rothstein, Joseph 'MIDI – A Comprehensive Introduction', (Oxford: Oxford University Press, 1992), 226pp.

Rumsey, Francis 'The Audio Workstation Handbook', (Oxford: Focal Press, 1996), 286pp.

Russ, Martin and Rumsey, Francis (Editor) 'Sound Synthesis and Sampling', (Oxford: Focal Press, 1996), 400pp.

Stavrou, Michael 'Mixing with your Mind', (Flux Research, 2004), 300pp. (available from: www.mixingwithyourmind.com)

Waugh, Ian 'Making Music with Digital Audio (Direct to disk recording on the PC)', (PC Publishing, 1997), 250pp

White, Paul 'Creative Recording 2 – Microphones and Recording Techniques', (Music Maker Books, 1995), 99pp.

White, Paul 'Home Recording Made Easy', (Sanctuary Publishing, 1997), 205pp.

White, Paul 'MIDI for the Technophobe', (Sanctuary Publishing, 1997), 184pp.

Useful websites

The internet is a very good resource for the latest information about Cubase and related products. The following lists some websites which may be of interest:

Steinberg Cubase
Steinberg website   www.steinberg.net

Plug-ins
Abbey Road Plug-ins   www.abbeyroadplugins.com
Antares   www.antarestech.com
Apulsoft   www.apulsoft.ch
Audio Ease   www.audioease.com
BBE Sound   www.bbesound.com
Bias   www.bias-inc.com
Blue Cat Audio   www.bluecataudio.com
Brainworx   www.brainworx-music.de
Celemony   www.celemony.com
dB-audioware   www.dB-audioware.com
DSP FX   www.dspfx.com
Flux   www.fluxhome.com
FXpansion   www.fxpansion.com
IK Multimedia   www.ikmultimedia.com
Izotope   www.izotope.com
Intelligent sounds and music   www.ismism.de
Kjaerhus   www.kjaerhusaudio.com
Melda Production   www.meldaproduction.com
Native Instruments   www.native-instruments.com
Nomad Factory   www.nomadfactory.com
Nugen Audio   www.nugenaudio.com
Princeton Digital   www.princetondigital.com
Prosoniq   www.prosoniq.com
PSP   www.pspaudioware.com
SIR (Impulse Response Processor)   www.knufinke.de/sir
Softube   www.softube.se
Sonalksis   www.sonalksis.com
Sonic Foundry   www.sfoundry.com

Sonnox	www.sonnoxplugins.com
Tascam	www.tascam.co.uk
URS	www.ursplugins.com
Virtos Audio	www.virtos-audio.com
Voxengo	www.voxengo.com
Wave Arts	www.wavearts.com
Waves	www.waves.com

DSP powered plug-ins

Focusrite Liquid Mix	www.focusrite.com
Solid State Logic Duende	www.solid-state-logic.com
T.C. Electronics Powercore	www.tcelectronic.com
UAD powered plug-ins	www.uaudio.com
MIDI plug-ins	
Franck's MIDI plug-ins	www.midi-plugins.de
Nicolas Fournel	www.nicolasfournel.com
Ntonyx MIDI effects	www.ntonyx.com
Tencrazy	www.tencrazy.com

VST Instrument developers

Applied Acoustics Systems	www.applied-acoustics.com
Arturia	www.arturia.com
Bojo	www.bojo-software.com
Cakewalk	www.cakewalk.com
Delaydots	www.delaydots.com
Edirol	www.edirol.com
Fxpansion	www.fxpansion.com
GForce Software	www.gforcesoftware.com
Green Oak	www.greenoak.com
Image Line	flstudio.image-line.com
Izotope	www.iztope.com
Lin Plug	www.linplug.com
LoftSoft	www.loftsoft.co.uk
Maz sound tools	www.maz-sound.de
mda	www.mda-vst.com
Muon Software	www.muon-software.com
Native Instruments	www.native-instruments.com
reFX	www.refx.net
Spectrasonics	www.spectrasonics.net
Steinberg	www.steinberg.net
Synapse Audio	www.synapse-audio.com
TC Works	www.tcworks.de
Ultimate Sound Bank	www.plugsound.com
VirSyn	www.virsyn.de

Audio cards / hardware

Apogee	www.apogeedigital.com
Echo	www.echoaudio.com

Edirol	www.edirol.com
E-MU	www.emu.com
ESI (Ego Systems Inc.)	www.esi-pro.com
Focusrite	www.focusrite.com
Korg	www.korg.com
Lexicon	www.lexiconpro.com
Lynx	www.lynxstudio.com
Mackie	www.mackie.com
Mark of the Unicorn (MOTU)	www.motu.com
M Audio	www.midiman.com
Metric Halo	www.mhlabs.com
Prism Sound	www.prismsound.com
RME	www.rme-audio.com
Sonic Core	www.sonic-core.net
T.C. Electronics	www.tcelectronic.com
Yamaha	www.yamaha.com

Soundbanks and samples

Convolution impulse responses	www.noisevault.com
Echo chamber	www.echochamber.ch
FM sounds	www.thedx7.co.uk
KVR VSTi sound libraries	www.kvraudio.com
Reaktor (Paul Swennenhuis)	www.midiworld.org/AuReality
Sample swap	www.sampleswap.org
Sonomic	www.sonomic.com
Sound ideas	www.sound-ideas.com
Tassman library	www.hvsynthdesign.com
Time and space	www.timespace.com
WizooSounds sample library	www.wizoosounds.com

Sound synthesis, synthesizers and music technology

Hammond organ	theatreorgans.com/hammond/faq
Mellotron	www.mellotron.com
Moog	www.moogmusic.com
Moog synthesizers	moogarchives.com
Synthesizers and synthesis	www.vintagesynth.org
Synthesizer history	www.obsolete.com/120_years
Synthesizer information and links	www.synthesizers.com
Synth zone	www.synthzone.com

General interest

Acousti Products	www.acoustiproducts.com
Acoustics	www.ethanwiner.com/acoustics.html
Acoustic analysis	www.etfacoustic.com
Analogx utilities	www.analogx.com
audio CD A/B tests	www.theabcd.com
audio comparison CDs	www.3daudioinc.com
Audio forums	www.audioforums.com

Audio production database	www.note2.com
Auralex acoustics	www.auralex.com
Apple website	www.apple.com
CD-Recordable FAQ website	www.cdrfaq.org
Computer Music Magazine	www.computermusic.co.uk
Computer isolation boxes	www.custom-consoles.com
Digital domain	www.digido.com
Electronic music publishing	www.raw42.com
Electronic music website	www.em411.com
Kustom PCs	www.kustompcs.co.uk
KVR Audio plug-in resources	www.kvraudio.com
Mac audio and music site	www.macmusic.org
Metal grille pop-shields	www.stedmancorp.com
MIDI Farm	www.hittrax.com.au
MIDI utilities	www.midiox.com
Millennium Music	www.millennium-music.co.uk
Musician's Tech Central	www.musicianstechcentral.com
Music XP website	www.musicxp.net
PC hardware analysis	www.cpuid.com
Plug-in Spot VSTi resources	www.pluginspot.com
Pro audio network	www.digitalprosound.com
Pro audio reference	www.rane.com/digi-dic.html
Professional recording resources	www.prorec.com
Project studio handbook	www.theprojectstudiohandbook.com/directory. htm
Quiet PC	www.quietpc.com
Rightmark audio analyser	audio.rightmark.org
Shareware Music Machine	www.hitsquad.com
Silent PC components/cases	www.antec.com
Silent PC components/cases	www.paq.ltd.uk
Silent PC review	www.silentpcreview.com
Softpedia general utilities	www.softpedia.com
Sonic Spot resources	www.sonicspot.com
Sound on Sound magazine	www.soundonsound.com
Studio design	www.johnlsayers.com
Studio design (SAE)	www.saecollege.de/reference_material
Studiospares	www.studiospares.com
Studio tips	www.studiotips.com
Tom's PC hardware guide	www.tomshardware.com
University of York	www.york.ac.uk/inst/mustech
Utilitygeek general utilities	www.utilitygeek.com
Virtual Guitarist website	www.bornemark.se
VST central VSTi listings	www.vstcentral.com
Windows optimisation	www.ccleaner.com

A/D converter Analogue-to-digital converter. A device which converts analogue data, such as an audio signal from the real world, into digital data (a sequence of numbers) which can be retained in computer memory or stored on digital media such as hard disk, CD and DVD.

ADSR Attack, Decay, Sustain, Release. A four-breakpoint envelope type used to control how the amplitude of a sound evolves over time. ADSR envelopes are also used to control the spectral evolution of a sound by modulating the cut-off frequency of a filter.

AES Audio Engineering Society. International organisation responsible for setting standards in the audio industry.

AES3 A digital signal interface standard agreed by the Audio Engineering Society and the European Broadcasting Union. Also known as AES-EBU, this uses 110 Ohm cable terminated in XLR connectors.

AES-EBU See AES3

Aftertouch The action of applying pressure to one or more keys of a musical keyboard after the onset of a note or chord. Also referred to as 'Channel Aftertouch' or 'Channel Pressure', it is transmitted via MIDI as Aftertouch messages and affects all notes present on the same MIDI channel by the same amount. It can be used to produce various real-time performance effects such as volume or brightness modulation and vibrato.

AGP Accelerated Graphics Port. Slot found on a computer's motherboard designed to accept graphics cards. Advantageous for audio since using an AGP graphics card optimises the use of the computer's resources and is unlikely to interfere with audio performance.

Algorithm A clearly defined, step-by-step set of instructions designed to achieve the completion of a specific task. Algorithms are invariably translated into computer programming languages and used as the building blocks for computer programs.

Aliasing Digital audio distortion which occurs when the sample rate is not more than twice the highest frequency to be sampled, or when unwanted frequencies higher than half the sample rate are somehow allowed into the digital audio system. This results in the addition of discordant frequencies when the sampled signal is reconstructed. The system is unable to reproduce the higher frequencies and instead reflects them around the half sampling rate as lower frequencies which can be heard within the audible part of the spectrum.

All-pass filter A filtering device which involves delaying frequency components by varying amounts and mixing the result with the original signal. Unlike conventional filtering, no attenuation in the amplitudes of the frequencies takes place.

AM Amplitude Modulation. A sound effect achieved by modulating the amplitude of one audio signal (the carrier) by another signal (the modulator). When the modulator is an LFO, tremolo effects are produced. When both signals are in the audible range, a more complex signal containing the carrier and the sum and difference frequencies of the carrier and modulator is produced (sometimes used for sound synthesis).

Amplifier A device which increases or decreases the amplitude of a signal which passes through it.

Amplitude A measure of the depth of the compression and rarefaction cycles of a sound signal where the peak amplitude is the point of maximum displacement from the mid-point of the signal's waveform. The amplitude contributes to the perceived loudness of the signal.

Analogue In audio, refers to a sound signal whose waveform has a value at every point in time. There are no discrete steps between each point and an analogue recording is usually that which has been made onto analogue tape. Also used to describe analogue synthesis (as opposed to digital synthesis).

Arpeggiator A device for automatically repeating a group of notes in a cyclic pattern, usually by stepping through the notes of a chord which is held down on the musical keyboard.

ASIO Audio Stream Input Output. Computer protocol developed by Steinberg for handling audio recording and playback in digital audio systems.

Attack The shape and duration of the first part of a sound event where the amplitude rises from zero to its peak level (as implemented in an ADSR envelope).

Attenuation The reduction of the amplitude of a sound signal (or of a component within the signal).

Balance i) describes the relative levels of two or more sound elements (for example, when setting up a mix on a mixing console). ii) MIDI Controller 8. Used to adjust the relative levels of two components of a sound.

Band-pass filter A filter which allows a band of frequencies between two cut-off points to pass through with little change while significantly attenuating frequencies both above and below the pass band.

Band-reject filter A filter which significantly attenuates a band of frequencies between two cut-off points while allowing the rest of the signal to pass through with little change.

Bandwidth i) The range between two frequency points within the spectrum of an audio signal. ii) The overall frequency range of the spectrum of an audio signal.

Bank Select A combination of MIDI Controllers 0 and 32. A Bank Select message is usually immediately followed by a Program Change and allows switching to as many as 16384 different Banks.

BIOS Basic Input / Output System. A program residing in a ROM memory or flash BIOS chip on a computer's motherboard, responsible for the basic initialisation of the processor, memory, I/O devices and operating system.

Bit Acronym for 'binary digit'. The smallest unit of information in a binary number, represented as a 1 or a 0.

Bit depth The number of levels of measurement available in a digital audio system during A/D and D/A conversion. For example, a 16-bit system features 65536 possible discrete values which can be used to measure the amplitude of an audio signal. Greater bit depth results in greater dynamic range.

Boot A term used to describe starting a computer. This can take the form of a 'cold start', when the computer is booted from its switched off state, and a 'warm start', when the computer is restarted in its switched on state.

BPM Abbreviation for Beats Per Minute. Musical tempo expressed as the number of beats which occur in one minute. For example, at a tempo of 60BPM each beat of the bar has a duration of one second.

Breath Controller A breath operated device connected to a synthesizer used to change the volume or timbre of a sound. It is transmitted via MIDI as Controller 2.

Byte An 8-bit binary number (e.g. 0011 1010), creating the fundamental unit of measurement for computer media. A kilobyte (Kb) is 1,024 bytes, a megabyte (Mb) is 1,024 kilobytes and a gigabyte (Gb) is 1,024 megabytes.

Buffer Temporary storage area used to store data as it flows in, out and through a computer system.

Carrier In frequency modulation, amplitude modulation and ring modulation, the carrier is the audio signal to which modulation is applied. The carrier normally governs the perceived pitch of the resulting tone.

CD ROM Compact Disc Read Only Memory. A read-only CD containing data which can only be read by a computer CD drive and not an audio CD player.

Cent One hundredth of a semitone. A unit in musical instrument tuning systems used for fine adjustments of pitch.

Centre frequency The centre point of the passband or stopband in a band-pass or band-reject filter.

Chorus An effect produced by passing a signal through one or more delay lines and modulating the delay time(s) with an LFO. The result is mixed with the original signal. The modulation of the delay times produces changes in the perceived pitch and timing, creating the illusion of an ensemble of sound sources.

Comb filter A filter comprised of multiple amplitude response curves (or resonances) located at harmonic intervals relative to a chosen fundamental frequency. Passing a signal through such a filter emphasises the chosen harmonics in the source sound and can often change its perceived pitch.

Compressor An automatic level adjustment device which normally results in loud parts of the signal becoming quieter and quiet parts becoming louder. Compression converts a large dynamic range into a smaller dynamic range.

Control Change A type of MIDI message used to control various parameters other than the musical notes. Control Change messages contain information about the Controller number (0 - 127) and its value (0 - 127). Each Controller number has a specific function and the more commonly used Controllers include modulation (01), breath control (02), main volume (07), pan (10), expression (11) and sustain pedal (64).

CPU Central Processing Unit. The main processor or chip controlling the operations of a computer, usually found on the main circuit board (motherboard).

Cross modulation The interconnection of the outputs of two oscillators to eachother's frequency inputs resulting in a complex frequency-modulated signal.

Cut-off The frequency at which the response of a filter passes from the pass band to the stop band (or vice versa), i.e. the frequency at which the filter starts to have an effect.

D/A converter Digital-to-analogue converter. A device which converts digital data into analogue data. For example, before we can hear the music on an audio CD, the digital information picked up by the read head of the CD player must first be converted into analogue form using a D/A converter.

DAT Digital Audio Tape. Digital audio recording format using 3.81mm wide tape in small cassettes. Began as a consumer format but later became widely accepted in the professional audio industry. DAT is now used less since mixing directly to hard disk and storage on other media is more convenient.

Decay i) As part of an envelope (e.g. ADSR), describes the shape and duration of a second part of a sound event where the amplitude falls from its peak level to its sustain level. ii) In general terms, describes how a sound fades away to silence.

Decibel (dB) A unit of relative measurement of sound level between audio signals on a logarithmic scale. For example, increasing the level of an input signal by 6dB results in an output which is double the amplitude of the original. Attenuating the level by 6dB results in an output which is half the amplitude.

Delay A replication of a signal which occurs at a set time after the original. Used in audio for delay, echo, chorus, flanging and other effects.

Digital Digital systems handle information as numerical data. For example, a digital waveform is measured as a succession of discrete points in time (samples), each of which is represented by a value (the maximum range of which forms the bit depth [or wordlength]). The quantity of these samples within a given time frame forms the sample rate. The audio on a CD is recorded at 16-bit / 44.1kHz, i.e. 44,100 16-bit wordlength samples per second.

Distortion A non-linear audio process which adds extra frequencies to the signal, thereby changing its waveform and harmonic structure.

Dither Audio processing technique which counteracts quantisation noise in digital audio recordings. Quantisation distortion occurs at very low levels when there are not enough bits in the system to accurately measure the signal. Noise shaped dithering involves converting the quantisation distortion into another kind of signal and re-distributing it to parts of the audio spectrum where it is less obvious to the human ear.

DMA Direct Memory Access. Describes access to RAM without passing through the main processor.

Download The process of loading a file from another system, such as from the internet or other network, into one's own computer.

Driver Software which provides the communication protocol between a hardware device and the operating system of the host computer. The hardware is usually set up and initialised via the driver software.

DSP i) Digital Signal Processing. The processing of signals using digital microprocessors. ii) Digital Signal Processor. A special computer chip which has been optimised for the high-speed numerical computations required for the processing of audio signals.

DVD Digital Versatile Disc. 5 inch diameter disc with around seven times the capacity of a regular compact disc, able to store data in computer, audio and video formats. DVD-A (DVD-Audio) is a high-quality format for stereo and multichannel audio.

EBU European Broadcasting Union. An organisation responsible for setting audio and broadcasting standards in Europe.

Echo A particular kind of delay where the delayed signal is clearly distinguishable from the original, often involving repeating echoes. Delay effects may be classed as echo when the delay time is increased to around 30ms or more, (i.e. when the ear begins to clearly differentiate the delayed and original signals).

EIDE Enhanced Integrated Drive Electronics. A standard for fast data transfer between the host computer and mass storage devices, such as hard drives and CD ROM drives.

Emphasis See Resonance

Envelope The shape of a sound's amplitude variations over time (usually plotted on a graph of amplitude against time with break-points for each stage in the sound's evolution). One of the most common envelope shapes is the ADSR envelope.

Envelope Generator (EG) A device which generates a time-varying control signal (envelope) used to modulate the amplitude of a sound (usually based upon a set of values entered by the user). Envelope generators are also commonly used to modulate the frequency of the cut-off point of a filter.

Equalisation (EQ) Boost / attenuation in the levels of different frequency bands within a signal (e.g. bass, mid and treble) for corrective or creative purposes.

Expression MIDI Controller 11. Used to change the volume of a note while it is sustaining.

FAT File Allocation Table. A small area of a computer's hard drive containing an index which is used to keep track of all data stored on the disk.

Feedback Circuit which allows the connection of the output signal back to the input, producing additional frequency components within the signal, (when used for overdrive and saturation effects), or for creating echo repeats, (when used for delay effects).

FFT Abbreviation for Fast Fourier Transform. An optimised version of the Fourier Transform (Joseph Fourier), a mathematical procedure for calculating the frequency components of a sound from the waveform.

Filter A device which attenuates one or more chosen frequency bands within a sound while allowing the others to pass through unchanged.

Firewire Data communication standard also referred to as IEEE-1394. Supports the serial transfer of data at 400Mbit/sec or 800Mbit/sec.

Flanging An audio effect created by mixing a delayed version of a signal with the original and modulating the delay time with an LFO while also applying an amount of feedback.

FM Frequency Modulation. A sound synthesis technique (or effect) where the frequency of one signal (the carrier) is modulated by another (the modulator). In the sound synthesis sense, FM implies that both frequencies are within the audible range and, when this is the case, multiple frequencies known as sidebands are added to the signal.

Frequency The number of times a periodic sound wave oscillates per second, measured in hertz (Hz).

Frequency domain The representation of a sound signal on a graph of amplitude versus frequency. This shows the spectrum of the signal.

Fundamental The lowest frequency component within a periodic sound wave and normally that which gives the tone its perceived pitch.

Gain A measure of the increase in relative amplitude level between the input and output of an amplifier.

Gate i) An audio device which radically attenuates the level of an input signal when it falls below a certain threshold. Used especially to filter out unwanted background noise and interference in the inactive parts of speech or musical performance. ii) The time between the moment a note is triggered by pressing a key on a musical keyboard (key on) and when the note is ended by releasing the key (key off).

General MIDI (GM) An addition to the MIDI protocol, (not formally a part of the MIDI Specification), providing a standard set of rules for patch mapping, drum and percussion note mapping, multi-timbrality, polyphony and various other elements. Roland introduced an enhanced version of the GM standard known as GS (General Standard) and Yamaha introduced similar enhancements known as XG (Extended General MIDI).

Harmonic Component within a sound whose frequency is a whole integer multiple of the fundamental.

Headroom The difference between the current level of a recorded signal and the maximum output level of the recording medium.

Hertz (Hz) A unit for measuring frequency. It expresses the number of oscillations per second of a periodic sound wave. The greater the number of hertz, the higher the perceived pitch of the sound.

Hexadecimal A base sixteen numbering system often used by computer programmers as an alternative to decimal or binary systems. The decimal numbers 0-9 are expressed as 0-9 in hexadecimal and decimal 10-15 are expressed as the letters A-F. Hexadecimal numbers have much more in common with the way that computers actually work than decimal numbers and they are less cumbersome than binary numbers. Thus they have proved extremely efficient for the analysis and understanding of computer data.

Hold pedal Middle foot pedal featured on acoustic pianos which, when pressed down, sustains the concurrently played note(s) but allows any subsequent notes to be played normally for as long as the pedal is held down. A similar foot pedal is featured on some electronic musical keyboards to create a similar effect. In MIDI-based applications the pedal action is transmitted using MIDI controller 66, (also referred to as sostenuto).

High-pass filter A filter which significantly attenuates the frequencies below a chosen cut-off point while allowing those above to pass through with little change.

HTML Hypertext mark-up language. A language used in the creation of web pages.

Internet Global network of computers interconnected via telephone lines. The internet is now the largest information resource in the world and provides a wide range of services and entertainment.

ISP Internet Service Provider. Internet users must subscribe to one of the ISPs which provide access to the internet.

Jumper A small clip for connecting pins on a circuit board to enable hardware re-configuration. Jumpers are found on such things as computer motherboards, extension cards and hard drives.

Latency The delay between the user input and the time it takes for a real-time digital audio system to respond and process the data through its hardware and software.

Level A measure of the amplitude of an audio signal.

LFO Abbreviation for low frequency oscillator. A type of oscillator which operates below the normal hearing range, often used for modulating a second oscillator to produce vibrato, tremolo and other modulation effects.

Limiter A peak level control device used to reduce the gain of the input signal when the input level exceeds the chosen threshold. A limiter is usually characterised by a very fast attack time and gain reduction which acts upon only the loudest peaks in the signal.

Logarithmic A manner in which to manage scales involving very large numbers and helpful in music and acoustics for understanding the human perception of sound intensity and frequency. The ear's response to these phenomena is logarithmic and not linear. For example, plotting frequency on a graph logarithmically shows equal pitch intervals (an equal distance between successive octaves) rather than a linear plot which shows equal frequency intervals (a doubling of the distance between successive octaves).

Loudness The subjective response of the ear to the amplitude and spectrum of a sound signal.

Loudness contour The shape of the amplitude of a sound as it evolves over time. The same meaning as envelope shape (see envelope, above).

Low-pass filter A filter which significantly attenuates the frequencies above a chosen cut-off point while allowing those below to pass through with little change.

Master keyboard A MIDI equipped keyboard (often with no sound generating circuitry) used to control a network of MIDI modules and devices. Sometimes referred to as a 'mother keyboard'.

MIDI Musical Instrument Digital Interface. A data communication standard, first established in 1983, for the exchange of musical information between electronic musical instruments and, subsequently, computers. This involves the serial transfer of digital information, (MIDI Messages), via 5 pin DIN connectors. MIDI Messages are governed by a predefined set of rules and syntax known as the MIDI Specification.

MIDI Channel A channel for the sending and receiving of MIDI messages between devices. MIDI specifies 16 separate channels and each MIDI device can be set to be receptive to messages on one of these channels or, in the case of a multi-timbral instrument, on several specified channels at the same time.

MIDI Clock A timing related MIDI Message embedded in the MIDI data stream. MIDI Timing Clocks are sent 24 times per quarter note and along with Song Position Pointer, Start, Stop and Continue messages are used to synchronize MIDI-based sequencers, drum machines and other MIDI devices. Unlike SMPTE/EBU Time Code, MIDI Timing Clock is tempo-dependent.

MIDI Controller A type of MIDI Message used to control various musical parameters other than the notes themselves, such as Modulation, Volume and Pan. Controllers are also referred to as 'Continuous Controllers' and 'Control Change messages'.

MIDI Event MIDI data once it has been recorded into a MIDI-based sequencer. This is in contrast to 'MIDI Message' which refers to the same data as it is being sent down the MIDI cable.

MIDI File A standardised file format providing a way of transferring MIDI data between different software sequencers, hardware sequencers and computer platforms. There are three types of MIDI File: Type 0 stores the data as a single stream of events, Type 1 contains multiple parallel tracks and Type 2 allows sets of independent sequences to be stored in a single file. Type 1 is the most popular format.

MIDI In 5 pin DIN socket found on all MIDI-equipped devices used to receive MIDI data.

MIDI interface A hardware interface which provides a link between a computer and external MIDI devices, normally providing at least one MIDI input and one MIDI output with more advanced units providing multiple MIDI sockets and synchronization facilities.

MIDI Machine Control (MMC) An addition to the MIDI Specification to facilitate the control of tape transports and other devices.

MIDI Message A short sequence of MIDI data which passes a discrete instruction or command to the receiving device. MIDI Messages include such things as Note On, Note Off, Polyphonic Pressure, Control Change, Program Change, Aftertouch, and System Exclusive messages.

MIDI Mode An operational mode governing how a MIDI device manages data on different MIDI Channels and whether it performs polyphonically or monophonically. There are 4 modes including Mode 1 (Omni On/Poly); response to messages on all MIDI channels and polyphonic, Mode 2 (Omni On/Mono); response to messages on all MIDI channels and monophonic, Mode 3 (Omni Off/Poly); response to messages on chosen MIDI channel(s) and polyphonic, Mode 4 (Omni Off/Mono); response to messages on chosen MIDI channel(s) and monophonic. Most units power up in Mode 3.

MIDI Out 5 pin DIN socket found on all MIDI equipped instruments used to send MIDI data.

MIDI Thru 5 pin DIN socket found on most MIDI equipped instruments providing a copy of the MIDI data received at the MIDI In. In other words, the data passes through the unit on to a further destination.

MIDI Time Code (MTC) A type of time code which is sent via MIDI, used to synchronize MIDI-based sequencers and other MIDI devices. Similar to SMPTE/EBU time code, MTC is an absolute timing reference measured in hours, minutes, seconds and fractions of a second and so does not vary with tempo.

Modulation i) The modification of one signal by another to produce effects (e.g. vibrato and tremolo). For realtime performance, the intensity of the modulation effect is controlled by the modulation wheel found on the control panel of electronic musical keyboards. Modulation is transmitted via MIDI as MIDI Controller 1. ii) The basis for FM and AM sound synthesis techniques.

Modulator i) The control signal which applies a modulating effect to a second signal. ii) The modulating part of a carrier:modulator pair of oscillators in FM synthesis.

Multi-timbral The ability of a synthesizer or module to produce several different sounds at the same time, controlled on different MIDI Channels.

Native processing Digital audio processing involving the computer's own processor and other resources rather than external digital signal processing hardware.

Noise A sound comprised of randomly distributed and inharmonic frequency components.

Notch filter A specialised type of band-reject filter which significantly attenuates a very narrow band of frequencies between two cut-off points while allowing the rest of the signal to pass through with little change.

Note On A MIDI message produced by pressing a key on a musical keyboard (or by the onset of a pre-recorded MIDI event). A Note On message starts the sounding of a musical event. It contains information about the Pitch and the Velocity of the note.

Note Off A MIDI message produced by releasing a key on a musical keyboard (or by the termination of a prerecorded MIDI event). A Note Off message starts the release phase of a musical event. It contains information about the Pitch of the note to be switched off and the Velocity with which the key was released.

Octave An interval in pitch between two tones corresponding with a doubling (or halving) of the frequency. In Western music there are 12 notes in each octave.

Operating system An organised collection of software at the next level up from BIOS which enables the user to communicate with the computer. The operating system provides the interface between BIOS and the applications running on the computer.

Oscillator A device which produces a periodic, alternating signal. Oscillators are used for generating periodic waveforms of a given amplitude and frequency.

Overtone Spectral component in a composite sound signal located at a higher frequency than the fundamental.

Pan The panoramic position of a sound within the stereo image. Most devices with two or more audio outputs feature a pan control. Pan data is transmitted via MIDI as Controller 10.

Parametric EQ Flexible signal filtering arrangement based upon a centre frequency selector, a Q control and a gain control. The centre frequency selector allows you to tune in to the frequency band you wish to process, the Q control regulates the width (filter slope characteristics) of this band and the gain control provides the means to boost or cut the chosen frequencies.

Patch A configuration of the controls of an electronic or software synthesizer which creates a specific sound. Also referred to as program, voice, sound or preset. Each patch can usually be stored in the instrument's memory for later recall.

PCI Peripheral Component Interconnect. PCI is a computer slot standard for the connection of expansion boards (including audio cards).

PCI Express A high-speed version of the standard PCI bus.

PCM Pulse Code Modulation. Coding scheme involving the conversion of binary numbers into electronic pulses and fundamental to the conversion of analogue signals into digital form during the sampling process.

Phase The relationship between two or more components of a waveform (or of separate signals) in terms of the relative position of the compression and rarefaction parts of their waveforms. Phase is expressed in degrees.

Phasing An audio effect created by mixing a phase shifted version of a signal with the original and modulating the phase shifting with an LFO while also applying an amount of feedback.

Pink noise A sound signal with equal acoustical energy per octave. In other words, there is the same energy output for the frequency bands 40Hz to 80Hz and 1kHz to 2kHz, or for any other octave band within the spectrum. Pink noise is useful in acoustic measurements since it produces a flat response when averaged on a constant Q spectrum analyser.

Pitch The subjective response of the ear to the frequency of a sound signal.

Pitch Bend Variation of the pitch of a sounding note (e.g. the bending of a note on a guitar). It is transmitted via MIDI as Pitch Bend data and on electronic keyboards is usually applied in real-time using a pitch wheel on the control surface of the instrument.

Plug and Play A standard developed by Microsoft and Intel to enable extension cards and peripheral hardware to be automatically recognised and installed in PC computer systems.

PMCD Pre-Master CD. A special format, originally developed by Sonic Solutions, to allow glass masters to be cut directly from CD-R. Sometimes used (wrongly) to describe any Red-Book-standard CD-R master from which a glass master can be made for mass CD duplication.

Pole An element in filter design responsible for the characteristics of the filter slope between the pass band and the stop band where a 1-pole filter results in a filter slope of 6dB per octave, a 2-pole filter gives a slope of 12dB per octave, a 4-pole filter gives a slope of 24dB per octave and so on.

Polyphonic Having the capacity to play more than one note simultaneously.

Portamento A sliding of pitch between consecutively played notes (similar to glissando).

Program Change A type of MIDI message used to remotely change the Program number or patch in a MIDI device. There are 128 available program numbers but when used in conjunction with Bank Select messages the number of possible program slots is significantly expanded.

Pulse wave A periodic sound wave containing odd numbered harmonics similar to a square wave but with certain harmonics in the series missing. Pulse waves are characterised by their pulse width which is the proportion of one complete cycle for which the waveform remains in the compression (or positive) part of its waveform. A pulse wave with a pulse width of $1/n$ lacks each nth harmonic.

PWM Pulse Width Modulation. The cyclic modulation of the pulse width of a pulse wave using an LFO as the modulator.

Q A measure of the selectivity and filter slope characteristics of a filter, where low Q values select a wide bandwidth and high Q values select a narrow bandwidth. Also referred to as resonance or emphasis.

Quantisation The process of transforming a continuous analogue signal into a series of discrete values during analogue-to-digital conversion.

Quantisation noise A noise produced when converting very low level audio signals, due to insufficient bit depth (lack of resolution). The noise results from the rounding up or down of some of the least significant bits used to express the signal. This may add a grainy quality to the sound.

Quantize A term used in hardware and software sequencers to describe the action of automatically moving recorded notes onto the nearest bar division according to a quantize value. For example, using a quantize value of 16 (meaning 1/16 notes) shifts all inaccurately played notes onto the nearest 1/16 division of the bar. More elaborate methods of quantizing material include moving notes towards a quantize value according to a percentage (iterative quantize) and moving notes according to a pre-recorded 'feel' template (groove quantize).

RAM Random Access Memory. Volatile memory for the temporary storage of data.

Real-time Instantaneous output (or result) from an input. Real-time digital audio processing refers to processing where there is virtually no delay between the input signal and the processed output signal. Recording music into a sequencer in real-time means that the performance is recorded instantaneously as it is played, much like recording onto a tape recorder.

Release The shape and duration of the final part of a sound event where the amplitude falls from its sustain level to zero.

Resonance The frequency or frequencies at which a device or object vibrates in sympathy with itself. Many filters are endowed with resonant behaviour normally characterised by a boost in the frequencies around the cut-off point. The shape and intensity of this boost in frequencies is regulated by a resonance control (often also referred to as Q or emphasis).

Resynthesis Analysis-synthesis technique where an existing sample is analysed and arranged into a set of parameters and values (e.g. pitch, amplitude and phase for each harmonic) which are used as the basis for synthesizing a new sound.

Reverberation Multiple series of reflections occurring after the original sound in an acoustic space. Also known as reverb, reverberation is characterised by three phases: the original sound which arrives directly from the source to the listener's ear, after a short pause the early reflections from

nearby surfaces and finally a complex mass of multiple reflections which fade to silence (known as the reverb tail).

Ring modulation Amplitude modulation technique where two oscillator signals are multiplied to produce the sum and difference of their frequencies in the output. The original frequency of the source signal is not present in the output.

ROM Read Only Memory. Memory with fixed contents which cannot be overwritten.

SACD Super Audio Compact Disc. A high fidelity CD format utilising DSD technology (Direct Stream Digital), developed by Sony and Philips. Rivals the DVD-A format.

Sample i) A snapshot of a digital audio signal at one moment in time. ii) A recorded segment of digital audio.

Sampler Musical instrument which allows the recording, editing, modifying and playback of segments of digitally recorded sound.

Sample rate In digital audio the sample rate is the number of times an analogue signal is measured per second during the process of analogue-to-digital conversion. The higher the sample rate, the greater the frequency bandwidth of the system. The audio on a CD is recorded at a sample rate of 44.1kHz, i.e.: 44,100 samples per second.

Sample resolution See 'Bit depth'.

Sawtooth wave A periodic sound wave containing all the harmonics in the natural harmonic series with the level of each harmonic at $1/n$ that of the fundamental (where $n =$ the harmonic number). A sawtooth wave has a saw shaped waveform, hence its name.

SCSI Small Computer System Interface. A communication bus system available in several standards, supporting fast data transfer speeds (up to around 240Mbit/second) and the connection of several devices on the same bus (usually hard drives).

Semitone A shift in pitch of half a tone. In mathematical terms, a change in pitch of one semitone is achieved by multiplying or dividing the frequency by 1.0595. The keys on a piano keyboard are arranged in one semitone steps.

Signal-to-noise (S/N) ratio The ratio of the signal level to the noise level in a system, usually expressed in decibels (dB's). The larger the value of the S/N ratio the lower the level of the background noise.

Sine wave A pure, periodic sound wave based upon the mathematical sine function containing a single component at the fundamental. A sine wave has a sinusoidal waveform.

SMPTE Society of Motion Picture and Television Engineers. An American organisation responsible for setting film and audio standards and recommended practices. For convenience, time code is often referred to as 'SMPTE' (pronounced 'simptee') but, in fact, this is only one type of time code.

Song Position Pointer A MIDI message often included when synchronizing MIDI devices using MIDI Timing Clocks. It allows the slaved instrument to be synchronized to the same position in the music as the master instrument after fast forward and rewind operations.

S/PDIF Sony Philips Digital InterFace. A digital signal interface standard using 75 Ohm cable terminated in RCA phono connectors.

Spectrum A representation of a sound in terms of its constituent components at one point in time or averaged over a chosen time frame. Expressed graphically in the frequency domain as vertical lines (or peaks) where each line represents a component at a different frequency and amplitude. A spectrum gives a good idea of a sound's timbral quality.

Square wave A periodic sound wave containing all the odd-numbered harmonics in the natural harmonic series with the level of each harmonic at 1/n that of the fundamental (where n = the harmonic number). A square wave has a square-shaped waveform, hence its name.

Steady-state The segment within the envelope of a sound event where the timbre and amplitude is relatively constant. It is within this part of the sound where a loop can be applied using sampling techniques for the artificial sustaining of a note.

Step-time A method of entering notes into a sequencer one step at a time (also referred to as Step input). The pitch, position and duration for each entry is predetermined and after input is complete the music can be played back at any tempo. Step-time provides a useful method of entering notes into a sequencer when real-time performance is either too fast or too complicated.

Sustain The part in the evolution of a sound event which determines the amplitude level which sustains for as long as the note is held.

Sustain Pedal A foot pedal on acoustic and electronic pianos used to produce a sustaining of all played notes for as long as the pedal is held down. MIDI Controller 64 (also known as the Damper pedal).

Synthesizer An electronic or software-based musical instrument specialised in the creation of a wide range of tones and sound textures beyond those encountered in conventional musical instruments. A synthesizer is normally endowed with a performance interface (a musical keyboard), a control interface (GUI or front panel controls) and a synthesis engine (sound processing circuitry).

System Exclusive A type of MIDI Message allowing non-standardised communication between MIDI devices. Used for the transfer of Manufacturer Specific System Exclusive and also Universal System Exclusive data. Manufacturer Specific System Exclusive includes a unique ID for each manufacturing company and might be used to change or control almost any parameter in the receiving device as deemed appropriate by the manufacturer. Universal System Exclusive data includes MIDI Machine Control, MIDI Show Control, Sample Dump Standard, MIDI File Dump, General MIDI On and General MIDI Off.

Timbre Tone colour, or harmonic structure which gives a sound its sonic identity.

Time Code A time encoded signal recorded onto audio or video tape for time and point location and synchronisation purposes. It is sometimes referred to as 'SMPTE' (pronounced 'simptee') but, in fact, SMPTE is only one standard, as used in the USA. The other is EBU Time Code as used in Europe. Time code is measured in hours, minutes, seconds, frames and subframes.

Time domain The representation of a sound signal on a graph of amplitude versus time. This shows the waveform of the signal.

Tremolo A periodic variation in the loudness of a tone produced by modulating its amplitude with a low frequency oscillator (LFO), usually set in the range between 1 and 10Hz.

Triangle wave A periodic sound wave containing all the odd-numbered harmonics in the natural harmonic series with the level of each harmonic at 1/n2 that of the fundamental (where n = the harmonic number). A triangle wave has a triangle-shaped waveform, hence its name.

Trigger A short pulse which instructs a synthesizer to start a process like the sounding of a note or the generating of an envelope.

USB Universal Serial Bus. High speed data communication standard allowing the serial transfer of data at up to 12Mbit/second for USB 1 and 480Mbit/second for USB 2.

VCA Voltage Controlled Amplifier. Type of amplifier used in analogue synthesis where the gain is regulated by a control voltage.

VCF Voltage Controlled Filter. Type of filter used in analogue synthesis where the cut-off frequency is regulated by a control voltage.

VCO Voltage Controlled Oscillator. Type of oscillator used in analogue synthesis where the frequency is regulated by a control voltage.

Velocity The speed (or force) with which a key is pressed or released on an electronic keyboard instrument. Normally, the harder a key is struck the louder the resulting note and the higher the velocity value. Velocity might also be used to affect the brightness, vibrato, sustain or some other expressive element within the sound. It forms part of the actual MIDI note data, (the third byte of Note On and Note Off messages), and does not assume a separate MIDI data category.

Vibrato A periodic variation in the pitch of a tone produced by modulating its frequency with a low frequency oscillator (LFO), usually set in the range between 1 and 10Hz. Vibrato produces a characteristic 'warbling' effect and is usually applied during the sustain part of the sound.

Virtual analogue Simulated analogue synthesis using digital signal processing techniques in software synthesis instruments.

Volume i) Generic term for loudness, amplitude or level. ii) MIDI Controller 7. Used to regulate the volume of notes in a MIDI recording. Also referred to as Main Volume.

VSTi Abbreviation for VST Instrument (Virtual Studio Instrument).

Waveform The shape of a sound wave when represented on a graph of time versus amplitude. Typical synthesized periodic waveforms include sawtooth, square, triangle and pulse.

White noise A sound signal with equal acoustical energy per frequency. The acoustical energy level at any one discrete frequency is the same as at every other frequency in the spectrum. White noise is perceived as a hissing sound.

Appendix 1
Computer hardware

Those with at least a superficial understanding of what goes on inside their computer are likely to get more out of Cubase. However, the first thing that Cubase users should bear in mind is that computer hardware and software changes extremely quickly and it is therefore difficult to keep up with the latest developments. While it is acknowledged that the specifications of your computer are important for system performance, this book is dedicated to Cubase itself and not to in-depth computer coverage. Any information contained in this appendix should therefore be regarded as additional to the main focus of the text. For more detailed coverage of computers readers are advised to consult the relevant books, magazines and websites. For precise computer recommendations for Cubase consult the Steinberg user documentation or the Steinberg website.

There now follows coverage of the basic hardware components of a computer and how these elements are likely to affect the Cubase user.

Motherboard concerns

The motherboard is a large circuit board inside the computer to which almost all other components are connected in some way. It is the central hub of activity and includes a wide range of slots and sockets. These generally include connectors for the CPU, RAM, hard drives, CD ROM / DVD drives, and serial and parallel ports. Also included are expansion ports for peripheral devices such as PCI, PCI Express, AGP, USB and Firewire, which may be used to connect audio hardware devices, MIDI interfaces, graphic cards, SCSI cards, printers and so on. The motherboard also contains the BIOS (Basic Input Output System).

Each motherboard features what is known as a chipset. Each chipset is endowed with the characteristics required to communicate with the latest processors, RAM and hardware devices. Motherboards and their chipsets are continually updated in order to maintain compatibility with the latest developments in computer hardware.

Processor choice

The processor or CPU (Central Processing Unit) is effectively the brain of the computer where the calculations and processing of data takes place. Processor speeds are measured in GHz (gigahertz) and guaged by the number of cores used (such as single-core, dual-core, quad-core and so on). In general, the faster the speed and the greater the number of cores, the shorter the performance time for any given operation. The processor choice dictates the choice of motherboard. Due to the rapid rate of change in the computer industry, you are advised to check the latest magazines and catalogues to find out the current state of affairs in the computer processor market.

RAM matters

With ever more memory-hungry operating systems and computer applications, lots of RAM is essential to run your system smoothly. RAM is an abbreviation for Random Access Memory. This is a temporary storage area and, when computations need to be performed, the data required is first stored there and then accessed at high speed by the computer's processor. If there is insufficient RAM the hard disk is used as a virtual memory expansion area. This slows things down since access to data on the hard drive is slower than access to RAM. Any such slowing down of the computer's performance may not be so important for non musical programs but for real-time applications which use native audio processing, like Cubase, optimal access to high speed RAM is essential for smooth operation. The amount of available RAM (among other things) directly affects how many audio tracks, plug-ins and virtual instruments your system can handle. It also affects the smooth operation of software sampling instruments which use RAM as a storage area for sample data. It therefore pays to have as much RAM as possible.

The hard disk

The hard disk is where the operating system, program applications (including Cubase) and all other important data is stored permanently. When it is needed, this data is retrieved from the hard disk and processed in other parts of the system. Large and fast hard drives are essential for optimum Cubase performance. Size is important for giving you enough space to record all your data and speed affects the rapidity with which data can be retrieved from the disk (which, in turn, affects the number of simultaneous audio tracks you can run in Cubase).

Digital audio eats up hard disk space extremely quickly. Recording 16-bit audio at 44.1kHz sampling rate (CD quality) takes up 5MB of disk space per mono minute. This means that a CD in its final stereo format would need around 600-700MB of disk space. When you record multiple tracks in Cubase your space requirements are likely to be much greater. If you intend to use high resolution 24-bit and 32-bit float audio then your disk space requirements are increased still further. However, size is not the only consideration when choosing a hard drive.

Multi-track digital audio puts heavy demands on the speed and efficiency of the drive. Large amounts of data must be transferred from the disk to the audio hardware in the fastest possible time. The data stream for each track is accessed in rotation and the data blocks on the disk may not always be found in convenient locations. For 16-track audio the read head of the drive is attempting to be in sixteen different places at the same time so that you can hear your audio with no delay and in perfect synchronisation. In reality, the data is stored in advance in a buffer which helps speed up the rate of data transfer. Add to this the fact that the hard disk may also be expected to simultaneously record during playback, then you can begin to appreciate why the hard drive needs to be particularly efficient. The main indicator of hard drive performance is the sustained data transfer rate (DTR). The DTR is the amount of data which can be read from the disk within a given time frame, measured in MB per second. Other indicators include the average access time, the average time it takes for the read head to find and retrieve a piece of data on the disk, and the rotation speed. Common rotations speeds include 5400, 7200 and 10,000rpm. 7200rpm or better is recommended for audio applications.

Although a single hard disk can produce adequate results, the use of two (or more) hard disk drives is highly recommended for audio-based computer systems. One drive is used for the system and program files, and the other is used for the project and audio files. This arrangement can significantly increase your track count and makes it easier to maintain and defragment the audio drive.

The choice of hard drive generally revolves around two types: Parallel ATA and Serial ATA. These are both from the same ATA / IDE interface standard which stands for Advanced Technology Attachment / Integrated Drive Electronics. There is also the slightly less popular SCSI standard (Small Computer Systems Interface).

ATA / IDE hard drives include controller hardware on the drive itself which manages the input and output of the data. ATA refers to the interface specification and IDE refers to the device type. Most drives are of an improved IDE type known as Enhanced IDE (EIDE) and their mode of data transfer is Ultra DMA (Ultra Direct Memory Access). Direct memory access allows data to be transferred to and from the hard drive without using the CPU. This results in a more efficient use of the system's resources since the CPU can engage in other calculations while the hard drive transfers data to and from RAM. Drives of this type are sometimes referred to as ultra ATA or ultra DMA. Traditional parallel ATA drives (PATA) are slowly being replaced by serial ATA drives (SATA). The latter use a serial interface which provides faster sustained transfer rates.

Whatever kind of hard drive you use for your Cubase setup, remember to organise a method of backing up your data. Hard drives can develop faults, and system crashes can result in damage to data on the disk. Popular back-up media include: spare internal hard drives, hard drives in removable caddies, external firewire drives, zip or jaz discs, recordable CD and DVD. Although hard disk failure is thankfully not a common occurrence, backing up your data is essential if you wish to avoid the potentially disastrous situation of losing all your files.

Audio hardware

Installing suitable audio hardware in your computer system is very important for the successful operation of Cubase. By audio hardware we mean a single audio card, a combined audio card with hardware interface or a separate audio device linked to the computer in some way (via USB or Firewire connectors, for example).

The audio hardware should be capable of recording and playing back digital audio using the hard drive to store the data. Audio hardware for computers commonly falls into the following categories:

- Budget stereo in/out devices – these normally feature digital audio recording capability, a MIDI interface, (usually on a dual joystick / MIDI port D-type socket) and MIDI synthesizer and/or sampling facilities. A card of this description is often a consumer card designed primarily for the games market.
- High-end audio cards and hardware featuring multiple inputs and outputs. These devices usually include an external rackmount unit or break-out box and have been designed with the professional recording industry in mind. Such devices are normally suitable for connection to both Mac and PC computers and they are the preferred choice for Cubase users.

For use with Cubase the audio hardware should:

- be able to record and play back stereo digital audio using the hard drive as the storage medium
- be a stereo or multiple input / output device with at least 16-bit resolution and 44.1 kHz sampling rate
- be equipped with a high-performance ASIO driver (Audio Stream Input Output)

The main factors to bear in mind before choosing your audio hardware can be summarised as follows: the signal-to-noise ratio (or dynamic range), the bit resolution of the A/D and D/A converters, the THD and frequency response figures, the number of line / mic inputs and outputs, the MIDI and digital I/O, the on-board synthesizer features (if you need them), the ADAT facilities (if you need them), ASIO driver availability, expected latency figures and so on. The presence of digital in and out sockets is also important, especially if you intend to record from or mix down to external digital media. Digital I/O improves the quality of both the record and playback path.

Low latency is essential if you are hoping to monitor your recordings via Cubase or if you are intending to trigger VST Instruments live via MIDI, and it also improves the general responsiveness of the software. All professional audio hardware is supplied with dedicated ASIO drivers which help reduce the latency figures to acceptable levels. A well written ASIO driver can reduce latency to around 3-10ms and those products quoting similar figures are preferable.

No matter how fast your processor and no matter how much RAM you have, the actual sound quality is finally governed by the audio hardware. However, this is not to say that if you have first class audio hardware you are guaranteed a high quality audio result – you also need to have a high quality microphone, (if you are recording vocals or live instruments), and, if the signal is passing through a mixing console, then this too must be of the highest quality possible. In addition, you must be monitoring the results through a good amplification and speaker system optimally placed in an acoustically balanced room. In other words, all stages in the recording and playback path should be of optimum quality. Your audio hardware might be viewed as a kind of cross-roads along this audio path – it is at the critical point in the recording and playback processes.

Graphics card

Computers require a graphics card in order to produce the image we see on the monitor screen. Graphics cards contain an amount of on-board RAM. The more RAM available, the greater the number of possible colours and the greater the potential resolution of the images produced. More importantly, more RAM means that graphics operations are less likely to interfere with audio operations. For Cubase, it is sufficient to use a 16-bit display quality but higher bit depths are unlikely to detract from the audio performance. Popular screen resolutions for Cubase might be anywhere between 1024 x 768 pixels to 1600 x 1200 pixels, depending upon the screen size and monitor specifications. Dual or triple monitor setups are popular among Cubase users and for this purpose a graphics card with dual or triple output ports is required. Output ports can be of the standard VGA variety or DVI. DVI is a digital interface which helps improve image quality. It is also recommended that you use a graphics card featuring passive cooling (i.e. no fan) since this helps cut down the overall noise of the computer.

The DVD/CD drive

A DVD-ROM drive is essential to install Cubase, since the program is supplied on a DVD-ROM disc. Luckily, DVD-ROM drives are standard in most computers, and most DVD-ROM drives can read both DVD-ROM and CD-ROM discs. DVD-ROM stands for Digital Versatile Disc Read Only Memory and describes a type of read-only disc similar to standard CD-ROMs (Compact Disc Read Only Memory). DVDs can store more data than CDs.

A variation on the DVD/CD-ROM drive is the DVD/CD-RW drive (DVD/CD Recorder). This allows you to write and read data to/from DVDs or CDs using DVD and CD recordable media. DVD/CD-R discs allow you to write data only once on the DVD/CD whereas DVD/CD-RW discs allow you to write data on the same disc many times. Recordable DVDs and CDs are extremely popular among Cubase users for backup purposes and for recording audio CDs. Cubase can directly import the data from standard audio CDs using the Import Audio CD option. To burn your own Red Book audio CD requires additional software (such as Wavelab, Sound Forge or Bias Peak).

A DVD/CD drive does not have to be enormously fast for Cubase. Drives are supplied in a variety of speeds such as 32 speed, 48 speed and so on, and most are adequate for general purpose use. The speed refers to the number of times faster the data is transferred to and from the disc when compared to an ordinary audio CD drive. However, for serious CD burning it is more the overall accuracy which is important. High precision drives supplied by Plextor (or similar) are recommended for this purpose.

The monitor

Monitor choice revolves around CRT (cathode ray tube) or TFT-LCD flat-screen types. Due to price considerations some are tempted to buy the smallest monitor but, for use with Cubase, this is a false economy. Cubase needs space to spread out and the use of multiple windows and their organisation on the screen demands a lot from the monitor.

TFT-LCD flat-screen monitors are an excellent alternative to CRT type computer monitors since their use results in less eye strain and general fatigue and they take up less space in cramped studios. In addition, CRT type monitors may cause significant hum when used near instruments such as electric guitar and electric bass, whereas TFT-LCD monitors do not produce this effect.

Remember that the monitor is one of the most important points of contact you have with the program and you may spend an awful long time gazing into it. As well as size, it is important to have a monitor capable of giving a crisp, clear image with good focus, brightness and colour controls. To enhance the visual interface still further, dual-monitor setups are always worth considering.

The keyboard and mouse

Of all the peripheral devices surrounding the computer, the humble keyboard and mouse are the most familiar. They provide points of tactile contact with the machine and methods by which we can give it instructions.

For Cubase, it pays to know how to use these basic tools and what to look for in the hardware sense. Most Cubase users would argue that learning to type has nothing to do with creating music and they are probably right. But if you are the kind of user who must search for each letter and symbol before you type it then you are going to be handicapped in your use of Cubase and, for that matter, most other computer software. Naming tracks, saving songs and using keyboard shortcuts all require some level of keyboard skill. So, if you are going to use the keyboard, you may as well choose one which is comfortable and then become very familiar with it. Some of the cheaper keyboards are not very pleasant to use and for the faster typist may not be sensitive enough. The final choice is a personal matter.

As for the mouse, the most comfortable shape and size depends on the characteristics of your hand. The final choice is, once again, a personal matter but it pays to make some comparisons between different models. Some users may prefer a trackball, where the cursor position is regulated by a rolling ball in the top part of the device. A wheel mouse is useful in Cubase for scrolling within the Project and other windows. Other possibilities include the use of wireless and optical keyboards and mice. These offer considerable flexibility if you need to move from one desktop or instrument location to another, and an optical mouse can be used on a wider range of surfaces than a standard mouse.

Noise issues

Unfortunately for computer users in general and particularly for musicians and recording studios, most computers make a certain amount of noise. This can prove extremely obtrusive when you are trying to listen to your latest musical masterpiece. Most of the noise comes from the various fans inside the computer case and the CD and hard drives.

A number of specialist PC computer suppliers provide computers which have been built specifically with noise minimisation and audio work in mind. These normally feature ultra quiet power supplies and hard drives housed in special acoustic enclosures. Computers of this type are the preferred option for Cubase users.

Appendix 2
MIDI messages

MIDI messages

The following table shows some of the most common MIDI messages. All data is shown in hexadecimal notation with the decimal equivalent below.

Table A2.1 MIDI messages

Message type	Function	Status byte	Data byte	Data byte	Data byte	Comments
Channel Voice messages						
Note off	Terminates a note event	8nH 128	kkH kk	vvH vv	–	kk = key number (0-127), vv = velocity (0-127)
Note on	Starts a note event	9nH 144	kkH kk	vvH vv	–	kk = key number (0-127), vv = velocity (0-127)
Polyphonic key pressure	Polyphonic key pressure	AnH 160	kkH kk	vvH vv	–	pressure for each individual key, kk = key number, vv = pressure
Control change	Generic control function	BnH 176	ccH cc	vvH vv	–	for wheels, switches, pedals etc. cc=controller no., vv =control value
Program change	Changes receiver's program number	CnH 192	ppH pp		–	pp = program number (0-127)
Channel key pressure	Channel key pressure (Aftertouch)	DnH 208	vvH vv		–	vv = amount of pressure applied (0-127)
Pitch bend	Changes pitch of notes on same channel	EnH 224	ffH ff	ccH cc	–	ff = fine changes (0-127), cc = coarse changes in pitch (0-127)

Table A2.1 MIDI messages (cont)

Message type	Function	Status byte	Data byte	Data byte	Data byte	Comments
Channel Mode messages						
Control change	Reset all controllers	BnH 176	79H 123	00H 0	–	resets all controllers to their default values
Control change	Local on/off	BnH 176	7AH 122	vvH vv	–	disconnects keyboard from sound-making circuitry (0=Off, 127=On)
Control change	All notes off	BnH 176	7BH 123	00H 0	–	terminates all currently playing notes
Control change	Omni mode off (all notes off)	BnH 176	7CH 124	00H 0	–	the receiver responds only to messages sent on its MIDI channel
Control change	Omni mode on (all notes off)	BnH 176	7DH 125	00H 0	–	the receiver responds to messages on all MIDI channels
Control change	Mono mode on/poly mode off (all notes off)	BnH 176	7EH 126	vvH vv	–	the receiver responds monophonically, vv = no of channels
Control change	Poly mode on/mono mode off (all notes off)	BnH 176	7FH 127	00H 0	–	the receiver responds polyphonically
System messages (a number of examples)						
System Exclusive	Manufacturer-specific	F0H 240	iiH ii	nnH-nnH nn-nn	F7H 247	ii = Manufacturer ID (0-127), nn - nn = almost any sequence of data dependent on function of message, F7H = end of the SysEx message
Active sensing	Transmitting instrument saying 'I am still here'	FEH 254	–	–	–	message transmitted every 300ms
MIDI clock	MIDI timing clock for sychronisation	F8H 248	–	–	–	message transmitted 24 times per quarter note
System reset	Resets receiver to power-up state	FFH 255	–	–	–	initialises all parameters to their default state

Table A2.1 MIDI messages (cont)

Message type	Function	Status byte	Data byte	Data byte	Data byte	Comments
Commonly used Control Change messages						
Control change	Modulation	BnH 176	01H 1	vvH vv	–	01H (1) = modulation, vv = modulation amount (0-127)
Control change	Breath controller	BnH 176	02H 2	vvH vv	–	02H (2) = breath control, vv = breath control amount (0-127)
Control change	Foot controller	BnH 176	04H 4	vvH vv	–	04H (4) = foot pedal control, vv = control amount (0-127)
Control change	Channel volume (Main volume)	BnH 176	07H 7	vvH vv	–	07H (7) = main volume, vv = volume level (0-127)
Control change	Pan	BnH 176	0AH 10	vvH vv	–	0AH (10) = pan, vv = pan value (0-127)
Control change	Expression	BnH 176	0BH 11	vvH vv	–	0BH (11) = expression, vv = control value (0-127)
Control change	Sustain pedal	BnH 176	40H 66	vvH vv	–	40H (66) = sustain pedal, vv = control value (0-63 = Off, 64-127 = On)

Notes

All message data is shown in hexadecimal notation with the decimal equivalent below.

n in the Status byte is a value between 0 and 15 designating one of the sixteen MIDI channels.

cc, ff, ii, kk, pp, vv are values between 0 and 127.

Appendix 3
MIDI controllers

No	Controller	No	Controller	No	Controller	No	Controller
0	Bank Select MSB	32	Bank Select LSB	64	Damper pedal on/off	96	Data increment
1	Modulation wheel	33	Mod wheel LSB	65	Portamento on/off	97	Data decrement
2	Breath control	34	Breath control LSB	66	Sustain pedal on/off	98	NRPN LSB
3	Undefined	35	Undefined	67	Soft pedal on/off	99	NRPN MSB
4	Foot controller	36	Foot controller LSB	68	Legato Footswitch	100	RPN LSB
5	Portamento time	37	Portamento time LSB	69	Hold 2	101	RPN MSB
6	Data Entry	38	Data entry LSB	70	Sound Variation	102	Undefined
7	Channel Volume	39	Channel Volume LSB	71	Timbre	103	Undefined
8	Balance	40	Balance LSB	72	Release Time	104	Undefined
9	Undefined	41	Undefined	73	Attack Time	105	Undefined
10	Pan	42	Pan LSB	74	Brightness	106	Undefined
11	Expression	43	Expression LSB	75	Sound Control #6	107	Undefined
12	Effect control 1	44	Effect control 1 LSB	76	Sound Control #7	108	Undefined
13	Effect control 2	45	Effect control 2 LSB	77	Sound Control #8	109	Undefined
14	Undefined	46	Undefined	78	Sound Control #9	110	Undefined
15	Undefined	47	Undefined	79	Sound Control #10	111	Undefined
16	Gen Purpose #1	48	Gen Purpose #1 LSB	80	Gen Purpose #5	112	Undefined
17	Gen Purpose #2	49	Gen Purpose #2 LSB	81	Gen Purpose #6	113	Undefined
18	Gen Purpose #3	50	Gen Purpose #3 LSB	82	Gen Purpose #7	114	Undefined
19	Gen Purpose #4	51	Gen Purpose #4 LSB	83	Gen Purpose #8	115	Undefined
20	Undefined	52	Undefined	84	Portamento Control	116	Undefined
21	Undefined	53	Undefined	85	Undefined	117	Undefined
22	Undefined	54	Undefined	86	Undefined	118	Undefined
23	Undefined	55	Undefined	87	Undefined	119	Undefined
24	Undefined	56	Undefined	88	Undefined	120	All Sound Off
25	Undefined	57	Undefined	89	Undefined	121	Reset All Controllers
26	Undefined	58	Undefined	90	Undefined	122	Local control on/off
27	Undefined	59	Undefined	91	FX 1 Reverb Depth	123	All notes off
28	Undefined	60	Undefined	92	FX 2 Trem Depth	124	Omni mode off
29	Undefined	61	Undefined	93	FX 3 Chorus Depth	125	Omni mode on
30	Undefined	62	Undefined	94	FX 4 Celeste Depth	126	Mono on/Poly off
31	Undefined	63	Undefined	95	FX 5 Phaser Depth	127	Poly on/Mono off

Appendix 4
General MIDI

For the convenience of those using General MIDI (GM) synths and modules and in order to avoid some of the confusion which can arise on the subject, this appendix outlines the essentials of the General MIDI protocol. There are three main types of General MIDI devices:

- GM – General MIDI. The first GM standard devised by Roland.
- GS – General Standard. The same as General MIDI but with additional features devised by Roland.
- XG – Extended General MIDI. The same as General MIDI but with additional features devised by Yamaha.

The essential idea of GM/GS/XG MIDI synths and sound modules is that they all share a common language. A MIDI sequence played back using one GM module will sound much the same on any other GM module. Cubase provides the Track Control MIDI effect plug-in which allows the editing of various GS/XG parameters. In addition, to select programs using GM names, activate the GM device in the MIDI Device manager window (Device menu) and select the GM device in the 'out' field of the MIDI track. You can now select GM programs by name rather than number.

    The following outlines the basic practical protocol for all GM/GS/XG devices, (note that the full GM protocol encompasses many more parameters than those described here):

- A minimum of 24-voice polyphony.
- Multi-timbrality on 16 MIDI channels where each channel can play a variable number of voices from the available polyphony.
- Drum sounds are always on MIDI channel 10, and each drum is allocated to a specific MIDI note number (as shown below in the 'Standard GM drum map' table).
- The sounds available comply with the program numbers and 128 presets of the standard bank of GM sounds, as in the following table:

Table A4.1 Standard bank of General MIDI sounds

No	Name	No	Name	No	Name	No	Name
1	Piano 1	9	Celesta	17	Organ 1	25	Nylon-str. Gt.
2	Piano 2	10	Glockenspiel	18	Organ 2	26	Steel-str. Gt.
3	Piano 3	11	Music box	19	Organ 3	27	Jazz Gt.
4	Honky-tonk P.	12	Vibraphone	20	Church organ	28	Clean Gt.
5	E. Piano 1	13	Marimba	21	Reed Organ	29	Muted Gt.
6	E. Piano 2	14	Xylophone	22	Accordion Fr	30	Overdrive Gt.
7	Harpsichord	15	Tubular bell	23	Harmonica	31	Distortion Gt.
8	Clav	16	Santur	24	Bandneon	32	Gt. harmonics
33	Acoustic Bass	41	Violin	49	Strings	57	Trumpet
34	Fingered Bass	42	Viola	50	Slow Strings	58	Trombone
35	Picked Bass	43	Cello	51	Syn. Strings 1	59	Tuba
36	Fretless Bass	44	Contrabass	52	Syn. Strings 2	60	Muted Trumpet
37	Slap Bass 1	45	Tremelo Str.	53	Choir Aahs	61	French Horn
38	Slap Bass 2	46	Pizzicato Str.	54	Voice Oohs	62	Brass 1
39	Synth Bass 1	47	Harp	55	SynVox	63	Synth Brass 1
40	Synth Bass 2	48	Timpani	56	Orchestral Hit	64	Synth Brass 2
65	Soprano Sax	73	Piccolo	81	Square Wave	89	Fantasia
66	Alto Sax	74	Flute	82	Saw Wave	90	Warm Pad
67	Tenor Sax	75	Recorder	83	Syn. Calliope	91	Polysynth
68	Baritone Sax	76	Pan Flute	84	Chiffer lead	92	Space Voice
69	Oboe	77	Bottle Blow	85	Charang	93	Bowed Glass
70	English Horn	78	Shakuhachi	86	Solo Vox	94	Metal Pad
71	Bassoon	79	Whistle	87	5th Saw Wave	95	Halo Pad
72	Clarinet	80	Ocarina	88	Bass & Lead	96	Sweep Pad
97	Ice Rain	105	Sitar	113	Tinkle Bell	121	Gt. Fret Noise
98	Soundtrack	106	Banjo	114	Agogo	122	Breath Noise
99	Crystal	107	Shamisen	115	Steel Drums	123	Seashore
100	Atmosphere	108	Koto	116	Wood Block	124	Bird
101	Brightness	109	Kalimba	117	Taiko	125	Telephone 1
102	Goblin	110	Bagpipe	118	Melo Tom 1	126	Helicopter
103	Echo Drops	111	Fiddle	119	Synth Drum	127	Applause
104	Star Theme	112	Shannai	120	Reverse Cymb.	128	Gun Shot

Table A4.2 Standard GM drum map

Note	No	Drum name	Note	No	Drum name
C1	36	Bass Drum	D3	62	Mute High Bongo
C#1	37	Side Stick	D#3	63	Open High Conga
D1	38	Acoustic Snare	E3	64	Low Conga
D#1	39	Hand Clap	F3	65	High Timbale
E1	40	Electric Snare	F#3	66	Low Timbale
F1	41	Low Floor Tom	G3	67	High Agogo
F#1	42	Closed Hi-Hat	G#3	68	Low Agogo
G1	43	High Floor Tom	A3	69	Cabasa
G#1	44	Pedal Hi-Hat	A#3	70	Maracas
A1	45	Low Tom	B3	71	Short Whistle
A#1	46	Open Hi-Hat	C4	72	Long Whistle
B1	47	Low Middle Tom	C#4	73	Short Guiro
C2	48	High Middle Tom	D4	74	Long Guiro
C#2	49	Crash Cymbal 1	D#4	75	Claves
D2	50	High Tom	E4	76	High Wood Block
D#2	51	Ride Cymbal 1	F4	77	Low Wood Block
E2	52	Chinese Cymbal	F#4	78	Mute Cuica
F2	53	Ride Bell	G4	79	Open Cuica
F#2	54	Tambourine	G#4	80	Mute Triangle
G2	55	Splash Cymbal	A4	81	Open Triangle
G#2	56	Cowbell	A#4	82	Shaker
A2	57	Crash Cymbal 2	B4	83	Castanets
A#2	58	Vibraslap	F0	29	Scratch Push
B2	59	Ride Cymbal 2	F#0	30	Scratch Pull
C3	60	High Bongo	A0	33	Metronome
C#3	61	Low Bongo	B0	35	Acoustic Bass Drum

Appendix 5
Additional software

While Cubase is undoubtedly a powerful music creation and audio editing tool, many users may wish to expand the possibilities with additional software. For music production and sounds effects creation popular choices include Native Instruments Kontakt and Reaktor, Propellerhead Reason, Applied Acoustics Systems Tassman, Tascam Gigastudio and Steinberg Halion. For audio editing, CD and DVD creation check out Steinberg Wavelab, Bias Peak or Sony Sound Forge. Wavelab (Figure A5.1) has established a very good reputation among mastering engineers. It includes leading edge audio editing, restoration and analysis tools, and for the creation of audio CDs and DVDs provides the intuitive and easy-to-use audio montage window. Other features include high quality DIRAC time stretching and pitch shifting, Crystal Resampler professional sample rate conversion, K system metering, effect morphing, batch processing and a Spectrum editor for surgical editing in both the time and frequency domains.

Figure A5.1
Steinberg Wavelab for audio editing, restoration, analysis and CD/DVD creation

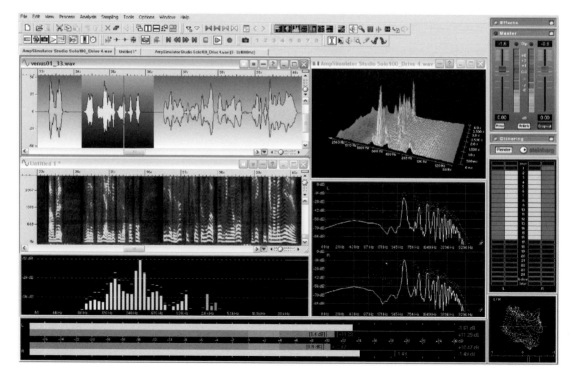

Index